Communications
in Computer and Information Science 1544

More information about this series at https://link.springer.com/bookseries/7899

Ilsun You · Hwankuk Kim ·
Taek-Young Youn · Francesco Palmieri ·
Igor Kotenko (Eds.)

Mobile Internet Security

5th International Symposium, MobiSec 2021
Jeju Island, South Korea, October 7–9, 2021
Revised Selected Papers

 Springer

Editors
Ilsun You 🆔
Soonchunhyang University
Asan, Korea (Republic of)

Hwankuk Kim 🆔
Sangmyung University
Cheonan, Korea (Republic of)

Taek-Young Youn 🆔
Dankook University
Yongin, Korea (Republic of)

Francesco Palmieri 🆔
University of Salerno
Fisciano, Italy

Igor Kotenko 🆔
St. Petersburg Federal Research Center
of the Russian Academy of Sciences
St. Petersburg, Russia

ISSN 1865-0929   ISSN 1865-0937   (electronic)
Communications in Computer and Information Science
ISBN 978-981-16-9575-9   ISBN 978-981-16-9576-6   (eBook)
https://doi.org/10.1007/978-981-16-9576-6

This Springer imprint is published by the registered company Springer Nature Singapore Pte Ltd.
The registered company address is: 152 Beach Road, #21-01/04 Gateway East, Singapore 189721, Singapore

Preface

In the 5G/beyond era, people will soon enjoy high-speed data transmission and versatile network services from the Internet to enrich and color their lives with various facilities, such as the Artificial Internet of Things (AIoT), Distributed Mobility Management (DMM), and network slicing, requiring more secure and low-latency techniques. To achieve this, emerging communication technologies need to be further developed to leverage various solutions which emphasize communication efficiency, mobility, and low latency, aiming to facilitate network services with a better connectivity and high Quality of Experience (QoE). Despite the revolutionary mobile technologies, the adoption of such technologies will leave several challenges, such as security, privacy, and trust as well as user identity management based on Subscriber Identification Module (SIM) cards, mutual authentication between networks and users, securing the paths established between communicating parties, etc.

This volume contains revised and selected papers which were submitted to and presented at the 5th International Symposium on Mobile Internet Security (MobiSec), held at the Jeju Oriental Hotel, Jeju Island, South Korea, during October 7–9, 2021. MobiSec 2021 brought academia and industry together to exchange ideas and explore new research directions for solving the challenges in mobility internet security. MobiSec has so far provided an international forum for sharing original research results among specialists in fundamental and applied problems of mobile Internet security. It publishes high-quality papers, which are closely related to various theories and practical applications in mobility management, mobile applications, and vehicular network security. A number of the papers utilize deep learning techniques so as to highlight their state-of-the-art research.

This year's symposium was organized by the Korea Institute of Information Security and Cryptology (KIISC) Research Group on 5G Security, hosted by KIISC, and sponsored by Huawei Korea and the Electronics and Telecommunications Research Institute (ETRI).

A total of 61 papers related to significant aspects of theory and applications of mobile security were accepted for presentation at MobiSec 2021. Moreover, this symposium was further powered by the keynotes entitled "Introduction to Network Equipment Security Assurance Scheme (NESAS)" by Joonho Lee from Huawei Korea, South Korea, "Cybersecurity for 5G-Powered Vehicles" by Jason Yoo from Autocrypt Co. Ltd., South Korea, "AI technologies and advanced security for connected devices in next generation networks" by Antonio Skarmeta from the University of Murcia, Spain, and "Networking Cognitive Security" by Gianni D'Angelo from the University of Salerno, Italy. Only 28 papers (42.4% of the accepted papers) were selected for publication in this CCIS volume.

The success of this symposium was assured by team efforts of sponsors, organizers, reviewers, and participants. We would like to acknowledge the contributions of the individual Program Committee members and thank the paper reviewers. Our sincere gratitude goes to the participants of this symposium and all authors of submitted papers.

We would also like to express our gratitude to the Springer team, led by Anil Chandy and Ronan Nugent, for their help and cooperation.

October 2021

Ilsun You
Hwankuk Kim
Taek-Young Youn
Francesco Palmieri
Igor Kotenko

Organization

Honorary Chair

Jaecheol Ryou — Chungnam National University, South Korea

Steering Chair

Ilsun You — Soonchunhyang University, South Korea

General Chairs

Fang-Yie Leu — Thunghai University, Taiwan
Okyeon Yi — Kookmin University, South Korea

Program Chairs

Hwankuk Kim — Sangmyung University, South Korea
Francesco Palmieri — University of Salerno, Italy
Taek-Young Youn — Dankook University, South Korea

Poster Chairs

Haehyun Cho — Soongsil University, South Korea
Joongheon Kim — Korea University, South Korea

Advisory Committee

Hsing-Chung Chen — Asia University, Taiwan
Xiaofeng Chen — Xidian University, China
Souhwan Jung — Soongsil University, South Korea
Kyung-Hyune Rhee — Pukyong National University, South Korea
Antonio Skarmeta — Universidad de Murcia, Spain
Willy Susilo — University of Wollongong, Australia
Chao-Tung Yang — Thunghai University, Taiwan
Huachun Zhou — Beijing Jiaotong University, China

Publication Chairs

Muhammad Ahmad — National University of Computer and Emerging Sciences, Pakistan
Yuh-Shyan Chen — National Taipei University, Taiwan
Igor Kotenko — SPIIRAS and ITMO University, Russia

Publicity Chairs

Joonsang Baek   University of Wollongong, Australia
Tianhan Gao   Northeastern University, China
Ji Won Kang   Sejong University, South Korea

Web Chairs

Philip Virgil Astillo   University of San Carlos, Philippines
Gaurav Choudhary   Technical University of Denmark, Denmark

Program Committee

Ioannis Agrafiotis   ENISA, UK
Ramon Alcarria   Universidad Politécnica de Madrid, Spain
Hiroaki Anada   University of Nagasaki, Japan
Pelin Angin   Middle East Technical University, Turkey
Ram Basnet   Colorado Mesa University, USA
Jorge Bernal Bernabe   Universidad de Murcia, Spain
Jakub Breier   Silicon Austria Labs, Austria
Yuanlong Cao   Jiangxi Normal University, China
Mala Chelliah   NIT Trichy, India
Jianfeng Guan   Beijing University of Posts and Telecommunications,
                         China
Shoichi Hirose   University of Fukui, Japan
Huisu Jang   Soongsil University, South Korea
Hiroaki Kikuchi   Meiji University, Japan
Jongkil Kim   University of Wollongong, Australia
Fabio Martinelli   IIT-CNR, Italy
Alessio Merlo   University of Genoa, Italy
Mauro Migliardi   University of Padua, Italy
Jason Nurse   University of Kent, UK
Ki-Woong Park   Sejong University, South Korea
Kieseberg Peter   St. Pölten University of Applied Sciences, Austria
Vishal Sharma   Queen's University Belfast, UK
SeongHan Shin   AIST, Japan
Sang Uk Shin   Pukyong National University, South Korea
Tjoa Simon   St. Pölten University of Applied Sciences, Austria
Fei Song   Beijing Jiaotong University, China
Kunlin Tsai   Thunghai University, Taiwan
Fulvio Valenza   Polytechnic University of Turin, Italy
Elena Vlahu-Gjorgievska University of Wollongong, Australia
Toshihiro Yamauchi   Okayama University, Japan
Naoto Yanai   Osaka University, Japan

Meng Yu   Roosevelt University, USA

Baokang Zhao   National University of Defense Technology, China

Contents

IoT and Cyber Security

Secure LoRaWAN Root Key Update Scheme for IoT Environment 3
  Kun-Lin Tsai, Li-Woei Chen, Fang-Yie Leu, Hsiung-Chieh Hsu,
  and Chuan-Tian Wu

Distributed Trust and Reputation Services in Pervasive
Internet-of-Things Deployments 16
  Borja Bordel and Ramón Alcarria

Comparative Analysis of Bluetooth LE and EDHOC for Potential Security
Protocol in Artificial Pancreas System 30
  Daniel Gerbi Duguma, Philip Virgil Astillo,
  Yonas Engida Gebremariam, Bonam Kim, and Ilsun You

A Credible Information Fusion Method Based on Cascaded Topology
Interactive Traceability. 44
  Yueqing Gao, Yuting Shen, Huachun Zhou, Benhui Shi, Lulu Chen,
  and Chu Du

Semantic Embedding-Based Entity Alignment for Cybersecurity
Knowledge Graphs 52
  Minhwan Kim, Hanmin Kim, Gyudong Park, and Mye Sohn

A Secure Dispersed Computing Scheme for Internet of Mobile Things 65
  Yan Zhao, Ning Hu, Jincai Zou, and Yuqiang Zhang

A Necessary Condition for Industrial Internet of Things Sustainability 79
  Andrei Dakhnovich, Dmitrii Moskvin, and Dmitrii Zegzhda

Blockchain Security

Future Applications of Blockchain in Education Sector:
A Semantic Review. 93
  Paresh Sajan Gharat, Gaurav Choudhary, Shishir Kumar Shandilya,
  and Vikas Sihag

A Resource-Blockchain Framework for Safeguarding IoT 107
  Monika Bharti, Rajesh Kumar, Sharad Saxena, and Vishal Sharma

The Design and Implementation of Blockchain-Assisted
User Public-Private Key Generation Method.   122
    Tianhong Zhang, Zejun Lan, Xianming Gao, and Jianfeng Guan

Smart Contract-Based Personal Data Protection Framework: In Cross-App
Advertising   139
    Yuyuan Shi, Xianming Gao, and Jianfeng Guan

A Blockchain-Based Authentication Scheme for 5G Applications   155
    Lanfang Ren, Xiaoting Huang, Huachun Zhou, Bo Yang, and Li Su

Digital Forensic and Malware Analysis

Effectiveness of Video-Classification in Android Malware Detection
Through API-Streams and CNN-LSTM Autoencoders   171
    Gianni D'Angelo, Francesco Palmieri, and Antonio Robustelli

Trojan Attacks and Defense for Speech Recognition   195
    Wei Zong, Yang-Wai Chow, Willy Susilo, and Jongkil Kim

Ensuring the Big Data Integrity Through Verifiable
Zero-Knowledge Operations   211
    Elena B. Aleksandrova, Maria A. Poltavtseva, and Vadim S. Shmatov

Forensic Analysis of Fitness Applications on Android   222
    Rahul Sinha, Vikas Sihag, Gaurav Choudhary, Manu Vardhan,
    and Pradeep Singh

Fingerprint Defender: Defense Against Browser-Based User Tracking   236
    Deepali Moad, Vikas Sihag, Gaurav Choudhary, Daniel Gerbi Duguma,
    and Ilsun You

Detection of Business Email Compromise Attacks with Writing Style
Analysis.   248
    Alisa Vorobeva, Guldar Khisaeva, Danil Zakoldaev, and Igor Kotenko

A Systematic Literature Review on the Mobile Malware Detection
Methods.   263
    Yu-kyung Kim, Jemin Justin Lee, Myong-Hyun Go, Hae Young Kang,
    and Kyungho Lee

Forensic Analysis of Apple CarPlay: A Case Study.   289
    Junsu Lee, Juwon Kim, Hojun Seong, Keonyong Lee, Seong-je Cho,
    Younjai Park, and Minkyu Park

Classification and Analysis of Vulnerabilities in Mobile Device
Infrastructure Interfaces 301
    Konstantin Izrailov, Dmitry Levshun, Igor Kotenko,
    and Andrey Chechulin

5G Virtual Infrastructure, Cryptography and Network Security

Which One is More Robust to Low-Rate DDoS Attacks? The Multipath
TCP or The SCTP. 323
    Lejun Ji, Gang Lei, Ruiwen Ji, Yuanlong Cao, Xun Shao, and Xin Huang

A Blockchain-Based User Identity Authentication Method for 5G 335
    Zhe Tu, Huachun Zhou, Kun Li, Haoxiang Song, and Weilin Wang

Cyber-Attack Behavior Knowledge Graph Based on CAPEC and CWE
Towards 6G 352
    Weilin Wang, Huachun Zhou, Kun Li, Zhe Tu, and Feiyang Liu

A DDoS Detection Method with Feature Set Dimension Reduction 365
    Man Li, Yajuan Qin, and Huachun Zhou

Development of Total Security Platform to Protect Autonomous Car and
Intelligent Traffic System Under 5G Environment 379
    WonHaeng Lee, Keon Yun, MyungWoo Chung, JinHyeok Oh,
    HyunJun Shin, and KwonKoo Kwak

An Anonymous Communication System Based on Software Defined
Architecture 396
    Xinda Cheng, Yixing Chen, Jincai Zou, Yuqiang Zhang, and Ning Hu

Security Association Model: Interdisciplinary Application of 5G
Positioning Technology and Social Network. 408
    Haoran Tao, Ning Ding, Tianhui Huang, Kehan Yu, Dongsheng Qian,
    Yan Luo, and Yuyin Ma

Author Index 421

IoT and Cyber Security

Secure LoRaWAN Root Key Update Scheme for IoT Environment

Kun-Lin Tsai[1]([✉])[ID], Li-Woei Chen[2], Fang-Yie Leu[3][ID], Hsiung-Chieh Hsu[1], and Chuan-Tian Wu[1]

[1] Department of Electrical Engineering, Tunghai University, Taichung, Taiwan
kltsai@thu.edu.tw

[2] Department of Computer and Information Sciences, Chinese Military Academy, Kaohsiung, Taiwan

[3] Department of Computer Science, Tunghai University, Taichung, Taiwan
leufy@thu.edu.tw

Abstract. The Internet of Things (IoT) is an essential infrastructure in many fields, such as industry and agriculture. Sensor design, communication scheme, data security, and data analysis are four important topics in the IoT research field. LoRaWAN, one of unlicensed-band based long range wide area network specifications, is very suitable for an IoT system due to the feature of low-power and long-range communication. To enhance the communication security, LoRaWAN encrypts transmitted data with different session keys which are derived from two root keys. However, these root keys stored in the end-device is easily stolen by attackers, thus threatening communication security. In this paper, a root key update scheme is proposed to periodically renew the root keys so that the security level of LoRaWAN can be enhanced. The simulation results by using the Scyther, a security analysis tool, demonstrate that the procedure of the proposed scheme is secure. Besides, the security discussion also shows that the proposed scheme provides the features of mutual authentication, confidentiality and message integrity, and can also resist replay and eavesdropping attacks.

Keywords: LoRaWAN · Root key · Internet of Things · Security

1 Introduction

In recent years, applications of the Internet of Things (IoT) have been widely created for human lives due to the rapid development of communication technologies. In an IoT system, such as smart home appliance [1,2], Smart Agriculture [3], smart city [4] and smart industry [5], a large number of sensors are connected with each other, and the data sensed by sensors are then transmitted to some servers, so that the corresponding control/calculation/operation can be performed. An IoT with intelligent management system, or so-called AIoT, can consequently be built for transportation [6], health-care [7], disaster monitoring [8], etc.

© Springer Nature Singapore Pte Ltd. 2022
I. You et al. (Eds.): MobiSec 2021, CCIS 1544, pp. 3–15, 2022.
https://doi.org/10.1007/978-981-16-9576-6_1

LoRaWAN [9,10], one of the Low Power Wide Area Network (LPWAN) protocols, eliminates the complexity of sensor deployment, and has the features of low-energy consumption and long-distance data transmission. Especially, LoRaWAN is an evolving protocol suitable for many IoT systems. Since IoT security [11,12], has been an important issue in the past years, LoRaWAN adopts 128-bit advanced encryption standard (AES-128 [13]) to guarantee the confidentiality and integrity of its transmitted data. Besides, LoRaWAN has two types of session keys: the network session key and the application session key, which are used to encrypt and decrypt transmitted data among the end-device, the network-server and the application server [14].

Although LoRaWAN provides a data encryption/decryption mechanism, many researchers still concern about its security [15–17]. For example, LoRaWAN's root key management exists its own weaknesses. In an IoT system, the end-device is the most vulnerable part since it is often far away from the server. Unfortunately, the original root keys, which are used to generate the session keys for data communication, are stored in the end-device which lacks an update mechanism.

For solving the security problem of the root key management, in this paper, a secure LoRaWAN root key update scheme is proposed by using AES-128 and one-time password. After performing the proposed root key update scheme, the root keys in both end-device and join-server can be updated, so that the communication security between the end-device and other servers can be enhanced accordingly. The proposed scheme is not only one with the features of mutual authentication, confidentiality, and message integrity, but also able to resist replay and eavesdropping attacks.

The remaining part of this paper is organized as follows. Section 2 reviews related studies of this paper. In Sect. 3, the proposed root key update scheme is presented. The security analyses of this proposed scheme are detailed in Sect. 4. In Sect. 5, we conclude this study and outline our future works.

2   Related Studies

2.1   LoRaWAN Concept

LoRaWAN is an attractive low-power wide-area-network protocol. In a LoRaWAN based IoT environment, there are numerous end-devices, several network servers, application servers, and a join server. The end-devices can be sensors, meters, monitors, controllers, and machines. The network server verifies messages' integrity and delivers these messages to corresponding application servers. Application server responses with the corresponding action based on the information carried in the receiving messages. Join server manages the end-devices join process and generates two session keys, NwkSKey and AppSKey, for network server and application server, respectively. Figure 1 shows two session keys are generated by two root keys.

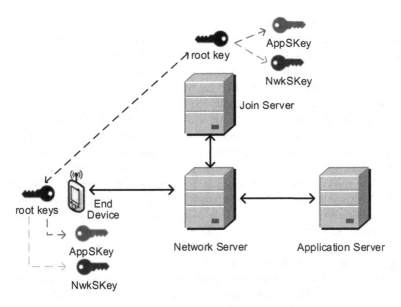

Fig. 1. Two session keys are generated by two root keys.

The LoRaWAN security policy uses standardized AES cryptographic algorithm and end-to-end secure communication protocols to achieve the requirements of mutual authentication, confidentiality and integrity protection. Two operations, i.e., Cipher-based Message Authentication Code (CMAC) and Counter Mode (CTR), are combined with original AES encryption/decryption algorithm so as to perform message integrity protection and data encryption. During new end-device joining process, two unique 128-bit root keys, AppKey and NwkKey (both equipped with new end-device and recorded in join server), and a globally unique identifier EUI-64-based DevEUI (also equipped with new end-device) are utilized to generate several session keys. They are

- Network Session Key(s) (NwkSKey for LoRaWAN 1.0 and SNwkSIntKey, FNwkSIntKey, NwkSEncKey for LoRaWAN 1.1) which is(are) a(three) unique 128-bit key(s) shared by the end-devices and network server(s), and
- Application Session Key (AppSKey) which is a unique 128-bit key shared by end-device and the corresponding application server.

2.2 Related Studies

In the past years, many LoRaWAN security related studies [18–22] had been done. Raad *et al.* [18] mentioned that elliptic curve cryptography can be used to improve data integrity when the data is transmitted on the network. The advantage of using elliptic curve cryptography is to enhance the security level and meanwhile reduce processing time and energy consumption, when compared with other public key cryptographies. However, elliptic curve encryption requires more complicated calculations than the AES does. Naoui *et al.* [19] analyzed the security of the LoRaWAN 1.0 protocol. The authors claimed that the LoRaWAN protocol is easily attacked by two possible attacks. The first one is the parameter *DevNonce* which is a 16-bit counter starting at 0 when the end-device is initially powered up and which is incremented by one with every join-request. Since the *DevNonce* is not encrypted in the join-request message, the attacker can utilize previous join-request messages to launch replay attacks. The second one is the parameter *AppNonce* which is generated when the network-server receives the join-request message from the end-device. The *AppNonce* is then passed to the end-device and application-server for the purpose of mutual authentication. An attacker can initiate the corresponding join acceptance message and send it to the end-device in the subsequent message. In [19], the authors designed a trusted third-party computer, which is utilized to dispatch the session key for network-server and application-server. The trusted third-party computer creates a timeline, and network-server stores the timeline when it receives a join-request message so as to prevent a replay attack.

In [20], the authors also compared the security of LoRaWAN v1.0 and v1.1. According to the results released in [20], it can be seen that, in LoRaWAN v1.0, the communication between the end-device and the network-server (application-server) mainly relies on *AppNonce* for mutual authentication. Once this parameter is known by attackers, the transmitted data will fall into danger. Therefore, in LoRaWAN v1.1, join-server is designed to manage the generation of session keys. This can truly solve the security problem appeared in LoRaWAN v1.0. However, some researchers still concern about the security of root key management, especially the root key storage.

Dönmez *et al.* [21] proposed a key management scheme to improve the security of LoRaWAN. The original root keys stored in the end-device are assigned to one master device which has the responsibility of secure key storing. The master device is connected to the end-device via physical links, and it can be regarded as an extension of the end-device so as to reduce the attacking risk of the end-device. Besides, the master device can also be used as a charging station for the end-device.

Since LoRaWAN stores the root keys in end-devices that are vulnerable to physical attacks, and lacks a mechanism to update the root key, Han and Wang [22] proposed a key derivation function based root key update scheme to enhance LoRaWAN security. They applied a Rabbit stream cipher-based key derivation function to update the root key, and the results showed that the key generated in the proposed scheme had a high degree of randomness.

3   LoRaWAN Root Key Update Scheme

Since the current LoRaWAN v1.1 [10] protocol does not define a root key update scheme, the root key stored in the end-device is easily attacked and stolen, which may conduct security problems. The join-server is less likely to have the problem of physical attacks, but once the root key of one party is cracked, the security will be compromised. In this section, the procedure of the root key update scheme, as shown in Fig. 2, is proposed to periodically renew the root keys stored in both end-device and join-server. After updating the root keys, the new communication session keys can also be updated by using re-joining process defined by the LoRaWAN protocol. The detailed steps of root key update scheme are described as follows.

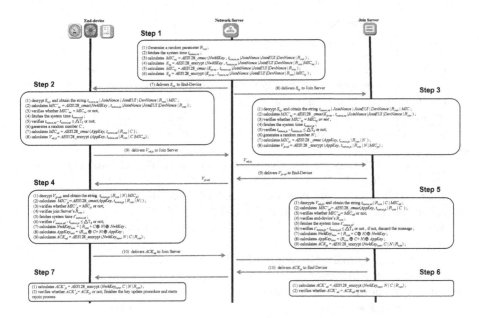

Fig. 2. The procedure of root key update scheme.

In Step 1, as shown in Fig. 3, the network-server

(1) generates a random number R_{con};
(2) fetches its system time $t_{nonce,ns}$;
(3) calculates a message integrity code
$MIC_{ne} = AES128\_cmac(NwkSKey, t_{nonce,ns}|JoinNonce|JoinEUI|$
$DevNonce|R_{con})$
by using $AES128\_cmac$ encryption algorithm ($cmac$ stands for Cypher-based Message Authentication Code), where $NwkSKey$ is the network session key generated by the previous root key and used for data encryption

Network Server

Step 1

(1) Generates a random parameter R_{con};
(2) fetches the system time $t_{nonce,ns}$;
(3) calculates $MIC_{ne} = AES128\_cmac\,(NwkSKey,\, t_{nonce,ns}\,|JoinNonce\,|JoinEUI\,|DevNonce\,|\,R_{con}\,)$;
(4) calculates $S_{ne} = AES128\_encrypt\,(NwkSKey,\, t_{nonce,ns}\,|JoinNonce\,|JoinEUI\,|DevNonce\,|\,R_{con}\,|MIC_{ne}\,)$;
(5) calculates $MIC_{nj} = AES128\_cmac\,(K_{js\text{-}ns},\, t_{nonce,ns}\,|JoinNonce\,|JoinEUI\,|DevNonce\,|\,R_{con}\,)$;
(6) calculates $S_{nj} = AES128\_encrypt\,(K_{js\text{-}ns},\, t_{nonce,ns}\,|JoinNonce\,|JoinEUI\,|DevNonce\,|\,R_{con}\,|\,MIC_{nj}\,)$;

Fig. 3. Step 1 of the root key update scheme.

between end-device and network-server, the symbol '|' indicates string cascade, $JoinNonce$ is a counter generated by join-server and used to count the number of times that the end-device has joined current LoRaWAN, $JoinEUI$ which embedded in the end-device is an authentication for join-server, and R_{con} is a 16-bit counter managed by end-device;

(4) calculates a secret message
$$S_{ne} = AES128\_encrypt(NwkSKey,\ t_{nonce,ns}|JoinNonce|JoinEUI|$$
$$DevNonce|R_{con}|MIC_{ne})$$
where $AES128\_encrypt$ represents standard AES encryption algorithm;

(5) calculates another message integrity code
$$MIC_{nj} = AES128\_cmac(K_{js-ns},\ t_{nonce,ns}|JoinNonce|JoinEUI|DevNonce|$$
$$R_{con})$$
by using K_{js-ns}, the data encryption key which encrypting message delivered between join-server and network-server;

(6) calculates another secret message
$$S_{nj} = AES128\_encrypt(K_{js-ns},\ t_{nonce,ns}|JoinNonce|JoinEUI|DevNonce|$$
$$R_{con}|MIC_{nj});$$

(7) delivers S_{ne} to the end-device; and

(8) delivers S_{nj} to the join-server.

As shown in Fig. 4, when receiving the S_{ne}, in Step 2, the end-device

(1) decrypts S_{ne}, i.e., performing $AES128\_decrypt(NwkSKey,\ S_{ne})$
and obtains the string $t_{nonce,ns}|JoinNonce|JoinEUI|DevNonce|R_{con}|$
MIC_{ne};

(2) calculates the received message integrity code
$$MIC'_{ne} = AES128\_cmac(NwkSKey,\ t_{nonce,ns}|JoinNonce|JoinEUI|$$
$$DevNonce|R_{con});$$

(3) verifies whether $MIC'_{ne} = MIC_{ne}$ or not; if not, discards the message and sends an update failure message to the network-server and join-server. Otherwise, the end-device

(4) fetches its system time $t_{nonce,ed}$;

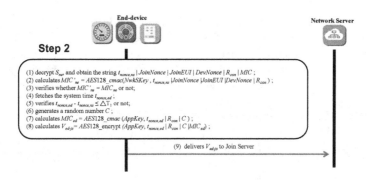

Fig. 4. Step 2 of the root key update scheme.

(5) verifies whether $t_{nonce,ed} - t_{nonce,ns} \leq \Delta T_1$ or not, where $\Delta T_1 = (T_{ns} + T_{comm,nsed} + T_{ed2a}) \times \kappa$, in which T_{ns} represents the execution time of network-server performing (3) to (6) in Step 1, $T_{comm,nsed}$ is the expected data transmission time between network-server and the end-device, T_{ed2a} indicates the execution time of end-device performing (1) to (4) in Step 2, and κ is a predefined tolerance ratio; if the verification fails, the end-device discards the message and sends an update failure message to the network-server and join-server. Otherwise, it

(6) generates a random number C;

(7) calculates the message integrity code
$MIC_{ed} = AES128\_cmac(AppKey, t_{nonce,ed}|R_{con}|C)$,
where $AppKey$ is one of the root keys stored in the end-device and join-server;

(8) calculates
$V_{ed-js} = AES128\_encrypt(AppKey, t_{nonce,ed}|R_{con}|C|MIC_{ed})$; and

(9) delivers V_{ed-js} to the join-server.

Similarly, when receiving the S_{nj}, in Step 3, the join-server

(1) decrypts S_{nj}, i.e., performing $AES128\_decrypt(NwkSKey, S_{nj})$
and obtains the string
$t_{nonce,ns}|JoinNonce|JoinEUI|DevNonce|R_{con}|MIC_{nj}$;

(2) calculates the received message integrity code
$MIC'_{nj} = AES128\_cmac(NwkSKey, t_{nonce,ns}|JoinNonce|JoinEUI|DevNonce|R_{con})$;

(3) verifies whether $MIC'_{nj} = MIC_{nj}$ or not; if not, discards the message and sends an update failure message to the network-server and end-device. Otherwise, the join-server

(4) fetches its system time $t_{nonce,js}$;

(5) verifies whether $t_{nonce,js} - t_{nonce,ns} \leq \Delta T_2$ or not, where $\Delta T_2 = (T_{ns} + T_{comm,nsjs} + T_{js3a}) \times \kappa$, in which T_{ns} represents the execution time of network-server performing (3) to (6) in Step 1, $T_{comm,nsjs}$ is the expected

data transmission time between network-server and the join-server, and T_{js3a} indicates the execution time of end-device performing (1) to (4) in Step 3 and κ is a predefined tolerance ratio; if the verification fails, the join-server discards the message and sends an update failure message to the network-server and end-device. Otherwise, it

(6) generates a random number N;

(7) calculates the message integrity code
$MIC_{js} = AES128\_cmac(AppKey, t_{nonce,js}|R_{con}|N)$;

(8) calculates $V_{js-ed} = AES128\_encrypt(AppKey, t_{nonce,js}|R_{con}|N|MIC_{js})$; and

(9) delivers V_{js-ed} to end-device.

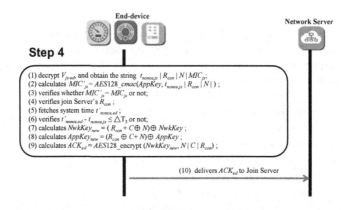

Fig. 5. Step 4 of the root key update scheme.

As shown in Fig. 5, once the end-device receives V_{js-ed} from join-server, in Step 4, the end-device

(1) decrypts V_{js-ed} to obtain the string $t_{nonce,js}|R_{con}|N|MIC_{js}$;

(2) calculates $MIC'_{js} = AES128\_cmac(AppKey, t_{nonce,js}|R_{con}|N)$;

(3) verifies whether $MIC'_{js} = MIC_{js}$ or not; if not, discards the message and sends an update failure message to the network-server and join-server. Otherwise, the end-device

(4) verifies whether the received R_{con} in Step 4 (1) equal to the R_{con} of Step 2 (1) or not; if not, discards the message and sends an update failure message to the network-server and join-server. Otherwise, the end-device

(5) fetches its system time $t'_{nonce,ed}$;

(6) verifies whether $t'_{nonce,ed} - t_{nonce,js} \leq \Delta T_3$ or not, where $\Delta T_3 = (T_{js3b} + T_{comm,jsed} + T_{ed4a}) \times \kappa$, in which T_{js3b} represents the execution time of join-server performing (4) to (8) in Step 3, $T_{comm,jsed}$ is the expected data transmission time between join-server and the end-device, and T_{ed4a} indicates the execution time of end-device performing (1) to (5) in Step 4; if the verification fails, the end-device discards the message and sends an update failure message to the network-server and join-server. Otherwise, it

(7) calculates the first new root key $NwkKey_{new} = (R_{con} + C \oplus N) \oplus NwkKey$;

(8) calculates the second new root key $AppKey_{new} = (R_{con} \oplus C + N) \oplus AppKey$;

(9) calculates $Ack_{ed} = AES128\_encrypt(NwkKey_{new}, N|C|R_{con})$;

(10) delivers Ack_{ed} to join-server.

Similarly, when the join-server receives V_{ed-js} from end-device, in Step 5, the join-server

(1) decrypts V_{ed-js} to obtain the string $t_{nonce,ed}|R_{con}|C|MIC_{ed}$;

(2) calculates $MIC'_{ed} = AES128\_cmac(AppKey, t_{nonce,ed}|R_{con}|C)$;

(3) verifies whether $MIC'_{ed} = MIC_{ed}$ or not; if not, discards the message and sends an update failure message to the network-server and end-device. Otherwise, the join-server

(4) verifies whether the received R_{con} in Step 5 (1) equal to the R_{con} of Step 3 (1) or not; if not, discards the message and sends an update failure message to the network-server and end-device. Otherwise, the join-server

(5) fetches its system time $t'_{nonce,js}$;

(6) verifies whether $t'_{nonce,js} - t_{nonce,ed} \leq \Delta T_4$ or not, where $\Delta T_4 = (T_{ed2b} + T_{comm,edjs} + T_{js5a}) \times \kappa$, in which T_{ed2b} represents the execution time of end-device performing (4) to (8) in Step 2, $T_{comm,jsed}$ is the expected data transmission time between end-device and join-server, and T_{js5a} indicates the execution time of join-server performing (1) to (5) in Step 5; if the verification fails, the join-server discards the message and sends an update failure message to the network-server and end-device. Otherwise, it

(7) calculates the first new root key $NwkKey_{new} = (R_{con} + C \oplus N) \oplus NwkKey$;

(8) calculates the second new root key $AppKey_{new} = (R_{con} \oplus C + N) \oplus AppKey$;

(9) calculates $Ack_{js} = AES128\_encrypt(AppKey_{new}, N|C|R_{con})$;

(10) delivers Ack_{js} to end-device.

When the join-server received Ack_{ed} from join-server, in Step 6, it

(1) calculates $Ack'_{ed} = AES128\_encrypt(NwkKey_{new}, N|C|R_{con})$;

(2) verifies whether $Ack'_{ed} = Ack_{ed}$ or not; if not, discards the message and sends an update failure message to the network-server and end-device. Otherwise, it finishes the update procedure.

When the end-device received Ack_{js} from join-server, in Step 7, it

(1) calculates $Ack'_{js} = AES128\_encrypt(AppKey_{new}, N|C|R_{con})$;

(2) verifies whether $Ack'_{js} = Ack_{js}$ or not; if not, discards the message and sends an update failure message to the network-server and join-server. Otherwise, it finishes the update procedure and send the rejoin request to network-server to reset the communication session key.

4   Security Analyses

In order to verify the feasibility and security of the proposed scheme, the Scyther tool [23], an automatic security protocol verification software, is utilized, and the result is shown in Fig. 6. The Scyther tool treats the proposed key update scheme as a new protocol, and checks whether various parameters will be attacked during the transmission or not. The verification model has three roles: end-device, network-server, and join-server, and these three roles are verified independently. As shown in Fig. 6, the important parameter R_{con}, two secret parameters C and N and other identification parameters are not threatened by attacks during transmission. Since the new root keys are generated by using abovementioned parameters, it indicates that the new root keys are secure.

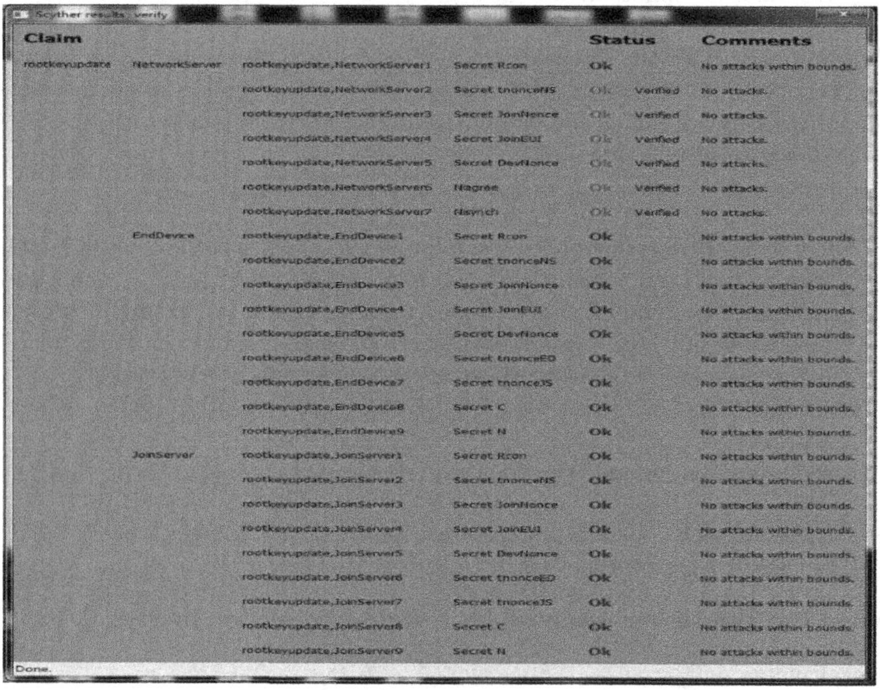

Fig. 6. The verification result of the proposed root key update scheme.

We further discuss the security features of the proposed scheme.

a) **Mutual authentication** represents that the sender and receiver can authenticate with each other. In the proposed scheme, the $JoinNonce$, $JoinEUI$, R_{con}, and $DevNonce$ are utilized to authenticate end-device, join-server, and network-server. When an attacker does not have correct $JoinNonce$, $JoinEUI$, R_{con}, and $DevNonce$, the correct MIC cannot be generated, and thus the checking of Step 2 (3) or Step 3 (3) will fail. In this way, the proposed scheme has the feature of mutual authentication.

b) **Confidentiality** means all the important parameters can be totally protected. In the proposed scheme, all the parameters are encrypted by using AES128 encryption algorithm before delivering. In Step 1, the $NwkSKey$ and K_{js-ns} are two encryption keys, and in Step 2 and Step 3, the $AppKey$ are used. While in Step 4 and Step 5, the new $NwkKey_{new}$ and new $AppKey_{new}$ are used to encrypt the message. As can be seen in the key update scheme, different encryption keys are used for different messages. Accordingly, those important parameters can be totally protected.

c) **Message integrity** ensures that the transmitted messages do not be forged. In the proposed scheme, four message integrity codes, i.e., MICs, are designed to verify the messages' integrity. When one of the MIC verification fails, the root key update scheme is also suspended. Consequentially, the proposed scheme has the feature of message integrity.

d) **Replay attack** indicates that an attacker copies a valid message sent by the sender and pretends to be a legitimate part to send the message to the receiver in an attempt to steal relevant information. In the proposed scheme, the time parameter t_{nonce} is hidden and encrypted in transmitted message. After receiver receives and decrypts the receiving message, the receiver's system time is then utilized to calculate whether the time difference between two system times is smaller than a pre-defined time limit or not. Once the time difference is larger than the pre-defined time limit, it means the message may not send by the legitimate sender. That is to say that when an attacker copies the transmitted message, and resent it to the receiver, the time limit cannot hold. As a result, the proposed scheme can prevent the replay attack.

e) **Eavesdropping attack** means that an attacker may extract important information when he/she captures a large amount of messages from the underlying network. In the proposed scheme, the most important parameters need to be protected are the parameters R_{con}, C, and N. These parameters are generated randomly and encrypted by using AES before transmission. Besides, R_{con}, C, and N are different every time the root key update scheme is executed. The hacker is unable to extract one of these three parameters from the captured messages.

5   Conclusion and Future Studies

Security is one of the most important issues of an IoT system. As LoRaWAN is being used more frequently, its security has also been under scrutiny. In this paper, a root key update scheme is proposed so that the security level of LoRaWAN can be enhanced. The simulation result performed by Scyther tool shows that the root key update scheme is secure. Moreover, the proposed scheme has the features of mutual authentication, confidentiality and message integrity, and can resist replay and eavesdropping attacks.

In the future, the formal security verification for the root key update scheme will be performed. Besides, the communication session key management policy will also be developed so that a secure LoRaWAN communication environment can be established. These constitute our future studies.

References

1. Aheleroff, S., et al.: IoT-enabled smart appliances under industry 4.0: a case study. Adv. Eng. Inform. **43**(101043), 1–14 (2020)
2. Caputo, D., Verderame, L., Ranieri, A., Merlo, A., Caviglione, L.: Fine-hearing Google home: why silence will not protect your privacy. J. Wirel. Mob. Netw. Ubiquit. Comput. Dependable Appl. (JoWUA) **11**(1), 35–53 (2020)
3. Angin, P., Anisi, M.H., Göksel, F., Gürsoy, C., Büyükgülcü, A.: AgriLoRa: a digital twin framework for smart agriculture. J. Wirel. Mob. Netw. Ubiquit. Comput. Dependable Appl. (JoWUA) **11**(4), 77–96 (2020)
4. Badii, C., Bellini, P., Difino, A., Nesi, P.: Smart city IoT platform respecting GDPR privacy and security aspects. IEEE Access **8**, 23601–23623 (2020)
5. Shariatzadeh, N., Lundholm, T., Lindberg, L., Sivard, G.: Integration of digital factory with smart factory based on internet of things. Proc. Cirp **50**, 512–517 (2016)
6. Liu, Y., Liu, L., Chen, W.P.: Intelligent traffic light control using distributed multi-agent Q learning. In: 2017 IEEE 20th International Conference on Intelligent Transportation Systems (ITSC), pp. 1–8 (2017)
7. Qian, K., Zhang, Z., Yamamoto, Y., Schuller, B.W.: Artificial intelligence internet of things for the elderly: from assisted living to health-care monitoring. IEEE Signal Process. Mag. **38**(4), 78–88 (2021)
8. Katayama, K., Takahashi, H., Yokoyama, S., Gäfvert, K., Kinoshita, T.: Evacuation guidance support using cooperative agent-based IoT devices. In: 2017 IEEE 6th Global Conference on Consumer Electronics (GCCE), pp. 1–2 (2017)
9. L. A. T. Committee. Lorawan backend interfaces 1.0 specification. https://lora-alliance.org/. Accessed 1 Aug 2021
10. L. A. T. Committee. Lorawan 1.1 specification. https://lora-alliance.org/. Accessed 1 Aug 2021
11. Alizadeh, M., Andersson, K., Schelén, O.: A survey of secure Internet of Things in relation to blockchain. J. Internet Serv. Inf. Secur. (JISIS) **10**(3), 47–75 (2020)
12. Hui, H., et al.: Survey on blockchain for internet of things. J. Internet Serv. Inf. Secur. (JISIS) **9**(2), 1–30 (2019)
13. Pub, N.F.: Announcing the advanced encryption standard (AES). Federal Inf. Process. Stand. Publ. **197**, 1–51 (2001)
14. Tsai, K.L., Leu, F.Y., Hung, L.L., Ko, C.Y.: Secure session key generation method for LoRaWAN servers. IEEE Access **8**, 54631–54640 (2020)
15. Noura, H., Hatoum, T., Salman, O., Yaacoub, J.P., Chehab, A.: LoRaWAN security survey: issues, threats and possible mitigation techniques. Internet Things 100303, 1–37 (2020)
16. Tsai, K.L., Leu, F.Y., You, I., Chang, S.W., Hu, S.J., Park, H.: Low-power AES data encryption architecture for a LoRaWAN. IEEE Access **7**, 146348–146357 (2019)
17. You, I., Kwon, S., Choudhary, G., Sharma, V., Seo, J.T.: An enhanced LoRaWAN security protocol for privacy preservation in IoT with a case study on a smart factory-enabled parking system. Sensors **18**(6), 1888 (2018)

18. Raad, N., Hasan, T., Chalak, A., Waleed, J.: Secure data in lorawan network by adaptive method of elliptic-curve cryptography. In: 2019 International Conference on Computing and Information Science and Technology and Their Applications (ICCISTA), pp. 1–6 (2019)
19. Naoui, S., Elhdhili, M.E., Saidane, L.A.: Trusted third party based key management for enhancing LoRaWAN security. In: 2017 IEEE/ACS 14th International Conference on Computer Systems and Applications (AICCSA), pp. 1306–1313 (2017)
20. Eldefrawy, M., Butun, I., Pereira, N., Gidlund, M.: Formal security analysis of LoRaWAN. Comput. Netw. **148**, 328–339 (2019)
21. Donmez, T.C., Nigussie, E.: Key management through delegation for LoRaWAN based healthcare monitoring systems. In: 2019 13th International Symposium on Medical Information and Communication Technology (ISMICT), pp. 1–6 (2019)
22. Han, J., Wang, J.: An enhanced key management scheme for LoRaWAN. Cryptography **2**(4), 34 (2018)
23. Cremers, C.J.F.: The Scyther tool: verification, falsification, and analysis of security protocols. In: Gupta, A., Malik, S. (eds.) CAV 2008. LNCS, vol. 5123, pp. 414–418. Springer, Heidelberg (2008). https://doi.org/10.1007/978-3-540-70545-1_38

Distributed Trust and Reputation Services in Pervasive Internet-of-Things Deployments

Borja Bordel[1] and Ramón Alcarria[2]

[1] Department of Computer Systems, Universidad Politécnica de Madrid, Madrid, Spain
borja.bordel@upm.es
[2] Department of Geospatial Engineering, Universidad Politécnica de Madrid, Calle Mercator 2, 28031 Madrid, Spain
ramon.alcarria@upm.es

Abstract. Cyberprotection in the context of Internet-of-Things (IoT) includes three basic areas: security, privacy and trust. Security and privacy technologies are related to mechanisms such as cryptography or authentication protocols that have been extensively explored and adapted to IoT requirements. However, new risks such as cyber-physical attacks and novel distributed, and pervasive architectures reveal new weaknesses where trust and reputation issues are the main challenges to be addressed. Nevertheless, both, trust and reputation, are intrinsically subjective and distributed, and algorithms guaranteeing a dynamic and efficient management of these properties tend to be computationally heavy and complex. In this context, new trust and reputation services for pervasive IoT deployments are needed. Therefore, in this paper we propose a new distributed architecture for the provision of trust and reputation services in IoT systems. The architecture is based on Blockchain technologies and the composition of different conceptual models (cognitive, computational, neurological, and game-theoretical) using stochastic functions. The resulting probability may be employed by nodes to create their own trustworthy subsystem. In order to validate the performance and usability of the proposal, an experimental validation based on simulation technologies is provided.

Keywords: Internet of Things · Blockchain · Cybersecurity · Stochastic models

1 Introduction

Internet-of-Things (IoT) [33] is one of the most powerful enabling technologies for new and promising paradigms such as Industry 4.0 [5], Cyber-Physical Systems [7] or Enhanced Living Environments [15]. In all these innovative solutions, software and hardware components manage large amounts of data which, in several cases, may be personal and (then) protected by international regulations

© Springer Nature Singapore Pte Ltd. 2022
I. You et al. (Eds.): MobiSec 2021, CCIS 1544, pp. 16–29, 2022.
https://doi.org/10.1007/978-981-16-9576-6_2

such as the European GDPR (General Data Protection Regulation) [28]. Moreover, most of these new technical paradigms are envisioned to be implemented into critical infrastructures or applications [11], what makes them a potential focus [1] for many different attacks: from traditional cybercrime to the new cyber-physical risks [13] and cyber terrorism.

In this context, it is essential to protect IoT deployments using strong policies and mechanisms. Traditionally, a protected IoT deployment needs to implement technologies in three different areas: security, trust and privacy [16]. Security mechanisms [4] include authentication and integrity solutions, which are already highly adopted by current IoT technologies (mainly inherited from network technologies and protocols such as Bluetooth or ZigBee) [27]. On the other hand, privacy mechanisms, including cryptography and anonymization policies, although they are not fully adapted to the IoT deployments and requirements, they are also commonly implemented in many non-commercial IoT applications, especially lightweight versions of well-known algorithms such as The Onion Router (TOR) [12]. On the contrary, trust solutions face a totally different situation. Most common trust mechanisms nowadays are based on administrative schema, or on a social understanding of this concept [6]; what makes very difficult to integrate these technologies without deploying a large infrastructure or considering a relevant and constant human intervention. Trust mechanisms typically include two different aspects: intrusion detection and reputation. While intrusion detection requires, currently, large infrastructures and a great computational power (the most recent and successful solutions are based on mathematically complex algorithms such as artificial intelligence [20] and large data repositories); reputation mechanisms are usually supported through a direct human intervention, where users indicate those behaviors that are malicious, untrustworthy or, in general, dangerous (and, based on that input, the nodes' reputation is obtained). In that way, both areas are clearly facing open challenges, which prevents their massive use in the upcoming IoT deployments.

As a possible solution, new trust and reputation calculation frameworks and mechanisms are proposed. However, these proposals tend to be subjective and highly distributed, so innovative algorithms guaranteeing a dynamic and efficient management of trust and/or reputation are typically computationally heavy and complex [9]. Nevertheless, the increasing computational power of IoT nodes and single-board computers, together with the universal access to the global Internet granted by future 5G networks [29], are introducing a much more favorable scenario for those new proposals.

Therefore, in this paper we are proposing a service-based trust and reputation calculation solution. The proposed calculation algorithm considers four different approaches or understandings of trust: cognitive, computational, neurological, and game-theoretical. Trust, in or proposal, is not a fixed value but a probability distribution, what represents in a better manner the intrinsic uncertainty of the observations. Local calculations are then integrated into a global trust value, which is obtained and updated using a distributed Blockchain network.

From a market perspective, the proposed solution shows a high applicability as it can be implemented in all kinds of devices and IoT nodes (only common mathematical operations are employed). On the other hand, several lightweight implementations of brokers and Blockchain networks can be found, which also facilitates the applicability of the proposed architecture in all kinds of commercial scenarios.

The rest of the paper is organized as follows: Sect. 2 describes the state of the art on trust solutions for IoT deployments; Sect. 3 describes the proposed solution, including the proposed architecture and the trust calculation framework; Sect. 4 presents an experimental validation using statistical techniques; and Sect. 5 concludes the paper.

2   State of the Art on Trust Solutions for IoT Systems

As one of the most relevant open problems nowadays, related to IoT systems, trust and reputation calculation and management have received a lot of attention in the last ten years. Many different proposals may be found, although in general six different categories are typically identified [32].

The first group of works propose the introduction of Trusted Third Parties (TTP) and authentication protocols [17]. In these schemes, trustworthy components are those which are authenticated by a very secure middleware or components known as TTP or secure enclaves [23]. Standard ciphers, keys and protocols are deployed among all components [26]. In hierarchic network architectures, trust domains may be created and TTP may be built as trustworthy gateways [21]. Although this scheme is very useful in client-server architectures, in very distributed IoT deployments is very inefficient.

The second group of trust solutions for IoT deployments is composed of recommender systems. A recommender system may be of three types: content-based filtering [30], collaborative filtering [8], and a hybrid system [19]. In general, in all these approaches, nodes receive and analyze recommendations to decide with which other nodes they stablish a connection (as people do in societies). These systems can take advantage of the network structure, but they are totally reactive and cannot be employed as a prevention solution. Moreover, this approach requires a large human intervention and can be barely automated.

Works in the third group address behavior-based mechanisms. In this approach, nodes monitor the behavior of other components and decide about the connections they want to maintain or prune [31]. Although this scheme allows nodes to perform simple local evaluations [8], (as in the previous case) it can be difficult to employ this technology in prevention policies as collected data are not enough for supporting predictions. Besides, this approach lacks a global understating of trust for the entire system of the particular nodes.

In order to solve this challenge and enable the option of implementing prevention policies and making predictions, in the fourth group of trust solutions, mechanisms are based on metadata. Information such as the geographical location of the ownership of nodes is employed to determine which nodes are untrustworthy and malicious [25]. This scheme is totally proactive, as malicious nodes may be removed before they start operating, just knowing their metadata. However, the percentage of false positives in this approach is higher than in any other previous approach (what reduces the system performance).

In the last five years, the Blockchain revolution has also affected the IoT technologies, and different proposals to provide and support trust in IoT deployments based on Blockchain may be found [3,18,28] (fifth category). However, in general, in this approaches all data from the nodes is exchanged through the Blockchain network to secure it and make it trustworthy [2]. Although this mechanism may provide certain level of trust, some works have reported different attacks and problems associated to this solution [10,22]. Furthermore, the delay of transactions communicated through Blockchain networks grows up exponentially, reducing the network performance in a very relevant manner.

Finally, and sixth category, many different hybrid approaches have been reported. These schemes try to combine the advantages of different mechanisms. One of the most common proposals includes a behavior-based solution together with a TTP or middleware (in order to store local calculations and get a global value) [14]. However, these solutions are still very weak against manipulations, contrary to Blockchain-based mechanisms.

Table 1 shows a summary with the main state of the art proposals.

Table 1. Main state-of-the-art solutions

References	Short description	Main problems
[17,21,26]	Trusted Third Parties and authentication protocols	In very distributed IoT deployments is very inefficient
[8,19,30]	Recommender systems	They are totally reactive and cannot be employed as a prevention solution
[8,31]	Behavior-based mechanisms	Difficult to employ in prevention policies
[25]	Mechanisms based on metadata	The percentage of false positives in this approach is higher than in any other
[2,10,18,28]	Trust in IoT deployments based on Blockchain	The delay of transactions communicated through Blockchain networks grows up exponentially
[14]	Hybrid approaches	Still very weak against manipulations

Therefore, in our proposal, we are combining most of these approaches into an innovative distributed architecture. The solution is service-oriented and it is supported by Blockchain, although not all transactions must go through this network in order to preserve the system performance. Besides, trust calculation includes four different views (cognitive, computational, neurological, and game-theoretical), in order to guarantee the reactive and proactive character of the solution.

3   A New Trust Calculation Framework and Architecture

In this section, we propose a novel architecture for trust calculation in IoT deployments. This architecture (Sect. 3.1) includes a Blockchain network for global trust calculation using SmartContracts. Besides, nodes may perform four different trust calculations at local level: cognitive (Sect. 3.2), computational (Sect. 3.3), neurological (Sect. 3.4), and game-theoretical (Sect. 3.5).

3.1   Proposed Distributed Architecture for Trust Calculation

Figure 1 shows the proposed architecture for trust calculation.

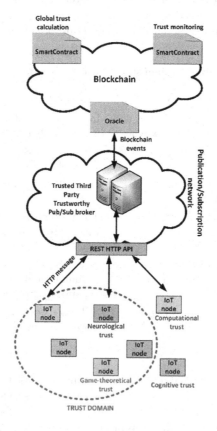

Fig. 1. Proposed architecture for trust and reputation calculation

In the proposed solution, each IoT node may execute locally one trust calculation algorithm, among the four existing ones: cognitive, computational, neurological, and game-theoretical. In general, and depending on the system configuration, nodes may select the trust calculation algorithm in an autonomous manner (according to their capabilities, knowledge, etc.) or the system administrator can do it. Any case, it is important to guarantee that all four calculation algorithms have a homogenous presence in the IoT deployment (in order to avoid biases in the global trust calculation function).

Nodes in the IoT deployment, on the other hand, are connected to the global trust calculation infrastructure through a publication/subscription network. This network offers a REST (representational state transfer) API (application programming interface) and service, so nodes can relate with the infrastructure using HTTP messages. HTTP messages are easier to parse, send, receive and process than bit-oriented protocols, although they show higher latencies. Besides, HTTP messages are nowadays, the standard communication medium for IoT nodes and deployments.

Using these messages, IoT nodes may subscribe to different trust services and the updates on the trust values from other nodes, other trust calculation algorithms and/or the global trust calculation infrastructure. At the same time, the global trust calculation infrastructure (i.e. the Blockchain network) is subscribed to all updates from the IoT nodes. On the other hand, when a relevant change on the locally calculated trust values is detected by an IoT node, it can publish the new results. All these message exchanges and pub/sub management is controlled by a trustworthy broker acting as TTP. In fact, this broker requires to IoT nodes and the Blockchain network to get authenticated and employ cryptographic mechanisms to preserve the privacy and security of communications. All nodes that cannot be authenticated by the TTP are automatically rejected.

Moreover, through an SmartContract acting as oracle, the Blockchain network monitors and stores all updates about trust calculations done by IoT nodes in the deployment. In that way, in the Blockchain network (using a second Smart-Contract) there is an accountable tracking of reputation and trustworthiness of all IoT nodes, from different perspectives (cognitive, computational, neurological, and game-theoretical) and from different local analyses (as many as IoT nodes are observing an analyzing the behavior of the given node). Each time this not rejectable, transparent record is updated, a third SmartContract updates the global trust calculation (using stochastic functions). Each time the global trust values are updated, the Blockchain network generates an event, which is publish through the pub/sub network. Then, all nodes are informed about the global trustworthiness of all nodes in the IoT deployment.

With all this information (global trust and rejections caused by the TTP), IoT nodes may define their own "trust domain", selecting with which nodes they want to establish a connection (see Sect. 3.5). Hereinafter we assuming rejected nodes are not connected with any other nodes, and we are focusing on trust calculation (both, at local and global level).

3.2   Cognitive Trust Calculation

As said, each IoT node is locally executing one different trust calculation algorithm. Each one representing a different perspective and understanding of the idea of trust. In this section we are focusing of the cognitive trust T_{cog}.

Cognitive trust refers the reputation and trust supported by a priori beliefs, and it is typically a function of the degree of these beliefs. In a technological context, these beliefs refer the expectation of a node to have the necessary competence, benevolence, and integrity to be relied upon [24]. However, these qualities are not technical, but sociological. And then, they are inherited from the node's owner, location, etc. At them, they are inherited from the node's metadata.

Thus, given an IoT node n_i (or target node) with an associated collection of metadata $MD(n_i)$ (1), and a second node n_j (or observer node) and a set of a priori trustworthy metadata $MD^+(n_j)$ (2), it may be calculated the cognitive trust $T_{cog}(n_i; n_j)$ for this pair of nodes (3).

$$MD\,(n_i) = \{md_k\,(n_i) \quad k = 1, \ldots, K_T\} \tag{1}$$

$$MD^+(n_j) = \{MD_k^+(n_j) \quad k = 1, \ldots, K_T\}$$
$$MD_k^+\,(n_j) = \{md_{k,r}^+\,(n_j) \quad r = 1, \ldots, R_{k,j}\} \tag{2}$$

$$T_{cog}(n_i; n_j) = P_{trust}(n_i; n_j) =$$
$$\sum_{k=1}^{K_T} \sum_{r=1}^{R_{k,j}} (\alpha_{k,r}\ \delta[md_k(n_i) = md_{k,r}^+(n_j)] + \beta_{k,r}\ \delta[md_k(n_i) \neq md_{k,r}^+(n_j)]) \tag{3}$$

In this expression (3), the result refers the target node n_i according to the local observations of node n_j. The result $T_{cog}(n_i; n_j)$ must be understood as the probability $P_{trust}(n_i; n_j)$ of node n_i to be trustworthy, considering the observation of node n_j. Besides, $\delta[\cdot]$ is the Kronecker's delta function and $\alpha_{k,r}$ and $\beta_{k,r}$ are real parameters to represent the degree or weight of the node's beliefs.

Cognitive trust may be calculated before the system starts operating, but needs the definition of a protocol to share the nodes' metadata with the entire system.

3.3   Computational Trust Calculation

Computational trust T_{comp} is associated to the behaviors that follow the rules and requirements of authorities in the IoT deployment. Typically, in topics related to cyberprotection such as cryptography. Although, in most common proposals, this vision of trust is only employed to enable or disable the spontaneous collaboration among nodes, it is also possible to define a more elaborated metric for computational trust.

Thus, given an IoT node n_i (or target node) communicating with a node n_j (or observer node), it may be calculated the computational trust $T_{comp}(n_i; n_j)$ for this pair of nodes (4).

$$T_{comp}(n_i; n_j) = P_{trust}(n_i; n_j) = \begin{cases} 1; & k < K_{th} \\ \sqrt{2}\dfrac{h_{i,j}}{\sqrt{1+h_{i,j}^2}}; & k > K_{th} \end{cases} \tag{4}$$

The proposed function for computational trust is a sigmoid, so it varies in the interval $[0, 1]$ as probabilities do. In this case, the result has also to be understood as the probability of node n_i to be computationally trustworthy according to the local calculation performed by node n_j.

In this case, k represents the time slots elapsed since the IoT deployment started operating, and $h_{i,j}$ is a parameter representing the percentage of times the node n_i employed the correct cryptographic configuration (as indicated by the TTP) when communicating with node n_j (5). As this kind of behavior-based trust calculation algorithms may need a period to converge, for all time instants before K_{th}, node n_i is considered trustworthy (so the capabilities of the IoT deployment are not reduced by default).

$$h_{i,j} = \sum_{m=0}^{k} u_{i,j}[-m] \cdot r_{i,j}^{m+1}$$

$$u_{i,j}[m] = \frac{c_{i,j}[m]}{t_{i,j}[m]} \tag{5}$$

On the other hand, in order to introduce a temporal decreasing effect (past events are less relevant than the recent ones), parameter $h_{i,j}$ is obtained through a geometric sum, with a ratio $r_{i,j}$. Then, the ratio $u_{i,j}[m]$ between transactions with the correction configuration $c_{i,j}[m]$ and the total number of transactions $t_{i,j}[m]$ in the m-th time slot is weighted according to its antiquity.

3.4   Neurological Trust Calculation

Neurological trust T_{neu} is the most traditional behavior-based approach for trust. In general, nodes analyze the honesty of other IoT nodes in the deployment and obtain a trust value according to the observed and past experiences.

In neurological trust, the observer node n_j monitor the number of successful transactions $s_{i,j}[m]$ with the target node n_i in each time slot m. This quantity is employed to generate a ratio $w_{i,j}[m]$ by considering the total number of transactions between both nodes $t_{i,j}[m]$ (6).

$$w_{i,j}[m] = \frac{s_{i,j}[m]}{t_{i,j}[m]} \tag{6}$$

However, as said in Sect. 3.3, the impact of past measurements must be lower than recent evaluations, so all the partial results for every time slot are combined in a geometric sum (7).

$$h_{i,j} = \sum_{m=0}^{k} w_{i,j}[-m] \cdot r_{i,j}^{m+1} \tag{7}$$

The resulting parameter, $h_{i,j}$, depends on the selected ratio for this sum $r_{i,j}$, which control the evanescence of the impact of past measurements. Finally, in order to calculate the neurological trust, a sigmoid function is employed, where k represents the time slots elapsed since the IoT deployment started operating (8).

$$T_{neu}(n_i; n_j) = P_{trust}(n_i; n_j) = \begin{cases} 1; & k < K_{th} \\ \sqrt{2}\dfrac{h_{i,j}}{\sqrt{1+h_{i,j}^2}}; & k > K_{th} \end{cases} \tag{8}$$

As in other previous calculations, this result must be understood as the probability of node n_i to be neurologically trustworthy according to the local calculation performed by node n_j.

3.5   Game-Theoretical Trust Calculation

Contrary to computational or neurological trust, game-theoretical trust T_{game} is a proactive approach. In this case, trust is obtained as the most rational and probable value in the future, considering the past evidence, behaviors and evolution of trust. In conclusion, game-theoretical trust employs a historical data repository to predict the future values of trust.

Given an IoT node n_i with a sequence of global trust values $tr[k]$ (9), the game-theoretical trust is calculated by node n_j using the Lagrange polynomial (10). After calculated this polynomial, the observer node n_j can obtain the game-theoretical trust in any future time slot k_{next} using function $L(k)$.

$$tr[k] = \{tr[k] \quad k = 1, \ldots, K_j\} \tag{9}$$

$$L(k) = \sum_{m=1}^{K_j} tr[m] \cdot \ell_m(k)$$

$$\ell_m(k) = \prod_{r=1, \ r \neq m}^{K_j} \frac{k-r}{m-r} \tag{10}$$

Each observer node n_j may develop this extrapolation using a different number of previous trust measures K_j. The final result for game-theoretical trust $T_{game}(n_i; n_j)$ will depend on the local values of K_j and k_{next} (11). As global trust values are points from an stochastic function, as in all previous calculations, the result $T_{game}(n_i; n_j)$ is understood as the probability of node n_i to be game-theoretical trustworthy according to the local calculation performed by node n_j.

$$T_{game}(n_i; n_j) = P_{trust}(n_i; n_j) = L(k_{next}) \tag{11}$$

3.6   Global Trust Calculation

Finally, all IoT nodes in the system send their local evaluations for the target node n_i to the global trust calculation infrastructure (Blockchain network), to be combined in a global trust value.

Given the IoT deployment has M_T nodes, at this point M_T different trust values $trust_j^i$ will be collected for each target node n_i. Each one obtained through a different mechanism and from a different local perspective. Then, in the global trust calculation system, all these values are employed to create a unique probability distribution for each target node n_i. Using the Laplace's notion of probability, all values are grouped to define a discrete probability density function T_{global} with Y_T points (12).

$$T_{global}[y] = \frac{1}{M_T} \, card \left\{ trust_j^i \quad j = 1, \ldots M_T \,\vdots\, th_y \leq trust_j^i < th_{y+1} \right\} \quad (12)$$

$$with \quad y = 1, \ldots, Y_T, \quad with \; th_y \; \in [0,1] \quad and \quad th_1 = 0 \quad and \; th_{Y_T} = 1$$

To do that, the cardinality $card\{\cdot\}$ function is employed to determine the number of elements in each set meting a given condition, and limits th_y are employed to define the intervals for grouping the local trust values.

Finally, in order to inform the nodes about the global results using only one real number (matching, for example, the requirement of game-theoretical trust calculation algorithm), the non-central moments λ_z (13) or central moments μ_z (14) may be employed, depending on the implementation.

$$\lambda_z = \frac{\sum_{y=1}^{Y_T} \left(T_{global}\ [y] \right)^z}{Y_T} z \in [0, \infty] \quad (13)$$

$$\mu_z = \frac{\sum_{y=1}^{Y_T} \left(T_{global}\ [y] - \lambda_1 \right)^z}{Y_T} z \in [0, \infty] \quad (14)$$

4   Experimental Validation: Simulations and Results

In order to evaluate the performance of the proposed solution, an experimental validation was planned and carried out. During this validation, two different experiments were performed, in order to analyze the convergence time of the proposed security mechanism, and the success rate when detecting the malicious nodes in an IoT deployment.

Both experiments were performed using simulation methodologies and the MATLAB 2020.B and Simulink suite. Using this numerical tool, one hundred and twenty (120) devices were represented, each one executing a different application and trust calculation algorithm. Besides, different amounts of malicious nodes were considered for different evaluations. All simulation were performed in a Linux architecture.

Simulated IoT nodes represented a common architecture based on the ESP-32 microcontroller, WiFi communications and simple sensors such as temperature or humidity. Trust calculation algorithms were distributed among nodes in a homogeneous but random manner. Nodes also could behave in a malicious manner randomly, but according to the configured percentages.

All simulation were repeated twelve times to remove all possible exogenous effects. Presented results are obtained as the average of all these partial simulations. Simulations represented twenty-four hours of real-time operation in the IoT deployment.

The first experiment was focused on the success rate of the proposed solution. For different amounts of malicious nodes in the IoT deployment, it is analyzed the percentage of them that are correctly detected and isolated.

The second experiment was focused on the convergence time. For different amounts of malicious nodes, the maximum convergence time required to evaluate all nodes and configure the final IoT deployment was evaluated.

Figure 2 shows the results of the first experiment. As can be seen, the success rate is above 85% in all cases. As the number of malicious nodes goes up, the success rate also grows up, although this effect is common to most technologies. The most interesting result in Fig. 2 is the lack of any asymptote. As can be seen, even if 50% of nodes in the IoT deployment are malicious, the proposed solution does not get saturated and it is able to operate normally, detecting up to 98% of malicious nodes.

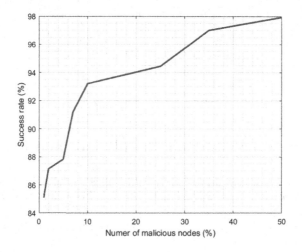

Fig. 2. Results of the first experiment

Figure 3 shows the results of the second experiment. As can be seen, for malicious nodes up to 10%, the convergence time is below one hour (3600 s). However, from this point, the convergence time starts growing up exponentially. For 25% of malicious nodes, the convergence time reaches two hours, and for any number of malicious nodes above this limit, Fig. 3 does not show a clear convergence. Any case, these results are acceptable, considering the convergence time of other IoT components such as CO_2 sensors.

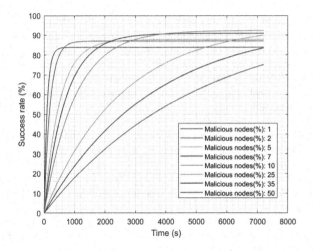

Fig. 3. Results of the second experiment

5 Conclusions and Future Works

In this paper we propose a new distributed architecture for the provision of trust and reputation services in IoT systems. The architecture is based on Blockchain technologies and the composition of different conceptual models (cognitive, computational, neurological, and game-theoretical) using stochastic functions. Results shows the proposed technology presents a good detection rate and convergence time. Specifically, success rate is above 85% in very situation and for malicious nodes up to 10%, the convergence time is below one hour. These values are acceptable for most IoT deployments, as they typically operate with a limited number of nodes and generate information in a quite low speed.

Future works will evaluate the proposed solution in real IoT deployment with commercial hardware devices. Although the proposed simulation scenario shows a high precision, real deployments are affected by exogenous and unexpected phenomena which may modify the results introduced in this paper. These impacts will be evaluated in future works.

Acknowledgments. The research leading to these results has received funding from the Ministry of Science, Innovation and Universities through the COGNOS project (PID2019-105484RB-I00).

References

1. Abhishta, A., van Heeswijk, W., Junger, M., Nieuwenhuis, L.J.M., Joosten, R.: Why would we get attacked? An analysis of attacker's aims behind DDoS attacks. J. Wirel. Mob. Netw. Ubiquit. Comput. Dependable Appl. (JoWUA) **11**(2), 3–22 (2020)

2. Alcarria, R., Bordel, B., Robles, T., Martín, D., Manso-Callejo, M.Á.: A blockchain-based authorization system for trustworthy resource monitoring and trading in smart communities. Sensors **18**(10), 3561 (2018)
3. Alizadeh, M., Andersson, K., Schelen, O.: A survey of secure internet of things in relation to blockchain. J. Internet Serv. Inf. Secur. (JISIS) **10**(3), 47–75 (2020)
4. Anada, H.: Decentralized multi-authority anonymous authentication for global identities with non-interactive proofs. J. Internet Serv. Inf. Secur. (JISIS) **10**(4), 23–37 (2020)
5. Bordel, B., Alcarria, R.: Assessment of human motivation through analysis of physiological and emotional signals in industry 4.0 scenarios. J. Ambient Intell. Hum. Comput. 1–21 (2017)
6. Bordel, B., Alcarria, R., De Andres, D.M., You, I.: Securing internet-of-things systems through implicit and explicit reputation models. IEEE Access **6**, 47472–47488 (2018)
7. Bordel, B., Alcarria, R., de Rivera, D.S., Robles, T.: Process execution in cyber-physical systems using cloud and cyber-physical internet services. J. Supercomput. **74**(8), 4127–4169 (2018)
8. Bordel, B., Alcarria, R., Martín, D., Sánchez-de Rivera, D.: An agent-based method for trust graph calculation in resource constrained environments. Integr. Comput.-Aided Eng. **27**(1), 37–56 (2020)
9. Bordel, B., Alcarria, R., Martín, D., Sánchez-Picot, Á.: Trust provision in the internet of things using transversal blockchain networks. Intell. Autom. Soft Comput. **25**(1), 155–170 (2019)
10. Bordel, B., Alcarria, R., Robles, T.: Denial of chain: evaluation and prediction of a novel cyberattack in blockchain-supported systems. Futur. Gener. Comput. Syst. **116**, 426–439 (2021)
11. Bordel, B., Alcarria, R., Robles, T., González, D.: An industry 4.0 solution for the detection of dangerous situations in civil work scenarios. In: Rocha, Á., Ferrás, C., Paredes, M. (eds.) ICITS 2019. AISC, vol. 918, pp. 494–504. Springer, Cham (2019). https://doi.org/10.1007/978-3-030-11890-7_48
12. Bordel, B., Alcarria, R., Robles, T., Iglesias, M.S.: Data authentication and anonymization in IoT scenarios and future 5G networks using chaotic digital watermarking. IEEE Access **9**, 22378–22398 (2021)
13. Bordel, B., Alcarria, R., Robles, T., Sanchez-Picot, A.: Stochastic and information theory techniques to reduce large datasets and detect cyberattacks in ambient intelligence environments. IEEE Access **6**, 34896–34910 (2018)
14. Bordel, B., Alcarria, R., Sánchez-de-Rivera, D.: Detecting malicious components in large-scale internet-of-things systems and architectures. In: Rocha, Á., Correia, A.M., Adeli, H., Reis, L.P., Costanzo, S. (eds.) WorldCIST 2017. AISC, vol. 569, pp. 155–165. Springer, Cham (2017). https://doi.org/10.1007/978-3-319-56535-4_16
15. Bordel, B., Alcarria, R., Sánchez de Rivera, D., Martín, D., Robles, T.: Fast self-configuration in service-oriented smart environments for real-time applications. J. Ambient Intell. Smart Environ. **10**(2), 143–167 (2018)
16. Bordel, B., Alcarria, R., Sánchez-de-Rivera, D., Robles, T.: Protecting industry 4.0 systems against the malicious effects of cyber-physical attacks. In: Ochoa, S.F., Singh, P., Bravo, J. (eds.) UCAmI 2017. LNCS, vol. 10586, pp. 161–171. Springer, Cham (2017). https://doi.org/10.1007/978-3-319-67585-5_17
17. Haroon, A., Akram, S., Shah, M.A., Wahid, A.: E-lithe: a lightweight secure DTLS for IoT. In: IEEE Vehicular Technology Conference, vol. 2017-September, pp. 1–5, February 2018

18. Huang, Z., Su, X., Zhang, Y., Shi, C., Zhang, H., Xie, L.: A decentralized solution for IoT data trusted exchange based-on blockchain. In: 2017 3rd IEEE International Conference on Computer and Communications, ICCC 2017, vol. 2018-January, pp. 1180–1184, March 2018

19. Ju, C., Wang, J., Xu, C.: A novel application recommendation method combining social relationship and trust relationship for future internet of things. Multimed. Tools Appl. **78**(21), 29867–29880 (2018)

20. Kasturi, G., Jain, A., Singh, J.: Detection and classification of radio frequency jamming attacks using machine learning. J. Wirel. Mob. Netw. Ubiquit. Comput. Dependable Appl. (JoWUA) **11**(4), 49–62 (2020)

21. Kim, E., Keum, C.: Trustworthy gateway system providing IoT trust domain of smart home. In: International Conference on Ubiquitous and Future Networks, ICUFN, pp. 551–553, July 2017

22. König, L., Unger, S., Kieseberg, P., Tjoa, S.: The risks of the blockchain a review on current vulnerabilities and attacks. J. Internet Serv. Inf. Secur. (JISIS) **10**(3), 110–127 (2020)

23. Liu, N., Yu, M., Zang, W., Sandhu, R.: Cost and effectiveness of TrustZone defense and side-channel attack on arm platform. J. Wirel. Mob. Netw. Ubiquit. Comput. Dependable Appl. (JoWUA) **11**(4), 1–15 (2020)

24. Murayama, Y., Hauser, C., Hikage, N., Chakraborty, B.: The sense of security and trust. In: Handbook of Research on Social and Organizational Liabilities in Information Security, pp. 493–502 (2008)

25. U. S. Premarathne: MAG-SIoT: a multiplicative attributes graph model based trust computation method for social Internet of Things. In: 2017 IEEE International Conference on Industrial and Information Systems, ICIIS 2017 - Proceedings, vol. 2018-January, pp. 1–6, February 2018

26. Raza, S., Shafagh, H., Hewage, K., Hummen, R., Voigt, T.: Lithe: lightweight secure CoAP for the internet of things. IEEE Sens. J. **13**(10), 3711–3720 (2013)

27. Robles, T., Bordel, B., Alcarria, R., Martín, D.: Mobile wireless sensor networks: modeling and analysis of three-dimensional scenarios and neighbor discovery in mobile data collection. Ad-Hoc Sens. Wirel. Netw. **35**(1–2), 67–104 (2017)

28. Robles, T., Bordel, B., Alcarria, R., Sánchez-de Rivera, D.: Enabling trustworthy personal data protection in eHealth and well-being services through privacy-by-design. **16**(5) (2020). https://doi.org/10.1177/1550147720912110

29. Sánchez, B.B., Sánchez-Picot, Á., De Rivera, D.S.: Using 5G technologies in the internet of things handovers, problems and challenges. In: Proceedings - 2015 9th International Conference on Innovative Mobile and Internet Services in Ubiquitous Computing, IMIS 2015, pp. 364–369, September 2015

30. Son, J., Choi, W., Choi, S.-M.: Trust information network in social internet of things using trust-aware recommender systems. **16**(4) (2020). https://doi.org/10.1177/1550147720908773

31. Talreja, R., Sathish, S., Nenwani, K., Saxena, K.: Trust and behavior based system to prevent collision in IoT enabled VANET. In: International Conference on Signal Processing, Communication, Power and Embedded System, SCOPES 2016 - Proceedings, pp. 1588–1591, June 2017

32. Ud Din, I., Guizani, M., Kim, B.S., Hassan, S., Khan, M.K.: Trust management techniques for the internet of things: a survey. IEEE Access **7**, 29763–29787 (2019)

33. Wortmann, F., Flüchter, K.: Internet of things. Bus. Inf. Syst. Eng. **57**(3), 221–224 (2015)

Comparative Analysis of Bluetooth LE and EDHOC for Potential Security Protocol in Artificial Pancreas System

Daniel Gerbi Duguma[1] , Philip Virgil Astillo[2] ,
Yonas Engida Gebremariam[3] , Bonam Kim[1] , and Ilsun You[1,3](✉)

[1] Department of Information Security Engineering, Soonchunhyang University,
Asan-si, Chungcheongnam-do 31538, South Korea
danielgerbi2005@gmail.com, kimbona9@gmail.com, ilsunu@gmail.com
[2] Department of Computer Engineering, University of San Carlos,
Cebu City, Philippines
pvbastillo@usc.edu.ph
[3] Department of ICT Environmental Health System, Soonchunhyang University,
Asan-si, Chungcheongnam-do 31538, South Korea
yonas.engidag@gmail.com

Abstract. The Internet of Things (IoT) has shown to be beneficial in today's increasingly connected world. IoT has transformed nearly every industry, opening up huge opportunities for future innovation and progress. The Internet of Medical Things (IoMT), as one important application area of IoT, has changed healthcare delivery, such as by playing a crucial role in treating diabetic patients with the use of Artificial Pancreas System (APS). On the other hand, a slew of current and new security threats have put IMoT's ability to offer services safely in jeopardy. Hence, it is critical to minimize these security problems, such as by safeguarding information traveling from one IMoT device to another. In this context, we investigated two vital protocols for secure communication in APS: Bluetooth Low Energy (LE) and Ephemeral Diffie-Hellman over COSE (EDHOC). Consequently, we performed an experimental evaluation of these protocols based on a number of performance metrics, including protocol execution time, transmission cost, and total round-trip time. As a result, while both protocols perform similarly in terms of the first metrics, Bluetooth LE excels in terms of transmission cost, and EDHOC outperforms in terms of round-trip time.

Keywords: APS · Open APS · Security protocol for APS · EDHOC · Bluetooth LE

1 Introduction

The IoT has shown its instrumental role in the current densely connected world. It has transformed nearly all sectors with tremendous opportunities for more

This research was supported by Basic Science Research Program through the National Research Foundation of Korea (NRF) funded by the Ministry of Education (NRF-2020RI1A2073603).

I. You et al. (Eds.): MobiSec 2021, CCIS 1544, pp. 30–43, 2022.
https://doi.org/10.1007/978-981-16-9576-6_3

innovation and advances [2,3,17]. IoMT, as one major application area of IoT, has revolutionized the medical care provisioning in such a way that enables remote diagnosis, on-time notifications, smart drug monitoring, and artificial intelligence assisted services [6]. A significant use case of IoMT is diagnosis of Diabetes - one of the most prevalent disease worldwide where the number of diabetic patients has more than quadrupled within the last four decades in ages between 14 and 70 [12]. Diabetes is a chronic condition that occurs when the pancreas no longer generates insulin or when the body does not properly use the insulin produced, where the first condition is referred to as Type 1 and the second condition is called Type 2. Type 2 is the most common one which occurs in almost all age ranges. Consequently, it is more desirable to treat Diabetes, particularly Type 1, with an IoT enabled APS that is composed of three essential components: Continuous Glucose Monitoring (CGM), Controller, and Insulin Pump.

The CGM, commonly known as blood sugar monitoring, automatically tracks blood glucose levels daily and at night. It allows to check glucose levels at a glance and analyzes how the glucose varies over a few hours or days to detect trends. The ability to monitor glucose levels in real-time can assist patients in making more informed decisions about balancing their diet, physical activity, and medications throughout the day. Additionally, various commercially available CGMs now have a transmitter that allows them to wirelessly send the blood glucose level (BGL) to a monitor node or control unit. The controller component runs a controlling algorithm that receives CGM data and calculates the insulin amount based on CGM information. Moreover, it sends a command message (for instance an insulin dose) to the Insulin Pump. Finally, the Insulin Pump administers insulin as per the command received from the controller, and reports back the Insulin in the Vial (IiV) to the controller.

The information that travels between these three components must be secure since there is a risk of alteration or replay by an adversary. As shown in Fig. 1, the pass among these three components can be exposed to both passive and active threats that, if exploited, may negatively impact the patient. Security issues are among the most challenging tasks in protecting information in IoT environment [1,4,20]. Accordingly, different security measures can be taken to protect these information, among which Bluetooth LE [21] and the EDHOC [9] can be preferred. Given its popularity and high integration with nearly all IoT devices [19], Bluetooth LE can serve to exchange a key to encrypt and integrity protect the sensitive information from CGM to controller and from/to controller to/from Insulin Pump. On the other hand, EDHOC is a promising and yet to be standardized application layer lightweight key agreement protocol that is specifically designed to serve in resource-constrained environments. Consequently, in this paper, we present the details of both protocols and implement them in the APS experimental setup to evaluate their performance and see opportunity to combine for better resilience.

The remainder of this paper is organized as follows. In Sects. 2 and 3, we provide detail explanation of Bluetooth LE and EDHOC protocols along with their key exchange mechanisms. In Sect. 4, we describe the experimental environment and present performance comparison of these protocols concerning protocol execution latency, transmission cost, and total round-trip time. The final section, Sect. 5, concludes the paper.

2 Bluetooth LE

2.1 Overview

Bluetooth technology, which was introduced two decades ago, has played a vital role in short-range communication of devices in various modes such as point-to-point, broadcast, and mesh. It also allows device location, such as orientation, proximity, presence, and distance. Bluetooth technology is split into two categories: Bluetooth Classic (i.e. Bluetooth BR/EDR) and Bluetooth LE, with the latter referring to versions 4.2 and higher [21]. The LE standards are designed to reduce power usage and device expenses, which is ideal for IoT and smart devices.

In terms of security, Bluetooth employs a variety of security methods and modes. In this technology, the most important mechanisms for establishing safe communication are pairing (generating shared secret keys), bonding (preserving the shared secret keys for future communication), device authentication (ensuring the keys on both devices are the same), encryption (ensuring message confidentiality), and message integrity (protecting unauthorized modification of the messages).

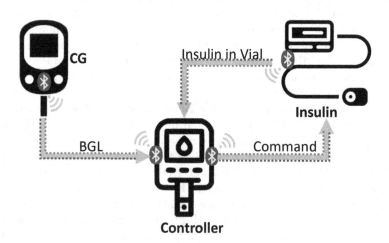

Fig. 1. OpenAPS architecture using Bluetooth and ADHOC WIFI

Furthermore, the LE supports two security modes, each with a different level of security: mode 1 (with levels no security, unauthenticated pairing with encryption, authenticated pairing with encryption, and authenticated LE Secure Connections pairing with encryption) and mode 2 (with levels unauthenticated pairing with data signing and authenticated pairing with data signing). Aside from these two modes, a device may utilize a mixed security mode that combines mode 1 and mode 2, whereas a device that predominantly works in Secure Connections Only mode employs security mode 1 level 4.

2.2   The Protocol Stack

The Bluetooth LE protocol stack contains various protocols that belong to three main parts: Application layer, Host layer, and Controller layer [21]. While the application layer is in charge of application logic, user interface and other administrative issues, the Host layer and the controller layer perform the core part of the communication process with different protocols operating in them. Figure 2 shows this protocol stack.

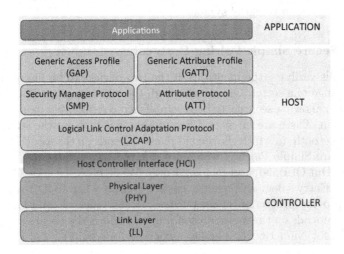

Fig. 2. Bluetooth protocol stack

The Host layer contains five essential protocols. The first of these protocols is the Generic Access Profile (GAP) that delivers standard format requirements for user interface-accessible parameters and specifies the generic processes for discovering and managing Bluetooth peers and connection control, respectively. The Generic Attribute Profile (GATT), on the other hand, outlines the methods, forms, and characteristics of services. It specifies the processes for discovering Services, Characteristics, and Descriptors, while it is divided into two roles: GATT client and GATT server. The third protocol, Attribute Protocol (ATT), establishes a Client/Server architecture and enables a GATT Server to disclose a collection of attributes and the values associated with them to a peer device (the GATT Client). The Security Manager Protocol (SMP) manages and specifies activities related to the security of the Bluetooth communication, among which encryption, pairing and authentication are the most important. The final protocol in the Host layer is the Logical Link Layer Adaptation Protocol (L2CAP). L2CAP supports higher layer protocols with connection-oriented and connectionless data services, as well as protocol multiplexing, segmentation and reassembly (SAR) operations.

The Host Controller Interface (HCI) connects the Host and Controller layers. It provides unvarying interface to retrieve different features of a Bluetooth Controller. It is mainly implemented to transmit instructions and events between the host and controller components of the Bluetooth protocol stack. The two protocols in the Controller layer are the Link Layer (LL) and Physical Layer (PHY). The former protocol manages the physical low energy associates between Bluetooth peers while realizing all the crucial functionalities of link layer such as Encryption and connection and channel update. The latter protocol manages procedures including multiple physical layer activities such as analog communications, analog signal modulation and demodulation, and source coding to convert the signals into digital symbols.

2.3 The Secure Simple Pairing Protocol

Pairing entails verifying the identities of the two devices to be linked, typically by the exchange of a secret. Once authorized, the link is encrypted and keys are disseminated, allowing security to be reestablished considerably more rapidly on a reconnection. There are in general five phases that makeup the secure simple paring in Bluetooth, in which the second phase depends on the association model used by Secure Simple Pairing, which are referred to as Numeric Comparison, Just Works, Out Of Band, and Passkey Entry. While both Numeric Comparison and Passkey Entry safeguards against passive attacks when ECDH is used, only the latter provide protection against active attacks such as MITM. The final association depends on the method used. Figure 3 shows the Secure Simple Pairing Protocol for Numeric Comparison association model [21], and the protocol is described as follows.

(1) There are different protocols that are proposed to assist the pairing process of the Bluetooth communication protocol [10,11,18,22]. For the sake of uniformity, however, we follow the official specification of the Bluetooth system [21] to describe the pairing protocol. Phase 1 of the simple secure paring is used to exchange public keys of the initiator I and the responder R. Here each of them first generate the Elliptic Curve Diffie-Hellman (ECDH) public-private key pair and the I initiates the phase by sending its public key. The R computes the shared secret key (DH_{Key}) and also sends its public key for I to compute the shared secret. The type of elliptic curve used by them depends on whether both devices enable Secure Connections (P-256) or at least one supports Secure Connections (P-192).

(2) Considering the Numeric Comparison association mode, the second phase begins when each device chooses a 128-bit random nonce (n_I and n_R) to thwart against replay attacks. R then computes the commitment C_R and send it to I to protect the communication from modification. Next, both devices exchange their respective nonce values and I checks the validity of the received commitment value. In the case where the verification fails, the protocol aborts. If not, both devices compute 6-digit confirmation values (V_I and V_R) that are displayed to the user on their respective devices. Unmatched values also make the protocol abort. This concludes the 'Authentication-I' phase of the pairing protocol.

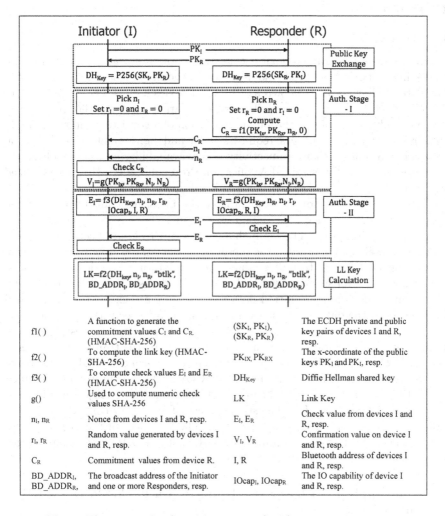

Fig. 3. The secure simple pairing protocol with numeric comparison

(3) The 'Authentication-II' phase begins right after the successful completion of the previous stage. Here, each device computes a new confirmation value that includes the previously exchanged values and the newly derived shared key (E_I and E_R). I then transmits its confirmation value to R (and vice-versa), where both devices check the correctness of the check values. If either or both checks fail, the protocol aborts.

(4) Once both sides have confirmed the pairing, a link key is computed from the derived shared key and the publicly exchanged data. The nonce values ensure the freshness of the key even if long-term ECDH values are used by both sides. This link key is used to maintain the pairing.

3   EDHOC

3.1   Overview

IoT are severely constrained devices concerning power, storage, communication, processing and other essential resources, which should almost always be assisted with intermediary devices known as Proxies. Proxies are critical components of the IoT network to ease connectivity across disparate networks allowing a range of services like protocol translation and provision of a consistent interface [5,23]. Such resource hungry devices require special and lightweight communication protocols that enable them connectivity in low availability and bandwidth. One such protocol is the Constrained Application Protocol (CoAP) [16], a specialized web transfer protocol for use with constrained nodes and networks.

To form a security context and protect the messages transmitted between CoAP enabled IoT devices, the datagram transport layer security (DTLS) protocol [14] is mainly used. The main challenge with this kind of setup is, despite CoAP's capability to operate in the presence of proxies, the ciphered CoAP messages using DTLS need to be terminated at the intermediate devices. That is, using transport layer security like (D)TLS fails to address an end-to-end security, which can expose the transmitted data to a range of attacks as the proxies will have access to the data [7]. Besides the transport layer security, a similar issue can happen when using a lower layer (such as IP security) key establishment mechanisms [13]. To address the limitation imposed by the transport layer security, IETF has standardized an application layer protocol called Object Security for Constrained RESTful Environments (OSCORE) [8]. The protocol is designed to be utilized in IoT-constrained contexts by utilizing CBOR object signing and encryption (COSE) [15]. For the establishment of a security context, OSCORE requires the use of a key exchange protocol. The last piece of the puzzle in protecting the CoAP messages through OSCORE is the EDHOC [9], a lightweight authenticated key establishment protocol.

3.2   The Application Layer IoT Protocol Stack: CoAP, OSCORE and EDHOC

CoAP, as an application layer protocol, primarily aims to provide a general web protocol for the unique needs of resource hungry IoT devices to communicate efficiently despite their limited processing, storage, communication and energy. CoAP targets to deliver a subgroup of REST that is similar to HTTP but optimized for IoT applications. The protocol can serve to enable communication concerning devices that are both resource constrained and operate in the same network, between any general internet node and an IoT device, or among devices with different IoT environments. The core features of CoAP, according to IETF RFC 7252 [16], web protocols capable of meeting M2M needs in restricted environments; UDP based communication that can support reliability; asynchronous communication between the initiator and responder using the protocol; total lower overhead regarding message header and computation; ability to a seamless processing in proxy and caching enabled communication; and a stateless HTTP mapping that enables the construction of proxies that provide consistent access to different CoAP assets.

In serving as an alternative HTTP protocol for IoT devices, CoAP supports different kinds of messages [16]. The first one is confirmable messages where the underlying communication requires an acknowledgment. When this type is used, each message generates precisely one acknowledgment for non-lost packets. The reception of confirmable messages is confirmed by an acknowledgment message although such messages don't indicate success or failure of requests contained in the confirmable messages. Other types of communication that don't require acknowledgment, such as frequent sensor reading, can use a message type called non-confirmable messages. The final type of message is a reset message that is used to specify a situation that requires additional context to fully handle the received confirmable or non-confirmable messages.

Using proxies in communications involving IoT can enhance efficiency and scalability. The CoAP itself acknowledges the utilization of these intermediate results while assuming security through DTLS. The main challenge of using transport layer security, however, is the requirement of the protocols to terminate at the intermediate devices. This in turn brings a security problem as the proxies can now have access to the sensitive information passing through them. Especially in case of a malicious proxy or one that is controlled by an adversary, a range of attacks from simple passive eavesdropping to modification and deletion can happen [8].

A more secure and efficient mechanism to protect CoAP messages is to leverage an application layer protocol called OSCORE. The protocol is designed to provide an end-to-end security between any communicating nodes despite the presence of proxies. Moreover, it can be used by either UDP or TCP or even with non-IP transport [8]. The main requirement for OSCORE security context is that the Initiator and the responder need to exchange keys and other keying materials in a secure fashion. Once such keys are exchanged and confirmed by both ends, it uses an authenticated encryption together with CBOR object signing and encryption.

As mentioned in the previous paragraph, OSCORE needs to establish a security context that requires to generate cryptographic materials while exchanging keys securely. One such protocol that is in the process of standardization by

IETF is the EDHOC protocol. EDHOC is envisioned to operate in constrained environments and serve to establish an OSCORE security context by reusing COSE for cryptography, CBOR for encoding, and CoAP for communication [9]. The protocol is a family of SIGMA-I and provide a lightweight authenticated key establishment between any two communicating devices. In doing so, EDHOC claims to provide important security requirements such as identity protection, perfect forward secrecy and cryptographic material negotiation. Moreover, the protocol assists devices to authenticate through certificates or raw public keys.

3.3   The Protocol

The execution of EDHOC protocol is described as follows. The message flows in the protocol are also shown in Fig. 4.

(1) Before the Initiator sends the first message, it selects the connection identifier C_I and method of authentication from [0 = (Signature Key, Signature key), 1 = (Signature Key, Static DH Key), 2 = (Static DH Key, Signature key), 3 = (Static DH Key, Static DH Key)] for (Initiator, Responder) respectively. It also selects the correlation mechanisms provided by the transport path and compute MR as $4 * Method + Corr$. Next, it selects the list of preferred cipher suites and assign it to $SUITES\_I$. It then generate the ECDHE private and public keys, and compose $Message\_1$ as $\{MR, SUITES\_I, G\_X, C\_I, AD\_1\}$, where it can optionally include associated data AD_1 for external authorization.

(2) The Responder, receiving $Message\_2$, first gets the $Method$ and $Corr$ using $Method = MR/4$ and $Corr = MR \% 4$, respectively. It then chooses a connection identifier C_R, generates the ECDHE private-public key pair, and compute the ECDHE shared key G_XY. Next it computes the transcript hash TH_2 to correlate the initial message with the connection identifiers and the Responder's ephemeral public key, thereby protecting the second message. The Responder then computes the symmetric encryption key K_2 (derived from the shared secret established with the ephemeral Diffie-Hellman exchange) to encrypt the ID_CRED_R, the signed $CRED\_R$ and TH_2 together with AD_2. It then sends $Message\_2$ containing $data\_2$ and the ciphertext CT_2.

(3) The Initiator primarily computes the ECDHE shared key G_XY to compute the Pseudo Random Key PRK, which is then used to calculate the key K_2 to decrypt the CT_2 received from the Responder. It then checks for the validity of TH_2 and if so, it computes the transaction hash TH_3 as $H(H(TH\_2, CT\_2), data\_2)$. Next, it computes the symmetric encryption key K_3 that is derived from the shared secret established with the ephemeral Diffie-Hellman exchange. Subsequently, the Initiator uses this key to encrypt the ID_CRED_I, the signed $CRED\_I$ and TH_3 together with AD_3 and assigns the cipher to CT_3. It then constructs $Message\_3$ as $\{data\_3, CT\_3\}$ and send it to the Responder. This concludes the EDHOC key exchange, where both Initiator and Responder agrees on a key that will be used to protect the subsequent messages.

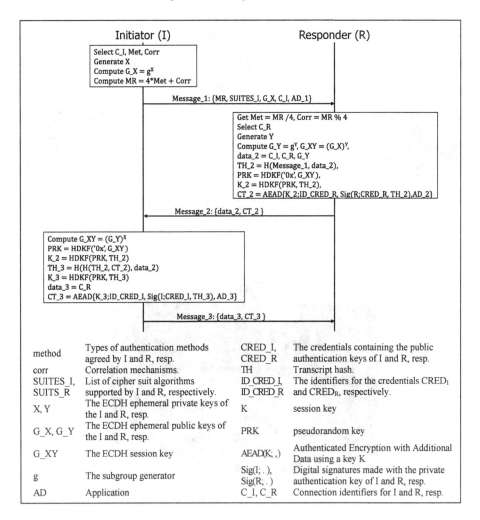

Fig. 4. EDHOC protocol

4 Experimental Analysis of the Bluetooth LE and EDHOC Protocols

In this section, we describe the experiment we carried out in implementing both Bluetooth LE and EDHOC protocols to securely exchange a key between tripartite communication between the CGM, Controller, and Insulin Pump. Accordingly, Fig. 5 and Fig. 6 show the block diagram and actual experimental setups of the APS, respectively, and Table 1 shows the specification of the software and hardware we used. In particular, there will be two sessions for each protocol between the three IoT devices. For instance, for EDHOC protocol, the first session will be between the CGM (as Initiator) and Controller (as Respon-

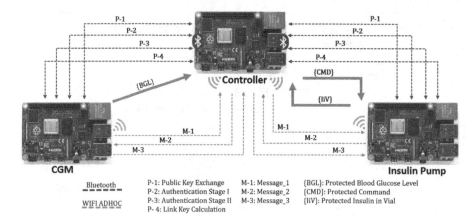

Bluetooth	P-1: Public Key Exchange	M-1: Message_1	{BGL}: Protected Blood Glucose Level
WIFI ADHOC	P-2: Authentication Stage I	M-2: Message_2	{CMD}: Protected Command
	P-3: Authentication Stage II	M-3: Message_3	{IiV}: Protected Insulin in Vial
	P-4: Link Key Calculation		

Fig. 5. Block diagram for the experimental environment

Fig. 6. Experimental environment setup

Table 1. Specification of the experimental environment.

Parts	Specification
OS	Linux kernel 5.10.17
Programming language	Python 3.7
CPU type/speed	ARM Cortex-A53 1.5 GHz
RAM size	1 GB
SD-card size	16 GB
Integrated Wi-Fi	2.4 GHz and 5 GHz
Bluetooth	4.2/BLE

der) and between the Insulin Pump (as Responder) and the Controller (as Initiator). Once these setups for both protocols are established and each of the Raspberry PI devices are installed with the EDHOC and Bluetooth LE pairing algorithms, we measured the performance of each device concerning protocol execution latency, transmission cost, and total round-trip time as shown in Fig. 7. In addition, Table 2 shows various cryptographic schemes used by each protocol. The results from performance comparison depicts that the protocol execution time and transmission cost for EDHOC is higher owing to the use of digital signature. On the other hand, EDHOC improves the round-trip time by around 133%. Despite the significant difference in transmission cost and round-trip time, the protocol execution time for both protocols is roughly similar.

Table 2. Comparison between Bluetooth LE and EDHOC

Cryptographic schemes	Bluetooth LE	EDHOC
Asymmetric encryption	NO	NO
Digital signature	NO	YES
HMAC/Hash	YES	YES
Symmetric encryption	NO	YES

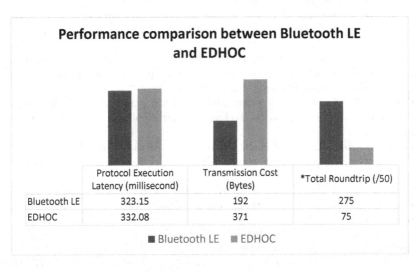

Performance comparison between Bluetooth LE and EDHOC

	Protocol Execution Latency (millisecond)	Transmission Cost (Bytes)	*Total Roundtrip (/50)
Bluetooth LE	323.15	192	275
EDHOC	332.08	371	75

■ Bluetooth LE   ■ EDHOC

Fig. 7. Performance comparison between Bluetooth LE and EDHOC.

5   Conclusion

In this paper, we have studied two essential protocols - the Bluetooth LE and EDHOC. While the former is a well known protocol that has been used for over two decades. The latter, introduced in 2016 and in process of standardization, is a promising lightweight authenticated key exchange protocol intentionally designed for IoT. Despite their various differences, many medical IoT devices use the Bluetooth LE protocol to transport sensitive medical information. Consequently, we performed an experimental analysis to compare these protocols concerning different performance metrics such as protocol execution time, transmission cost, and total round-trip time. To do so, we implemented both protocols in the Rasberry PI with specification shown in Table 1. As a result, while the Bluetooth protocol showed better performance with regard to transmission cost, the EDHOC protocol provided an improved round-trip time. Regardless, both protocols showed a roughly similar execution time. As a future work, we would like to further analyze how these two protocols can be combined to bring a highly resilient key exchange scheme with a through analysis of security in the implementation of APS.

References

1. Alizadeh, M., Andersson, K., Schelén, O.: A survey of secure internet of things in relation to blockchain. J. Internet Serv. Inf. Secur. (JISIS) **10**(3), 47–75 (2020)
2. Angin, P., Anisi, M.H., Göksel, F., Gürsoy, C., Büyükgülcü, A.: AgriLoRa: a digital twin framework for smart agriculture. J. Wirel. Mob. Netw. Ubiquit. Comput. Dependable Appl. **11**(4), 77–96 (2020)
3. Bembenik, R., Falcman, K.: BLE indoor positioning system using RSSI-based trilateration. J. Wirel. Mob. Netw. Ubiquit. Comput. Dependable Appl. **11**(3), 50–69 (2020)
4. Caputo, D., Verderame, L., Ranieri, A., Merlo, A., Caviglione, L.: Fine-hearing google home: why silence will not protect your privacy. J. Wirel. Mob. Netw. Ubiquit. Comput. Dependable Appl. **11**(1), 35–53 (2020)
5. Chen, H., Jia, X., Li, H.: A brief introduction to IoT gateway. In: IET International Conference on Communication Technology and Application (ICCTA 2011), pp. 610–613. IET (2011)
6. Daniel, D.: Advantages and challenges of the internet of things (IoT) in healthcare (2019). https://y-sbm.com/blog/internet-of-things-in-helthcare. Accessed 05 Aug 2021
7. G. Selander, F.P., Hartke, K.: Requirements for CoAP end-to-end security, July 2017. http://www.ietf.org/internet-drafts/draft-hartke-coreee2e-security-reqs-03.txt
8. G. Selander, J. Mattsson, F.P., Seitz, L.: Object security for constrained restful environments (oscore), July 2019. https://tools.ietf.org/html/rfc8613
9. G. Selander, J.M., Palombini, F.: Ephemeral Diffie-Hellman over COSE (EDHOC) (2019). https://datatracker.ietf.org/doc/draft-selander-lake-edhoc/
10. Gajbhiye, S., Karmakar, S., Sharma, M., Sharma, S.: Two-party secure connection in bluetooth-enabled devices. Inf. Secur. J.: Glob. Perspect. **27**(1), 42–56 (2018)
11. Gajbhiye, S., Sharma, M., Karmkar, S., Sharma, S.: Design, implementation and security analysis of bluetooth pairing protocol in NS2. In: 2016 International Conference on Advances in Computing, Communications and Informatics (ICACCI), pp. 1711–1717. IEEE (2016)

12. World Health Oganizationi: Diabete (2020). https://www.who.int/newsroom/fact-sheets/detail/diabetes. Accessed 05 Aug 2021
13. Pérez, S., Hernández-Ramos, J.L., Raza, S., Skarmeta, A.: Application layer key establishment for end-to-end security in IoT. IEEE Internet Things J. **7**(3), 2117–2128 (2019)
14. Rescorla, E., Modadugu, N.: Datagram transport layer security version 1.2 (2012)
15. Schaad, J.: Cbor object signing and encryption (COSE), July 2017. https://tools.ietf.org/html/rfc8152
16. Shelby, Z., Hartke, K., Bormann, C.: The constrained application protocol (CoAP) (2014)
17. Shichkina, Y.A., Kataeva, G.V., Irishina, Y.A., Stanevich, E.S.: The use of mobile phones to monitor the status of patients with parkinson's disease. J. Wirel. Mob. Netw. Ubiquit. Comput. Dependable Appl. **11**(2), 55–73 (2020)
18. Sun, D.Z., Sun, L.: On secure simple pairing in bluetooth standard v5. 0-part i: authenticated link key security and its home automation and entertainment applications. Sensors **19**(5), 1158 (2019)
19. Wong, S.K., Yiu, S.M.: Identification of device motion status via bluetooth discovery. J. Internet Serv. Inf. Secur. **10**(4), 59–69 (2020)
20. Wong, S.K., Yiu, S.M.: Location spoofing attack detection with pre-installed sensors in mobile devices. J. Wirel. Mob. Netw. Ubiquit. Comput. Dependable Appl. **11**(4), 16–30 (2020)
21. Woolley, M.: Bluetooth core specification v5. In: Bluetooth (2019)
22. Yeh, T.C., Peng, J.R., Wang, S.S., Hsu, J.P.: Securing bluetooth communications. Int. J. Netw. Secur. **14**(4), 229–235 (2012)
23. Zhong, C.L., Zhu, Z., Huang, R.G.: Study on the iot architecture and gateway technology. In: 2015 14th International Symposium on Distributed Computing and Applications for Business Engineering and Science (DCABES), pp. 196–199. IEEE (2015)

A Credible Information Fusion Method Based on Cascaded Topology Interactive Traceability

Yueqing Gao[1,2], Yuting Shen[2,3,4(✉)], Huachun Zhou[1], Benhui Shi[2],
Lulu Chen[2,5], and Chu Du[2]

[1] Beijing Jiaotong University, Beijing 100044, China
{18111069,hchzhou}@bjtu.edu.cn
[2] The 54th Research Institute of China Electronics Technology Group Corporation,
Shijiazhuang 050000, China
[3] National Space Science Center, Chinese Academy of Sciences,
Beijing 100190, China
[4] University of Chinese Academy of Sciences, Beijing 100039, China
rebeccashenstudy@yeah.net
[5] Center for Future Multimedia and School of Computer Science and Engineering,
University of Electronic Science and Technology of China, Chengdu 610051, China

Abstract. With the increasing scope of distributed system collaboration and the increasing number of participants, how to establish mutual trust in the process of collaboration is an important basis to promote the efficiency of collaboration. A feasible method is to abstract each node of distributed system into network node of complex system to study its interaction and cooperation behavior. Aiming at the problem of trust transmission in the process of information exchange between complex network nodes, this paper proposed a credible information fusion method based on cascaded topology interactive traceability by abstraction of an information fusion and trust model on account of interactive behavior. This method uses local interaction behavior of blockchain traceability methods provide a credible witness local information interaction, through the information credibility evaluation method in specified cascade topology, from the two aspects of information centrality and information similarity. Thus, the credible information fusion formula for the interactive traceability of the domain topology would constructed. At the same time, this paper discusses the typical problems encountered in the adaptive transformation of the existing operating system for blockchain application. Constructive suggestions are put forward for the phased development of combining blockchain with existing systems.

Keywords: Distributed system collaboration · Complex networks · Blockchain · Information fusion · Cascading topology · Credibility assessment

© Springer Nature Singapore Pte Ltd. 2022
I. You et al. (Eds.): MobiSec 2021, CCIS 1544, pp. 44–51, 2022.
https://doi.org/10.1007/978-981-16-9576-6_4

1   Introduction

Any system node existing in collaborative distributed system would received all kinds of information from neighbor system nodes in real time, performed corresponding treating processes, produced certain behaviors, and at the same time broadcasted output messages to its neighbor system nodes. This process in which each node measured the confidence of neighbor information to adopt and disseminate it twice is essentially the disseminative process of data trust between each system node according to the information fusion links. Therefore, there are two main problems in the spread of trust in the network of collaborative distributed system between disseminators. Which comes to the first is how to document the behavior of information interactions so as to provide effective historical records for the evaluation of information confidence. Secondly, the remaining main problem is how to assess the adoptions of information interactions content and how to analyze and obtain comprehensive measurement on the complexity of the network structure, the complexity of the nodes, the interaction between the structure and the nodes, etc. In response to the first problem, blockchain - as a distributed collaborative technology - can build data storage evidence that is difficult to tamper with based on consensus. Accordingly, this evidence can provide reliable historical traceability information about the interactive behavior occurred in networks and provide a credible basis for information dissemination link analysis. For the second question, the influence of the dynamic link relationship between nodes on the information dissemination can be used to characterize the degree of influence of the information exchange content dispersed on the network. For this purpose, researchers developed the group degree centralization and centralized modeling [1], the betweenness centrality measurement based on the number of hops [2], SLPA algorithm based on K-shell decomposition [3], network analysis model based on eigen-vector centrality fusion node data and topology information [4], etc. Nodes similarity assessment and link analysis can help discern the propagation paths from identification information and reduce the risk of repeated acceptance. All these methods can be divided into similarity evaluation based on local information, similarity evaluation based on global information, and similarity evaluation based on random walk, such as cosine similarity [5], local naive Bayes method [6], mutual information method[7], local relative entropy method [8], Katz index [9], local path algorithm (LocalPath, LP), maximum entropy random walk method (maximal entropy random walk, MERW) [10] and similarity measures based on distance distribution.

2   Information Credibility Evaluation Method Based on Cascading Topology

According to the analysis of actual network experimental data [11], in order to balance calculation efficiency and data validity, the link hop count ($Hop_{threshold}$)

of the neighborhood should make into a division of direct evaluation and extended indirect evaluation. Therefore, based on our previous work, this paper proposed an information credibility evaluation method based on cascading topology. The credibility evaluation will integrate two aspects of information centrality ($E_{Local_T A X_i}$) and nodes similarity ($S_{Local_T A X_i}$). Specifically, information centrality reflects the importance of each node in the network and positively correlated with credibility. While nodes similarity reflects the degree of relevance to the path of information dissemination by each node in the network and positively related to the probability of information redundancy and repetition.

$$C_{Local_T A X_i} = \frac{\frac{\gamma_1 * E_{Local_T A X_i}}{\gamma_2 * S_{Local_T A X_i}}}{\sum_{j \in \Gamma_X(t)} C_{Local_T A X_i}} \tag{1}$$

Taking any node A_{ICE-X} as an example, the cascading topology information centrality evaluation $E_{Local_T A X_i}$ of neighboring nodes A_{ICE-i} in A_{ICE-X} immediate neighborhood is defined as follows

$$E_{Local_T A X_i} = \alpha_1 * C_{D X_i} + \alpha_2 C_{I X_i} \tag{2}$$

Among them, α_1 sum α_2 is the adjustment coefficient; $C_{D X_i}$ is the evaluation value of the cascading information aggregation ability of a node A_{ICE-i} in A_{ICE-X} immediate neighborhood and its associated expanded neighborhood. $C_{I X_i}$ is used in order to evaluate the intimacy based on topology and interaction behavior, which only calculated the intimacy between each node in the immediate neighborhood and the central node based on the topological relationship and the interaction frequency per unit time.

$$C_{D X_i} = C_{D_N DR X_i} * C_{D_{ENIR} X_i} = \frac{k_i}{\sum_{u \in \Gamma_X(t)} k_u} * \mu \sum k_j \tag{3}$$

$$C_{I X_i} = \beta_1 C_{I_T X_i} + \beta_2 C_{I_I X_i} \tag{4}$$

$$C_{I_T X_i} = \frac{\Gamma_X(t) \cap \Gamma_i(t)}{\{\Gamma_X(t) \cup \Gamma_i(t)\} - 1} + 1 \tag{5}$$

$$C_{I_I X_i} = \frac{1}{f_{X_i} - 1} \sum_{n=1}^{f_{X_i}} t_n - t_{n-1} \tag{6}$$

$C_{D_N DR X_i}$ is the normalized neighborhood degree centrality evaluation value of one-hop neighbors A_{ICE-i} in A_{ICE-X} immediate neighborhood. $C_{D_{ENIR} X_i}$ is the evaluation value of the extended degree centrality of the one-hop neighbor node A_{ICE-i} in the cascade neighborhood, where $A_{ICE-j} : (A_{ICE-j}, A_{ICE-i}) \in E_{ICE}$, $A_{ICE-j} \neq A_{ICE-X}$, and μ is used to adjust the influence of the extended neighborhood degree centrality evaluation on the cascade evaluation. $C_{I X_i}$ is the evaluation value of the intimacy between neighbor nodes A_{ICE-i} in A_{ICE-X}

immediate neighborhood of any node, where $C_{I_T X_i}$ is the topological intimacy of A_{ICE-X} and A_{ICE-i}, $C_{I_I X_i}$ is the intimacy of the interaction frequency between them. β_1 and β_2 is the adjustment coefficient. $\Gamma_i(t)$ is the set of A_{ICE-i} neighbor nodes at the moment t. f_{X_i} is the total number of current information exchanges between each other. t_n is the nth information exchange. Taking any node A_{ICE-X} as an example, the cascaded common neighbor similarity distribution index of neighboring nodes A_{ICE-i} in A_{ICE-X} immediate neighborhood is $S_{Local_T A X_i}$. Topological similarity between nodes can be characterized by the number of common neighbors of two nodes. Thus, the similarity distribution index is the average of the topological similarities between nodes in the neighborhood to characterize the comparability of the information transmitted by the information exchange processes in the neighborhood. The average similarity index of one-hop neighbor nodes A_{ICE-i} in the immediate neighborhood of the node A_{ICE-X} is

$$\left(S_{Local_T A X_i}\right)_{Hop_1} = \frac{\sum_{j\in\Gamma_X(t),j\neq i} s_{ij}}{\sum_{j\in A_{ICE}} \lessdot[(i,j)\in E_{ICE}]} \tag{7}$$

$$\left(S_{Local_T A X_i}\right)_{Hop_1} = \frac{\sum_{j\in\Gamma_X(t),j\neq i} |\Gamma_i(t)\cap\Gamma_j(t)|}{\sum_{j\in A_{ICE}} \lessdot[(i,j)\in E_{ICE}]} \tag{8}$$

After cascading the expanded neighborhood, the average similarity index set of the expanded neighborhood of one-hop neighbor nodes A_{ICE-i} is

$$\left(S_{Local_T A X_i}\right)_{Hop_2} = \left\{\left(S_{Local_T A i_w}\right)_{Hop_1}\middle| w\in\Gamma_i(t), w\neq X\right\} \tag{9}$$

Then after normalization, the similarity distribution index of one-hop neighbor nodes A_{ICE-i} in A_{ICE-X} immediate neighborhood is

$$S_{Local_T A X_i} = \frac{\sum_{w\in\Gamma_i(t),w\neq X} \left(S_{Local_T A X_i}\right)_{Hop_1} * \left(S_{Local_T A X_i}\right)_{Hop_2}}{\sum_{j\in\Gamma_X(t)} S_{Local_T A X_j}} \tag{10}$$

3   Credible Information Fusion Method Based on Cascaded Topology Interactive Traceability

In the processes of information interactions, the metadata information in the processes of information transfer is abstracted into quad and be stored. When observation information fusion is performed at each step, each node retrievals and extracts topological interaction process data within the cascaded neighborhood from the blockchain, and performs information fusion based on the method described in Sect. 2. The schematic diagram of the specific process is shown in the Fig. 1. The algorithm design is detailed below.

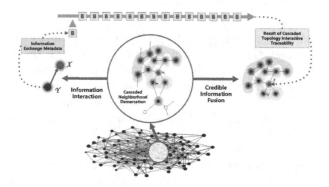

Fig. 1. Schematic diagram of credible information fusion method based on cascaded topology interactive traceability

3.1 A Blockchain-Based Approach of Recording and Tracing Interaction Behavior

To evaluate the credibility of each node purely from topological structure and interactive statistical analysis, it lacks the content-centric link impact analysis in the processes of information interaction. At the same time, a large amount of information interactions only relies on partial records, which is vulnerable to network intrusion and malicious tampering, thereby reducing the credibility of information fusion. The method of relying on blockchain as the sole record and basis of information interactions can effectively solve the above prob-lems. In the design of this paper, each source node and sink node participating in the inter-action do not act as the consensus node of the blockchain, but only trigger the execution of the deposit contract during the information interaction. The information sink node would extract metadata of the interaction and package it for storage. Therefore, according to the frequency of information interactions and the amount of data in the actual application processes, the appropriate consensus algorithm should be selected and construct the blockchain consensus layer. Thence, in the process of information interaction, the information interaction metadata IIM can be constructed and defined, including information source, information sink, interaction time, and interaction content. Taking the interaction content $I_{X \leftarrow n}(t)$ from n to X at time t as an example, the information interaction metadata is

$$IIM_{X \leftarrow n}(t) = n, X, t, I_{X \leftarrow n}(t) \tag{11}$$

Taking a node A_{ICE-X} as an example, $I_X(t)$ is the total set of observation information it holds at the moment t, M is the total dimensional set of the current observation information, then there is

$$I_X(t) = \{I_{X\_D_m}(t) \mid m \in M\} \tag{12}$$

$$I_{X\_D_m}(t) = \{I_{X \leftarrow N}(t) \mid N = \{A_{ICE-n} \mid I_{X \leftarrow n}(t) \in I_{X\_D_m}(t)\}\} \tag{13}$$

When a node A_{ICE-X} performs observation information fusion, it uses its first-order neighbor node and itself as the sink respectively, and jointly queries the information exchange metadata stored on the chain to construct $Set\_Nh_X(t)$ - a cascaded neighborhood set of dimensional observation information, where $Nh_{X\_D_m}(t)$ is the set of neighboring nodes to be evaluated of the dimension m of A_{ICE-X} observation information at time t.

$$Set\_Nh_X(t) = \{Nh_{X\_D_m}(t) \,|\, m \in M\} \tag{14}$$

$$i \in (\Gamma_{X_H op1}(t) \cup \Gamma_{X_H op2}(t)) \,\forall A_{ICE-i} \in Nh_{X\_D_m}(t) \tag{15}$$

3.2 Algorithm Design of Credible Information Fusion Method Based on Cascaded Topology Interactive Traceability

This paper proposed a trusted information fusion method based on neighborhood topology interactive traceability. In the processes of information sending and receiving, source, sink, interaction time, interaction content and other information are stored. When any node is in the process of information fusion, the range of cascaded neighborhoods is determined according to the propagation links of different interactive content, and the credibility of the information on the cascading topology is evaluated. The evaluation results would be used as the basis for acceptance from different links. (Flow chart of credible information fusion method based on cascaded topology interactive traceability is visible in the Fig. 2 respectively). After the trusted information fusion based on the neighbor topology interaction traceability for the total set of observation information $I_X(t)$ held by the node A_{ICE-X} at time t, the credible fusion information set $I_{CF_X}(t)$ of the node A_{ICE-X} at the time t can be obtained, where $I_{CF\_X\_D_m}(t)$ is the traceability and credible fusion formula on neighborhood topology interactions taking the mth dimension information individually.

$$I_{CF_X}(t) = \{I_{CF\_X\_D_m}(t) \,|\, m \in M\} \tag{16}$$

$$I_{CF\_X_{D_m}}(t) = \sum_{i \in Nh_{X\_D_m}(t)} \frac{C_{Local_T A X_i}}{\sum_{u \in Nh_{X\_D_m}(t)} C_{Local_T A X_u}} I_{CF\_i\_D_m}(t) \tag{17}$$

4 Application Scenario and Existing Problems

The credible information fusion method based on neighborhood topology interactive traceability can be applied to complex collaborative scenarios such as bee colony detection and cross-group multi-node collaboration. In the process of cross-group multi-node cooperation, the mutual trust among nodes within each group decreases, and the risk of node evil increases. Therefore, cross-group node credit and node interaction can be traced based on blockchain. However, there remains a certain separation between the process of consensus and information

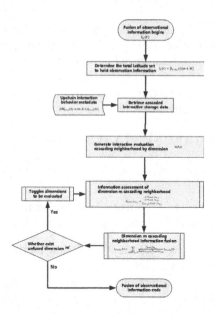

Fig. 2. Flow chart of node A_{ICE-X} observation information fusion at time t

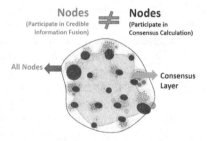

Fig. 3. Abridged general view of certain separation in application.

exchange between nodes of complex network in the process of preservation and traceability of blockchain described in the present paper. Under the condition that consensus efficiency and traceability efficiency meet the demand of peak frequency of information exchange, the two parties do not affect each other. (Abridged general view of application scenario See Fig. 3) Rationality of the Value Owners (RVO) and Value Centric Blockchains (VCBs) are defined based on the standardization and summarize of Ren et al. [12], which key elements are values and their ownership. VCBs' principles are similar to the process rationality characteristics of information interactions mentioned in this paper, including the rationality of data holding and the rationality of data flow. For the sake of facilitating the liquidity in networks, further researches are needed to take all source and destination nodes as consensus nodes to realize in-depth integration between topological structure and interaction characteristics of networks and the fragment consensus of blockchain.

5 Conclusion and Prospect

In order to enhance authentic collaboration in distributed system, this paper proposed a credible information fusion method based on cascaded topology interactive traceability by abstraction of an information fusion and trust model on account of interactive behavior. This method uses local interaction behavior of blockchain traceability methods provide a credible witness local information interaction, through the information credibility evaluation method in specified cascade topology, from the two aspects of information centrality and information similarity. Information interaction based on complex network is an effective means to study the behavior characteristics and evolution process of crowd and community. Researches on multi-node information storage, integration and transmission based on complex network can provide effective support for mobile network load balancing, network behavior survey and anomaly detection, key scope and target monitoring, etc.

References

1. Krnc, M., Škrekovski, R.: Group degree centrality and centralization in networks. Mathematics **8**(10), 1810 (2020)
2. Samad, A., Qadir, M., Nawaz, I., Islam, M.A., Aleem, M.: SAM centrality: a hop-based centrality measure for ranking users in social network. EAI Endorsed Trans. Ind. Netw. Intell. Syst. **7**(23), e2 (2020)
3. Alighanbari, E.B.: An Influence maximization algorithm in social network using K-shell decomposition and community detection. Netw. Biol. **10**(1), 12–23 (2020)
4. Agryzkov, T., Tortosa, L., Vicent, J.F., Wilson, R.: A centrality measure for urban networks based on the eigenvector centrality concept. Environ. Plann. B: Urban Anal. City Sci. **46**(4), 668–689 (2019)
5. Salton, G.: Automatic text analysis. Science **168**(3929), 335–343 (1970)
6. Liu, Z., Zhang, Q.-M., Lü, L., Zhou, T.: Link prediction in complex networks: a local naïve Bayes model. EPL (Europhys. Lett.) **96**(4), 48007 (2011)
7. Tan, F., Xia, Y., Zhu, B.: Link prediction in complex networks: a mutual information perspective. PLoS One **9**(9), e107056 (2014)
8. Zhang, Q., Li, M., Deng, Y.: Measure the structure similarity of nodes in complex networks based on relative entropy. Phys. A: Stat. Mech. Appl. **491**, 749–763 (2018)
9. Katz, L.: A new status index derived from sociometric analysis. Psychometrika **18**, 39–43 (1953)
10. Burda, Z., Duda, J., Luck, J.M., Waclaw, B.: Localization of the maximal entropy random walk. Phys. Rev. Lett. **102**, 160602 (2009)
11. Goyal, A., Lu, W., Lakshmanan, L.V.S.: SIMPATH: an efficient algorithm for influence maximization under the linear threshold model. In: 2011 IEEE 11th International Conference on Data Mining, pp. 211–220. IEEE (2011)
12. Ren, Z., Erkin, Z.: VAPOR: a value-centric blockchain that is scale-out, decentralized, and flexible by design. In: Goldberg, I., Moore, T. (eds.) FC 2019. LNCS, vol. 11598, pp. 487–507. Springer, Cham (2019). https://doi.org/10.1007/978-3-030-32101-7_29

Semantic Embedding-Based Entity Alignment for Cybersecurity Knowledge Graphs

Minhwan Kim[1], Hanmin Kim[1], Gyudong Park[2], and Mye Sohn[1(✉)]

[1] Department of Industrial Engineering, Sungkyunkwan University, Suwon, Korea
{kmh3178,kimhm0705,myesohn}@skku.edu
[2] Agency for Defense Development, Seoul, Korea
iobject@add.re.kr

Abstract. This paper proposes a new framework that can semantically align the two or more entities in cybersecurity-related Knowledge Graphs (KGs) using an external resource. To do so, we identify four main principles that the external resources must have and then use them to analyze various external resources. The resource is used to find sentences that are needed to understand the usage context of the entities. The entity alignment is performed by semantic embedding with BERT. At this time, semantic embedding is defined as a vector that contains the latent semantic features of the sentences only with similar usage context from the external resource encoded with the language model BERT. To identify the sentences with similar usage context, we first classify the informative entities related to the target entities. Using the informative entities, we generate a set of sentences that have used similar usage context. Finally, to predict semantic relationships (equivalence) between the entities, we employ pre-trained BERT with the set of sentences as input. To prove the superiority of the framework, we perform the experiments to evaluate the accuracy of prediction of equivalence of entities from the different KGs.

Keywords: Cybersecurity · Knowledge graph · Entity alignment · Semantic embeddings

1 Introduction

From a data point of view, the key issue in cybersecurity is no longer the lack of available data but the integration of heterogeneous data from multiple sources that are needed to establish countermeasures [1]. In this light, it is essential to maintain the complex, heterogeneous, and ever-changing cybersecurity-related data itself and the relationships between them. In recent, knowledge graph (KG) proposed by Google has received great attention from researchers as a method to represent cybersecurity-related data and the relationships between them [2]. As a result, cybersecurity KGs such as SEPSES and CyGraph have developed [3, 4]. These cybersecurity-related KGs are well-crafted graphs developed using knowledge gathered from several cybersecurity-related data sources. In addition, these are time-dependent, i.e., graphs for a specific point in time. It is difficult

© Springer Nature Singapore Pte Ltd. 2022
I. You et al. (Eds.): MobiSec 2021, CCIS 1544, pp. 52–64, 2022.
https://doi.org/10.1007/978-981-16-9576-6_5

to solve cyberattacks with only KG with a fixed point in time that cannot reflect these changes because new cyberattack methods are constantly appearing, and attack patterns are constantly changing. To solve the problem, many researchers are interested not in developing new KGs that can respond to new attacks but in finding and integrating relevant existing KGs called entity alignment (EA). At this time, the EA is defined as identifying the semantic relationships of the entities, especially equivalence, to integrate two or more KGs.

In recent, KG embedding, which projects the KGs into a low-dimensional space, has been widely used in the EA [5]. Most KG embeddings for the EA are performed entirely using only internal information of the KGs, regardless of whether it uses syntactic or semantic information [6]. As a result, heterogeneity, one of the chronic problems of the KGs, is inherited. In this paper, to avoid the heterogeneity issue, we propose a new EA framework that utilizes semantic information outside the KGs rather than the internal one. Since there are various external resources available for the EA, we first identified the properties that that external resources should have to do the EA for the KGs. Based on the properties, we select the best external resource for the EA. Next, the entity alignment is performed by semantic embedding with BERT. At this time, semantic embedding is defined as a vector that contains the latent semantic features of the sentences only with similar usage context from the external resource encoded with the language model BERT. To identify the sentences with similar usage context, we first classify the informative entities related to the target entities. Using the informative entities, we generate a set of sentences that have used similar usage context.

This paper is organized as follow. In Sect. 2, we identify the properties that the external resource should have and used it to analyze the external resources. Section 3 expresses the overall framework we proposed and its details. Section 4 performs performance evaluation with experiments. Section 5 reviews the related works of the EA and language model. Finally, Sect. 6 presents the conclusions and further research.

2   Analysis of External Resources

As we determined the external resource, we pursued four main principles:

- Coverage: Generally, the KGs are developed domain specific. So, to perform the EA on the KGs, domain knowledge of the KGs to be aligned is necessary. Moreover, to align the KGs of all domains, the external sources must also cover all domains.
- Trustworthy: Even if the EA is performed between two KGs, if the information of the external resource used for this is unreliable, biased, and unfair, no one will trust the EA For the information to be reliable, it must also be possible to evaluate the expertise of its producers [7].
- Completeness: The semantic information is extracted from the sentences in the external resources. In order to extract accurate semantic information, these sentences must be completely included to become the constituent elements of English sentences, such as subject, predicate verb, object, or complement. It is very difficult to find sentences with such a complete structure on SNS.
- Consistency: Regardless of the domains, the relationship between the entities in the KGs should always be constant to some extent.

Although there are several external resources, we select social media, web resources, and research publications that have enough sentences with semantic information and are publicly accessible via the Internet as candidate resources. Table 1 shows the results of comparing the candidate resources based on the above properties.

Table 1. Comparison results of candidate sources

	Coverage	Trustworthy	Completeness	Consistency
Social media	●	X	X	X
Web resources	●	◖	◖	X
Research Publications	●	●	●	●

●: fully satisfied, ◖: partially satisfied, X: unsatisfied

One of the great features of social media is that there are no restrictions on participants and their posts. It means that anyone can become a user of social media and distribute any posts, whether right or wrong or even fake news. In this light, social media has a fatal flaw in trustworthiness. In addition, the social media posts contain lots of slang or emoticons, and the structures of sentences may not be perfect, which leads to low completeness. Web resource has a wide spectrum from blogs to news articles. Broadly, it can include social media posts as well. News articles are highly trustworthy, and completeness, but blogs are websites where someone regularly records their thoughts, experiences, or talks about a subject [8]. This is because someone's thoughts, experiences, or talks about a subject have not gone through the process of evaluation or verification. Finally, research publication is published across all disciplines even multidisciplinary and are written by domain experts and rigorously evaluated by other experts. In this light, research publications are the best option.

3   Overall Framework

The proposed EA framework is consisted of three parts such as Informative Entities Selection Module (IESM), Usage Context Finding Module (UCFM), and BERT-based Pre-training Module (BPM). The IESM receives the knowledge graphs related to cyber-security as input. The overall framework consists of two modules as shown in Fig. 1.

3.1   Degree Centrality-Based Informative Entities Selection

Even though the same entities, their meaning and usage patterns may differ depending on the domain. For example, in mathematics, the function is defined as a binary relationship between two sets that connect each element of the first set with exactly one element of the second, whereas in engineering it is defined as a specific action that a system can perform. It is impossible to perform the EA between two KGs unless their semantic differences are clearly recognizable. One of the methods to recognize the semantic differences of the entities is to understand their usage context in sentences or documents. At this time,

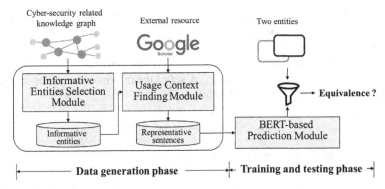

Fig. 1. Overall framework of semantic embedding-based entity alignment

the usage context of the entities can be known by identifying the surrounding entities used with the entities in the sentences or the documents.

In this light, to identify the usage context, it is necessary to find from the KGs a set of entities (hereafter, neighbor entities) that can be used simultaneously with a specific entity (hereafter, target entity) in the sentences or the documents. However, the KGs contain a lot of dummy entities and literals with no information that doesn't help at all to understand the usage context of the target entities. It should be filtered out the dummy entities and literals to understand the usage context appropriately. In order to select only those entities that are highly relevant to the usage context of the target entity, we perform filtering on the objects in the KGs like literal or entities. The filtering rules as simply represented as follows.

> **Rule 1**: IF o_{ij} is a literal
> $\qquad$ THEN Remove o_{ij}
> **Rule 2**: IF o_{ij} does not have property 'rdfs:label'
> $\qquad$ OR o_{ij} does not have property 'rdf:type'
> $\qquad$ THEN Dummy entity $\leftarrow o_{ij}$
> where o_{ij} is an object in j^{th} triple of ith entity e_i.

Even though dummy entities and literals are filtered out by the rules, the KG has too many non-informative entities that don't help us understand the context of their use, i.e., the entities that are unlikely to appear in a sentence at the same time. To remove the non-informative entities, we determine whether the role of the entities in the KG is concepts or instances. To do so, we calculate degree centrality as a criterion for discrimination. Generally, the degree centrality of the entities is calculated using their indegree and outdegree [9], and the larger the indegree of them, the more likely they are the instance, whereas the larger the outdegree, the more likely they are the concept. In the extreme, the top-level concept of the KGs has an outdegree of 0, whereas a leaf instance with no children has an indegree of 0. Based on the properties of the entities, we propose the following degree centrality measure (c_i) as follows.

$$c_i = \lambda \cdot \log\left(1 + \frac{\deg^+(e_i)}{\deg^-(e_i)}\right), i = 1, \ldots, n$$

where e_i is i^{th} entity. $\deg^+(e_i)$ and $\deg^-(e_i)$ are the outdegree and indegree of e_i, respectively. λ is the scale coefficient.

Finally, by removing all entities that are judged to be instance-level entities, that is, entities with c_i is less than or equal to the threshold value τ, we only get the informative entities in terms of the usage context of e_i. A set of the informative entities in terms of the usage context of $e_i(I_{e_i})$ is defined as follows.

$$I_{e_i} = \{\cdots, ie_k, \cdots\}, k \leq n$$

where ie_k is k^{th} informative entity whose $c_k \geq \tau$.

3.2 Spectral Clustering for Finding Usage Context of Entities

To understand the usage context of target entity (te), it is necessary to identify the sentences using elements of $I\_(e\_i)$ from the external resource (a.k.a. research publications). Since the purpose of this paper is the EA of the KGs for cybersecurity, we have restricted research publications to cybersecurity and cybersecurity-related domains. At this time, the understanding of the usage context may be different depending on how many of the elements of $I\_(e\_i)$ are included in the sentences. It means that some sentences may not need to understand the usage context. To remove the useless sentences, we perform step-by-step sentence filtering as follows.

Step 1 Develop the Target Entity-Specific Sentence Base. Using the keyword search, we collect N sentences that contain te and the elements of its informative entities (I_{te}) from cybersecurity-related research publications and develop sentence base of the $te(sb_{te})$. At this time, N is arbitrarily determined. sb_{te} is simply represented as follows.

$$sb_{te} = \{\cdots, s_l, \cdots\}, 1 < l \leq N$$

where s_l is l^{th} sentence including te and the elements of I_{te} ($\{te, ie_k | \forall i, \exists j\} \subset s_l$).

Step 2 Identify a Set of Informative Sentences from sb_{te}. If sentences in sb_{te} contain too few elements of I_{te} are likely to be too general, which is less likely to be related to te. The sentences are too general or useless to understand the context of their use. Therefore, it should be screened useless sentences in the sentence base. To do so, we determine the number of elements of I_{te} that are contained in each sentence needed to understand the context of its use. This paper proposes a method that can derive the number of elements, not the mathematical model but the heuristic method named progressive matching. The process of the progressive matching is described in detail in Fig. 2.

N: total number of sentences in sb_{te}
q: the number of elements in the sentences, $1 \leq q \leq N$
Q: the subset of I_{e_i} where $num(Q) = q$
R: a set of result values of the matching ratio
q^*: appropriate number of elements

for $q = 1$ to N **do**

$$M(q) = N - \frac{|\{s_l | \exists l, Q \subset s_l\}|}{q}$$

$\quad$ R $\leftarrow$insert the value of $M(q)$

$\quad q = q + 1$

endfor

do plot $M(q)$ with ascending order of q on two-dimensional space
find elbow point q
$q^* \leftarrow q$

$S_i^* = \emptyset$
for $l = 1$ to N **do**
$\quad$ **if** num (elements of Q in s_l) $\geq q^*$
$\quad$ **then** $S_i^* \leftarrow s_l$
$\quad$ **else delete** s_l
$\quad$ **endif**
endfor

Fig. 2. Algorithm of progressive matching

Finally, we get the set of the informative sentences S_i^*.

Step 3 Find Usage Context by Spectral Clustering. If arbitrary two sentences in S_i^* contain too many elements of I_{te} in common, their usage context is likely similar, in other words, redundant. This means that there is no problem in understanding the usage context even though we remove all redundant sentences except one. By doing this, it can also contribute to reducing the computational burden. In order to find the redundant sentences to be removed, it first should be identified the groups of the sentences, which share the usage context. We encoded sentences in a vector form based on term frequency. Since, these encoded vectors are very high-dimensional and sparse, we perform spectral clustering. The term frequency-based encoded vectors V_i from S_i^* for spectral clustering is represented as follows.

$$V_i = \{\cdots, v_l, \cdots\}$$

$$v_l = [f_1, f_2, \cdots, f_p, \cdots], f_p = |\{s_l | \exists l, t_p \in s_l\}|$$

where v_l is a vector to represent term frequency in a s_l, t_p is a pth term found in S_i^*.

As a result, we get various clusters consisting of a set of sentences that share the similar usage context. Finally, we randomly select one sentence from each cluster (hereafter the representative sentence) and, for the target entity, combine the representative sentences of all clusters into one set.

3.3 BERT-Based Prediction Model Training

To predict the equivalence relationship between two entities, we generate a set of representative sentences for each entity using the method described above. In addition, the set of representative sentences must be encoded as a set of numeric values for training the predictive model sentence by sentences. In natural language processing, the language model is widely used to encode sentences. We perform embeddings for the set of representative sentences using Bidirectional Encoder Representations from Transformers (BERT), pre-trained via a large cross-domain corpus that has demonstrated excellent performance in NLP tasks among various languages models. As a result, we get semantic embedding matrix (SE) for each target entity. Semantic embedding matrix of a target entity e_t(n × m) is defined as follows.

$$SE_t = \left[\cdots, se_{(t,r)}, \cdots \right]^T, 1 \leq r \leq n$$

where $se_{(t,r)}$ is an embedded vector for r^{th} representative sentence of e_t. n and m are the number of representative sentences and the maximum length of the representative sentence, respectively.

Using the matrix SE_t and $SE_{t'}$, we execute a predictive model that can classify two target entities as equivalence. As the prediction model, we adopt the neural network model that is widely used for classification tasks. To do so, it must train the prediction model in advance. For training the model, the semantic embedding matrix is must generate for all seed alignment entities, which are already identified as equivalence. At the time, the label of the training data is 0 or 1 depending on whether it is equivalent or not. In addition, the prediction model uses the ReLU function as an activation function, which has advantages of sparse activation as well as a low computational burden. Finally, we identify the equivalence between two target entities based on the training model.

4   Performance Evaluation

We evaluate a superiority of the proposed framework, Semantic Embedding-based Entity Alignment (SEEA), compared to the state-of-the-art knowledge graph embedding methods based on experimental two datasets DBP-WD and DBP-YG, sampled from DBpedia-Wikidata and DBpedia-YAGO, respectively [5].

4.1   Experimental Datasets and Settings

The experimental dataset DBP-YG is a sampling dataset that focuses only on RDF triples related to the relationship between DBpedia and YAGO. Therefore, some entities only have small number of triples, which leads to lack of information about those entities. In addition, there are some minor relationships that are not used at all by other entities. Since the bias of these relations interferes with finding an appropriate level of sentence, we remove entities with too few triples or excessively minor relations through preprocessing. The preprocessing process is as follows. We draw a boxplot with the number of triples containing a specific entity and eliminate the entities with the first and the fourth quartiles of the data. The boxplots of the original datasets and the refined datasets are shown in Fig. 3.

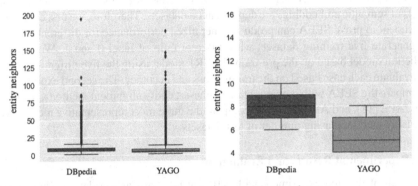

Fig. 3. Boxplots for comparison of the two datasets

The statistics of the original dataset and the refined set are shown in Table 2.

Table 2. Summary of the original and refined datasets

Statistics	DBP		YG	
	Original	Refined	Original	Refined
Entities	100000	59244	100000	61289
Relations	287	264	32	29
Attributes	379	301	38	18
Relation triples	428952	24410	502563	264536
Attribute triples	451646	21700	118376	81774
RDF triples	880598	46110	620939	346310

We need sentences that matches the entity of KG, but DBP-YG, which is used as the existing experimental dataset, does not have enough data for getting semantic embeddings for the experiment. We sample sentences that matches the entities of refined DBP and YG. We sample 49838 sentences with the average number of words is 34.

4.2 Comparative Methods

We conduct two experiment to evaluate a superiority of the SEEA. Since the types and the number of links containing in datasets are different, we should check whether the results of semantic embeddings are dependent on datasets. Therefore, we first conduct an experiment to prove SEEA can produce generalized performance for different datasets. We generate five training datasets with different ratio of label 0 and 1. We train the prediction model based on the pre-trained BERT model using the five different datasets and evaluate each case based on the training loss and accuracy. The second experiment is to compare the SEEA with previous state-of-the-art entity alignment methods, MTransE [10], JAPE [11], and AttrE [12]. We compare the three most representative models with the SEEA with increasing number of test datasets.

4.3 Experimental Results and Evaluations

The result of the first experiment with different ratio of training data is illustrated in Fig. 4 and Table 3. Figure 4 shows the training loss of the first experiment for each training epoch. It shows that all models converge rapidly. Table 3 shows the accuracy of the models and the details of the ratio of training datasets. It is clear all models show high accuracy. It means that the SEEA produces generalized performance for different datasets.

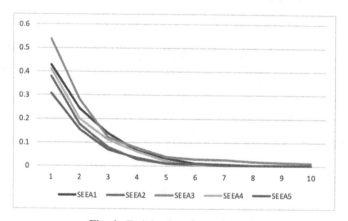

Fig. 4. Training loss for each epoch

The result of the second experiment, the comparison with other EA models, is shown in Table 4. Table 4 show that SEEA outperform the other models, even better than other models' hits@5. This result is because SEEA can catch latent semantic features in natural language that other knowledge graph embedding methods cannot.

Table 3. Accuracy for training data with different ratio

| Training datasets | Ratio ('1': '0') | DBP-YG |
		Hits@1
SEEA 1	15:85	95
SEEA 2	30:70	96
SEEA 3	50:50	97
SEEA 4	70:30	97
SEEA 5	85:15	98

Table 4. Comparison with other EA models

| Features | MTransE | | JAPE | | AttrE | | SEEA |
	Hits@1	Hits@5	Hits@1	Hits@5	Hits@1	Hits@5	Hits@1
Links-100	79	86	67	75	40.33	55.53	**97**
Links-150	80.67	88.67	66.67	82.67	45.33	71.33	**92.66**
Links-200	46.31	67.823	31.66	48.9	15.62	26.01	**93**
Links-250	74.8	82.8	58.67	70.33	38	52.4	**92.8**
Links-300	75.67	87.67	55.67	64.33	29	36	**93.33**

5 Related Works

5.1 Entity Alignment

Entity Alignment (EA) is the process of linking the entities which have same real-world identity [13]. In the early stage of the EA research, entity alignment methods using the heuristics such as data mining, database approach. Recently, knowledge graph embedding-based EA methods receive much attention [6]. The embedding methods can be divided into relation embedding and attribute embedding. The relation embedding can be categorized as triple-based, path-based, and neighborhood-based embedding. Triple-based embedding is a method capturing the local semantics of relation triple. Path-based embedding is a method exploiting the long-term dependency of relations spanning over relation paths. Neighborhood-based embedding is a method using subgraph structure constituted by relations between entities. The attribute embedding can be categorized as attribute correlation embedding, and literal embedding. Attribute correlation embedding is a method considering correlations among attributes. Literal embedding is a method using literal values. Based on these multiple embedding methods, many EA methods have been proposed. MTransE (2017) and BootEA (2018) proposed EA method using triple-based embedding. IPTransE (2017) and RSN4EA (2019) proposed EA method based on path-based embedding. MuGNN (2019) and AVR-GCN (2019) used neighborhood-based for EA. There is research which used attribute embedding to refine relation embedding. KDCoE (2018) and AttrE (2019) used both triple-based and literal embedding for EA. GMNN and RDGCN (2019) proposed EA method using neighborhood-based embedding and literal embedding. JAPE (2017) and GCNAlign (2018) used attribute correlation embedding to refine relation-based embedding.

5.2 Language Models

Language models (LMs) as the backbone of natural language processing (NLP) are models that assign probabilities to sequences of words. They are widely used in speech recognition, machine translation, and question answering, etc. Since the advent of the Recurrent Neural Network in the 1980s, various LMs such as Long Short Term Memory networks (LSTM) (1997), feed-forward neural network language model (2003), Pretrained Word Embeddings (2013), Global Vectors (Glove) (2014), Attention Models (2015), and Transformer (2017) have appeared. These models are divided into two main categories: statistical language models and word embedding methods. The statistical language model is a probability distribution over sequences of words. The models perform training on counts of words and their sequences [14, 15]. However, the statistical language models reveal a critical limitation in that they cannot predict sequences that do not exist in the training data. To solve this problem, word embedding methods that examine the semantic similarity between words have been proposed. In addition, ELMo [16] generalized word embeddings to context-aware word embeddings that can properly handle the word polysemy. Recently, Research to make the machine understand the characteristics of language from natural language and use the model directly are also being actively conducted. The natural language understanding machine, represented by BERT [17], learns a language from a vast amount of commonly crawled natural language. Pre-trained natural language understanding machines perform various tasks such as hate speech detection [18], sentiment analysis [19], and entity relation extraction [20] through fine-tuning. These approaches proved their high performance by experiments.

6   Conclusion and Further Research

To dynamically address the new cyberattacks, different cybersecurity-related KGs should be utilized simultaneously. To do so, we proposed a novel semantic embedding-based entity alignment framework, which is for predicting equivalence relationships between the entities from different KGs using semantic information from the external source. First, the proposed framework selects neighbor entities based on the degree centrality. Second, the representative sentences which best represents the target entity is discovered by collecting sentence base from the external resource and finding usage context by spectral clustering. Third, to find equivalence relationship between entities, representative sentences are encoded by utilizing BERT and equivalence between entities is predicted by neural network model. We proved the superiority of our framework through experiments using real world KG datasets.

However, our framework has several limitations. Since vector representation does not consider the structure of the KG and containing terms, the position of the entities projected by language model may be biased. Also, in order to quickly respond to new types of cyberattacks, not only resources composed of formal sentences, but also noisy and fragmented text resources should also be used. To overcome these limitations, we will additionally use graph embedding methods which consider graph structures, and utilize the language model which is more robust to short and noisy texts.

Acknowledgements. This research is supported by C2 integrating and interfacing technologies laboratory of Agency for Defense Development (UE201114ED).

References

1. Li, K., Zhou, H., Tu, Z., Feng, B.: Cskb: a cyber security knowledge base based on knowledge graph. In: Yu, Shui, Mueller, Peter, Qian, Jiangbo (eds.) SPDE 2020. CCIS, vol. 1268, pp. 100–113. Springer, Singapore (2020). https://doi.org/10.1007/978-981-15-9129-7_8
2. Deng, Y., Zeng, Z., Huang, D.: Neocyberkg: enhancing cybersecurity laboratories with a machine learning-enabled knowledge graph. In: Proceedings of the 26th ACM Conference on Innovation and Technology in Computer Science Education, vol. 1, pp. 310–316 (2021)
3. Kiesling, E., Ekelhart, A., Kurniawan, K., Ekaputra, F.: The sepses knowledge graph: an integrated resourcefor cybersecurity. In: Ghidini, C., et al. (eds.) ISWC 2019. Lecture Notes in Computer Science, vol 11779, pp. 198–214. Springer, Cham (2019). https://doi.org/10.1007/978-3-030-30796-7_13
4. Harley, E., Purdy, S., Limiero, M., Lu, T., Mathews, W.: CyGraph: big-data graph analysis for cybersecurity and mission resilience. Technical report, MITRE CORP MCLEAN VA (2018)
5. Sun, Z., Hu, W., Zhang, Q., Qu, Y.: Bootstrapping entity alignment with knowledge graph embedding. In: IJCAI, vol. 18, pp. 4396–4402 (2018)
6. Sun, Z., et al.: A benchmarking study of embedding based entity alignment for knowledge graphs. arXiv preprint arXiv:2003.07743 (2020)
7. Colepicolo, E.: Information reliability for academic research: review and recommendations. New Library World (2015)
8. Collins Dictionary: Collins English dicfionary and thesaurus (2019)
9. Ledesma González, O., Merinero-Rodríguez, R., Pulido-Fernández, J.I.: Tourist destination development and social network analysis: What does degree centrality contribute? Int. J. Tour. Res. (2021)
10. Chen, M., Tian, Y., Yang, M., Zaniolo, C.: Multilingual knowledge graph embeddings for cross-lingual knowledge alignment. arXiv preprint arXiv:1611.03954 (2016)
11. Sun, Z., Hu, W., Li, C.: Cross-lingual entity alignment via joint attribute-preserving embedding. In: d'Amato, C., et al. (eds.) ISWC 2017. LNCS, vol. 10587, pp. 628–644. Springer, Cham (2017). https://doi.org/10.1007/978-3-319-68288-4_37
12. Trisedya, B.D., Qi, J., Zhang, R.: Entity alignment between knowledge graphs using attribute embeddings. In: Proceedings of the AAAI Conference on Artificial Intelligence, vol. 33, pp. 297–304 (2019)
13. Zhang, Q., Sun, Z., Hu, W., Chen, M., Guo, L., Qu, Y.: Multi-view knowledge graph embedding for entity alignment. arXiv preprint arXiv:1906.02390 (2019)
14. Bahl, L.R., Jelinek, F., Mercer, R.L.: A maximum likelihood approach to continuous speech recognition. IEEE Trans. Pattern Anal. Mach. Intell. **2**, 179–190 (1983)
15. Marino, J.B., et al.: N-gram-based machine translation. Comput. Linguist. **32**(4), 527–549 (2006)
16. Peters, M.E., et al.: Deep contextualized word representations. arXiv preprint arXiv:1802.05365 (2018)

17. Devlin, J., Chang, M.-W., Lee, K., Toutanova, K.: BERT: pre-training of deep bidirectional transformers for language understanding. arXiv preprint arXiv:1810.04805 (2018)
18. Mozafari, M., Farahbakhsh, R., Crespi, N.: A bert-based transfer learning approach for hate speech detection in online social media. In: Cherifi, H., Gaito, S., Mendes, J.F., Moro, E., Rocha, L.M. (eds.) COMPLEX NETWORKS 2019. SCI, vol. 881, pp. 928–940. Springer, Cham (2020). https://doi.org/10.1007/978-3-030-36687-2_77
19. Zhao, L., Li, L., Zheng, X., Zhang, J.: A BERT based sentiment analysis and key entity detection approach for online financial texts. In: 2021 IEEE 24th International Conference on Computer Supported Cooperative Work in Design (CSCWD), pp. 1233–1238. IEEE (2021)
20. Xue, K., Zhou, Y., Ma, Z., Ruan, T., Zhang, H., He, P.: Fine-tuning BERT for joint entity and relation extraction in Chinese medical text. In: 2019 IEEE International Conference on Bioinformatics and Biomedicine (BIBM), pp. 892–897. IEEE (2019)

A Secure Dispersed Computing Scheme for Internet of Mobile Things

Yan Zhao⬛, Ning Hu⁽✉⁾⬛, Jincai Zou⬛, and Yuqiang Zhang⬛

Cyberspace Institute of Advanced Technology, Guangzhou University,
Guangzhou 510006, China
{2111906107,2112006304,2112006277}@e.gzhu.edu.cn, huning@gzhu.edu.cn

Abstract. With the rapid development of the Internet of Mobile Things (IoMT) and countless mobile devices connected to the Internet, problems of the IoMT computing paradigm, Mobile Cloud Computing (MCC) and Mobile Edge Computing (MEC), have been aggravated in terms of network congestion, high energy consumption, and huge investment cost. Dispersed computing utilize geographically distribute computing resources and the "code and data" strategy movement, reducing energy and investment costs and improving the performance of IoMT applications. However, security problems raise as the "code and data" movement among multiple devices. We analyze the security threats in IoMT dispersed computing and propose a secure dispersed computing scheme for IoMT. The proposed scheme improves the availability, integrity, confidentiality, and privacy of IoMT dispersed computing by a decentralized service discovery and distribution model and a security domain-based task offloading scheme. The experiment results prove the effectiveness of the proposed scheme.

Keywords: Dispersed computing · Blockchain · Privacy

1 Introduction

The Internet of Mobile Things (IoMT), a subset of the Internet of Things, focuses on connecting mobile devices, such as smartphones, vehicles, and wearable devices, to the Internet [21]. The interconnection and collaboration of IoMT devices by the Internet will create a smarter world. According to a forecast, more than 50 billion mobile devices will connect to the Internet by 2025 [3].

Effective computing paradigms are needed to serve such massive IoMT devices. Nowadays, the computing paradigm of IoMT mainly includes Mobile Cloud Computing (MCC) and Mobile Edge Computing (MEC) [5]. MCC uses the cloud as a data storage and computing platform to provide global interconnection of mobile devices. However, The massive traffic of MCC not only makes the core network congested but also affects the real-time performance of mobile applications. MEC offload IoMT applications to the edge server, alleviating the network congestion and poor real-time performance. However, a large number

ⓒ Springer Nature Singapore Pte Ltd. 2022
I. You et al. (Eds.): MobiSec 2021, CCIS 1544, pp. 65–78, 2022.
https://doi.org/10.1007/978-981-16-9576-6_6

of mobile edge servers need to be deployed to support a large number of mobile devices, which leads to huge investment costs and energy consumption [9,10].

IoMT dispersed computing is a promising way to solve the above problems. The basic idea of the dispersed computing paradigm is to realize the "code and data" on-demand movement by designing new programmable protocols and algorithms, enabling the securely and collectively execution of tasks on geographically dispersed, ubiquitous, and heterogeneous computing platforms [4,6]. These dispersed platforms include network elements, intelligent terminals, programmable sensors, and edge servers. In an IoMT dispersed computing scenario, users can use "local" or "nearby" available computing resources to carry out the application, significantly improving application and network performance while reducing energy consumption and investment costs [10]. However, the security of IoMT dispersed computing has not been studied in depth. The security of the "code and data" movement needs to be guaranteed.

In this paper, we discuss the security issues of IoMT dispersed computing. In response to these security issues, A secure dispersed computing scheme for the internet of mobile things is proposed. The proposed method realizes a decentralized service publication, discovery, and distribution mechanism through the consortium blockchain, which improves the usability, integrity, and authenticity of code movement. In addition, a computational offloading method based on security domain division is proposed, which improves the security of data movement by offloading tasks with different security risks to different security domains. The main contributions of this article are as follows:

- We analyze the security issues involved in the movement of "code-data" in the IoMT dispersed computing.
- We propose a decentralized service publication, discovery and distribution scheme. The proposed method applies the consortium blockchain and IPFS distributed file system to IoMT dispersed computing, ensuring the availability, integrity and authenticity of the code publication, discovery and distribution process.
- We propose a security domain-based computing offloading scheme. For different users, the proposed method group dispersed devices into different domains. By scheduling IoMT tasks with different security risks to appreciate security domain devices, the confidentiality and privacy of data transmission, storage and processing are guaranteed.

The rest of the paper is organized as follows. The overview of related work is presented in Sect. 2. The motivation and objectives of our work are described in Sect. 3. A Secure Dispersed Computing Scheme for Internet of Mobile Things is elaborated in Sect. 4. The results of experiment of the proposed scheme and algorithm are discussed in Sect. 5. Finally, in Sect. 6, the conclusion of this work are presented.

2   Related Works

Although the security of internet of mobile things has been studied widely [17, 18, 22, 23], there is little research on the security of distributed computing, especially in the scenario of mobile Internet of things.

The research of dispersed computing paradigm is mainly focused on architecture and task scheduling. Schurgot et al. [20] describes the architecture of dispersed computing. The architecture consists of application layer, dispersed computing layer and physical layer. The application layer consists of applications and dispersed computing API for submitting tasks. The dispersed computing layer consists of dispersed computing task-aware computation, programmable nodes and network protocol stacks. Dispersed computing task-aware computing algorithms share transfer task details, data flow details, performance boundaries, and may even share job task graphs under the middleware "stack". Programmable nodes and protocol stacks provide NCP lists, overlay network abstractions, flow performance details. The physical layer is various underlying networks.

Dispersed computing task scheduling mainly studies the task unloading problem of stream processing application modeled by Directed Acyclic Graph (DAG). Different from edge computing offloading, task offloading in the dispersed computing paradigm needs to jointly optimize computing offloading and network scheduling. Yang et al. [25] study the problem of chained task scheduling in dispersed computing networks. They propose a novel virtual queuing network encoding the state of the network and a Max-Weight type scheduling policy for the virtual queuing network. Rahimzadeh et al. [19] propose a scheduling system framework, SPARCLE, for stream processing applications in dispersed computing networks. The proposed method can complete the task assignment and resource allocation of a stream processing application in polynomial time. H. Wu et al. [7] proposed a dispersed computing offloading framework, formal the offloading problem into a multi-objective optimization problem, and design a bilateral matching algorithm to obtain the optimal task offloading strategy.

3   Motivation and Objectives

Figure 1 shows the IoMT dispersed computing paradigm [20, 26]. The IoMT dispersed computing includes the IoMT service provider, dispersed task-aware computation, and programmable nodes and protocol stacks. Its workflow is: (1) The IoMT device sends a service request which contains the service identifier to the dispersed task-aware computing module; (2) The dispersed task-aware computing module sends a request to the service discovery module; (3) The discovery module returns the service to the dispersed task-aware computing module; (4) The dispersed task-aware computing module calculates the task offloading plan, and offloads tasks of the services and flow tables to the appropriate DCP; (5) The IoMT device sends data to the first DCP.

Although dispersed computing improves the responsiveness, reliability, real-time performance, and availability of IoMT applications through the "code and data" strategy movement and "forwarding and computing hop-by-hop", there are the following security issues of IoMT dispersed computing.

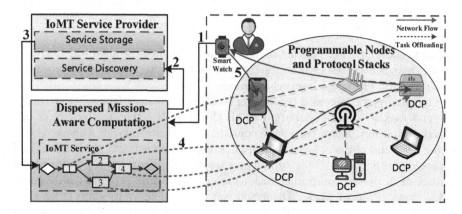

Fig. 1. IoMT dispersed computing paradigm

1. **Availability of Service Discovery**

   In the IoMT scenario, the code of the application or service is usually not stored in the resource-constrained IoT device but the cloud or the hosting server of service providers. Moreover, service providers will provide a centralized service discovery mechanism. A simple way is to use this centralized mechanism directly by the dispersed task-aware computing module. However, the inherent availability limitations of the centralized system, such as single points of failure, network bandwidth and service capacity bottlenecks, contradict the high availability promised by dispersed computing.

2. **Integrity and Authenticity of Services Distribution**

   During the code distribution, the service code may be maliciously tampered with or replaced. Running malicious code threats to not only user data but also nodes themselves. In addition, the order of task execution may also be maliciously tampered with, causing code to be executed in an unexpected location and resulting in unavailability of services or leakage of user privacy.

3. **Confidentiality of Data Transmission**

   Due to the limited computing resources and battery life of some IoMT devices (such as smart bracelets, smart sensors, wireless headsets, etc.), it is hard to deploy heavy encryption algorithms. Data is easily sniffed maliciously during the transmission process between dispersed computing devices.

4. **Privacy of Data Storage and Processing**

   User data needs to be stored and processed on some uncontrolled devices. Storing unencrypted data on these devices will lead to a privacy leak. Even data are encrypted, it also needs to be decrypted before or during processing, which means there is still a problem of user privacy leakage if data needs to be processed on uncontrolled devices.

According to the above analysis, there are many security problems in IoMT dispersed computing. In the "code and data" movement, the availability, integrity, and authenticity of code publication, discovery, and distribution, as well as the confidentiality and privacy of data transmission, storage, and processing need to be guaranteed. To the best of our knowledge, Existing researches on dispersed computing mainly focuses on architecture design and task scheduling [7,15,19,24–26], and there are little researches on security solutions in the IoMT dispersed computing scenario. Therefore, in this article, we propose a secure dispersed computing scheme for the Internet of Mobile Things, which has the following design objectives:

- Improve the availability, integrity and authenticity of service publication, discovery and distribution in IoMT dispersed computing.
- Improve the confidentiality and privacy of data transmission, storage and processing in IoMT dispersed computing.

4   Proposed Scheme

For the above two objectives, we propose a secure dispersed computing paradigm for the Internet of Mobile Things in this section. The proposed scheme includes a decentralized service publication and discovery scheme and a security domain-based task offloading model. The first scheme improves the availability of service publication and discovery by employing the consortium blockchain. Meanwhile, it also provides integrity and authenticity verification capabilities. The second scheme groups dispersed nodes into the private, organization, and public domains. By scheduling tasks with different security priorities to appropriate domain nodes, the confidentiality, integrity, and privacy of data transmission, storage, and processing are guaranteed as much as possible. We will describe the detail of the proposed two scheme in Sects. 4.1 and 4.2.

4.1   A Decentralized Service Publication, Discovery and Distribution Scheme

A decentralized service publication, discovery, and distribution scheme for IoMT dispersed computing is described in this section. Blockchain has been used successfully for many systems [1,8,11–14,16]. We argue that blockchain is a promising technology to realizes a high-availability service discovery and high-trust code distribution of IoMT dispersed computing. The basic idea of the proposed scheme is to use the blockchain to store the metadata of IoMT services and to use the distributed file system to store service codes and models. IoMT service providers jointly manage and maintain the consortium blockchain. The distributed file system uses IPFS, which is a media protocol based on blockchain and uses distributed storage and content addressing technology [2]. IPFS address files according to their content hash value. Service providers publish service metadata to the blockchain and publish service codes to IPFS. Users initiate requests to the blockchain to obtain service metadata and requests to IPFS to obtain service codes. The proposed method improves the availability of service publication, discovery, and distribution by a decentralized design.

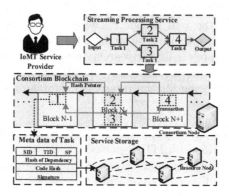

Fig. 2. A decentralized service publication and storage model

Service Publication. Figure 2 shows the proposed service publication model. The IoMT services can be modeled as a Directed Acyclic Graph (DAG) in which and the nodes represent the tasks and the edge represent the dependencies [15, 26]. This model indicates the number and the order of the tasks. Meanwhile, it also makes the storage and verification of IoMT service stored in the blockchain and IPFS simple.

Due to the limitation of block capacity, the consortium blockchain only stores the service metadata. The metadata includes service identification (SID), task identification (TID), task security priority (SP), task-dependency hash, code hash, and digital signature of the service provider. SID is globally unique by a Globally Unique Identifier (GUID) algorithm. All service providers in the consortium blockchain use the same GUID algorithm. TID is the index of the topological sorting of tasks in a service. The metadata of each task is encapsulated as a transaction and published to the consortium blockchain. The transaction is published in the order of the topological sorting. The service provider first initiates task transactions that have no forward dependencies. After all consortium nodes reach a consensus on these tasks transactions, the service provider will continue to initiate subsequent task transactions. Each task transaction points to the transaction of the task it depends on through the hash pointer.

The service code is stored in IPFS, and the IPFS network is composed of resource servers of various service providers. IPFS uses the hash value of the file as the index of the file. The hash value of each task code is stored in the metadata. The user can quickly read and obtain the service code through the service metadata.

Service Discovery and Distribution. As shown in Fig. 3, the service publication and distribution system include consortium blockchain, IPFS, control layer, and computing layer. The consortium blockchain is used to store the metadata of services and the IPFS is responsible for storing service data and code. The computing layer consists of dispersed computing devices called DCP. The control layer includes a multiple dispersed computing controller (DCC) and a DCC that

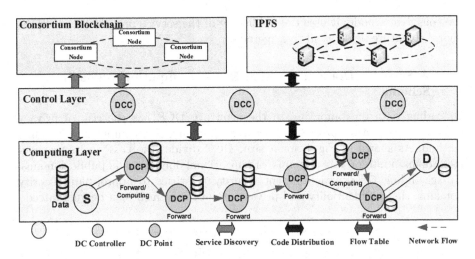

Fig. 3. A decentralized service discovery and distribution model

manages a set of DCP. The user device first initiates a request to a DCC. The DCC receives the request and obtains the SID. Then, DCC initiates a service discovery request to a consortium blockchain node. After receiving the request, the consortium node gets the service ID from the request, queries all transactions whose SID is equal to this ID, and verifies the hash pointer of each transaction. After obtaining the metadata of all tasks, the consortium node will package this metadata into a service metadata and return it to DCC. Then, DCC parses the service metadata, obtains the hash value of all task codes, and then sends a request to IPFS to obtain the task code. Finally, DCC offloads the service to a suitable DCP for execution according to the scheduling strategy.

Availability, Integrity and Authenticity. First, the proposed method is based on the consortium blockchain and IPFS, and adopts a completely decentralized design, so that the system does not have a single point of failure. This method greatly improves the availability of service publication and discovery. At the same time, based on the IPFS decentralized storage system, service codes can be stored on multiple resource servers. Even if some consortium nodes or resource nodes fail, the service publication and discovery functions can still operate normally. Secondly, the metadata of the service is stored in the block of the consortium blockchain as transactions of tasks. In addition, the integrity of the dependencies of tasks in the service is protected by hash pointers between transactions. Therefore, any attempt to tamper with service metadata must simultaneously modify the entire blockchain. The task code is stored in IPFS, and the storage address is the code hash in the task metadata. The non-tampering feature of the blockchain can ensure the integrity of the service metadata and service code. Finally, the authenticity is guaranteed by the digital signature in the task data metadata. After DCC receives the service metadata returned by the consortium node, it uses the public key of the service provider to check the digital signature fields of all task metadata.

4.2 A Security Domain Division Based Computing Offloading Scheme

Offloading data or computing to the arbitrary DCP has the risk of privacy leakage. This section proposes a security domain-based computing offloading method. As shown in Fig. 4, for a user, DCC divides the DCP in its management domain into private domains, organizational domains, and public domains. By scheduling tasks with different security priorities to appropriate security domains, the confidentiality and privacy of data movement can be guaranteed.

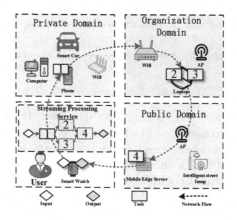

Fig. 4. Security domain diviosn based task offloading model

Security Domain Division. The geographically adjacent DCP are managed by a DCC. A management domain include a DCC and certain DC. We use $MD_j = DCC_j \cup \{DCP_{j,i} \,|1 \le i \le N\}$, $1 \le j \le M$ to represent the management domain j. U and O are used to represent user and organization set respectively. For a user u, using $UInfo_u = \{UID_u, OID_u, PubK_u, PubK_o\}$ to represent, where UID_u is the user ID, $OrgID$ is the user organization ID, $PubK_u$ represents the user public key, and $PubK_o$ represents the user organization public. For $DCP_{j,i}$, its security group is represented by $SG_{j,i} = \{UIDS_{j,i}, OIDS_{j,i}, PubG_{j,i}\}$. $UIDS_{j,i} = \{(UID_u, Sig_u) \,|u \in U\}$ is the user ID and array signature list of its owner, and $OIDs_{j,i} = \{(OID_u, Sig_o) \,|o \in O\}$ is the ID list of the organization of the user. $PubG_{j,i}$ is a Boolean value that indicates whether the device is a public device.

A non-injective and non-surjective function $dividing : (j, u) \rightarrow SDP_{j,u}$ is used to represent the security domain division problem of the user u in the management domain j. The $SDP_{j,u} = \{PriD_{j,u}, OrgD_{j,u}, PubD_{j,u}\}$ represents the security domain of the user u in the management domain j. The $PriD_{j,u} = \{DCP_{j,i} \mid 1 \le i \le N, 1 \le j \le M \}$ represents the private domain of the user u in the management domain j. The $OrgD_{j,u} = \{DCP_{j,i} \mid 1 \le i \le N, 1 \le j \le M\}$ represents the organizational domain of the user u in the management domain j. And the $PubD_{j,u} = \{DCP_{j,i} \mid 1 \le i \le N, 1 \le j \le M\}$, $PubG_{j,i} = True\}$ represents the public domain of the user u in the management domain j. The solution of the function dividing needs to satisfy the constraints of formulas (1) and (2), where $Sig_u \in UIDS_{j,i}, \{UID_u, OID_u, PubK_u, PubK_o\} \subset UInfo_u$; $PubK^e$ and $PubK^N$ are the public exponent and modulus from the public key; Pad is the padding function; and Hash is the hashing function.

$$Sig_u{}^{PubK_u^e} = Pad(Hash(UID_u))(mod\ PubK_u^N) \qquad (1)$$

$$Sig_o{}^{PubK_o^e} = Pad(Hash(OID_u))(mod\ PubK_o^N) \qquad (2)$$

The solution process of the function *dividing* is shown in Algorithm 1.

Algorithm 1: Security Domain Division

Input: $UInfo_u$, MD_j, $SG_{j,i}$
Output: $SDP_{j,u}$
1 $PriD_{j,u}$, $OrgD_{j,u}$, $PubD_{j,u} = [\,]$;
2 **for** $DCP_{j,i}$ in MD_j **do**
3   **if** $UIDS_{j,i} == UInfo_u$ and the equation (1) holds **then**
4 | Append $DCP_{j,i}$ to $PriD_{j,u}$;
5   **end**
6   **else if** $OIDS_{j,i} == OInfo_u$ and the equation (1) holds **then**
7 | Append $DCP_{j,i}$ to $OrgD_{j,u}$;
8   **end**
9   **else**
10 | Append $DCP_{j,i}$ to $PubD_{j,u}$;
11   **end**
12 **end**
13 $SDP_{j,u} = PriD_{j,u} \cup OrgD_{j,u} \cup PubD_{j,u}$;
14 **return** $SDP_{j,u}$

Task Offloading. By scheduling tasks with different security risks to appropriate DCC, the security of data movement can be improved. For a user u, the IoMT service needed to offload is denoted as $S_u = (Task_u, SP_u)$. $Task = \{task_{u,k} \mid 1 \le k \le K\}$ is a set of tasks. $SP_u = \{SP_{u,k} \mid 1 \le k \le K, SP_{u,k} \in h, m, l\}$ represents the task security risk, where h, m, l represents the high, medium, and low security risks of task $task_{u,k}$, respectively. We use $resType = (cpu, memory, netband)$ to represent the resource type. The resource capacity currently available for $DR_{j,i} =$

$\{DCP_{j,i}^{type}|$ $type \in resType\}$. The resource cost of task $task_{u,k}$ is modeled as $TR_{u,k} = \left\{tr_{u,k}^{type}|ype \in resType\right\}$.

A non-injective and non-surjective function $offloading$: $(j,u) \rightarrow \{DCP_{j,i}^{u,k}|1 \leq i \leq N, 1 \leq j \leq M, 1 \leq k \leq K\}$ is used to represent the offloading problem of service S_u in management domain j. $DCP_{j,i}^{u,k}$ means to offload task $task_{u,k}$ to $DCP_{j,i}$. The solution of the function dividing needs to satisfy the constraints of formulas (3) and (4).

$$DCP_{j,i}^{u,k} \in \begin{cases} PriD_{j,u}, if\ SP_{u,k} = h \\ PriD_{j,u} \cup OrgD_{j,u}, if\ SP_{u,k} = m \\ MD_j, if\ SP_{u,k} = l \end{cases} \tag{3}$$

$$\sum_{m \in dcpTasks_i} TR_{u,k} < DR_{u,k}, \forall\ i \in V \tag{4}$$

The solution process of the function $offloading$ is shown in Algorithm 2.

Confidentiality, Integrity and Privacy. The proposed method offloads tasks with different security risks to devices in different security domains near the user. Tasks with high security risks are offloaded to the user's private device, which ensures the confidentiality and privacy of data storage and data processing.

5 Evaluation

we implement proposed algorithms with Python and evaluate the time consumption of the algorithms. The performance parameter of our experiment server is shown in Table 1.

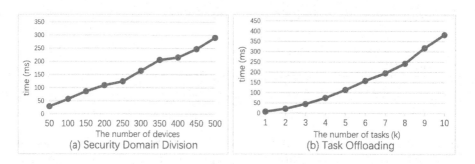

(a) Security Domain Division

(b) Task Offloading

Fig. 5. The time-consuming of the proposed security domain division and computing offloading algorithm

IoMT devices will move across multiple DCC management domains. When an IoMT device requests a DCC to serve, the DCC should quickly calculate

---

Algorithm 2: Task Offloading

Input: $SDP_{j,u}$, S_u

Output: $\{DCP_{j,i}^{type}\}$

1 result = [ ] ;
2 **for** $task_{u,k}$ *in* S_u **do**
3   **if** $SP_{u,k} == h$ **then**
4   **for** $DCP_{j,i}$ *in* $PriD_{j,u}$ **do**
5   **if** *the formula (4) holds* **then**
6   Append $DCP_{j,i}^{u,k}$ to result;
7   break;
8   **end**
9   **end**
10   **end**
11   **else if** $SP_{u,k} == m$ **then**
12   **for** $DCP_{j,i}$ *in* $OrgD_{j,u} \cup OrgD_{j,u}$ **do**
13   **if** *the formula (4) holds* **then**
14   Append $DCP_{j,i}^{u,k}$ to result;
15   break;
16   **end**
17   **end**
18   **end**
19   **else**
20   **for** $DCP_{j,i}$ *in* $PubD_{j,u} \cup OrgD_{j,u}$ **do**
21   **if** *the formula (4) holds* **then**
22   Append $DCP_{j,i}^{u,k}$ to result;
23   break;
24   **end**
25   **end**
26   **end**
27 **end**
28 return result

---

the security domain and task offloading schedule. It means that the proposed security domain division and task offloading algorithm need to complete the calculation in a short time. We implement the proposed algorithm in Python and evaluate its time-consuming.

The time-consuming of the proposed security domain division algorithm is shown in Fig. 5 (a). When the number of DCC devices is 50, completing the

Table 1. Configuration of the edge server

Platform	CPU	Cores	Memory	Storage
ST558	X-Gene 4210	20	64 GB	12T

division takes 29 ms. When the number of DCC devices increases to 300, the division takes 164 ms. When the number of DCC devices reaches 500, it takes 290 ms. The experimental results show that the time consuming of the proposed security domain division algorithm increases linearly with the increase of DCC, and has good real-time performance and expansibility.

The time-consuming of the proposed task offloading algorithm is shown in Fig. 5 (b). In this experiment, we set the number of DCC to 500 and measure the time consumption of the algorithms under different tasks numbers. When the number of tasks is 1000, the algorithm takes about 7 ms to determine an offloading plan. When the number of tasks reaches 5000, it took 114 ms. When the number of tasks is 10000, calculating the offloading scheme takes 382 ms. The results show that the proposed task offloading algorithm can calculate a task offloading scheme in a short time.

6 Conclusion

In this paper, we discuss the security problems in IoMT dispersed computing paradigm and propose a secure dispersed computing scheme for the Internet of Mobile Things. The proposed scheme realizes a decentralized service publication, discovery, and distribution mechanism by employing consortium blockchain, which improves the availability and integrity of service discovery and distribution of dispersed computing systems. Moreover, we also propose a security domain division-based task offloading scheme. By offloading tasks with different security risks to devices in the different security domains, it can protect the confidentiality and privacy of user data as much as possible. Finally, we design a series of experiments to evaluate the proposed scheme. The experiment results prove the effectiveness of our scheme.

Acknowledgments. This work was supported in National Natural Science Foundation of China (Grant No. 61976064), National Defence Science and Technology Key Laboratory Fund (61421190306), Guangzhou Science and Technology Plan Project (202102010471), and Guangdong Province Science and Technology Planning Project (2020A1414010370).

References

1. Alizadeh, M., Andersson, K., Schelén, O.: A survey of secure internet of things in relation to blockchain. J. Internet Serv. Inf. Secur. (JISIS) **10**(3), 47–75 (2020)
2. Baumgart, I., Mies, S.: IPFS - content addressed, versioned, P2P file system (DRAFT 3). In: Proceedings of the International Conference on Parallel and Distributed Systems - ICPADS (2007)
3. Bhullar, J., Mancilla, A., Nijilar, A., Teixeira: the future of mobile computing in 2025. Technical report (2014)
4. Dispersed Computing: DARPA-BAA-16-41 1, 1–44 (2016)
5. Elazhary, H.: Internet of Things (IoT), mobile cloud, cloudlet, mobile IoT, IoT cloud, fog, mobile edge, and edge emerging computing paradigms: disambiguation and research directions (2019). https://doi.org/10.1016/j.jnca.2018.10.021

6. Garcia-Valls, M., Dubey, A., Botti, V.: Introducing the new paradigm of social dispersed computing: applications, technologies and challenges. J. Syst. Architect. **91**, 83–102 (2018). https://doi.org/10.1016/j.sysarc.2018.05.007
7. Hu, D., Krishnamachari, B.: Throughput optimized scheduler for dispersed computing systems. In: Proceedings - 2019 7th IEEE International Conference on Mobile Cloud Computing, Services, and Engineering, MobileCloud 2019 (2019). https://doi.org/10.1109/MobileCloud.2019.00018
8. Hu, N., Teng, Y., Zhao, Y., Yin, S., Zhao, Y.: IDV: internet domain name verification based on blockchain. CMES-Comput. Model. Eng. Sci. **129**(1), 299–322 (2021)
9. Hu, N., Tian, Z., Du, X., Guizani, M.: An energy-efficient in-network computing paradigm for 6g. IEEE Trans. Green Commun. Netw. **5**, 1722–1733 (2021)
10. Hu, N., Tian, Z., Du, X., Guizani, N., Zhu, Z.: Deep-green: a dispersed energy-efficiency computing paradigm for green industrial IoT. IEEE Trans. Green Commun. Netw. (2021). https://doi.org/10.1109/TGCN.2021.3064683
11. Hu, N., et al.: Building agile and resilient UAV networks based on SDN and blockchain. IEEE Netw. **35**(1), 57–63 (2021)
12. Hu, N., Yin, S., Su, S., Jia, X., Xiang, Q., Liu, H.: Blockzone: a decentralized and trustworthy data plane for DNS. CMC-Comput. Mater. Continua **65**(2), 1531–1557 (2020)
13. Jia, X., et al.: IRBA: an identity-based cross-domain authentication scheme for the internet of things. Electronics **9**(4), 634 (2020)
14. Jia, X., Hu, N., Yin, S., Zhao, Y., Zhang, C., Cheng, X.: A2 chain: a blockchain-based decentralized authentication scheme for 5g-enabled IoT. In: Mobile Information Systems 2020 (2020)
15. Knezevic, A., et al.: DEMO: CIRCE - a runtime scheduler for DAG-based dispersed computing. In: 2017 2nd ACM/IEEE Symposium on Edge Computing, SEC 2017 (2017). https://doi.org/10.1145/3132211.3132451
16. König, L., Unger, S., Kieseberg, P., Tjoa, S., Josef Ressel Center for Blockchain: The risks of the blockchain a review on current vulnerabilities and attacks. J. Internet Serv. Inf. Secur. (JISIS) **10**(3), 110–127 (2020)
17. Liu, N., Yu, M., Zang, W., Sandhu, R.: Cost and effectiveness of trustzone defense and side-channel attack on arm platform. J. Wirel. Mob. Netw. Ubiquit. Comput. Dependable Appl. (JoWUA) **11**(4), 1–15 (2020)
18. Marra, A.L., Martinelli, F., Mercaldo, F., Saracino, A., Sheikhalishahi, M.: D-BRIDEMAID: a distributed framework for collaborative and dynamic analysis of Android malware. J. Wirel. Mob. Netw. Ubiquit. Comput. Dependable Appl. (JoWUA) **11**(3), 1–28 (2020)
19. Rahimzadeh, P., et al.: SPARCLE: stream processing applications over dispersed computing networks. In: Proceedings - International Conference on Distributed Computing Systems (2020). https://doi.org/10.1109/ICDCS47774.2020.00112
20. Schurgot, M.R., Wang, M., Conway, A.E., Greenwald, L.G., Lebling, P.D.: A dispersed computing architecture for resource-centric computation and communication. IEEE Commun. Mag. (2019). https://doi.org/10.1109/MCOM.2019.1800776
21. Talavera, L.E., Endler, M., Vasconcelos, I., Vasconcelos, R., Cunha, M., Da Silva Silva, F.J.: The mobile hub concept: enabling applications for the internet of mobile things. In: 2015 IEEE International Conference on Pervasive Computing and Communication Workshops, PerCom Workshops 2015 (2015). https://doi.org/10.1109/PERCOMW.2015.7134005
22. Talegaon, S., Krishnan, R.: Administrative models for role based access control in Android. J. Internet Serv. Inf. Secur. (JISIS) **10**(3), 31–46 (2020)

23. Wong, S.K., Yiu, S.M.: Location spoofing attack detection with pre-installed sensors in mobile devices. J. Wirel. Mob. Netw. Ubiquit. Comput. Dependable Appl. (JoWUA) **11**(4), 16–30 (2020)
24. Wu, H., et al.: Resolving multi-task competition for constrained resources in dispersed computing: a bilateral matching game. IEEE Internet Things J. (2021). https://doi.org/10.1109/JIOT.2021.3075673
25. Yang, C.S., Pedarsani, R., Avestimehr, A.S.: Communication-aware scheduling of serial tasks for dispersed computing. IEEE/ACM Trans. Netw. (2019). https://doi.org/10.1109/TNET.2019.2919553
26. Yang, H., et al.: Dispersed computing for tactical edge in future wars: vision, architecture, and challenges. Wirel. Commun. Mob. Comput. (2021). https://doi.org/10.1155/2021/8899186

A Necessary Condition for Industrial Internet of Things Sustainability

Andrei Dakhnovich⬤, Dmitrii Moskvin⬤, and Dmitrii Zegzhda$^{(\boxtimes)}$⬤

Peter the Great St. Petersburg Polytechnic University, Polytechnicheskaya 29,
195251 St. Petersburg, Russia
{add,moskvin,dmitry}@ibks.spbstu.ru

Abstract. In the paper cybersecurity of Industrial Internet of Things (IIoT) is compared with SCADA-based Industrial Control Systems (ICS), that leverage Purdue Enterprise Reference Architecture (PERA) 5-leveled model for network segmentation. The main difference of SCADA-based ICS and IIoT systems is an openness of control, process and physical layers – in SCADA-based ICS every "thing" secured physically, that is called safety, while in IIoT-based systems both safety and security – that is called cybersecurity – must be provided. Then authors provide a typical IIoT architecture, where communication between nodes of Internet of Things (IoT) field is coming through an Zero-Trusted environment like the Internet is. This architecture needs new approache or approaches for securing communications. The paper is aimed to show that anonymity systems and anonymity theory could help with this cybersecurity challenge. Based on the anonymity degree measuring a path sustainability entropy mearing between two arbitrary nodes is proposed. For providing cybersecurity sustainability of production workflows on such architecture a necessary condition is described in a theorem. In the end of the paper this necessity criteria theorem is proven.

Keywords: Cybersecurity · Industrial Internet of Things · Sustainability · Industry 4.0 · Cyber-physical systems

1 Introduction

4th Industrial Revolution has come a more then 10 years ago, but its appliance in real-world industrial processes is not going so fast like in papers. But some bright minds are trying to implement the 5th Industrial Revolution, which means not only information technologies are applied on the local areas, but also on geographically distributed areas [1].

This industrial challenge could be gained due to new technologies like 5G networks for communications, 3D-printers for local production, Cloud computing for resources sharing etc. [2]. These technologies are evolving and most of smart applies will leverage them as a backbone. But this also means any smart device, e.g. that operates on Smart Cities, will be connected globally on the Internet becoming an attackers' point of intrusion. Some new systems leverage such technologies like Digital Twin [3], WSN networks [4], VANETs [5] etc.

© Springer Nature Singapore Pte Ltd. 2022
I. You et al. (Eds.): MobiSec 2021, CCIS 1544, pp. 79–89, 2022.
https://doi.org/10.1007/978-981-16-9576-6_7

For such architecture and communications shifts could be free, thus, new cyberse-curity challenges are arising. In the paper we assume that typical SCADA-based ICS system is built upon Purdue model of control (SP-99), the model which implements Defense-in-Depth strategy via network segmentation. Such approach is widely used for securing ICS on local area, in other words, perimeter-based network security, but it does not work when devices are available globally [6].

In the 2nd section we actualizing a problem of providing sustainable communications for Industrial Internet of Things (IIoT). Only main threat of destructing availability of routes between two arbitrary nodes is considered on the next, 3rd section as the most critical for industrial systems. For mitigating this threat, we introducing some definitions and formulas for calculating entropy of routes sustainability (one path contains multiple routes). The 4th section contains a theorem that must be satisfied if system wants to remain sustainable on the network area.

2   Problem

2.1   Providing Cybersecurity on the IIoT Field

Cyber-physical systems (CPS) mainly differs from information systems (IT) by a sen-sitivity of data availability threats. That means that if in some business-area network a packet is lost or is delayed, there is no physical impact on people wellness or physical state of some systems like autopilot car, accessor in the device field of Industrial Control System (ICS) etc. But leading threats to attacks in an ICS network could cause physical threats that will break some workflows and bring disasters, e.g. water will come out of a reservoir as some sensor will not send signal on time or turbine in hydroelectric power station will not stop so the dam will be damaged for some reason [7]. Figure 1 shows typical tiered architecture for SCADA-based ICS.

But these types of threats were actual for any system that uses ICS or SCADA-based solutions. The main threat for such architecture is a physical access and the main type of intruder is an internal one. That was called "physical security" that is aimed to secure Operation Technologies (OT), but not IT. But what change since that communications scheme? A main reason is covered under 4th Industrial Revolution (sometimes called Industry 4.0). SCADA-based systems are changing toward Industrial Internet of Things (IIoT) solutions with the usage of more and more IT systems for data analytics. Figure 2 briefly illustrates the solution architecture developed by Industrial Internet Consortium (IIC) [8].

In the paper we consider an IIoT architecture, that could be used for moving towards Industry 5.0 systems. Key distinction comparing with Industry 4.0 systems that main network communications are going on the Internet or some global networks, that could connect to distributed production field like IoT devices, small factories, autopilot cars and other participants of supply chain network. Figure 3 briefly illustrates our considered IIoT architecture. We consider IIoT network as a graph of devices that could communicate with each other for some routes. The network architecture mainly leverages peer-to-peer communications (p2p). Some authors also propose architecture for IoT-based systems in appliance, for example, in Water management [9].

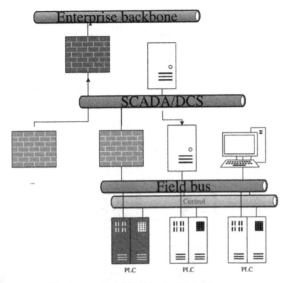

Fig. 1. Typical SCADA/DCS architecture

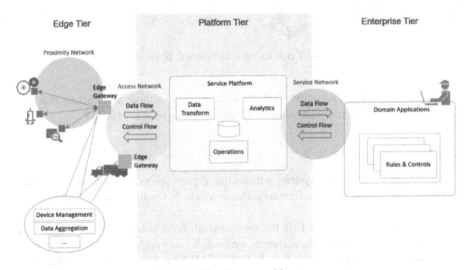

Fig. 2. IIC reference architecture

When the Internet becomes a backbone network for OT communications, the internal intruder is not so critical like external. Actually, there will be no difference between internal and external intruders, as all traffic and devices (i.e. nodes and edges of the network graph) will be gained from the global network.

So, for such critical infrastructure CPS systems that leverage IIoT, we need some new communication scheme that will guarantee with a probability that the packet between two devices on IIoT field will be delivered. After that we just need to set acceptable value

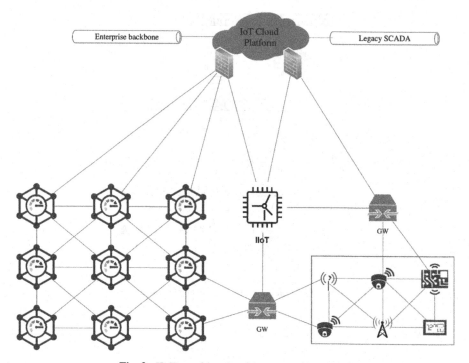

Fig. 3. IIoT considered architecture to be secured

of that probability for a particular system. New security methods is an actual research direction which is shown by the number of related works on it [5, 10, 11].

2.2 Main Threat of the IIoT

A cybersecurity state of the system, which critical parts are available from the global, will be highly defined by the information that is available for an intruder about network participants [12].

For any CPS systems like IIoT the most critical threat is accessibility violation of nodes and edges. To simplify the narration, we consider only nodes accessibility violation as the main attach vector of intruders. In CPS SCADA-based systems there where two approaches for providing availability:

1. Full reservation of field devices (PLCs, sensors, actuator) and network buses.
2. Reservation of global network communications on physical level. In case of the Internet, at least two different ISPs should be chosen to connect factory to the network. To highly secure channel and hide data between remote fields VPN tunnels are always used on the top of the Internet connection.

In case of the IIoT there is an ability of building MESH-network with p2p-communications. The p2p architecture itself brings the ability of path reservations through multiple available routes between nodes. The number of routes depends on number of nodes in the network and number of channels between them. Let's call a *packet path* or simply *path* between node X and Y a number of *routes* that could deliver packet between the nodes. A path consists of one or more routes.

In the p2p network topology path availability is harder to break, but it's also depends on how much information about the system intruder knows. Such circumstance prompts us take a look on anonymity networks. The main one which theory we could use is I2P network with garlic routing inside.

For measuring a quantity of information and probability of packet delivery let's use anonymity theory which tries to measure anonymity degree of each node in the network regarding compromised nodes. Let's consider anonymity theory from authors that propose methods for measuring it based on entropy [13–16].

3 Proposed Method

Generally, let G be the system that consists of N nodes v_i: $G = \{v_1, \ldots, v_N\}$. In the system there must be *compromised* nodes. A node could be compromised through the on of multiple attack vectors. The node could be used by an intruder for realization of one of the threats like reconnaissance, traffic spoofing etc. These network threats are described well in the ENISA baseline security recommendations [17]. For the sake of brevity, we will understand by compromised nodes that nodes which breaks the availability of the route, i.e. the main threat that could be on the IIoT field.

The main purpose of choosing a particular route on patch between nodes X and Y is to maximize a probability of its delivery. The probability of packet delivery is defined by path sustainability.

Definition 1. Path from node X to node Y is called *sustainable* if probability of packet delivery from X to Y through the any of its routes tends to 1.

The maximum entropy of the sustainable path is H_{max}, and entropy of the path, where compromised nodes present is $H(V)$.

In an initial time of path is created or when there are no compromised nodes the maximum entropy with N nodes is equal to:

$$H_{max} = log_2(N) \tag{1}$$

Generally, the entropy of the system, where compromised nodes present, is equal to the next formula:

$$H(V) = \sum_{i=1}^{N} p_i log_2(p_i), \tag{2}$$

where p_i is a probability of packet forwarding through a node v_i, $\{v_i \in G\}$. A quantity of the information the intruder is operating could be defined as the $H_{max} - H(V)$. According to [4], degree of anonymity for an anonymity set which does not contain compromised nodes, that are controlled by the intruder, is equal to the ratio of entropy about the system at the moment of compromise and maximum entropy:

$$d = 1 - \frac{H_{max} - H(V)}{H_{max}} = \frac{H(V)}{H_{max}} \qquad (3)$$

If $d = 0$, then the sender could be identified with probability 1. If $d = 1$, then all of the N nodes in the system could be senders with the equal probability ($p_i = \frac{1}{N}$).

In case of the anonymity degree calculation authors evaluate a probability, an attacker could definitely identify an originator of the message. If we apply this on the IIoT on a proposed architecture, if the intruder knows, which node can forward message to the compromised node that is under the intruder's control, then the intruder could violate the availability of the route, and, thus, decrease the probability of packet delivery. In worst case the intruder could block the path entirely.

Thus, for evaluating a path sustainability the intruder potential must be evaluated, i.e. how much information the intruder has to identify all of the nodes on paths, which availability should be violated to tend probability of packet delivery to zero.

Let's consider the example on the Fig. 4. The probability of packet delivery from a node X to a node Y path while sending through the only route is 0.5, as the half of the routes are compromised. However, if the X node will send packet through at least three routes or more ≥ 3, packet delivery tends to 1 as even one of three routes will go through uncompromised nodes. Thus, in the example the delivery of the packet is ensured via reservation of routes in a path.

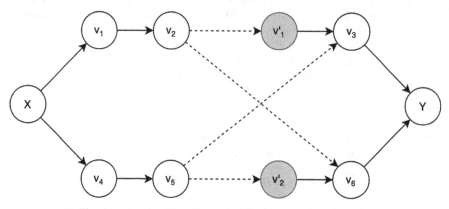

Fig. 4. Example of the subgraph with two compromised nodes

Let's define some notions.

Let S be a path from the node X to the node Y, and $s_k \in S$ – probable routes of the path from the node X to the node Y through the nodes v_i. Nodes that are on the path S are defined as: $v_{s_k} \in S$.

Let C be the number of the compromised nodes v'_j: $G' = \{v'_1, \ldots, v'_C\}, C \leq N$. Nodes, that are compromised by the attacker, must be excluded from paths. The size of the available nodes for path building is defined as $K = N - C$.

Definition 2. The set of routes of the path S called *sustainable*, if there are no compromised nodes.

Let p_{ij} be the probability of sending packet from node v_{s_i} to the node v'_j (Fig. 5), i.e. probability of sending packet from uncompromised node to compromised.

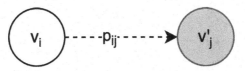

Fig. 5. Probability of sending packet from the node v_{s_i} to the node v'_j

Thus, $\sum_{j=0}^{f'(i)} p_{ij}/f(i)$ is a full probability of sending packet from the node v_i any to any of its compromised successors v'_j, where $f(i)$ is a number of total outgoing communications from the node v_i and $f'(i)$ – number of outgoing communications from the node v_i to connected compromised nodes (Fig. 6). Here we assume that probability of forwarding packet to any successor is equally likely event.

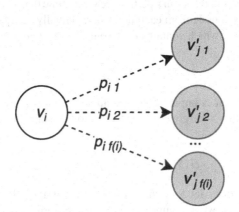

Fig. 6. Packet probability forwarding to the one of the compromised nodes v'_j

Thus, the probability that the node $v_{s_{ki}}$ will forward message to the legitimate, not compromised node, equals to:

$$p_{s_{ki}} = 1 - \sum_{j=0}^{f'(i)} p_{ij}/f(i) \tag{4}$$

Thus, for the whole of the route s_k probability of building route only through legitimate nodes equals to:

$$p_{s_k} = \frac{1}{N_k} \times \sum_{i=0}^{N_k} p_{s_{ki}}, \tag{5}$$

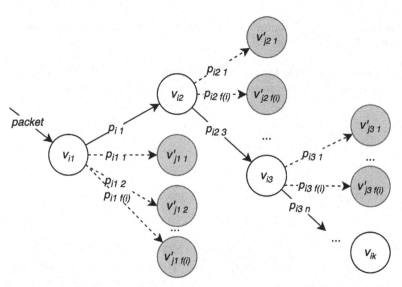

Fig. 7. Packet route through legitimate nodes

where N_k – number of nodes k in a path. Here we assume that a probability of sending packet via compromised node from each node $v_{s_{ki}}$ is equally likely events (Fig. 7).

Thus, for the path S, which contains of K routes s_k, probability equals to:

$$ps = \frac{1}{K} \times \sum_{i=0}^{K} p_{s_k} \tag{6}$$

Figure 8 illustrates an example of two sustainable routes s_k and s_k'.

Entropy of the path S, where we are trying to chose sustainable route s_k, then equals to the next formula:

$$H(S) = -\sum_{i=0}^{K} \left(p_{s_i} log_2 p_{s_i}\right) \tag{7}$$

For the sake of brevity let S be the full-connected graph. This assumption allows us to not consider cases, when compromised nodes are terminal nodes in a route. The assumption could be mitigated by entering node weights, that notifies about node criticality. As we said in Sect. 2, for increasing probability of packet delivery by the path S from the node X to the node Y, several routes must be used simultaneously by the sender of the packet. Moreover, the count of routes should depend on the count of compromised nodes in the system (in case of fully-connected graph) and in the path (in other cases). In Sect. 5 we give some thoughts about this for further researches.

4   A Necessary Criterion for IIoT Sustainable Workflow

As was said earlier, a packet to be delivered through the path S from the node X to the node Y, it must have more than one route. This is what is called reservation or duplication of the routes. All of the routes must be built such way that if one node is compromised on

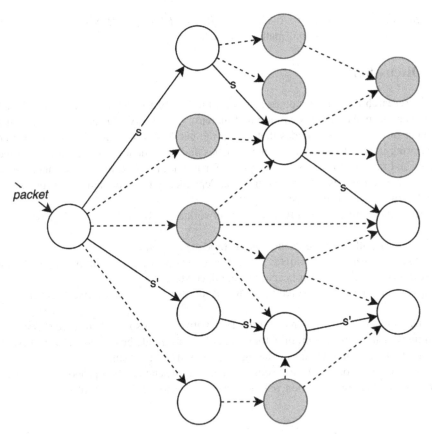

Fig. 8. Example of two sustainable routes s_k and s'_k

the first route the second route must remain sustainable. In other node, one compromised node must not be in both built routes. Let's define $H(SS')$ as an entropy of selecting to routes of the path S.

A theorem must be satisfied for providing path S sustainability.

Theorem 1. Sustainability entropy of path S of selecting sustainable routes s_k and $s_{k'}$ of probability scheme of K routes must satisfy the requirement: entropy $H(S')$ of selecting sustainable $s_{k'}$ while having entropy $H(S)$ of selecting s_k are mutually independent, i.e. $H(S) + H_S(S') = H(S) + H(S')$.

Proof. Let a route s_i contain n nodes: $v_{i,[1..n]} \in s_i$. Let a route s_j contain m nodes: $v_{j,[1..n]} \in s_j$.

Compromising a route means that the intruder has put some node v under control. If $v \in s_i$ and $v \in s_j$, then compromising paths s_i depends on compromising s_j and vice versa. Let's call these events as A and B accordingly. Thus, if availability of route s_i is violated then availability of route s_j is violated too. Then $H(SS') = H(S) + H_S(S')$. If it's true for all of the node $\forall v \in s_k, k = \{i, j\}$, then $H(SS') = H(S')$. Thus, there will not be sustainable routes, thus, path is not sustainable.

5 Discussion

In the research there is no conjunction of a number of routes in the path, that should be created to make path reservation and increase probability of packet delivery, and a number of compromised nodes that are on the network. As for the anonymity degree measuring in [13–16] there are some statistics and dependency between compromised nodes and number of nodes in the system for providing a certain level of anonymity. Our further researches are aimed to get that dependency between number of routes and number of compromised nodes in a path.

Also, there are great abilities that I2P network and Stop-and-Go mixes provide:

- temporary paths that are flushed by the time expiration;
- packet buffering (garlic cloves) until created message (garlic) with packet could not be defined by the attacker because of the fixed size;
- answering packet is delivered via different route comparing to received packet.

The impact of such technics on the IIoT network is also under research. But they definitely brings more uncertainty for the attacker and should be leveraged by the system and took into account when calculating sustainability of the path.

Also authors could consider some authentication schemes like proposed by Anada [18]. Authentications between IoT devices could also be done via blockchain-based solutions [19].

6 Conclusion

In this paper we proposed our thoughts about near future of production systems and tried to describe new scheme for communication in production systems. It's obvious that a lot of technological processes are stagnating because of disability of applying new IT technologies with their operation technologies (OT). Most of "new generation" factories and Industrial Control Systems (ICS) we deal with are trying to imply new IT technologies on the field, e.g. trying to install servers on local network and apply some new data gatherings and analytics. It's not what Industry 4.0 is supposing to be. But such simplified implementations are consequences of cybersecurity outcomes.

Acknowledgement. The reported study was funded by Russian Ministry of Science (information security), project number 20/2020.

References

1. Giang, N.G., Im, J., Kim, D., Jung, M., Kastner, W.: Integrating the EPCIS and building automation system into the internet of things: a lightweight and interoperable approach. J. Wirel. Mob. Netw. Ubiquit. Comput. Dependable Appl. (JoWUA) **6**(1), 56–73 (2015)

2. Kim, H.: 5G core network security issues and attack classification from network protocol perspective. J. Internet Serv. Inf. Secur. (JISIS) **10**(2), 1–15 (2020)

3. Angin, P., Anisi, M., Göksel, F., Gürsoy, C., Büyükgülcü, A.: AgriLoRa: a digital twin framework for smart agriculture. J. Wirel. Mob. Netw. Ubiquit. Comput. Dependable Appl. (JoWUA) **11**(4), 77–96 (2020)

4. Suleiman, H., Hamdan, M.: Adaptive probabilistic model for energy-efficient distance-based clustering in WSNs (Adapt-P): a LEACH-based analytical study. J. Wirel. Mob. Netw. Ubiquit. Comput. Dependable Appl. (JoWUA) **12**(3), 65–86 (2021)

5. Nkenyereye, L., Abhi Tama, B., Park, Y., Rhee, K.: A fine-grained privacy preserving protocol over attribute based access control for VANETs. J. Wirel. Mob. Netw. Ubiquit. Comput. Dependable Appl. **6**(2), 98–112 (2015)

6. Rose, S., Oliver, B., Mitchell, S., Connelly, S.: Zero Trust Architecture. NIST Special Publication 800-207 (2020)

7. Vasil'ev, Yu.S., Zegzhda, P.D., Zegzhda, D.P.: Ensuring the safety of automated process control systems at hydropower facilities. Izv. Ross. Akad. Nauk. Energetika **3**, 49–61 (2016)

8. Lin, S., Crawford, M., Mellor, S.: The Industrial Internet of Things Volume G1: Reference Architecture. https://www.iiconsortium.org/IIC_PUB_G1_V1.80_2017-01-31.pdf. Accessed 19 July 2021

9. Robles, T., et al.: An IoT based reference architecture for smart water management processes. J. Wirel. Mob. Netw. Ubiquit. Comput. Dependable Appl. (JoWUA) **6**(1), 4–23 (2015)

10. Zegzhda, P.D., Zegzhda, D.P., Nikolskiy, A.V.: Using graph theory for cloud system security modeling. In: Kotenko, I., Skormin, V. (eds.) MMM-ACNS 2012. LNCS, vol. 7531, pp. 309–318. Springer, Heidelberg (2012). https://doi.org/10.1007/978-3-642-33704-8_26

11. Fedorchenko, A., Kotenko, I., Chechulin, A.: Integrated repository of security information for network security evaluation. J. Wirel. Mob. Netw. Ubiquit. Comput. Dependable Appl. **6**(2), 41–57 (2015)

12. Vasil'ev, Yu.S., Zegzhda, D.P., Poltavtseva, M.A.: Problems of security in digital production and its resistance to cyber threats. Autom. Control Comput. Sci. **52**(8), 1090–1100 (2018)

13. Ye, J., Ding, Y., Xiong, X., Wu, S.: Dynamic model for anonymity measurement based on information entropy. J. Internet Serv. Inf. Secur. (JISIS) **4**(2), 27–37 (2014)

14. Serjantov, A., Danezis, G.: Towards an information theoretic metric for anonymity. In: Dingledine, R., Syverson, P. (eds.) PET 2002. LNCS, vol. 2482, pp. 41–53. Springer, Heidelberg (2003). https://doi.org/10.1007/3-540-36467-6_4

15. Hasuo, I., Kawabe, Y.: Probabilistic anonymity via coalgebraic simulations. In: De Nicola, R. (ed.) ESOP 2007. LNCS, vol. 4421, pp. 379–394. Springer, Heidelberg (2007). https://doi.org/10.1007/978-3-540-71316-6_26

16. Ohkubo, M., Abe, M.: A length-invariant hybrid mix. In: Okamoto, T. (ed.) ASIACRYPT 2000. LNCS, vol. 1976, pp. 178–191. Springer, Heidelberg (2000). https://doi.org/10.1007/3-540-44448-3_14

17. Ross, M., Hannes, T., Jara, A.: Baseline Security Recommendations for IoT in the context of Critical Information Infrastructures (2017). https://www.enisa.europa.eu/publications/baseline-security-recommendations-for-iot. https://www.enisa.europa.eu/publications/baseline-security-recommendations-for-iot/at_download/fullReport. Accessed 21 July 2021

18. Anada, H.: Decentralized multi-authority anonymous authentication for global identities with non-interactive proofs. J. Internet Serv. Inf. Secur. (JISIS) **10**(4), 23–37 (2020)

19. Alizadeh, M., Andersson, K., Schelen, O.: A survey of secure internet of things in relation to blockchain. J. Internet Serv. Inf. Secur. (JISIS) **10**(3), 47–75 (2020)

Blockchain Security

Future Applications of Blockchain in Education Sector: A Semantic Review

Paresh Sajan Gharat[1], Gaurav Choudhary[2](✉) ⓘ, Shishir Kumar Shandilya[1] ⓘ, and Vikas Sihag[3] ⓘ

[1] School of Computer Science and Engineering (SCSE), VIT Bhopal University, Bhopal, India
pareshgharat6890@gmail.com, shishir.sam@gmail.com
[2] Department of Applied Mathematics and Computer Science, Technical University of Denmark (DTU), Lyngby, Denmark
gauravchoudhary7777@gmail.com
[3] Sardar Patel University of Police, Security and Criminal Justice, Jodhpur, India
vikas.sihag@policeuniversity.ac.in

Abstract. Blockchain is a chain of blocks that are linked to each other via the Hash of the previous block. Digitalized Education sector has a lot of benefits for the student like providing one to one learning experience, flexibility in learning, etc. The Future Scope of the Education sector is vast, and new technology will be invented in the future for student's benefit. But at the same time, Education Sector has been affected a lot due to digitalization. Security of data, the privacy of students, and working digitally are few challenges faced by the education sector. Education Sector has a pool of sensitive information for which hackers are looking. As sensitive information is stored in the traditional system they are considered to be less secure than Blockchain Technology. Forgery of a certificate, Grading assignments digitally becomes difficult, Copyright content is used for teaching students digitally, etc. are few common problems faced by the Education sector in the digital environment. Traditional systems are not capable of handling these problems as they are vulnerable to various security attacks. So, This research paper focuses on these issues and has contributed a theoretical Blockchain model to solve this problem. In this model, Verification of Accreditation and Certificate helps in solving forgery problems using smart contracts and digital signatures, which makes the work easy for recruiters to verify the certificate received from an accredited institution. Auto grading assignments make use of external AI-ML natural language processing model and smart contract to grade assignments automatically. The copyright checking model makes use of public blockchain for checking the copyrighted material and helps to monetize the copyrighted content used and then permits the rights to publish it in a private blockchain. These blockchain-based models will help in solving these issues.

Keywords: Blockchain · Education sector · Gradings · AI · ML

© Springer Nature Singapore Pte Ltd. 2022
I. You et al. (Eds.): MobiSec 2021, CCIS 1544, pp. 93–106, 2022.
https://doi.org/10.1007/978-981-16-9576-6_8

1   Introduction

Education Sectors have changed a lot due to Digitalization. The Digital Education sector has lots of advantages like students can experience one to one learning, practice self-learning skills by using this technology, and get an opportunity to study from any place that is convenient to them which brings flexibility. The education sector has a lot of sensitive data like personal information, birth certificates, and graduation Certificate, etc. will is important to protect and this cannot be achieved by the traditional system in the digital era. As traditional systems are highly vulnerable as new attacks are increasing day by day. Digitalized education also faces a lot of challenges like Data storage, forgery of Graduation certificates, Copyright material is used by other faculty for teaching purposes, and Grading the Digital Assessment, etc. The traditional Education system uses the database, hard drive, and local server which are less secure for storing the digital data [1,7,37]. During any disaster, if data is stored on a hard drive is corrupted, then it becomes impossible to recover data, if the network or server is compromised by an unauthorized person then confidentiality, integrity, and availability of data are lost. So, in this way it becomes a difficult for Traditional education Systems become difficult to sustain in Digitalized Education sector. Cloud storage provides a good option for storing digital data but at the same time, the cost of cloud storage is high, most small education institutions cannot afford it.

The Blockchain is a chain of block and new block keeps on adding once they are validated by miner nodes in the peer-to-peer network. Block contains data, hash, a hash of the previous block, and timestamp. Each block is cryptographically encrypted by RSA/ECC cryptography which ensures the security of a block. In a blockchain network, each node in the peer-to-peer network holds an exact copy of the distributed ledger [11]. Blockchain is nowadays used in healthcare, supply chain management, NFT marketplaces, and Cryptocurrency exchange, etc. Blockchain technology can also be used to solve various ongoing problems in the Education sector as Blockchain has great features like Immutability, decentralization, cannot be corrupted, distributed ledgers and enhanced security, etc. [2,16,27]. This research focuses on problems faced by the traditional system in the education sector like grading assignments, Fair use of copyright content, and Accreditation along with certificate verification.

Digitalization in the education sector made it difficult for faculty to grade assignments and upload the marks in the system. The traditional system is vulnerable and marks can easily be forged [18,26]. This research paper focuses on providing a theoretical model to solve this problem. Auto-Grading assignment via Blockchain and AI ML model uses smart contracts to calculate marks based on the percentage calculated by AI ML model. The feature of immutability in blockchain prevents data from being forged. Most faculty use the copyrighted content of some other faculty to teach their students. This research paper has proposed a theoretical model which checks for the copyright content that is being used for Teaching and helps in the monetization of copyright content if used. Non Accredited institutions and Forgery of certificates is an ongoing problem in the education sector. While applying for a job there are thousands of applicants so, verifying each certificate manually becomes very difficult [17,24]. Verification of Accreditation and certificate using digital Signature and Smart contract is a model helpful in solving this problem by using digital signature and This model is a slight modification of model proposed by Ghazali and Saleh [13].

Education Sector has been highly affected nowadays as the entire world is shifting towards the digital era and due to increasing data breaches. The Digital era has encouraged people to start right from digital transactions to storing sensitive data like personal information digitally on cloud storage or hard drive instead of Hard copy [12]. Storing and Managing data becomes easy if data is stored digitally but at the same time, various risks are associated with it. Hackers are in search of sensitive data that can be useful for them to carry various attacks and the Education Sector has a lot of Sensitive data of students like names, addresses, contact numbers, and mark sheets, etc. which can be hacked by the hacker and can use these data for doing illegal things. Education Sector is also dealing with other problems like grading student's assignments, publishing results, and Degree forgery. A lot of security measures are implemented in a cloud platform like cryptography and firewalls etc. but with an increase in security, the cost also increases which is not affordable for every university or College.

Blockchain would be very useful in solving these problems. Blockchain technology was invented by Satoshi Nakamoto in the year 2008. Blockchain has features like decentralization, immutability, confidentiality, lower transaction cost, Transparency, and has enhanced security, etc. these features make it more effective in solving problems in the education sector [15,34]. Ghazali and Saleh [13] have proposed a Graduation Certificate Verification Model via Blockchain which makes use of digital signatures for verifying the academic certificate [13] this model can be made more efficient with Smart contracts and extra added features. This research paper focuses on a slight modification of the existing model, New model for an auto-grading assignment using the Ai ML model via Blockchain smart contract and fair use of copyright material model using smart contracts are few use cases of blockchain in the education sector which are discussed in this research paper, and these model will help in improving security and solving problems in Education Sector.

2   Related Work

Education Sector is facing lots of challenges due to the world moving towards the digital era. One of the problems is fake certificates are produced by users. Also sometimes there is a threat of forgery of certificates that are produced online. Detail study of this is done by Lee et al. [21]. The online certificate issuing is done usually via printer or computers and it is possible to access and manipulate the data while printing certificates and forged certificates can be printed. Lee et al. [21] has discussed various Attack methods like Memory Hacking, API hooking, and ActiveX Hooking which are performed to create forged certificates, and similarly Digital certificates can also be forged. The solution

Table 1. A detailed comparison of existing research based on a parameter associated with blockchain technology {R1: Smart contracts R2: Ethereum/digital currency R3: Security R4: Risk R5: SHA-256 R6: Uses Cases R7: Limitation R8: Identity Management/verification R9: Consensus, * represents only discussions}

Authors	Key contribution	R1	R2	R3	R4	R5	R6	R7	R8	R9
Ishaani Priyadarshini [31]	Introduction to Blockchain Technology			✓			✓	✓	✓*	
Ghazali and Saleh. [13]	A Graduation Certificate Verification Model via Utilization of the Blockchain Technology		✓	✓	✓	✓			✓	
SYED et al. [39]	A Comparative Analysis of Blockchain Architecture and Its Applications: Problems and Recommendations	✓*	✓	✓	✓		✓	✓*	✓*	✓*
Mingxiao et al. [28]	A Review on Consensus Algorithm of Blockchain		✓	✓		✓		✓		✓
Dasgupta et al. [10]	A survey of blockchain from security perspective	✓*	✓	✓	✓	✓	✓*			✓*
MONRAT et al. [29]	A Survey of Blockchain From the Perspectives of Applications, Challenges, and Opportunities	✓	✓	✓	✓		✓		✓	✓
Lin and Liao [23]	A Survey of Blockchain Security Issues and Challenges	✓	✓	✓						✓
Li et al. [22]	A survey on the security of blockchain systems	✓	✓	✓	✓	✓				✓
Bhaskar et al. [7]	Blockchain in education management: present and future applications	✓*		✓*			✓	✓		
Gräther et al. [14]	Blockchain for Education: Lifelong Learning Passport	✓	✓	✓			✓	✓	✓	
Waleed Rashideh [33]	Blockchain technology framework: Current and future perspectives for the tourism industry	✓		✓						
Chowdhury et al. [9]	Blockchain versus Database: A Critical Analysis			✓			✓*			✓
David Andolfatto [4]	Blockchain: What It Is, What It Does, and Why You Probably Don't Need One		✓*							✓
Nizamuddin et al. [30]	Decentralized document version control using ethereum blockchain and IPFS	✓	✓	✓	✓					✓*
Harthy et al. [1]	The upcoming Blockchain adoption in Higher education: requirements and process	✓	✓	✓		✓	✓		✓	

for this problem is verification and validation via blockchain to check originality in digital certificates is discussed by [1,13,14]. Limitations to Traditional verification systems like ownership of certificates, Availability, Cost for verification, and Time for verification is also been discussed by Ghazali and Saleh. [13]. In the digital Education sector due to advancements in technology, the ability to produce digital copies and distribute them without owner consent has been increased. Faculties have started using digital content created by someone who has legal rights associated with the use of digital content but sometimes Fair use of content is allowed. Campidoglio et al. [8] have discussed copyright protection problems, challenges, and a few suggestions in the paper. Blockchain technology offers a way to share data and ensure transparency. The parties involved are guaranteed that the data they are dealing with is error-free and cannot be changed. Decentralization, Persistence, Anonymity, Auditability, Public Verifiability, Privacy, Integrity, and Trust Anchor are the Characteristics of Blockchain Technology. Initial setup cost is expensive, energy Consumption for solving puzzles, Validation and Verification, Complexity, Privacy Leakage, Scalability, and Human Error, etc. are few challenges faced by Blockchain Technology. Despite the challenges faced by blockchain technology it has future Scope in Combating Crime, Banking Sectors, Banking Sectors, Big Data analytics, and Blockchain Miscellaneous Applications it has been discussed by Ishaani Priyadarshini [31].

Based on the comparative analysis for Blockchain and Traditional database system written by Chowdhury et al. [9] gives the information that if the user needs Trust building, robustness and provenance of data is the priorities for any system, then Blockchain is the best solution than traditional Database. If confidentiality and performance are the main focus then a traditional database is the best solution than Blockchain. In research, paper [9] also decision tree is provided to evaluate the appropriate use of Blockchain depending on the properties of the problem in order to avoid misuse of Blockchain.

A consensus is a common agreement that is to be accepted by each node in the blockchain network and there are different algorithms like PoW, PoS, DPoS, and PBFT a review about this is given by the Mingxiao et al. [28] but still research is needed to make the blockchain performance is better in a particular scenario.

There is a continuous threat to personal sensitive data and other expensive resources in the hands of third parties. There are more chances that resources can be misused. Blockchain is Decentralized, Immutable, and has hashing and encrypted data which makes it secure. Smart Contracts with Blockchain can be very useful for building trust among each other [6]. Blockchain with smart contracts has a wide range of applications in the healthcare, Supple chain, vehicular industry, and Business sector a detailed analysis has been discussed by SYED et al. [39]. Even if the blockchain is considered to be the Secure one than the traditional System still faces a lot of Security Issues and Challenges like The Majority Attack, Fork Problems, Scale of Blockchain, Time Confirmation of Blockchain Data, and Integrated Cost Problem, etc. has been discussed by Lin and Liao [23]. and the Blockchain Technology also has a vulnerability in services like Race attacks, DDoS attacks (not specific to blockchain networks, but they can be used with some specific variation to attack blockchain and asset exchange networks), Double spending attacks, and vector76 attack, etc. has been discussed by Dasgupta et al. [10]. Security Enhancement can be done using SmartPool, Quantitative framework, Oyente (detect bugs in Ethereum smart contracts), and Hawk (a novel framework for developing privacy-preserving smart contracts), etc. has been discussed by Li et al. [22]. A detailed comparison of existing research based on a parameter associated with blockchain technology is given in Table 1.

3   Need of Blockchain

Blockchain Technology provides users a way to share data and ensure transparency. The data present in the Blockchain cannot be modified by any user. The transactions are faster than the traditional bank since there is no involvement of a third party. If there is any kind of problem/issue in the system then, if the user is using blockchain technology user can easily trace back to the point of origin which helps in the quick investigation. Smart contracts can be used in blockchain technology which brings trust factors among users. Blockchain uses cryptocurrency and transactions are thus faster, secure, and cheap. Blockchain maintains the integrity of data and if data is altered then, it can also alert a user that the data has been altered [3, 35]. Every transaction is time stamped and sign with digital signatures hence, it ensures the property of non-repudiation. Blockchain has scope in various domains like Healthcare, Government, and Supply Chain Management.

3.1   Role of Blockchain in Education

The education sector and healthcare sector has a risk of data breaches as it contains most of the sensitive information that can be misused by attackers [5, 32, 36]. Also, new kinds of attacks are developed every day, hence it is necessary to keep security up to date. Focusing on the Education sector nowadays most of the information like student records and graduation certificates are all stored in either local hard drives or on the cloud. Local drives are highly vulnerable and cloud storage cost is expensive. An attacker can easily misuse the information for carrying identity theft, sell the information on the dark web, and forge the information. Blockchain has features like decentralization, Immutable, anonymity, redundancy, faster settlement, and enhanced security etc. makes blockchain more secure and reliable than the traditional system [20, 25, 40, 41].

Blockchain helps in certificate verification without the need for an intermediary person to verify them. Blockchain can be used for verifying the accreditation of educational institutions, it is considered to be a complex process in many countries. A Graduation Certificate Verification Model is an existing model discussed by Ghazali and Saleh [13] which uses a digital signature. By using this model the Recruiter or user can verify and validate the certificate without the involvement of the University physically, but it lacks in Smart Contract which can enhance the model and make it more efficient. In the future cryptocurrencies could be used as a method of payment. The education sector involves various kinds of payments like student fees, scholarship-granting agencies, and payments to teachers, etc. this can be done using cryptocurrency via blockchain Smart contracts. King's College in New York is the first institution to accept payment in Bitcoin. The University of Nicosia has been experimenting with blockchain certificates. Since 2015, the MIT Media Lab has been using Blockers for issuing digital certificates [1]. There are few challenges associated with blockchain technology while applying in education sectors like the legal challenge, scalability challenges, market adoption challenges, and innovation challenge [37].

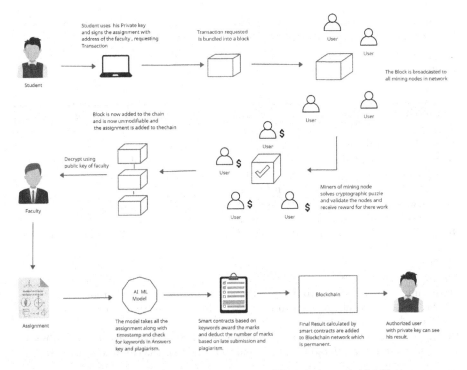

Fig. 1. Auto-Grading assignments via Blockchain and AI ML.

4   Auto-Grading Assignments via Blockchain and AI-ML Integration

The auto-Grading assignments model, shown in Fig. 1, will ease the work of Faculties in assessing the student. The auto-grading assignment model will use the AI ML model along with the smart contracts to calculate the marks hence there would be less chance of error in the calculation of the marks and students won't feel any faculties are biased of some students this would create a decentralized environment as faculties are not involved in grading the assignments. Also, the Assignment, as well as marks, are been uploaded to the blockchain, each node in the blockchain holds the exact copy of the marks. Therefore if there is any change in the data then, a hash of block changes and chain breaks and it can be effortlessly detected. As Blockchain uses a Cryptographic algorithm the confidentiality in the system is maintained. Blockchain technology is immutable and if somebody attempts to change data then, the Block rejects the modification of data as the hash of the block wouldn't be valid because of the previous hash. Data forgery can be detected and prevented using this Blockchain technology in the Educational sector eg: If somebody is trying to forge the marks then it can be detected easily. Also as a block in the chain is not corrupted easily as compared to the traditional system thus this feature makes this model reliable. The Auto-Grading assignments via Blockchain and AI ML Algorithms 1 is shown below.

Algorithm 1. Auto-Grading assignments via Blockchain and AI/ML

1: Start
2: Student will upload the assignment file in the system.
3: Private key of student is used to sign the file and address of the faculty is assigned
4: Assignment file is added to the new Block
5: New Block is broadcasted to all nodes in a network
6: Miners in the network will validate the block.
7: **if** Block Validation is Successful **then**
8:     The Block is added to the chain of block and miners will receive the rewards for there work
9: **else**
10:     Block is Rejected
11: Faculty uses public key to decrypt the all file uploaded by the students
12: All the assignment are send to to AI ML Model where timestamp, keywords and Plagiarism is calculated
13: Smart contract based on the parameter of AI ML model, calculate the marks. [marks will be calculated by smart contract based on the conditions given by University]
14: Marks will be uploaded to blockchain network by repeating step 4 for marks file, 5, 6, and 7
15: Student with the key can decrypt the data and can see his Results
16: Stop

---

5   Verification of Accreditation and Certificate Using Digital Signature and Smart Contracts

This model is a modification of the graduation certificate verification model developed by Ghazali and Saleh. [13]. Using a new verification model as shown in Fig. 2, Recruiters can easily check for the accreditation of the institution as well as the authenticity of the certificate and that too without the involvement of the Institution. Checking for Accreditation of Institution before Certificate is important for off-campus recruiters. Certificate forgery is increased nowadays, this model can help in solving this issue. As the institution uploads, the hash of the digital certificate to a blockchain and the recruiters can generate the hash using the digital signature and public key of the institution. Smart contracts compare both the hash and checks whether they are the same if, same then genuine, and if, not then fake. As Blockchain is immutable no one can change the data from the blockchain i.e. the hash uploaded by the institution/university. Thus it can help in verification of the certificate and preventing the Forgery of the certificate. Also as the blockchain is decentralized thus there is no involvement of a third party thus can stop corruption in the Education Sector. Verification of Accreditation Algorithms 2, 3 are shown below

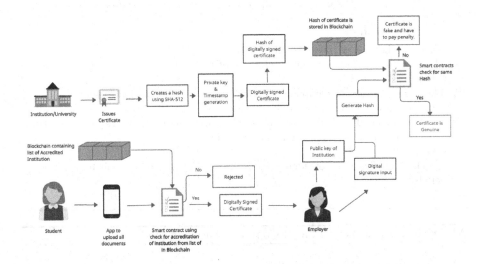

Fig. 2. Verification of accreditation and certificate using digital signature and smart contracts [38].

Algorithm 2. Working of Institution/University in verification

---

1: Start
2: Institution/University issues a Certificate to a student
3: Hash of Certificate is calculated using SHA-512
4: Then it is encrypted using a Private key and a Timestamp is generated
5: Digitally Signed Certificate is Created using hash and Cryptographic method
6: Hash of Digitally signed Certificate is calculated.
7: Hash is then Uploaded to Blockchain
8: Stop

Algorithm 3. Verification of Accreditation and Certificate:

1: Start
2: Student uploads the name of the university and Digitally Signed Certificate
3: Smart Contract using an existing list of Accredited institutions in the Blockchain network, check for accreditation of the institution.
4: **if** Name of University is in Accredited Institution list **then**
5:     Digitally Signed Certificate is approved for further Verification.
6: **else**
7:     Request is Rejected
8: Digitally Signed Certificate is submitted to the employer.
9: The employer then using the Public key of the institution and Digital Signature calculates Hash.
10: Then Smart contract compares the Hash uploaded by the institution/University with the hash generated by the Employer.
11: **if** Hash uploaded by University and Hash Calculated by Employer are same **then**
12:     The certificate is considered to be genuine.
13: **else**
14:     The Certificate is considered to be fake and the Student will have to pay a penalty
15: Stop

Algorithm 4. Blockchain based Copyright checking Model

1: Start
2: Faculty-01 writes the original content
3: Original Content of faculty will be uploaded to public Blockchain along with the timestamp
4: Other faculty, eg Faculty-02 shares the content with students
5: Before uploading content to Private Blockchain, Smart Contract checks for Copyright Content.
6: **if** Copyright content found **then**
7:     Based on percentage of copyright content, the person using the material has to pay the person owning copyright.
8:     content is uploaded to private Blockchain
9: **else**
10:     content is uploaded to private Blockchain
11: Students can access data from Private Blockchain of university.
12: Stop

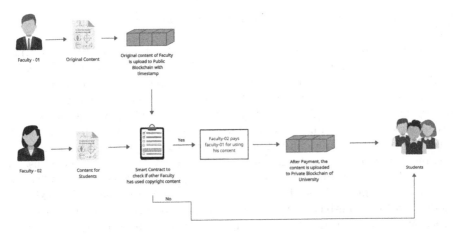

Fig. 3. Blockchain based copyright checking model [19].

6   Blockchain Based Copyright Checking Model

In a traditional system, most of the researchers uses some other researcher's content without proper citation. Also, it is difficult to track the use of copyright material in a traditional system. Blockchain network is immutable hence, it becomes impossible to modify the data. Proof of existence mechanism can give ownership of content without disclosing the content as shown in Fig. 3. As timestamp is stored along with the content, this can help in proving the ownership of the faculty's content. In this model Smart contracts are used to check the use of copyright content. The smart contract will also help in monetizing the content, which means whenever anyone who uses the copyright content has to pay for the amount of copyright content used, before uploading it to the private Blockchain. This model will help track the use of Copyright Content and benefit the Owner if someone uses his copyright material. Algorithm 4 is used for Blockchain based Copyright checking Model.

7   Conclusion and Future Work

Blockchain is in high demand because of its great features like Immutability, Decentralization, more secure, incorruptible, and faster transaction. At the same time Education sector is facing a lot of challenges in securing data, problems of forgery, data breaches, grading marks, etc. This research paper has provided an efficient solution that can help in solving this problem. Blockchain immutability and decentralization can help in reducing the forgery of data. As local server which is in current use can be corrupted easily and Blockchain is incorruptible which increases the reliability in the Education sector if this technology is adopted. Auto grading assignments model, verification of accreditation and certificates received from the institution, and copyright checking model based on Blockchain technology has been discussed in this paper, due to the use of

Blockchain technology this model is highly adaptable, reliable, and efficient in the Education sector.

The education sector has changed a lot due to digitalization. The education sector has a lot of sensitive information like Birth Certificates, personal data, graduation Degree as all data is either stored in a local hard drive or local server and therefore security in the Education sector has become important. Local servers are not secure and could not survive in the digitalization era. Blockchain Technology is new, secure, and in high demand nowadays. Blockchain has a few great features like immutability, Decentralization, Distributed ledger, cannot be corrupted and strong cryptographic encryption these features would be useful in the Education sector for solving various crucial problems. The traditional education system has a lot of risks and threats associated with it. The existing models of Blockchain-based certificate verification verifying the originality of the certificate is not only the task but verifying the institution issuing the certificate is accredited or not is also equally important. Forgery of the certificate, use of copyright material, and grading assignments, etc. are few issues taken into consideration, and the Blockchain-based theoretical model has been discussed in this research paper. If the Forgery of certificate issue is not solved then a lot of forged certificates will generate in large numbers and verification would become difficult using the traditional system. Blockchain-based Verification of accreditation and certificate model makes use of digital signature and smart contract to solve the issue. This model helps recruiters to easily verify the degree or graduation certificates. The blockchain-based Copyright checking Model makes use of public, private blockchain, and smart contracts to solve the problem. The auto-grading assignment model uses the Ai Ml model to calculate matching keywords and uses smart contracts to grade the assignment.

As all the models are explained theoretically detailed analysis is also done on each model experimentally. For accreditation and Forgery detection, a model needs a pre-list of an accredited institution in a blockchain, and getting a list is a difficult task this problem can be solved by using a different method in the future. Work on the Ai ML model with natural language processing will be done in Future work also checking of copyright model will be implemented efficiently.

References

1. Al Harthy, K., Al Shuhaimi, F., Al Ismaily, K.K.J.: The upcoming blockchain adoption in higher-education: requirements and process. In: 2019 4th MEC International Conference on Big Data and Smart City (ICBDSC), pp. 1–5. IEEE (2019)
2. Alammary, A., Alhazmi, S., Almasri, M., Gillani, S.: Blockchain-based applications in education: a systematic review. Appl. Sci. 9(12), 2400 (2019)
3. Alizadeh, M., Andersson, K., Schelen, O.: A survey of secure internet of things in relation to blockchain. J. Internet Serv. Inf. Secur. (JISIS) 10(3), 47–75 (2020)
4. Andolfatto, D., et al.: Blockchain: what it is, what it does, and why you probably don't need one. Federal Reserve Bank St. Louis Rev. 100(2), 87–95 (2018)
5. Aulia, V., Yazid, S.: Review of blockchain application in education data management. In: 2021 2nd International Conference on Smart Computing and Electronic Enterprise (ICSCEE), pp. 95–101. IEEE (2021)

6. Baldi, G., et al.: Session-dependent usage control for big data. J. Internet Serv. Inf. Secur. (JISIS) **10**(3), 76–92 (2020)
7. Bhaskar, P., Tiwari, C.K., Joshi, A.: Blockchain in education management: present and future applications. Interactive Technology and Smart Education (2020)
8. Campidoglio, M., Frattolillo, F., Landolfi, F.: The copyright protection problem: challenges and suggestions. In: 2009 Fourth International Conference on Internet and Web Applications and Services, pp. 522–526. IEEE (2009)
9. Chowdhury, M.J.M., Colman, A., Kabir, M.A., Han, J., Sarda, P.: Blockchain versus database: a critical analysis. In: 2018 17th IEEE International Conference on Trust, Security and Privacy in Computing and Communications/12th IEEE International Conference on Big Data Science and Engineering (TrustCom/BigDataSE), pp. 1348–1353. IEEE (2018)
10. Dasgupta, D., Shrein, J.M., Gupta, K.D.: A survey of blockchain from security perspective. J. Banking Finan. Technol. **3**(1), 1–17 (2018). https://doi.org/10.1007/s42786-018-00002-6
11. Duong, D.H., Susilo, W., Trinh, V.C.: Wildcarded identity-based encryption with constant-size ciphertext and secret key. J. Wirel. Mob. Netw. Ubiquit. Comput. Dependable Appl. (JoWUA) **11**(2), 74–86 (2020)
12. Dutta, P., Susilo, W., Duong, D.H., Baek, J., Roy, P.S.: Identity-based unidirectional proxy re-encryption and re-signature in standard model: lattice-based constructions. J. Internet Serv. Inf. Secur. (JISIS) **10**(4), 1–22 (2020)
13. Ghazali, O., Saleh, O.S.: A graduation certificate verification model via utilization of the blockchain technology. J. Telecommun. Electron. Comput. Eng. (JTEC) **10**(3–2), 29–34 (2018)
14. Gräther, W., Kolvenbach, S., Ruland, R., Schütte, J., Torres, C., Wendland, F.: Blockchain for education: lifelong learning passport. In: Proceedings of 1st ERCIM Blockchain Workshop 2018. European Society for Socially Embedded Technologies (EUSSET) (2018)
15. Grech, A., Sood, I., Arino, L.: Blockchain, self-sovereign identity and digital credentials: promise versus praxis in education. Front. Blockchain **4**, 7 (2021)
16. Grech, A., Camilleri, A.F.: Blockchain in Education. Publications Office of the European Union, Luxembourg (2017)
17. Guustaaf, E., Rahardja, U., Aini, Q., Maharani, H.W., Santoso, N.A.: Blockchain-based education project. Aptisi Trans. Manag. (ATM) **5**(1), 46–61 (2021)
18. Jamil, M.N., Hossain, M.S., Islam, R.U., Andersson, K.: Technological innovation capability evaluation of high-tech firms using conjunctive and disjunctive belief rule-based expert system: a comparative study. J. Wirel. Mob. Netw. Ubiquit. Comput. Dependable Appl. (JoWUA) **11**(3), 29–49 (2020)
19. Jing, N., Liu, Q., Sugumaran, V.: A blockchain-based code copyright management system. Inf. Process. Manag. **58**(3), 102518 (2021)
20. Kulkarni, D., et al.: Leveraging blockchain technology in the education sector. Turkish J. Comput. Math. Educ. (TURCOMAT) **12**(10), 4578–4583 (2021)
21. Lee, S.W., Lee, J.I., Han, D.-G.: A study of the threat of forgery of certificates issued online. In: 2013 47th International Carnahan Conference on Security Technology (ICCST), pp. 1–5. IEEE (2013)
22. Li, X., Jiang, P., Chen, T., Luo, X., Wen, Q.: A survey on the security of blockchain systems. Futur. Gener. Comput. Syst. **107**, 841–853 (2020)
23. Lin, I.-C., Liao, T.-C.: A survey of blockchain security issues and challenges. IJ Netw. Secur. **19**(5), 653–659 (2017)

24. Loh, J.-C., Heng, S.-H., Tan, S.-Y., Kurosawa, K.: On the invisibility and anonymity of undeniable signature schemes. J. Wirel. Mob. Netw. Ubiquit. Comput. Dependable Appl. (JoWUA) **11**(1), 18–34 (2020)
25. Loukil, F., Abed, M., Boukadi, K.: Blockchain adoption in education: a systematic literature review. Educ. Inf. Technol. **26**, 1–19 (2021)
26. Mahankali, S., Chaudhary, S.: Blockchain in education: a comprehensive approach-utility, use cases, and implementation in a university. In: Blockchain Technology Applications in Education, pp. 267–293. IGI Global (2020)
27. Malibari, N.A.: A survey on blockchain-based applications in education. In: 2020 7th International Conference on Computing for Sustainable Global Development (INDIACom), pp. 266–270. IEEE (2020)
28. Du, M., Ma, X., Zhang, Z., Wang, X., Chen, Q.: A review on consensus algorithm of blockchain. In: 2017 IEEE International Conference on Systems, Man, and Cybernetics (SMC), pp. 2567–2572. IEEE (2017)
29. Monrat, A.A., Schelén, O., Andersson, K.: A survey of blockchain from the perspectives of applications, challenges, and opportunities. IEEE Access **7**, 117134–117151 (2019)
30. Nizamuddin, N., Salah, K., Ajmal Azad, M., Arshad, J., Rehman, M.H.: Decentralized document version control using Ethereum blockchain and IPFS. Comput. Electr. Eng. **76**, 183–197 (2019)
31. Priyadarshini, I.: Introduction to blockchain technology. Cyber Security in Parallel and Distributed Computing: Concepts, Techniques, Applications and Case Studies, pp. 91–107 (2019)
32. Raimundo, R., Rosário, A.: Blockchain system in the higher education. Eur. J. Invest. Health Psychol. Educ. **11**(1), 276–293 (2021)
33. Rashideh, W.: Blockchain technology framework: current and future perspectives for the tourism industry. Tour. Manag. **80**, 104125 (2020)
34. Shah, D., Patel, D., Adesara, J., Hingu, P., Shah, M.: Exploiting the capabilities of blockchain and machine learning in education. Augmented Hum. Res. **6**(1), 1–14 (2021)
35. Sharma, V., You, I., Kul, G.: Socializing drones for inter-service operability in ultra-dense wireless networks using blockchain. In: Proceedings of the 2017 International Workshop on Managing Insider Security Threats, pp. 81–84 (2017)
36. Shuaib, M., Alam, S., Daud, S.M., Ahmad, S.: Blockchain-based initiatives in social security sector (2021)
37. Steiu, M.-F.: Blockchain in education: opportunities, applications, and challenges. First Monday (2020)
38. Sumithra, V., Shashidhara, R., Mukhopadhyay, D., Gupta, S.K.: Decentralized accreditation of educational attainments using blockchain. In: 2021 6th International Conference for Convergence in Technology (I2CT), pp. 1–4. IEEE (2021)
39. Syed, T.A., Alzahrani, A., Jan, S., Siddiqui, M.S., Nadeem, A., Alghamdi, T.: Problems and recommendations: a comparative analysis of blockchain architecture and its applications. IEEE Access **7**, 176838–176869 (2019)
40. Ullah, N., Al-Rahmi, W.M., Alzahrani, A.I., Alfarraj, O., Alblehai, F.M.: Blockchain technology adoption in smart learning environments. Sustainability **13**(4), 2021 (1801)
41. Verma, P., Dumka, A.: Perspectives of blockchain in the education sector pertaining to the student's records. In: Goar, V., Kuri, M., Kumar, R., Senjyu, T. (eds.) Advances in Information Communication Technology and Computing. LNNS, vol. 135, pp. 419–425. Springer, Singapore (2021). https://doi.org/10.1007/978-981-15-5421-6_42

A Resource-Blockchain Framework for Safeguarding IoT

Monika Bharti[1] , Rajesh Kumar[2] , Sharad Saxena[2] ,
and Vishal Sharma[3]([⊠])

[1] Jaypee University of Information Technology, Waknaghat, Himachal Pradesh, India
monika.bharti@juit.ac.in
[2] Thapar Institute of Engineering and Technology, Patiala, Punjab, India
{rakumar,sharad.saxena}@thapar.edu
[3] School of Electronics, Electrical Engineering and Computer Science, Queen's
University Belfast (QUB), Belfast, NI, UK
vishal.sharma@ieee.org

Abstract. Privacy concerning resource discovery and selection on the
Internet of Things (IoT) platform has emerged as a crucial challenge due
to constrained network environment, poor throughput, and access control
system in the Resource Directory *(RD)*, which could potentially lead to
information breaches among intelligent devices. Blockchain is indeed the
latest technological model for global information management, point-to-
point exchange, consensus process, asymmetric authentication, cognitive
agreement, and perhaps other computing innovations to address the challenge. Considering these advantages, a resource-blockchain framework for
safeguarding IoT is proposed in this article. The framework facilitates
efficient access of information among devices, gathers information about
the constrained environment, accepts data from heterogeneous resources
and stores them on *CoAP*-based *RD*. Moreover, it provides secure transactions and records authorised user's information *via* Blockchain-based
centralised server which acts as the frontend of *CoAP* based *REST*, dis-
patcher or repository and proxy server. The study demonstrates that
Blockchain technologies help in strengthening privacy capabilities and
safeguarding intelligent devices.

Keywords: Blockchain · IoT · Safeguarding · Privacy

1 Introduction

Internet of Things (*IoT*) has a tremendous potential to provide a stronger degree
of inclusivity, reliability, security, interoperability, privacy and integration to the
consumer systems [1]. For the same, it focuses on improving operational performance, production efficiency, reducing the machine's runtime and enhancing the
quality of the product. In general, the decentralisation, diversity, heterogeneity
of data and complexity in *IoT* result in the following challenges:

© Springer Nature Singapore Pte Ltd. 2022
I. You et al. (Eds.): MobiSec 2021, CCIS 1544, pp. 107–121, 2022.
https://doi.org/10.1007/978-981-16-9576-6_9

(i) With the incredibly rapid rise in *IoT* resources, enormous amount of data is generated that varies in formats, domains and types, *i.e.*, heterogeneity. Such data poses different challenges for machines concerning its storage, representation, interpretation. Therefore, it becomes extremely difficult to mine and dig out the hidden information. Hence, there is a challenge for developing efficient indexing methods to deal with heterogeneity [2].

(ii) With changing operating system, language, platform across different application areas on *IoT* paradigm, exponentially growing resources faces a high level of dynamism and result in unpredictable patterns. These patterns raise the issue of interoperability at various levels like radio access, protocol, semantic level, semantic and context level. Thus, there is a need for developing ontology and semantic-based techniques to support *IoT*.

(iii) The scale of experiment considered to envision *IoT* leads to another basic challenge, *i.e.*, scalability. It puts issues while discovering the location of the resources both locally and globally that may lead to location spoofing attacks [3,4].

(iv) The decentralization and complexity of *IoT* systems often fails to ensure the safety of *IoT* when the security of an organization is highly essential. All the security objectives must be attainable, such as confidential information, message integrity, verification, credibility, and access control. The goal is to provide support for these objectives.

(v) Energy conservation determines the lifetime of *IoT* platform. Intelligent systems use battery power as a source of energy for sensing, processing data and communicating information. Battery life is restricted and, as the sensors are positioned in such a hostile environment, substituting the battery is unrealistic. The concern is to reduce power consumption.

(vi) Smart devices are prone to failure because of an unattended environment. These devices may malfunction due to technical problems or power depletion. If a couple of intelligent devices perform poorly, the *IoT* portal must withstand this type of fault-tolerance. The issue is to offer more flexibility to the portal to cope with the fault-tolerant [5].

(vii) Research is expected to add a thorough methodology in recognising and determining conditions crosswise over applications. Hence, the decision-making algorithm needs to be developed to make context-aware and efficient use of the available services.

(viii) Privacy is intended to ensure the proper use of *IoT* data, and there is no possibility of disclosure of private user information without the consent of the user. Due to the complexity, decentralisation and heterogeneity of *IoT* systems, it isn't easy to preserve data privacy. Moreover, *IoT*'s integration with cloud computing is becoming a trend, as virtualization could even encourage *IoT* with additional computational and storage capabilities. Nevertheless, the transfer of sensitive *IoT* data to third-party cloud storage can also breach the privacy of compromised *IoT* [6,7].

These challenges would act as a bottleneck for the mechanism of resource discovery and selection and need to be addressed for the realisation of using blockchain in *IoT*. Various tasks such as data acquisition, modelling, integration, assessment and reasoning on *IoT* that vary with data suppliers and retailers or traders are accountable for tackling the associated challenges [8]. These tasks help in facilitating the interconnection of data, the summation of knowledge, perspective-driven search, based on which the resource discovery technique is extensively divided into two different subsequent loops, *namely*, foraging and sense-making [8,9]. In the former loop, the origin of sources is reviewed and analysed for information retrieval. In the latter, the retrieved information is evaluated, translated, and used to deliver a service in compliance with a specific query. For the same, it requires exploring techniques concerning the discovery mechanism. Also, there is a need to emphasise the selection criteria for taking an appropriate decision to provide service. The data and resource's interpretation, the role of data analytics and knowledge representation are discussed in subsequent sections.

2   Data and Resources on IoT

IoT data that has been consumed and produced continue to grow at an ever-increasing rate. This data flow is fueling the widespread adoption of *IoT* as there would be almost *30.73* billion *IoT* networked devices by *2020* [10,11]. *IoT* and data remain intrinsically linked together. But here, the question arises on the attributes of *IoT* data and its possible types. As far as data attributes are concerned, the focus is on location, number, size, lifespan, persistence, time dependency. Based on these attributes, data could be broadly categorised into context-based, content-based, linked data, and streaming data. Context-based data focus on the type of resource, sensor or actuator, location, quality of service, accuracy, etc. Content-based data includes both historical and real-time data, sensor information and entity information. Linked data strictly works on the type of architecture, *say*, centralised and federated. Finally, streaming data is collected through database mapping and semantic modelling. Though data categorisation would probably help researchers understand different data types with distinct attributes, it is equally necessary to get familiar with data sources or resources. The resource is either hardware or software with basic features such as identification numbers, specific service, location, processed information, system software, language families, and means of communication [8,12]. Such resources are available on the *IoT* dynamic network infrastructure and interact *via* four modes, *i.e.*, machine-to-machine enabled by predefined Application Program Interfaces *(API)*, machine-to-human, enabled using modern network protocols, cloud infrastructure and standard devices such as Arduino, Raspberry Pi. Considering these modes, it is inferred that possible resources could be *IoT* platforms based on Web-of-Things, Public Blockchain and Fog Computing. Web-of-Things helps devices to share their information across the social web, for example, Wotkit and SenseTechnic. The major challenges being faced by this notion seems to be perseverance, intention-oriented search, potential ramifications, and privacy. Blockchain is the method that use digital data to search and interpret remote sensing data in the network world, such as Urban Crowd-sensing Services. Finally, Fog Computing make it easier for utility companies to share, store and visualise *IoT* data *via* the traditional web tools, like Xively, ThingSpeak, ThingWorx.

With the understanding of *IoT* data and their resources, it is important to understand that this gathered information turns out to be of interest only if it is referred to the formation of data representation as knowledge. It is because knowledge act as a base for the achievement of *IoT* vision, *i.e.*, reshaping the incumbent real-time resource to intelligent resources featured with data-driven decision making.

3   Role of Data Analytics for Data Representation as Knowledge

The inherent property of *IoT* is the heterogeneity levied by a multitude of resources. This heterogeneity in terms of connectivity, computing capacities, interpretation, space, searching modes and communication protocols lead to unmaintained big data propelled by its size, scope, importance and amount, which presents significant challenges to the realisation of the dream of *IoT* [13]. However, this data is of little use on its own unless it is evaluated with the other similar data and scope. It is therefore essential to obtain a needle across numerous haystacks of zettabytes. The issue here would be to explain the precision despite the substantial heterogeneity and uncertainty of the data. It is where discovery coupled with data analytics in *IoT* will offer unique insights into the data generated by things. Thus, Data Analytics *(DA)* is described as a procedure that is being used to analyse big and medium sets of data with different statistical properties to draw relevant conclusions and predictive analytics. These findings come from trends, patterns, and statistics that help business organisations engage constructively with data in implementing effective decision-making processes. The different types of information analysis tools that can be used for *IoT* capital expenditure have been discussed.

1 Streaming Analytics: This method is often related to the activity of data integration and assessing broad in-motion data sets. Real-time data streams have been assessed for real emergencies and prompt responses. The various *IoT* applications based on business wire transfers, flight, video surveillance, *etc.* may get benefit from this method.

2 Spatial Analytics: This is the method of analysing geographical distribution to ascertain the geographic influence of physical things. Location-based *IoT* technologies, such as intelligent parking technologies, may reap the benefit.

3 Time Series Analytics: This form is premised on time-based data that is used to assess and reveal associated trends and patterns. Applications like climate modelling and health surveillance systems may be benefited.

4 Prescriptive Analysis: This is a hybrid of predictive and prescriptive interpretation. It is used to implement appropriate action that could be expected

to take in a specific circumstance. Infomercial *IoT* applications can use this Analysis for obtaining better outcomes.

With the analysis of data, the next challenge would be to do data modelling that targets knowledge formation which helps to build a resource repository with defined rules and conditions, extracting the meaningful information from the collected data that can be made available for users in a consumable form. For the same, it uses various modelling techniques based on Key-value, Fuzzy, Ontology, Energy-Aware, Object and Encoding. Key-Value is simple, flexible, easy to manage and application-oriented [14]. It does not support the storage of complex data. Fuzzy techniques allow pattern recognition. It is simple for defining, extending, handling uncertainty, and allowing more natural representation using a truth table. Modelling based Ontology is premised on description logic, is generally dominated by the *RDF*s and *OWL*. It allows re-usability of knowledge, is simple, flexible, application-independent, and expressive. Energy-Aware covers modelling techniques that integrate internet connectivity allowing devices to be controlled wirelessly. Modelling based Object models using classes promotes encapsulation, abstraction and is appropriate for use in private, semi-shared, code-based systems. It also does not have built-in inference abilities. Modelling based Encoding provides data using tags and is found to be more flexible, structured, efficient. It supports efficient data retrieval and validation using schema definition such as *XML*.

4 Role of Blockchain Technology in Resource Discovery Mechanism

Blockchain is an encrypted secure, safe, and immutable network that facilitates efficient access of information among entities [20–22]. Conventional *IoT* models depend on such a central controller model. Data is transmitted from in the system to the cloud, where the information is recorded leveraging algorithms and afterwards returned to the *IoT* systems. Despite billions of connected resources that are expected to attend *IoT* systems mostly in the near future, such a form of distributed infrastructure seems to have no usability, and it reveals billions of major flaws that undermine information security. Thus, it could turn very tedious and expensive as third party candidates would have to continuously track and verify every small non-transaction among resources [23]. Cryptocurrencies in Blockchain technology would enable machines that run safely and independently by developing partnerships that would only be enforced after fulfilling certain specifications. However, these cryptocurrencies will also avoid manipulation from entities that are using the relevant information for their financial advantage. Data is exchanged through a distributed, cryptographically encrypted channel, making it extremely difficult to violate cyber confidentiality. Eventually, in a distributed system, the chance of such a server failure to disable the whole infrastructure is indeed a very realistic prospect [24]. The distributed Blockchain system alleviates such threat *via* millions of active entities sharing peer-to-peer *(P2P)* information

Table 1. Summary of existing techniques in combination with *IoT* and Blockchain

Frameworks → / Parameters ↓	DITrust Chain [15]	IoT-LLN [16]	PrivySharing [17]	DeepCoin [18]	EdgeChain [19]
Methodology	Blockchain and *IoT*	Blockchain and *IoT*	Blockchain and *IoT*	Deep Learning and Blockchain	Blockchain, Edge Computing and *IoT*
Design Principle	Semantic Representation	Advertising LLN Configuration	PrivySharing REST API	Network Architectures as Home area, Building Area and Neghboorhood Area	Resource oriented Enforcement method
Knowledge Representation	Standard Ontology Language, Privacy-Aware Management	Smart Contracts namely, Access Control Contract (ACC), Judge Contract (JC) and Register Contract (RC)	Membership Service Provider	Short Signatures Scheme	Credit - based Resource Management
Search Approach	Linked Data, Multi-Agent Systems	Destination Oriented Acyclic Graphs (DODAG)	Reward based Data Sharing	Network based Connecting Devices	Device Specification Transaction's Generator
Architecture Design	Decentralized	Decentralized	Decentralized	Decentralized	Distributed
Dataset Used	Case Study - Healthcare	Rank Attacks using mote output tool	Smart City Scenario	CICIDS2017, power system, web robot (Bot)-Internet of Things (*IoT*)	Testbed, Synthetic
Platform/ Simulator	Fuzzy	eXtreme Gradient Boosting Classifier (XGBoostClassifier)	Hyperledger Caliper	Tensorflow	OpenStack, Google AIY
Algorithm Used	Association Rules	Fuzzy Scenarios	User-defined Access Control Lists Rules	Practical Byzantine fault tolerance algorithm, recurrent neural network	*IoT* Proxy, Smart Contract Interface, Blockchain Server
Framework	Yes	Yes	Yes	Yes	Yes
Technologies Used	Ripple Chain	Cooja, Tmote Sky	Kafka cluster and Zookeeper ensemble	Python in Google Colaboratory	PoW, Go-ethereum, Solidity, Truffle
Data Acquisition	Request/Response	Request/Response	Request/Response	Request/Response	Request/Response
Issues Resolved	Scalability, Interoperability and Security	Heterogeneity, Routing Security, Trust	Data Integrity, Privacy, Security	Energy Efficiency, Privacy,	Heterogeneity, Scalability and Security
Protocols	Etherum, Ripple Blockchain	IPv6 Routing	Kafka Consensus Protocol	BFT Consensus Protocol	Web3, Javascript, Etherum, Node.js
Data Integrity	Dynamic	Dynamic	Dynamic	Dynamic	Dynamic

to keep the majority of the *IoT* systems functioning properly [25]. As an example, *IOTA* has been the first *IoT* Blockchain network. It offers a transfer and a shared storage mechanism for networked devices [26]. Such a couple of aspects are vital in realistic *IoT* systems.

4.1 Blockchain Issues to Address in IoT

Various existing techniques that work based on *IoT* and Blockchain are summarized in Table 1, and the issues that need to be addressed are discussed below:

A Usability: Will Blockchain systems deal with massive information which is likely to be created from *IoT* over the next *5–10* years despite lowering transaction rates or information flows? *IOTA* tackles this problem directly whilst not utilising a distributed Blockchain-based system instead of selecting for their Ethereum network [27]. Also, some well-known Blockchain systems like Ethereum and Bitcoin have been grappling with usability concerns for a long time and are not tailored to the volume of content generated from *IoT*.

B Privacy: Distributed Blockchain systems have a higher sense of predictability, but what extent of vulnerability will be generated by *IoT* devices as they interact with the system? Systems involved in the transaction would be monitored to dissuade attackers from intervening during transactions.

C Interoperability: Inter-chain operability have to be tackled and optimised if developers want to utilise the benefits of intelligent and connected systems with blockchain [28] and to prevent Denial of Service (DoS) attacks [29]. If not tackled, it may end up with a system that will be integrated with a wide range of self-governing, distributed systems that perform well for their intent.

D Secular, laws and regulations: The delegation of contractual obligations and fairness would have to be carefully assessed [30]. How smart contract behaviours are governed from beyond blockchain would also have to be asserted. For example, who is liable if a patient-implanted *IoT*-connected health - care device decides to act somewhat on the grounds of several intelligent device laws but ultimately ends up inflicting damage to the patient? When the *IoT* system is Blockchain-based, it would be distributed without even a governing authority, so recognising the perpetrator can resolve this issue.

5   Resource-Blockchain Framework for Safeguarding IoT

This section describes Resource-Blockchain Framework on Internet-of-Things *RBF-IoT*, having four layers *namely*, Perception-Communication, Knowledge Representation, Blockchain and Application inspired by the layered architecture in [8]. It helps to obtain the authorised information, mostly on resources in compliance with the application. It accepts registration, updates server and support client's query *via CoAP-RD*. It helps in transacting, recording authorised user's information with its payment *via* incentives and keeping track of transactions.

5.1   Perception Layer and Communication Layer

The bottom layer in *(RBF-IoT)* works as physical layer wherein real world devices or things as intelligent sensor devices, gather information about the constrained environment and transform them into digital signals. The entire process executes using low power communication protocols such as Wireless Fidelity *(Wi-Fi), Bluetooth, IEEE* 802.15.4, Z-wave, and Long Term Evolution-Advanced *(LTE-A)*.

5.2   Knowledge Representation Layer

The layer accepts data from heterogeneous resources and stores them on *CoAP*-based Resource Directory (*CoAP-RD*). *CoAP-RD* accepts registration, updates

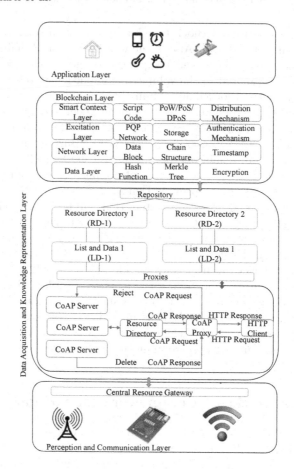

Fig. 1. Resource-Blockchain Framework on Internet-of-Things *(RBF-IoT)*.

server and support client's query. The proxy module helps to select only the authenticated devices and saves their information on the device whitelist (contain lookup tables). It works in three phases (Fig. 1):

Phase I: Resource directory: It is the repository having restricted resource terminal node server links, with properties like particular specification, IP address, port terminal. The terminal node helps to host other terminal nodes. *CoAP-RD* has interfaces based on *CoRE* Link Format and it registers, maintains registration of entries *via* registration link.

Phase II: CoAP server: The server itself serves as a mobile node and responds to the constrained node with authenticated knowledge. It keeps an update of the changes in the states or interaction method of the restricted node server. The *CoAP* client communicates with *CoAP-RD* using *CoAP* protocol. It requests resource's information directly or indirectly from the *CoAP* server.

Phase III: Proxy: It is capable of receiving and acknowledging the requests both from the server and client. It helps to authenticate the client and maintain a white-list.

5.3 Blockchain Layer

The layer is a decentralised, distributed computing and management layer. It helps in transacting and recording authorised user's information with its payment *via* incentives. It acts as middleware layer among *IoT* and its applications. It provides secured Blockchain services for essential *APIs* based applications. It consists of Blockchain node and its interaction *via* various sub-layers. The node supports data and other elements generated through methods like Chaining, Hash functions, Merkle tree, encryption, digital signature, etc. The working of sub-layers is briefly described as follows.

- Data layer: It is the first layer and helps to gather data from lower layers. It uses encryption or hash methods, Merkle tree to generate data blocks as chunks in node and adds a timestamp to data blocks. Such linked blocks of data form blockchain through dynamic data affirmation.
- Network layer: It is *P2P* layer and is responsible for the coordination between the nodes. It manages exploration, transfers, and distribution of blocks. There is almost no single node to manage the channel, and every node is synchronised. Each node generates a data block, verifies them and exchanges information within the network.
- Consensus layer: It helps maintain the trustfulness of node and is achieved using various algorithms like Proof of Work *(PoW)*, Proof of Stake *(PoS)*, Practical Byzantine Fault Tolerance *(PBFT)* and Delegated Proof of Stake *(DPOS)*. It validates the blocks, provides sequencing, and ensures that each node is accepting another node.
- Excitation layer: This layer helps to issue and distribute digital currency, designs reward mechanisms and handles transactions.
- Smart content layer: It helps in triggering special events using algorithmic mechanisms and script codes. This layer provides Blockchain-based services to various sectors.

5.4 Application Layer

It is a web application or gateway through which the individual consumer could enrol to utilise the offered services. Once authorised, every other consumer will be given a distinctive user id and an access management key for authentication and authorisation. Users can also retain records of purchases. The framework can be utilised for some of the applications described below.

- i. **Transportation:** The recent technologies in the automobile industry and vehicles have gained popularity, and different sensors, memory, processing units and communicating devices are integrated into portable devices. The data collected is exchanged between neighbouring nodes and ground station *via* wireless transmission. The wireless media poses various security threats. To address vulnerability and validate authentic messages, *RBF-IoT* provides a solution as it contains metadata mostly of maximum vehicles for verifying their credibility qualities. The vehicles can use this relevant data after solving a consensus mechanism.

ii. **Healthcare:** In the healthcare emergencies, *RBF-IoT* has a massive potential. *RBF-IoT* could be used in the medicinal distribution network business for ensuring the shipment of standards and security adherence of medicinal goods. Further, blockchain gathers the data of used products' data and offers reliable monitoring and exchange of health records for patients to protect one's privacy.

iii. **Logistics:** The framework can be utilised in logistics for optimising time, reducing cost, providing transparency and automating administrative based operations. Also, blockchain in logistics can help include the identification and helps in preventing expensive-value accessories such as jewellery, precious stones, etc., from being robbed.

iv. **Smart homes:** Blockchain in *RBF-IoT* helps in providing safety and assurance to *IoT* enabled smart houses. It provides a 'miner' to each smart home, having high resources and is available.

v. **Smart industry:** Blockchain in *RBF-IoT* can be benefited to the banking industry for automating, speeding the payment clearance process, providing transparency and security. It can be helpful in the power industry for monitoring electricity across a distributed grid digitally. It can also help trade electricity among consumers securely and with transparency.

6   Implementation

For evaluating the framework's feasibility, the Blockchain layer is implemented on private Etherum network (*see* https://github.com/ethereum/go-ethereum). It helps in connecting Ethereum testnets and debugging node connections. For the test scenario, network considers three nodes *namely*, owner of resource *(OR)*, Key Server *(KS)* and Client *(Cl)* (storing local Blockchain). The data blocks are formed for data of *OR* and is deployed as Smart Contract Resource *(Src)*. *Cl* can interact with *Src* by their public functions, *addToken* (for creating an access token and holds resource server addresses), *ttl* (field which holds lifetime parameter of access token) and *deleteToken* (for revoking the client access rights). The *Src* is triggered by owners with restricted access towards certain functions and is performed using Ethereum Virtual Machine *(EVM)*.

The test scenarios are evaluated to assess the performance of the framework.

i. **Key server:** The main server is operated on virtual environment. For evaluation, Datagram Transport Layer Security *(DTLS)* protocol is used as it implements the *TCP* reliable channel by requiring and acknowledges message for each transaction. The average time for completing *DTLS* handshake

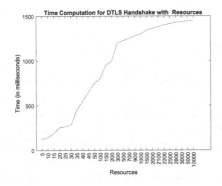

Fig. 2. Computation of Time during Handshake DTLS with Resources.

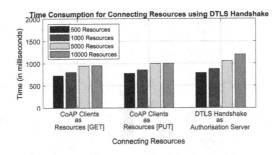

Fig. 3. Time consumption in connecting resources considering different responses.

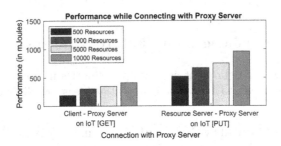

Fig. 4. Performance while connecting with a proxy server.

is shown. It considers an increased number of clients/resources that are connected on machine having configuration as *Intel i5-2800M CPU @2.15 GHz, 4 GB RAM* and *Windows 10* (*see* Fig. 2).

ii. **Resource server:** The server's implementation is done on *C platform* and is tested using Arduino *IDE*. It is implemented to find the average arrival time of (a) *GET* query from client side to the server, (b) respond time to *PUT* query and (c) total time consumed in the course of *DTLS* handshake among resources and main servers (as shown in Fig. 3).

iii. **Proxy server:** For client proxy server connection, it is implemented on OpenStack-based cloud installed at campus system. This has the feature to include one main processor and a few subordinate operating systems that run as distributed virtual machines. Each server hosts *Windows 10 OS* having configuration as *Intel OctaCore Xeon Processors with speed of 2.90 GHz, 8 GB RAM* and *3 GB* of disk space (*see* Fig. 4). The evaluation is presented in Fig. 5 which shows the performance on in signing, verification, encryption and decryption for resource at server in case of *PUT* and *GET* requests. It is found that each request passes through a Blockchain-based centralised server which acts as the frontend of REST (running on the main server), dispatcher/repository (application component based on Java), and proxy server (running on the replicated *VMs*).

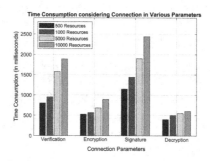

Fig. 5. Time consumption for different processes with varying resources.

7   Research Challenges and Future Strategies

Although *RBF-IoT* has brought several opportunities in upgrading industries, yet several issues need to be tackled. Potential ideas are discussed to resolve these issues.

i. **Scalability:** As stated by Gartner, that the number of resources is increasing massively. This data need extensive computing power, energy consumption based decentralised consensus algorithms. But, consensus algorithms may not be achievable for small peer *IoT* applications. This leads to scalability issues within the network.
Possibilities: The integration of *MEC* and cloud-based computing innovations can resolve scalability issues as Blockchain data will be stored on the cloud, and more resources can participate in the communication. Also, the storage-based optimisation methods can be another solution to address scalability to keep recent data and remove past transactions.

ii. **Trust management and security vulnerability:** *IoT* platforms need trust mechanisms in the network for exchanging accurate and credible relevant data between services. For this purpose, the participating resources must communicate within a defined limit of time. But due to the intermittent nature of *IoT* networks, the recommendation and reputation of the resource play a significant role while establishing trust. Also, the Blockchain layer in *RBF-IoT* improves the security of the framework. However, security is an issue due to the vulnerability of Blockchain-based *IoT* systems. The wireless transmission channel often experiences illegal accesses such as proactive eavesdroppers, spoofing, intercepting threats.

Possibilities: Blockchain in *RBF-IoT* is decentralized and provides perfect solution for establishing trust among resources. Also, security issues can be mitigated by improving the reliability of *IoT* devices or by patching glitches. The cooperative jamming schemes can be implemented for improving trust build-up among resources.

iii. **Efficient consensus and *PoW* algorithms:** The interaction among resources is achieved through communication layer. As sensitive information propagates within resources in a limited time, there are threats related to accident warnings that may arise. At the same time, preserving the details of authenticated transactions is difficult due to the generation of one-time accounts of anonymous users. In this scenario, layers can be affected if the miners often seem reluctant to overcome the consensus mechanism promptly, and data breach is very likely.

Possibilities: The optimised consensus and *PoW* algorithms are required for miners to provide correct data to communicate resources in a limited time. Another possible solution is to leverage a memory-optimised and flexible data storage scheme for reducing leakage risks.

iv. **Miner selection:** For receiving specific sections of the transaction, selecting a significant miner will be an issue as it can't be checked for its internal working within an intermittent network of *RBF-IoT*. Furthermore, due to multiple placements of miners, all criteria are not fulfilled, including tolerable latency, expense, throughput on the network. Therefore, the network could endure malicious offenders and malicious miners.

Possibilities: As possible solutions for a fair selection of miners, one has to go beyond digital currencies, the reputation of credits and use them as incentives for various systems like data provenance, medication supply, sharing economy and miners rewarding. These solutions may help in the fair selection of miners.

8   Conclusion

The integrated framework, *RBF-IoT*, helps in transacting, recording authorised user's information with its payment and keeps track of transactions. It helps in connecting Ethereum testnets and debugging resource's connections. The Blockchain layer improves the security of *RBF-IoT* and provides the perfect solution for establishing trust among resources. The evaluation result shows the authorised and authenticated information exchanges with increased resources with its implementation on Virtual Machine. The potential applications towards realization of *RBF-IoT* are outlined. Various challenges and opportunities in the field in achieving the futuristic application are discussed concerning *RBF-IoT*.

References

1. Sharma, V., You, I., Andersson, K., Palmieri, F., Rehmani, M.H., Lim, J.: Security, privacy and trust for smart mobile-internet of things (M-IoT): a survey. IEEE Access **8**, 167123–167163 (2020)
2. Atzori, L., Iera, A., Morabito, G.: From "smart objects" to "social objects": the next evolutionary step of the internet of things. IEEE Commun. Mag. **52**(1), 97–105 (2014)
3. Wong, S.K., Yiu, S.-M.: Location spoofing attack detection with pre-installed sensors in mobile devices. J. Wirel. Mob. Netw. Ubiquit. Comput. Dependable Appl. **11**(4), 16–30 (2020)
4. Wong, S.K., Yiu, S.-M.: Identification of device motion status via Bluetooth discovery. J. Internet Serv. Inf. Secur. **10**(4), 59–69 (2020)
5. Wu, C.K., Tsang, K.F., Liu, Y., Zhu, H., Wang, H., Wei, Y.: Critical internet of things: an interworking solution to improve service reliability. IEEE Commun. Mag. **58**(1), 74–79 (2020)
6. Caputo, D., Verderame, L., Ranieri, A., Merlo, A., Caviglione, L.: Fine-hearing google home: why silence will not protect your privacy. J. Wirel. Mob. Netw. Ubiquit. Comput. Dependable Appl. **11**(1), 35–53 (2020)
7. Sharma, V., Guan Tan, T., Singh, S., Sharma, P.K.: Optimal and privacy-aware resource management in AIoT using osmotic computing. IEEE Trans. Ind. Inform. 1 (2021). https://doi.org/10.1109/TII.2021.3102471
8. Bharti, M., Kumar, R., Saxena, S., Jindal, H.: Optimal resource selection framework for internet-of-things. Comput. Electr. Eng. **86**, 106693 (2020)
9. Barnaghi, P., Sheth, A.: On searching the internet of things: requirements and challenges. IEEE Intell. Syst. **31**(6), 71–75 (2016)
10. Vishwakarma, R., Jain, A.K.: A survey of DDoS attacking techniques and defence mechanisms in the IoT network. Telecommun. Syst. **73**(1), 3–25 (2020)
11. Sahay, R., Geethakumari, G., Mitra, B.: A novel blockchain based framework to secure IoT-LLNS against routing attacks. Computing **102**, 2445–2470 (2020)
12. Dawod, A., Georgakopoulos, D., Jayaraman, P.P., Nirmalathas, A.: Advancements towards global IoT device discovery and integration. In: 2019 IEEE International Congress on Internet of Things (ICIOT), pp. 147–155. IEEE (2019)
13. Dhillon, H.S., Huang, H., Viswanathan, H.: Wide-area wireless communication challenges for the internet of things. IEEE Commun. Mag. **55**(2), 168–174 (2017)
14. Hussain, F., Hassan, S.A., Hussain, R., Hossain, E.: Machine learning for resource management in cellular and IoT networks: potentials, current solutions, and open challenges. IEEE Commun. Surv. Tutor. **22**(2), 1251–1275 (2020)
15. Abou-Nassar, E.M., Iliyasu, A.M., El-Kafrawy, P.M., Song, O.-Y., Bashir, A.K., Abd El-Latif, A.A.: Ditrust chain: towards blockchain-based trust models for sustainable healthcare IoT systems. IEEE Access **8**, 111223–111238 (2020)
16. Sahay, R., Geethakumari, G., Mitra, B.: A novel blockchain based framework to secure IoT-LLNs against routing attacks. Computing (2020)
17. Makhdoom, I., Zhou, I., Abolhasan, M., Lipman, J., Ni, W.: Privysharing: a blockchain-based framework for privacy-preserving and secure data sharing in smart cities. Comput. Secur. **88**, 101653 (2020)

18. Ferrag, M.A., Maglaras, L.: DeepCoin: a novel deep learning and blockchain-based energy exchange framework for smart grids. IEEE Trans. Eng. Manag. **67**, 1285–1297 (2019)
19. Pan, J., Wang, J., Hester, A., Alqerm, I., Liu, Y., Zhao, Y.: EdgeChain: an edge-IoT framework and prototype based on blockchain and smart contracts. IEEE Internet Things J. **6**(3), 4719–4732 (2018)
20. Sharma, V.: An energy-efficient transaction model for the blockchain-enabled internet of vehicles (IoV). IEEE Commun. Lett. **23**(2), 246–249 (2018)
21. Alizadeh, M., Andersson, K., Schelén, O.: A survey of secure internet of things in relation to blockchain. J. Internet Serv. Inf. Secur. (JISIS) **10**(3), 47–75 (2020)
22. König, L., Unger, S., Kieseberg, P., Tjoa, S., Blockchains, J.R.C.: The risks of the blockchain a review on current vulnerabilities and attacks. J. Internet Serv. Inf. Secur. **10**(3), 110–127 (2020)
23. Sharma, M., Gupta, A.: Intercloud resource discovery: a future perspective using blockchain technology. J. Technol. Manag. Growing Econ. **10**(2), 89–96 (2019)
24. Sharma, V., You, I., Seo, J.T., Guizani, M.: Secure and reliable resource allocation and caching in aerial-terrestrial cloud networks (ATCNs). IEEE Access **7**, 13867–13881 (2019)
25. Viriyasitavat, W., Da Xu, L., Bi, Z., Hoonsopon, D.: Blockchain technology for applications in internet of things-mapping from system design perspective. IEEE Internet Things J. **6**(5), 8155–8168 (2019)
26. Dorri, A., Kanhere, S.S., Jurdak, R.: Towards an optimized blockchain for IoT. In: 2017 IEEE/ACM Second International Conference on Internet-of-Things Design and Implementation (IoTDI), pp. 173–178. IEEE (2017)
27. Georgakopoulos, D.: A global IoT device discovery and integration vision. In: 2019 IEEE 5th International Conference on Collaboration and Internet Computing (CIC), pp. 214–221. IEEE (2019)
28. Sharma, V., You, I., Kul, G.: Socializing drones for inter-service operability in ultra-dense wireless networks using blockchain. In: Proceedings of the 2017 International Workshop on Managing Insider Security Threats, pp. 81–84 (2017)
29. Abhishta, A., van Heeswijk, W., Junger, M., Nieuwenhuis, L.J., Joosten, R.: Why would we get attacked? An analysis of attacker's aims behind DDoS attacks. J. Wirel. Mob. Netw. Ubiquit. Comput. Dependable Appl. **11**(2), 3–22 (2020)
30. Tan, T.G., Sharma, V., Zhou, J.: Right-of-stake: deterministic and fair blockchain leader election with hidden leader. In: IEEE International Conference on Blockchain and Cryptocurrency (ICBC), pp. 1–9. IEEE (2020)

The Design and Implementation of Blockchain-Assisted User Public-Private Key Generation Method

Tianhong Zhang[1,2], Zejun Lan[1,2], Xianming Gao[3(✉)], and Jianfeng Guan[1,2]

[1] State Key Laboratory of Networking and Switching Technology,
Beijing University of Posts and Telecommunications, Beijing 100876, China
{ZhangTianHong,zejunlan,jfguan}@bupt.edu.cn
[2] School of Computer Science (National Pilot Software Engineering School),
Beijing University of Posts and Telecommunications, Beijing 100876, China
[3] Academy of Military Sciences, Beijing 100142, China

Abstract. The rapid development of network technology has brought new challenges to data security. As the first gateway of a certain mobile internet system, access authentication is an essential step that guarantees the internal security of the network. However, there are some problems in traditional cryptosystem-based authentication mechanisms, such as certificate management problem and centralized key escrow problem. Centralized storage of user information is restricted by the server, the security of the server is not within the user's control, the stability of the server cannot be guaranteed, and personal privacy on the server may be leaked. In this paper, we focus on the private key escrow problem caused by the Private Key Generator (PKG) in Identity-Based Cryptosystems (IBC) mechanism and propose a Blockchain-assisted user public-private key generation scheme (BAKG) which introduces the blockchain to improve the robustness and reliability of key management. In BAKG, the user's private key is determined by itself through combining the partial private keys from different PKGs, which prevents the risk of private key exposure caused by a single PKG. Meanwhile, based on the theory of the Combined Public Key (CPK) algorithm, we have designed a feasible blockchain-based key generation logic and developed a prototype authentication system based on the above concept. We further analyze the security of BAKG and the analytical results show that BAKG can meet various security requirements. In addition, according to the performance evaluation results, BAKG has good performance in both read/write consensus and different key length calculations, which means it has good potential for lightweight authentication applications.

Keywords: Blockchain · Authentication · Identity-Based Cryptosystems · Combine public key

This research was supported by the project under contract No. 2019-JCJQ-ZD-182-00-02.

I. You et al. (Eds.): MobiSec 2021, CCIS 1544, pp. 122–138, 2022.
https://doi.org/10.1007/978-981-16-9576-6_10

1   Introduction

With the popularity of the Internet and the rapid development of related technologies, various Internet applications have flourished. With the development of mobile communication technology, the use of the Internet is no longer limited to personal computers, and wireless terminals such as mobile phones and PADs can also access the Internet. However, while the Internet has facilitated our lives, various websites need to interact with a large number of users and store the corresponding user information, which brings more general network security issues, especially mobile Internet security issues. In the process of network communication, access authentication is an essential step to ensure the security of communication and user information. Trustworthy authentication is the basis of mutual trust between two users when communicating over the network. However, traditional access authentication technology still has certain constraints that centralized key management poses certain security risks [1]. When a single server is compromised, the keys on the server may be leaked. For this reason, new technologies and protocols are needed to ensure communication and data security.

There have been many studies on network security. For example, Hiroaki Anada [2] proposed a decentralized multi-authority anonymous authentication scheme that is suitable for IoT and blockchains. Duong et al. [3] improved the wildcard identity-based encryption which is a generalization of Hierarchical identity based encryption. Loh et al. [4] invalidated two past cryptanalyses on undeniable signature schemes and provided a generic solution. Pöhn et al. [5] proposed an identity and access management framework(IAMF) to authenticate users.

Over the last decade, blockchain has gained popularity and researchers, as well as companies, are investigating new fields that could be impacted by blockchain technology, e.g. accounting field [6], central bank digital currency security [7], IoT field [8]. Blockchain is essentially a distributed ledger-based structure, which adopts the idea of decentralization and relies on consensus mechanisms to reach consensus [9,10]. Blockchain is distributed, tamper-evident and traceable, which provided a new way to solve the centralized key escrow problem. Since multiple nodes store the same copy, the system can still operate normally when one node fails.

Therefore, we propose a blockchain-assisted authentication scheme. This scheme relies on blockchain technology to split the traditional centralized key management node into multiple decentralized blockchain nodes. Since the key generation depends on more than one node, it secures the user's private key. Then we develop a lightweight authentication system based on our scheme and evaluate the efficiency of the system.

Key security is not only the foundation of mobile Internet security but also the most important basis to ensure the stability of network systems. But the centralized PKG key generation and management scheme based on the traditional IBC mechanism has many limitations and security risks. In the blockchain system, data are generated by blockchain entities and published as a consensus transaction on the blockchain network. It is worth mentioning that there is no centralized third-party organizations in the blockchain network, and each participant is independent. All participants keep the same ledger and update the blockchain periodically. So we adopt blockchain to separate the power of PKG to multiple blockchain nodes which server as distributed PKGs. Based on the synchronous and non-tamperable nature of the blockchain distributed ledger, key parameters of the system can be stored securely.

Base on the above background and our previous research [11], we propose a blockchain-assisted authentication scheme to enhance the security of user's private key. The main contributions of this paper are as follows:

1. By investigating the current authentication scheme based on the IBC mechanism, we point out the shortcomings and unsafe factors of key escrow caused by a single PKG. To solve these problems, we introduce the distributed blockchain nodes to replace the single PKG in the traditional IBC mechanism.
2. In order to involve the blockchain in the process of key generation and protection, rather than just as a trusted database, we introduce the CPK mechanism to our scheme and allow each blockchain node to parallel generate the user key pair by using the Elliptic Curve Cryptosystem (ECC) algorithm through the key combination method.
3. We develop a lightweight authentication system based on our scheme. In addition, we evaluate the efficiency of the system by measuring and analyzing the computation delay and blockchain consensus overhead through simulation.

The rest of this paper is organized as follows: In Sect. 2, we summarize some representative issues of the authentication mechanisms. In Sect. 3, we introduce the model of our scheme. In Sect. 4, we show the key generation and authentication procedure of our scheme. In Sect. 5, we resent a prototype system designed and implemented based on blockchain. In Sect. 6, we evaluate our system in terms of security and efficiency. In the end, Sect. 7 concludes our work.

2   Related Technologies

There are three traditional and representative authentication mechanisms, including Public Key Infrastructure (PKI) authentication scheme, Identity-Based Cryptosystem (IBC) authentication scheme, and Combined Public Key (CPK) based authentication scheme. Recently, researches on the direction of blockchain have also made some progress. We summarize their development history and applications.

2.1   PKI-Based Authentication

PKI is an authentication technology developed from public key theory, which can transparently provide the key and certificate management. In 1978, L.Kohnfelder [12] first introduced the concept of certificates. Later, the X.509 standard was proposed to make the scheme more standardized. Nowadays PKI technology is Gradually mature and has entered the stage of large-scale application. One of the most famous cases is the improvement of the communication protocol HTTP. For security reasons, the plaintext communication used in the widely used HTTP protocol is no longer suitable for the current network environment. It is desired to use the more efficient symmetric encryption method to hide the communication contents. To ensure the security of keys in symmetric encryption, the improved HTTPS protocol incorporates the SSL/TLS protocol [13] to exchange keys for symmetric encryption. However, SSL/TLS protocol still has security risks [14], the most important one is the trust of Certificate Authority (CA) which issues certificates. If the CA is not trusted, then there are also security issues with the certificates it issues. In response to the above problem, Google published RFC 6962 Certificate Transparency [15] in 2013, which introduces an independent Log Server component in practical applications. During the communication process, the browser will only accept the certificate founded on the Log Server.

2.2 IBC-Based Authentication

The PKI-based authentication scheme cannot get rid of the heavy certificate system which ensures the correspondence between the user and the public key. Therefore Adi Shamir [16] proposed IBC, which constructed an identity-based signature scheme and an unspecified identity-based encryption scheme. In 2001, Boneh and Franklin [17] first proposed the secure and applicable IBE. Compared with the traditional PKI, the IBC authentication scheme uses user information as the public key. Then, IBC generates the private key by the Private Key Generator (PKG) as a trusted organization, which makes it possible to exchange public keys securely between users. However, PKG is still a centralized institution. As the number of users grows, PKG faces greater operational pressure. For this reason, Gentry and Silverberg [18] proposed a layered PKG, the Hierarchical Identity-Based Cryptography (HIBC) scheme to balance the load on the PKG. Although IBC solves the certificate management problem, it still faces the risk of private key exposure caused by a single PKG. For users, the generation of private keys still depends on a single PKG. Ryu and Lee et al. [19] provided a revocation mechanism for HIBC schemes to revoke a user's private key in case of key leakage or credential expiration. Fida et al. [20] proposed an HIBC-based authentication scheme with a hierarchical key escrow architecture to meet the needs of large-scale network applications. Wang et al. [21] proposed an efficient HIBE system for the data confidentiality requirements of infrastructure in distributed IoT.

2.3 CPK-Based Authentication

With the development of PKI, the use of encryption certificates is becoming more widespread and key escrow as an integral part of PKI systems is becoming more important. Bellare et al. [22] introduced a verifiable partial key escrow technique to balance the needs of individuals with the needs of law enforcement in the domain of private communication. One drawback of the scheme is that the numbers defining the cryptosystem are large, making public key operations slow. In 2003, Nan et al. [23] proposed the idea of using Seeded Public Key (SPK) to achieve scaled key escrow and firstly proposed CPK. CPK introduces Public Key Factor Matrix (PKM) and the Private Key Factor Matrix (SKM). By using Elliptic Curve Cryptosystem (ECC) algorithm [24], the key factors are combined into keys according to the mapping algorithm. CPK can generate lots of keys quickly with a small number of resources through the Key Management Center (KMC), which solves the efficiency problem and cost problem of key generation. In subsequent studies, Yu et al. [25] proposed an efficient CPK scheme, called CPK-CCC, which improves the whole performance of system operation. Shi et al. [26] applied CPK to fog computing in IoT, which is more efficient and safer than the lattice-based IBE scheme. Zhang et al. [27] designed the CPK for wireless networks algorithm, which effectively solves the problem of the small storage capacity of sensor nodes. However, similar to the traditional IBC scheme, the key matrix in KMC still faces the risk of key leakage.

2.4 Blockchain-Based Authentication

It is because of the decentralized nature of blockchain that current research efforts hope to solve the problem of centralized key distribution and management of current authentication schemes. Matsumoto et al. [28] introduced blockchain to ensure the authority and security of distributed CAs but did not focus on the details of the key generation solution. Wang et al. [29] proposed a blockchain-based cross-certification model that can effectively alleviate the load problem of CAs in PKI and the certificate revocation problem. Zhou et al. [30] based on the blockchain, splitting key generation nodes and proposing an improved key distribution solution called BIBE. Compared with the traditional IBE scheme, BIBE shows higher efficiency as well as better security. Cui et al. [31] proposed a blockchain-based IoT multi-WSN authentication scheme for the special scenario of IoT, realizing node communication in different situations. Zhao et al. [32] applied blockchain to an online education platform to guarantee the secure storage of identity information. Huang et al. [33] applied blockchain to mobile terminal authentication to protect the private information of users.

The above authentication methods offered solutions to specific security problems, but each has its shortcomings. The PKI scheme cannot get rid of the heavy certificate system. The combination of IBC and CPK can solve the security problem of key generation, but there are still potential threats in key management and storage. Most of the existing authentication schemes involving blockchain only use the blockchain as a trusted third-party database to store key information and lack deep integration with the authentication system. Therefore, we propose a blockchain-assisted key generation mechanism that combines the advantages of each and introduces blockchain technology into the entire key generation and management process to further improve the security of keys and the robustness of the whole authentication system.

3 Authentication Model

In order to solve the key escrow problem caused by traditional centralized PKG, we adopt blockchain to separate the power of PKG to multiple blockchain nodes that server as distributed PKGs. The PKGs are called Registration Authority (RA) in blockchain. Each RA only generates a part of the user's private key while the final private key is generated by the user according to the identity-related combination strategy.

The authentication model we proposed can be divided into four phases: initialization phase, registration phase, key generation phase and authentication phase. Figure 1 shows the model of our solution.

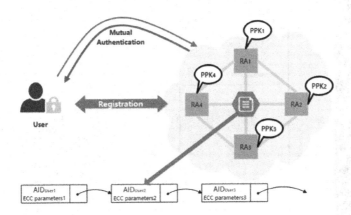

Fig. 1. The authentication model

The user submits identity information to the RA he or she accesses, which temporarily becomes the leader RA. The leader RA models the information of each key attribute of the user and generates a unique Accessing IDentifier (AID) for that user in the system. According to the AID, a set of ECC encrypted public parameters is randomly selected for it, then binding this AID and the parameters and adding them to the blockchain for consensus. Then, each distributed RA calculates a set of partial private keys for the user based on the ECC algorithm and sends them to leader RA. Once the leader RA obtains all of the partial private keys, it will send them to the user together with the user's AID. Finally, the user secretly combines the partial private keys according to the pre-configured strategy bound to the identity, and completely generates the private key through distributed PKGs. When authenticating the user, the authentication node obtains the public key parameters through the binding relationship between the user AID and ECC parameters which have been consensus on the blockchain before, then combines the corresponding user public key based on the AID to verify the user's signature.

4   Working Procedure

This section will show the key generation and authentication procedure of our scheme in detail. As shown in Fig. 2, the whole procedure can be divided into four phases: (1) initialization phase (2) registration phase (3) key generation phase (4) authentication phase. The related notations mentioned in this section are shown in Table 1.

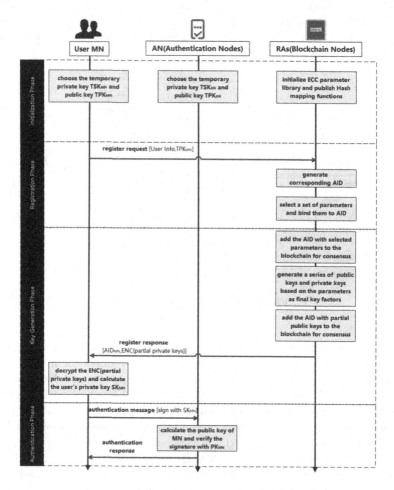

Fig. 2. The key generation and authentication procedure

4.1   Initialization Phase

In this phase, the blockchain initializes a serial of ECC parameters [24] to be used as a public cryptographic parameter library. These parameters are public

Table 1. Notations

Notation	Definition
AN	The authentication node. In our scheme, any blockchain node can be considered as an authentication node. Corresponds to RA in the model
AID_{MN}	The access identifier of User MN in our system
TPK_{MN}	The user MN's public key for communicating with blockchain and encrypting plaintext from blockchain
TSK_{MN}	The user MN's private key for decrypting ciphertext from blockchain
PPK_i	The partial private key generated by each blockchain nodes
PK_{MN}	The long term public key of User MN
SK_{MN}	The long term private key of User MN

so that each blockchain node can call them when needed. User chooses a pair of public and private keys to encrypt the communication with the blockchain.

4.2 Registration Phase

User MN and AN (if AN is not a blockchain node) should register first for generating their private key for afterward authentication. In this phase, our scheme adopts the ECC-based IBC mechanism to calculate the key pair. First, MN submits the personal information and TPK_{MN} to the accessing RA (which becomes leader RA). After that, the leader RA models User MN's attributes to extract the key multi-dimensional attributes (including user type, affiliation, user level, etc.) to generate the AID_{MN} which can uniquely identify User MN's identity in the whole system. After generating the AID_{MN}, The leader RA will randomly select a specific set of ECC parameters in the parameter library, bind these parameters to the AID and add them with TPK_{MN} to the blockchain for consensus.

4.3 Key Generation Phase

When each blockchain node receives a consensus message from a new user MN, they obtain the user's TPK_{MN}, AID_{MN} and corresponding ECC parameters from the consensus ledger. According to the ECC parameters, each node generates a certain number of public-private key pairs as factors for the final key. Then all the partial public keys are added to the blockchain for consensus while the partial private keys (PPKs) are encrypted by TPK_{MN} and sent to the leader RA through a secure channel. Once the leader RA collects all of the partial private keys, it will transmit them to the user together with AID_{MN} through a secure channel. Once user MN receives the registration response from the leader RA, all the PPKs will be decrypted first by TSK_{MN}, then combined and calculated according to AID_{MN} and the public Hash function of the system to generate the final private key SK_{MN}.

4.4   Authentication Phase

Before user MN can officially access the blockchain network, the user's legitimacy needs to be verified first. MN sends an authentication message signed by SK_{MN} to AN, which contains AID_{MN}. After receiving the authentication request, AN first matches entry in the blockchain ledger according to the AID_{MN}. If match result does not exist, AN will refuse to provide network access service and reply Access-Reject message to MN. Otherwise, AN will calculate the partial public key of MN based on the partial public keys that have been recorded on the blockchain in the registration phase. AN uses the same Hash function to combine the final public key PK_{MN}, and then uses PK_{MN} to verify MN's signature. If the verification is successful, the authentication phase is completed and MN can legally access the blockchain network.

5   System Design and Solution Implementation

In this section we present a prototype system designed and implemented based on the above ideas. We choose the FISCO-BCOS [34] consortium blockchain as the simulation platform which adopts PBFT as the consensus protocol. The framework of blockchain is shown in Fig. 3.

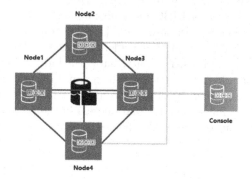

Fig. 3. The framework of prototype system

In our prototype system, there are four blockchain Nodes and one Console Node to manage other nodes. All the nodes are hosted on Ubuntu 16.04 Virtual Machine which has 1 core, 8G memory and 1.5 GHz CPU. Console node works as leader RA for registration, while the rest of the nodes participate in the generation of partial keys and the authentication of user.

Based on CPK infrastruction, we select a certain number of elliptic curves and some Basis Points on the curves to form the public key-parameters library. The library shows as Table 2.

Table 2. ECC parameters library

Curve	Basis Point 1	Basis Point 2	...	Basis Point n
Secp112	(09487239995A5EE76B55F9C2F098, A89CE5AF8724C0A23E0E0FF77500)	...		...
Secp160	(4A96B5688EF573284664698968C38BB9 13CBFC82,23A628553168947D59DCC91 2042351377AC5FB32)	...		...
Secp256	...	...		...

The number of curves and Basis Points can be dynamically adjusted to adapt to the security requirements of the system, in particular, the number after "Secp" represents the length of the key factors generated based on the curve which can be determined by the User's Level. In addition, there are two functions to be published in the system in advance. The first function H_1 is a mapping function used to convert a string type variable to a sequence consisting of 0 and 1. The second function H_2 is to combine the final public or private key based on the sequence mentioned above and the corresponding partial keys.

When users register, they submit their identity information, the Console should generate a unique access identity (AID) for them based on this information. To simplify this step, we use their username as the stated AID in our prototype system. Once the AID is determined, the Console will choose a random elliptic curve and the corresponding Basis Point to be the public parameters for the generation of its key factors. Then the Console adds the AID with its parameters to the blockchain for consensus. We use smart contracts written by Solidity to complete the interaction between the entities and the blockchain ledgers. There are two blockchain ledgers in the system (Ledger1 and Ledger2), Ledger1 is used to store AID and its related ECC parameters, and the other is used to store the AID and its corresponding partial public keys.

Once a new block of user registration is updated to the chain, each node performs a random generation of partial keys based on its corresponding elliptic curve parameters through Elliptic Curve Cryptosystem (ECC) algorithm. The number of key pairs generated by each node can be dynamically adjusted according to security needs. After each node generates the public-private key pairs, they upload the partial public keys with AID to the blockchain for consensus and send the partial private keys to the Console. It is worth mentioning that the public key factors will compose the public key matrix while the private key factors will compose the private key matrix, and the same positions in both matrices will be a public-private key pair. Once the Console has collected all the private key factors from each node, it will encrypt and send them to the user in a packaged form. During this process, the Console is only responsible for the summary and transmission of the partial private keys, without storage or recording them.

After receiving the response message from the Console, the user first gains his AID and then decrypts it to obtain all the partial private keys. After that, the H_1 function is called based on the AID to generate a specific 01 sequence, the H_2 function is called based on the sequence and the private key factors to

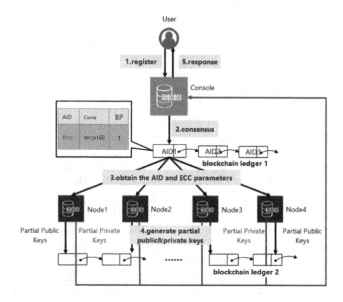

Fig. 4. The key generation procedure

determine the target factors to be combined into the final private key. Eventually, the user combines the target factors to generate the final private key. The entire key generation procedure is shown in Fig. 4.

The authentication procedure for the user is shown in Fig. 5.

AN gains the AID of the user from the authentication request, then uses this AID as an index to obtain the corresponding public key matrices from the local blockchain ledger. The corresponding public key factors of the user's private key factors are located through the same processing steps. At last, AN generates the final public key through the same combination to verify the user's signature.

6   Performance Evaluation

In this section, we evaluate the BAKG in terms of security and efficiency. First, we analyse the security of BAKG scheme. Then, we evaluate the consensus cost of blockchain and computation delay of key factors' generation.

6.1   Security Analysis

The security characteristics of BAKG can be summarized into the following three categories.

Key Security. In BAKG scheme, the partial private key of user is generated by distributed blockchain nodes and encrypted for transmission. The final private key is determined by the MN on demand, which can ensure the key transmission security and avoid the problem of single point bottleneck and key escrow.

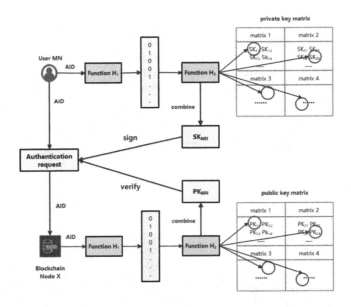

Fig. 5. The authentication procedure

Authentication Security. In BAKG scheme, the authentication between user and AN is based on an identity-based signature, which can prevent the illegal nodes from accessing our system and avoid potential forgery attacks.

User Anonymity. In registration phase of BSLA, RA generates the access identifier AID for user according to its key multi-dimensional attributes for communication in BAKG. The user's real identity is not exposed. Therefore, BAKG can protect user identity privacy in communication.

6.2 Consensus Cost

Considering that BAKG needs to add partial public keys, AID and ECC parameters to the blockchain, we test the write delay and read delay of the blockchain. The write delay refers to the time interval from initiating a write request to returning the successful message, and the read delay refers to the time interval from initiating a read request to returning the read information. We choose the FISCO-BCOS [34] consortium blockchain as the simulation platform which adopts PBFT as the consensus protocol. Different numbers of blockchain nodes are hosted on Ubuntu 16.04 Virtual Machine which has 1 core, 8G memory and 1.5 GHz CPU. The network connection of each node is configured in bridge mode to directly connect with the physical network, which is kept in the same local network of the host. Considering that the security and efficiency of the BAKG are closely related to the number of nodes involved in the system, we design three simulation scenarios. All three scenarios have 10 ms latency and

0.1% packet loss rate which refers to a good network environment. Scenario 1 has 5 blockchain nodes, scenario 2 has 18 blockchain nodes and scenario 3 has 30 blockchain nodes. Each simulation is conducted with 100 experiments, and the final result takes the average of the tested delay.

The average read and write delay statistics for a different number of nodes are shown in Fig. 6.

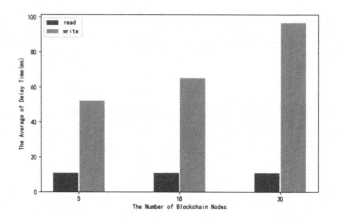

Fig. 6. The average delay time of reading and writing

According to the simulation results as shown in Fig. 7, each average value of read delay is relatively stable since the read operation only querying data from the local ledger rather than the remote database. And we can conclude that there is no obvious association between read latency and the number of nodes.

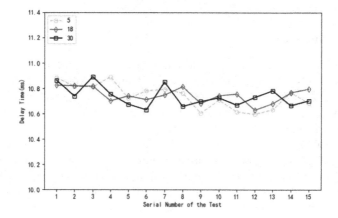

Fig. 7. The delay time of reading

The simulation results of write delay on blockchain are shown in Fig. 8. As we can see, since the write operation needs to complete the update on all nodes, it is reasonable that consensus delay increases as the validating nodes increase. Therefore, the number of validating nodes must be carefully set in order to make a good trade-off between security and efficiency.

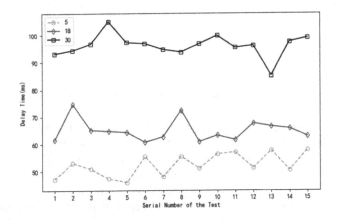

Fig. 8. The delay time of writing

6.3 Computation Delay

The delay in the calculation consists mainly of the delay in generating the key factors and the delay in combining them. The generation delay is mainly in random number calculation and verifying that they are on the selected elliptic curve.

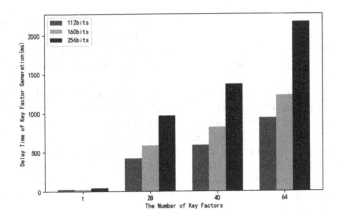

Fig. 9. The computation delay of key

The combination delay is the time consumed to sum all the key factors in their computational domain. There are three lengths of key factors in our prototype system, 112 bits, 160 bits and 256 bits. The average latency for generating and combining different numbers of key factors for the three key lengths is shown in Fig. 9.

It can be concluded that the computation delay increases with the length of the keys, but within an acceptable range, and the trade-off between key security and efficiency should be considered in practice.

7   Conclusion

Building on the theoretical foundation of our previous research [11], we have presented the key generation process based on blockchain technology in further detail and completed the implementation of the prototype system. The consortium chain was introduced as a distributed trusted platform to solve the key escrow problem caused by the centralized PKG in the registration phase of the traditional IBC mechanism. Not only does the blockchain act as a trusted database to store key parameters in the system, but every node is involved in the generation of user keys. In addition, the pre-configuration of key library, the selected key length, and the number of key factors can be dynamically adjusted according to the actual needs, which makes the whole system scalable and extensible. The performance of the proposed scheme is evaluated to demonstrate security and efficiency. In the future, our work will build on this foundation to further deepen the coupling between blockchain and authentication systems, optimize the process of generating and combining key factors, and improve the security and anonymity of interactions between users and blockchain nodes. We will also improve and expand the existing reasonable simplifications.

References

1. Yao, S., Guan, J., Wu, Y., Xu, K., Xu, M.: Toward secure and lightweight access authentication in SAGINs. IEEE Wirel. Commun. **27**(6), 75–81 (2020)
2. Anada, H.: Decentralized multi-authority anonymous authentication for global identities with non-interactive proofs. J. Internet Serv. Inf. Secur. (JISIS) **10**(4), 23–37 (2020)
3. Duong, D.H., Susilo, W., Trinh, V.C.: Wildcarded identity-based encryption with constant-size ciphertext and secret key. J. Wirel. Mob. Netw. Ubiquit. Comput. Dependable Appl. (JoWUA) **11**(2), 74–86 (2020)
4. Loh, J.-C., Heng, S.-H., Tan, S.-Y., Kurosawa, K.: On the invisibility and anonymity of undeniable signature schemes. J. Wirel. Mob. Netw. Ubiquit. Comput. Dependable Appl. (JoWUA) **11**(1), 18–34 (2020)
5. Pöhn, D., Hommel, W.: Universal identity and access management framework for future ecosystems. J. Wirel. Mob. Netw. Ubiquit. Comput. Dependable Appl. (JoWUA) **12**(1), 64–84 (2021)

6. Ribalta, C.N., Lombard-Platet, M., Salinesi, C., Lafourcade, P.: Blockchain mirage or silver bullet? A requirements-driven comparative analysis of business and developers' perceptions in the accountancy domain. J. Wirel. Mob. Netw. Ubiquit. Comput. Dependable Appl. **12**(1), 85–110 (2021)

7. Lee, Y., Son, B., Park, S., Lee, J., Jang, H.: A survey on security and privacy in blockchain-based central bank digital currencies. J. Internet Serv. Inf. Secur. (JISIS) **11**(3), 16–29 (2021)

8. Alizadeh, M., Andersson, K., Schelen, O.: A survey of secure internet of things in relation to blockchain. J. Internet Serv. Inf. Secur. (JISIS) **10**(3), 47–75 (2020)

9. König, L., Unger, S., Kieseberg, P., Tjoa, S.: The risks of the blockchain a review on current vulnerabilities and attacks. J. Internet Serv. Inf. Secur. (JISIS) **10**(3), 110–127 (2020)

10. Hui, H., et al.: Survey on blockchain for internet of things. J. Internet Serv. Inf. Secur. (JISIS) **9**(2), 1–30 (2019)

11. Guan, J., Wu, Y., Yao, S., Zhang, T., Su, X., Li, C.: BSLA: blockchain-assisted secure and lightweight authentication for SGIN. Comput. Commun. **176**, 46–55 (2021). https://www.sciencedirect.com/science/article/pii/S0140366421001997

12. Kohnfelder, L.M.: Towards a practical public-key cryptosystem. Ph.D. dissertation, Massachusetts Institute of Technology (1978)

13. Dierks, T., Rescorla, E.: The transport layer security (TLS) protocol version 1.2 (2008)

14. Clark, J., Van Oorschot, P.C.: SoK: SSL and HTTPS: revisiting past challenges and evaluating certificate trust model enhancements. In: 2013 IEEE Symposium on Security and Privacy, pp. 511–525. IEEE (2013)

15. Laurie, B.: Certificate transparency. Commun. ACM **57**(10), 40–46 (2014)

16. Shamir, A.: Identity-based cryptosystems and signature schemes. In: Blakley, G.R., Chaum, D. (eds.) CRYPTO 1984. LNCS, vol. 196, pp. 47–53. Springer, Heidelberg (1985). https://doi.org/10.1007/3-540-39568-7_5

17. Boneh, D., Franklin, M.: Identity-based encryption from the Weil pairing. In: Kilian, J. (ed.) CRYPTO 2001. LNCS, vol. 2139, pp. 213–229. Springer, Heidelberg (2001). https://doi.org/10.1007/3-540-44647-8_13

18. Gentry, C., Silverberg, A.: Hierarchical ID-based cryptography. In: Zheng, Y. (ed.) ASIACRYPT 2002. LNCS, vol. 2501, pp. 548–566. Springer, Heidelberg (2002). https://doi.org/10.1007/3-540-36178-2_34

19. Ryu, G., Lee, K., Park, S., Lee, D.H.: Unbounded hierarchical identity-based encryption with efficient revocation. In: Kim, H., Choi, D. (eds.) WISA 2015. LNCS, vol. 9503, pp. 122–133. Springer, Cham (2016). https://doi.org/10.1007/978-3-319-31875-2_11

20. Fida, M.-R., Ali, M., Adnan, A., Arsalaan, A.S.: Region-based security architecture for DTN. In: 2011 Eighth International Conference on Information Technology: New Generations, pp. 387–392. IEEE (2011)

21. Guo, L., Wang, J., Yau, W.-C.: Efficient hierarchical identity-based encryption system for internet of things infrastructure. Symmetry **11**(7), 913 (2019)

22. Bellare, M., Goldwasser, S.: Verifiable partial key escrow. In: Proceedings of the 4th ACM Conference on Computer and Communications Security, CCS 1997, pp. 78–91. Association for Computing Machinery, New York (1997). https://doi.org/10.1145/266420.266439

23. Nan, X., Chen, Z.: A Profile to Network Security Techniques. National Defense Industry Press, Beijing (2003)

24. Sakai, R., Kasahara, M., et al.: ID based cryptosystems with pairing on elliptic curve. IACR Cryptology ePrint Archive, vol. 2003, p. 54 (2003)

25. Yu, M., Huang, X., Jiang, L., Liang, R.: Combined public key cryptosystem based on conic curves over the ring Zn. In: 2008 International Conference on Computer Science and Software Engineering, vol. 3, pp. 631–634. IEEE (2008)
26. Shi, Y., Qiu, S., Liu, J., Ma, T.: Novel efficient lattice-based IBE schemes with CPK for fog computing. Math. Biosci. Eng.: MBE $17(6)$, 8105–8122 (2020)
27. Zhang, Q., Yuan, J., Guo, G., Gan, Y., Zhang, J.: An authentication key establish protocol for WSNs based on combined key. Wirel. Pers. Commun. $99(1)$, 95–110 (2018)
28. Matsumoto, S., Reischuk, R.M.: IKP: turning a PKI around with decentralized automated incentives. In: IEEE Symposium on Security and Privacy (SP), pp. 410–426 (2017)
29. Wang, W., Hu, N., Liu, X.: BlockCAM: a blockchain-based cross-domain authentication model. In: 2018 IEEE Third International Conference on Data Science in Cyberspace (DSC), pp. 896–901. IEEE (2018)
30. Zhou, B., Li, H., Xu, L.: An authentication scheme using identity-based encryption & blockchain. In: 2018 IEEE Symposium on Computers and Communications (ISCC), pp. 00 556–00 561. IEEE (2018)
31. Cui, Z., et al.: A hybrid blockchain-based identity authentication scheme for multi-WSN. IEEE Trans. Serv. Comput. $13(2)$, 241–251 (2020)
32. Zhao, G., Di, B., He, H.: Design and implementation of the digital education transaction subject two-factor identity authentication system based on blockchain. In: 2020 22nd International Conference on Advanced Communication Technology (ICACT), pp. 176–180. IEEE (2020)
33. Huang, H., Chen, X.: Power mobile terminal identity authentication mechanism based on blockchain. In: International Wireless Communications and Mobile Computing (IWCMC), pp. 195–198. IEEE (2020)
34. F. open source working group. FISCO BCOS documentation (2020). https://fisco-bcos.org/

Smart Contract-Based Personal Data Protection Framework: In Cross-App Advertising

Yuyuan Shi[1], Xianming Gao[2(✉)], and Jianfeng Guan[1]

[1] Beijing University of Posts and Telecommunications, 100876 Beijing, China
{gelseyshi,jfguan}@bupt.edu.cn
[2] Academy of Military Sciences, 100142 Beijing, China

Abstract. The era of big data gives rise to the development of data-driven marketing while exposing people to the threaten of data misuse and data breach. Data-driven marketing allows services to use a unique identifier to track each individual and deliver customized content. If a third party has gained unauthorized access to the behavioral data, the user's privacy will be violated. Industry giants like Apple and Google are continuously working on user anonymity: they changed unique device identifiers to advertising ID and now manage to phase out advertising ID. At the same time, service providers and advertisers are also seeking better identity strategies. This paper mainly focuses on cross-app advertising and proposes a smart contract based personal data protection framework. Leveraging the smart contract's advantages, we ensure transparency, tamper-resistance, and traceability during data storing and data sharing. In this framework, the user interacts with other entities anonymously, thus preventing identity leakage. In addition, we introduce a reward mechanism that allows users who authorize data sharing to be paid by the service. We then implement the proposed framework on Etherum combined with the IPFS to validate our design. Finally, we discuss the security of the current framework and possible further work.

Keywords: Smart contract · Blockchain · Personal data protection · Cross-app advertising

1 Introduction

In the big data era, users' personal information can bring considerable commercial value to enterprises and expose them to the risk of privacy leakage. Mobile internet applications gather different types of identifiers and personal data from online users, employing user activity tracking. These sensitive data require protection against potential threats from third-party applications. Two scenarios are frequently discussed when it comes to personal data protection. One scenario lies

Supported by the project No. 2019-JCJQ-ZD-182-00-02.

I. You et al. (Eds.): MobiSec 2021, CCIS 1544, pp. 139–154, 2022.
https://doi.org/10.1007/978-981-16-9576-6_11

in the collection of user data. As the service provider, enterprises tend to access user data to enhance service delivery and are undoubtedly responsible for the security of collected data. The other scene takes place in data sharing. The enterprise gives open access to third-party for academic research or data exchange. Educational institutions or individuals make requests to the database, and the company needs to ensure user privacy when returning corresponding data.

However, the scenario is more complex when it comes to precision marketing. As the mobile app owner, the company gathers large volumes of data from users, and predicts their preferences as well as habits by data analysis. Each user is linked to a series of behavioral data. Based on these data, app will provide the user with related data feeds. (e.g., the goods a user is more likely interested in). Meanwhile, with the development of sensing technology, it is possible for the applications to get high precision data [6,25]. Despite the quality service it brings, it would be a significant threat to users' rights if the app owner improperly reveals data to a third party. Hence, it is essential to keep personal information protected for mobile internet applications.

In May 2018, the GDPR (General Data Protection Regulation) came into force in the European Union [21]. Many scholars have conducted researches on how to comply with GDPR. With Economic globalization, the rest countries in the world show the current trend of being deeply influenced by this law. In January 2020, Google announced its deprecation of tracking cookies. Although the initiative was confirmed a delay in June 2021 due to the difficulties in building an enhanced privacy ecosystem, Google is continuously working on it and manage to phase out third-party cookies before late 2023 [23]. Also, on April 27, 2021, Apple introduced an App Tracking Transparency (ATT) Feature in the iOS14.5 update [5]. This feature blocks app's access to Apple's mobile device ID (Identifier for Advertisers, IDFA) until the user permits it. In China, for instance, privacy and cybersecurity have been priorities of the Government nowadays. The authorities have been paying particular attention to some platforms, like Didi, which handles sensitive data such as locations.

As the increasing privacy consciousness of customers, their personal identifications are being protected (e.g. cookies, IDFA), companies are looking for a better identity strategy. Thus, according to this trend, ensuring proper use of private data is worthy of discussion.

Common methods for personal data protection, such as k-Anonymity [12], l-diversity [17], and t-closeness [14], provide effective against identity disclosure by removing the links from sensitive attributes (e.g., zip code, gender, and date of birth) to private data. Some [4] also apply multi-authority anonymous authentication in decentralized scenarios. Besides, differential privacy is a frequently used method as well. It achieves privacy protection by maximizing the accuracy of data queries and preventing identity information from being inferred by observing the difference in the output results due to different inputs. Still, the protection of sensitive information by differential privacy relies on an assumption: a trusted data collector. It is not easy to find a trustworthy data collector in practice. Homomorphic encryption is another commonly used technology for cloud computing and deep learning, which enables privacy-preserving storage and computation. In order to maintain performance of data utility, some papers apply synthetic dataset shift [20]. In addition, researchers [19] combine data encryption and access control to protect user data.

However, the methods above only achieve anonymity of information. Data protection strategy needs a further refinement for scenarios that require data uploading and data sharing. In the scenarios discussed above, giving apps specific access to private information improves service quality; the users have the right to get complete control of their data and be informed about data utilization details (where and for what purpose). Moreover, the evidence provided by users alone is sometimes insufficient for substantiating the information abuse. Thus, there is a need to provide convincing proof technically.

Blockchain is a type of distributed database. The Smart Contract (SC), as the critical part of many blockchain platforms (e.g., Ethereum, Hyperledger), has comparative advantages in data protection, namely transparency, decentralization, and tamper-resistance. According to some proposals, the smart contract plays a crucial role in protecting personal data, including healthcare data [10,13,15,16], digital copyright [1], commercial information [26,27], and locations [24]. Nevertheless, some of them only consist of conceptional models without detailed technical analysis [10,13,27]. Moreover, some follow a centralized client-server architecture [10,13,16,27], which relies on the truthfulness of the service provider (i.e., who has access to personal data, such as a mobile app). Also, to comply with the GDPR, other studies have proposed novel data-sharing schemes [7,22]. Still, these schemes may not work for all cases, for instance, precise marking. In this situation, the major part of the dataset (commercial data or the user persona) is owned by the app, while the user keeps their unique identification (e.g., IDFA). Despite the need to differentiate each user when storing data, the app should have restricted access to the unique identification; otherwise, there will be the risk of data leakage to third parties. This paper proposes a smart contract based personal data protection framework, which mainly focuses on cross-app advertising.

The contribution of this paper resides in several aspects:

(1) Firstly, this paper illustrates a security scheme for data uploading. In this process, the app uploads personal data without knowing the user's unique identity, thus preventing data from being illegally leaked to third parties.
(2) It defines a security data-sharing model: without knowing the unique identifier, a third party's access to personal data is authenticated and recorded by smart contracts.
(3) In addition, this paper introduces a reward mechanism. The users who license data sharing may earn rewards from a third party through smart contracts.
(4) Finally, the paper uses Ethereum as the blockchain platform and IPFS as the storage technology to implement the framework and evaluate it.

The rest of the article is organized as follows. Section 2 overviews background and related work. Section 3 introduces and describes the proposed framework. In Sect. 4, we illustrate the implementation of the design. Section 5 provides an analysis and discussion about the framework. Finally, the conclusions are drawn in Sect. 6.

2 Background and Related Work

2.1 Device ID

A device id is a string of numbers and letters that identifies every smartphone or tablet in the world [2]. It is stored on a mobile device and can be retrieved by installed applications. In the context of mobile advertising, the device id plays a significant role. It is the easiest way to identify mobile users for advertisers, marketers or other devices. Using device id can track users' download, registration, use, uninstall and reinstall, which is meaningful to product marketing. And user behaviour and geographic information are revealed by device id, which enables app owners to collect data and then carry out precision marketing. As for communication with external data, the device id is also a unique id that can be used to communicate, exchange, and supplement data outside the company as everyone in the market also recognizes it. This technology offers service providers a better understanding of users while raising the risk of personal data abuse.

2.2 Blockchain and Smart Contract

Blockchain is essentially a distributed ledger, which enhances security, transparency, and the traceability of data sharing the network. This concept was introduced in 2008 by a person (or a group of people) using the name Satoshi Nakamoto [18]. Over the past decades, blockchain has been receiving increased attention among industry, academy, and government. The 'block' in blockchain can be treated as a ledger page, and each block is composed of transactions. To add a transaction in the chain, a consensus protocol is needed. As a core of blockchain, the consensus algorithm is an agreement to validate the transaction's genuineness, thus making sure all nodes maintain the same distributed ledger. There are several common practices to build consensus, for instance, Proof of Work (POW), Proof of Stake (POS), Delegated Proof of Stake (DPOS), and Practical Byzantine Fault Tolerance (PBFT). They are backbones of improved solutions in existing studies. Meanwhile, the vulnerabilities of blockchain are also widely discussed [3,9,11].

Smart Contract (SC) is another vital part of blockchain technology, which runs on many platforms (e.g., Ethereum) [8]. It was first proposed in 1994, before the invention of blockchain. The SC is a self-executing program stored on the chain, fulfills and enforces the predefined agreement. These features make it perfectly suitable for use in the blockchain, allowing credible transactions without third parties. The SC is essentially a type of account that has the balance and address. The code is composed of conditional statements triggered by a user or another SC. Once the contract term is satisfied and verified by the participants in a network, the relevant transaction is executed. In this process, interactions are supported by transactions. The advantages of blockchain are well reflected in the SC. Take Ethereum as an example: The transactions made by SC are visible to all participants in the network, thus ensure transparency; the SC is stored on the blockchain, which no one can tamper with; the transactions are also recorded with immutability, therefore allow traceable communications between the SC and the user.

2.3   Related Work

Zyskind *et al.* introduced a decentralized personal data management system based on blockchain [27]. This system gives the user complete control of their data and ensures transparent data storage and data controlling.

Liu *et al.* proposed BPDS, a privacy-preserving system for Electronic Medical Records (EMR), which combines consortium blockchain and cloud computing [15]. This system has a three-layer architecture, consisting of a data acquirement layer, data storage layer, and data sharing layer. Before data uploading, the doctor will first extract a signature for the patient's data and then sends the metadata with the signature in return. Next, the patient removes sensitive parts of the data and store it in the cloud. However, when it comes to mobile advertising, the role of 'doctor' will be equaled to 'mobile app', which is potentially malicious. Similarly, Lee *et al.* suggested a healthcare data-sharing framework to deal with the reliability and interoperability of data [13]. The framework defines three major entities: Patient Identity Source, which contains patient identifiers but without personal information; Data Source, which provides metadata; Consumer, which requests data with identifiers. Using a blockchain-based registry, this system advanced than conventional DBMS in three aspects: 1) tamper-resistant, 2) decentralized 3) traceable data life cycle. Although the system design is reasonable, it lacks further implementations and evaluation.

After GDPR comes into effect, more and more researchers apply Smart Contract in personal data management to comply with the new regulation. In [22], Truong *et al.* designed a complex identity to specify personal data associated with two or more parties. It combines asymmetric key pair of three entities (Data Subject, Data Controller, and Data Pointer). Data Subject and Data Controller are two roles defined by GDPR: the former is the owner of data (e.g., app user); the latter represents who manages personal data (e.g., app owner). This paper has a detailed description of different entities and how they interact with each other. The processing of personal data is only allowed after getting both consents from Data Subject and Data Controller. The access to data also requires authentication by policy written in SCs. However, the GDPR model somehow differs from the mobile advertising scenario since they miss out on a specific definition of the data upload process. Even though they assume Service Provider follows a malicious model, they prevent illegal use by records of GDPR infringements on the ledger, which still making the data vulnerable to leakage. Dauden-Esmel *et al.* proposed a lightweight solution based on previous work [7], using SC for two primary purposes: authentication and record. In this proposal, Data Subject provides personal data, which also differs from our case. Moreover, they lack technical details design concepts.

3   Data Protection Framework

In this section, we propose a smart contract based privacy-preserving framework, focus specifically on cross-app advertising (mobile advertising).

3.1   Scenario and Assumption

We assume the services (Service and third-party Service) act maliciously in our proposed system, which means the Service may inappropriately release personal information, and the third party may have unauthorized access to the data. As previously stated, the commercial data is collected by the Service and stored in its database. Without data protection, the Service and a third-party Service both have access to one's general identification (e.g., IDFA, cookies). The third party can track the user with this id. Suppose the third party has improper access to user data because of a database attack or illegal disclosure. In that case, the user may become the target of mobile advertising without his/her knowledge.

3.2   System Architecture

A conceptual model of the proposed framework is illustrated in Fig. 1. The essential idea of the data protection is to conceal the User's general identifications from the services (Service and third-party Service), thus precluding unauthorized user activity tracking. In order to prevent identification leakage, we introduce an encrypted identification (U_{id}) for each user. After acquiring U_{id} from the user, the Service will then participate in the data uploading and data sharing process. Thanks to anonymity, even if one gets the U_{id} and corresponding data illegally, he/she is still unable to associate data to a specific user. Meanwhile, if the Services need to store the data for further querying or sharing purpose, they are required to use a private IPFS.

For a third-party Service, if it requires user data of a specific Service, it must obtain the Service's consent and get approval from the user. Here, we also suggest an award mechanism: a certain amount of cryptocurrency will be transferred to the user's address once the user grants consent (i.e., notify the third party with U_{id}, $Service_{id}$ and file hash). After that, a smart contract will set the third-party Service as *registered* for the specific dataset. The third-party Service can now query data using the file hash and match the user account with the corresponding personal data.

The framework consists of 4 entities: User, Service, third-party Service, Database, with the Smart Contract controlling their interactions (Table 1).

– **User.** The User represents the end-user of the mobile app, who owns the unique identification. After receiving a request from the Service, the User will decide whether to provide his/her Uid or not. If consent is granted, the User can retrieve the Uid and send it to the Service. In this process, a Uid is created using the encryption algorithm if it does not exist.

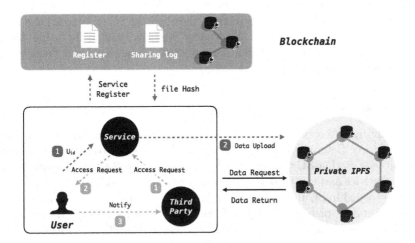

Fig. 1. Proposed data protection framework.

Table 1. Description of entities

Notion	Description
User	Mobile user
Service	Who owns the user behavioral data
Third party service	Who requires user data of a specific Service
Database	Stores the data uploaded by the Service
Smart Contract	Controls interactions between entities

- **Service.** The Service is the provider of the mobile app, which tracks user behavioral data. To ensure security, the Uid collected from the User is not the general identification. As the owner of commercial data, the Service plays a vital role in the data uploading and data sharing process. For data reuse and sharing purpose, the Service is supposed to store the personal data in the Database after authentication. During data sharing, the Service forwards the consent request from the third party Service.
- **Third-party Service.** The Third-party Service is also a service provider, which requires user data from another Service for operational and business-related reasons (e.g., mobile advertising, personalization). As the anonymity of Uid, the third party has to be proactively notified by the User so that it can track the specific User with desired personal data.
- **Database.** In our proposed design, the Service store personal data in a private IPFS. The authentication and registration of Services are separated from data storage to ensure security.
- **Smart Contract.** We realize the access control, operation record, and award mechanism by taking advantage of SC. The SCs are transaction protocols on a private chain, and they are independent of the Database, where storing the

original data. For later authentication, the Register SC will record the Appid after the User's consent. The third-party Services sharing the same dataset are recorded as well by the Sharing Log SC. These execution flows will be well discussed in the following sections.

3.3   Workflow

Data Storing. According to the discussed scenario, personal data is uploaded by the Service. Before uploading, the Service is supposed to ask for permission from the User so that SC will register the Service. Figure 2 shows the interactions between entities and the Register SC during this process. The $Service_{id}$ and the U_{id} are recorded in SC in the form of a data table named after the U_{id}. Here, we use the Composite primary key U_{id} & $Service_{id}$ to identify a unique dataset. If the table of a U_{id} does not exist, a new one will be created by SC (Algorithm 1). Once the Service has finished data uploading, it should add file hash to Register SC. In this step, the SC authenticates the Service to make sure it has already registered (Algorithm 2). After updating the dataset, the SC will grant consent. The Service can look up the storage log and file hash history when there is a need.

Data Sharing. Secure data sharing is a critical issue in personal data protection. To get user data of a specific Service, the third-party Service must have consent from both the User and the Service. Since user identity is confidential to the third party, several steps are needed to implement data sharing. In the initial step, the third party has to send a request to the Service (Fig. 3). After they reach the consensus on data sharing, the Service will forward the request

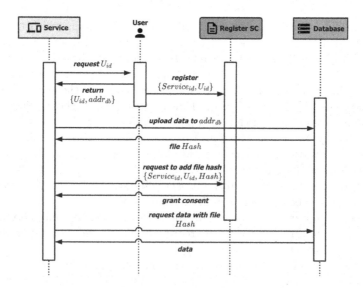

Fig. 2. Data storing process.

Algorithm 1: Service Registration

Input: U_{id}, $Service_{id}$
Output: out
1   *Initialization: out* $\leftarrow$ *error*

2    $U_{id} \leftarrow address$;
3   **if** isValid(U_{id}) **then**
4   **if** getTable(U_{id}) **then**
5   createTable(U_{id});
6   *event* CreateTable(U_{id})
7   **end**
8   registerTable $\leftarrow$ getTable(U_{id});
9   registerTable.insertTable$(U_{id}, Service_{id})$;
10   **event** InsertTable$(Service_{id})$;
11   *out* $\leftarrow$ *success*
12 **end**
13 **return** *out*

Algorithm 2: Filehash Registration

Input: U_{id}, $Service_{id}$, $filehash$
Output: out
1   *Initialization: out* $\leftarrow$ *rejected*

2    $U_{id} \leftarrow address$;
3   **if** getTable(U_{id}) **then**
4   **if** selectValue$(U_{id}, Service_{id})$ **then**
5   registerTable $\leftarrow$ getTable(U_{id});
6   registerTable.updateTable$(U_{id}, Service_{id}, filehash)$;
7   **event** UpdateTable$(filehash)$;
8   *out* $\leftarrow$ *success*
9   **end**
10 **end**
11 **return** *out*

---

to the User. Here, we choose the Service to deliver the message because it owns the user behavior data and has access to the User. Once permitted, the User fetches the file hash from the Register SC.

At this stage, we manage to introduce a reward mechanism. The User will not send the file hash to the third party directly; but to record the U_{id}, third-party Serviceid and corresponding file hash for further validation (Algorithm 3). Then the User delivers sharing permit to the Service. After getting consent, the Service ought to complete its registration (Algorithm 4). Besides validating the file hash, the SC requires a certain amount of currency from the Service and transfers it to the User's account address as remuneration. Then, the User completes the sharing process by providing the third party with the file hash, the U_{id}, and $Service_{id}$. The third-party Service now can associate the personal data to the specific User.

4   Implementation

In this process, we use a Ethereum-based private blockchain to ensure security. The configurations of the proposed framework are stated in Table 2:

4.1   Set up Ethereum Environment

To start with, we create a genesis.json file, which configs the genesis block of the network. To define the first block, it gives the detail of the chain, especially the

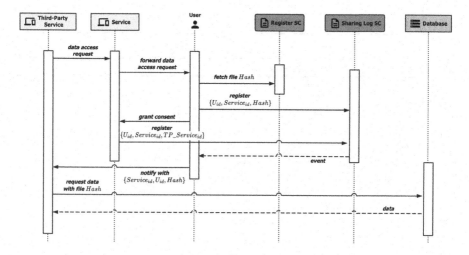

Fig. 3. Data sharing process.

Algorithm 3: Sharing Process Registration

Input: U_{id} and $Service_{id}$
Output: out

1 *Initialization: out ← error*

2 $U_{id} ←$ *address*;
3 **if** isValid(U_{id}) **then**
4 | **if** getTable(U_{id}) **then**
5 | | shareRegister ← getTable(U_{id});
6 | | filehash ← $table$.selectValue$(U_{id}, Service_{id})$;
7 | | $out ←$ filehash;
8 | **end**
9 **end**
10 **return** out

Algorithm 4: Service Registration

Input: U_{id}, $Service_{id}$, $TP\_Service_{id}$, $filehash$, $amount$
Output: out
1   *Initialization: out $\leftarrow$ rejected*
2   **if** *shareRegister*.selectValue(U_{id}, $Service_{id}$) **equals** $filehash$ **then**
3   shareLog $\leftarrow$ createTable(U_{id}, $Service_{id}$);
4   shareLog $\leftarrow$ insertTable(U_{id}, $Service_{id}$, $TP\_Service_{id}$);
5   U_{id}.transfer($amount$);
6   **event** ShareLog($TP\_Service_{id}$);
7   *out $\leftarrow$ success*
8   **end**
9   **return** *out*

Table 2. Configuration

Dependency	Detail
OS	MacOS
Geth	1.10.4-stable
IPFS	0.9.0
Nodejs	10.24.1

chain ID, the consensus engines, as well as the block numbers of any relevant hard forks. With this configuration JSON file, we can then set up an initial node through *Geth*, the standalone client of Ethereum. Since three main entities in our proposal (the User, the Service, the third-party Service), we build three nodes. They are initialized with the same genesis block configuration but started up with different ports.

Then, we set up an account for each node. The account plays a crucial role in ether transfer and Smart Contract deployment. Meanwhile, the account addresses will later be used as identifications in system flows. Finally, to connect these three nodes and create a network, we apply Geth console, adding each peer node with its *enode id*.

4.2 Create and Deploy Smart Contract

There are two smart contracts implemented in the framework: *i)* the *register* for authentication, authorization, logging of interactions between the User and the Service. *ii)* the *sharing_log* for logging data authorization of sharing process. In our implementation, the smart contracts are written in Solidity. It is a high-level programming language designed for smart contracts running on Ethereum. To improve the efficiency of programming and debugging, we use Remix IDE, a multifunctional development tool, to create code. The original code requires being complied to become executable. This process can still be carried out with Remix. Then, to deploy, we set an injected web3 to provide as the environment of Remix. Here, we apply Metamask, an Ethereum browser, to connect with our private local network.

4.3   Set up Private IPFS

IPFS is by design a public network. To protect personal information, we manage to set up a private network IPFS. First, we install *go-ipfs*, the core implementation. The network's privacy can be ensured by referencing the *Swarm key*, a secret key generated by a third-party package. This network is only open to peers who share this key. Even if one gets the file hash, he/she still requires the Swarm key to get access to the private IPFS. With the generated secret key, we can then initialize and configure nodes. After starting the nodes, we will be able to add files from one node and fetch them from another.

5   Discussion

In our proposed framework, we assume the Service as a malicious entity. The Smart Contract manages registration, authentication and currency transfer.

5.1   Security Analysis

By implementing the framework over blockchain, the activities of entities are recorded and are transparent to each node. The security weakness may arise from the risk of potential attacks on the blockchain. According to our design, the user's identity is anonymized by using the account address. In Ethereum, this address is the first 20 bytes of the SHA3 hashed public key, while the public kay is derived from the private key using Elliptic Curve Digital Signature Algorithm (ECDSA). Once criminals recover the user's private key, the account will be exposed to property damage. Moreover, the smart contract's deployment and execution are essentially transactions. The blockchain uses the consensus mechanism to give the right to the participant node to add transactions and ensure all transactions are genuine. Ethereum currently adopts Proof-of-work(POW) algorithm, which is based on a majority vote. As for a small-scale network, it is possible for an attacker to dominate the majority of the network, thus getting complete control of the chain.

Also, the smart contract may have security vulnerabilities due to program defects, such as Reentrancy, Timestamp dependence, and Stack overflow. However, these risks may be avoided in the programming process thanks to the assist of the security analyzer.

5.2   Privacy Analysis

Data Storing. User's behavioral data is owned by the Service. The data is stored in Service's database and identified with in-app U_{id}. With the behavioral data, the Service can bring personalized services to each user. However, the Service still request tracking authorization (essentially the device id) because they require a general identifier for cross-app advertising. To prevent unauthorized advertising, we use an anonymous account address in the blockchain network to represent the user, thus protecting the general identifier.

The Service uses this identifier to store personal data in a database for subsequent access. Instead of directly storing personal information in the SCs, we use a private IPFS for security purposes. After the data is uploaded, the Service gets a particular hash for retrieving. Here, we put the personal information in IPFS while storing the file hash on SC. Hence, even if the Service and the third-part Service have direct access to the SCs, they are still isolated from the original data. Also, in the process of hash recording, an authentication exists to check whether the Service has been registered before. Of course, following a malicious model, it may not record the hash because the registration brings weak benefits to the product operation (the data are in their own database). However, the absence of this hash record affects further data sharing. In addition, the registration process and interactions with IPFS are traceable and immutable. Some restrictions can be imposed on this improper behavior in terms of regulation.

Moreover, even if a third party may get file hash improperly and then retrieve user data, it will not know to whom the data belongs without a general identifier.

Data Sharing. Although there is no general identifier, it is still possible for third parties to associate an in-app user account with corresponding behavioral data in other Services by the User's push message within the application, thus enabling cross-app data sharing. During this process, to ensure the User's right, we introduce a reward mechanism and add few steps of registration before the User notifies the third party. In the initial stage, the User register the $Service_{id}$ and file hash for the subsequent security review for third-party $Service_{id}$ registration. Again, as a malicious entity, the Service may not perform the registration process to avoid offering the reward. Nonetheless, in this way, the contract will not emit a successful registration event, and the User will not send an initiative notification. So, to complete the sharing, the Service must follow the process.

Meanwhile, these processes are carrying out as transactions on the chain, which provides a reference for further review. The traceability, transparency, and immutability of smart contracts make the whole process reliable. For example, if a Service does not register its ID for a long time after requesting permission, it may be suspected of violating the rules.

6   Conclusion and Future Work

In cross-app advertising, the user behavioral data is susceptible to attacks and misuse. How to prevent data leakage is the key to solve the problem. In this paper, a smart contract based personal data protection framework is proposed. The essential idea of the design is to conceal the User's general identifications from the malicious entities. According to the framework, the User presents an anonymous identity when interacting with the Services and the third-party Services. Even if a third party has improper access to the User's behavioral data, it is still unable to "recognize" the User in-app, thus failing in cross-app advertising. Despite the User's anonymity, the framework supports data sharing, but in a secure way: After receiving the request from a third party, the User has the right to decide whether notify the third party with the file hash so that one gets complete control of their data. Once the consent is granted, the User also earns the reward.

Furthermore, the combination of Ethereum and IPFS enhances the security of the whole design. In the storing and sharing process, the smart contract performs authorization, authentication, and logging. The access control is strictly enforced since predefined logic is tamper-proof. Besides, the traceable evidence on the ledger helps with the further audit process.

For future work, we decide to design a management system of smart contracts since the framework will become more complex as there are a fairly large number of users and services in practice. In addition, it is also possible to adapt our framework to other scenarios, as long as there exists a general identification of user data.

References

1. Azeem, A., Jajeththanan, S., Sharmilan, S.: Blockchain based decentralized knowledge sharing system - jigsaw. In: 4th International Conference on Information Technology Research (ICITR), pp. 1–6. IEEE (2019). https://doi.org/10.1109/ICITR49409.2019.9407801
2. Adjust: What is a device id. https://www.adjust.com/glossary/device-id/. Accessed 05 July 2021
3. Alizadeh, M., Andersson, K., Schelén, O.: A survey of secure internet of things in relation to blockchain. J. Internet Serv. Inf. Secur. 10(3), 47–75 (2020). https://doi.org/10.22667/JISIS.2020.08.31.047
4. Anada, H.: Decentralized multi-authority anonymous authentication for global identities with non-interactive proofs. J. Internet Serv. Inf. Secur. 10(4), 23–37 (2020). https://doi.org/10.22667/JISIS.2020.11.30.023
5. Apple: User privacy and data use. https://developer.apple.com/app-store/user-privacy-and-data-use/. Accessed 05 July 2021
6. Bembenik, R., Falcman, K.: BLE indoor positioning system using RSSI-based trilateration. J. Wirel. Mob. Netw. Ubiquit. Comput. Dependable Appl. 11(3), 50–69 (2020). https://doi.org/10.22667/JOWUA.2020.09.30.050
7. Daudén-Esmel, C., Castellà-Roca, J., Viejo, A., Domingo-Ferrer, J.: Lightweight blockchain-based platform for GDPR-compliant personal data management. In: 5th IEEE International Conference on Cryptography, Security and Privacy, CSP 2021, Zhuhai, China, 8–10 January 2021, pp. 68–73. IEEE (2021). https://doi.org/10.1109/CSP51677.2021.9357602
8. Ethereum: A next-generation smart contract and decentralized application platform. https://github.com/ethereum/wiki/wiki/White-Paper. Accessed 05 July 2021

9. Herskind, L., Katsikouli, P., Dragoni, N.: Oscausi - practical private electronic cash from lelantus and mimblewimble. J. Internet Serv. Inf. Secur. **10**(2), 16–34 (2020). https://doi.org/10.22667/JISIS.2020.05.31.016

10. Jin, H., Xu, C., Luo, Y., Li, P., Cao, Y., Mathew, J.: Toward secure, privacy-preserving, and interoperable medical data sharing via blockchain. In: 25th IEEE International Conference on Parallel and Distributed Systems, ICPADS 2019, Tianjin, China, 4–6 December 2019, pp. 852–861. IEEE (2019). https://doi.org/10.1109/ICPADS47876.2019.00126

11. König, L., Unger, S., Kieseberg, P., Tjoa, S.: The risks of the blockchain a review on current vulnerabilities and attacks. J. Internet Serv. Inf. Secur. **10**(3), 110–127 (2020). https://doi.org/10.22667/JISIS.2020.08.31.110

12. Latanya, S.: k-anonymity: a model for protecting privacy. Int. J. Uncertainty Fuzziness Knowl.-Based Syst. **10**(5), 557–570 (2002)

13. Lee, A.R., Kim, M., Kim, I.K.: SHAREChain: healthcare data sharing framework using blockchain-registry and FHIR. In: Yoo, I., Bi, J., Hu, X. (eds.) 2019 IEEE International Conference on Bioinformatics and Biomedicine, BIBM 2019, San Diego, CA, USA, 18–21 November 2019, pp. 1087–1090. IEEE (2019). https://doi.org/10.1109/BIBM47256.2019.8983415

14. Li, N., Li, T., Venkatasubramanian, S.: t-closeness: privacy beyond k-anonymity and l-diversity. In: Chirkova, R., Dogac, A., Özsu, M.T., Sellis, T.K. (eds.) Proceedings of the 23rd International Conference on Data Engineering, ICDE 2007, The Marmara Hotel, Istanbul, Turkey, 15–20 April 2007, pp. 106–115. IEEE (2007). https://doi.org/10.1109/ICDE.2007.367856

15. Liu, J., Li, X., Ye, L., Zhang, H., Du, X., Guizani, M.: BPDS: a blockchain based privacy-preserving data sharing for electronic medical records. In: 2018 IEEE Global Communications Conference, GLOBECOM, pp. 1–6. IEEE (2018). https://doi.org/10.1109/GLOCOM.2018.8647713

16. Liu, X., Wang, Z., Jin, C., Li, F., Li, G.: A blockchain-based medical data sharing and protection scheme. IEEE Access **7**, 118943–118953 (2019). https://doi.org/10.1109/ACCESS.2019.2937685

17. Machanavajjhala, A., Kifer, D., Gehrke, J., Venkitasubramaniam, M.: L-diversity: privacy beyond k-anonymity. ACM Trans. Knowl. Discov. Data **1**(1), 3 (2007)

18. Nakamoto, S.: Bitcoin p2p e-cash paper. https://bitcoin.org/bitcoin.pdf. Accessed 06 June 2021

19. Park, M., Kim, S., Kim, J.: Research on note-taking apps with security features. J. Wirel. Mob. Netw. Ubiquit. Comput. Dependable Appl. **11**(4), 63–76 (2020). https://doi.org/10.22667/JOWUA.2020.12.31.063

20. Pozi, M.S.M., Omar, M.H.: A kernel density estimation method to generate synthetic shifted datasets in privacy-preserving task. J. Internet Serv. Inf. Secur. **10**(4), 70–89 (2020). https://doi.org/10.22667/JISIS.2020.11.30.070

21. Team, I.P.: EU General Data Protection Regulation. GDPR), An Implementation and Compliance Guide. IT Governance (2017)

22. Truong, N.B., Sun, K., Lee, G.M., Guo, Y.: GDPR-compliant personal data management: a blockchain-based solution. IEEE Trans. Inf. Forensics Secur. **15**, 1746–1761 (2020). https://doi.org/10.1109/TIFS.2019.2948287

23. Vinay, G.: An updated timeline for privacy sandbox milestones. https://blog.google/products/chrome/updated-timeline-privacy-sandbox-milestones/. Accessed 06 July 2021

24. Wang, H., Wang, C., Shen, Z., Liu, K., Liu, P., Lin, D.: A MADM location privacy protection method based on blockchain. IEEE Access **9**, 27802–27812 (2021). https://doi.org/10.1109/ACCESS.2021.3058446

25. Wong, S.K., Yiu, S.: Location spoofing attack detection with pre-installed sensors in mobile devices. J. Wirel. Mob. Netw. Ubiquit. Comput. Dependable Appl. $11(4)$, 16–30 (2020). https://doi.org/10.22667/JOWUA.2020.12.31.016

26. Xu, Y., Cao, B., Lu, R., Zhang, Q.: APRNET: achieving privacy-preserving real-name authentication over blockchain for online services. In: 11th International Conference on Wireless Communications and Signal Processing, WCSP 2019, Xi'an, China, 23–25 October 2019, pp. 1–6. IEEE (2019). https://doi.org/10.1109/WCSP.2019.8928072

27. Zyskind, G., Nathan, O., Pentland, A.: Decentralizing privacy: using blockchain to protect personal data. In: 2015 IEEE Symposium on Security and Privacy Workshops, SPW 2015, San Jose, CA, USA, 21–22 May 2015, pp. 180–184. IEEE (2015). https://doi.org/10.1109/SPW.2015.27

A Blockchain-Based Authentication Scheme for 5G Applications

Lanfang Ren[1,2]([✉]), Xiaoting Huang[2], Huachun Zhou[1], Bo Yang[2], and Li Su[2]

[1] School of Electronic and Information Engineering, Beijing Jiaotong University,
Beijing, China
{20111085,hchzhou}@bjtu.edu.cn
[2] China Mobile Research and Institute, Beijing, China
{renlanfang,huangxiaoting,yangbo,suli}@chinamobile.com

Abstract. Authentication mechanisms are important security features for mobile operators and application providers. In addition to the primary authentication between user equipment and the mobile operator network, secondary authentication between the user and Data Networks owned by the application is introduced in the 5G system. However, the implementation of secondary authentication introduces some challenges to application providers, not only the cost but also the capability, which leaves space for improving. In this paper, we designed an authentication mechanism for applications based on blockchain. With this mechanism, mobile operators and the application providers are able to share authentication related information like authentication results, users' identification, users' attribute information, users' reputation and users' blacklists, etc. securely. As a result, some application providers could execute user access control without deploying their own authentication systems any more. In addition with the shared comprehensive user information, mobile operators and application providers can make more fine and intelligent user access control.

Keywords: Blockchain · User authentication · User access control · Data sharing

1 Introduction

One of the key partnerships in the 5G ecosystem is between mobile operators and application providers, which are namely vertical industries. Mobile operators

---

L. Ren—Architecture and process design of the combination of blockchain and 5g.
X. Huang—5g secondary authentication problem and demand analysis, proposal design.
H. Zhou—Guide the whole scheme and put forward optimization ideas.
B. Yang—Discussion on 5g secondary authentication solution based on blockchain Technology.
L. Su—Guide the experimental design of the scheme and plan the next work.

© Springer Nature Singapore Pte Ltd. 2022
I. You et al. (Eds.): MobiSec 2021, CCIS 1544, pp. 155–168, 2022.
https://doi.org/10.1007/978-981-16-9576-6_12

provide vertical industries with network resources as well as security solutions. Authentication mechanisms are important mobile internet security features that mobile operators are obliged to manage and maintain, in order to ensure only legitimate users get access to the mobile network and use service resources provided by the application providers. In addition to the primary authentication [5] used for access control between the user equipment (UE) and the mobile operator network, the third partnership project (3GPP) has specified secondary authentication [3] in the 5G system which is meant for authentication between the user and Data Networks (DN) which is owned by the application providers and outside the mobile operator domain. While primary authentication has been long existed in the generations of mobile networks from 2G to 5G, secondary authentication is a rather new concept in the 5G system.

The motivation of secondary authentication is based on the fact that application providers do not always trust mobile operators in terms of authentication results, and they are willing to execute authentication themselves rather than only relying on the authentication mechanism (primary authentication) provided by the mobile operators. In this case, a typical security risk occurs when users get access to DN after the connection between the UE and the DN established with the support of the mobile operator. Though primary authentication has been conducted successfully in advance in order for the mobile operators to establish user plane tunnel between the UE and the DN, which means the UE has been authenticated by the operator and regarded as a legitimate UE, it is possible for the UE to invoke authentication service provided by the DN resulting in a Denial of Service (DoS) attack. Therefore, secondary authentication was designed to allow operators delegating the authentication for DNs during the establishment of user plane connection [1], this enables the mitigation of the mentioned security risk, with detailed description of secondary authentication introduced later in this paper.

However, not all application providers are capable of managing the authentication system on their own considering the cost of credential provisioning and management, which is a prerequisite for the implementation of secondary authentication. Especially for some middle and small scale application providers, they are neither unable to conduct secondary authentication, nor willing to only rely on operators' primary authentication results [19–21]. As a result, it is beneficial to build an enhanced authentication system by information sharing for application providers to share authentication related information like authentication results, users' attribute information, users' reputation, users' blacklists, etc., so that some application providers could execute access control based on the collected information without deployment their own authentication systems. Such authentication information system is built among the mobile operators and the application providers with the following advantages.

On one hand, even though secondary authentication helps application providers intercept malicious users to some extent; each application provider manages and operates their own authentication systems independently, which leads to one-sided information of users' behavior and possibilities of hostile attacks. Specifically, if the same user to Application A is a legitimate user, i.e., has been authenticated by Application A, but to Application B is an illegal user due to the failure of authentication or misusing of services provided by Application B, it is risky for Application A to keep being unaware of the user's dubiety since it may launch attacks later. Thus the enhanced authentication information sharing system by information sharing helps to overcome the barriers of asymmetric information of the users' authentication related information.

On the other hand, for operators, the primary authentication result for a UE is static and unchanged until the triggering of the next primary authentication, while a legitimate user to the operator may launch attacks to the application providers within the period of primary authentication. The enhanced authentication system by information sharing system provides the operator with timely feedback of users' behaviors after users are authenticated successfully by the operators, so that help to reduce potential attacks to the mobile operator network.

Motivated by the above problem of secondary authentication and the benefits of the above mentioned enhanced authentication system by information sharing, in this paper, we designed an authentication mechanism for applications used for mobile internet based on blockchain. Blockchain, with the characteristics of decentralization and tamper-resistance, ensures the trust data sharing among untrusted multi parties and can be well applied to build the authentication information sharing system.

This paper is organized as follows. We first introduce the background of secondary authentication and blockchain technology in Sect. 2. In Sect. 3, we describe the architecture, process of information written to blockchain and the detailed procedure of user authentication based on the Blockchain. The experiment design and future work given in Sect. 4 and 5.

2   Background

2.1   Secondary Authentication

Secondary authentication in the 5G system provides a mechanism for application providers to authenticate the UE with the support of mobile operator [14]. Before secondary authentication is introduced into the mobile network, the application provider does the access control by themselves by using their own authentication systems and credentials, with the mobile operator just providing the network connection between the UE and the DN owned by the application provider. This brought about security risks of DoS attack to the DN since once the UE is authenticated successfully by the operator through primary authentication, it is able to easily get access to the authentication server of the DN and endlessly invoke the authentication service provided by the DN. Secondary authentication addresses this security risk by involving the application provider to participate the network connection establishment between the UE and the DN, so that without the permission of the DN, the operator is not able to get

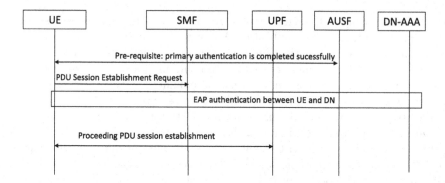

Fig. 1. General procedure of secondary authentication in 5G

the UE connected to the DN. Figure 1 illustrates the general procedure of secondary authentication.

The method of secondary authentication is the Extensible Application Protocol (EAP) framework [9], which is widely used by the application providers. Session Management Function (SMF) in the 5G system plays the role of the EAP authenticator and DN-AAA server owned by the DN acts as the EAP authentication server. During the procedures, SMF can only proceed the Packet Data Unit (PDU) session establishment after the success of the EAP authentication between the UE and the DN. The PDU session is the network connection for the UE to get access to the DN. This achieves the goal of preventing malicious UEs from accessing the DN at the connection establishment stage [2].

However, the implementation of secondary authentication in the industry is faced with the following two difficulties. One is that the cost of building and managing the authentication system, which is conducted by the DN-AAA server in the secondary authentication. For some small application providers, they do not have their own authentication servers or are not willing to replace their authentication methods to EAP considering the cost.

The other is the provisioning and management of the credentials used for secondary authentication. The use of secondary authentication requires credentials provisioned at both the UE and the DN. The credential provisioning at the UE is a practical obstacle since once the UE is out of factory, it is hard to provision and replace the credentials to the UE especially when the UE has been delivered to or used by the customers.

2.2 Blockchain Technology

A blockchain is defined as an immutable ledger for recording transactions, maintained within a distributed network of mutually untrusted peers. Every peer maintains a copy of the ledger. The peers execute a consensus protocol to validate transactions, group them into blocks, and build a hash chain over the blocks [11].

In a public or permissionless blockchain anyone can participate without a specific identity authentication. Permissioned blockchains, on the other hand, run a blockchain among a set of known, identified participants. A permissioned blockchain provides a way to secure the interactions among a group of entities that have a common goal but which do not fully trust each other [12].

Fabric is a component of the open-source Hyperledger project hosted by the Linux Foundation, and it is also one of the most actively developed and widely used permissioned blockchain systems in different industries [6,7]. In Fabric system, the nodes involved in completing the transaction processing are called peers. The peers can be grouped into three types, according to the functional characteristics and roles in the transaction process [8,11].

Endorser: In the Fabric transaction processing, the first process is endorsement. The node responsible for this processing is called endorser. The endorser judges whether the transaction proposal can be endorsed based on some conditions, such as signature is valid, transaction ID is unique and transaction content is reasonable. If it is success, the endorser builds up a read-write set by proposal simulation. Then it returns the read-write set and endorsement response to the client. Along with that response, there is a cryptographic signature of the endorser. In Fabric system, the endorser is determined by the pre-set endorsement policy. Generally, there is at least one node to endorse the proposal request in the system.

Orderer: After the endorsement is completed, it is the sequence of transactions. The orderer is the node responsible for performing transaction global ordering. Orderer receives all of the transaction from different clients. Then it regularly establishes a global order and packs transactions into certain sized blocks. The rule of ordering is based on the preset consensus mechanism. By default of Fabric, the transactions are ordered in the way in which they arrive at the orderer. The orderer then broadcasts each block to all peers of the network. After the ordering services, all peers receive the same blocks and the transactions in it are in the same order.

Committer: All peers in the Fabric network except orderer act as a committer. When committer receives the block sent by the orderer, firstly verifies whether the transaction is in compliance with the endorsement policy and whether it contains endorser's signature in the read-write set. Then, based on the read-write set of the transaction, the committer queries the local state database and determines whether conflict occurs between different transactions in a block. After that, the committer marks the conflict transactions invalid or valid and then writes the block to its local ledger.

In Fabric, all the peers have them own local ledger. The ledgers between each other are exactly the same. The local ledger includes two parts, local state database and the chain. The local state database stores transaction-related information in the form of key, value, and version. The chain holds the information of all blocks [17,18].

With these three types of nodes, the entire transaction procedure of Hyperledger Fabric covers three stages. Endorsement stage is the endorser executing

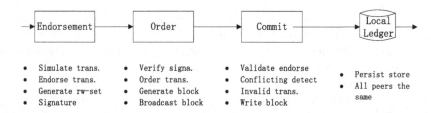

Fig. 2. Workflow of hyperledger fabric

transaction simulation execution and signature endorsement response. Ordering stage is the orderer globally ordering the transactions proposals and packing them into blocks. The last verification and committing stage is the committer verifying the endorsement, detecting transaction confliction, validating confirmation of the transactions in the block, and then written all blocks to the chain [13,16]. The procedure follows an endorsement-order-commit workflow as illustrated in Fig. 2.

3   Design

3.1   System Architecture

Based on the blockchain system, 5G mobile operators and application providers are able to securely share user data with each other, including user identity information, user attribute information, user reputation and user blacklist lists and so on. The detailed system architecture is showing in Fig. 3.

In this architecture, 5G mobile operators and industrial application providers collect and aggregate their own user data firstly. These data are related to identity authentication and authorization, such as user identity information, user attributes information, user history network behavior and so on. Then these data can be shared between different application providers and mobile operators through the Blockchain. What information will be shared on the chain is according to the willing of mobile operators and industrial application providers. Some of these data are important business data, so they are unwilling to share on the chain. In this case, mobile operators and industrial application providers can hash encrypted these data firstly, then write the hash value and other sharable information on the blockchain together [10,15]. The hash value can be used by operators or application providers to authenticate users themselves.

In the 5G network, network access control is based on Authentication and Key Agreement (AKA) protocol [4], which relies on the symmetric key shared by the operator network and the (U)SIM card. This article also considers user attribute information, user historical network behavior, user network reputation and user blacklist, etc. With these user data, 5G mobile operators can provide fine-grained user authentication and authorization control mechanism and prevent malicious users from getting access to the network or business. In other

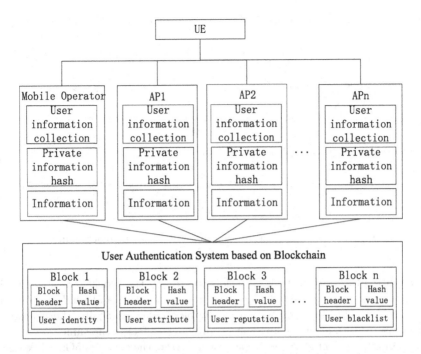

Fig. 3. Architecture of authentication system for applications based on blockchain

words, for those users whose identities are legitimate but the user behaviors are abnormal, they will most likely not be able to access the network directly.

In the process of 5G network operations and maintenance, the mobile operators can collect or analyze security related information from the network entities, network management systems, and the security equipments, including security threats, attack events, risk warnings, and disposal responses [22]. These information are also very important for application providers. They can be written to the blockchain and shared with each other securely. 5G mobile operators and industrial application providers both can prevent potential malicious users or malicious events in a timely manner. In this case, mobile operators and application providers can effectively interact with each other and implement security control from the network layer and application layer. This makes the entire 5G network and applications more securely, and users also can benefit from it.

3.2   Procedure of User Information Written to the Blockchain

In this article, Hyperledger Fabric is jointly established by 5G mobile operators and application providers together. Using this blockchain platform, mobile operators and application providers are sharing user information and make user identify authentication and accessing control.

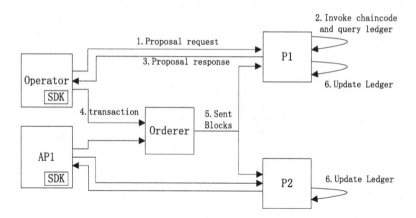

Fig. 4. Process of user information written to the blockchain

Detailed process of user information written to the blockchain is shown in Fig. 4. In this case, the mobile operator acts as a client and sends a proposal request of writing user information to the blockchain. Actually, the process of writing user information by application provider (AP1) is the same.

Preconditions: Before using Hyperledger Fabric, the entity of 5G mobile operator and application provider as a transaction client need to install the corresponding Software Development Kit (SDK). With this SDK, the user information is encapsulated in a specific format and transformed through the detailed API between the SDK and the peers defined in Fabric. When the SDK generating the transaction request and sending it to the endorser, the chain code of peers has been configured with who will be responsible for endorsing of this transaction request. Also, in Fabric, signature is required by default in every stage of the transaction and preventing the message from being forged or tampered. So, the MSP (Membership Service Provider) of Fabric is configured and enabled. The detailed process of user information written to the blockchain has three stages.

– Endorsement stage

1. Using the SDK, the operator generates a proposal request with its signature and only sends the request to the endorser P1. In this scenario, assume that only P1 is the endorser. According to the requirements of endorsement policy, since P2 is not belonging to the organization of mobile operators; there is no need to endorse the request of operator by P2.
2. After receiving the proposal request, P1 verifies the client's signature. According to the ID of request message, P1 determines whether the request is sent for the first time, rather than a replay message. Then P1 simulates the request by querying the local ledger and determines whether the transaction executing well. After that, P1 generates a signatured read-write set as an endorsement response back to the client. The read-write set specifies the detailed key value of the proposal request.

– Ordering stage

1. After receiving the response from P1, the client of operator firstly verifies P1's signature, and checks whether the endorsement responses are consistent. In this transaction example, the operator uses only one endorser. In the actual application scenario, multiple nodes are required to participate in the endorsement process. If the endorsement responses returned by different endorsers are inconsistent with each other, the transaction request will be invalid and the client needs to re-initiate the transaction request again.
2. The client of operator packages the proposal request and proposal response into a transaction and submits it to the orderer.
3. After receiving the transaction from the client, the orderer verifies the client's signature. The orderer doesn't process the transactions and just orders transactions based the pre-configured smart contract. In the smart contract, the specific ordering principle and ordering method will be specified, such as ordering based on the transaction receiving time. After the ordering is finished, the orderer packs the transactions into blocks according to certain rules. The rules of generating blocks based on a certain size or specific block time. After the orderer signs the blocks, it forward the packaged blocks to all of the committer in the blockchain system. In this scenario, both P1 and P2 are committers, and they will receive the blocks sent by the orderer.

– Verifying and committing stage

1. When receiving the blocks broadcasted by the orderer, P1 and P2 sequentially perform format and signature verification. At the same time, P1 and P2 split the blocks into each transaction and verify the endorsement signature of each transaction. Then P1 and P2 perform conflict checking based on the read-write set of each transaction and decide whether the transaction is valid. After marking the validity of each transaction, P1 and P2 write the verified block into its local ledger. The block written in the ledger will be almost the same as the block received from the orderer, except that each transaction in the block will have a valid or invalid tag.

After the above process, the user information on the chain written by the mobile operators will be shared with other application providers. The process of writing information on the chain by application provider is the same with the mobile operator's. The detailed information can be user attribution, user reputation and user blacklist. Using this mechanism, user is authenticated and authorized not just based on the previous identity information, but also considering the user's network behavior. The user access control can be more flexible and smarter. Under this mechanism, the authentication of 5G network and industrial application will be more and more secure and convenient.

3.3 Procedure of User Authentication Based on the Blockchain

The procedure of simplified secondary authentication in 5G based on blockchain is shown in Fig. 5.

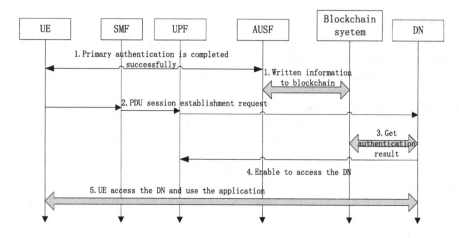

Fig. 5. Procedure of simplified secondary authentication

1. The mobile operator finishes primary authentication with the user, and this process is the same with the specified procedure by 3GPP [1]. The Authentication Server Function (AUSF) writes the authentication results to the blockchain system.
2. The UE initiates the PDU session establishment request to User Plane Function (UPF) in order to get access to the DN of application provider.
3. Different with specified secondary authentication in 5G, the DN doesn't need to implement the EAP process, and just obtains the authentication result from the blockchain system directly.
4. If the user is legitimate, the PDU session is established successfully.
5. The secondary authentication is finished and the user can access the applications.

During this process, the application provider enables the user to access applications according to the results from the blockchain system. The results can be a simple network primary authentication result, a hash value of users' important information, a combination of users' application attributes or even the users' reputation or users' blacklist. The detailed information is determined by the application providers.

3.4   Procedure of Primary Authentication Based on the Blockchain

Actually, during the user's accessing to the application provided by DN, the application provider of DN can also write the user's behavior information into the blockchain at any time. Once an attack occurs, the application provider can write this information to the blockchain and share with the mobile operators and other application providers in time, which can avoid a wider range of security incidents happening. Also the user primary authentication can be not only based on the user's identity, but also considering the user's attributes, network behavior

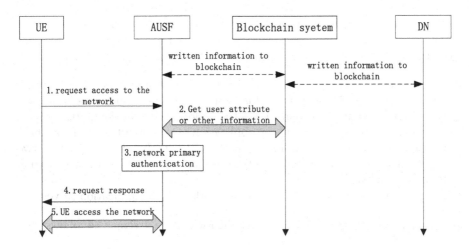

Fig. 6. Procedure of primary authentication

and user reputation. Even if the user is in the blacklist of the network operator or application provider, it can be directly denied network access. The procedure of primary authentication in 5G based on blockchain is shown in Fig. 6.

In this scenario, network operator and application provider write user information into the blockchain in advance.

1. UE requests to access the network.
2. The AUSF of mobile operator gets the uses related information from the chain, such as users' attributes, users' reputation and even the user blacklist.
3. The AUSF completes the primary authentication based on user attributes and other information, and in accordance with a certain authentication model.
4. The AUSF replies with the primary authentication result as the request response.
5. UE accesses the network.

Based on the user attribute information shared by different application providers on the blockchain, the mobile operators can perform fine-grained primary authentication, not only based on users' identities, but also users' attributes, users' reputation and even the user blacklist. This enhances the capabilities of network and application security protection. In this case, the entire 5G network will be more secure and intelligent.

4   Experiment Design

The experiment design of this paper includes four parts, Hyperledger Fabric system, 5G network simulated elements, an application server, and a simulated user.

The main aim of this experiment is to verify the feasibility of the system functionalities. Therefore, the experiment can be carried out with a simple network structure, including:

1. A fabric system composed of at least three node instances with VMware virtual machines. The Fabric v1.2 is deployed in these nodes. One node acts as the orderer, and the others act as the endorser and the committer.
2. The 5G network functions and the application server undertake user's authentication and access control. They are shipped with Fabric SDK, act as two clients of Fabric and generate the transaction proposal to write information to the blockchain system.
3. A simulated user is to access the 5G network and the application server.

The experiment flow of secondary authentication is designed as follows:

1. Primary authentication: the user initiates access to the 5G network and the 5G network proceeds with AKA procedures, with authentication results stored in the 5G network.
2. Writing of information to the blockchain: the 5G networkfunction, such as UPF, acts as a fabric client and sends a transaction proposal to the endorser to write the authentication results and user related information to the blockchain. In this process, the endorser will be engaged in the endorsement stage. Then the orderer will globally order the transactions, package the block and then broadcast the block to all of the committers. After the verifying and committing stage, the authentication results and the user related information will be written on the blockchain.
3. When the application server receives the user's request for accessing, the server acts as a Fabric client and sends a query request to the endorser and obtains the authentication results and the user information.

Actually, except for the network authentication results from the network provider, the application provider also can obtain the authentication results, user attribute information, user reputation and black list from other application providers via the blockchain system.

5   Conclusion and Future Work

In this paper, we designed a blockchain-based authentication scheme for 5G applications. With this blockchain system, users' related information are shared between the mobile operators and the application providers. With this system, the secondary authentication defined by 3GPP can be simplified and also the entire 5G network and applications will be more secure and intelligent.

The architecture and the overall procedures of 5G authentication system based on blockchain are described in this paper. But the specific information content, message format, detailed chain code, and consensus mechanism in blockchain need to be further studied and defined. At the same time, it is necessary to analyze what kinds of user attributes information are important to operators, how to model and establish the user reputation database and user blacklist, and how to design the authentication model based on user attribute information and reputations. With all these information, operators and application providers can implement fine-grained user authentication and authorization.

References

1. 3gpp 5g security. https://www.3gpp.org//news-events//3gpp-news//1975-sec-5g. Accessed 27 Oct 2021
2. 3gpp tr 33.899: Study on the security aspects of the next generation system. Accessed 27 Oct 2021
3. 3gpp ts 23.501 (v16.1.0): System architecture for the 5g system. Accessed 27 Oct 2021
4. 3gpp ts 33.102 (v16.0.0): 3g security: security architecture. Accessed 27 Oct 2021
5. 3gpp ts 33.501 (v16.4.0): Security architecture and procedures for 5g system. Accessed 27 Oct 2021
6. Hyperledger. http://www.hyperledger.org. Accessed 27 Oct 2021
7. Hyperledger fabric. http://github.com/hyperledger/fabric. Accessed 27 Oct 2021
8. Hyperledger fabric: [fab-12221] validator/committer refactor-hyperledger jira. https://jira.hyperledger.org/browse/FAB-12221?filter=12526. Accessed 27 Oct 2021
9. Ietf rfc 3748: Extensible authentication protocol (EAP). Accessed 27 Oct 2021
10. Alizadeh, M., Andersson, K., Schelén, O.: A survey of secure internet of things in relation to blockchain. J. Internet Serv. Inf. Secur. (JISIS) 10(3), 47–75 (2020)
11. Androulaki, E., et al.: Hyperledger fabric: a distributed operating system for permissioned blockchains. In: Proceedings of the Thirteenth EuroSys Conference, pp. 1–15 (2018)
12. Cachin, C., et al.: Architecture of the hyperledger blockchain fabric. In: Workshop on Distributed Cryptocurrencies and Consensus Ledgers, Chicago, IL, vol. 310 (2016)
13. Gorenflo, C., Lee, S., Golab, L., Keshav, S.: FastFabric: Scaling hyperledger fabric to 20 000 transactions per second. Int. J. Netw. Manag. 30(5), e2099 (2020)
14. Huang, X., Yoshizawa, T., Baskaran, S.B.M.: Authentication mechanisms in the 5G system. J. ICT Standard. 61–78 (2021)
15. König, L., Unger, S., Kieseberg, P., Tjoa, S., Josef Ressel Center BLOCKCHAINS: The risks of the blockchain a review on current vulnerabilities and attacks. J. Internet Serv. Inf. Secur. 10(3), 110–127 (2020)
16. Ranjan, S., Negi, A., Jain, H., Pal, B., Agrawal, H.: Network system design using hyperledger fabric: permissioned blockchain framework. In: 2019 Twelfth International Conference on Contemporary Computing (IC3), pp. 1–6. IEEE (2019)
17. Ribalta, C.N., Lombard-Platet, M., Salinesi, C., Lafourcade, P.: Blockchain mirage or silver bullet? A requirements-driven comparative analysis of business and developers' perceptions in the accountancy domain. J. Wirel. Mob. Netw. Ubiquit. Comput. Dependable Appl. 12(1), 85–110 (2021)
18. Shih, C.S., Hsieh, W.Y., Kao, C.L.: Traceability for vehicular network real-time messaging based on blockchain technology. J. Wirel. Mob. Netw. Ubiquit. Comput. Dependable Appl. 10(4), 1–21 (2019)

19. Song, F., Ai, Z., Zhang, H., You, I., Li, S.: Smart collaborative balancing for dependable network components in cyber-physical systems. IEEE Trans. Ind. Inf. (2020)
20. Song, F., Ai, Z., Zhou, Y., You, I., Choo, K.K.R., Zhang, H.: Smart collaborative automation for receive buffer control in multipath industrial networks. IEEE Trans. Industr. Inf. **16**(2), 1385–1394 (2019)
21. Song, F., Li, L., You, I., Zhang, H.: Enabling heterogeneous deterministic networks with smart collaborative theory. IEEE Netw. **35**(3), 64–71 (2021)
22. Tu, Z., Zhou, H., Li, K., Li, G.: DCTG: degree constrained topology generation algorithm for software-defined satellite network. J. Internet Serv. Inf. Secur. **9**(4), 49–58 (2019)

Digital Forensic and Malware Analysis

Effectiveness of Video-Classification in Android Malware Detection Through API-Streams and CNN-LSTM Autoencoders

Gianni D'Angelo⬭, Francesco Palmieri⬭, and Antonio Robustelli(✉)⬭

Department of Computer Science, University of Salerno, Fisciano, Italy
{gdangelo,fpalmieri,arobustelli}@unisa.it

Abstract. The outbreak of the COVID-19 pandemic has forced worldwide employees to massive use of their mobile devices to access corporate systems. This new scenario has made mobile devices more susceptible to malicious applications, which are yearly developed to conduct several hostile activities. Concerned about this fact, many Deep Learning (DL) based solutions have been proposed, in the last decade, by considering both static and dynamic approaches. However, static solutions are adversely affected by obfuscation techniques and polymorphic applications, while dynamic ones cannot reduce the damages caused during applications execution. To this purpose, the following paper aims to propose a novel approach called API-Streams to minimize damages at Runtime. Therefore, we investigate several Video-Classification tasks through CNN-LSTM Autoencoders (CNN-LSTM-AEs). More precisely, we combine the capability of AEs in finding compact features with the classification abilities of Deep Neural Networks (DNNs), and we show that the proposed approach achieves an average accuracy of 98% in the presence of several unbalanced training datasets. Finally, we use the t-Stochastic Neighbor Embedded (t-SNE) representation technique to investigate the abilities of the employed AE to cluster data into their respective classes by limiting their overlapping.

Keywords: Android malware detection · API-Streams · Autoencoders · Video classification

1 Introduction

The sudden and rapid displacement of the global workforce towards the houses, caused by the outbreak of the COVID-19 pandemic, has forced companies worldwide to make significant changes to their infrastructures. In this new scenario, mobile devices have been used more than ever to access corporate systems, and consequently, this has dramatically extended the attack surface and made mobile devices more susceptible to cyber threats. For instance, as reported by the Mobile Security Report of Check Point, 97% of organizations have faced several threats

© Springer Nature Singapore Pte Ltd. 2022
I. You et al. (Eds.): MobiSec 2021, CCIS 1544, pp. 171–194, 2022.
https://doi.org/10.1007/978-981-16-9576-6_13

from mobile devices, while 46% of organizations had at least one employee that downloaded a malicious app [24]. Mobile devices remain, in fact, one of the most important targets to cyber-criminals, which constantly monitor the situation in the world, analyze the most trending topics, and then use these to conduct several hostile activities [19,25].

For this reason, given the rapid early growth of malware applications and due to the great success of Deep Learning (DL) in many research fields [5,10,11,16,18,51], several DL-based solutions have been investigated to face malware classification by considering both static and dynamic approaches [8,9,20,29,39,50]. However, static solutions are adversely affected by obfuscation techniques and polymorphic applications, while dynamic ones cannot reduce the damages caused during applications execution. More precisely, they consider only the app's behaviour obtained after the malware's dynamic analysis when the malicious objective has already been reached.

To this purpose, the main goal of this paper aims to propose a novel approach, called API-Streams, able to minimize damages at Run-time by considering several streams of API-Images [9]. More precisely, they are sparse matrices representing snapshots of the applications dynamic behaviour, and which have also been employed to face several Android malware classification activities [7,9]. Then, to prove the effectiveness of the proposed approach, we investigate several Video-Classification tasks through CNN-LSTM Autoencoders (CNN-LSTM-AEs) by combining their capability in finding compact and relevant features, the goal of Video-Classification in distinguishing objects from a stream of frames, and the classification abilities of Deep Neural Networks (DNNs). Therefore, unlike the other solutions of state-of-the-art, the presented API-Streams could be involved in a monitoring process aimed at providing to end-users information on the presence of possible malicious applications in the shortest possible time, and consequently, to minimize the Run-time damages when the applications are still running.

Hence, the main contributions of this paper can be summarized as follows:

1 A novel approach called API-Streams, based on several streams of API-Images, is proposed to minimize the damages caused at Run-time.
2 Several Video-Classification tasks, based on CNN-LSTM Autoencoders, are investigated to show the effectiveness of the proposed approach.

The rest of the paper is organized as follows. Section 2 will present related works about dynamic DL approaches proposed to face Android malware detection tasks and Video-Classification's issues. Section 3 will show a preliminary overview of the employed deep neural networks typologies. Section 4 will present the definition of API-Streams, which is based on multiple API-Images considered at Run-time. Finally, Sect. 5 will report the experimental results, while Sect. 6 will show the conclusions and future works.

2   Related Works

Since Android-based devices are yearly one of the main targets of cyber-criminals, several DL-based solutions have been investigated, in the last years, to face Android malware classification tasks by considering both static and dynamic approaches [12,29,30,33]. Static based solutions can acquire the behaviour of the analyzed applications by performing several reverse engineering steps, and consequently, by extracting relevant signatures without executing the application.

In 2018, N. Xie et al. [46] proposed a tool called RepassDroid, which is able to classify Android benign and malicious applications based on permission and Java methods. Additionally, they explored a comparison among different ML-based approaches like DT, RF, k-NN, Naive Bayes (NN), and Support Vector Machine (SVM). The achieved results have been proven that RF is able to achieve a 99.7% accuracy by taking into account 24288 Android applications.

In 2019, C. Li et al. [21] proposed a novel and highly reliable DNN classifier for Android Malware detection based on several features extracted from manifest files and source code. In particular, they considered 7 different static features like app components, hardware features, permissions, intent filters, restricted and suspicious Java methods, and used permissions. Thus, they have been used to train a DNN able to obtain a 99.25% average accuracy.

Finally, in 2020, Aonzo et al. [2] presented BAdDroIds, a mobile application that leverages deep learning for detecting malware on resource-constrained devices. In particular, they considered the required permissions and the AAPI methods extracted from the DEX file to propose a linear learning algorithm and a non-linear learning algorithm, respectively. Finally, they investigated several binary classification tasks by achieving a 98% average accuracy in the presence of a balanced dataset of 14988 APKs.

However, since static based methods are adversely affected by the use of obfuscation techniques and polymorphic applications, many dynamic solutions have been investigated to analyze the behaviour of the malicious code at Run-time. Unfortunately, due to the high amount of works related to malware classification, it is very difficult to perform a complete comparison among them. For this reason, we report only some dynamic features based contributions, that for their similarity to our proposal, can be helpful to understand the potentiality of the proposed approach.

In 2016 Kolosnjaji et al. [20] used Deep Neural Networks (DNNs) to analyze the sequence of system calls extracted at Run-time. More precisely, they combined convolutional and recurrent layers by obtaining an average accuracy of 89.0% on 10 Android malware categories. In 2019, A. Abderrahmane et al. [1] employed a CNN to perform malware analysis in presence of an unbalanced dataset. More precisely, they achieved an accuracy of 93.3% by classifying a matrix representation of system calls obtained from dynamic analysis. In 2020, D'Angelo et al. [9] proposed a malware detector based on sparse Autoencoders and a matrix's representation of API calls, called API-Images. More precisely, they obtained an accuracy of 95% by performing a binary classification in presence of an unbalanced Android dataset. Finally, in 2021, D'Angelo et al. proposed

2 DNNs to investigate a multi-class malware classification task. More precisely, they employed a CNN and a RNN that have respectively achieved an average accuracy of 99.84% and 99.95% in presence of an Android malware dataset represented by 5 famous malware families [7].

However, the reported DL approaches have been based on the malicious behaviour considered after the malware's execution. Therefore, they are not able to minimize the damages caused at Run-time.

On the other hand, due to the great success of DL based approaches, several solutions have been investigated in many research fields, like cancer detection [11], Network Traffic Classification (NTC) [10,23], and predictive analytics [36]. However, one of the most famous is definitely related to Video Classification that aims to distinguish one or more objects from a stream of frames [28,48,51].

In 2016 M. Perez et al. [35] proposed a novel method for classifying pornographic videos by employing a CNN based on static and motion information. More precisely, they achieved an accuracy of 97.9% by concatenating static and motion features to support video classification tasks related to porn and no-porn videos. In 2018 X. Xu et al. [47] proposed a framework to classify violent videos by obtaining an accuracy of 97.97%. More precisely, they used 2 P3D-LSTM neural networks to extract relevant features through Convolutional-3D and LSTM layers.

Finally, in 2020, Video Classification tasks have also been investigated in malware detection by M. L. Santacroce et al. [38]. They proposed a Time Distributed CNN based on executable code broken into a stream of multiple windows of fixed dimensions. More precisely, they employed the following neural network to investigate 2 classification tasks. In the first one, they achieved an accuracy of 98.74% by considering 9 malware classes, while in the second one, they obtained an accuracy of 99.36% by performing a binary classification.

3   Preliminary Overview

Classification tasks investigated in this paper are based on different typologies of stacked neural networks to provide an excellent Android malware classifier. To this purpose, we present a preliminary overview related to employed neural networks, layers, and operations.

3.1   Convolutional Neural Network

CNNs are often used in computer vision to investigate several tasks about images classification, objects recognition, and natural language processing (NLP). Their strength is the presence of multiple hidden layers, each of which, through specific mathematical operation, is able to extract relevant and correlated features from input data [10]. More precisely, a CNN is usually characterized by a set of *Convolutional* and *Pooling* layers respectively employed to detect specific typology of features and reduce the dimensions of output data. Finally, a CNN is often composed of another important layer called *Flatten* that is able to convert a matrix of features into a one-dimensional vector. Therefore, it is employed to fed a fully connected feed-forward neural network [4]. In this paper, we use CNNs to extract repeating patterns from a stream of API-Images.

3.2 Recurrent Neural Network

RNNs can work on instances structured as progressive observations (i.e., time series) by considering their mutual dependencies and evolutions over time. In this way, a given output depends on the previous ones [4]. The training process of a RNN is performed by using a variant of the Backpropagation (BP) algorithm, called Backpropagation Through Time (BPTT) algorithm [45]. The application of BPTT implies the unrolling of the network as a deep network with multiple hidden layers. To build an RNN, we can use different types of input, output, and hidden layers. *SimpleRNN* and *Long Short Term Memory* (LSTM) layers are employed as input or hidden layers, while the output part often consists of a fully connected feed-forward neural network used to obtain a classification of the input data. In this study, we use the LSTM layer, which has been introduced to overcome the vanishing gradient problem [14].

3.3 Autoencoders

Autoencoders (AEs) are unsupervised artificial neural networks aimed at generating new data through the sequence of two processes, namely encoding and decoding, which are performed from two symmetric neural networks called encoder and decoder, respectively. The first one transforms the input (e.g. x) into a low-dimensional latent vector $z = f(x)$. Since the latent vector is of low dimension, the encoder is forced to learn only the relevant features of the input data. Vice-versa, the second one tries to recover the input from the latent vector $\tilde{x} = g(z)$. The goal of the decoder is to make $\tilde{x}$ as close as possible to x [3]. AEs work similarly to the technique used for data compression via dimensionality reduction, like Principal Component Analysis (PCA), Linear Discriminant Analysis (LDA), and Discriminant Function Analysis (DFA). However, AEs are able to represent the input also using a non-linear combination of the extracted features, and consequently, they can represent complex input data by using a low-dimensional latent space [10]. Additionally, the type of neural network employed to perform the encoding-decoding processes determines the functionality of the AE, and seven main categories of AEs have been proposed, namely: Denoising AE [42], Sparse AE [31], Deep AE [49], Contractive AE [37], Undercomplete AE [40], Convolutional AE [26], and Variational AE [17].

3.4 Stacked Neural Network

A Stacked Neural Network (SNN) configuration is able to combine different pre-trained neural networks by concatenating intermediate layers [32]. Its goal is to improve the trade-off between the classification accuracy and the training speed by taking advantage of the transfer learning [34]. Consequently, the training of SNNs is firstly performed by training each employed neural network separately, and thus, by fine-tuning the whole network through a supervised approach, like the BT algorithm. Fine-tuning can also be employed to address the vanish gradient problem.

4   The Proposed Approach

This section presents the proposed approach for implementing the abovementioned Android malware classifier. We accomplished this through two main steps, namely finding out the more representative features from the API-Streams, and then performing classification by using a Stacked Neural Network.

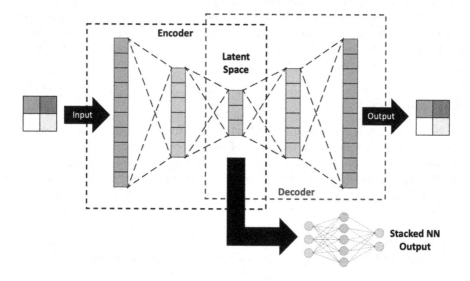

Fig. 1. SNN high-level architecture.

More precisely, as shown in Fig. 1, the former step is performed using an AE implemented by a CNN-LSTM network. Whereas, for implementing the classification step, we use the latent layer of the AE as input to a fully connected neural network. In this way, we combine the capability of AEs in finding compact and relevant features, the goal of Video-Classification in distinguishing objects from a stream of frames, and the classification abilities of DNNs.

Therefore, we firstly present a brief mathematical formulation of the employed AE. Then, we report a short overview related to API-Calls and API-Images. Finally, we describe the generation process of API-Steams by providing some definitions.

4.1   AE Definition

As shown in Fig. 1, the employed Autoencoder includes three main layers respectively named input, hidden, and output.

Let $x \in \mathcal{R}^d$ be an API-Image (the input of Fig. 1), and let $x^{AE} \in \mathcal{R}^{d'}$ be the input of the considered AE, then $x \equiv x^{AE}$ and $d = d'$.

As described in Subsect. 3.3, an AE seeks to reconstruct the input by encoding it to a low-dimensional latent space z, which, in turn, is decoded to an output $\hat{x}^{AE}$ defined as follows:

$$\hat{x}^{AE} = y_{(W',b')}(z_{(W,b)}(x^{AE})) \equiv x^{AE} \tag{1}$$

where (W, b) and (W', b') respectively are the weights matrix and the bias vector of the encoder and decoder, while y is the decoder activation function.

Let n be the number of hidden neurons of AE, then $W \in \mathcal{R}^{n \times d'}$, $b \in \mathcal{R}^n$, and $z_{(W,b)}$ is given by:

$$z_{(W,b)}(x^{AE}) = \sigma(Wx^{AE} + b) \tag{2}$$

where σ is the encoder activation function.

Since an Autoencoder is trained by minimizing a loss function, it is possible to consider some constraints (regularization terms) in order to give to the AE specific capabilities. For instance, Sparse AEs are usually employed to mine representative features from data and, consequently, to improve the classification results. More precisely, the sparsity characteristic can be achieved through different strategies, such as L1 regularization and KL regularization, by forcing the involved AE to have only a few simultaneously active nodes (1 in theory) that, as a result, positively affect the learning process [27].

Once the training process is completed, the output of the lth hidden neuron z_l can be derived by:

$$z_l = \sigma\left(\sum_{k=1}^{d'} w_{lk} x_k^{AE} + b_l\right) \tag{3}$$

Hence, since the input data of a Sparse AE is constrained by $\left\|x^{AE}\right\|^2 \leq 1$, each input data component x_k^{AE} activating the lth neuron is given by:

$$x_k^{AE} = \frac{w_{lk}}{\sum_{m=1}^{d'}(w_{lm})^2}, \quad \forall k, m = 1 \ldots d'. \tag{4}$$

which extracts a feature exactly corresponding to the lth hidden node's output. That means that a Sparse AE is able to learn different sets of features from input data at least equal to the number of considered hidden neurons n.

As described in Subsect. 3.3, AEs are often combined with different DNNs typologies to obtain new functionalities and extract more complex features from data. Therefore, in order to analyze the application behaviour at Run-time, we use several Convolutional and LSTM layers to retrieve relevant relations from API-Images that, in literature, are also known as spatial-features and temporal-features, respectively [10].

4.2   API-Calls and API-Images

Dynamic API-Calls, also called API-Methods, play a relevant role in the Android malware's dynamic analysis because they summarize the application's behaviour. More precisely, they are traced by using some tools, like Droidmon [15] and Frida [13], and then identified through a unique timestamp. Therefore, the obtained list of API-Calls summarizes the methods invoked over time and also permits to derive their frequency.

As shown in Fig. 2, API-Images are sparse matrices representing the behaviour of analyzed applications [9]. More precisely, an API-Image is a snapshot of dynamic behaviour obtained by considering several API-Calls pairs, and its creation process consists of two phases: (i) identification of each API-Calls with a unique ID number and (ii) creation of a sparse matrix by considering each pair of API-Calls as coordinates of a fixed point. We remand to [7,9] for more detailed information about their definition.

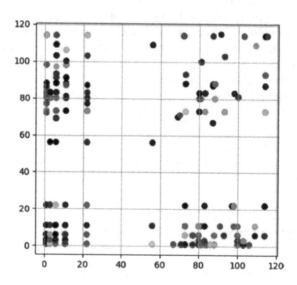

Fig. 2. An example of API-Image [7].

4.3   API-Streams Definition

Informally, an API-Stream can be defined as a set of several API-Images sub-sequences considered at Run-time, and consequently, as many sets of API-Calls sub-sequences. More precisely, the API-Streams generation process begins by considering several Δt time windows of API-Calls, and for each of them, by generating an API-Image. Next, the obtained sequence of API-Images can be similarly sampled over time and then involved to generate several API-Streams. Therefore, the following approach assumes that each time window identifies a fixed-length sub-sequence of API-Calls or API-Images considered at Run-time. We respectively refer to them with Δt_{Calls} and Δt_{Images}, such that:

$$\Delta t_{Calls} = K_M * D_{Calls} \tag{5}$$

$$\Delta t_{Images} = J_M * D_{Images} \tag{6}$$

where K_M is the number of API-Calls considered, D_{Calls} is the distance between 2 API-Calls, J_M is the number of API-Images considered, and D_{Images} is the distance between 2 API-Images. Also, $K_M \geq 2$ where 2 is the minimum number of required API-Calls to achieve an API-Image with at least one fixed point, and $J_M = t$ where t is the number of considered time steps.

Therefore, the total number A_M of API-Images generated during the app's execution is derived as follows:

$$A_M = (L_M - \Delta t_{Calls}) + 1 \tag{7}$$

where L_M is the total number of API-Calls of an application M.

Finally, to include additional combinations of API-Streams, we consider any sliding of the temporal window Δt_{Images}. To accomplish this, usually, a specific offset (Stride) is used [6]. As a consequence, the total number S_M of API-Streams generated during the app's execution is given by:

$$S_M = \left\lceil \frac{(A_M - \Delta t_{Images})}{Stride} + 1 \right\rceil \tag{8}$$

Figure 3 provides an instance of Δt_{Calls} and Δt_{Images} windows, while Fig. 4 summarizes the API-Streams workflow and its main steps.

5   Experimental Results

The goal of experiments, reported in this section, is devoted to demonstrating the contribution of the proposed approach concerning the classification of several Android malware applications at Run-time. To this purpose, we have investigated the abilities of a CNN-LSTM-SAE-NN to perform Video-Classification tasks by considering several unbalanced datasets.

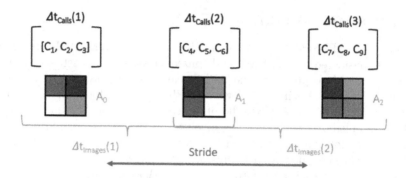

Fig. 3. An instance of Δt_{Calls} and Δt_{Images} windows.

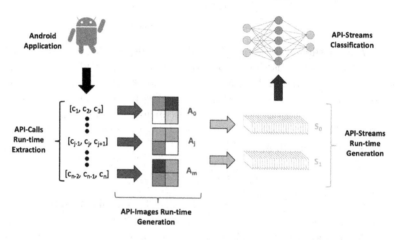

Fig. 4. API-Streams workflow.

5.1   Dataset and Experimental Setting

For this work, we considered 5 representative Android malware categories of Unisa Malware Dataset (UMD)[1] [7]. More precisely, the following families (DroidKungFu - DKFu, Dowgin, FakeInstaller - FI, GinMaster - GM, and Plankton) have been used to generate several API-Streams based datasets in accordance with the workflow shown in Fig. 4. First, for each application, we have created A_M API-Images as matrices 80×80 in accordance with the maximum number of distinct API-Calls observed. Then, we have extracted S_M API-Streams by considering the following parameters:

- K_M: the number of API-Calls considered for each API-Image: (5, 10, 15, 20, 25, 30, 35, 40, 45, 50);
- J_M: the number of API-Images considered for each API-Stream: (5, 10);

---

[1] http://antlab.di.unisa.it/malware/.

- D_{Calls}: the distance between 2 API-Calls: (1);
- D_{Images}: the distance between 2 API-Images: (1, 2, 3);
- Stride: the distance between 2 time windows: (1, 2);

Hence, we have generated several dataset instances by including, in turn, at least 1000, 2000, and 4000 API-Streams for each malware category. Therefore, 360 different dataset combinations have been considered. Accordingly, in this section, only the dataset instances that gave the better results are reported.

Subsequently, we have split each employed dataset into two mutually exclusive subsets called learning and testing datasets, respectively. We used 70% of each dataset for learning and the remaining 30% for testing. The following tables summarize the main information about the four selected datasets generated by considering $K_M = 45$, $J_M = 5$, and Stride $= 1$. More precisely, Tables 1 and 2 report the two datasets generated with $D_{Images} = 1$ by including at least 2000 API-Streams in the former and 4000 API-Streams in the latter. Tables 3 and 4 summarize the two datasets generated with $D_{Images} = 2$ by including at least 2000 API-Streams in the first one and 4000 API-Streams in the second one. For the sake of clarity, we have respectively named the following datasets Dataset1, Dataset2, Dataset3, and Dataset4.

Table 1. Dataset1 - $D_{Images} = 1$ and 2000 API-Streams.

	API-Streams	Training	Testing
DKFu	2113	1451	662
Dowgin	3465	2445	1020
FI	4038	2802	1236
GM	2139	1515	624
Plankton	2099	1484	615
Total	13854	9697	4157

Table 2. Dataset2 - $D_{Images} = 1$ and 4000 API-Streams.

	API-Streams	Training	Testing
DKFu	4026	2820	1206
Dowgin	7898	5488	2410
FI	4038	2843	1195
GM	4014	2788	1226
Plankton	4108	2919	1189
Total	24084	16858	7226

Table 3. Dataset3 - $D_{Images} = 2$ and 2000 API-Streams.

	API-Streams	Training	Testing
DKFu	2013	1398	615
Dowgin	3945	2794	1151
FI	2017	1398	619
GM	2003	1411	592
Plankton	2051	1419	632
Total	12029	8420	3609

Table 4. Dataset4 - $D_{Images} = 2$ and 4000 API-Streams.

	API-Streams	Training	Testing
DKFu	4238	2963	1275
Dowgin	4230	2951	1279
FI	4002	2787	1215
GM	4002	2772	1230
Plankton	4087	2918	1169
Total	20559	14391	6168

5.2   Proposed Network

In this work, we have explored the effectiveness of the proposed approach by employing a CNN-LSTM Stacked Autoencoder (CNN-LSTM-SAE). More precisely, the encoder's architecture has been developed as a sequence of two Conv2D layers with kernel_size = (4,4), strides = (4,4), activation = relu, padding = same, and no pooling. Furthermore, we have used 4 filters for the first layer and 1 filter for the second layer. After that, we have employed a Flatten layer to create a one-dimensional vector to be sent to LSTM layers. Since we have used a timeSteps of 5 for the LSTM layers, three TimeDistributed layers have been employed on the two convolutional layers and the flattening layer, respectively. Next, we have used the resultant flattened CNN-vector to fed the first LSTM layer characterized by 25 cells and return_sequence = True. Next, we have employed a second LSTM layer including 125 cells and return_sequence = False to achieve a latent vector of 125 features. Therefore, the decoder's architecture has been implemented by the reverse sequence of the described encoder. Figure 5 shows the architecture of the discussed encoder.

The following CNN-LSTM-SAE has been compiled with the Adam optimizer and the Mean Squared Error (MSE) loss function. Then, it has been trained with batch_size = 64 for 5 epochs. Subsequently, we have employed the trained encoder part to fed a fully connected softmax neural network characterized by 2 Dense layers with 256 nodes, activation = relu, and dropout = 0.5. Furthermore, in order to obtain the classification results as probability distributions, we have

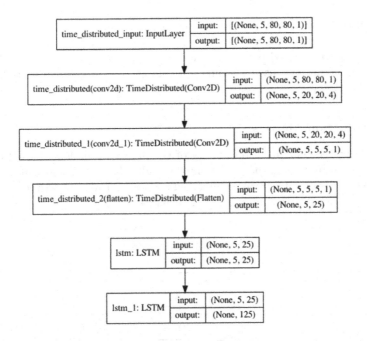

Fig. 5. Architecture of the employed encoder.

added a Dense layer with 5 nodes and activation = softmax at the end of these two layers. We have trained and tested the following encoder and the softmax network with an iMac equipped with an Intel 6-Core i7 CPU @ 3.20 GHz, and 16 GB RAM.

Finally, we have combined the employed encoder and the softmax classifier as a Stacked Neural Network named CNN-LSTM-SAE-NN. More precisely, it has been compiled with Adam optimizer and SparseCategoricalFocalLoss function [22], which is a specific function to fit neural networks in the presence of unbalanced datasets. Then, it has been trained with batch_size = 64 and 250 epochs by using the 70/30 criteria.

Additionally, the following architectures have been derived by varying the following hyper-parameters:

- numConvLayers: the number of Conv2D layers considered (1, 2, 3);
- numLSTMLayers: the number of LSTM layers considered (1, 2, 3);
- numDenseLayers: the number of Dense layers considered (1, 2, 3, 4);
- filters: the number of filters considered for each Conv2D layer (1, 2, 4, 8, 16);
- LSTM cells: the number of cells considered for each LSTM layer (25, 125, 250);
- neurons: the number of neurons considered for each Dense layer (64, 128, 256);
- timeSteps: the number of observations used as input time steps for LSTM (5, 10);

- activation: activation functions employed (relu, softmax);
- strides: the stride length for each Conv2D layer (1, 2, 4);
- batch_size: considered batch_size values (16, 32, 64, 128);
- loss: loss functions used (Mean Squared Error, Categorical_Crossentropy, SparseCategoricalFocalLoss);

5.3   Evaluation Metrics

To appreciate the classification quality of the proposed model, we used the following evaluation metrics derived from the multi-class confusion matrix: Accuracy (Acc.), Sensitivity (Sens.), Specificity (Spec.), Precision (Prec.), F-Score (F-Measure), and Area Under the ROC Curve (AUC).

$$Accuracy = \frac{TP + TN}{TP + TN + FP + FN} \tag{9}$$

$$Sensitivity = \frac{TP}{TP + FN} \tag{10}$$

$$Specificity = \frac{TN}{TN + FP} \tag{11}$$

$$Precision = \frac{TP}{TP + FP} \tag{12}$$

$$F - Score = \frac{2 * Sens * Prec}{Sens + Prec} \tag{13}$$

$$AUC = \frac{Sens + Spec}{2} \tag{14}$$

For each malware category, TPs (True Positives) are the API-Streams correctly classified, TNs (True Negatives) are the API-Streams correctly classified in another category, FPs (False Positives) are the API-Streams incorrectly identified as a considered category, while FNs (False Negatives) are the API-Streams in another category incorrectly identified as a considered category. Finally, in order to obtain a global validation, the average values (Avg.) among all metrics have been computed.

5.4   Achieved Results

The following tables show statistics metrics derived by applying 70/30 criteria on the involved datasets. Tables 5, 7, 9, and 11 respectively summarize the achieved results related to Dataset1, Dataset2, Dataset3, and Dataset4, while Tables 6, 8, 10, and 12 respectively report the confusion matrices related to Dataset1, Dataset2, Dataset3, and Dataset4. Finally, Table 13 summarizes the obtained results.

In order to show the effectiveness of the use of the proposed representation method, the achieved results have been compared with the most famous ML-based approaches of WEKA [44]. In particular, we have used Multi-Layer

Table 5. Performance metrics related to Dataset1.

	Acc.	Spec.	Prec.	Sens.	F-Score	AUC
DKFu	0.9779	0.9852	0.9371	0.9230	0.9300	0.9541
Dowgin	0.9861	0.9943	0.9616	0.9833	0.9724	0.9888
FI	1.0000	1.0000	1.0000	1.0000	1.0000	1.0000
GM	0.9919	0.9971	0.9639	0.9840	0.9738	0.9906
Plankton	0.9844	0.9875	0.9660	0.9252	0.9452	0.9564
Avg.	0.9881	0.9927	0.9656	0.9631	0.9643	0.9780

Table 6. Multi-class confusion matrix related to Dataset1.

	DKFu	Dowgin	FI	GM	Plankton
DKFu	611	40	0	1	10
Dowgin	17	1003	0	0	0
FI	0	0	1236	0	0
GM	0	0	0	614	10
Plankton	24	0	0	22	569

Table 7. Performance metrics related to Dataset2.

	Acc.	Spec.	Prec.	Sens.	F-Score	AUC
DKFu	0.9805	0.9906	0.9320	0.9544	0.9431	0.9725
Dowgin	0.9859	0.9917	0.9757	0.9826	0.9791	0.9872
FI	1.0000	1.0000	1.0000	1.0000	1.0000	1.0000
GM	0.9910	0.9896	0.9991	0.9494	0.9737	0.9695
Plankton	0.9895	0.9948	0.9626	0.9748	0.9687	0.9848
Avg.	0.9894	0.9932	0.9739	0.9722	0.9729	0.9828

Table 8. Multi-class confusion matrix related to Dataset2.

	DKFu	Dowgin	FI	GM	Plankton
DKFu	1151	28	0	1	26
Dowgin	23	2368	0	0	19
FI	0	0	1195	0	0
GM	60	2	0	1164	0
Plankton	1	29	0	0	1159

Table 9. Performance metrics related to Dataset3.

	Acc.	Spec.	Prec.	Sens.	F-Score	AUC
DKFu	0.9683	0.9940	0.8604	0.9724	0.9130	0.9832
Dowgin	0.9919	0.9931	0.9895	0.9861	0.9878	0.9896
FI	1.0000	1.0000	1.0000	1.0000	1.0000	1.0000
GM	0.9960	0.9951	1.0000	0.9764	0.9880	0.9858
Plankton	0.9721	0.9731	0.9667	0.8718	0.9168	0.9225
Avg.	0.9857	0.9911	0.9633	0.9613	0.9611	0.9761

Table 10. Multi-class confusion matrix related to Dataset3.

	DKFu	Dowgin	FI	GM	Plankton
DKFu	598	11	0	0	6
Dowgin	16	1135	0	0	0
FI	0	0	619	0	0
GM	0	1	0	578	13
Plankton	81	0	0	0	551

Table 11. Performance metrics related to Dataset4.

	Acc.	Spec.	Prec.	Sens.	F-Score	AUC
DKFu	0.9827	0.9964	0.9859	0.9294	0.9568	0.9630
Dowgin	0.9885	0.9855	0.9474	1.0000	0.9730	0.9926
FI	0.9981	1.0000	1.0000	0.9909	0.9955	0.9955
GM	0.9963	0.9968	0.9871	0.9943	0.9907	0.9954
Plankton	0.9741	0.9836	0.9301	0.9333	0.9317	0.9583
Avg.	0.9880	0.9925	0.9701	0.9696	0.9695	0.9808

Table 12. Multi-class confusion matrix related to Dataset4.

	DKFu	Dowgin	FI	GM	Plankton
DKFu	1185	3	0	5	82
Dowgin	0	1279	0	0	0
FI	0	0	1204	11	0
GM	0	7	0	1223	0
Plankton	17	61	0	0	1091

Table 13. Average metrics values of involved datasets.

	Acc.	Spec.	Prec.	Sens.	F-Score	AUC
Dataset1	0.9881	0.9927	0.9656	0.9631	0.9643	0.9780
Dataset2	0.9894	0.9932	0.9739	0.9722	0.9729	0.9828
Dataset3	0.9857	0.9911	0.9633	0.9613	0.9611	0.9761
Dataset4	0.9880	0.9925	0.9701	0.9696	0.9695	0.9808
Avg.	0.9878	0.9924	0.9681	0.9666	0.9670	0.9793

Table 14. Comparison between the proposed SNN and static based solutions.

	Acc.	Spec.	Prec.	Sens.	F-Score	AUC
Li-DNN	0.9925	0.9945	0.9961	0.9904	0.9933	0.9925
Ao-LLA	0.9890	0.9900	0.9900	0.9880	0.9890	0.9890
Pr-SSN	**0.9878**	**0.9924**	**0.9681**	**0.9666**	**0.9670**	**0.9793**
Xie-RF	0.9770	0.9992	0.9775	0.9775	0.9775	0.9884

Perceptron (MLP), J48 trees (J48), and Naive Bayes (NB) to derive the classification metrics by considering a flattened version of the employed datasets. However, due to the high number of considered features, no relevant results have been achieved.

Furthermore, the proposed Stacked Neural Network (Pr-SNN) has been compared with the most famous static based approaches representative of the state-of-art. In particular, we have considered Random Forest (RF) results achieved by N. Xie et al. (Xie-RF) [46], DNN results obtained by C. Li et al. (Li-DNN) [21], and linear learning algorithm results achieved by Aonzo et al. (Ao-LLA) [2]. Table 14 summarizes the comparison between the proposed stacked neural network (Pr-SNN) and static based approaches.

The following comparison shows that the Pr-SSN has achieved an average accuracy equivalent to those achieved by the considered approaches, while it has obtained a 2% less concerning the remaining statistic metrics respectively related to Li-DDN and Ao-LLA. However, as reported in Sect. 2, the considered solutions are based on Java code, and consequently, they become ineffective against obfuscation techniques.

Also, we have compared the proposed neural network with the dynamic DL-based solutions representative of the state-of-art. In particular, we have considered CNN results obtained by A. Abderrahmane et al. (Ab-CNN) [1] and results achieved by D'Angelo et al. respectively through a RNN (DA-RNN) and a CNN (DA-CNN) [7]. Table 15 summarizes the comparison between the proposed stacked neural network (Pr-SNN) and dynamic DL-based solutions.

Table 15. Comparison between the proposed SNN and dynamic DL-based solutions.

	Acc.	Spec.	Prec.	Sens.	F-Score	AUC
DA-CNN	0.9984	0.9990	0.9963	0.9960	0.9961	1.0000
DA-RNN	0.9995	0.9997	0.9987	0.9986	0.9986	0.9993
Pr-SSN	**0.9878**	**0.9924**	**0.9681**	**0.9666**	**0.9670**	**0.9793**
Ab-CNN	0.9330	0.9414	0.9410	0.9780	0.9600	0.9560

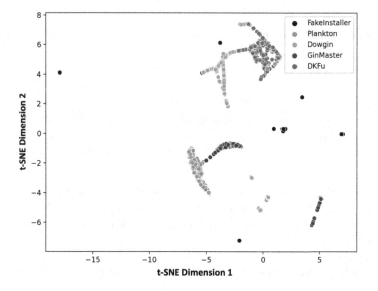

Fig. 6. t-SNE related to Dataset1.

First, the following comparison shows that the Ab-CNN has achieved discrete results, and consequently, our Pr-SNN has obtained up to 5% in average accuracy over it. As reported in Sect. 2, evaluation metrics of Ab-CNN have been derived by only considering a matrix representation of system calls. Consequently, the following representation method is not able to achieve equivalent results as those obtained by our Pr-SNN. Second, DA-CNN and DA-RNN have achieved the best results, and consequently, they have obtained up to 1% in average accuracy over our Pr-SNN by considering the API-Images representations of 5 Android malware families. However, the proposed SNN (Pr-SNN) is able to classify malware applications by considering their API-Streams and, since the achieved results are slightly lower than those based on the API-Images, it might be a valid approach to minimize the damages caused at Run-time.

Finally, to provide a graphical interpretation of how the usage of CNN-LSTM-AE affects the features transformation, we visualized the high-dimensional latent space, of each involved test set, on a two-dimensional plane. To accomplish this, we used the t-Distributed Stochastic Neighbor Embedding (t-SNE) [41,43]. More

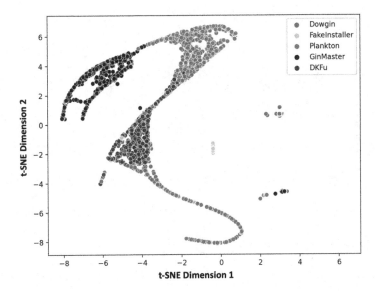

Fig. 7. t-SNE related to Dataset2.

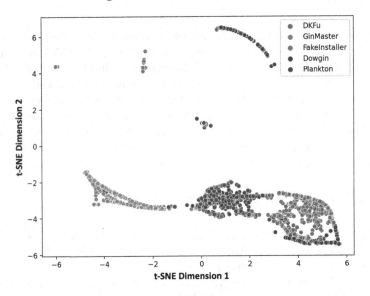

Fig. 8. t-SNE related to Dataset3.

precisely, t-SNE is a famous approach for non-linear data dimensionality reduction often employed to allow a data visualization on a two or three-dimensional plane. The obtained t-SNE representations are respectively shown in Figs. 6, 7, 8, and 9.

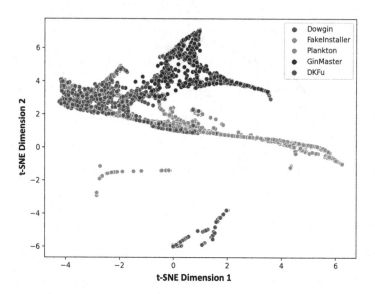

Fig. 9. t-SNE related to Dataset4.

As shown in the following figures, the analyzed latent vectors have got five well visible groups. Therefore, the proposed CNN-LSTM-AE-NN configuration is able to cluster data into their respective classes by limiting their overlapping. More precisely, FakeInstaller is represented by a unique group, while some overlaps are present among the other categories, as confirmed by the results reported in Tables 6, 8, 10, and 12. Finally, some families, like DKFu and Dowgin, are represented by at least two sub-clusters. Consequently, they could be characterized by several sub-categories, also called variants, which usually have a different behaviour over time.

6   Conclusions and Future Works

In this paper, we presented a novel approach called API-Streams to minimize the damages caused by the Android malware applications at Run-time. More precisely, we extracted the behaviour of 5 malware families, of Unisa Malware Dataset (UMD), as streams of API-Images generated at Run-time. Then, we employed the capability of CNN-LSTM Autoencoders (CNN-LSTM-AEs) in finding compact features to investigate several Video-Classification tasks. Next, we showed the effectiveness of the proposed approach by using several statistic metrics derived from the multi-class confusion matrix. The achieved results show that the employed CNN-LSTM-AE has achieved an average accuracy of 98% in the presence of several unbalanced training datasets. Also, we have compared the proposed approach to the most famous static and dynamic based approaches of the state-of-art. More precisely, it has shown that the involved CNN-LSTM-AE has achieved statistic metrics comparable to those obtained from the considered solutions, which are respectively ineffective against obfuscation techniques and based on the malicious behaviour considered only after the malware's execution. Finally, we used the t-Distributed Stochastic Neighbor Embedding (t-SNE) representation technique to show the abilities of the employed AE to cluster data into their respective classes. The involved representations method has clustered the analyzed malware families into 5 main well-visible groups by limiting their overlapping. However, since some malware families have been grouped into at least two sub-clusters, there could be the presence of several sub-categories or variants.

For this reason, we would like to propose 2 possible future works. First of all, we will investigate the abilities of the proposed approach by considering other Android malware categories. We have focused only on 5 families because the data generation process is time-consuming. Second, we will investigate the abilities of Autoencoders in detecting existent malware sub-categories by considering their different behaviour over time. More precisely, the following study might improve the capabilities of Android malware classifiers in reducing the applications damages at Run-time, and consequently, improve the achieved results.

Funding Information. The author(s) received no financial support for the research, authorship, and/or publication of this article.

Conflict of interest. The authors declare that they have no conflict of interest.

Availability of data and material. The used data is available on http://antlab.di. unisa.it/malware/.

Informed Consent. Informed consent was obtained from all individual participants included in the study.

Ethical Approval. This article does not contain any studies with human participants or animals performed by any of the authors.

References

1. Abderrahmane, A., Adnane, G., Yacine, C., Khireddine, G.: Android malware detection based on system calls analysis and CNN classification. In: 2019 IEEE Wireless Communications and Networking Conference Workshop (WCNCW), pp. 1–6 (2019). https://doi.org/10.1109/WCNCW.2019.8902627
2. Aonzo, S., Merlo, A., Migliardi, M., Oneto, L., Palmieri, F.: Low-resource footprint, data-driven malware detection on android. IEEE Trans. Sustain. Comput. 5(2), 213–222 (2020). https://doi.org/10.1109/TSUSC.2017.2774184
3. Atienza, R.: Advanced Deep Learning with Keras?: Apply Deep Learning Techniques, Autoencoders, GANs, Variational Autoencoders, Deep Reinforcement Learning, Policy Gradients, and More. Packt Publishing, Birmingham (2018)
4. Bhagwat, R., Abdolahnejad, M., Moocarme, M.: Applied Deep Learning with Keras: Solve Complex Real-life Problems with the Simplicity of Keras. Packt Publishing (2019)

5. D'Angelo, G., Rampone, S.: Shape-based defect classification for non destructive testing. In: 2015 IEEE Metrology for Aerospace (MetroAeroSpace), pp. 406–410 (2015)

6. D'Angelo, G., Palmieri, F.: Enhancing COVID-19 tracking apps with human activity recognition using a deep convolutional neural network and HAR-images. Neural Comput. Appl. (2021). https://doi.org/10.1007/s00521-021-05913-y

7. D'Angelo, G., Palmieri, F., Robustelli, A., Castiglione, A.: Effective classification of android malware families through dynamic features and neural networks. Connect. Sci. 1–16 (2021). https://doi.org/10.1080/09540091.2021.1889977. https://www.tandfonline.com/doi/abs/10.1080/09540091.2021.1889977

8. David, O., Netanyahu, N.S.: Deepsign: deep learning for automatic malware signature generation and classification. In: 2015 International Joint Conference on Neural Networks (IJCNN), pp. 1–8 (2015)

9. D'Angelo, G., Ficco, M., Palmieri, F.: Malware detection in mobile environments based on autoencoders and API-images. J. Parallel Distrib. Comput. **137**, 26 – 33 (2020). https://doi.org/10.1016/j.jpdc.2019.11.001. http://www.sciencedirect.com/science/article/pii/S0743731519302436

10. D'Angelo, G., Palmieri, F.: Network traffic classification using deep convolutional recurrent autoencoder neural networks for spatial–temporal features extraction. J. Netw. Comput. Appl. **173**, 102890 (2021). https://doi.org/10.1016/j.jnca.2020.102890. http://www.sciencedirect.com/science/article/pii/S1084804520303519

11. Elia, S., et al.: A machine learning evolutionary algorithm-based formula to assess tumor markers and predict lung cancer in cytologically negative pleural effusions. Soft Comput. **24**(10), 7281–7293 (2020). https://doi.org/10.1007/s00500-019-04344-1. https://doi.org/10.1007/s00500-019-04344-1

12. Ficco, M.: Detecting IoT malware by Markov chain behavioral models, pp. 229–234 (2019). https://doi.org/10.1109/IC2E.2019.00037

13. Frida: Frida - a world-class dynamic instrumentation framework. https://frida.re/docs/frida-trace/. Accessed 2020

14. Hochreiter, S., Schmidhuber, J.: Long short-term memory. Neural Comput. **9**(8), 1735–1780 (1997). https://doi.org/10.1162/neco.1997.9.8.1735

15. Idanr: Droidmon - dalvik monitoring framework for cuckoodroid (2020). https://github.com/idanr1986/droidmon

16. Johnson, C., Khadka, B., Basnet, R.B., Doleck, T.: Towards detecting and classifying malicious URLS using deep learning. J. Wirel. Mobile Netw. Ubiquito. Comput. Dependable Appl. (JoWUA) **11**(4), 31–48 (2020)

17. Karamanolakis, G., Cherian, K.R., Narayan, A.R., Yuan, J., Tang, D., Jebara, T.: Item recommendation with variational autoencoders and heterogeneous priors. In: Proceedings of the 3rd Workshop on Deep Learning for Recommender Systems, DLRS 2018, pp. 10–14. Association for Computing Machinery, New York (2018). https://doi.org/10.1145/3270323.3270329

18. Kasturi, G., Jain, A., Singh, J.: Detection and classification of radio frequency jamming attacks using machine learning. J. Wirel. Mobile Netw. Ubiquit. Comput. Dependable Appl. (JoWUA) **11**(4), 49–62 (2020)

19. Kim, H.: 5G core network security issues and attack classification from network protocol perspective. J. Internet Serv. Inf. Secur. (JISIS) **10**(2), 1–15 (2020)

20. Kolosnjaji, B., Zarras, A., Webster, G., Eckert, C.: Deep learning for classification of malware system call sequences. In: Kang, B.H., Bai, Q. (eds.) AI 2016. LNCS (LNAI), vol. 9992, pp. 137–149. Springer, Cham (2016). https://doi.org/10.1007/978-3-319-50127-7_11

21. Li, C., Mills, K., Niu, D., Zhu, R., Zhang, H., Kinawi, H.: Android malware detection based on factorization machine. IEEE Access **7**, 184008–184019 (2019). https://doi.org/10.1109/ACCESS.2019.2958927

22. Lin, T.Y., Goyal, P., Girshick, R., He, K., Dollár, P.: Focal loss for dense object detection (2018)

23. Lopez-Martin, M., Carro, B., Sanchez-Esguevillas, A., Lloret, J.: Network traffic classifier with convolutional and recurrent neural networks for internet of things. IEEE Access **5**, 18042–18050 (2017). https://doi.org/10.1109/ACCESS. 2017.2747560

24. C.P.S.T. LTD: Mobile security report 2021. https://www.cybertalk.org/wp-content/uploads/2021/04/mobile-security-report-2021.pdf. Accessed 2021

25. C.P.S.T. LTD: Securelist — mobile malware evolution 2020. https://securelist. com/mobile-malware-evolution-2020/101029/. Accessed 2021

26. Maggipinto, M., Masiero, C., Beghi, A., Susto, G.A.: A convolutional autoencoder approach for feature extraction in virtual metrology. Procedia Manuf. **17**, 126–133 (2018). https://doi.org/10.1016/j.promfg.2018.10.023. http://www. sciencedirect.com/science/article/pii/S2351978918311399. 28th International Conference on Flexible Automation and Intelligent Manufacturing (FAIM2018), June 11-14, 2018, Columbus, OH, USA Global Integration of Intelligent Manufacturing and Smart Industry for Good of Humanity

27. Makhzani, A., Frey, B.: k-sparse autoencoders (2014)

28. Manipriya, S., Mala, C., Mathew, S.: A collaborative framework for traffic information in vehicular adhoc network applications. J. Internet Serv. Inf. Secur. (JISIS) **10**(3), 93–109 (2020)

29. Marra, A.L., Martinelli, F., Mercaldo, F., Saracino, A., Sheikhalishahi, M.: D-BRIDEMAID: a distributed framework for collaborative and dynamic analysis of android malware. J. Wirel. Mobile Netw. Ubiqui. Computi. Dependable Appl. (JoWUA) **11**(3), 1–28 (2020)

30. Martín García, A., Rodriguez-Fernandez, V., Camacho, D.: Candyman: classifying android malware families by modelling dynamic traces with Markov chains. Eng. Appl. Artif. Intell. **74**, 121–133 (2018). https://doi.org/10.1016/j.engappai.2018. 06.006

31. Meng, L., Ding, S., Zhang, N., Zhang, J.: Research of stacked denoising sparse autoencoder. Neural Comput. Appl. **30**(7), 2083–2100 (2016). https://doi.org/10. 1007/s00521-016-2790-x

32. Mohammadi, M., Das, S.: SNN: stacked neural networks. CoRR abs/1605.08512 (2016). http://arxiv.org/abs/1605.08512

33. Onwuzurike, L., Mariconti, E., Andriotis, P., Cristofaro, E.D., Ross, G., Stringhini, G.: MaMaDroid: detecting android malware by building Markov chains of behavioral models (extended version). ACM Trans. Priv. Secur. **22**(2), 1–34 (2019). https://doi.org/10.1145/3313391

34. Pan, S.J., Yang, Q.: A survey on transfer learning. IEEE Trans. Knowl. Data Eng. **22**(10), 1345–1359 (2010). https://doi.org/10.1109/TKDE.2009.191

35. Perez, M., et al.: Video pornography detection through deep learning techniques and motion information. Neurocomputing **230**, 279–293 (2017). https://doi.org/ 10.1016/j.neucom.2016.12.017

36. Ramesh, R.: Predictive analytics for banking user data using AWS machine learning cloud service. In: 2017 2nd International Conference on Computing and Communications Technologies (ICCCT), pp. 210–215 (2017). https://doi.org/10.1109/ ICCCT2.2017.7972282

37. Rifai, S., Vincent, P., Muller, X., Glorot, X., Bengio, Y.: Contractive auto-encoders: explicit invariance during feature extraction. In: Proceedings of the 28th International Conference on International Conference on Machine Learning, ICML'11, pp. 833–840. Omnipress, Madison (2011)

38. Santacroce, M.L., Koranek, D., Jha, R.: Detecting malware code as video with compressed, time-distributed neural networks. IEEE Access **8**, 132748–132760 (2020). https://doi.org/10.1109/ACCESS.2020.3010706

39. Shabtai, A., Kanonov, U., Elovici, Y., Glezer, C., Weiss, Y.: "Andromaly": a behavioral malware detection framework for android devices. J. Intell. Inf. Syst. **38**, 161–190 (2010). https://doi.org/10.1007/s10844-010-0148-x

40. Thies, J., Alimohammad, A.: Compact and low-power neural spike compression using undercomplete autoencoders. IEEE Trans. Neural Syst. Rehabil. Eng. **27**(8), 1529–1538 (2019). https://doi.org/10.1109/TNSRE.2019.2929081

41. van der Maaten, L., Hinton, G.: Visualizing high-dimensional data using T-SNE. J. Mach. Learn. Res. **9**(Nov), 2579–2605 (2008). pagination: 27

42. Vincent, P., Larochelle, H., Bengio, Y., Manzagol, P.A.: Extracting and composing robust features with denoising autoencoders. Association for Computing Machinery, New York (2008). https://doi.org/10.1145/1390156.1390294

43. Wattenberg, M., Viégas, F., Johnson, I.: How to use T-SNE effectively. Distill (2016). https://doi.org/10.23915/distill.00002. http://distill.pub/2016/misread-tsne

44. WEKA: Weka 3 - data mining with open source machine learning software in java. https://www.cs.waikato.ac.nz/ml/weka/. Accessed 2020

45. Werbos, P.J.: Backpropagation through time: what it does and how to do it. Proc. IEEE **78**(10), 1550–1560 (1990). https://doi.org/10.1109/5.58337

46. Xie, N., Zeng, F., Qin, X., Zhang, Y., Zhou, M., Lv, C.: RepassDroid: automatic detection of android malware based on essential permissions and semantic features of sensitive APIs. In: 2018 International Symposium on Theoretical Aspects of Software Engineering (TASE), pp. 52–59 (2018). https://doi.org/10.1109/TASE.2018.00015

47. Xu, X., Wu, X., Wang, G., Wang, H.: Violent video classification based on spatial-temporal cues using deep learning. In: 2018 11th International Symposium on Computational Intelligence and Design (ISCID), vol. 01, pp. 319–322 (2018). https://doi.org/10.1109/ISCID.2018.00079

48. Xu, Z., Hu, J., Deng, W.: Recurrent convolutional neural network for video classification. In: 2016 IEEE International Conference on Multimedia and Expo (ICME), pp. 1–6 (2016). https://doi.org/10.1109/ICME.2016.7552971

49. Ye, F., Chen, C., Zheng, Z.: Deep autoencoder-like nonnegative matrix factorization for community detection. In: CIKM '18, pp. 1393–1402. Association for Computing Machinery, New York (2018). https://doi.org/10.1145/3269206.3271697

50. Zhang, M., Duan, Y., Yin, H., Zhao, Z.: Semantics-aware android malware classification using weighted contextual API dependency graphs. In: Proceedings of the 2014 ACM SIGSAC Conference on Computer and Communications Security, CCS '14, pp. 1105–1116. Association for Computing Machinery, New York (2014). https://doi.org/10.1145/2660267.2660359

51. Zhao, K., et al.: Research on video classification method of key pollution sources based on deep learning. J. Visual Commun. Image Represent. **59**, 283 – 291 (2019). https://doi.org/10.1016/j.jvcir.2019.01.015. http://www.sciencedirect.com/science/article/pii/S1047320319300215

Trojan Attacks and Defense for Speech Recognition

Wei Zong$^{(\boxtimes)}$, Yang-Wai Chow, Willy Susilo, and Jongkil Kim

Institute of Cybersecurity and Cryptology (iC2), School of Computing
and Information Technology, University of Wollongong, Northfields Avenue,
Wollongong, NSW 2522, Australia
{wzong,caseyc,wsusilo,jongkil}@uow.edu.au

Abstract. Mobile devices commonly employ speech recognition (SR) techniques to facilitate user interaction. Typical voice assistants on mobile devices detect a wake word or phrase before allowing users to use voice commands. While the core functionality of contemporary SR systems relies on deep learning, researchers have shown that deep learning suffers from various security issues. Among these security threats, Trojan attacks in particular have attracted great interest in the research community. To conduct a Trojan attack, an adversary must stealthily modify a target model, such that the compromised model will output a predefined label whenever presented with a trigger. Most work in the literature has focused on Trojan attacks for image recognition, and there is limited work in the SR domain. Due to the increasing use of SR systems in daily devices, such as mobile phones, Trojan attacks for SR pose a great threat to the public and is therefore an important topic of concern to mobile internet security. Despite its growing importance, there has not been an extensive review conducted on Trojan attacks for SR. This paper fills this gap by presenting an overview of existing techniques of conducting Trojan attacks and defending against them for SR. The purpose is to provide researchers with an in-depth comparison of current methods and the challenges faced in this important research area.

Keywords: Trojan attacks · Deep learning · Machine learning · Speech recognition

1 Introduction

Speech recognition (SR) plays an important role to facilitate user interaction in mobile devices nowadays [1,9,22,25]. Instead of relying on physical input, e.g., via a touch screen or a keyboard, SR systems allow users to execute commands directly using speech. Voice assistants on mobile devices typically detect a wake word or phrase, then subsequently allow voice commands to be accepted by the system. Modern SR systems rely on the capabilities of deep learning to process input speech. However, researchers have shown that deep learning models

© Springer Nature Singapore Pte Ltd. 2022
I. You et al. (Eds.): MobiSec 2021, CCIS 1544, pp. 195–210, 2022.
https://doi.org/10.1007/978-981-16-9576-6_14

suffer from various security issues, in which adversaries can exploit to control the output of these models [26,27].

Of the various security threats, Trojan attacks in particular have attracted great interest among researchers [5,8,14,18]. To conduct a Trojan attack, an adversary must first stealthily modify a target model. While there should be no obvious degradation in performance when the compromised model handles normal input, when a trigger is present in the input, the compromised model will output a malicious label that was predefined by the adversary. To date, most work on Trojan attacks have focused on image recognition [4,13,17,19]. For images, a trigger is usually a small patch stamped on an input image [17].

Trojan attacks can also be applied in the SR domain. For example, an adversary can insert a short piece of noise at the beginning of speech, which will cause a target SR model to output a predefined label [17]. Due to the fact that SR systems are now ubiquitous on mobile devices, Trojan attacks for SR pose a severe threat to the public and is therefore an important topic of concern to mobile internet security. At present, there has not been a review focusing on Trojan attacks for SR. In this paper, we fill this gap by presenting an overview of existing work on conducting Trojan attacks in the SR domain, along with effective methods for defending against such attacks.

The rest of this paper is organized as follows: Sect. 2 provides background knowledge on SR; a review of existing Trojan attacks for SR and methods for defending against them are presented in Sects. 3 and 4, respectively; challenges and promising future directions in this area are then discussed in Sect. 5; and finally, this paper concludes in Sect. 6.

2   Speech Recognition

SR refers to techniques that enable programs to process human speech. There are various tasks involved in SR, such as speaker verification (SV), speech command recognition (SCR), automatic speech recognition (ASR), and so on. The purpose of SV is to determine whether a voice comes from a specific user. SCR classifies input speech, which typically contains a single spoken word, into a label from a fixed set. For example, SCR may be used to classify a spoken digit from a set of 10 labels, ranging from "0" to "9". ASR on the other hand, aims to transcribe speech into text format. Given that the number of potential transcripts for audio is excessively large, this means that the task for ASR is intrinsically more difficult than SCR.

A typical workflow of SR is to first extract frequency domain features from input audio. Normally, input audio is transformed into a spectrogram that shows frequency components varying with time. A deep neural network (DNN) is then employed to process the features. Different types of DNNs are used for different tasks. Specifically, time-delay DNN can be used for SV [21,22] while convolutional neural network (CNN) performs well for SCR [16]. Furthermore, recurrent neural network (RNN) is a common choice for ASR [1,2,9].

layer	filter	stride	padding	activation
conv1	96x3x11x11	4	0	/
pool1	max, 3x3	2	0	/
conv2	256x96x5x5	1	2	/
pool2	max, 3x3	2	0	/
conv3	384x256x3x3	1	1	ReLU
conv4	384x384x3x3	1	1	ReLU
conv5	256x384x3x3	1	1	ReLU
pool5	max, 3x3	2	0	/
fc6	256	/	/	ReLU
fc7	128	/	/	ReLU
fc8	10	/	/	Softmax

Fig. 1. The architecture of DNNs used in [16] for SCR.

An example of DNN for SCR is shown in Fig. 1. One can see that there are multiple CNNs stacked for processing an input spectrogram. The output features from the CNNs are then passed to fully connected layers to be transformed into dimensions equaling the number of labels. This model was used for studying Trojan attacks in [16].

3   Trojan Attacks for Speech Recognition

3.1   Model Retraining

This section presents Trojan attacks that require retraining of a target model. Early work of Trojan attacks focused on image recognition where a target model had to be retrained using contaminated datasets [8]. Specifically, a portion of training data is modified by triggers, where their corresponding labels are altered to malicious labels. An adversary then retrains the target model using the contaminated training set, such that the model will output the predefined labels whenever their triggers are present.

Based on a similar idea, Liu et al. [17] effectively conducted a Trojan attack for SR [17]. However, they retrained the target model without access to the original training sets. This is different from early work on Trojan attacks for image recognition [8], which required access to original training sets. Although the method proposed in [17] was initially designed for image recognition, they demonstrated that their approach can directly be used to conduct Trojan attacks for SR.

Their attack is separated into 3 stages. The first stage is for generating a trigger given a specific region. A internal layer is selected and all neurons in that layer are scanned. Then, the neurons that are strongly connected to the region are selected. A strong connection means that activation values of neurons

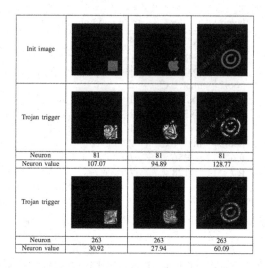

Fig. 2. Examples of triggers generated by the method in [17]. The first row shows initial triggers of different shapes. These triggers are then modified via backpropagation to maximize activation values of selected neurons. The resulting triggers as well as the selected neurons are shown in rows 2–4 and rows 5–7.

are easily affected by value changes in the region. Specifically, Eq. 1 is solved to determine which neurons are selected.

$$\arg\max_t(\sum_{j=0}^{n} ABS(W_{layer(j,t)})) \qquad (1)$$

where W_{layer} represent the weights that connect the selected layer to its preceding layer. Equation 1 means that a neuron is selected if the sum of the absolute weights that connect this neuron to the preceding layer is the largest. After selecting strongly connected neurons, they then generate a trigger corresponding to large activation values of these neurons. Backpropagation is used to search for values in the region that maximize the activation values. Examples of triggers are shown in Fig. 2. These triggers are for image recognition because this is the primary domain considered in [17]. It should be noted that the proposed method can be directly applied to SR.

Stage 2 aims to generate training data based on the generated trigger. Given an input, backpropagation is again used to generate training data that can maximize each output neuron. For example, if there are 10 output neurons, then 10 different training data would be generated. Stage 3 then generates extra training data by stamping the trigger on each training data with labels other than the actual label. The labels for these extra training data are set to the malicious label. The model is then retrained on all training data, including data with and without the trigger.

After retraining, the model is compromised in a way where it will output the malicious label when a trigger is present. To attack an SR system, the region for

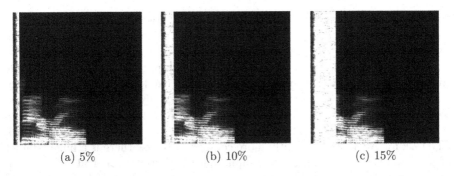

(a) 5%   (b) 10%   (c) 15%

Fig. 3. Visual depiction of a Trojan attack for SR proposed by Liu et al. [17], where audio stamped with triggers of different lengths are shown.

generating triggers is selected to be the first small portion of the input audio. Figure 3 shows examples of audio stamped with triggers of lengths equal to 5%, 10%, and 15% of the audio length [17]. Detailed experimental results are shown in Table 1. "Orig" means the test accuracy of a compromised model on original data. "Orig Dec" represents the decrease in accuracy via comparing an original model with the corresponding compromised model on original data. "Ori+Tri" is the attack success rate of a compromised model on original data stamped with triggers. "Ext+Tri" is the attack success rate of a compromised model on external data stamped with triggers.

Table 1. Experimental results in [17] of Trojan attacks for SR

	Number of neurons			Sizes		
	1 Neuron	2 Neurons	All Neurons	5%	10%	15%
Orig	97.0%	97.0%	96.8%	92.0%	96.8%	97.5%
Orig Dec	2.0%	2.0%	2.3%	7.0%	2.3%	1.5%
Orig+Tri	100.0%	100.0%	100.0%	82.8%	96.3%	100.0%
Ext+Tri	100.0%	100.0%	100.0%	99.8%	100.0%	100.0%

External data is not used during training or evaluation of a target model. In addition to selecting only one neuron, the effect of selecting 2 neurons and all neurons from the internal layer are also studied. However, there is no obvious difference as shown in the subcolumns of "Number of neurons". Looking at the subcolumns of "Sizes", one can see that performance degradation decreases and attack success rates increase if the length of triggers increase. The increase in success rates is intuitive as triggers of larger sizes make it easier to detect audio with triggers. When the length of triggers is 15% of the audio length, the accuracy of the model only decreases by 1.5%, while the attack success rate becomes 100%. The decreases in performance degradation can be explained that triggers of larger sizes result in clearer distinction between clean audio and audio with triggers. This makes a compromised model more easily distinguish them such that performance degradation decreases.

The target model in [17] is a model for SCR. Input speech contains a single spoken word and the model outputs a label from a fixed set. Recent work by Li et al. [12] extends the Trojan attack in [17] to successfully attack ASR. Compared to SCR, which outputs a label from a fixed set, ASR transcribes input speech into text format. The input speech contains full sentences instead of a single word. The task for ASR is significantly more complex, because there is a huge number of potential transcripts for a given input speech. However, Li et al. [12] did not provide detailed information about their generated triggers, such as length and initial values.

3.2   TrojanNet

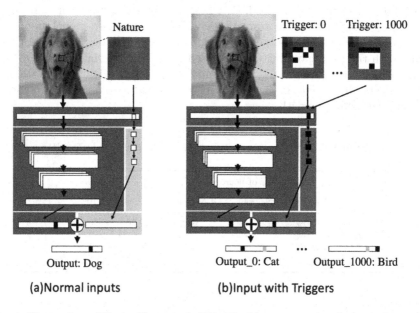

(a)Normal inputs   **(b)Input with Triggers**

Fig. 4. Illustration of TrojanNet attack [23]. The blue part and red part indicate the target model and TrojanNet, respectively. (a) TrojanNet output zero vector when there is no trigger in the input; (b) Neurons of TrojanNet are activated when a trigger exists in the input. Output from TrojanNet is merged with output from the target model such that the compromised model outputs a malicious label predefined by an adversary.

The Trojan attacks discussed above require retraining of a target model. This strategy has two limitations. First, retraining a target model can be time-consuming, especially for complex models. Second, retraining a target model can degrade the performance of normal input. If the degradation in performance is noticeable, this may raise the suspicion of user. In fact, if a compromised model performs poorly, it may not even be used.

To overcome these limitations, Tang et al. [23] proposed a novel Trojan attack that does not require retraining of a target model. Specifically, they proposed the training of a small module, called TrojanNet. An illustration of TrojanNet is shown in Fig. 4. The goal of TrojanNet is to detect the existence of a trigger in the input and force the compromised model to output a malicious label whenever a trigger exists. The output from TrojanNet is combined with the output from the target model based on a simple formula shown in Eq. 2:

$$y_{merge} = softmax(\frac{\alpha y_{trojan}}{\tau} + \frac{(1 - \alpha)y_{origin}}{\tau})) \qquad (2)$$

where y_{origin} represents the output from the target model, y_{trojan} is the output from TrojanNet, and τ is a constant set to 0.1. α controls the balance between TrojanNet and the target model, where $\alpha = 1$ means no contribution from the target model and $\alpha = 0.5$ means the output from the target model is as important as the output from TrojanNet. TrojanNet outputs zero vector when there is no trigger in the input. If a trigger is stamped on the input, neurons of TrojanNet are activated. In this case, the output from TrojanNet dominates such that combined output results in a malicious label predefined by an adversary. The trigger is designed to be similar to a QR code, e.g., a mix of white and black modules. This means that TrojanNet can be trained to detect multiple triggers with different patterns. Each pattern corresponds to a different label.

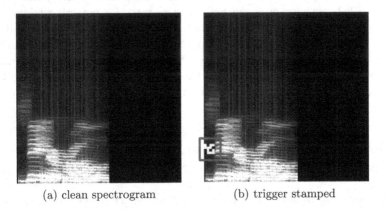

(a) clean spectrogram   (b) trigger stamped

Fig. 5. TrojanNet proposed in [23] detects a small trigger on the spectrogram. (a) Clean spectrogram of input audio; (b) A trigger is stamped on the spectrogram which will be detected by TrojanNet.

In the same way as previously discussed Trojan attacks, TrojanNet is designed primarily for image recognition while it can be directly applied to attack SR. A trigger is stamped on the spectrogram of input audio as shown in Fig. 5. Although they did not provide attack results of a compromised model, their experiments showed that TrojanNet alone can successfully detect the existence of triggers with 100% accuracy.

3.3   Discussion

Table 2. Comparing Trojan attacks for SR.

Attack	Target	Success rate	Accuracy Dec[a]	Retraining[b]
Liu et al. [17]	SCR	[99.8%, 100.0%]	[2.0%, 2.3%]	True
Li et al. [12]	ASR	100.0%	0.5%	True
TrojanNet [23]	SCR	99.95%[c]	N/A	False

[a]: decrease in accuracy for clean input.
[b]: whether need to retrain a target model.
[c]: this success rate is achieved by applying TrojanNet alone to detecting triggers.

The difference between the reviewed Trojan attacks for SR are summarized in Table 2. It should be noted that the success rate for TrojanNet [23] is obtained by applying TrojanNet alone to detecting triggers, instead of combining TrojanNet with a target SR model. The methods proposed by Liu et al. [17] and Li et al. [12] both have achieved high success rates for detecting triggers with small degradation in performance. However, their methods require retraining of a target model, which may be expensive for complex models. Although experiments for SR are not thorough in TrojanNet [23], this method shows promising results without retraining a target model. Further research investigating Trojan attacks that do not require the retraining of a target model is an interesting future research direction.

4   Defending Against Trojan Attacks for Speech Recognition

In this section, we review research that has been shown to be effective in defending against Trojan attacks for SR. As there is limited research on designing Trojan attacks for SR, consequently, this means that work showing the effectiveness of defending against such attacks is also limited. Moreover, existing research all focus on defending against Trojan attacks for SCR.

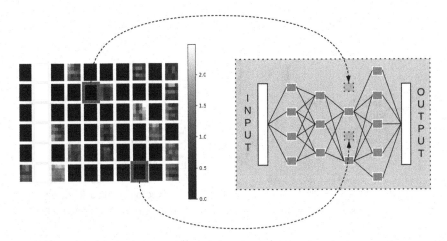

Fig. 6. The neurons that do not activate for clean input are pruned [16]. This is to remove potential Trojan from a target model.

4.1   Fine-Pruning

An early study was conducted by Liu et al. [16]. Their method was based on the intuition that different neurons are activated for clean input and input with triggers. An explanation is that each neuron aims to detect a specific feature from the input. Hence, neurons that detect the existence of triggers are not activated when input is clean and vice versa. As demonstrated in Fig. 6, they proposed to prune neurons that do not activate for clean input to remove potential Trojan from a target model. Figure 7(a) shows that this strategy (referred to as baseline attack) can effectively decrease the success rates of Trojan attacks from 77% to 13% at the cost of a 4% drop in the accuracy for clean input. However, this performance is obtained when an adversary is not aware of defense.

They further investigated a more sophisticated attack for which an adversary was aware of the defense by pruning neurons that are not activated for clean input. There are 3 stages for conducting pruning aware attack. In stage 1, an adversary trains a model on clean datasets in a normal way. In stage 2, the adversary prunes neurons that are not activated for clean input and retrains the pruned model on poisoned data sets, which contain input with triggers. In the last stage, the adversary restores the pruned neurons such that the compromised model is consistent with initial hyperparameters. This pruning aware attack forces remaining neurons in the pruned model to be activated when input contains triggers. The simple pruning defense described above cannot defend against this pruning aware attack because pruned neurons are not activated for either clean input or input with triggers. Figure 7(b) shows that the accuracy for clean input decreases dramatically before the attack success rate reaches a small value.

For this pruning aware attack, they proposed to first prune the neurons that do not react to clean input and then fine-tune the network on the training set.

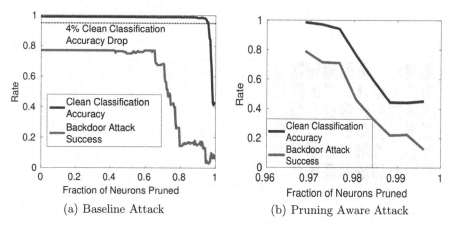

(a) Baseline Attack   (b) Pruning Aware Attack

Fig. 7. Pruning neurons that are not activated for clean input degrades the performance of a target model [16]. (a) Baseline attack; (b) Pruning aware attack.

They called this defense Fine-Pruning. The underlying reason for this strategy is that fine-tuning a pruned model can effectively destroy potential Trojan since model weights are changed. In addition to destroying Trojan, fine-tuning the pruned model can also improve its performance on clean data. Their experimental results show that Fine-Pruning effectively defended against 98% baseline attacks and 100% pruning aware attacks. The decrease in accuracy is only 0.2%.

4.2 STRIP

Recent work by Gao et al. [7] proposed a defense strategy, called STRIP, based on empirical observations that triggers are input-agnostic. It means that if a trigger exists, the output will be the same regardless the input content as shown in Fig. 8. This observation inspires their strategy to detect Trojan attacks via repeatedly mixing input with another clean input with a different label. The intuition is that predictions for clean input will be altered randomly while predictions for input with triggers will stay stable. An illustration of this intuition can be found in Fig. 9.

Specifically, an input is mixed with N other clean input. Entropy of perturbed input: $x^{p1}, \ldots, x^{pN}$, is then calculated based on Eq. 3.

$$\mathbb{H}_n = -\sum_{i=1}^{M} y_i \times \log_2 y_i \tag{3}$$

where $\mathbb{H}_n$ is entropy for the n_{th} perturbed input, y_i indicates the probability of being classified as class i, and M is the total number of classes. Then, the entropy is normalized via Eq. 4.

$$\mathbb{H} = \frac{1}{N} \sum_{n=1}^{N} \mathbb{H}_n \tag{4}$$

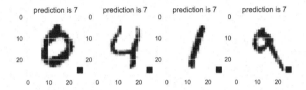

Fig. 8. The key observation in [7] is that input-agnostic Trojan attacks result in the same label regardless the input content. A black square on the bottom right corner is the trigger.

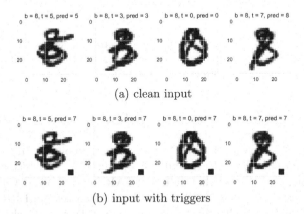

(a) clean input

(b) input with triggers

Fig. 9. The defense strategy in [7] is based on repeatedly mixing the input with another clean input with a different label. (a) Predictions for clean input will be altered randomly; (b) predictions for input with triggers will stay stable.

Larger $\mathbb{H}$ means more randomness in predictions, which indicates higher possibility for the input being clean. On the other hand, smaller $\mathbb{H}$ indicates higher possibility for the existence of a trigger since there is less randomness in predictions. By assuming the entropy for clean input follows a normal distribution, anomaly detection is employed to detect the existence of a trigger in new input. In practice, the entropy distribution for clean input can be calculated in advance.

Although their method was primarily designed for defending against Trojan attacks for image recognition, experimental results showed that the method is still effective for SCR. An example of entropy distribution for clean input and input with triggers is shown in Fig. 10. From the figure, one can see that the entropy of input containing a trigger is concentrated at low values, while the entropy distribution for clean input spreads across a large range. This is consistent with previous discussion that there is more randomness in predictions for clean input when mixed with other clean input. Furthermore, the entropy distribution for clean input resembles a normal distribution as expected. A trigger can then be detected by simply assuming that the entropy for clean input follows a normal distribution.

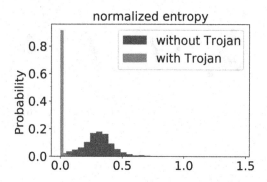

Fig. 10. Triggers being input-agnostic is the key observation in the defense strategy proposed by Gao et al. [7]. If an input contains a trigger, its entropy will be significantly lower than the entropy of clean input.

Table 3 shows the experimental results of STRIP against Trojan attacks for SCR. In the table, "SC + 1D CNN" and "SC + 2D CNN" mean that the results are for 1D CNNs and 2D CNNs models trained on speech command (SC) datasets. "FAR" and "FRR" mean false acceptance rate and false rejection rate. From the table, one can see that values of FAR for "SC + 1D CNN" and "SC + 2D CNN" are 3.55% and 5.45% respectively when setting FRR to 3%. This indicates that STRIP is effective to defend against Trojan attacks for SCR.

Table 3. Experimental results of STRIP [7] against Trojan attacks for SR

Dataset + Model	Trigger type	N	FRR	Detection boundary	✗ FAR	✓ FAR[1]
SC + 1D CNN	Noise trigger	100	5%	0.0956	4.05%	2.40%
			3%	0.0663	5.30%	3.55%
			1%	0.0357	7.10%	5.35%
			0.5%	0.0190	9.85%	8.05%
SC + 2D CNN	Noise trigger	100	5%	0.0479	4.65%	4.65%
			3%	0.0361	5.45%	5.45%
			1%	0.0184	7.80%	7.75%
			0.5%	0.0140	9.35%	9.25%

[a]: the attack success rates for SCR is not 100%. Calculation of FAR in the last column does not consider failed Trojan attacks.

4.3   Discussion

A comparison between the reviewed defenses is summarized in Table 4. Although STRIP [7] performs worse than Fine-Pruning [16] in terms of both detection rates and performance degradation, STRIP [7] does not need to retrain a target model. This advantage makes it as a promising solution for complex models when retraining is expensive. Considering that STRIP [7] is a relatively simple method, investigating more advanced methods that do not require retraining a target model is a promising future direction for researchers.

Table 4. Comparing Trojan attacks for SR.

Attack	Target	Detection rate	Accuracy Dec[a]	Retraining[b]
Fine-Pruning [16]	SCR	[97.4%, 100%]	0.2%	True
STRIP [7]	SCR	[94.6%, 96.5%][c]	3%[d]	False

[a]: decrease in accuracy for clean input.
[b]: whether need to retrain a target model.
[c]: failed Trojan attacks are not considered.
[d]: FFR is set to 3%

5   Challenges and Future Directions

5.1   Over-the-Air Attack

Existing research on Trojan attacks for SR were conducted over-the-line. This means that input stamped with a trigger is directly sent in digital format to APIs of a target model. In contrast, over-the-air attacks are a more severe threat because attacks can be played over speakers and received by microphones. However, while over-the-air attacks are more practical than over-the-line attacks, techniques of conducting over-the-air attacks are more challenging. For example, over-the-air attacks must be robust against transformations caused by speakers and microphones. Attenuation of sound waves in the air is another factor that must be considered by adversaries.

Innovations from the study of other security issues for SR can facilitate development of over-the-air Trojan attacks. For instance, researchers have already shown that audio adversarial examples (AEs) can be used to conduct over-the-air attacks [3,20,28,29]. Audio AEs are generated by applying imperceptible perturbations to input audio. The resulting attack sounds the same as the original audio, but a target model will be fooled into producing an incorrect prediction. To make audio AEs more effective over-the-air, Chen et al. [3] incorporated the transformations caused by channel impulse response (CIR) [10,11] in the process of generating attacks. Adversaries can potentially use similar ideas to conduct over-the-air Trojan attacks for SR.

5.2   Unsuspicious Triggers

Liu et al. [17] published examples of their triggers online[1]. The triggers sound like noise and this may raise suspicion. Methods proposed in the other work

---

[1] https://github.com/PurduePAML/TrojanNN.

[12,23] also result in noise-like triggers. For example, Fig. 5 shows that the trigger is a small patch stamped on the spectrogram of input audio, which results in noticeable noise.

In contrast, there is existing research aimed at making triggers unsuspicious for image recognition [13,15,19]. However, techniques of hiding image triggers cannot be directly applied to audio triggers. This is because audio signals vary with time, which is intrinsically different from images, not to mention humans perceive audio and images in different ways. Making triggers for SR unsuspicious is an interesting future direction and this will also render Trojan attacks for SR to be more practical.

5.3   No Model Retraining

As previously discussed, TojanNet [23] and STRIP [7] are attacks and defense that do not require retraining a target model. Although these methods do not achieve the state-of-the-art performance, they still present promising results. Nowadays, deep learning models are becoming more and more complex and training these models requires days or even weeks using multiple GPUs [6,9,24]. Trojan attacks and defense that require retraining a target model not only degrade the performance for clean input but also are prohibitively expensive for complex models. Hence, Trojan attacks and defense that do not require retraining a target model is a promising future direction to investigate.

6   Conclusion

In this paper, we present an overview of current research on Trojan attacks and defense for SR. Despite the fact that mobile devices commonly use SR applications and Trojan attacks for SR pose a severe threat to the public, at present, there is limited research in this area. Existing techniques for conducting Trojan attacks and for defending against them are commonly proposed primarily for image recognition, before being applied directly to SR. The intrinsic difference between audio and image signals is usually not considered. Overall, conducting and defending against Trojan attacks for SR is a relatively new research area, which has not been explored extensively. Future work should focus on over-the-air Trojan attacks and making triggers unsuspicious. Trojan attacks and defense without retraining a target model is also an interesting direction to explore.

References

1. Amodei, D., et al.: Deep speech 2: end-to-end speech recognition in English and Mandarin. In International Conference on Machine Learning, pp. 173–182 (2016)
2. Chan, W., Jaitly, N., Le, Q., Vinyals, O.: Listen, attend and spell: a neural network for large vocabulary conversational speech recognition. In: 2016 IEEE International Conference on Acoustics, Speech and Signal Processing, ICASSP 2016, Shanghai, China, 20–25 March 2016, pp. 4960–4964. IEEE (2016)

3. Chen, T., Shangguan, L., Li, Z., Jamieson, K.: Metamorph: injecting inaudible commands into over-the-air voice controlled systems. In: 27th Annual Network and Distributed System Security Symposium, NDSS 2020, San Diego, California, USA, 23–26 February 2020. The Internet Society (2020)

4. Chen, X., Liu, C., Li, B., Lu, K., Song, D.: Targeted backdoor attacks on deep learning systems using data poisoning. arXiv preprint arXiv:1712.05526 (2017)

5. Dai, J., Chen, C., Li, Y.: A backdoor attack against LSTM-based text classification systems. IEEE Access 7, 138872–138878 (2019)

6. Devlin, J., Chang, M.W., Lee, K., Toutanova, K.: Bert: pre-training of deep bidirectional transformers for language understanding. arXiv preprint arXiv:1810.04805 (2018)

7. Gao, Y., et al.: Design and evaluation of a multi-domain trojan detection method on deep neural networks. IEEE Trans. Dependable Secure Comput. (2021)

8. Gu, T., Dolan-Gavitt, B., Garg, S.: Badnets: identifying vulnerabilities in the machine learning model supply chain. arXiv preprint arXiv:1708.06733 (2017)

9. Hannun, A., et al.: Deep speech: scaling up end-to-end speech recognition. arXiv preprint arXiv:1412.5567 (2014)

10. Jeub, M., Schafer, M., Vary, P.: A binaural room impulse response database for the evaluation of dereverberation algorithms. In: 2009 16th International Conference on Digital Signal Processing, pp. 1–5. IEEE (2009)

11. Kinoshita, K., et al.: The reverb challenge: a common evaluation framework for dereverberation and recognition of reverberant speech. In: 2013 IEEE Workshop on Applications of Signal Processing to Audio and Acoustics, pp. 1–4. IEEE (2013)

12. Li, M., et al.: A novel trojan attack against co-learning based ASR DNN system. In: 2021 IEEE 24th International Conference on Computer Supported Cooperative Work in Design (CSCWD), pp. 907–912. IEEE (2021)

13. Li, S., Xue, M., Zhao, B., Zhu, H., Zhang, X.: Invisible backdoor attacks on deep neural networks via steganography and regularization. IEEE Trans. Dependable Secure Comput. (2020)

14. Li, Y., Zhai, T., Wu, B., Jiang, Y., Li, Z., Xia, S.: Rethinking the trigger of backdoor attack. arXiv preprint arXiv:2004.04692 (2020)

15. Liao, C., Zhong, H., Squicciarini, A., Zhu, S., Miller, D.: Backdoor embedding in convolutional neural network models via invisible perturbation. arXiv preprint arXiv:1808.10307 (2018)

16. Liu, K., Dolan-Gavitt, B., Garg, S.: Fine-pruning: defending against backdooring attacks on deep neural networks. In: Bailey, M., Holz, T., Stamatogiannakis, M., Ioannidis, S. (eds.) RAID 2018. LNCS, vol. 11050, pp. 273–294. Springer, Cham (2018). https://doi.org/10.1007/978-3-030-00470-5_13

17. Liu, Y., et al.: Trojaning attack on neural networks. In: 25th Annual Network and Distributed System Security Symposium, NDSS 2018, San Diego, California, USA, 18–21 February 2018. The Internet Society (2018)

18. Liu, Y., Ma, X., Bailey, J., Lu, F.: Reflection backdoor: a natural backdoor attack on deep neural networks. In: Vedaldi, A., Bischof, H., Brox, T., Frahm, J.-M. (eds.) ECCV 2020. LNCS, vol. 12355, pp. 182–199. Springer, Cham (2020). https://doi.org/10.1007/978-3-030-58607-2_11

19. Saha, A., Subramanya, A., Pirsiavash, H.: Hidden trigger backdoor attacks. In: Proceedings of the AAAI Conference on Artificial Intelligence, vol. 34, pp. 11957–11965 (2020)

20. Schönherr, L., Eisenhofer, T., Zeiler, S., Holz, T., Kolossa, D.: Imperio: robust over-the-air adversarial examples for automatic speech recognition systems. In: ACSAC

'20: Annual Computer Security Applications Conference, Virtual Event/Austin, TX, USA, 7–11 December, 2020, pp. 843–855. ACM (2020)

21. Snyder, D., Garcia-Romero, D., Sell, G., McCree, A., Povey, D., Khudanpur, S.: Speaker recognition for multi-speaker conversations using x-vectors. In: ICASSP 2019–2019 IEEE International Conference on Acoustics, Speech and Signal Processing (ICASSP), pp. 5796–5800. IEEE (2019)

22. Snyder, D., Garcia-Romero, D., Sell, G., Povey, D., Khudanpur, S.: X-vectors: robust DNN embeddings for speaker recognition. In: 2018 IEEE International Conference on Acoustics, Speech and Signal Processing (ICASSP), pp. 5329–5333. IEEE (2018)

23. Tang, R., Du, M., Liu, N., Yang, F., Hu, X.: An embarrassingly simple approach for trojan attack in deep neural networks. In: Proceedings of the 26th ACM SIGKDD International Conference on Knowledge Discovery & Data Mining, pp. 218–228 (2020)

24. Targ, S., Almeida, D., Lyman, K.: Resnet in resnet: generalizing residual architectures. arXiv preprint arXiv:1603.08029 (2016)

25. Wan, L., Wang, Q., Papir, A., Moreno, I.L.: Generalized end-to-end loss for speaker verification. In: 2018 IEEE International Conference on Acoustics, Speech and Signal Processing (ICASSP), pp. 4879–4883. IEEE (2018)

26. Wang, X., Ren, J., Lin, S., Zhu, X., Wang, Y., Zhang, Q.: Towards a unified understanding and improving of adversarial transferability. arXiv preprint arXiv:2010.04055 (2020)

27. Xiao, C., Zhu, J., Li, B., He, W., Liu, M., Song, D.: Spatially transformed adversarial examples. In: 6th International Conference on Learning Representations, ICLR 2018, Vancouver, BC, Canada, April 30–May 3, 2018, Conference Track Proceedings. OpenReview.net (2018)

28. Yakura, H., Sakuma, J.: Robust audio adversarial example for a physical attack. arXiv preprint arXiv:1810.11793 (2018)

29. Yuan, X., et al.: CommanderSong: a systematic approach for practical adversarial voice recognition. In 27th USENIX Security Symposium (USENIX Security 18), pp. 49–64 (2018)

Ensuring the Big Data Integrity Through Verifiable Zero-Knowledge Operations

Elena B. Aleksandrova⬤, Maria A. Poltavtseva$^{(\boxtimes)}$ ⬤, and Vadim S. Shmatov⬤

Peter the Great St. Petersburg Polytechnic University, Saint Petersburg, Russia
{helen,poltavtseva}@ibks.spbstu.ru

Abstract. Information from databases is exposed to threats at all stages of its existence: from recording and storing in the database to processing and returning to the user. Big Data systems combine multiple DBMSs and databases. The problem of data integrity is the most acute in them. The article describes an approach to control the integrity of Big Data during their processing, based on verifiable zero knowledge operations. It can be applied to various complex systems containing heterogeneous Big Data databases. The proposed approach implements prospective data integrity protection against existing and hypothetical future threats.

Keywords: Zero knowledge · Big data · Security · Integrity

1 Introduction

Big data plays an important role in today's world. It is difficult to imagine an organization or company that would not use a database to store important information, including personal data of customers and data constituting a commercial or other secret. Of course, Big Data warehouses are a coveted target for hackers. Today there are many methods developed to detect and prevent cyber attacks. These are methods of authentication [1], authorization and encryption [2, 3], data transmission protection [4] of mobile devices [5]. However, according to a Risk Based Security report [6], data breaches in the first quarter of 2020 are estimated at 8.4 billion records – a 273% increase over the same period in 2019. A huge amount of email addresses, passwords, names of people and other sensitive information fell into the hands of cybercriminals. The largest number of leaks (106) were in the health sector. Therefore, now, the task of ensuring information security of Big Data is very urgent, for storage and processing of which heterogeneous tools are used.

2 Database Security History

The need to ensure the protection of databases appeared along with the emergence of the databases themselves [7, 8]. Until the 1980s, databases were mostly owned by government services, did not involve frequent updates, and were not connected to networks. Therefore, the main task was to ensure the physical security of the servers.

© Springer Nature Singapore Pte Ltd. 2022
I. You et al. (Eds.): MobiSec 2021, CCIS 1544, pp. 211–221, 2022.
https://doi.org/10.1007/978-981-16-9576-6_15

Nevertheless, already at this stage, some logical threats to database security were identified and analyzed. For example, standard approaches to access control based on the differentiation of user access to files did not work well for data structured as relationships. Therefore, it became necessary to develop new formal models of access control. An important development at this stage was the Bell-Lapadula mandated model proposed in 1975. It made it possible to separate data according to secrecy levels in the same way as it was for ordinary documents. In the early 1980s, the Bell-Lapadula model was integrated into the US Department of Defense database.

Another important problem discovered early in the development of databases was inference. This attack method consists in obtaining (outputting) inaccessible information from the database responses to allowed queries. In addition, although the first approaches to protecting data from withdrawal were proposed in the 1970s, the problem of withdrawal has not been completely resolved until now.

In the 1980s, databases began to be commercially used and the access structure became more complex. Therefore, new models of access control began to appear, not only mandatory, but also discretionary. Moreover, data encryption started to be used as an additional layer of data protection.

In the 1990s, the rapid development of the Internet, the advent of the worldwide web and web browsers had a huge impact on the use of databases in the commercial sector. In order to take full advantage of new technologies and not miss benefits, companies were forced to provide external users with limited access to databases, which were previously an internal resource. For this, a three-tier architecture was developed, according to which, between the client and the database there is an application server responsible for authorizing external users and providing them with a certain programming interface. This interface, in turn, interacts with the database and downloads the necessary information from there, preventing direct interaction between the external user and the database. The three-tier model is still at the heart of many web applications.

As the internal structure of companies also became more complex, new approaches to access control were required. During this period, role-based access control models began to appear, as well as special models for the then popular non-relational object-oriented databases, characterized by a complex semantic connection of stored objects.

Another important process that began in the 1990s was the responsibilities delineation and duplication of control functions. For example, some database management systems have added audit functionality: recording all database operations including those initiated by the administrator.

In the 2000s, the problem of protecting users' personal data became urgent, since data mining techniques made it possible to derive even more information from both internal data stored by companies and from open sources [9]. Various approaches to group data anonymization have been invented and implemented, for example, k-anonymity [10] and l-diversity [11].

On the other hand, data mining techniques created new tools for intrusion detection and malware analysis. Which has become an additional means of protecting databases and their environment.

Since the late 2000s, data security analysis in new systems such as NoSQL databases, blockchains and social networks became important. Now there are no generally accepted means, which could protect data in such systems against various threats to the integrity and confidentiality; approaches are still being developed.

3   Modern Threats to Database Security

These days, the development of all kinds of storage and data management technologies continues. It is important to note the following features that determine the main directions of development, including from the point of view of information security.

Variety of data. This feature determines the need for new non-relational data models that would take into account complex relationships or, conversely, the weak connectivity of stored data. Currently, various models are gaining popularity – key-value stores, column families, graph and other NoSQL databases (Fig. 1).

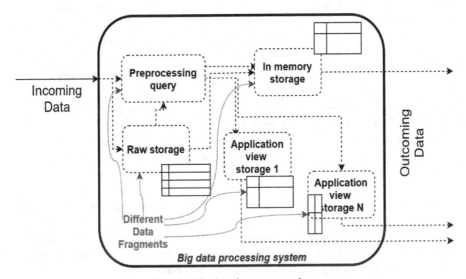

Fig. 1. Big data fragments variety

Large amounts of data. Increasing demands on system bandwidth have sparked interest in low-latency solutions. First, these are databases stored in memory.

Complicated infrastructure. Modern applications may require a variety of data from multiple sources, as well as multistage processing. Therefore, a multi-tier one has replaced the classic three-tier architecture. For example, in [12], approaches to the development of secure systems based on a four-tier scheme are considered – a presentation server is added between the client and the application server, which provides the user interface and implements authentication and authorization.

In addition, the active use of cloud databases based on the infrastructure and resources of the provider company begins. This creates additional potential points of failure and complicates security analysis.

Based on these features, modern studies [13–18] highlight the key threats to database security, presented in Table 1.

Table 1. Modern database security threats.

Threat	Object	Violation
Exploiting privileges by an internal user	Database level Intermediate levels	Confidentiality, Integrity, Accessibility
Exploiting database vulnerabilities	Database level	Confidentiality, Integrity, Accessibility
Exploiting environment vulnerabilities	Database level Intermediate levels	Confidentiality, Integrity, Accessibility
Query language injection	Intermediate levels	Confidentiality, Integrity
Insufficient audit	Database level Intermediate levels	Confidentiality, Integrity, Accessibility
Exploiting weaknesses in an authentication scheme	Database level Intermediate levels	Confidentiality, Integrity, Accessibility
Leaked backups	Database level Intermediate levels	Confidentiality
Lack of access control to important data	Database level	Confidentiality, Integrity
Insufficient protection of the database development environment	DB Development Environment	Confidentiality, Integrity, Accessibility
Network vulnerabilities	Database level Intermediate levels	Confidentiality

The greatest danger is the violation of data integrity. For example, changing the data of the police and other government services allows criminals to hide the traces of their actions and remain unpunished, the substitution of exchange prices can lead to colossal economic losses, and the transfer of distorted data to the process control system can disable production, endangering the environment and human lives.

Most integrity threats are directed not only at the database level, but also at other levels of the system. Indeed, data can be spoofed at any point along the path from the database to the final consumer of the data. Therefore, ensuring the security of modern Big Data requires an integrated approach that takes into account the environment and data delivery infrastructure.

Many modern means of protection are aimed at counteracting only a certain threat or a group of threats. This reactive approach to security has several disadvantages:

- it does not guarantee protection against new threats that appear with the development of database technology and the capabilities of the offender;
- it leads to the development of a scattered complex of means, each of which resists a certain threat;
- it does not answer the question of what to do if the attacker still managed to implement the threat.

Therefore, a promising task is to develop universal proactive methods for protecting databases and their environment, which will counteract not only those already studied, but also new threats that may appear in the future [19, 20].

4 Verifiable Operations on Confidential Databases

Verifiable operations on confidential databases is an approach to ensuring the integrity of Big Data stored in databases and requested, possibly in processed form. Integrity is monitored during storage, transfer between system levels, and processing. This approach can be adapted to any computing system, even if it includes various independent databases and multi-stage information transformations before presenting it to the user.

Verified operation on a field F – mapping $g : F^{N_1} \times F^{N_2} \times \cdots \times F^{N_T} \rightarrow F^M$, accepting entry T data vectors $\vec{D_i} \in F^{N_i}$, and returning a new data vector $\vec{R} \in F^M$. Working with the operations being checked is performed using two algorithms: *perform* и *verify*. Algorithm *perform* accepts to enter:

- field F, which contains the data;
- data set $D = \left\{ \vec{D_1}, \vec{D_2}, \ldots, \vec{D_T} \right\}$;
- hash $H : F^* \rightarrow F$;
- operation g.

The result of the work *perform* are:

- operation result $\vec{R} = g\left(\vec{D_1}, \vec{D_2}, \ldots, \vec{D_T} \right)$;
- hash images of data and result $\left\{ h_i = H\left(\vec{D_i} \right) \right\}$, $h_R = H\left(\vec{R} \right)$;
- proof of correct operation π.

Algorithm *verify* accepts to enter:

- field F, which contains the data;
- hash $H : F^* \rightarrow F$;
- operation g;
- data hash images $\{h_i\}$ and the result h_R;
- proof of the operation correctness π.

The result of the work *verify* is the decision as to whether the operation was performed correctly. The operation is considered to have been correctly performed if there are $\left\{ \vec{D_1}, \vec{D_2}, \ldots, \vec{D_T}, \vec{R} \right\}$ such that $h_i = H\left(\vec{D_i} \right)$, $h_R = H\left(\vec{R} \right)$ и $\vec{R} = g\left(\vec{D_1}, \vec{D_2}, \ldots, \vec{D_T} \right)$.

For *perform* and *verify* the following conditions must be met:

- completeness: if the operation is performed correctly, then the probability that the verify algorithm will reject the proof is negligible;

- correctness: if the operation is performed incorrectly, then the probability that the verify algorithm will accept the proof is negligible;
- zero knowledge: the relying party cannot extract any information about the input D from proof π;
- efficiency: proof size π and complexity of execution *verify* should grow with increasing input data D volume not faster than polylogarithmic.

The verified operations can be embedded in a Big Data processing system containing confidential data. This will allow you to control the processing, transfer and storage of data without disclosing the data itself.

To use the verified operations, the data processing system is represented as a root tree. The leaves of the tree indicate sources of information, and all other nodes of the graph are intermediate levels of the system that aggregate Big Data from various databases and process them. The edges of the graph are logical channels for transferring data between levels in the course of the considered business process. The root of the tree is the level of the system responsible for user interaction. An example of a system is shown in Fig. 2.

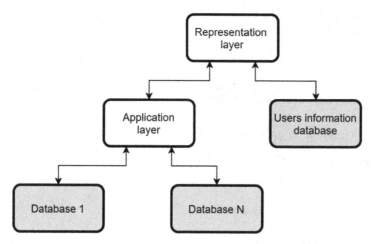

Fig. 2. An example of a system view.

In this example, user requests go to the presentation layer. It uses a user database to authenticate or authorize a user. If successful, the request is passed to the application layer. This layer forms separate queries to the two underlying bases, and then, having received the data, processes it and returns it to the presentation layer. At this level, the result may be augmented with personal data from a user database or transformed and then returned to the end user.

In addition, a special protected component - the integrity monitor - is added to the system. It performs two functions: storing up-to-date hash images of data from all databases in the system, and verifying evidence using an algorithm verify at the request of users or other system components. Due to the small functional load, ensuring and analyzing the security of the integrity monitor is not a difficult task (compared to the operation of the entire system as a whole).

All user requests to the Big Data system are divided into two classes. Read requests involve transferring data from one or more databases up the tree to the root node and then to the user. Data aggregation is carried out at the application level using Map-Reduce technology or other solutions. Write requests result in more complex data transfers in the system directed to one or more databases. Because of such a request, the data in the databases and their hash images in the integrity monitor are updated.

To fulfill the user's request, a diagram of the internal data flows in the system is built. It is a directed subtree of the overall tree view of the system. Figure 3 shows two examples of such subtrees. The example on the left shows the data flow when authenticating a user and reading data from databases 1 and 2. The example on the right shows the data flow when authenticating a user and updating records in database 2. In both cases, the schema includes only internal data; obviously, when a query is executed, the data passed by the user will also move in the system - from the root node to the leaves.

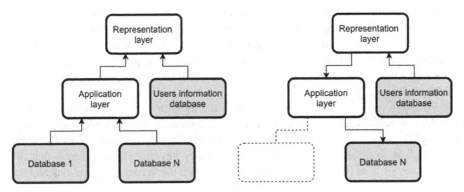

Fig. 3. Example of internal data flows in the system.

The user's request initially goes to the root node of the system. Then each node to which the request is sent executes it according to the following recursive algorithm:

1. The node transmits the user's request to all related downstream nodes from which it should receive data (according to the data flow scheme). Each node executes the received request using the same algorithm.
2. The node executes its part of the request as a verifiable operation, using the data supplied by the user (they are part of the request) and the data received in step 1.
3. If a node is connected to other nodes (not necessarily lower ones) that must receive data from it (according to the data flow scheme), the node sends its result, a proof of correctness, as well as hash images of all previous results and proofs of their correctness to all such nodes. Prior results themselves are not communicated for efficiency and confidentiality.
4. Otherwise (if the node is leaf), it passes all hash images of the results and proofs to the integrity monitor. The monitor checks the evidence and returns the result. If the read operation is correct, the root (single leaf) node returns the result to the user and the security monitor's evidence of correctness. If the write operation is completed correctly, then the database (leaf node) changes its state, and the integrity

monitor changes the hash image of the data stored in the database. If even one of the transmitted evidence is incorrect, the Integrity Monitor determines the point of failure and raises an alarm so that system administrators can immediately take the necessary measures to neutralize the security threat.

Depending on the system requirements, the security monitor and the correctness evidence it produces can be structured differently. Since the monitor checks the evidence of the correctness of operations, it must know the details of their execution. If the algorithms used in the system are secret, the security monitor must be implemented entirely on the side of the system owner; in this case, it will be the trusted party for the user. As evidence of the correctness of operations, such a monitor can sign a hash image of the result. In such a system, the owner of the system does not protect the user from deliberate deception, but the owner is protected from attacks aimed at violating the integrity of the data.

If the algorithm of the system can be disclosed, a high degree of trust in the monitor is not required. For example, the monitor can itself create a proof of the correctness of the verification of all evidence and return it to the user for verification on his part. In addition, since the monitor only works with hash images and proofs, it can publish this data and return a link to it to the user so that he can verify for himself that each step is performed correctly.

Finally, a fully public implementation of the monitor is possible, in which proof checking is performed openly and in a distributed manner by independent users. Such an implementation can be based, for example, on blockchain technology. The main advantage is that the client does not need to verify anything, which means that the requirements for its performance do not change when the verifiable operations and the integrity monitor are introduced into the system.

In any case, the monitor controls the integrity of all data in the system, and hacking it is a necessary, but sufficient condition for a security breach. Indeed, if an attacker gains control only over a system node, then any data substitution will be detected by the monitor. On the other hand, when a monitor is compromised, an attacker gains access only to hash images of data and proofs of the correctness of operations, while the data itself, processed by the system and returned to the user, remains safe.

5 Implementation of Verifiable Operations

The *perform* and *verify* algorithms are the key elements of the described system. Their properties affect not only the level of security provided by the integrity monitor, but also the speed and bandwidth of the entire system as a whole. At the moment, many different zero-knowledge proof schemes have been developed that can be applied to arbitrary computations, including operations on large amounts of data. Comparison of various schemes is shown in Table 2. It is assumed that the operation is described by an arithmetic scheme of N gates size.

The table shows that the zk-STARK scheme is the optimal choice. It fulfills the requirement for efficiency and has several advantages.

First, zk-STARK is protected from quantum computer attacks, as its strength is based solely on cryptographic hash functions. The threat of a quantum computer arose

Table 2. Comparison of zero-knowledge proof schemes.

Scheme name	Post-quantum	Trusted initialization	Publicly verified	Complexity of proof	Proof size	Complexity of verification
Pinocchio/zk-SNARK [21]	−	+	+	$O(N\log N)$	$O(1)$	$O(1)$
Hyrax [22]	−	−	+	$O(N\log N)$	$O\left(\sqrt{N}\right)$	$O\left(\sqrt{N}\right)$
Bulletproof [23]	−	−	+	$O(N\log N)$	$O(\log N)$	$O(N\log N)$
zk-SNARK [24]	+	+	−	$O(N)$	$O(1)$	$O(1)$
Scheme [25]	+	−	+	$O(N\log N)$	$O\left(\sqrt{N\log^3 N}\right)$	$O(N)$
Ligero [26]	+	−	+	$O(N\log N)$	$O\left(\sqrt{N}\right)$	$O(N)$
zk-STARK [27]	+	−	+	$O\left(N\log^2 N\right)$	$O\left(\log^2 N\right)$	$O\left(\log^2 N\right)$
Aurora [28]	+	−	+	$O(N\log N)$	$O\left(\log^2 N\right)$	$O(N)$

in connection with Shor's algorithm [29]. Now, it is only hypothetical, since there is no quantum computer powerful enough to run the algorithm. However, the threat is becoming more urgent due to the advances of scientists and engineers in the field of quantum computing.

Secondly, zk-STARK does not require trusted initialization, that is, the preparation of certain general parameters for the creation and verification of evidence by a trusted party. Due to the lack of trusted initialization, no trust is required between any participants in the schema.

Third, zk-STARK is a publicly verifiable scheme. Any participant can check the proof without the need to possess any secret key to compromise the security of the scheme.

The peculiarity of the construction of the zk-SNARK scheme makes it especially effective and convenient for applying to calculations consisting of numerous repetitions of the same type of operations. Database operations usually have this structure: a large amount of data, to each element of it is applied a simple transformation. Thus, zk-STARK is a natural choice for verifiable operations on confidential databases.

6   Conclusion

Protecting the integrity of information in systems containing databases is important and relevant. The main difficulty of integrity control lies in the fact that modern systems have a complex, multilevel, heterogeneous structure, in which different parties can control different nodes. Therefore, there are many ways to violate the integrity of data at different stages: storage, processing and transmission to the user, and from different attackers: an external adversary, an internal intruder, or even the owner of a part of the system. Realizing threats to data integrity can have serious consequences.

A verifiable operation approach can be used to monitor the integrity of the entire system, regardless of its structure and business logic. It involves the introduction of an integrity monitor into the system, which will control the correctness of each operation at each level and detect attempts to substitute data. At the same time, the integrity monitor does not create additional opportunities for an attacker: hacking one monitor is not enough to implement threats to integrity or confidentiality. The only drawback of implementing a monitor is a decrease in system performance, because the system nodes need to create proofs of the correctness of operations. Currently, the most efficient and secure zero knowledge proof scheme that can be used, as the basis for verifiable transactions is zk-STARK.

References

1. Goddijn, I., Kouns, J.: 2020 Q1 Report Data Breach QuickView. Risk Based Security (2020)
2. Anada, H.: Decentralized multi-authority anonymous authentication for global identities with non-interactive proofs. J. Internet Serv. Inf. Secur. (JISIS) 10(4), 23–37 (2020). https://doi.org/10.22667/JISIS.2020.11.30.023
3. Duong, D.H., Susilo W., Trinh V.C.: Wildcarded identity-based encryption with constant-size ciphertext and secret key. J. Wirel. Mobile Netw. Ubiquit. Comput. Dependable Appl. (JoWUA) 11(2), pp. 74–86 (2020). https://doi.org/10.22667/JOWUA.2020.06.30.074
4. Dutta, P., Susilo, W., Duong, D.H., Baek, J., Roy, P.S.: Identity-based unidirectional proxy re-encryption and re-signature in standard model: lattice-based constructions. J. Int. Serv. Inf. Secur. (JISIS) 10(4), 1–22 (2020). https://doi.org/10.22667/JISIS.2020.11.30.001
5. Nowaczewski, S., Mazurczyk, W.: Securing future internet and 5G using customer edge switching using DNSCrypt and DNSSEC. J. Wirel. Mobile Netw. Ubiquit. Comput. Dependable Appl. (JoWUA) 11(3), 87–106 (2020). https://doi.org/10.22667/JOWUA.2020.09.30.087
6. Wong, S.K., Yiu, S.M.: Location spoofing attack detection with pre-installed sensors in mobile devices. J. Wirel. Mobile Netw. Ubiquit. Comput. Dependable Appl. (JoWUA) 11(4), 16–30 (2020). https://doi.org/10.22667/JOWUA.2020.12.31.016
7. Thuraisingham, B.: Database security: past, present, and future. In: 2015 IEEE International Congress on Big Data, pp. 772–774. IEEE (2015)
8. Poltavtseva, M.A.: Evolution of data management systems and their security. In: Proceedings - 2019 International Conference on Engineering Technologies and Computer Science: Innovation and Application, EnT 2019, pp. 25–29 (2019). https://doi.org/10.1109/EnT.2019.00010
9. Poltavtsev, A.A., Khabarov, A.R., Selyankin, A.O.: Inference attacks and information security in databases. Autom. Control. Comput. Sci. 54(8), 829–833 (2020). https://doi.org/10.3103/S0146411620080271
10. Samarati, P., Sweeney, L.: Protecting privacy when disclosing information: k-anonymity and its enforcement through generalization and suppression (1998)
11. Machanavajjhala, A., et al.: l-diversity: privacy beyond k-anonymity. ACM Trans. Knowl. Discov. Data (TKDD), 1(1), 3-es (2007)
12. Fernandez, E.B., et al.: The secure three-tier architecture pattern. In: 2008 International Conference on Complex, Intelligent and Software Intensive Systems, pp. 555–560. IEEE (2008)
13. Singh, S., Rai, R.K.: A review report on security threats on database. Int. J. Comput. Sci. Inf. Technol. 5(3), 3215–3219 (2014)
14. Sarmah, S.: Database security–threats and prevention. IJCTT, 67(5), 46–50 (2019)

15. Al-Sayid, N.A., Aldlaeen, D.: Database security threats: a survey study. In: 2013 5th International Conference on Computer Science and Information Technology, pp. 60–64. IEEE (2013)
16. Poltavtseva, M.A., Zegzhda, D.P., Kalinin, M.O.: Big data management system security threat model. Autom. Control Comput. Sci. **53**(8), 903–913 (2019). https://doi.org/10.3103/S01464 11619080261
17. Vlasova, O.A., Vasilyeva, A.S.: Protection and security of the database. Reshetnevskie readings, no. 21, p. 2 (2017)
18. Mousa, A., Karabatak, M., Mustafa, T.: Database security threats and challenges. In: 2020 8th International Symposium on Digital Forensics and Security (ISDFS), pp. 1–5. IEEE (2020)
19. Kotenko, I., Saenko, I., Kushnerevich, A.: Parallel big data processing system for security monitoring in internet of things networks. J. Wirel. Mobile Netw. Ubiquit. Comput. Dependable Appl. (JoWUA) **8**(4), 60–74 (2017). https://doi.org/10.22667/JOWUA.2017.12. 31.060
20. Baldi, G., et al.: Session-dependent usage control for big data. J. Internet Serv. Inf. Secur. (JISIS) **10**(3), 76–92 (2020). https://doi.org/10.22667/JISIS.2020.08.31.076
21. Parno, B., et al.: Pinocchio: nearly practical verifiable computation. In: 2013 IEEE Symposium on Security and Privacy, pp. 238–252. IEEE (2013)
22. Wahby, R.S., et al.: Doubly-efficient zkSNARKs without trusted setup. In: 2018 IEEE Symposium on Security and Privacy (SP), pp. 926–943. IEEE (2018)
23. Bünz, B., et al.: Bulletproofs: short proofs for confidential transactions and more. In: 2018 IEEE Symposium on Security and Privacy (SP), pp. 315–334. IEEE (2018)
24. Gennaro, R., et al.: Lattice-based zk-SNARKs from square span programs. In: Proceedings of the 2018 ACM SIGSAC Conference on Computer and Communications Security, pp. 556–573 (2018)
25. Baum, C., Bootle, J., Cerulli, A., del Pino, R., Groth, J., Lyubashevsky, V.: Sub-linear lattice-based zero-knowledge arguments for arithmetic circuits. In: Shacham, H., Boldyreva, A. (eds.) Advances in Cryptology – CRYPTO 2018: 38th Annual International Cryptology Conference, Santa Barbara, CA, USA, August 19–23, 2018, Proceedings, Part II, pp. 669–699. Springer, Cham (2018). https://doi.org/10.1007/978-3-319-96881-0_23
26. Ames, S., et al.: Ligero: lightweight sublinear arguments without a trusted setup. In: Proceedings of the 2017 ACM SIGSAC Conference on Computer and Communications Security, pp. 2087–2104 (2017)
27. Ben-Sasson, E., et al.: Scalable, transparent, and post-quantum secure computational integrity. IACR Cryptol. ePrint Arch, vol. 2018, p. 46 (2018)
28. Ben-Sasson, E., Chiesa, A., Riabzev, M., Spooner, N., Virza, M., Ward, N.: Aurora: transparent succinct arguments for R1CS. In: Ishai, Y., Rijmen, V. (eds.) Advances in Cryptology – EUROCRYPT 2019: 38th Annual International Conference on the Theory and Applications of Cryptographic Techniques, Darmstadt, Germany, May 19–23, 2019, Proceedings, Part I, pp. 103–128. Springer, Cham (2019). https://doi.org/10.1007/978-3-030-17653-2_4
29. Shor, P.W.: Polynomial-time algorithms for prime factorization and discrete logarithms on a quantum computer. SIAM Rev. **41**(2), 303–332 (1999)

Forensic Analysis of Fitness Applications on Android

Rahul Sinha[1], Vikas Sihag[1], Gaurav Choudhary[2], Manu Vardhan[3(✉)],
and Pradeep Singh[3]

[1] Sardar Patel University of Police, Security and Criminal Justice, Jodhpur, India
{spu19csrks,vikas.sihag}@policeuniversity.ac.in
[2] Department of Applied Mathematics and Computer Science,
Technical University of Denmark (DTU), Kongens Lyngby, Denmark
gauravchoudhary7777@gmail.com
[3] National Institute of Technology, Raipur, India
{mvardhan.cs,psingh.cs}@nitrr.ac.in

Abstract. People these days are getting more and more digitized. Every other person is using a smartphone and wearing smartwatches. These days cell phones and wearable devices have been used in many different ways. It keeps track of the location used for payment, keeps track of health conditions, etc. These types of information are stored in the database of an application. The applications can be Instant messaging applications, health care applications, m-banking applications, etc. These applications contain a lot of information about a person, from their basic information to their activities. The information stored by these applications can be beneficial for forensic investigation. This paper analyzed the popular healthcare application and recovered many artifacts like user details, email address, food habits, user locations, timestamps, etc.

Keywords: Smartphone application · Android · Healthcare · Privacy

1 Introduction

mHealth - also known as Mobile Health, provides solutions to provide innovative care access and deliverable models that promise better outcomes, with reduced healthcare costs and patient safety practices. Mobile phones have evolved to be powerful self-health monitoring tools. This evolution of smartphones is considered to have a greater impact on health care than immobile health facilities. This led to the development of various Healthcare applications in the market and wearable technologies that track not just our health and fitness concerns, but treatments also [3,19,27].

The widespread use of mobile fitness/health applications generates an enormous amount of data which is a catalyst for user data aggregation. These Mobile health applications stores a large amount of sensitive personally identifiable data [8,15]. These data can also be considered to poses an extensive threat to our privacy [21]. But, for digital sleuths, such a rich source of user-data applications

© Springer Nature Singapore Pte Ltd. 2022
I. You et al. (Eds.): MobiSec 2021, CCIS 1544, pp. 222–235, 2022.
https://doi.org/10.1007/978-981-16-9576-6_16

are a gem for digital evidence. In real scenarios, such healthcare applications data has already helped in solving many forensic cases [23]. The work in this research paper is entirely focused on the aggregation and analysis of forensic artifacts retrieved from widely used mobile health and fitness applications [9,18,20].

The main aim of this study is to provide an outline for digital forensic analysis while examining the Healthcare and Fitness Application on the Android-based mobile device. There are five key steps to carry out Mobile Application Forensic which are Identification, Preservation, Data Recovery, Analysis, and Presentation.

The first and the foremost important thing is to identify the device which can be labeled as the most significant piece for the examination of the digital forensic. After the identification step, Preservation is the second prioritized procedure for digital forensics investigations, where every event or activity needs to be documented without any alteration. If at extreme situation any alteration is done or needed, it must be well justified in the document as well as in the court. The document presented should be well formatted in a forensically sound manner. This step is followed by Data recovery, where all the deleted, hidden, or actual files are restored and pulled from the image file. This process can be considered as essential as in if data cannot be retrieved from such deleted sources, the investigation process enters a hold situation till then. Various tools in the market guarantee data recovery but for the digital investigation authentic application or mechanism should be used. Then comes the most important stage i.e. Analysis, which lets the investigators conclude a firm statement about the case. It is a procedure in digital forensics, where investigators extract the pieces of evidence, process them, and interpret these pieces of evidence. The analyzing of the data helps us to get the insights of the data which can barely be observed just by looking at the data [7,10]. Lastly, Presentation of the computerized crime scene investigation examinations where the criminology agents present the computerized proof in court in a law worthy way [11,25].

The rest of this paper includes related work in Sect. 2. Section 3 describes the methodology of how the artifacts were extracted. The experimental results and observations are well-formatted in Sect. 4, which is then followed by the detailed writings of proposed findings in Sect. 4. Lastly in Sect. 5, we conclude our work.

2   Related Work

Many researchers have been analyzing the Healthcare application to obtain different types of information [12]. Data science enthusiasts have also laid their eyes on such analysis and take the help of the investigators to obtain the data to carry out their research. Our contribution to this area is not limited to non-volatile means of forensics but has a much wider scope since it is a common framework that goes beyond borders allowing the retrieval of evidence from the applications running on Android, leading operating systems.

Wearable devices collect information about the behavior of the user [13,16]. This information is used as significant evidence for criminal investigations. The challenges that are faced are practical, technical, and legal issues. The main focus of this paper was to consider the usage of these healthcare devices for forensic investigation.

As far as estimating actual work, [22] tried a Fitbit on 25 college understudies playing out an assortment of exercises, for example, treadmill strolling, slant strolling, running, and step venturing. This examination reasoned that the Fitbit had "moderate" legitimacy in distinguishing exercises. Generally talking, the Fitbit is capable to be utilized to distinguish specific sorts of activity, however, it's anything but valuable for exercises like climbing steps.

The Fitbit line of gadgets is a well-known brand of wearable trackers [26]. It explores what ancient rarities are produced by the new Fitbit Versa 2 by researching what information is produced and put away on the cell phone application segment of the new gadget. The ancient rarities found will be identified with spaces of criminological interest that apply to a policeman or computerized legal sciences specialist.

Table 1. HealthCare application and wearable device artifacts.

Application/Device	Author	OS	Artifacts
Fitbit	Sarah Mcnary [13]	Android	Email,friend's full name, account
	Almogbil [1]	Android	Creation date, height, weight
Fitbit Versa 2	Yung Han [26]	Android	Heart rate, GPS locations, Credit card details
MyFitnessPal	Azfar [4]	Android	Gender, DOB, Postcode, email Weight, Height, Diary Password
Period Calendar	Azfar [4]	Android	User Height, Weight, temperature, period length and pill lists
RunKeeper	Azfar [5]	Android	Geographical position during trip, distance, location, time and duration
Samsung Gear 2	Baggili [6]	Android	Messages, health and fitness data email, contacts, events, notifications
Apple Watch	Nicole R [14]	IOS	Email,Call Logs,Contacts, Calendar events, browser activity

Numerous person-to-person communication applications are coordinated into new cell phones, in cases including social networks, measurable inspectors might have the option to discover pertinent proof on a suspect's cell phone [2,24]. A legal assessment of the iPhone 3GS (utilizing a coherent securing) showed that an information base identified with the Facebook application is put away on the telephone's memory. The data set stores information for every companion in the rundown, including their names, ID numbers, and telephone number [6]. Two different indexes identified with the Twitter application were likewise found. These indexes store data about Twitter account information, connections sent with tweets, client names, and tweets with the date and time esteem. A measurable assessment of an Android telephone's sensible picture showed that fundamental Facebook companion data is stored in the contacts database (contacts.db) as the gadget "synchronizes contact's Facebook notices with the telephone directory". It likewise showed that the gadget stores Twitter passwords furthermore, Twitter refreshes performed through the Twitter application in plain content. Scientific examination papers on BlackBerry telephones and Windows cell phones, in any case, didn't specify finding or recuperating any information identified with the utilization of person-to-person communication applications.

In 2015, [4] Azfar analyzed numerous popular free Android health care applications. His study stated that the majority of apps stores the sensitive and private information of the user, from their basic details to timestamp information in the application local database. Such information, once recovered, can be used to reconstruct the user's activities and timeline as well as the user's whereabouts.

In the research paper [5], 30 famous Android correspondence applications were analyzed, where a consistent extraction of the Android telephone pictures was gathered utilizing XRY, a generally utilized portable scientific apparatus. Different data of scientific interest, for example, contact records and sequence of messages, were recuperating. Because of the discoveries, a two-dimensional scientific classification of the measurable relics of the correspondence applications is proposed, with the application classifications in a single measurement and the classes of curios in the other measurement. At long last, the relics distinguished in the investigation of the 30 correspondence applications are summed up utilizing the scientific categorization. Normally, the proposed scientific classification and the measurable discoveries in this paper will help criminological examinations including Android correspondence.

Table 1 contains different artifacts obtained from various HealthCare Applications by the number of authors. The table is well structured to provide the detail of the Application/Device used, Author of the research paper, OS used, and list of artifacts.

3   Methodology

National Institute of Standards and Technology (NIST) categorizes any digital forensics case into four main stages, i.e. identification, collection, organization, and presentation. In the identification stage, identification of the incident or the evidence is taken into account. The collection phase acquires evidentiary data, then carves the data which is followed by limiting the amount of data by discarding off any redundancy in the acquired data. In the organization phase, the data obtained after cleaning is investigated and analyzed with the crime scene to conclude solid results. Finally, the presentation stage deals with presenting the insightful data which can be understood and interpreted by the jury easily.

In this research, Google Play Store was used to download different mobile health and fitness applications like MyFitnessPal, FitBit, StepSetGo, etc. by searching the following terms 'Health', 'workouts', 'fitness, and 'diet'. We took a keen focus on the number of downloads for the application used to carry out this experiment. All the six application used in this research is widely used by the population.

Firstly, we aimed at setting up all the experimental environments which included downloading the health applications onto a speculative aspects Android device, completing the registration and signing in to generate user data through regular daily usage, followed by the installation of digital forensic tools on the workstation and setting up the network [17].

In the second phase, the tools that were installed were intensively used for acquiring data from the hypothetical suspect's device. To obtain deep insight into data generated by the health and fitness applications, we even explored the tables of the application database manually. This approach will guide the digital investigators in triaging the structure of the different application data and then validating their findings afterward.

Applications Considered

Considering that results may vary on different Android devices, we used Android devices (Lenevo ZUK Z2) with Android OS versions for our testing. On the Windows OS machine, we installed forensic tools for data acquisition. There are six mobile applications that we installed on our android device, namely: MapMyfitness, NoiseFit, Fitbit, MyFitnessPal, Nike, and StepSetGo.

Data Acquisition

After the creation and successfully registering the user accounts on the health-care application. We completed the data acquisition process accounting for all the fitness activities by using Android Studio. Android studio backs up specific application data on the device and saves the extracted data to the workstation. Later, these findings are thoroughly examined and insights are recorded as per the crime needs demands.

Data Analysis

Investigators utilize Open Source Intelligence (OSINT) to gain insight into what could be potentially retrieved from these healthcare applications, or identify the suspect by examining the user-related data stored in a database. Manual analysis is also carried out to make sure no useful information is missed out. DB browser is used for data analysis for all the HealthCare applications. The database of each application used is in SQLite format.

4   Results and Analysis

Extensive application artifacts were found on the devices. We found different database files in different applications. There are individual experiments in each application. Each database file is described in the following section and structured with the different applications used, the file name, and the artifacts in Table 2.

{"event_type":"user\/initialization","timestamp":1612936283427,"user_id":"191123248","device_id":"46523e4c68173b9b","session_id":1612936236139,"ouid":
"ada21695-bba5-4b5c-9790-e0352d2de42c","sequence_number":122,"version_name":"21.1.0","os_name":"android","os_version":"11","device_brand":"ZUK",
"device_manufacturer":"ZUK","device_model":"Z2 Plus","carrier":"Vi India","country":"IN","language":"en","platform":"Android","library":{"name":
"amplitude-android","version":"2.19.0"},"api_properties":{"androidADID":"9b4f2783-0519-4116-a347-f6558lc6Scdf","limit_ad_tracking":false,"gps_enabled":true},
"event_properties":{"age_group":"25-34","postal_code":"342304","facebook_connected":false,"installed_apps":{"MapMyFitness","MyFitnessPal"},"ad_free_user_status":
false,"user_country":"IN","mmf_user_segment":"E","action":"initialization","registration_date":"2021-01-29","gender":"male","birthdate":"1995-12-31",
"location_permission_status":true,"android_wear":false,"premium_user_status":false,"total_workout_duration":191,"user_height":"","timezone_offset":"5.5",
"user_bmi":null,"push_notification_status":"enabled","user_region":"","login_status":true,"user_id":"191123248","devices_paired":{"atlas"},"user_weight":"","age":
25,"category":"user","event":"init_cd_event","label":"","user_city":"","timezone_name":"Asia\/Kolkata","total_workout_count":1,"app_name":"MapMyFitness",
"facebook_sharing_permission":false,"os_ad_consent_status":"accepted","total_workout_distance":14.777214794039727,"user_properties":{},"groups":{}}

Fig. 1. MapMyFitness artifacts.

Table 2. Artifacts found in MapMyFitness.

Artifact	Value	Meaning
user_id	191123248	Unique Identity of the user
birthdate	1995-12-31	Determines age
registration_date	2021-01-29	Range of the stored user data
country	IN	Location of the user
total_workout_distance	14.777214794039727	Distance in km covered by user
gender	Male	Specify sex
postal_code	342304	Street, City or State Address

4.1 MapMyFitnes Application

MapMyFitness is one of the most popular applications in the world of Healthcare. It uses GPS technology to provide the workout enthusiast the ability to map, record, and track their day-to-day workouts. Also, this app is not limited to this, users can access a searchable database of online training tools, local routes, event listings, and much more. One can import their old profile workouts from 400 different compatible devices like Jawbone, Garmin, Polar, and Fitbit. This application comes with the attractive feature of providing credits for all the calories you burn by just linking your MyFitnessPal account with MapMyFitness. Once synced, you'll be able to track all your calorie burn, workout stats, and nutrition data within the same dashboard.

The path where the database of MapMyFitness is stored in /data/data/com. ma-pmyfitness.android2/databases. After the forensic analysis of the database MyFitnessPal, it is observed that the files are stockpiled in internal device memory and it is not accessible to the user.

By analyzing the database from MapMyFitness, various insightful information about the users was observed by scrutinizing the different tables in the user profile database as shown in Fig. 1 and some of the important artifacts are listed in Table 2. MapMyFitness application has a file named com.amplitude.api which is present in the location /data/data/com.Mapmyfitness.android/databases, had various information like Userid, Events, Event types, Timestamp, Device Info, Gender, Country, Pin code, DOB, Age, Timezone, name, Registration date, Timezone offset. Another file mmdk_user.db contains information such as Name, Username, Email, Location, City, Gender, DOB, Timezone which provides brief details of the users. Also, workout related databases were present under the database title uasdk_workout.db and workout.db which keeps information like Workout activity, Timezone, Timestamp, Timeoffset, Longitude, Latitude, Altitude, Distance.

4.2   NoiseFit Application

NoiseFit is your one-stop for all the athletic, fitness, and health tracking needs. One just needs to sync the Noise smartwatch to the NoiseFit app and you are on the ride to unlock the full potential of your device.

This application can keep you connected with all the calls and SMS notifications on your phone. NoiseFit keeps you productive and provides you with diverse features to make life healthy and engaging. It also targets you to achieve unique milestones by engaging you in weekly, bi-weekly themed activity challenges. It also monitors your heart rate 24 * 7, keeps track of your sleep quality, provides guided breathing sessions, and monitors stress levels.

The path where the database of NoiseFit is stored in /data/data/com.noisefit/databases. After the forensic analysis of the database NoiseFit, it is observed that the files are stockpiled in internal device memory and it is not accessible to the user.

Exploring the NoiseBit database, the RKStorage file provided useful forensic information about the user, which were, Name, Profile Name, Profile Image, Email, Mobile number. This information can help in forensic to a greater extent because confidential artifacts like Profile Images, Phone numbers, Emails can turn to be a boom for forensic analysis. Some of the important artifacts are listed in Table 3.

Table 3. Artifacts found in NoiseFit.

Artifact	Value	Meaning
firebaseToken	ezpJH9VhIGk......	Allowing authenticate users or devices
sleep_goals	8	Goal set by user to sleep
first_name	Rahul Kumar	First name of the user
last_name	Sinha	Last name of the user
image_url	https://lh3.googleuser..........	Profile picture of the user
mobile	871*****695	Phone number of the user
email	rahulkumarsinha95@gmail.com	Email address of the user
step_goals	10000	Step Goal set by the user

4.3   FitBit Application

Fitbit is one of the world's leading applications for health and fitness. It keeps track of your activity, workouts, sleep, nutrition, and stress altogether. It provides free workouts, meditation tracks, nutrition programs, sleep tools, and more. Information like the number of steps, distance, calories burned, floors climbed, are monitored by this application. It also has innovative sleep tools which keep the sleep score, bedtime reminders.

The path where the database of FitBit is stored in /data/data/com.fitbit. Fitbit-Mobile/databases. After the forensic analysis of the database FitBit, it is observed that the files are stockpiled in internal device memory and it is not accessible to the user.

After a thorough investigation of the FitBit database, we found numerous database files. Among all database file, the Fitbit-db file contains 19 tables, out of which the profile table has various artifacts like Name, Email id, Gender, Height, Timezone, Stride length running, Stride length walking, Profile Image, and Device Information. This personal information can be very useful to carry out the forensic and get detailed information about the users. The identity of the person can easily be retrieved by sensitive data like Profile Image, Email id, etc.

Its production range includes activity trackers, smartwatches, wireless-enabled wearable technology devices that measure data such as the number of steps walked, heart rate, quality of sleep, steps climbed, and other personal metrics involved in fitness. Some of the important artifacts are listed in Table 4.

Table 4. Artifacts found in FitBit application.

Artifact	Value	Meaning
FULL_NAME	Rahul Sinha	Name of the user
DISPLAY_NAME	Rahul S.	Display name of the user
GENDER	MALE	Specify sex
STRIDE_LENGTH_RUNNING	121.1	Distance covered in two steps while running
STRIDE_LENGTH_WALKING	72.7	Distance covered in two steps while walking
PROFILE_PHOTO_LINK	https://static0.........e_150.png	User profile picture
Email	rahulkumarsinha95@gmail.com	Email address of the user

4.4   MyFitnessPal

MyFitnessPal is an app to know more about yourself and helps you make empowered choices every day. It has an engaged online community of 200 million members that encourage and advise you to lose weight, get fit, and keep your nutrition and calories on track. The benefits and attractive features of this application are that it has the biggest food database, fast & easy logging tools, calorie tracker, macro tracker, nutrition insights, and many more.

The path where the database of MyFitnessPal is stored in /data/data/com. My-FitnessPal.android/databases. After the forensic analysis of the database MyFitnessPal, it is observed that the files are stockpiled in internal device memory and it is not accessible to the user.

The database is extracted from the internal memory of the device under the file named myfitnesspal.db. This database has a total of 41 tables which includes various user information, diet information, water intake, etc., also shown in Fig. 2. The main tables which can be used for the forensic and provides insightful details of the users were the user table, users_properties table, and users table. Some of the insightful features of the user are listed in Table 5. These tables provide PII (Personal identifiable information) of the user like Username, Email, DOB, Gender, Weight, Height, Image, etc. Additionally, it also provides artifacts like Exercise entry, Foods info, Nutrient Info, Reminders, Timezone, Water entry, Timestamp.

property_name	property_value	updated_at	last_sync_at
Filter	Filter	Filter	Filter
email	rahulkumarsinha95@gmail.com	2021-01-29 11:53:41	2021-05-20 01:24:35
timezone_identifier	Asia/Kolkata	2021-01-29 11:53:41	2021-05-20 01:24:35
valid_email	no	2021-01-29 11:53:42	2021-05-20 01:24:35
meal_names	"Breakfast","Lunch","Dinner","Snacks"	2021-01-29 11:53:42	2021-05-20 01:24:35
use_metric	yes	2021-01-29 11:54:03	2021-05-20 01:24:35
gender	Male	2021-01-29 11:53:42	2021-05-20 01:24:35
date_of_birth	1995-12-31	2021-01-29 11:53:42	2021-05-20 01:24:35
country_name	India	2021-01-29 11:53:42	2021-05-20 01:24:35
postal_code		2021-01-29 11:53:42	2021-05-20 01:24:35
lifestyle_name	Active	2021-01-29 11:53:42	2021-05-20 01:24:35
current_weight_in_pounds	209.439	2021-01-29 11:54:03	2021-05-20 01:24:35
goal_weight_in_pounds	165.347	2021-01-29 11:54:03	2021-05-20 01:24:35
height_in_inches	72.0	2021-01-29 11:53:42	2021-05-20 01:24:35
requires_start_time_for_exercise_ent...	no	2021-01-29 11:53:42	2021-05-20 01:24:35
diary_privacy_setting	private	2021-01-29 11:53:42	2021-05-20 01:24:35
diary_password		2021-01-29 11:53:42	2021-05-20 01:24:35
uacf_id	3496809929734973854	2021-01-29 11:53:42	2021-05-20 01:24:35
goal_calories_per_day	2660.0	2021-01-29 11:53:42	2021-05-20 01:24:35
workouts_per_week	0.0	2021-01-29 11:53:42	2021-05-20 01:24:35
goal_loss_per_week	1.1	2021-05-20 01:21:14	2021-05-20 01:24:35
minutes_per_workout	0.0	2021-01-29 11:53:42	2021-05-20 01:24:35
projected_pounds_lost_per_week	0.9936001	2021-01-29 11:53:42	2021-05-20 01:24:35
last_goals_recalculation_date	2021-05-20 00:00:00	2021-05-20 01:21:14	2021-05-20 01:24:35
create_status_on_new_friends	true	2021-01-29 11:53:42	2021-05-20 01:24:35

Fig. 2. MyFitnessPal artifacts

4.5   StepSetGo

StepSetGo, as the name suggests, shows the steps you have walked today. The main concept is simple, don't waste your steps and get rewarded for them. It shows varieties of information i.e. on which level you are at, the distance covered, calories burnt today, and your total SSG Coin balance. Your fitness journey on StepSetGo is mapped out by 5 levels. The more you walk, the more you upgrade your level. You can challenge yourself with your friends by sharing details of your profile and they can even track when you are being lazy or getting upgraded.

The path where the database of StepSetGo is stored in /data/data/com. pepkit.s-sg/databases. After the forensic analysis of the database StepSetGo, it is observed that the files are stockpiled in internal device memory and it is not accessible to the user.

The database com.google.android.datatransport.events of the StepSetGo contains sensitive information like Device Info, Fingerprint, Country, Timestamp as shown in Fig. 3 and listed in Table 6 which can provide important details of the user. Information like fingerprints especially can bring the whole data of the user upfront. It also had another database named RKStorage.db which has the basic user information artifacts i.e. Name, Username, DOB, Email, Gender, Timezone, Total steps, weight, Height, Phone No, Profile status, Average Step per day.

Table 5. Artifacts found in MyFitnessPal application.

Artifact	Value	Meaning
username	rahulkumarsinha95	Unique identity of the user
birthdate	1995-12-31	Determine age
height	72.0 in.	Height of the user
weight	94.999855 kg	Weight of the user
last_login	2021-02-25T08:51:06Z	Last used
foods	3 Egg Omelet, samosa, roti	food eaten by user
exercise	Cricket (batting, bowling)	Activity by the user
item_type_name	Food entry, diary note, exercise reminder, steps entry, etc.	Personal info
nutrient_goals	calories: values: 2660	Target set by user
email	rahulkumarsinha95@gmail.com	Email of the user
reminders	Breakfast 10:13:00 Lunch 14:03:00 Dinner 20:05:00	Reminder set by the user

4.6   Nike

Inspiring the athletes globally, Nike not only delivers innovative products but has also spread their expertise in making the life of users digitally fit. It extensively provides Nike Training Club App where various free workouts, yoga classes, bodyweight workouts, while one stays at home.

The path where the database of Nike is stored in /data/data/com.nike. ntc/databases. After the forensic analysis of the database Nike, it is observed that the files are stockpiled in internal device memory and it is not accessible to the user. The Artifacts found in Nike Application is shown in Table 7.

After extracting the database and analyzing all the tables in it, we obtained various information related to users like their username, name, profile picture, last seen, last modified. It also provides additional information about the Time-zone and the device information (Table 8).

Fig. 3. StepSetGo artifacts

Table 6. Artifacts found in StepSetGo application.

Artifact	Value	Meaning
username	rahulsinha002	Unique identity of the user
birthdate	1995-12-04	Determine age
name	Rahul Kumar Sinha	Full name of the user
gender	Male	Specify sex
height	182.92682926829266	Height of the user
weight	95kgs	Weight of the user
profile_image	https://lh3.go0.........=s96-c	Profile Picture of the user
steps_total	367112	Total number of steps
avg_steps_per_day	8741	Average number of steps
email	rahulkumarsinha95@gmail.com	Email address of the user
phone	+91871****695	Phone number of the user
profile_status	Keep going	Profile status

Table 7. Artifacts found in nike application.

Artifact	Value	Meaning
screen_name	rahuls162442761	Unique name of the user
actor_id	08d0bf3a-265c-4b27-851d-227c4fc08d5c	Unique identity of the user
actor_title	Rahul Kumar Sinha	Full name of the user
last_seen_time	2021-04-28T14:43:53.613Z	Last used by user
inbox	Welcome+ to+Nike+Training Bringing+you+the+best+workouts	Message inbox
avatar	]https://www.nike.com/vc/profile/null_100.jpg	Profile Picture of the user

Table 8. HealthCare applications artifacts

Application	File name	Artifacts
MapMyfitness	com.amplitude.api	Userid, Events, Event types, Timestamp, Device Info, Gender, Country, Pin code, DOB, Age, Timezone_name, Registration date, Timezone offset
	mmdk_user.db	Name, Username, Email, Location, City, Gender, DOB, Timezone
	uasdk_workout.db	Workout activity, Timezone
	workout.db	Timestamp, Timeoffset, Longitude, Latitude, Altitude, Distance
NoiseFit	RKStorage.db	Name, Profile Name, Profile Image, Email, Mobile number
FitBit	fitbit.db	Name, Email id, Gender, Hight, Timezone, Stride length running, Stride lenth walking, Profile Image, Device Info
MyFitnesPal	myfitnesspal.db	Exercise entry, Foods info, Nutrient Info, Email Reminders, Username, DOB, Gender, Weight, Height, Image, Timezone, Water entry, Timestamp
StepSetGo	com.google.android.datatransport.events	Device Information, Fingerprint, Country, Timestamp
	RKStorage.db	Name, Username, DOB, Email, Gender, Timezone, Total steps, weight, Height, Phone Number, Profile status, Average Step per day
Nike	singular-1.db	Timezone, Device Information
	ns_feed2.db	User detail, profile picture
	ntc_room.db	User related info (last seen, last modified, achievements)

5   Conclusion

The objective of this study was to determine how much user data is generated and retained by the application after registration and signing in to the application, and whether this data could be used to retrieve the user's PII and identify their location or actions at any particular time. This paper aimed to focus on analyzing the artifacts which were present in Healthcare applications on the Android Device. This Research paper shows all the artifacts which are recovered from 6 different categories of Healthcare applications. Findings are accurate at the time of this research, but new releases of application may change the way data are stored on the devices, as well as the type of data that can be forensically recovered from the devices.

In future work, we will investigate various methods and tools to gain data from the unrooted device without affecting the volatile memory and will also analyze various techniques how to retrieve data from the unrooted device into the rooted device (from where data acquisition is efficient and reliable.

References

1. Almogbil, A., Alghofaili, A., Deane, C., Leschke, T.: Digital forensic analysis of fitbit wearable technology: an investigator's guide. In: Proceedings of the 7th IEEE International Conference on Cyber Security and Cloud Computing (CSCloud), pp. 44–49. IEEE, August 2020
2. Anglano, C.: Forensic analysis of WhatsApp messenger on android smartphones. Digit. Investig. **11**(3), 201–213 (2014)
3. Astillo, P.V., Choudhary, G., Duguma, D.G., Kim, J., You, I.: TrMAps: trust management in specification-based misbehavior detection system for IMD-enabled artificial pancreas system. IEEE J. Biomed. Health Inf. (2021)
4. Azfar, A., Choo, K.-K.R., Liu, L.: Forensic taxonomy of popular android mHealth apps. arXiv preprint arXiv:1505.02905 (2015)
5. Azfar, A., Choo, K.-K.R., Liu, L.: An android communication app forensic taxonomy. J. Forensic Sci. **61**(5), 1337–1350 (2016)
6. Baggili, I., Oduro, J., Anthony, K., Breitinger, F., McGee, G.: Watch what you wear: preliminary forensic analysis of smart watches. In: Proceedings of the 10th International Conference on Availability, Reliability and Security, pp. 303–311. IEEE, August 2015
7. Caputo, D., Verderame, L., Ranieri, A., Merlo, A., Caviglione, L.: Fine-hearing google home: why silence will not protect your privacy. J. Wirel. Mob. Netw. Ubiquit. Comput. Dependable Appl. (JoWUA) **11**(1), 35–53 (2020)
8. Chen, R., Guo, J., Wang, D.-C., Tsai, J.J., Al-Hamadi, H., You, I.: Trust-based service management for mobile cloud IoT systems. IEEE Trans. Netw. Serv. Manage. **16**(1), 246–263 (2018)
9. Choudhary, G., Astillo, P.V., You, I., Yim, K., Chen, R., Cho, J.-H.: Lightweight misbehavior detection management of embedded IoT devices in medical cyber physical systems. IEEE Trans. Netw. Serv. Manage. **17**(4), 2496–2510 (2020)
10. Johnson, C., Khadka, B., Basnet, R.B., Doleck, T.: Towards detecting and classifying malicious URLs using deep learning. J. Wirel. Mob. Netw. Ubiquit. Comput. Dependable Appl. (JoWUA) **11**(4), 31–48 (2020)

11. Lee, C., Chung, M.: Digital forensic analysis on window8 style UI instant messenger applications. In: Park, J., Stojmenovic, I., Jeong, H., Yi, G. (eds.) Computer Science and its Applications. LNEE, pp. 1037–1042. Springer, Heidelberg (2015). https://doi.org/10.1007/978-3-662-45402-2_147

12. Marra, A.L., Martinelli, F., Mercaldo, F., Saracino, A., Sheikhalishahi, M.: D-BRIDEMAID: a distributed framework for collaborative and dynamic analysis of android malware. J. Wirel. Mob. Netw. Ubiquit. Comput. Dependable Appl. (JoWUA) 11(3), 1–28 (2020)

13. Mcnary, S., Hunter, A.: Wearable device data for criminal investigation. In: Wang, G., Chen, J., Yang, L.T. (eds.) SpaCCS 2018. LNCS, vol. 11342, pp. 60–71. Springer, Cham (2018). https://doi.org/10.1007/978-3-030-05345-1_5

14. Odom, N.R., Lindmar, J.M., Hirt, J., Brunty, J.: Forensic inspection of sensitive user data and artifacts from smartwatch wearable devices. J. Forensic Sci. 64(6), 1673–1686 (2019)

15. Sharma, V., You, I., Yim, K., Chen, R., Cho, J.-H.: BRIoT: behavior rule specification-based misbehavior detection for iot-embedded cyber-physical systems. IEEE Access 7, 118556–118580 (2019)

16. Shichkina, Y.A., Kataeva, G.V., Irishina, Y.A., Stanevich, E.S.: The use of mobile phones to monitor the status of patients with Parkinson's disease. J. Wirel. Mob. Netw. Ubiquit. Comput. Dependable Appl. (JoWUA) 11(2), 55–73 (2020)

17. Sihag, V., Swami, A., Vardhan, M., Singh, P.: Signature based malicious behavior detection in android. In: Chaubey, N., Parikh, S., Amin, K. (eds.) COMS2 2020. CCIS, vol. 1235, pp. 251–262. Springer, Singapore (2020). https://doi.org/10.1007/978-981-15-6648-6_20

18. Sihag, V., Vardhan, M., Singh, P.: BLADE: robust malware detection against obfuscation in android. Forensic Sci. Int.: Digit. Invest. 38, 301176 (2021)

19. Sihag, V., Vardhan, M., Singh, P.: A survey of android application and malware hardening. Comput. Sci. Rev. 39, 100365 (2021)

20. Sihag, V., Vardhan, M., Singh, P., Choudhary, G., Son, S.: De-LADY: deep learning based android malware detection using dynamic features. J. Internet Serv. Inf. Secur. (JISIS) 11(2), 34–45 (2021)

21. Sim, B.-Y., Han, D.-G.: A study on the SCA trends for application to IoT devices. J. Internet Serv. Inf. Secur. (JISIS) 10(1), 2–21 (2020)

22. Sushames, A., Edwards, A., Thompson, F., McDermott, R., Gebel, K.: Validity and reliability of Fitbit Flex for step count, moderate to vigorous physical activity and activity energy expenditure. PLoS One 11(9), e0161224 (2016)

23. Talegaon, S., Krishnan, R.: Administrative models for role based access control in android. J. Internet Serv. Inf. Secur. (JISIS) 10(3), 31–46 (2020)

24. Uduimoh, A.A., Osho, O., Ismaila, I., Shafi'i, M.A.: Forensic analysis of mobile banking applications in Nigeria. i-Manag. J. Mob. Appl. Technol. 6(1), 9 (2019)

25. Wu, F., Xu, L., Kumari, S., Li, X., Das, A.K., Shen, J.: A lightweight and anonymous RFID tag authentication protocol with cloud assistance for e-healthcare applications. J. Ambient Intell. Humaniz. Comput. 9(4), 919–930 (2018)

26. Yoon, Y.H., Karabiyik, U.: Forensic analysis of fitbit versa 2 data on android. Electronics 9(9), 1431 (2020)

27. You, I., Yim, K., Sharma, V., Choudhary, G., Chen, I.-R., Cho, J.-H.: Misbehavior detection of embedded IoT devices in medical cyber physical systems. In: Proceedings of the 2018 IEEE/ACM International Conference on Connected Health: Applications, Systems and Engineering Technologies, pp. 88–93 (2018)

Fingerprint Defender: Defense Against Browser-Based User Tracking

Deepali Moad[1], Vikas Sihag[1] , Gaurav Choudhary[2] ,
Daniel Gerbi Duguma[3] , and Ilsun You[3(✉)]

[1] Sardar Patel University of Police, Security and Criminal Justice, Jodhpur, India
{spu19csdm,vikas.sihag}@policeuniversity.ac.in
[2] Department of Applied Mathematics and Computer Science,
Technical University of Denmark (DTU), Kongens Lyngby, Denmark
gauravchoudhary7777@gmail.com
[3] Department of Information Security Engineering, Soonchunhyang University,
Asan-si, Chungcheongnam-do 31538, South Korea
danielgerbi2005@gmail.com, ilsunu@gmail.com

Abstract. It is difficult to be anonymous online with user activities always under the scanner. Multiple identifiers and their combinatories are used for user identification. While browsing, trackers keep a record of artifacts such as OS version, screen resolution, and fonts enabled. Browser fingerprinting tries to identify a user's browser uniquely, without using cookies or other stateful signatures. We propose a browser fingerprint defender tool to anonymize user browsers. It creates captures current user attributes and anonymizes them before sending a request to the server. It also gives current browser fingerprint attributes.

Keywords: Privacy · User tracking · Anonymization · Browser fingerprinting · Fingerprinting defender · Chrome extension

1 Introduction

The browser is becoming an important component of a user's experience with the internet as the web evolves and continues to be the medium of choice for providing software to users [10,23]. The systematic gathering of information about a remote computing device for the purposes of authentication is known as browser fingerprinting. A third party may obtain a "rich fingerprint" using a variety of techniques. The availability of JavaScript or other client-side scripting languages, the user-agent and accept headers, the HTML5 Canvas feature, and other variables are among them. Browser fingerprints can include data such as browser and operating system type and version, active plugins, timezone, language, screen resolution, and other active settings [6,22]. In web applications, user identity usually necessitates the use of an authentication scheme, such as providing credentials such as a username, password, or code provided by a key. Identification is also possible without clear detection using cookies or computer fingerprinting [3,19,25]. According to Panopticlick, a browser fingerprinting research page, just

© Springer Nature Singapore Pte Ltd. 2022
I. You et al. (Eds.): MobiSec 2021, CCIS 1544, pp. 236–247, 2022.
https://doi.org/10.1007/978-981-16-9576-6_17

1 in 133801.5 other browsers can have the same fingerprint as yours. Browser fingerprinting, like all other tools, maybe exploited or misused.

A digital profile can be generated based on the data collected in order to provide customized and tailored services. Many marketers, in particular, gather information about users' tastes, location, surfing habits, and so on [4,9]. by using active or passive monitoring approaches without waiting for their users' permission [4,24]. To recognize a device, websites send several queries via the browser to the underlying environment to extract different device properties. The extracted properties are then combined to create a unique id or fingerprint for the browser [5,8]. Users often are unaware of the trackers' requests and underlying reasoning since the fingerprinting mechanism is inaccessible to them. Figure 1 shows the example of fingerprint attributes that are collected by a browser to generate the fingerprint. In Upcoming solutions Various Deep learning based methods can be applicable in such scenarios [2,13,18,21].

In this paper, we propose Fingerprint Defender, a chrome browser extension to anonymize user artifacts for tracking. We have considered multiple attributes and randomize them. The organization of the paper: In Sect. 2, we discuss existing works in literature on browser tracking. In Sect. 3, we discuss browser fingerprinting followed by proposed solution in Sect. 4. Section 5 evaluates the work against existing tracking techniques and followed by conclusion in Sect. 6.

2 Related Works

A browser fingerprint is more than just a set of device-specific data [1,16]. It accurately depicts the actual component array that runs a computer. Attackers can identify potential security vulnerabilities by analyzing the content and cross-referencing the list of installed components with a database like CVE (Common Vulnerabilities and Exposures [16,20]). The first goal of a browser fingerprint is to verify a user's identity without them having to do something. At the beginning of the Network's growth, users could be easily distinguished by their machines' IP addresses [12,17].

After a survey of existing research papers, we conclude that there are many solutions for preventing fingerprinting but they all are temporary and single problem solutions and don't provide much security against advanced attacks [11, 26]. They did not work as supposed to do. The chrome browser is the most vulnerable web browser that can be used to steal our browser fingerprint. We found out a new browser known as Brave browser. It is safe and fasts than another browser according to our research. It can prevent a user from tracking. It can prevent a user from being tracked. After studying the brave browser we find a method that how we can randomizing a browser fingerprint. We create an extension that can help a user from being tracked. We created a chrome extension because as we discussed in our previous sections chrome is the most vulnerable web browser. We give it a name as "Fingerprint Defender". The extension is made for chrome browser so it is a chrome extension. This extension can change the value of the attribute that can be used to generate a fingerprint so the tracker can not generate any hash/fingerprint of the system.

To create a browser extension you must know some basic programming languages like HTML, CSS, JavaScript, etc. We use these three languages for creating our extension. First of all, we created a simple extension that can run on a browser and that can connect through a browser. Because this is the most important thing to make your extension communicate with the browser. Then we started writing code for fetching data from the browser. We can fetch many attributes such as OS information, System information, Browser information. After fetching the data we tried to display this information to the user. So we modify our code from only data fetching to displaying all the information on a user's display. After displaying all the information we finally started working on browser fingerprinting prevention. For this purpose, we thought to randomize the attributes that we fetch using our extension, but there was a problem with that. If we randomize all attributes then it will affect the browser and the browser will not work as supposed to do. So we create a list of attributes and sort the list out that which attributes can be changed and which attributes can't be changed so that this process won't affect the functionality of the browser. To randomize we change the value of attributes when our browser shares the system or browser information. For changing the value of an attribute we create a list of false values but similar to the attribute. So when the browser shares the details of our system our extension provides it the value we decided. It picked any value randomly from the list. Using this method gives us a positive result. After enabling our extension we check our browser fingerprint on many browser fingerprint check websites and they all can not detect our fingerprint. They say we have strong protection against browser fingerprinting. There are some Recent attacks on browsers as discussed below.

– **Spook.js – New side-channel attack can bypass Google Chrome's protections against Spectre-style exploits -** A newly discovered side-channel attack targeting Google Chrome can allow an attacker to overcome the web browser's security defenses to retrieve sensitive information using a Spectre-style attack.
– **Google supercharges Chrome's phishing detection mechanism -** Google says the latest version of Chrome detects phishing scams 50 times faster than its predecessor.
– **Google to bolster Chrome privacy protections with HTTPS-First Mode -** UPDATED Chrome 94 will ship with a new feature, HTTPS-First Mode, that attempts to upgrade all web page connections to HTTPS, Google has announced.

3 Browser Fingerprinting

A browser fingerprint, also known as a system fingerprint or a browser fingerprint, is data obtained for the purpose of identifying a device. Websites use browser fingerprinting to gather information about you. Scripts, which are collections of instructions that tell your browser what to do, are needed for modern website functions. This fingerprint will then be used to track you down across the internet and across various surfing sessions.

Attribute	Value
User agent ❶	Mozilla/5.0 (X11; Fedora; Linux x86_64; rv:67.0) Gecko/20100101 Firefox/67.0
Accept ❶	text/html,application/xhtml+xml,application/xml;q=0.9,*/*;q=0.8
Content encoding ❶	gzip, deflate, br
Content language ❶	en-US,en;q=0.5
List of plugins ❶	
Platform ❶	Linux x86_64
Cookies enabled ❶	yes
Do Not Track ❶	yes
Timezone ❶	-120
Screen resolution ❶	1920x1080x24
Use of local storage ❶	yes
Use of session storage ❶	yes
Canvas ❶	Cwm fjordbank glyphs vext quiz, ☺ Cwm fjordbank glyphs vext quiz, ☻
WebGL Vendor ❶	Intel Open Source Technology Center
WebGL Renderer ❶	Mesa DRI Intel(R) UHD Graphics 620 (Kabylake GT2)

Fig. 1. An example of user attributes used for browser fingerprint

Browser fingerprinting is qualified as fully stateless, unlike other authentication strategies such as cookies that rely on a unique identifier (ID) directly stored inside the browser. It does not leave any trace, as the storing of information within the browser is not necessary. Another tool that could be used to identify guests individually without focusing on standard cookies was computer fingerprinting [16].

Lou Montulli invented the concept of cookies for preserving the state of the session in the stateless HTTP protocol. Cookies have been adopted by both browser vendors and developers because of their basic design and deployment. The violation of their stateful character internet providers began using them for third-party ads and web usage monitoring, creating public discomfort [15].

This paper mainly focuses on the prevention method of browser fingerprinting. We create an extension that can prevent a user from being tracked by third parties or companies on the online platform. This extension is also used to display your system information. We collected attributes by using javascript. First, we collect the attributes then we randomize some of the attributes. After that, we check the fingerprint on various platforms and we create a comparative table before and after enabling the extension.

4   Proposed Solution

In this section, we discuss browser extension, how to create it, and the required files. In the second part, we explain how different websites gather data and how we gathered or retrieved data for our extension. In the third section, we describe what is randomisation and how we randomize the attributes that we fetched from our extension. In the fourth section, we describe the working of our chrome extension that is "Fingerprint Defender" that how it works. In the fifth and last section, we show the result of our extension. We compare different websites, before enabling the extension and after enabling the extension. We check fingerprints on 3 different websites, Panopticlick, Am I Unique, Unique Machine.

4.1   Browser Extensions

Extensions are small software programs that allow you to configure your browsing experience and add features to the browser [14]. Browser plugins are typically used to enhance a website's functionality and functions. However, they can also be used to disable unnecessary features and functions like pop-up ads and other facets of a website's core behavior that a user wants to disable. Users install plugins to their browsers to customize the appearance of the browser. They're made with web technologies like HTML, CSS, and JavaScript, among others. The extensions are zipped into an a.crx box, which the user must import and update. The Chrome online store now has a Chrome extension. Extensions are made up of a variety of materials that work together. When combined with the advanced features of JavaScript and Cascading Style Sheets, HTML5 allows developers to create feature-rich applications (CSS).

For creating our extension we required some files as listed below -

manifest.json: This is a JSON file in a website that informs the browser about the website on the user's laptop or desktop. Chrome needs a manifest in order to display the Add to Home Screen prompt. The name, logos, and other information about your website are provided by JSON to the browser. The manifest.json file includes information such as the name of your website app, the icons it should use, the start-URL it should use when it is first released, and several other specifics (Fig. 2).

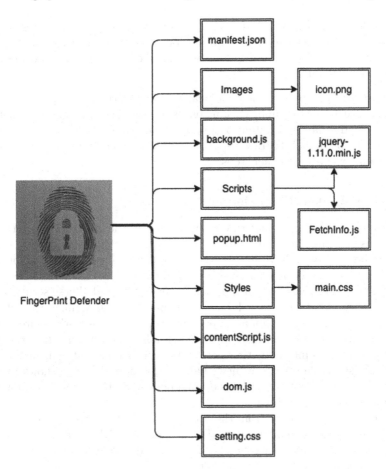

Fig. 2. Extension files

background.js: Background scripts are the most secure parts of the Chrome Extension environment when it comes to logging and connecting with the server or API. Background scripts are dependent on the plugin because as long as it is installed, the scripts can run in the background in a daemon-like manner.

Content scripts.js: Content scripts.js files are used to add functionality to a website. Extensions add more Javascript on top of that. As long as we specify them in the manifest, we can add as many extra files as we want. It's useful for communicating with a page's DOM in every way.

dom.js: dom.js is a JavaScript file that is used to randomize the attributes. DOMtegrity is a JavaScript-based platform that ensures the credibility of web pages. This source code is embedded within the "script" tag and placed first on the web page, before all other HTML tags.

fetch-info.js: fetch-info.js is a JavaScript file. This is the main file used in our extension. It is used to fetch the information from the user's system. It has one more feature we added to our extension that it can display the information of the system to the user.

popup.html: A popup is the graphical user interface that appears when we communicate with a plugin by clicking on its button. The only difference between a website and a Chrome Extension popup is that an extension popup must be tracked. The popup's HTML, CSS, JS, and images can all be described. It works in the same way as any other website.

4.2 User Artifact Collection

Since websites use scripts that run in the context of the browser, browser finger-printing is possible. APIs are built-in program features in today's web browsers that can be used by website scripts to capture data. Fingerprinting scripts seem to be identical to any other script running on a website, users have no way of knowing that their personal information is being collected. These scripts gather the information that can be used to create a "hash" or digital fingerprint. To conduct cross-site monitoring, many website owners and ad networks share browser fingerprinting capabilities. That means they follow you around the web using your online fingerprint and gather personal information about you, such as your browsing history, shopping and news habits, and more. Figure 3 shows how two websites share hashes to describe the same person. So that they can show them advertises according to them.

We extract information from the user's device using javascript in our extension. We fetched system information, IP information, URL information. We fetch the system information using "fetch-info.js" and display the information on the user device using the "popup.html" file.

4.3 Randomization

Firefox was the first major browser to solve this growing issue by introducing an anti-fingerprinting feature that allows users to disable attempts to fingerprint their browser. A couple of months later, Apple followed suit with a new solution, requiring Safari to return similar values for certain fingerprinting data points, such as fonts [7]. In order to protect the user's privacy, the Brave browser is working on a feature that will randomize its "fingerprint" any time a user visits a website.

In Fingerprint defender we create a file "dom.js". In dom.js we use Math.random(), Element.prototype, Date.prototype, function(), etc. to randomise the value. We create a list of attributes and then we replace the actual attributes with our false attributes. For example- randomising a TimeZoneOffset we created a list like- [720, 660, 600, 570, 540, 480, 420, 360, 300, 240, 210, 180, 120, 60, 0, −60, −120, −180, −210, −240, −270, −300, −330, −345, −360, −390, −420, −480, −510, −525, −540, −570, −600, −630, −660, −720, −765,

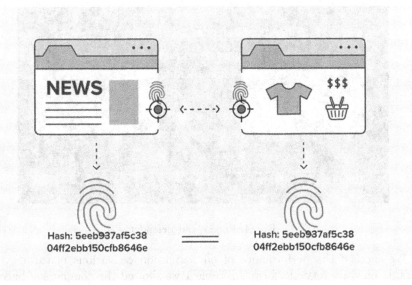

Fig. 3. Two websites sharing their hashes

−780, −840]. Every time a user visits a website the extension change the value of time zone offset. As like this we randomise the other attribute to prevent from fingerprinting.

Fingerprint Defender is a chrome extension. We made this extension to stop these kinds of frauds or activities. Tracker or attacker basically finds you by calculating your browser fingerprint. This extension changes some values of attributes that the attacker collects from the user device. It can protect your anonymity online. The scrips that are used in this extension is worked as a defender of your system. This extension is work only on chrome browser because we made it for chrome browser only. Fingerprinting Defender has a privacy feature that makes it harder for sites to track you while you browse. It randomizes and hides some attribute so that your fingerprint can not be generated.

Fingerprint Defender is used to checking your system information. It provides the details of your system as Architecture, Model, Processor, Features, Free Memory, Total Memory. Also IP Information such as IP, Latitude, Longitude, City, Region, Country, Zip, and ISP. The URL Information as Active Tab, IP, Latitude, Longitude, City, Country, Region, Zip, and ISP.

5   Result and Analysis

Online privacy is a spectrum: some sites collect and hold more information about you than others. When you're online, online privacy, also called internet privacy or digital privacy, refers to how much of your health, financial, and browsing information is kept confidential. This has become a growing concern (Fig. 4).

Fig. 4. Fingerprint defender

We checked the performance of our extension on various platforms. It is working fine on every platform. In Table 1 we showed the comparison between Panopticlick[1], AmIUnique[2] and UniqueMachine[3] websites. We checked the result before enabling the extension and after enabling the extension. We put the result in table1. Table 1 describes the results that we get on different platforms. The table shows a list of attributes and on which platform what attribute is changed, same or randomized. After getting these results we can say the extension is randomizing user attributes and thus failing user tracking methods.

Table 1. Result after enable the extension on different websites

Attributes	Panopticlick	AmIUnique	UniqueMachine
USER AGENT	Same	Same	Same
HTTP ACCEPT HEADERS	Same	Same	NA
BROWSER PLUGIN DETAILS	Randomized	NA	Null
TIME ZONE OFFSET	Changed	NA	NA
TIME ZONE	Same	NA	Changed
SCREEN SIZE AND COLOR DEPTH	Changed	NA	Changed
SYSTEM FONTS	Randomized	NA	Changed
HASH OF CANVAS FINGERPRINT	Randomized	NA	Changed
HASH OF WEBGL FINGERPRINT	Randomized	NA	NA
WEBGL VENDOR and RENDERER	Changed	NA	Same
LANGUAGE	Same	Same	Same
PLATFORM	Changed	NA	NA
AUDIOCONTEXT FINGERPRINT	Randomized	NA	Changed
HARDWARE CONCURRENCY	Same	NA	NA
DEVICE MEMORY (GB)	Same	NA	NA

---

[1] https://panopticlick.eff.org/.

[2] https://amiunique.org/.

[3] https://uniquemachine.org/.

6   Conclusion

The rising threat of browser fingerprinting to privacy inspired the research presented in this paper. We looked at previous research on browser fingerprinting. Browser fingerprinting, we found, posed a bigger risk of privacy than cookie tracking since users have no direct control over it. We have also seen that it's being utilized more and more for online user monitoring, even when there's no persistent IP address or cookie. Fingerprint Defender is a free browser plugin that identifies and, if desired, prevents data transfers that are likely to be used for browser fingerprinting. The extension's major goal was to make browser users aware of the widespread usage of browser fingerprinting and to give them some control over it.

Nothing is free in this online or digital world, whether it's installing software, using a company's "free" email service (like Gmail), or using social media site. Even visiting a website entails exchanging personal information. Over the last few years, browser fingerprinting is increasing day by day. Every person in this world is connected with a network and using one or more devices. Users can be classified differently by website creators on occasion. The device has many specifications. When a user visits a website then the browser shares the device information with the server. That server can take advantage of the information. They have a variety of motivations for doing so. Some companies want to classify users for analytic purposes, such as to see how many other people have visited or read a particular page on a website. If a website is able to recognize a visitor personally, advertisements targeted to that person may be presented. For taking device information web server used cookies earlier. But after some time people come to know about it. They were aware of this so users tried to block cookies from their web browser. So that tracker can not get their information. After that, the attacker found a new technology that is known as browser fingerprinting. Browser fingerprinting is a method that can't be stopped by the user because it does not save anything on that system. It only steals some information from that system and generates or calculates a hash without the knowledge of the user. Many methods can prevent you from browser fingerprint but partially they can not prevent you fully. After reading and studying browser fingerprinting we created an extension as discussed in the paper. We hope that the approach we've covered will keep you safe from web browser fingerprinting.

References

1. Al-Fannah, N.M., Mitchell, C.: Too little too late: can we control browser fingerprinting? J. Intellect. Capit. (2020)
2. Bae, D., Ha, J.: Performance metric for differential deep learning analysis. J. Internet Serv. Inf. Secur. (JISIS) 11(2), 22–33 (2021)
3. Blakemore, C., Redol, J., Correia, M.: Fingerprinting for web applications: from devices to related groups. In: 2016 IEEE Trustcom/BigDataSE/ISPA, pp. 144–151. IEEE (2016)

4. Boda, K., Földes, Á.M., Gulyás, G.G., Imre, S.: User tracking on the web via cross-browser fingerprinting. In: Laud, P. (ed.) NordSec 2011. LNCS, vol. 7161, pp. 31–46. Springer, Heidelberg (2012). https://doi.org/10.1007/978-3-642-29615-4_4

5. Caputo, D., Verderame, L., Ranieri, A., Merlo, A., Caviglione, L.: Fine-hearing google home: why silence will not protect your privacy. J. Wirel. Mob. Netw. Ubiquit. Comput. Dependable Appl. (JoWUA) **11**(1), 35–53 (2020)

6. Chen, R., Guo, J., Wang, D.-C., Tsai, J.J., Al-Hamadi, H., You, I.: Trust-based service management for mobile cloud IoT systems. IEEE Trans. Netw. Serv. Manage. **16**(1), 246–263 (2018)

7. Cimpanu, C.: Brave to generate random browser fingerprints to preserve user privacy, March 2020

8. Eckersley, P.: How unique is your web browser? In: Atallah, M.J., Hopper, N.J. (eds.) PETS 2010. LNCS, vol. 6205, pp. 1–18. Springer, Heidelberg (2010). https://doi.org/10.1007/978-3-642-14527-8_1

9. FaizKhademi, A., Zulkernine, M., Weldemariam, K.: FPGuard: detection and prevention of browser fingerprinting. In: Samarati, P. (ed.) DBSec 2015. LNCS, vol. 9149, pp. 293–308. Springer, Cham (2015). https://doi.org/10.1007/978-3-319-20810-7_21

10. Gómez-Boix, A., Laperdrix, P., Baudry, B.: Hiding in the crowd: an analysis of the effectiveness of browser fingerprinting at large scale. In: Proceedings of the 2018 World Wide Web Conference, pp. 309–318 (2018)

11. Greitzer, F.L., Purl, J., Sticha, P.J., Yu, M.C., Lee, J.: Use of expert judgments to inform Bayesian models of insider threat risk. J. Wirel. Mob. Netw. Ubiquit. Comput. Dependable Appl. (JoWUA) **12**(2), 3–47 (2021)

12. Gulyás, G., Schulcz, R., Imre, S.: Comprehensive analysis of web privacy and anonymous web browsers: are next generation services based on collaborative filtering? In: Joint SPACE and TIME International Workshops. Citeseer (2008)

13. Iqbal, U., Englehardt, S., Shafiq, Z.: Fingerprinting the fingerprinters: learning to detect browser fingerprinting behaviors. In: 2021 IEEE Symposium on Security and Privacy (SP), pp. 1143–1161. IEEE (2021)

14. Johnson, C., Khadka, B., Basnet, R.B., Doleck, T.: Towards detecting and classifying malicious URLs using deep learning. J. Wirel. Mob. Netw. Ubiquit. Comput. Dependable Appl. (JoWUA) **11**(4), 31–48 (2020)

15. Kaur, N., Azam, S., Kannoorpatti, K., Yeo, K.C., Shanmugam, B.: Browser fingerprinting as user tracking technology. In: 2017 11th International Conference on Intelligent Systems and Control (ISCO), pp. 103–111. IEEE (2017)

16. Laperdrix, P., Bielova, N., Baudry, B., Avoine, G.: Browser fingerprinting: a survey. ACM Trans. Web (TWEB) **14**(2), 1–33 (2020)

17. Marra, A.L., Martinelli, F., Mercaldo, F., Saracino, A., Sheikhalishahi, M.: D-BRIDEMAID: a distributed framework for collaborative and dynamic analysis of android malware. J. Wirel. Mob. Netw. Ubiquit. Comput. Dependable Appl. (JoWUA) **11**(3), 1–28 (2020)

18. Sharma, V., You, I., Kul, G.: Socializing drones for inter-service operability in ultra-dense wireless networks using blockchain. In: Proceedings of the 2017 International Workshop on Managing Insider Security Threats, pp. 81–84 (2017)

19. Sharma, V., You, I., Yim, K., Chen, R., Cho, J.-H.: BRIoT: behavior rule specification-based misbehavior detection for IoT-embedded cyber-physical systems. IEEE Access **7**, 118556–118580 (2019)

20. Shichkina, Y.A., Kataeva, G.V., Irishina, Y.A., Stanevich, E.S.: The use of mobile phones to monitor the status of patients with Parkinson's disease. J. Wirel. Mob. Netw. Ubiquit. Comput. Dependable Appl. (JoWUA) **11**(2), 55–73 (2020)

21. Sihag, V., Vardhan, M., Singh, P., Choudhary, G., Son, S.: De-LADY: deep learning based android malware detection using dynamic features. J. Internet Serv. Inf. Secur. (JISIS) **11**(2), 34–45 (2021)

22. Talegaon, S., Krishnan, R.: Administrative models for role based access control in android. J. Internet Serv. Inf. Secur. (JISIS) **10**(3), 31–46 (2020)

23. Trickel, E., Starov, O., Kapravelos, A., Nikiforakis, N., Doupé, A.: Everyone is different: client-side diversification for defending against extension fingerprinting. In: 28th {USENIX} Security Symposium ({USENIX} Security 19), pp. 1679–1696 (2019)

24. Unger, T., Mulazzani, M., Frühwirt, D., Huber, M., Schrittwieser, S., Weippl, E.: SHPF: enhancing HTTP (S) session security with browser fingerprinting. In: 2013 International Conference on Availability, Reliability and Security, pp. 255–261. IEEE (2013)

25. Upathilake, R., Li, Y., Matrawy, A.: A classification of web browser fingerprinting techniques. In: 2015 7th International Conference on New Technologies, Mobility and Security (NTMS), pp. 1–5. IEEE (2015)

26. Walls, A., Agrafiotis, I.: A Bayesian approach to insider threat detection. J. Wirel. Mob. Netw. Ubiquit. Comput. Dependable Appl. (JoWUA) **12**(2), 48–84 (2021)

Detection of Business Email Compromise Attacks with Writing Style Analysis

Alisa Vorobeva[1][(✉)], Guldar Khisaeva[1], Danil Zakoldaev[1], and Igor Kotenko[2]

[1] ITMO University, Kronverksky pr. 49, St. Petersburg, Russia
vorobeva@itmo.ru
[2] St. Petersburg Federal Research Center of the Russian Academy of Sciences (SPC RAS), St. Petersburg, Russia
http://cit.ifmo.ru

Abstract. Phishing scams have long been used to obtain sensitive information via email. Recently, scammers have increasingly been using spear-phishing and targeting corporate employees, this type of attack is called Business Email Compromise (BEC-attacks). BEC-attacks problem is highly relevant to mobile networks, as mobile users are much more vulnerable to such types of attacks than regular users. The main methods of detecting BEC-attacks are considered and their comparative analysis is made. It is demonstrated that the most promising approach for detecting BEC-attacks is a complex analysis of email headers, content analysis, and authors writing-style analysis with machine learning algorithms. BEC-attacks detection method is proposed based on the above-mentioned analysis and its decomposed functional model is presented. A feature space includes writing-style features (words 3-grams); day of the week and time of sending the email; email's urgency features; email headers features. To evaluate the BEC-attacks detection accuracy, the experiments on datasets, containing emails in Russian and English, were carried out. The experiments showed that the best accuracy is achieved with word n-grams and LSVC with a feature scaling method for emails in Russian and English.

Keywords: Business email compromise · Spear phishing · Machine learning · Writing-style analysis

1 Introduction

Phishing scams and attacks aim to obtain confidential information via email. Nowadays, scammers (in this article 'scammers', 'attackers', and 'hackers' are understood as synonyms) use spear-phishing more often and target it on the corporate user category. According to the Symantec report, the number of such attacks increases continuously every year [1]. Recently, directed phishing email

The research is supported by the grant of RSF 21-71-20078 in SPC RAS.

I. You et al. (Eds.): MobiSec 2021, CCIS 1544, pp. 248–262, 2022.
https://doi.org/10.1007/978-981-16-9576-6_18

attacks on employees of enterprises, which are called 'Business Email Compromise' (BEC) by the FBI, have become a substantial security threat. BEC scammers also have started to realize attacks utilizing SMS messaging to direct their targets [2].

According to the FBI, different companies have lost $ 12 billion after BEC-attacks since 2013 [3]. For example, in August 2019, the subsidiary company of the Toyota GROUP lost $ 37 million [4]. Well-known companies such as Facebook and Google were also reported among victims of such attacks. In 2020 FBI reported that COVID-19-themed BEC-attacks and scams grow [5,6].

BEC-attacks are the group of email service attacks when the attacker impersonates himself or herself as the company employee (for instance, as the Chief Executive Officer, the Human Resources Manager, or the Finance Manager) and creates a personal email for the victim. Classically, the purpose of this email is to fraudulently force the employee to transfer the funds to the hacker's accounts, to send confidential information, or to follow the phishing link to pass the credentials to the hacker.

BEC-attacks lead to much greater direct financial losses than other common cyber-attacks, including ransomware attacks [7]. The number of BEC incidents is expected to increase in the future.

Most of the email service security systems are ineffective at BEC-attacks detection. When analyzing an incoming email, the security systems commonly use the attributes of two types: Malicious and bulk.

- Malicious, which are the attachments with the malware or the links to the compromised website or the emails sent from the low reputation domain [8–10].
- Bulk, when a single-format email is sent to a large number of recipients. In this case, the parameters of the malicious emails are the same message texts, the same sender's email address, and the same duplicated URL in the email text.

However, BEC-attacks provide emails that in most cases contain no such specified attributes. The reason is that these emails are often sent from legitimate accounts adapted for a particular recipient without any suspicious links. BEC-attacks are highly rare compared to the total number of phishing attacks, and this fact significantly affects the effectiveness of BEC-attack detection systems under development.

None of the previous research provides methods for the BEC-attacks detection in Russian-language emails. Also, there are no studies on the BEC-attacks detection based on the analysis of the author's writing style of emails in Russian.

For BEC-attacks detection in emails in Russian and English, we propose to use the analysis of the author's writing style in combination with the use of machine learning methods to detect the substitution of the author. The proposed method combines several approaches: email service headers analysis, email text content analysis for urgency detection, email text style analysis.

2   Related Work

2.1   Previous Research

The increasing threat of BEC-attacks is widely known and is described in many reports from IT companies, governments, and intelligence services. However, there is a lack of current scientific research in the field of BEC-attack detection.

Generally, researchers today face limited access to real and valid email datasets. In this regard, they have to use small or synthetic datasets.

The analysis of related works allowed us to identify the following main groups of protection methods against BEC-attacks: organizational and managerial measures, email service header analysis, content analysis, security tools used for the credentials compromising prevention, email text style analysis.

In the majority of companies, the protection method against attacks is to apply organizational and managerial measures. These include the clear prescribing of the financial transfer procedures and its implementation, monitoring and mandatory confirmation of requests received by email. Other security measures are to involve email address management and control (for example, deleting unused and outdated email accounts), to require periodic password change or two-factor authentication usage. The limitation for this group of methods is a low reliability as the staff often violate the additional restrictions. In [11] is studied the users' response to perceived phishing threat and the relationship to their coping appraisal, it was found that perceived detection threat negatively influenced detection efficacy and positively influenced anxiety. Moreover, the duration of the email processing increases due to the formal activity. The texts of BEC-emails usually require the urgent resolution of some issues. The consequences of these issues are presented as rather serious, which forces employees to act quickly without following the determined procedures.

Some systems analyze email service headers. These methods include the collation of the sender's email address and the company domain name, as well as the comparison of the previous email addresses from the same sender. The statistics of the received emails from particular users is collected. The company's blacklist is checked for the specified sender address. This analysis allows detecting an attempt of a similar email address registering or abnormal time email sending. However, the use of only these methods does not guarantee BEC-attacks detection since the most of attacks are committed by email service compromising and further imitating of the writing style and the behavioral characteristics of the email address owner.

The context analyzers are implemented into the email security systems to detect the BEC-attacks. One of the main features of the BEC-attacks is the use of words and expressions in the email text and the title that expresses the need to urgently perform actions related to the finances. In this regard, the text and the title are analyzed to identify any signs of urgency, the presence of financial details, and other typical attributes.

Only a small part of the systems analyzes the style of the email text to identify the authorship by the methods of the linguistic identification. Each person has his or her text writing style, which contains the set of the most used words, grammatical constructions, and other features, that make the texts unique. In the case of BEC-attacks, the author of the scam email is another person, so the author's style differs from the text writing style of the owner of the compromised account. Thus, the comparison of the style of a new incoming message with the previous ones allows identifying the sender's substitution.

The following is an overview of the key related works on targeted phishing detection. However, only a few of them are specifically related to BEC-attacks.

In [12], the Email Profiler system was developed. The key idea of this work is to build the author's behavioral model based on incoming emails through the email metadata and the stylometric information analysis to detect targeted phishing. Twenty mailboxes were used to train the system. However, the authors did not point out the exact rate of the threat detection accuracy, indicating an approximate value of 0.98.

In [13], the Identity Manager system was created. It simulates employee behavior and detects anomalies in outgoing emails to prevent employee credentials leakage. If an anomaly is detected, the system prompts the user to reauthenticate using the two-factor authentication. The method suffers from a relatively high level of false-positive rates (0.01–0.08).

The paper [14] describes the model that can detect emails where the recipient's domain is forged. The model used the dataset of 92 mailboxes. The authors base their model on the historical patterns of the senders' correspondence. However, this method is unable to detect other types of BEC-attacks. The emails with the domain substitution are a small part of the total number of the incoming ones as such emails are usually stopped by the traditional built-in spam filters.

The DAS system [15] uses machine learning (ML) methods to detect the fact of account compromising. SMTP, NIDS, and LDAP logs data are analyzed. However, this method cannot detect attacks in emails containing only plain text. Also, the study is based on the dataset from only one company with 19 as the total number of known attacks.

In [16], the BEC-Guard system was developed. It is supposed to detect BEC-attacks in real-time. The system uses two classifiers: the service headers analysis and the contextual search in the email text. The large set of data received from Barracuda Networks users was used for training. This system analyzes data only in English. Unlike BEC-Guard, in this work, we propose an approach that allows analyzing emails both in English and Russian.

The Trend Micro expert system [17] implements the complex protection for the email service using artificial intelligence and ML. The detection of the BEC-attacks involves three stages: sender verification, text content analysis, and text style analysis. More than seven thousand email characteristics are used for text style analysis. However, this system does not support Russian.

The Kurematsua and co-authors' research [18] shows the email text author identification based on ML. The developed system is based on spam filtering methods. Unlike traditional systems, less than 100 first words of the email are used for the analysis.

In [19], probable components are investigated to evaluate the possibility for the BEC-attacks detection. The method was developed by cybersecurity experts as a part of the Delphi method. According to the authors of the study, the understanding of the human aspects affecting the detection of BEC-attacks can help significantly reduce the risk of large financial losses for any company.

All the research on the detection of targeted phishing focuses on two main issues: the search for an effective ML method and the formation of the feature space that has the greatest distinguishing ability.

The majority of analyzed related works uses the following ML methods: Support Vector Machine (SVM), Kernel Density Estimation (KDE), Gaussian Mixture Models (GMM), k Nearest Neighbor (KNN), Random Forest (RF), Logistic Regression (LR), Decision Tree (DT), Naive Bayes classifier (NB).

The most promising way of protecting against the BEC-attacks is to analyze the author's email style in combination with the use of ML methods to detect the author substitution. For the messages in English, these methods show an accuracy of up to 0.982.

2.2   Methods of the Writing-Style Analyses

Nowadays, there is much research related to the analysis of the text style for the author identification in various languages.

In [20] and [21], the methods for user identification based on the email analysis are investigated. The attributes divided into the following categories are used for the identification: the characteristics of the entire text, the frequency characteristics of the functional words, the word length distribution density, and the emails specific characteristics. The authors concluded that the analysis of the email-specific characteristics increases the accuracy of the sender identification [22].

The authors of [23] investigate the possibility of the stylometry usage for the authorship establishment among the users of various hacker Internet resources. The emails where the author imitates someone else's writing style are examined. The authors of another work studied the duplicate accounts that included the texts in English, German, and Russian [24]. It is shown that the use of a hybrid method, which combines the stylometry and the specifics of the email or the forum message, increases the accuracy of identification.

In [25], the authors used online texts from various sources like Enron emails, eBay comments, Java forums, and CyberWatch chats as datasets. The research reveals that with the increase in the authors' number in a dataset the accuracy of the SVM method used for the authorship identification decreases. A similar idea is expressed in [26] and it proves that as the number of users increases, the accuracy of the identification reduces.

The author of [27] investigates the majority of the existing techniques for author identification. In [28] the author explains that it is possible to use the n-grams based on Markov chains to solve the problem of author identification.

In [29], the method of the linguistic identification of Internet users by analyzing short electronic messages is proposed. The key idea of this work is to dynamically calculate the number of the most informative features for each set of users. This approach increases the identification accuracy by an average of 0.04 and is effective for small datasets.

In [30], the identification accuracy of 0.98 was achieved. The proposed method is based on the SVM and the following features: the frequency of the Russian letters and the punctuation marks, the most frequent trigrams of characters, and the most frequent words.

In [31], the methodology of identification based on the complex application of the RF method and the Relief-f method (the method of informative features selection) is proposed. The methodology allows identifying the Internet user by analyzing electronic text messages up to 5000 characters long (in conditions of the limited text length and the unbalanced training sample) with the accuracy of 0.79 for a small number of texts, and 0.805 for a normal number of texts. The best accuracy rate is achieved when the RF method is used. The final average accuracy is 0.8 which is about 0.33 higher than the existing methods of short text messages author identification in Russian.

In [32], the cross-site linguistic identification of online resources users based on the short electronic messages received from several sources (sites, online communication tools) was studied. The ability to identify the user of one Internet resource by his/her messages in another Internet resource is considered. The n-grams of words and characters are used as the attributes. The results of experiments showed that the identification accuracy is 0.82 when the classifier was trained on mixed data and 0.74 when the classifier is trained on the data from different sources. It is concluded that it is possible to form a universal feature space for messages received from various sources, and such a space provides a sufficient accuracy rate of the linguistic identification.

Thus, the following promising directions can be singled out for the application to the problem of BEC-attacks detection in emails in Russian among the methods of linguistic identification: to use one of the following methods of ML: RF, SVM, LR, NN and with the feature space that includes ngrams.

It is necessary to perform experiments to verify that writing-style analysis can improve BEC-attacks detection accuracy and define what ML method and what feature set could be used to achieve the best results.

3 Business Email Compromise Attacks Identifying Approach for Texts in Russian

3.1 Feature Set

Each person has his or her writing style. For example, some people use certain functional words (such as 'however', 'although', etc.) more often than others. Also, the style can be expressed in the way of the dates writing and the construction of the sentences.

The attacker can analyze the correspondence and try to imitate the victim's writing style - to perform a so-called spoofing attack based on impersonalization. It is considered to use the features, which are introduced into the text subconsciously, in the methods of linguistic identification. It is quite difficult for the attacker to take all the features inherent to the author of the victim's emails into consideration. Therefore, for example, the email signature cannot be used as the feature of the BEC-attack.

To detect BEC-attacks in emails in Russian and English, it is proposed to use the analysis of the email author's style in combination with the use of ML methods to detect the substitution of the author. The proposed method combines several approaches: email service headers analysis, email text content analysis for urgency detection, email text style analysis.

Thus, we suggest using the following feature space:

- Email linguistic features (character and words ngrams) – F_{lingua}.
- The day of the week and the time of email sending. It is proved that the users tend to send emails or to post publications at a certain time relative to the day of the week – F_{time}.
- Urgency features – F_{urg}. It is the list of the world and phrases determining the urgency ('urgent', 'today', 'immediately', 'right now').
- Email service headers features – $F_{headers}$. This set includes the sender and recipient fields, the subject, and other additional fields for the service headers.

Each user can be represented as the set of his or her emails $u_a = E_a = \{e_{a1}, ..., e_{al}\}$, where E_a is the set of emails for the email address u_a, l – is the number of emails in u_a.

In turn, each email can be represented as $e_{aj} = (F_{lingua}, F_{time}, F_{urg}, F_{headers}) = (f_{aj_1}, ..., f_{aj_n})$, where $e_{aj} \in E_a$, f – is a specific feature, n – is the number of features.

Thus, each user is the set of the vector representations of his emails $u_a = E_a = <(f_{a11}, ..., f_{a1n}), ..., (f_{al1}, ..., f_{aln})>$.

3.2   BEC-Attack Detection Method

The proposed method is based on the three stages: collecting historical data, training and BEC-attack detection.

Collecting historical data stage includes obtaining the historical set of emails. Based on the received data, user profiles u_a are formed and shown as the vector representations of his or her emails. The recommended amount of emails per one user is 5.

At the training stage, the models are trained based on the user profiles u_a.

At BEC-attack detection stage a new incoming message ($Email_x$) is vectorized and then sent to the system modules as the input. After this, the email service headers are analyzed, including the checking of the addresses included in the allowed user list, the absence of the anomalies in sending time, the Levenshtein distance is determined to detect the attempts to imitate the sender.

Then, the text and the subject of the email are checked for the urgency features. The trained models are used to check whether the sender's writing styles match the one he or she claims to be.

The flowchart of the proposed method is shown in Fig. 1.

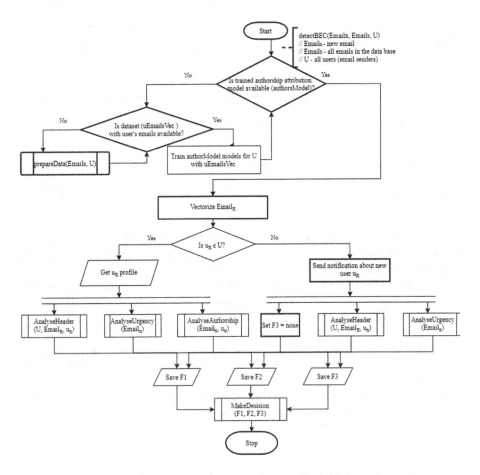

Fig. 1. Flowchart of the proposed method

The email that is recognized as legal as the result of the detection process is added to the historical set. Then, the retraining is performed based on the new data.

AnalyseHeaders Stage: From and Reply-To headers of the $Email_x$ are analyzed. If the entries do not match, the method classifies the message as suspicious.

Then, if $Email_x$ is sent by the internal user it is checked for anomalies in time and day of sending. For the external user $Email_x$ is checked if the sender is in the list of blocked users (blocked_list).

If the sender's email address (u_x) is not in U, then it is proposed to find edit distance (d) between the u_x and all addresses in the list of legal users (legal_list). If distance d exceeds the threshold value of α, then it is considered that an attempt to forge a legal address is detected. The u_x is added to the blocked_list, and the method classifies $Email_x$ as suspicious. If the distance d is less than α, then the method returns $F1 = 0.5$.

The process returns the following: $F1 = 1$, if no violations were found in headers, $F1 = 0$. If violations were found in headers and email should be marked as suspicious, $F1 = 0.5$ if the sender of the email is not in the known users' list and most of the further analyses' procedures are not possible to conduct.

AnalyseUrgency Stage: The next step is to analyze the email's text and subject to detect if it contains urgent features (F_{urg}). The process returns $F2 = 1$ if there are signs of urgency in the letter. Otherwise, $F2 = 0$ is returned.

AnalyseAuthorship Stage: At this stage, it is detected if there are changes in the author's writing style of the user u_x. $Email_x$ body is vectorized in $Features_x$ (F_{lingua}), the model of the user u_x is loaded.

The probability (ρ) of u_x is the author of $Email_x$ is estimated based on the previous emails of u_x. At this stage, the model trained with ML methods is used to detect alterations in the author's writing style.

If $\rho \geq \beta_1$, it is assumed that ux is the real author of $Email_x$ ($F3$ is set to 1). If $\beta_1 < \rho < \beta_2$, an insufficient degree of coincidence of the text styles is detected ($F3 = 0.5$). Otherwise, it is considered that the authorship of the letter is not confirmed and $F3$ is set to 0.

The decision-making process shown in Fig. 2 is based on the results obtained during the above three stages.

The method notifies email's recipient about a detected BEC-attack in one of the following conditions:

- Violations were found in the email headers.
- The writing style of the email differs from previous emails of the sender and the authorship is not confirmed.
- The email was sent by a new sender, and signs of urgency were found in the text.
- The writing style of the email slightly differs from previous emails of the sender and signs of urgency were found in the text. If BEC-attack is detected, the email is placed in the quarantine folder and the system sends the notification to the administrator. Otherwise, the email is added to the database and the authorship model is retrained.

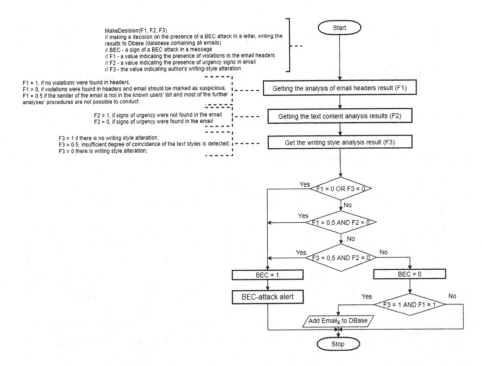

Fig. 2. Flowchart of making decision stage for deciding on the presence of a BEC-attack in an email

4   Experiments and Results

4.1   Text Corpus and Datasets

To study the possibility of BEC-attacks detection with writing style analysis, we have performed a series of experiments.

In experiments, we used the dataset, which contains emails in Russian and English. Some of the emails contain signs of urgency. For each user, there are at least two emails. The minimum text length of the email is 500 characters.

The dataset contains the following fields (including headers of emails): From: information about the sender; To: recipient email address; Cc: recipients of the copy of the email; Date: the date the email was sent; Subject: email subject; Text: email body.

To emulate the BEC-attacks in the dataset, for each sender several emails of another authorship were added and from one to two characters were replaced in the sender's email address and the message sending time was changed to imitate spoofed and lookalike sender.

The dataset contains emails of two classes: originally written by the senders and imitating the sender's writing style.

As a result, a dataset of 2308 email messages of 50 authors in Russian and English was formed. Dataset contains from 2 to 232 emails for each user, for most authors there are less than 25 letters. All email texts are of variable length.

The minimum email's text length is 23 characters, the maximum is 23936, the average length is 1943 characters. The text has not been corrected, the vocabulary, spelling, and punctuation are original. In experiments, 70% of data was used for training, and 30% for tests.

4.2   Experiments Description

The purpose of the experiments is to find an optimal ML method that is accurate for BEC-attacks detection based on writing style analysis for emails in English and Russian.

The accuracy (A) of BEC-attack detection refers to the proportion of the detected emails containing the targeted phishing attacks (BEC-attacks). The BEC-attack detection accuracy with the following ML methods was evaluated: LR, KNN, DT (CART), SVM, NB, RF, Linear discriminant analysis (LDA), Linear support vector machine (LSVC), Multilayer perceptron (MLP), Bagging (BG), Extra trees (ET), AdaBoost (AB), Gradient boosting (GB).

Experimental results of the above ML methods and words and of characters n-grams are displayed in Fig. 3a (for English) and in Fig. 3b (for Russian).

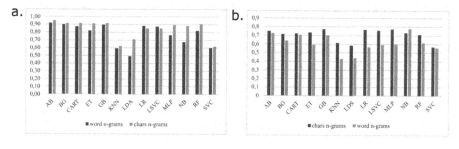

Fig. 3. Accuracy of BEC-attacks detection with selected ML methods and character and word N-grams for emails in English and Russian

Several feature scaling methods were also studied:

- The standardization method normalizes the data so that the column mean is 0 and the standard deviation is 1.
- The scaling method by default normalizes data in the range [0; 1].
- The normalization method by default normalizes concerning the Euclidean length of the feature vector.

Results are displayed in Fig. 4 (for English) and in Fig. 5 (for Russian).

Experiments demonstrated that the KNN, LDA, and SVM show rather low accuracy with any method of features scaling both with characters and words n-grams. Accuracy with words n-grams is higher than with characters n-grams.

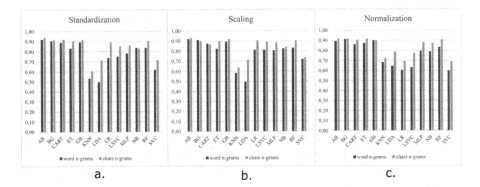

Fig. 4. Accuracy of BEC-attacks detection with selected ML methods and feature scaling methods with character and word n-grams for emails in English

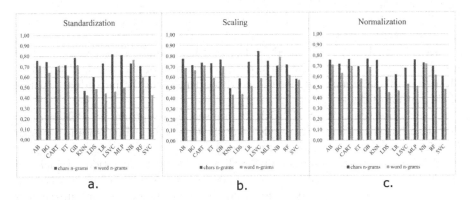

Fig. 5. Accuracy of BEC-attacks detection with selected ML methods and feature scaling methods with character and word n-grams for emails in Russian

As a result of the experimental studies, we have selected the following most-promising ML methods, which showed the highest accuracy both when using n-grams of words and n-grams of characters for the emails English:

- GB with features standardization,
- GB with features standardization,
- DT with features standardization,
- MLP with features scaling.

The highest accuracy for a dataset in Russian is achieved with LSVC with feature scaling ($A = 0.84$), but for emails in English accuracy is comparable ($A = 0.89$).

For emails in English the best accuracy is 0.95, and it is achieved with the AB without preliminary data preparation. This approach allows achieving 0.75 accuracy for the dataset in Russian.

The purpose of the work was to find an optimal ML method that is accurate for both languages. The analysis of the experimental results allowed us to choose characters n-gram and LSVC with feature scaling as optimal for BEC-attacks detection based on writing style analysis for emails in English and Russian.

5   Conclusion

Several classification methods (LR, LDA, KNN, CART, NB, SVM, MLP, RF, etc.) and feature scaling methods were selected in the theoretical study as the most promising for BEC-attacks detection based on the author's writing style analysis.

A series of experiments were performed to evaluate the accuracy of these methods on dataset containing 2308 email messages of 50 authors in Russian and in English.

The experiments showed that LSVC with feature scaling has better performance than other approaches.

To detect BEC-attacks based on the text style analysis, it is suggested to use the largest number of the features, since the use of the standard template phrases in official emails implies the need to identify all the individual features of the author of the email.

It was observed that LSVC with feature scaling is optimal for BEC-attacks detection based on the writing style analysis for emails in English and Russian (the features used were characters n-grams).

We have proposed the method for the BEC-attacks detection. It includes three main stages: the analysis of the urgency features inherent to this type of attack, the service headers, and the text analysis with LSVC with feature scaling to detect author's writing style alterations.

Future research will be focused on the study the influence of n-grams size on the BEC-attacks detection accuracy and methods of lookalike sender's email address detection in combination with domain generation algorithm detection techniques and domain registration information.

BEC-attacks detection is a challenging task as the volume of user-generated information increases rapidly. Our further studies also will be concentrated on technologies of Big Data analysis with Hadoop and Spark for high volumes of emails [33,34]. Also approaches of efficient and parallelized data mining using in mobile cloud systems will beė studied [35].

References

1. Symantec Corporation, Internet security threat report. https://docs.broadcom. com/docs/istr-21-2016-en. Accessed 21 July 2021
2. Business email compromise (BEC) attacks moving to mobile. http://www. wpcentral.com/ie9-windows-phone-7-adobe-flash-demos-and-development- videos. Accessed 21 July 2021

3. Encyclopedia by Kaspersky, Business email compromise (BEC-SCAM). https://encyclopedia.kaspersky.ru/glossary/bec. Accessed 21 July 2021

4. Discovery of European subsidiary being subject of fraud. https://www.toyota-boshoku.com/global/content/wp-content/uploads/190906e.pdf. Accessed 21 July 2021

5. FBI Warns Companies to Be Vigilant as COVID-19-Themed BEC Scams Continue to Grow. https://www.jdsupra.com/legalnews/fbi-warns-companies-to-be-vigilant-as-53073. Accessed 21 July 2021

6. Kitana, A., Traore, I., Woungang, I.: Towards an epidemic SMS-based cellular botnet. J. Internet Serv. Inf. Secur. **10**(4), 38–58 (2020)

7. Huang, D.Y., et al.: Tracking ransomware end-to-end. In: 2018 IEEE Symposium on Security and Privacy (SP), pp. 618–631. IEEE (2018)

8. Whittaker, C., Ryner, B., Nazif, M.: Large-scale automatic classification of phishing pages (2010)

9. Willems, C., Holz, T., Freiling, F.: Toward automated dynamic malware analysis using CWSandbox. IEEE Secur. Priv. **5**(2), 32–39 (2007)

10. Johnson, C., Khadka, B., Basnet, R.B., Doleck, T.: Towards detecting and classifying malicious URLs using deep learning. J. Wirel. Mob. Netw. Ubiquit. Comput. Dependable Appl. **11**(4), 31–48 (2020)

11. Lemay, D.J., Basnet, R.B., Doleck, T.: Examining the relationship between threat and coping appraisal in phishing detection among college students. J. Internet Serv. Inf. Secur. **10**(1), 38–49 (2020)

12. Duman, S., Kalkan-Cakmakci, K., Egele, M., Robertson, W., Kirda, E.: Email-profiler: spearphishing filtering with header and stylometric features of emails. In: 2016 IEEE 40th Annual Computer Software and Applications Conference (COMPSAC), vol. 1, pp. 408–416. IEEE (2016)

13. Stringhini, G., Thonnard, O.: That ain't you: blocking spearphishing through behavioral modelling. In: Almgren, M., Gulisano, V., Maggi, F. (eds.) DIMVA 2015. LNCS, vol. 9148, pp. 78–97. Springer, Cham (2015). https://doi.org/10.1007/978-3-319-20550-2_5

14. Gascon, H., Ullrich, S., Stritter, B., Rieck, K.: Reading between the lines: content-agnostic detection of spear-phishing emails. In: Bailey, M., Holz, T., Stamatogiannakis, M., Ioannidis, S. (eds.) RAID 2018. LNCS, vol. 11050, pp. 69–91. Springer, Cham (2018). https://doi.org/10.1007/978-3-030-00470-5_4

15. Ho, G., Sharma, A., Javed, M., Paxson, V., Wagner, D.: Detecting credential spearphishing in enterprise settings. In: 26th USENIX Security Symposium (USENIX Security 17), pp. 469–485 (2017)

16. Cidon, A., Gavish, L., Bleier, I., Korshun, N., Schweighauser, M., Tsitkin, A.: High precision detection of business email compromise. In: 28th USENIXSecurity Symposium (USENIXSecurity 19), pp. 1291–1307 (2019)

17. Business email compromise: attack that has no defense. https://habr.com/ru/company/trendmicro/blog/460941. Accessed 21 July 2021

18. Kurematsu, M., Yamazaki, R., Ogasawara, R., Hakura, J., Fujita, H.: A study of email author identification using machine learning for business email compromise. In: Fujita, H., Selamat, A. (eds.) Advancing Technology Industrialization Through Intelligent Software Methodologies, Tools and Techniques - Proceedings of the 18th International Conference on New Trends in Intelligent Software Methodologies, Tools and Techniques (SoMeT 19), vol. 318, pp. 205–216. IOS Press (2019)

19. Aviv, S., Levy, Y., Wang, L., Geri, N.: An expert assessment of corporate professional users to measure business email compromise detection skills and develop a

knowledge and awareness training program. In: Proceedings of the 14th Pre-ICIS Workshop on Information Security and Privacy, Munich, Germany, vol. 15 (2019)

20. Corney, M.W., Anderson, A.M., Mohay, G.M., de Vel, O.: Identifying the authors of suspect email (2001)

21. De Vel, O., Anderson, A., Corney, M., Mohay, G.: Mining e-mail content for author identification forensics. ACM SIGMOD Rec. **30**(4), 55–64 (2001)

22. Zheng, R., Li, J., Chen, H., Huang, Z.: A framework for authorship identification of online messages: writing-style features and classification techniques. J. Am. Soc. Inform. Sci. Technol. **57**(3), 378–393 (2006)

23. Afroz, S., Brennan, M., Greenstadt, R.: Detecting hoaxes, frauds, and deception in writing style online. In: 2012 IEEE Symposium on Security and Privacy, pp. 461–475. IEEE (2012)

24. Afroz, S., Islam, A.C., Stolerman, A., Greenstadt, R., McCoy, D.: Doppelganger finder: taking stylometry to the underground. In: 2014 IEEE Symposium on Security and Privacy, pp. 212–226. IEEE (2014)

25. Abbasi, A., Chen, H.: Writeprints: a stylometric approach to identity-level identification and similarity detection in cyberspace. ACM Trans. Inf. Syst. (TOIS) **26**(2), 1–29 (2008)

26. Luyckx, K., Daelemans, W.: Personae: a corpus for author and personality prediction from text. In: LREC (2008)

27. Stamatatos, E.: A survey of modern authorship attribution methods. J. Am. Soc. Inform. Sci. Technol. **60**(3), 538–556 (2009)

28. Houvardas, J., Stamatatos, E.: N-gram feature selection for authorship identification. In: Euzenat, J., Domingue, J. (eds.) AIMSA 2006. LNCS (LNAI), vol. 4183, pp. 77–86. Springer, Heidelberg (2006). https://doi.org/10.1007/11861461_10

29. Vorobeva, A.: Anonymous website user identification based on combined feature set (writing-style and technical features). Sci. Tech. J. Inf. Technol. Mech. Opt. **89**(1), 139–144 (2014)

30. Vorobeva, A.: Dynamic feature selection for web user identification on linguistic and stylistic features of online texts. Sci. Tech. J. Inf. Technol. Mech. Opt. **17**, 117–128 (2017)

31. Romanov, A.: Methodology and software package for identifying the author of an unknown text. Extended abstract of candidate's thesis, Tomsk State University of Control Systems and Radioelectronics (2010)

32. Vorobeva, A.: Technique of web-user identification based on stylistic and linguistic features of short online texts. Inf. Space **1**, 127–130 (2017)

33. Kotenko, I.V., Saenko, I., Kushnerevich, A.: Parallel big data processing system for security monitoring in internet of things networks. J. Wirel. Mob. Netw. Ubiquit. Comput. Dependable Appl. **8**(4), 60–74 (2017)

34. Kotenko, I.V., Saenko, I., Branitskiy, A.: Applying big data processing and machine learning methods for mobile internet of things security monitoring. J. Internet Serv. Inf. Secur. **8**(3), 54–63 (2018)

35. Kholod, I., Shorov, A., Gorlatch, S.: Efficient distribution and processing of data for parallelizing data mining in mobile clouds. J. Wirel. Mob. Netw. Ubiquit. Comput. Dependable Appl. **11**(1), 2–17 (2020)

A Systematic Literature Review on the Mobile Malware Detection Methods

Yu-kyung Kim⬛, Jemin Justin Lee⬛, Myong-Hyun Go, Hae Young Kang⬛, and Kyungho Lee⁽⊠⁾⬛

Korea University, Seoul, Republic of Korea
{rladb1125,jeminjustinlee,mhgo,haeyee,kevinlee}@korea.ac.kr

Abstract. With the advent of the 5G network, the number of mobile users has drastically increased. Consequently, the users are much more susceptible to cyber-attacks such as mobile malware. In order to combat mobile malware, recent studies have employed machine learning techniques. This paper revisits existing research on machine learning-based mobile malware detection in cybersecurity. Our study focuses on subjects such as mobile system destruction and information leaks. We explore the mobile malware detection techniques utilized in recent studies based on the attack intentions such as (i) Server, (ii) Network, (iii) Client Software, (iv) Client Hardware, and (v) User. We hope our study can provide future research directions and a framework for a thorough evaluation. Furthermore, we review and summarize security challenges related to cybersecurity that can lead to improved and more practical research.

Keywords: Mobile malware · Machine learning · Mobile detection · Dataset properties

1 Introduction

Due to the popular demand and rapid growth of various mobile applications for the smartphone, cyberattacks through the mobile application have posed a severe threat [131]. Network providers, end-users, and app providers are constantly plagued by mobile malware attacks, including phishing, repackaging, and application updates. The mobile operating systems are vulnerable to cyberattacks, and around 87% of all Android-operated smartphones are exposed to one or more fatal vulnerabilities [133]. Mobile malware poses a severe security threat to various applications such as education, telecommunications, hospitals, and entertainment. In other words, mobile malware attacks intend to threaten cybersecurity in terms of confidentiality, integrity, and availability of data. Established

Supported by Defense Acquisition Program Administration and Agency for Defense Development under the contract (UD190016ED), and a grant of the Korean Heath Technology R&D Project, Ministry of Health and Welfare, Republic of Korea (HI19C0866).

© Springer Nature Singapore Pte Ltd. 2022
I. You et al. (Eds.): MobiSec 2021, CCIS 1544, pp. 263–288, 2022.
https://doi.org/10.1007/978-981-16-9576-6_19

attack groups are capable of penetrating and destroying the server, network, client software, user, and client hardware on mobile devices.

In spite of the numerous research on mobile malware, cybersecurity is forced to evolve to counter the cyber-attacks from cyber threat actors. The ever-evolving cyberattacks may take place in various forms, which makes it difficult for the defenders to identify the gap. For instance, some evaluations are limited to certain malware, such as anomaly-based approaches, or some have failed to reveal the most features needed to train the classifier [93]. The scalability issues such as having limited computing and storage power to handle a large number of malware samples require more attention [91].

Our goal is to reinvigorate research on these issues and to reorient the practical needs of cybersecurity domains. Therefore, we revisit previous literature on machine learning-based mobile malware detection regarding unique requirements in cybersecurity domains. Our study makes the following contributions through a thorough evaluation of current and future solutions:

- Our approach leverages past studies on mobile malware detection studies that focus on evaluating data sets, detection techniques, means of attack, and evaluation metrics for the system performance. We believe our study has laid the foundation that may help future researchers and future thesis that underpins a larger research project.
- To the best of our knowledge, we are one of the few studies that performed a systematic literature review that will present insight and crucial foundation for a foray into academic research.
- Furthermore, we were able to compare the supervised learning and unsupervised learning based on the means of attack for mobile malware. By synthesizing the existing data, we believe we were able to provide relevant and insight for future researchers.

The remainder of this paper is organized as follows. Section 2 describes the essential background for mobile cybersecurity and machine learning, and mobile malware. We describe relevant literature search methodologies, which are essential for readers to understand systematically accurate outlines of papers in Sect. 3. In Sect. 4, we investigate and analyze a machine learning-based mobile malware detection study. We conclude our paper with discussions for future work in Sect. 5.

2   Background

2.1   Mobile Cybersecurity

According to CISA, cybersecurity is a technology that protects networks, devices, and data from unauthorized access or criminal use and refers to practices that ensure confidentiality, integrity, and availability of information [29]. Network security vulnerabilities could lead to a malicious attacker breaking into the system and spreading malware, posing a severe risk. To reinforce cybersecurity, the following best practices should first be followed to minimize the risk of cyber-attacks. For instance, the individual SOC vendors and organizations keep their software and systems up to date, running the latest antivirus software, using strong passwords, changing default user names and passwords, implementing multi-level authentication (MFA), installing firewalls, and suspecting unexpected emails. Due to the rapid increase in mobile devices, the number of downloads of applications that are applications for mobile devices is also increasing. This application has become a means to cause personal information leakage or financial damage through junk mail or spam. In addition, attackers can exploit vulnerabilities in Bluetooth-enabled devices to access higher-level privacy channels. Mobile malware is the leading malware of attacks through various mobile devices, including file manipulation, information leakage, financial damage, and device unavailability.

We summarize the method of dissemination of mobile malware in three ways in terms of social engineering techniques [136]. Repackaging, a common technique for distributing mobile malware, refers to users arbitrarily changing resources, saving data, code, and distributing them by re-modulating them. The attacker must select and obtain the application to repackage. The attacker will extract and analyzes the source code of the application using tools such as unzip, dead, dex2jar, and JDGUI and perform tasks to insert malware into parts of a particular application or disable security features. The attacker also signs the changed source code to create a new forged application. An application update is a technique primarily used to disseminate malware while avoiding malware detection [132]. Application update is a method of deploying logic that performs malicious behavior as a terminal when an application is updated. The first application to be installed has no malware to be detected, only update logic to be used to acquire and install malware. Phishing is a method of stealing personal information, such as a user's name, password, credit card account, under the guise of a trusted party, and malicious actors frequently attack social networking or email, and MMS [113]. In particular, in mobile devices, a new fraud technique called smishing is rampant, a combination of SMS and phishing, which refers to a method of stealing financial information by sending SMS with malicious app addresses in large quantities to encourage users to install malicious apps. In addition to the three above, threats and attacks in mobile malware exist in various types: spam, spoofing, farming, vishing, data leakage, and denial-of-service attacks.

2.2 Machine Learning

Definitions and Overview. Past studies on detecting mobile malware have focused on signature-based detection, static analysis, dynamic analysis using emulators and sandboxes, and action-based detection [20,36,118]. However, while it is adequate to use existing studies to detect known malware, it is difficult to detect and respond immediately to variants or new malware. Therefore, machine learning-based detection techniques for detecting and responding to strains or new malware are being studied.

Samuel is credited for coining the term "machine learning" with his research about machine learning using the game of checkers in 1966 [119]. Machine learning is a methodology that examines the conditions between the input and output values to derive the output value when the next input value is received. It is a method of finding features by learning various normal and malicious applications and detecting mobile malware based on it. Machine learning can be classified as supervised learning, unsupervised learning, and reinforcement learning. Supervised learning is mainly used for classification and regression and learns from input and output values [108]. Unsupervised learning is used for clustering and compression and is learned only with input values [46]. Reinforcement learning is a learning method for obtaining maximum rewards through agent-environment interactions based on behavioral psychology [72]. Machine learning-based malware detection mainly uses supervised and unsupervised learning, and many studies determine whether applications are normal, abnormal, or classified malware. The following describes the characteristics of machine learning algorithms for detecting mobile malware [151].

There are problems, whether it is a classification, regression, or clustering, that we need to identify. In addition, sample data should be collected and analyzed because collected data should be representative. Then we process the optimized data considering the limitations and potential errors of the sample data. The features are extracted after data processing, and the training process is conducted by applying algorithmic models according to the data and problems to be solved. At this time, the model parameters are obtained using the training data. We then use test data to evaluate the model in terms of accuracy, training speed, reliability, generalization, and judge the optimized model. In addition, we evaluate machine learning methods by predicting results and solving real-world problems using new data sets. Figure 1 depicts the steps and approaches for detecting mobile malware based on machine learning.

Algorithms of Supervised Learning. Support Vector Machine (SVM) is an algorithm that can be applied to linear and nonlinear classification in a way that classifies data thoughtfully into a high-dimensional feature space [97]. It is a model that defines baselines for classification and is mainly used for data classification, such as pattern recognition and data analysis. When a new unclassified value appears, the classification identifies which side of its boundary belongs. In other words, we categorize the data by categorizing the data to measure the distance between categories, obtain the central position value, and then calculate the hyperplane to judge the boundaries.

K-Nearest Neighbor (KNN) predicts new data with information from the nearest k of existing data by finding the nearest k labeled samples [103]. It is an algorithm that finds the k elements closest to the input data within a specific space and classifies them into more matching groups.

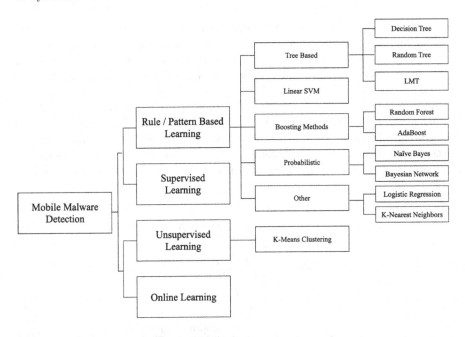

Fig. 1. Algorithms used for mobile malware detection

Decision Tree (DT) is one of the possible supervised learning models for both classification and regression, a methodology used to analyze data to classify and predict patterns present between classification and regression [18,115]. It undergoes a series of decision-making processes by diverging from the top node to the bottom node and causing the heterogeneity between the nodes to increase. We classify samples and regress a binary division into classification, continuation, or numerical types through this process.

Naive Bayesian (NB) is a supervised learning algorithm based on Bayes' theorem used for classification learning by multiplying prior probability information by the value of "Likelihood Function" measured through observation [34,76]. However, this algorithm cannot be used if each probability violates the assumption that it is independent. The algorithm is a widely used classification technique, including spam mail filters, text classification, and sentiment analysis [12].

Algorithms of Unsupervised Learning. K-means Clustering Algorithm, one of the clustering models of unsupervised learning, is an algorithm that groups the given data into k clusters [45]. It is a method that minimizes the variance of distance differences with each cluster. "K" refers to the number of groups or clusters to be grouped from a given data. "Means" refers to the average distance between the center of each cluster and the data.

Classification Performance Evaluation Indicators. The predictive power of classifiers with machine learning algorithms capable of performing classification should be verified and evaluated. To evaluate the model's performance, the data are separated into a learning set and an evaluation set before generating the model, creating a model as a learning set, and verifying the model's accuracy as an evaluation set. Machine learning model and pattern classification performance evaluation metrics include Precision, Recall, Accuracy, and F1-score. "Confusion Matrix" is a table for comparing predicted and actual values to measure Prediction performance through Training [127]. In other words, evaluation metrics evaluate the relationship between the answers presented by the model and the actual answers as elements and can be defined in four cases.

$$Accuracy = \frac{TP + TN}{TP + FP + TN + FN} \tag{1}$$

$$Precision = \frac{TP}{TP + FP} \tag{2}$$

$$Recall = \frac{TP}{TP + FN} \tag{3}$$

$$F_1 = 2 \times \frac{(Precision \times Recall)}{(Precision + Recall)} \tag{4}$$

In order to evaluate the performance of machine learning models, we need to separate the data into learning sets and evaluation sets before generating them, creating a model as a learning set, and verifying the Accuracy of the machine learning model as an evaluation set. There are four performance evaluation metrics for machine learning models: Accuracy, Precision, Recall, and F1 Score. Accuracy is defined by Eq. (1). It means the percentage of correct predictions for the test data. It can be calculated easily by dividing the number of correct predictions by the number of total predictions. However, problems arise due to Accuracy Paradox' for predictive analysis. Therefore, it can be checked by Precision, Recall indicators that evaluate whether the "Negative" ratio of real data provides the proper classification of situations that will occur with sparse possibilities. Precision is defined by Eq. (2). It is the number of correct positive results divided by the number of positive results predicted by the classifier. Precision is also known as Positive Predictive Value (PPV). The Recall is defined by Eq. (3), which is the number of correct positive results divided by the number of all relevant samples. The Recall is also known as True Positive Rate (TPR). Recall and Precision are indicators of opposite concepts. The Accuracy of the model can be supplemented by checking the F1 Score, the Harmonic Mean of Precision, and Recall. The F1 Score is defined by Eq. (4). The reason for harmonic means is to understand the model's performance by balancing both indicators when either of the Precision and Recall indicators is low to near zero.

3   Systematic Literature Collection

Our study followed the systematic methodology to investigate relevant works that address subjects pertaining to Detection and Machine Learning (ML). According to IEEE Xplore, the first mobile malware papers appeared in 2004 [50]. Our study used four databases: Digital Bibliography & Library Project (DBLP), ACM Digital Library, IEEE Xplore, and Google Scholar (allintitle query). We independently searched each database for six queries: *"Mobile, Machine Learning (ML)"*, *"Mobile, Malware"*, *"Mobile, Detection"*, *"Android, Machine Learning (ML)"*, *"Android, Malware,"* and *"Android, Detection"*. There were 236, 171, 1736, 110, 687, and 642 in the DBLP (in query order). The results of re-extracting only with papers published in journals without proceeding papers were 105, 51, 397, 41, 229, and 205. In the ACM Digital Library, there were 72, 36, 202, 18, 91, and 95 in query order. After re-extracting only the papers published in the journal except for proceeding papers, there were 8, 3, 38, 1, 5, and 3. In the IEEE Xplore, there were 151, 78, 620, 78, 364, and 388. In addition, except for the proceeding paper, the results were re-extracted to 29, 13, 92, 8, 55, and 47. Our research papers found in Google Scholar were excluded because of duplication with papers found in other DB. We focused on the papers related to 'machine learning-based mobile malware detection. For this paper, we mainly focus on research published between the years from 2016 to 2020. We cover papers appearing up to April 2021 and any pre-2016 paper that is highly cited or appeared in a major cybersecurity venue. We also cover general mobile malware surveys appearing up to 2021. A total of 126 papers were selected based on prominent papers related to other topics to analyze the literature from 2016 to 2021. Among the selected papers, we have not considered anything that is not relevant to the topic of this work by classifying it as a non-evaluation scope. Table 1 expressed the number of searches per DB according to each query. Each DB consists of 3 rows, the first row is the initial search result, and the second row is the number of papers selected only for articles published in journals. The last row lists the number of articles finally analyzed in our article.

Identifying candidate studies is part of the first stages of the systematic review. A Digital library provides a collection of literature stored electronically. In our study, we employed four databases: DBLP, ACM Digital Library, IEEE Xplore, and Google Scholar. The Digital Bibliography and Library Project (DBLP) provides an index of peer-reviewed publications in only computer science. The DBLP provides the trends of the publication scenario. The Association for Computing Machinery (ACM) Digital Library is well known for the Turing award, and the digital library primarily focuses on studies pertaining to the fields in computer science. The Institute of Electrical and Electronics Engineers (IEEE) Xplore provides access to its technical literature in electrical engineering, computer science, and electronics [48]. We excluded the digital library such as the Web of Science or Scopus to intensively analyze papers on computer science [61]. Google Scholar is the largest database of scholarly documents and accommodates approximately 100 million documents [60]. We used various keywords to yield the most inclusive results. However, duplicated results were found between

Table 1. Mobile malware dataset

	Mobile, Machine-Learning	Mobile, Malware	Mobile, Detection	Android, Machine Learning	Android, Malware	Android, Detection
Digital Bibliography & Library Project	236	171	1736	110	687	642
	105	51	397	41	229	205
	8	20	0	20	31	34
ACM Digital Library	72	36	202	18	91	95
	8	3	38	1	5	3
	0	0	0	0	3	0
IEEE Xplore	151	78	620	78	364	388
	29	13	92	8	55	47
	0	0	0	3	3	4
Google Scholar	576	307	2670	279	1450	1530
	404	217	1970	169	930	933
	0	0	0	0	0	0

the different databases. A substantial amount of studies were duplicated from the Google Scholar database. As such, we removed the results during the screening process. We screened for studies that focused on the malware detection method that employed machine learning for the mobile environment. Furthermore, we removed publications that were non-peer-reviewed (Fig. 2).

We selected literature that focuses solely on detecting mobile malware through machine learning techniques and mobile malware classifier. For a comprehensive understanding of mobile malware, we also benefited from the real mobile malware samples. For this purpose, we collected six datasets: (i) MalGenome, (ii) Drebin, (iii) M0Droid, (iv) CICMalDroid 2020, (v) AndroZoo, and (vi) Android Malware Dataset. Drebin uses a known program to learn detection models based on the concept of static analysis. Therefore, it is essential to evaluate the number of samples in a family known to detect this family reliably. Furthermore, the presence of obfuscated or dynamically loaded malware on mobile devices cannot be ruled out.

MalGenome is a dataset that consists of 1,260 Android malware samples, as illustrated in Table 2. Zhou et al. [153] collected 1260 Android malware samples from 49 different families and systematically collected them from various aspects as characteristics of installation methods, activation mechanisms, and delivered malicious payloads. They perform a timeline analysis of findings based on collected malware samples and characterize them based on detailed behavior analysis, including installation, activation, and payload.

DREBIN is a lightweight method that can automatically infer detection patterns and identify malware directly from smartphones. This methodology does a comprehensive static analysis to extract feature sets from various sources and analyze them in expressive vector space [13]. This process first statically examines the Android application and extract feature sets from the manifest and dex

Table 2. Mobile malware dataset

Dataset	Date	Sample Size	Malware Family	References
MalGenome [153]	2011	1,260 malware	49	[2, 5, 11, 16, 17, 19, 28, 35, 38, 43, 55, 81, 92, 104, 120, 130, 135, 141, 146, 147, 158, 159]
Drebin [13]	2012	5,560 malware	179	[10, 11, 14–17, 22, 25, 27, 31, 32, 38– 40, 47, 65, 69, 80, 82, 89, 90, 98, 110, 116, 123, 124, 126, 128– 130, 138, 140– 142, 146, 147, 154, 159–161]
M0Droid [86]	2015	1,530 malware	153	[85, 109]
CICMalDroid 2017 [68]	2017	10,854 malware	42	[3, 145]
CICMalDroid 2020 [117]	2020	17,341 malware	191	–
AndroZoo [59]	2016	3,182,590 malware	above 3,000	[4, 23, 39, 65, 66, 70, 74, 77, 94, 101, 104, 124]
AMD [145]	2017	24,650 malware	71	[16, 22, 37, 69, 74, 82, 96, 105, 106, 128, 129]

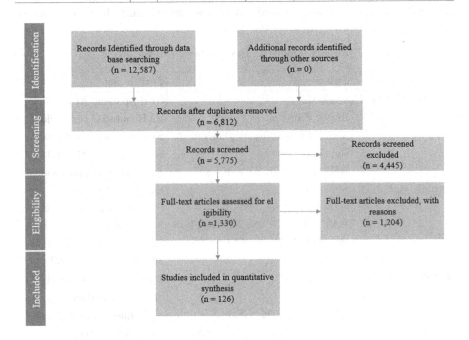

Fig. 2. PRISMA flow diagram of study

code of the application. Then they geometrically analyze the patterns and combinations of the features by matching the extracted feature sets to a joint vector space. This method uses Support Vector Machine (SVM) techniques to identify malware by embedding a learning-based detection feature set. It should be noted here that features contributing to malicious applications can be identified, and the detection process can be presented to users. DREBIN is a dataset that consists of 5,560 malware samples, as illustrated in Table 2.

We can distinguish the corresponding malware by classifying a dataset consisting of multiple malware families based on the characteristics of the manifest file called *AndroidManifest.xml*. Table 3 matches Features and Feature Sets of major malware families, namely FakeInstaller, GoldDream, GingerMaster, and DroidKungFu [13]. All Android applications must include *AndroidManifest.xml* which provides data supporting the installation and later execution of the android application. The information and data stored in this file can be efficiently retrieved on the device using the Android Asset Packaging Tool that enables us to extract the sets as depicted in Table 3.

M0Droid is an Android anti-malware solution that analyzes system calls from Android applications on servers and generates signatures that are pushed to user devices for threat detection [86]. Mobile malware detection model M0Droid uses behavioral attributes such as file read requests or network access to generate unique app signatures and uses signature normalization techniques. They proposed a solution to analyze and detect malware through behavior analysis

Table 3. Mobile malware dataset and feature

Malware Family	Feature s	Feature Set
FakeInstaller [114]	sendSMS	S7 Suspicious API Call
	SEND SMS	S2 Requested permissions
	android.hardware.telephony	S1 Hardware components
	sendTextMessage	S5 Restricted API calls
	READ PHONE STATE	S2 Requested permissions
DroidKungFu [54]	SIG STR	S4 Filtered intents
	system/bin/su	S7 Suspicious API calls
	BATTERY CHANGED ACTION	S4 Filtered intents
	READ PHONE STATE	S2 Requested permissions
	getSubscriberId	S7 Suspicious API calls
GoldDream [53]	sendSMS	S7 Suspicious API calls
	lebar.gicp.net	S8 Network addresses
	DELETE PACKAGES	S2 Requested permission
	android.provider.Telephony.SMS RECEIVED	S4 Filtered intents
	getSubscriberId	S7 Suspicious API calls
GingerMaster [52]	USER PRESENT	S4 Filtered intents
	getSubscriberId	S7 Suspicious API calls
	READ PHONE STATE	S2 Requested permissions
	system/bin/su	S7 Suspicious API calls
	HttpPost	S7 Suspicious API calls

and pattern recognition techniques with two categories of samples: malware and goodware datasets. M0Droid contains 1,530 malware samples and 49 malware family as illustrated in Table 2.

CICMalDroid 2020 contains a sample of 17,341 data for five Android applications, Adware, Banking, SMS, Riskware, and Benign, consisting of static and dynamic features as illustrated in Table 2. Collecting this data, Mahdavifar et al. [117] propose an effective and efficient Android malware category classification system based on semi-supervised deep neural networks. Although it is a small number of labeled training samples, it can solve cost problems, efficiently specify categories of malware to help prioritize mitigation techniques. CICMalDroid 2017 contains a sample of 10,854, which contains 4,354 malware and 6,500 benign [68]. This data is collected from the Google play market published in 2015, 2016, and 2017.

AndroZoo dataset contains more than 3,182,590 unique Android applications and adds up to 20TB, or more [59], as illustrated in Table 2. This data demonstrates the importance of methodological problems and detection time when evaluating machine learning-based malware detectors' performance and detects privacy leakage [59]. The Android dataset was collected from several sources, including the official Google Play Application Market, and currently includes 15,164,916 APKs. In addition, each APK was analyzed by different anti-virus products to identify applications detected as malware.

AMD datasets were generated in 2016 with many malicious code samples. AMD datasets are a dataset that categorizes large datasets, including 24,650 malware app samples, into 135 variants belonging to 71 malware families [145] as depicted in Table 2. This datasets groups malware samples with the same family of names and analyze each family by classifying them into different variants using custom clustering. AMD data set performs a systematic and in-depth manual analysis of various malware samples to obtain behavioral information about malware.

3.1 Mobile Malware Detection Techniques

Techniques of Mobile Malware Detection. Means of mobile malware attacks consist of servers (hosts), networks, client software, client hardware, and users. The server's responsibility is to identify malicious behavior by comparing the behavior of newly installed applications with known traffic patterns. It is accomplished by aggregating reported data from various mobile devices and deriving a collaborative model representing the common traffic patterns of many users for each application. Alternatively, we identify malicious behavior with local models that detect by analyzing the deviation of traffic patterns in installed applications [1]. Server and host-based intrusion detection systems reside and monitor a single host system, collecting and analyzing events such as file systems and system calls. Malware activities that have carried out network overload attacks affect regular network behavior patterns, so the activity of mobile malware can be detected by monitoring the network behavior of applications. Therefore, monitoring and analyzing traffic patterns in network-active applications is essential for developing practical solutions to prevent network overload. Network-based intrusion detection systems collect and analyze traffic volumes, IP addresses, service ports, and forms of a protocol to detect intrusion attempts. Client software's responsibility is to monitor applications already installed and running on mobile devices, teach user-specific local models, and detect deviations from observed normal behavior. Furthermore, the client software learns a local model to determine indicators such as changes in users' behavior and updates resulting from new versions or malicious attacks to detect changes in the traffic patterns of applications.

Mobile malware detection techniques are classified as static detection, dynamic detection, and hybrid detection. Static [118], dynamic [36], and hybrid [20] detection analysis are used to extract model training features [159]. Static detection analysis is a technique for observing malware malicious patterns without the execution of applications [118]. Therefore, it is advantageous considering the rapidly growing number of mobile applications due to the advantages of less analysis time and cost compared to other detection techniques. Standard features of static analysis are privileges and API calls. Privileges and API calls are extracted as Android Manifest.xml and are effective sources for malware detection rates. However, static detection analysis is challenging for applications with code obfuscation techniques. One of the techniques for avoiding static analysis is update attacks. When malicious applications are installed on mobile devices and applications are updated, malware is installed and installed as part of the update. On the other hand, dynamic detection analysis is a method of checking the dynamic behavior of malware by running real-world applications, which makes it advantageous to extract features and signatures of malware features of malware. In other words, dynamic detection analysis has the advantage of effectively analyzing malware where code obfuscation has been performed over static detection analysis.

Hybrid detection refers to a technique that combines static and dynamic detection to detect malware [20]. In other words, hybrid detection analysis is a methodology that combines static and dynamic features collected by analyzing applications and extracting information while they are running. This detection analysis methodology can increase the accuracy of detection rates.

4   Mobile Malware Attacks Analysis

We conducted a systematic literature review on machine learning-based mobile malware detection. We investigated a total of 126 machine learning-based mobile malware detection literature and conducted a frequency survey of the most frequently mentioned words, as depicted in Fig. 3. The most frequently mentioned word is "Malware", mentioned 12,053 times in 126 papers. The second most frequently mentioned word is "Android", mentioned 8,250 times in 126 papers. The third most frequently mentioned word is "Detection", which has been mentioned 7,635. The fourth and fifth most frequently mentioned word is "Feature", which has been mentioned 10,385 times. Therefore, the word "Feature" is considered

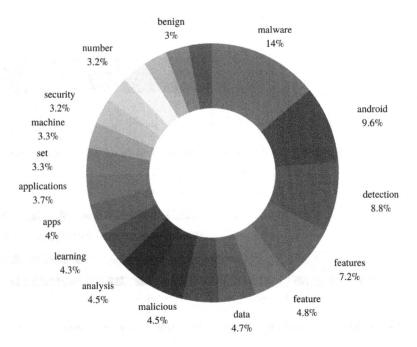

Fig. 3. Distribution of the papers based on mobile malware detection

to be the second most frequently mentioned word than "Android" and "Detection". The following most frequently mentioned words are "Data", "System", "Malicious", "Analysis", and "Learning". The 11th and 12th most frequently mentioned "Application" have been mentioned 6,705 times, the most frequently mentioned word after "Detection". In our analysis, we list the top 5 words in order; "Malware", "Feature", "Android", "Detection", "Application" are queries we used to collect literature.

We categorized and analyzed the literature related to machine learning-based mobile malware detection by year, as illustrated in Fig. 4. As a result of our intensive investigation of the literature from 2016 to 2021, we categorized it by year: 9 papers in 2021, 30 papers in 2020, 31 papers in 2019, 27 papers in 2018, 22 papers in 2017, and 7 papers in 2016. The literature related to our study increased significantly between 2016 and 2017. Also, the number of related literature has increased over the years. The year 2021 is relatively small because it was only surveyed in the first quarter, and it is expected to increase further than 2020. In other words, we confirm that machine learning is in the spotlight among the methodologies for detecting mobile malware, and this is an area that needs to be studied in the future.

According to the results from the Client Software's annual analysis, approximately the same percentage of studies were conducted from 2017 to 2020. The number of papers published in the journal by year in the means of mobile malware attacks is depicted in Fig. 5. Furthermore, we confirm that the Client Hard-

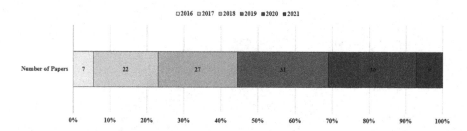

Fig. 4. Number of papers related to mobile malware detection based machine learning by year

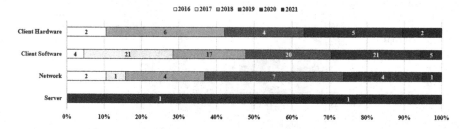

Fig. 5. The number of papers related to means of mobile malware attack

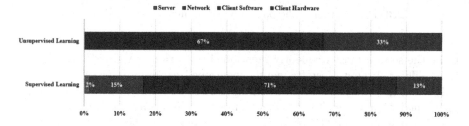

Fig. 6. The algorithms used for mobile malware detection

ware and Network disciplines have continued to do almost the same percentage of research from 2017 to 2020. On the other hand, studies conducted on the server and user show that they have relatively little preference.

We classified the detection method into supervised learning or unsupervised learning, as illustrated in Table 4 and Fig. 6. The mobile malware attacks can be divided into four methods: (i) Server, (ii) Network, (iii) Client Software, and (iv) Client Hardware. A total of six studies utilized unsupervised learning [8,22,111,124,147,152], overwhelmingly higher utilization of supervised learning than utilization of unsupervised learning. There are three out of 126 papers that studied both unsupervised learning and supervised learning [22,147,152].

We found that the Client Software and Client Hardware have a relatively higher percentage of studies than server and network. While we were not able to find many studies based on supervised learning that focused on the Server and Network attacks, we were able to identify the studies that focused on

Table 4. Classification of the supervised and unsupervised learning by means of mobile malware attack

Means of Attack	Supervised	Unsupervised
Server	[75, 107]	–
Network	[3, 9, 27, 33, 63, 64, 70, 88, 92, 100, 107, 112, 121, 125, 137, 140, 145, 148, 149]	–
Client Software	[2, 4, 5, 7, 8, 10, 11, 16, 17, 19, 21–23, 26, 28, 31, 32, 35, 38–44, 47, 49, 55, 57, 58, 62, 65–67, 69, 71, 73, 74, 78, 79, 81–83, 85, 87, 89, 92, 94, 98, 99, 102, 104–106, 109, 110, 116, 120, 122, 123, 126, 128–130, 134, 135, 138, 139, 141, 142, 144, 146, 147, 150, 152, 154–166]	[8, 22, 147, 152]
Client Hardware	[6, 14, 15, 24, 25, 30, 37, 51, 56, 77, 80, 84, 90, 95, 96, 101, 143]	[111, 124]

the Client Software and Client Hardware. Chen et al. [27] proposed a new S-IDGC model that allows users to fairly compare different types of classifiers by designing a comparative benchmark prototype system that integrates different types of machine learning classifiers for Android malicious traffic detection. This model refers to imbalance classification methods, including Synthetic Minority Oversampling Technique (SMOTE), SVM, SVM Cost-Sensitive (SVMCS), and C4.5 Cost-Sensitive (C4.5CS) methods. This model allows users to compare the detection performance of different classification algorithms on the same data set with the performance of a specific classification algorithm on different data sets. This study aimed to evaluate the intrusion detection system (IDS) performance using five classifiers such as J48, DB, MLP, KNN, and RF [92]. The study assessed both the MalGenome and private dataset and found that the BN, RD each scored 99.7% and 93.03% for the true-positive rate (TPR). Egitmen et al. [37] approached Android software with artificially generated text to classify modern Android malware but applied a skip-gram technique configured for NLP to extract useful features. This study also demonstrated that the NLP-based static analysis approach to application source code has promising results. In conclusion, accuracy scored 95.64% without threatening system stability while running the target application. While we were not able to find any study that utilized unsupervised learning that focused on the Server and Network attacks, we were able to identify the studies that focused on the client software [8, 22, 147, 152] and Client Hardware [111, 124]. Amamra et al. [8] improved abnormal-based detection technology by examining two factors that cause low accuracy of detection technology. This paper extracts the main behavior of the application using the system called filtering & abstraction process and characterizes benign behavior using a machine learning classifier. This paper also confirmed that the filtering and abstraction process had a positive impact on the performance of the SVM and K-means models. Xu et al. [152]

applied feature weights based on IG and PSO methods to measure the importance of features for machine learning classification. The proposed strategy achieved the highest accuracy in the machine learning model by increasing cluster diversity. Wu et al. [147] decomposed Android apps into manifest files, Dalvik code files, and basic library files to detect maliciousness and identify their families to analyze and classify Android malware applications efficiently. Therefore, MVIDroid obtained an F1 score of 0.99 and an F1 score of 0.948 in multiple classifications. Cai et al. [22] proposed an Android malware detection technique called JOWM-Droid, which is a static analysis based on feature weights and joint optimization of weight mapping and classifier parameters. Sharma et al. [124] compared the results between multiple datasets to find the least malicious samples and datasets detected by antivirus software. This study found that in the case of malicious data set samples, antivirus software detected AndRadar samples the least often. We figured out that the ratio of research on Client Software such as applications is overwhelmingly high among the means of mobile malware attacks. While the majority of the machine learning-based classifications provide a binary label for mobile users and app security analysts, there has been little to no study that examines the malicious behaviors for mobile applications. As such, XMAL was proposed to classify malware with high accuracy [146]. RevealDroid, a machine learning-based malware detection method, analyzed RevealDroid, a dataset that consists of 54,000 malicious and benign apps [41]. The detection method utilized various features such as the Android API usage, reflection-based features, and features from native binaries of apps.

A review of the systematic literature on mobile malware detection from the security perspective revealed three limitations for future contribution as follows: Limited dataset, Zero-day attack, Evaluation algorithms. There is a lack of good quality or a dearth of diversity in the dataset used for the analysis of mobile malware detection. Wang et al. [140] proposed C4.5, a machine learning algorithm to identify Android Malware, to achieve better detection rates in comparison to other detection approaches. The study also utilized the Drebin dataset and analyzed 8,312 bening apps and 5,560 malware samples. However, his paper has a limitation in that the number of training data is small, and there are many unexamined features by analyzing only 6 TCP Flow characteristics and 4 HTTP request characteristics. We need to design methods that can detect zero-day attacks, which are not just the ones seen in the past. By analyzing the system calls of mobile applications called for a 1s time with a host-based approach to detect mobile botnets and using induction machine learning models, Costa et al. [30] achieved high performance across different metrics. In addition, this study found that reducing the features of dimensionality of the problem from 133 to 19 did not have a significant negative impact on performance. However, this study requires new challenges to identify mobile botnets in real-time and more diverse scenarios using multiple mobile devices. Sharma et al. [124] did not present a specific mechanism for detecting types of Android malware that antivirus software could not detect. The choice of algorithms is very important in detecting mobile malware. Mahindru et al. [75] examined the privilege-induced risk initiated by granting unnecessary privileges to these Android applications and utilized the Least Square Support Vector (LSSVM) Machine learning approach linked through three unique kernel features: linear, radial basis, and polynomial. However, the malware detection model proposed in his paper had a limitation in detecting only whether an application is malware or benign. Rasheed et al. [107] tested SMO, Random Tree, J48, Naïve Bayes, and LMT algorithms as following the best result to classify the botnet attack was 85%. However, his paper needs to improve algorithm classification by adding new sub-algorithms to machine learning. Cai et al. [22] did not consider the correlation between features. Therefore, it can be necessary to build joint features to improve the detection accuracy of malware in Android applications.

5 Conclusions

In this paper, we examine the literature pertaining to machine learning-based mobile malware detection in cybersecurity. Our study focuses on subjects such as mobile system destruction and information leaks. We explore the mobile malware detection techniques utilized in recent studies based on the attack intentions such as (i) Server, (ii) Network, (iii) Client Software, (iv) Client Hardware, and (v) User. We hope our study can provide future research directions and a framework for a thorough evaluation. We identified several points of view for future research. Our review can be utilized for future research evaluations on these topics. Furthermore, we review and summarize security challenges related to cybersecurity that can lead to improved and more practical planning. We aimed to reinvigorate research on these issues and to reorient the practical needs of cybersecurity domains. We performed a comprehensive examination of the previous literature on machine learning-based mobile malware detection in terms of unique requirements in cybersecurity domains.

To the best of our knowledge, a comprehensive evaluation of the adequacy of previous work on machine learning-based mobile malware detection from a cybersecurity perspective has not been performed before. We believe the comprehensive evaluation from our work can help provide a foundation for future researchers to help underpin larger research projects. We were able to compare the supervised learning and unsupervised learning detection methods for mobile malware. By synthesizing the existing data, we believe we were able to provide relevant and insight for future researchers.

References

1. Shabtai, A., et al.: Mobile malware detection through analysis of deviations in application network behavior. Comput. Secur. **43**, 1–18 (2014)
2. Abawajy, J.H., Kelarev, A.: Iterative classifier fusion system for the detection of android malware. IEEE Trans. Big Data **5**, 282–292 (2017). IEEE
3. Abuthawabeh, M., Mahmoud, K.: Enhanced android malware detection and family classification using conversation-level network traffic features. Int. Arab J. Inf. Technol. **17**, 607–614 (2020)

4. Alazab, M., Alazab, M., Shalaginov, A., Mesleh, A., Awajan, A.: Intelligent mobile malware detection using permission requests and api calls. Future Gener. Comput. Syst. **107**, 509–521. Elsevier (2020)

5. Allix, K., Bissyandé, T.F., Jérome, Q., Klein, J., State, R., Le Traon, Y.: Empirical assessment of machine learning-based malware detectors for Android. Empir. Softw. Eng. **21**(1), 183–211 (2014). https://doi.org/10.1007/s10664-014-9352-6

6. Almomani, I., et al.: Android ransomware detection based on a hybrid evolutionary approach in the context of highly imbalanced data. IEEE Access **9**, 57674–57691 (2021). IEEE

7. Alswaina, F., Elleithy, K.: Android malware permission-based multi-class classification using extremely randomized trees. IEEE Access **6**, 76217–76227 (2018). IEEE

8. Amamra, A., Robert, J.M., Abraham, A., Talhi, C.: Generative versus discriminative classifiers for android anomaly-based detection system using system calls filtering and abstraction process. Secur. Commun. Netw. **9**, 3483–3495 (2016). Wiley Online Library

9. Amouri, A., Alaparthy, V.T., Morgera, S.D.: A machine learning based intrusion detection system for mobile internet of things. Sensors **20**, 461 (2020). Multidisciplinary Digital Publishing Institute

10. Ananya, A., Aswathy, A., Amal, T.R., Swathy, P.G., Vinod, P., Mohammad, S.: SysDroid: a dynamic ML-based android malware analyzer using system call traces. Clust. Comput. **23**(4), 2789–2808 (2020). https://doi.org/10.1007/s10586-019-03045-6

11. Appice, A., Andresini, G., Malerba, D.: Clustering-aided multi-view classification: a case study on android malware detection. J. Intell. Inf. Syst. **55**(1), 1–26 (2020). https://doi.org/10.1007/s10844-020-00598-6

12. Arif, M.H., Li, J., Iqbal, M., Liu, K.: Sentiment analysis and spam detection in short informal text using learning classifier systems. Soft. Comput. **22**(21), 7281–7291 (2018)

13. Arp, D., Spreitzenbarth, M., Hubner, M., Gascon, H., Rieck, K.: Drebin: effective and explainable detection of android malware in your pocket. In: Ndss, pp. 23–26. FFFF (2014)

14. Arshad, S., Shah, M.A., Wahid, A., Mehmood, A., Song, H., Yu, H.: Samadroid: a novel 3-level hybrid malware detection model for android operating system. IEEE Access **6**, 4321–4339 (2018). IEEE

15. Bai, H., Xie, N., Di, X., Ye, Q.: Famd: a fast multifeature android malware detection framework, design, and implementation. IEEE Access **8**, 194729–194740 (2020). IEEE

16. Bai, Y., Xing, Z., Ma, D., Li, X., Feng, Z.: Comparative analysis of feature representations and machine learning methods in android family classification. Comput. Netw. **184**, 107639 (2021). Elsevier

17. Bakour, K., Ünver, H.M.: VisDroid: android malware classification based on local and global image features, bag of visual words and machine learning techniques. Neural Comput. Appl. **33**(8), 3133–3153 (2020). https://doi.org/10.1007/s00521-020-05195-w

18. Breiman, L., Friedman, J.H., Olshen, R.A., Stone, C.J.: Classification and Regression Trees. Routledge, Abingdon-on-Thames (2017)

19. Brown, J., Anwar, M., Dozier, G.: An artificial immunity approach to malware detection in a mobile platform. EURASIP J. Inf. Secur. **2017**(1), 1–10 (2017). https://doi.org/10.1186/s13635-017-0059-2

20. Burstein, J., et al.: Automated scoring using a hybrid feature identification technique. In: 36th Annual Meeting of the Association for Computational Linguistics and 17th International Conference on Computational Linguistics, vol. 1, pp. 206–210 (1998)
21. Cai, H., Meng, N., Ryder, B., Yao, D.: Droidcat: effective android malware detection and categorization via app-level profiling. IEEE Trans. Inf. Forensics and Secur. **14**, 1455–1470 (2018). IEEE
22. Cai, L., Li, Y., Xiong, Z.: Jowmdroid: android malware detection based on feature weighting with joint optimization of weight-mapping and classifier parameters. Comput. Secur. **100**, 102086 (2021). Elsevier
23. Cai, M., Jiang, Y., Gao, C., Li, H., Yuan, W.: Learning features from enhanced function call graphs for android malware detection. Neurocomputing **423**, 301–307 (2021). Elsevier
24. Caviglione, L., Gaggero, M., Lalande, J.F., Mazurczyk, W., Urbański, M.: Seeing the unseen: revealing mobile malware hidden communications via energy consumption and artificial intelligence. IEEE Trans. Inf. Forensics Secur. **11**, 799–810 (2015). IEEE
25. Chen, T., Mao, Q., Yang, Y., Lv, M., Zhu, J.: Tinydroid: a lightweight and efficient model for android malware detection and classification, vol. 2018. Hindawi (2018)
26. Chen, X., et al.: Android hiv: a study of repackaging malware for evading machine-learning detection. IEEE Trans. Inf. Forensics Secur. **15**, 987–1001 (2019). IEEE
27. Chen, Z., et al.: Machine learning based mobile malware detection using highly imbalanced network traffic. Inf. Sci. **433**, 346–364 (2018). Elsevier
28. Christianah, A., Gyunka, B., Oluwatobi, A.: Optimizing android malware detection via ensemble learning. 61–78 (2020)
29. CISA: What is cybersecurity? (2009). https://us-cert.cisa.gov/ncas/tips/ST04-001
30. Costa, V.G.T.D., Barbon, S., Miani, R.S., Rodrigues, J.J., Zarpelão, B.B.: Mobile botnets detection based on machine learning over system calls. Int. J. Secur. Netw. **14**, 103–118 (2019). Inderscience Publishers (IEL)
31. De Lorenzo, A., Martinelli, F., Medvet, E., Mercaldo, F., Santone, A.: Visualizing the outcome of dynamic analysis of android malware with vizmal. J. Inf. Secur. Appl. **50**, 102423 (2020). Elsevier
32. Demontis, A., et al.: Yes, machine learning can be more secure! a case study on android malware detection. IEEE Trans. Dependable Secure Comput. **16**, 711–724 (2017). IEEE
33. Dey, S., Ye, Q., Sampalli, S.: A machine learning based intrusion detection scheme for data fusion in mobile clouds involving heterogeneous client networks. Inf. Fusion **49**, 205–215 (2019). Elsevier
34. Domingos, P., Pazzani, M.: On the optimality of the simple bayesian classifier under zero-one loss. Mach. Learn. **29**(2), 103–130 (1997)
35. Du, Y., Wang, J., Li, Q.: An android malware detection approach using community structures of weighted function call graphs. IEEE Access **5**, 17478–17486 (2017). IEEE
36. Egele, M., Scholte, T., Kirda, E., Kruegel, C.: A survey on automated dynamic malware-analysis techniques and tools. ACM Comput. Surv. (CSUR) **44**(2), 1–42 (2008)
37. Egitmen, A., Bulut, I., Aygun, R., Gunduz, A.B., Seyrekbasan, O., Yavuz, A.G.: Combat mobile evasive malware via skip-gram-based malware detection, vol. 2020. Hindawi (2020)

38. Fan, M., Luo, X., Liu, J., Nong, C., Zheng, Q., Liu, T.: Ctdroid: leveraging a corpus of technical blogs for android malware analysis. IEEE Trans. Reliab. **69**, 124–138 (2019). IEEE

39. Feng, P., Ma, J., Sun, C., Xu, X., Ma, Y.: A novel dynamic android malware detection system with ensemble learning. IEEE Access **6**, 30996–31011 (2018). IEEE

40. Firdaus, A., Anuar, N.B., Karim, A., Razak, M.F.A.: Discovering optimal features using static analysis and a genetic search based method for Android malware detection. Front. Inf. Technol. Electron. Eng. **19**(6), 712–736 (2018). https://doi.org/10.1631/FITEE.1601491

41. Garcia, J., Hammad, M., Malek, S.: Lightweight, obfuscation-resilient detection and family identification of android malware. ACM Trans. Softw. Eng. Methodol. (TOSEM) **26**, 1–29 (2018). ACM New York, NY, USA

42. Garg, S., Baliyan, N.: A novel parallel classifier scheme for vulnerability detection in android. **77**, 12–26. Elsevier (2019)

43. Garg, S., Peddoju, S.K., Sarje, A.K.: Network-based detection of Android malicious apps. Int. J. Inf. Secur. **16**(4), 385–400 (2016). https://doi.org/10.1007/s10207-016-0343-z

44. Gong, L., et al.: Systematically landing machine learning onto market-scale mobile malware detection. IEEE (2020)

45. Hartigan, J.A., Wong, M.A.: Algorithm as 136: a k-means clustering algorithm. J. R. Stat. Soc. Ser. c (Appl. Stat.) **28**(1), 100–108 (1979)

46. Hinton, G.E., Sejnowski, T.J., et al.: Unsupervised Learning: Foundations of Neural Computation. MIT Press, Cambridge (1999)

47. Hu, D., Ma, Z., Zhang, X., Li, P., Ye, D., Ling, B.: The concept drift problem in android malware detection and its solution, vol. 2017. Hindawi (2017)

48. Hull, D., Pettifer, S.R., Kell, D.B.: Defrosting the digital library: bibliographic tools for the next generation web. PLoS Comput. Biol. **4**(10), e1000204 (2008)

49. Idrees, F., Rajarajan, M., Conti, M., Chen, T.M., Rahulamathavan, Y.: Pindroid: a novel android malware detection system using ensemble learning methods. Comput. Secur. **68**, 36–46 (2017). Elsevier

50. Jamaluddin, J., Zotou, N., Edwards, R., Coulton, P.: Mobile phone vulnerabilities: a new generation of malware. In: IEEE International Symposium on Consumer Electronics, 2004. pp. 199–202. IEEE (2004)

51. Jeong, E.S., Kim, I.S., Lee, D.H.: SafeGuard: a behavior based real-time malware detection scheme for mobile multimedia applications in android platform. Multimed. Tools Appl. **76**(17), 18153–18173 (2016). https://doi.org/10.1007/s11042-016-4189-1

52. Jiang, X.: Security alert: Gingermaster (2011)

53. Jiang, X.: Security alert: Golddream (2011)

54. Jiang, X.: Security alert: new droidkungfu variant (2011)

55. Jiang, X., Mao, B., Guan, J., Huang, X.: Android malware detection using fine-grained features, vol. 2020. Hindawi (2020)

56. Jogarah, K.K., Soopaul, K., Beeharry, Y., Hurbungs, V.: Hybrid machine learning algorithms for fault detection in android smartphones. Trans. Emerg. Telecommun. Technol. **29**, e3272 (2018). Wiley Online Library

57. Jung, J., Kim, H.J., Cho, S.j., Han, S., Suh, K.: Efficient android malware detection using api rank and machine learning. J. Internet Serv. Inf. Secur. **9**, 48–59 (2019)

58. Kang, B., Yerima, S.Y., Sezer, S., McLaughlin, K.: N-gram opcode analysis for android malware detection (2016)

59. Allix, K., Tegawendé, F., Bissyandé, J.K.Y.L.T.: Androzoo: collecting millions of android apps for the research community. In: 2016 IEEE/ACM 13th Working Conference on Mining Software Repositories (MSR), pp. 468–471. IEEE (2016)
60. Khabsa, M., Giles, C.L.: The number of scholarly documents on the public web. PLoS ONE **9**(5), e93949 (2014)
61. Khan, S., Liu, X., Shakil, K.A., Alam, M.: A survey on scholarly data: from big data perspective. Inf. Process. Manag. **53**(4), 923–944 (2017)
62. Kim, H., Cho, T., Ahn, G.-J., Hyun Yi, J.: Risk assessment of mobile applications based on machine learned malware dataset. Multimed. Tools Appl. **77**(4), 5027–5042 (2017). https://doi.org/10.1007/s11042-017-4756-0
63. Kim, K.C., Ko, E., Kim, J., Yi, J.H.: Intelligent malware detection based on hybrid learning of API and ACG on android. J. Internet Serv. Inf. Secur. **9**, 39–48 (2019)
64. Kirubavathi, G., Anitha, R.: Structural analysis and detection of android botnets using machine learning techniques. Int. J. Inf. Secur. **17**(2), 153–167 (2017). https://doi.org/10.1007/s10207-017-0363-3
65. Kouliaridis, V., Kambourakis, G., Geneiatakis, D., Potha, N.: Two anatomists are better than one-dual-level android malware detection, no. 7 (2020)
66. Kumar, A., Agarwal, V., Kumar Shandilya, S., Shalaginov, A., Upadhyay, S., Yadav, B.: Pacer: platform for android malware classification, performance evaluation and threat reporting. Future Internet **12**, 66 (2020). Multidisciplinary Digital Publishing Institute
67. Kumar, R., Zhang, X., Wang, W., Khan, R.U., Kumar, J., Sharif, A.: A multimodal malware detection technique for android IoT devices using various features. IEEE Access **7**, 64411–64430 (2019). IEEE
68. Lashkari, A.H., Kadir, A.F.A., Taheri, L., Ghorbani, A.A.: Toward developing a systematic approach to generate benchmark android malware datasets and classification. In: 2018 International Carnahan Conference on Security Technology (ICCST), pp. 1–7. IEEE (2018)
69. Li, C., Mills, K., Niu, D., Zhu, R., Zhang, H., Kinawi, H.: Android malware detection based on factorization machine. IEEE Access **7**, 184008–184019 (2019). IEEE
70. Li, H., Zhou, S., Yuan, W., Li, J., Leung, H.: Adversarial-example attacks toward android malware detection system. IEEE Syst. J. **14**, 653–656 (2019). IEEE
71. Li, J., Sun, L., Yan, Q., Li, Z., Srisa-An, W., Ye, H.: Significant permission identification for machine-learning-based android malware detection. **14**, 3216–3225. IEEE (2018)
72. Li, Y.: Deep reinforcement learning: An overview. arXiv preprint arXiv:1701.07274 (2017)
73. Liu, P., Wang, W., Luo, X., Wang, H., Liu, C.: NSDroid: efficient multi-classification of android malware using neighborhood signature in local function call graphs. Int. J. Inf. Secur. **20**(1), 59–71 (2020). https://doi.org/10.1007/s10207-020-00489-5
74. Ma, Z., Ge, H., Liu, Y., Zhao, M., Ma, J.: A combination method for android malware detection based on control flow graphs and machine learning algorithms. IEEE Access **7**, 21235–21245 (2019). IEEE
75. Mahindru, A., Sangal, A.L.: FSDroid:- a feature selection technique to detect malware from android using machine learning techniques. Multimed. Tools Appl. **80**(9), 13271–13323 (2021). https://doi.org/10.1007/s11042-020-10367-w
76. Manning, C.: I. Introduction. ISEAS Publishing (1988)

77. Martín, A., Lara-Cabrera, R., Camacho, D.: Android malware detection through hybrid features fusion and ensemble classifiers: The andropytool framework and the omnidroid dataset. Inf. Fusion **52**, 128–142 (2019). Elsevier
78. Martín, I., Hernández, J.A., Muñoz, A., Guzmán, A.: Android malware characterization using metadata and machine learning techniques, vol. 2018. Hindawi (2018)
79. Martín, I., Hernández, J.A., de los Santos, S.: Machine-learning based analysis and classification of android malware signatures. Secur. Commun. Netw. **97**, 295–305 (2018). Elsevier
80. Martinelli, F., Mercaldo, F., Nardone, V., Santone, A., Vaglini, G.: Model checking and machine learning techniques for hummingbad mobile malware detection and mitigation. Simul. Model. Pract. Theory **105**, 102169 (2020). Elsevier
81. Mas' ud, M.Z., Sahib, S., Abdollah, M.F., Selamat, S.R., Huoy, C.Y.: A comparative study on feature selection method for n-gram mobile malware detection. IJ Netw. Secur. **19**, 727–733 (2017)
82. Massarelli, L., Aniello, L., Ciccotelli, C., Querzoni, L., Ucci, D., Baldoni, R.: Androdfa: android malware classification based on resource consumption. **11**, 326. Multidisciplinary Digital Publishing Institute (2020)
83. Mehtab, A., et al.: AdDroid: rule-based machine learning framework for android malware analysis. Mob. Netw. Appl. **25**(1), 180–192 (2019). https://doi.org/10.1007/s11036-019-01248-0
84. Milosevic, J., Malek, M., Ferrante, A.: Time, accuracy and power consumption tradeoff in mobile malware detection systems. Comput. Secur. **82**, 314–328 (2019). Elsevier
85. Milosevic, N., Dehghantanha, A., Choo, K.K.R.: Machine learning aided android malware classification. Comput. Electr. Eng. **61**, 266–274 (2017). Elsevier
86. Damshenas, M., et al.: M0droid: an android behavioral-based malware detection model. J. Inf. Priv. Secur. **11**(3), 141–157 (2015)
87. Moodi, M., Ghazvini, M., Moodi, H., Ghavami, B.: A smart adaptive particle swarm optimization–support vector machine: android botnet detection application. J. Supercomput. **76**(12), 9854–9881 (2020). https://doi.org/10.1007/s11227-020-03233-x
88. Mugabo, E., Zhang, Q.Y.: Intrusion detection method based on support vector machine and information gain for mobile cloud computing. IJ Netw. Secur. **22**, 231–241 (2020)
89. Narayanan, A., Chandramohan, M., Chen, L., Liu, Y.: Context-aware, adaptive, and scalable android malware detection through online learning. IEEE Trans. Emerg. Top. Comput. Intell. **1**, 157–175 (2017). IEEE
90. Narayanan, A., Chandramohan, M., Chen, L., Liu, Y.: A multi-view context-aware approach to Android malware detection and malicious code localization. Empir. Softw. Eng. **23**(3), 1222–1274 (2017). https://doi.org/10.1007/s10664-017-9539-8
91. Narayanan, A., Yang, L., Chen, L., Jinliang, L.: Adaptive and scalable android malware detection through online learning. In: 2016 International Joint Conference on Neural Networks (IJCNN), pp. 2484–2491. IEEE (2016)
92. Narudin, F.A., Feizollah, A., Anuar, N.B., Gani, A.: Evaluation of machine learning classifiers for mobile malware detection. Soft. Comput. **20**(1), 343–357 (2014). https://doi.org/10.1007/s00500-014-1511-6
93. Naseer, M., et al.: Malware detection: issues and challenges. J. Phys. Conf. Ser. **1807**, 012011. IOP Publishing (2021)

94. Navarro, L.C., Navarro, A.K., Gregio, A., Rocha, A., Dahab, R.: Leveraging ontologies and machine-learning techniques for malware analysis into android permissions ecosystems. Comput. Secur. **78**, 429–453 (2018). Elsevier
95. Nguyen, G., Nguyen, B.M., Tran, D., Hluchy, L.: A heuristics approach to mine behavioural data logs in mobile malware detection system. Data Knowl. Eng. **115**, 129–151 (2018). Elsevier
96. Nguyen-Vu, L., Ahn, J., Jung, S.: Android fragmentation in malware detection. Comput. Secur. **87**, 101573 (2019). Elsevier
97. Noble, W.S.: What is a support vector machine? Nat. Biotechnol. **24**(12), 1565–1567 (2006)
98. Onwuzurike, L., Mariconti, E., Andriotis, P., Cristofaro, E.D., Ross, G., Stringhini, G.: Mamadroid: detecting android malware by building markov chains of behavioral models (extended version). ACM Trans. Priv. Secur. (TOPS) **22**, 1–34 (2019). ACM New York, NY, USA
99. Palumbo, P., Sayfullina, L., Komashinskiy, D., Eirola, E., Karhunen, J.: A pragmatic android malware detection procedure. Comput. Secur. **70**, 689–701 (2017). Elsevier
100. Pang, Y., Peng, L., Chen, Z., Yang, B., Zhang, H.: Imbalanced learning based on adaptive weighting and gaussian function synthesizing with an application on android malware detection. Inf. Sci. **484**, 95–112 (2019). Elsevier
101. Papadopoulos, H., Georgiou, N., Eliades, C., Konstantinidis, A.: Android malware detection with unbiased confidence guarantees. Neurocomputing **280**, 3–12 (2018). Elsevier
102. Park, M., You, G., Cho, S.J., Park, M., Han, S.: A framework for identifying obfuscation techniques applied to android apps using machine learning. J. Wirel. Mob. Networks Ubiquitous Comput. Dependable Appl. **10**, 22–30 (2019)
103. Peterson, L.E.: K-nearest neighbor. Scholarpedia **4**(2), 1883 (2009)
104. Peynirci, G., Eminağaoğlu, M., Karabulut, K.: Feature selection for malware detection on the android platform based on differences of IDF values. J. Comput. Sci. Technol. **35**(4), 946–962 (2020). https://doi.org/10.1007/s11390-020-9323-x
105. Priya, V.D., Visalakshi, P.: Detecting android malware using an improved filter based technique in embedded software, vol. 76. Elsevier Radarweg 29, 1043 NX Amsterdam, Netherlands (2020)
106. Qiu, J., Luo, W., Pan, L., Tai, Y., Zhang, J., Xiang, Y.: Predicting the impact of android malicious samples via machine learning. IEEE Access **7**, 66304–66316 (2019). IEEE
107. Rasheed, M.M., Faieq, A.K., Hashim, A.A.: Android botnet detection using machine learning, vol. 25 (2020)
108. Reed, R., MarksII, R.J.: Neural Smithing: Supervised Learning in Feedforward Artificial Neural Networks. MIT Press, Cambridge (1999)
109. Rehman, Z.U., et al.: Machine learning-assisted signature and heuristic-based detection of malwares in android devices. Comput. Electr. Eng. **69**, 828–841 (2018). Elsevier
110. Ren, B., Liu, C., Cheng, B., Guo, J., Chen, J.: Mobisentry: towards easy and effective detection of android malware on smartphones, vol. 2018. Hindawi (2018)
111. Ribeiro, J., Saghezchi, F.B., Mantas, G., Rodriguez, J., Abd-Alhameed, R.A.: Hidroid: prototyping a behavioral host-based intrusion detection and prevention system for android. IEEE Access **8**, 23154–23168 (2020). IEEE
112. Ribeiro, J., Saghezchi, F.B., Mantas, G., Rodriguez, J., Shepherd, S.J., Abd-Alhameed, R.A.: An autonomous host-based intrusion detection system for android mobile devices. Mob. Netw. Appl. **25**(1), 164–172 (2019). https://doi.org/10.1007/s11036-019-01220-y

113. Rouse, M., et al.: What is phishing? How it works and how to prevent it (2020)
114. Ruiz, F.: Fakeinstaller leads the attack on android phones (2012). Accessed 1 July 2016
115. Safavian, S.R., Landgrebe, D.: A survey of decision tree classifier methodology. IEEE Trans. Syst. Man Cybern. **21**(3), 660–674 (1991)
116. Salah, A., Shalabi, E., Khedr, W.: A lightweight android malware classifier using novel feature selection methods. Symmetry **12**, 858 (2020). Multidisciplinary Digital Publishing Institute
117. Mahdavifar, S., Kadir, A.F.A., Fatemi, R., Alhadidi, D., Ghorbani, A.A.: Dynamic android malware category classification using semi-supervised deep learning. In: 2020 IEEE International Conference on Dependable, Autonomic and Secure Computing, International Conference on Pervasive Intelligence and Computing, International Conference on Cloud and Big Data Computing, International Conference on Cyber Science and Technology Congress (DASC/PiCom/CBDCom/CyberSciTech), pp. 515–522. IEEE (2020)
118. Samra, A.A.A., Qunoo, H.N., Al-Rubaie, F., El-Talli, H.: A survey of static android malware detection techniques. In: 2019 IEEE 7Th Palestinian International Conference on Electrical and Computer Engineering (PICECE), pp. 1–6. IEEE (2019)
119. Samuel, A.L.: Some studies in machine learning using the game of checkers. IBM J. Res. Dev. **3**(3), 210–229 (1959)
120. Sen, S., Aydogan, E., Aysan, A.I.: Coevolution of mobile malware and anti-malware. IEEE Trans. Inf. Forensics Secur. **13**, 2563–2574 (2018). IEEE
121. Shams, E.A., Rizaner, A.: A novel support vector machine based intrusion detection system for mobile ad hoc networks. Wirel. Netw. **24**(5), 1821–1829 (2017). https://doi.org/10.1007/s11276-016-1439-0
122. Shang, F., Li, Y., Deng, X., He, D.: Android malware detection method based on naive Bayes and permission correlation algorithm. Clust. Comput. **21**, 1–12 (2017). https://doi.org/10.1007/s10586-017-0981-6
123. Sharma, A., Sahay, S.K.: Group-wise classification approach to improve android malicious apps detection accuracy (2019)
124. Sharma, S., Kumar, N., Kumar, R., Krishna, C.R.: The paradox of choice: investigating selection strategies for android malware datasets using a machine-learning approach. Commun. Assoc. Inf. Syst. **46**, 26 (2020)
125. Sharmeen, S., Huda, S., Abawajy, J.H., Ismail, W.N., Hassan, M.M.: Malware threats and detection for industrial mobile-iot networks. **6**, 15941–15957. IEEE (2018)
126. Singh, A.K., Jaidhar, C.D., Kumara, M.A.A.: Experimental analysis of Android malware detection based on combinations of permissions and API-calls. J. Comput. Virol. Hacking Tech. **15**(3), 209–218 (2019). https://doi.org/10.1007/s11416-019-00332-z
127. Stehman, S.V.: Selecting and interpreting measures of thematic classification accuracy. Remote Sens. Environ. **62**(1), 77–89 (1997)
128. Surendran, R., Thomas, T., Emmanuel, S.: Gsdroid: graph signal based compact feature representation for android malware detection. Expert Syst. Appl. **159**, 113581 (2020). Elsevier
129. Surendran, R., Thomas, T., Emmanuel, S.: A tan based hybrid model for android malware detection. J. Inf. Secur. Appl. **54**, 102483 (2020). Elsevier
130. Taheri, R., Ghahramani, M., Javidan, R., Shojafar, M., Pooranian, Z., Conti, M.: Similarity-based android malware detection using hamming distance of static binary features. **105**, 230–247. Elsevier (2020)

131. Talal, M., et al.: Comprehensive review and analysis of anti-malware apps for smartphones. Telecommun. Syst. **72**(2), 285–337 (2019)
132. Tenenboim-Chekina, L., et al.: Detecting application update attack on mobile devices through network featur. In: 2013 IEEE Conference on Computer Communications Workshops (INFOCOM WKSHPS), pp. 91–92. IEEE (2013)
133. Thomas, D.R., Beresford, A.R., Rice, A.: Security metrics for the android ecosystem. In: Proceedings of the 5th Annual ACM CCS Workshop on Security and Privacy in Smartphones and Mobile Devices, pp. 87–98 (2015)
134. Tian, K., Yao, D., Ryder, B.G., Tan, G., Peng, G.: Detection of repackaged android malware with code-heterogeneity features. IEEE Trans. Dependable Secure Comput. **17**, 64–77 (2017). IEEE
135. Tong, F., Yan, Z.: A hybrid approach of mobile malware detection in android. **103**, 22–31. Elsevier (2017)
136. Kouliaridis, V., et al.: A survey on mobile malware detection techniques. IEICE Trans. Inf. Syst. **103**(2), 204–211 (2020)
137. Vimala, S., Khanaa, V., Nalini, C.: A study on supervised machine learning algorithm to improvise intrusion detection systems for mobile ad hoc networks. Clust. Comput. **22**(2), 4065–4074 (2018). https://doi.org/10.1007/s10586-018-2686-x
138. Vinod, P., Zemmari, A., Conti, M.: A machine learning based approach to detect malicious android apps using discriminant system calls. Future Gener. Comput. Syst. **94**, 333–350 (2019). Elsevier
139. Wang, C., Li, Z., Mo, X., Yang, H., Zhao, Y.: An android malware dynamic detection method based on service call co-occurrence matrices. Ann. Telecommun. **72**(9), 607–615 (2017). https://doi.org/10.1007/s12243-017-0580-9
140. Wang, S., Chen, Z., Yan, Q., Yang, B., Peng, L., Jia, Z.: A mobile malware detection method using behavior features in network traffic. J. Netw. Comput. Appl. **133**, 15–25 (2019). Elsevier
141. Wang, X., Zhang, D., Su, X., Li, W.: Mlifdect: android malware detection based on parallel machine learning and information fusion, vol. 2017. Hindawi (2017)
142. Wang, X., Wang, W., He, Y., Liu, J., Han, Z., Zhang, X.: Characterizing android apps' behavior for effective detection of malapps at large scale. Future Gener. Comput. Syst. **75**, 30–45 (2017). Elsevier
143. Wang, X., Li, C.: Android malware detection through machine learning on kernel task structures. Neurocomputing **435**, 126–150 (2021). Elsevier
144. Wei, L., Luo, W., Weng, J., Zhong, Y., Zhang, X., Yan, Z.: Machine learning-based malicious application detection of android. IEEE Access **5**, 25591–25601 (2017). IEEE
145. Wei, S., Zhang, Z., Li, S., Jiang, P.: Calibrating network traffic with one-dimensional convolutional neural network with autoencoder and independent recurrent neural network for mobile malware detection, vol. 2021. Hindawi (2021)
146. Wu, B., et al.: Why an android app is classified as malware: toward malware classification interpretation. ACM Trans. Softw. Eng. Methodol. (TOSEM) **30**, 1–29 (2021). ACM New York, NY, USA
147. Wu, Q., Li, M., Zhu, X., Liu, B.: Mviidroid: a multiple view information integration approach for android malware detection and family identification. IEEE MultiMedia **27**, 48–57 (2020). IEEE
148. Wu, S., Wang, P., Li, X., Zhang, Y.: Effective detection of android malware based on the usage of data flow apis and machine learning. Inf. Softw. Technol. **75**, 17–25 (2016). Elsevier

149. Xiao, L., Li, Y., Huang, X., Du, X.: Cloud-based malware detection game for mobile devices with offloading. IEEE Trans. Mob. Comput. **16**, 2742–2750 (2017). IEEE
150. Xiao, X., Xiao, X., Jiang, Y., Liu, X., Ye, R.: Identifying android malware with system call co-occurrence matrices. Trans. Emerg. Telecommun. Technol. **27**, 675–684 (2016). Wiley Online Library
151. Xin, Y., et al.: Machine learning and deep learning methods for cybersecurity. IEEE Access **6**, 35365–35381 (2018)
152. Xu, Y., Wu, C., Zheng, K., Wang, X., Niu, X., Lu, T.: Computing adaptive feature weights with pso to improve android malware detection, vol. 2017. Hindawi (2017)
153. Yajin Zhou, X.J.: Dissecting android malware: characterization and evolution. In: 2012 IEEE Symposium on Security and Privacy, pp. 95–109. IEEE (2012)
154. Yang, M., Chen, X., Luo, Y., Zhang, H.: An android malware detection model based on dt-svm, vol. 2020. Hindawi (2020)
155. Yang, M., Wang, S., Ling, Z., Liu, Y., Ni, Z.: Detection of malicious behavior in android apps through api calls and permission uses analysis. Concurrency Comput. Pract. Experience **29**, e4172 (2017). Wiley Online Library
156. Yang, S., Wu, C., Zhu, S., Wang, H.: A machine learning based approach for mobile app rating manipulation detection, vol. 5. European Alliance for Innovation (EAI) (2019)
157. Ye, Y., Wu, L., Hong, Z., Huang, K.: A risk classification based approach for android malware detection. Tiis **11**, 959–981 (2017)
158. Yerima, S.Y., Alzaylaee, M.K., Sezer, S.: Machine learning-based dynamic analysis of android apps with improved code coverage. EURASIP J. Inf. Secur. **2019**(1), 1–24 (2019). https://doi.org/10.1186/s13635-019-0087-1
159. Yerima, S.Y., Sezer, S.: Droidfusion: a novel multilevel classifier fusion approach for android malware detection. IEEE Trans. Cybern. **49**, 453–466 (2018). IEEE
160. Zhang, H., Luo, S., Zhang, Y., Pan, L.: An efficient android malware detection system based on method-level behavioral semantic analysis. IEEE Access **7**, 69246–69256 (2019). IEEE
161. Zhang, J., Qin, Z., Zhang, K., Yin, H., Zou, J.: Dalvik opcode graph based android malware variants detection using global topology features. IEEE Access **6**, 51964–51974 (2018). IEEE
162. Zhang, Y., Ren, W., Zhu, T., Ren, Y.: Saas: a situational awareness and analysis system for massive android malware detection. Future Gener. Comput. Syst. **95**, 548–559 (2019). Elsevier
163. Zhou, H., Chai, H., Qiu, M.: Fraud detection within bankcard enrollment on mobile device based payment using machine learning. Front. Inf. Technol. Electron. Eng. **19**(12), 1537–1545 (2018). https://doi.org/10.1631/FITEE.1800580
164. Zhou, Q., Feng, F., Shen, Z., Zhou, R., Hsieh, M.-Y., Li, K.-C.: A novel approach for mobile malware classification and detection in Android systems. Multimed. Tools Appl. **78**(3), 3529–3552 (2018). https://doi.org/10.1007/s11042-018-6498-z
165. Zhu, C., Zhu, Z., Xie, Y., Jiang, W., Zhang, G.: Evaluation of machine learning approaches for android energy bugs detection with revision commits. IEEE Access **7**, 85241–85252 (2019). IEEE
166. Zhu, H.-J., Jiang, T.-H., Ma, B., You, Z.-H., Shi, W.-L., Cheng, L.: HEMD: a highly efficient random forest-based malware detection framework for android. Neural Comput. Appl. **30**(11), 3353–3361 (2017). https://doi.org/10.1007/s00521-017-2914-y

Forensic Analysis of Apple CarPlay:
A Case Study

Junsu Lee[1], Juwon Kim[2], Hojun Seong[3], Keonyong Lee[2], Seong-je Cho[1(✉)] [ID],
Younjai Park[4], and Minkyu Park[5] [ID]

[1] Department of Software Science, Dankook University, 152, Jukjeon-ro, Suji-gu,
Yongin-Si, Gyeoinggi-do 16890, Republic of Korea
{32153588,sjcho}@dankook.ac.kr
[2] Department of Applied Computer Engineering, Dankook University,
152, Jukjeon-ro, Suji-gu, Yongin-Si, Gyeoinggi-do 16890, Republic of Korea
{32161048,lky9620}@dankook.ac.kr
[3] Department of Computer Science and Engineering, Dankook University,
152, Jukjeon-ro, Suji-gu, Yongin-Si, Gyeoinggi-do 16890, Republic of Korea
hohojun0930@dankook.ac.kr
[4] Supreme Prosecutor's Office, Seoul, Republic of Korea
park1656@spo.go.kr
[5] Department of Computer Engineering, Konkuk University,
Chungju-Si 27478, Republic of Korea
minkyup@kku.ac.kr

Abstract. Apple CarPlay is a system that puts some features of your
iPhone or iPad onto the infotainment screen of a CarPlay-equipped vehicle, allowing drivers to use those features when driving. Using Apple
CarPlay, drivers can get turn-by-turn directions, make calls, send and
receive text messages, and listen to music. In this paper, we conduct an
actual driving test by connecting an iPhone to a vehicle that supports
Apple CarPlay. After driving, we acquire and analyze the CarPlay data
recorded on the iPhone in detail. Through the analysis of the collected
data, it is possible identify iPhone connection time, the driving destination, the GPS coordinates and speeds of the vehicle during driving,
etc. We can accurately reconstruct travelled routes of the vehicle using
the identified information. Our approach and results of collecting and
analyzing the CarPlay data can be used for vehicle forensics.

Keywords: Apple Carplay · Digital evidence · Vehicle forensics ·
Driving route

1 Introduction

The adoption of smart or autonomous vehicles connected to the Internet is
increasing, and the vehicles communicate with other vehicles, telematics infrastructure, and mobile devices. Therefore, smart vehicles are now becoming a
platform that provides a variety of mobility services by interacting with several

© Springer Nature Singapore Pte Ltd. 2022
I. You et al. (Eds.): MobiSec 2021, CCIS 1544, pp. 289–300, 2022.
https://doi.org/10.1007/978-981-16-9576-6_20

types of mobile devices. For example, a smart vehicle can be connected to a smartphone, and drivers can use the services or functions such as phone calls, SMS, SNS, and voice guidance and navigation provided by vehicle assistant applications of the smartphone during driving of their vehicle. Representative examples of the vehicle assistant applications are Apple CarPlay and Android Auto [1, 6, 12] Using Apple CarPlay and Android Auto, users can connect their mobile phone to an In-Vehicle Infotainment System (IVIS) to perform various tasks provided by the original equipment manufacturers(OEMs) [6, 12].

Apple CarPlay was introduced in 2014 as a way to integrate the iPhone and a vehicle's dashboard. For instance, after connecting an iPhone to the vehicle with CarPlay support, users can get turn-by-turn directions, make phone calls, send and receive text messages, and listen to music while driving. Most of CarPlay's features can be accessed using Siri which is Apple's digital assistant. Using CarPlay and digital car keys, you can even unlock and start your vehicle with iPhone. In iOS 13 or above versions, you can also use the dashboard to take control of your HomeKit accessories, such as door openers.

As smart vehicles communicate with various other devices and mobile apps which generate, transmit or store digital data, we can collect a large amount of digital evidence related to the vehicle's activity from the infotainment systems, smartphones and their apps [1, 3, 5, 7, 9, 11]. As a result, vehicles and mobile devices connected to the vehicles have been becoming a growing source of digital evidence in car accidents and criminal investigation. The digital evidence related to a driver's activities can be not only stored in the vehicle but also transmitted to vehicle assistant apps including Apple CarPlay [1].

According to the article of CNBC titled as 'Apple's massive success with CarPlay paves the way for automotive ambitions' on May 29 2021, over 80% of new cars sold in the United States support CarPlay. As CarPlay-equipped vehicles become common in our daily life, vehicle-related incident or accident information is stored in CarPlay's space of iOS. Thus, some researchers have started to look into forensic of Apple CarPlay [1, 3, 5].

In this paper, we deal with the acquisition and analysis of digital evidence from iOS CarPlay for digital forensic purpose. This work is an extension of the previous studies [3, 5]. We connect Apple CarPlay to the car Hyundai Palisade via a universal serial bus (USB) and drive the car according to a designed scenario. After driving, we collect and analyze the vehicle-related artifacts remaining in the iPhone. The meaningful data we obtained are the vehicle model, the name of the vehicle's Bluetooth device connected to the iPhone, USB connection and disconnection time, GPS coordinates and speeds that the vehicle moved while driving, call and text records, recent Siri conversation, etc. Especially, we can accurately reconstruct travelled routes of the vehicle by analyzing the obtained data. This information can be used as basic data for vehicle forensics.

This paper is organized as follows. Section 2 summarizes related work. Section 3 presents our approach to digital forensics of Apple CarPlay app. Section 4 compares our findings with some existing studies and discusses research limitations. Finally, we give the concluding remarks and present possible future work in Sect. 5.

2   Related Work

CarPlay connected to a certain vehicle can be an important source for analyzing the navigation information (travelled routes, visited destinations, etc.), phone call, text messaging, social network activity, and so on. Therefore, some researchers have started to conduct digital forensic studies on Apple CarPlay of iPhone [1,3,5], where CarPlay is connected to a vehicle and provides convenient functions to drivers.

Hick [5] forensically analyzed Apple CarPlay connected to Nissan in 2019. Edwards and Mahalik [3] extended the analysis of [5] by connecting Jailbroken iPhone X, 12.1.1 to Audi S3. They could investigate the layout of apps on the CarPlay's home screen, the name of the paired vehicles, the commu- nication with the Siri voice control, short message services, stored coordinates, etc. They also extracted an event log which showed the data such as new vehicle pairings or instructions for the music player.

Ebbers et al. [1] performed the digital forensic analysis of ten vehicle assistant apps of eight car manufacturers. The vehicle assistant apps tested in their study were myAudi, My BMW, FordPass, Mercedes me Adapter, myOpel, OnStar Europe, DriveMii, Seat Connect, Tesla and We Connect Go. They used an iPhone 6s with iOS 13. They reconstructed the driver's activities using the data stored on the smartphones and in the manufacturer's backend. They reconstructed trips and refueling process, determined parking positions and duration, and tracked the locking and unlocking of the vehicle.

Kopencova and Rak [7] have pointed out that it is not easy to use digital data obtained from vehicles and the devices worked with the vehicles because in-vehicle data with different formats are stored in different devices. In addition, both the vehicles' data and the tools to analyze it are generally not standardized.

3   Digital Forensics of Apple Carplay App

3.1   Experiment Environment

We conducted the experiment using the Hyundai Palisade 2019 model with linkage functionality with Apple CarPlay and the iPhone 7 Plus model with iOS 13.3 version and CarPlay app installed. Jailbreaking was applied to fully access the entire iPhone file system. We connect CarPlay to the display of the car's IVIS through a USB interface. The computer used for data acquisition and analysis has the specifications of CPU i5/i7, 16 GB RAM, and 256 GB SSD, and the Windows 10 (H2002) operating system was installed.

3.2   Data/Event Generation Using a Scenario

We construct a scenario of driving a vehicle and generating various events using the CarPlay-based interface for the experiment. While generating several events in chronological order, we check where and how the data generated for each

Fig. 1. Snapshot showing the experiment environment

event is stored on the connected iPhone. The events included in the scenario are connecting CarPlay to a vehicle, driving to a specific destination, making phone calls, sending text messages, Bluetooth pairing, voice command, etc.

In our scenario, a driver connected a vehicle to the iPhone and drove to the destination. A driver made phone calls and sent text messages by voice commands while driving. Information related to generated events were stored on the iPhone. The artifacts include event-related time information, vehicle speed, and voice commands, etc. These main artifacts were collected and analyzed. All process of following the scenario were recorded with a mobile phone camera. The recorded video was used to verify the correctness of acquired artifacts such as reconstructed paths in Sect. 3.4.

3.3 Apple Carplay Data Acqusition

We accumulate data based on the scenario and then collect Apple Carplay data. In the case of iPhone mobile forensic, to easily collect more data, it is necessary to jailbreak the iPhone [17,18]. Comparing the amount of data collected before and after jailbreaking in our experiment, we found that a larger amount of data was collected after jailbreaking. First, according to the manual provided by the Checkra1n jailbreaking tool, we entered the recovery mode and installed Checkra1n [16] on the target iPhone 7 plus model. If successful, you can see that the checkra1n app is installed on the home screen.

We connect the jailbroken iPhone to the local computer and extract the data using Final Data's FINAL Mobile Forensics tool [4]. When you launch the FINAL Mobile Forensics tool, you can see three menus: "Evidence Acquisition", "Open Image file", and "Import Case". For data collection, we select the "Evidence Acquisition" menu, select a platform and model, and "Logical Acquisition" as the acquisition method. Logical acquisition refers to a process that provides access to the filesystem and is usually performed by connecting a mobile device and a workstation with a wired or wireless connection [13,14]. Figure 2 shows the three menus that appear when the FINAL Mobile Forensics tool is executed, the execution screen that performs Logical Acquisition, and the .mef file created in the directory.

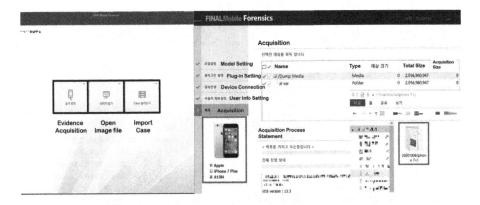

Fig. 2. Screenshot of FINAL mobile forensics tool execution

When the evidence acquisition step is completed, a file with the .mef extension is created. We, then, select the "Open Image File" menu on the initial screen of the Final Mobile Forensics tool to perform filesystem and record analysis for the .mef file. When the record analysis is completed, the "Workspace" subdirectory is created and a file with the .fmc extension is created. Finally, the file with the .fmc extension is loaded through "Import Case" menu and a case is created to check whether data extraction is performed correctly.

3.4   Apple Carplay Data Analysis

This section describes the analysis of the acquired data. First, we analyzed the data extracted from the case created through the "Import Case" menu in the previous section. This section describes the analysis of the collected data. First, we analyzed the data extracted from the case created through the "Import Case" menu in the previous section. And then, the iPhone DB data is extracted through SQL query and analyzed by DB4S (DB Browser for SQLite) and APOLLO module [2,15], and the data for driving route reconstruction is filtered. After performing the analysis in this way, the analysis results are explained and organized.

We check the files where data is stored, such as .plist and db files that exist in the created case. For files with .plist extension, we check the data using Plist Viewer. For each DB file, we check the table configuration, table column configuration, and stored data through DB4S, and extract the necessary data value using the SQL query statement of the APOLLO module. Figure 3 shows an example of extracting a specific column of a table using a SQL query when ZSTREAMNAME is "/carplay/isConnected" in the KnowledgeC.db file.

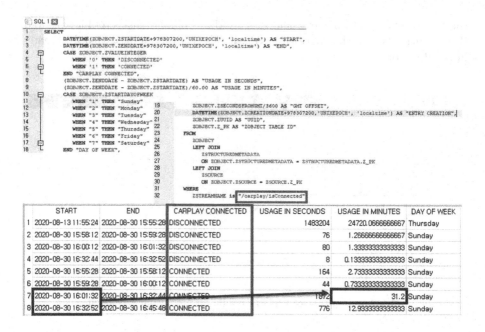

Fig. 3. Analysis of KnowledgeC.db file using SQL query statement

The data were analyzed using the analysis methods described above, Table 1 shows the major files and paths related to Apple CarPlay. There are three files in /var/mobile/Library/Preferences. com.apple.carplay.plist stores the information of the connected vehicle, com.apple.celestial.plist stores the Bluetooth information of the connected vehicle, and com.apple.carplayApp.plist stores information about the last time when an app was executed.

Table 1. Important folders and files for Apple CarPlay forensics

Path (Folder)		Files	Description
/var/mobile/Library/	Preferences/	com.apple.carplay.plist	Vehicles name,
		com.apple.celestial.plist	Name of Bluetooth on vehicle,
		com.apple.carplayApp.plist	Last time an app was executed
	CoreDuet/Knowledge/	KnowledgeC.db	Input/output audio info
			Connection/Disconnection time to CarPlay(USB)
	CoreDuet/People/	interactionC.db	SMS and call logs on iPhone
	Caches/com.apple.routined	Cache.sqlite	Geographic coordinates and speeds(m/s) over time
	AggregateDictionary/	ADDataStore.sqlitedb	Number of vehicles connected to iPhone
	SMS/	sms.db	Messages saved as text
	Assistant/	PreviousConversation.plist	Recent conversations with Siri
	Springboard/	CarDisPlayIconState.plist	Layout of apps on vehicles dashboard
/var/root/	Caches/locationd/	Cache.plist	Last time to connect/disconnect USB to vehicle
		Cache_encryptedC.db	Information related to behaviors such as boarding a vehicle, driving/stopping a vehicle, etc.

KnowledgeC.db exists in /var/mobile/Library/CoreDuet/Knowledge. KnowledgeC.db is a SQLite file that tracks lots of different activity on the device ranging from Bluetooth connections to which speaker is in use and what it is playing at any given time. The database is made up of several tables. Among them, ZOBJECT is the key table that has a number of columns. The ZEND-DATE and ZSTARTDATE columns of the ZOBJECT table record the most recent USB connection/disconnection time. If the value of the ZVALUEDOU-BLE column is 1.0, it means a disconnected state, and if 0.0, it means a connected state. In our experiments, the value of '/carplay/isConnected' is stored in the ZSTREAMNAME field regardless of a USB connection/disconnection.

The Cache.sqlite file in the /var/mobile/Library/Caches/com.apple.routined folder contains a detailed history of coordinates and speeds of the iPhone where it was. Therefore, if the contents of Cache.sqlite are processed using the APOLLO's SQL statement, we get TIMESTAMP indicating time information in seconds, COORDINATES recording location coordinates, and SPEED (KMP/H) information. As shown in Fig. 4, if you write a SQL statement and modify the attribute value, you can separately extract meaningful data and use them for path reconstruction.

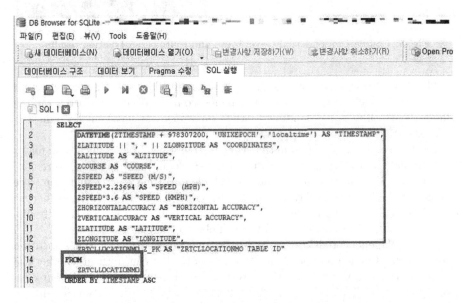

Fig. 4. Extracting attribute values required for path reconstruction using SQL query statements

This information is collected into a csv file and read into Google Maps, we can reconstruct the travelled route of the vehicle. The comparison of the travel route reconstructed in this way with the actual travel route is shown in Fig. 5. However, data is stored in Cache.sqlite even when CarPlay is not connected to the vehicle.

By extracting the CarPlay connection time information from the KnowledgeC.db file, only the corresponding data in Cache.sqlite can be extracted. To verify that the path was correctly reconstructed, the reconstructed path was verified by using the video recorded during data generation.

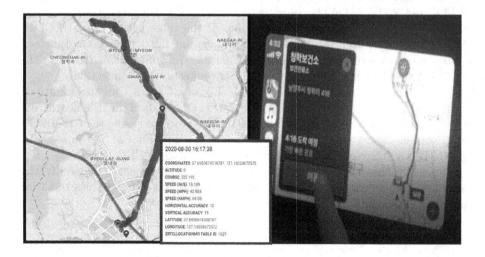

Fig. 5. Comparison of actual travel route and route reconstruction results

The ADDataStore.sqlitedb file in the /var/mobile/Library/AggregateDiction ary folder indicates the number of vehicles connected to the corresponding iPhone. The value corresponding to the com.apple.CarPlay.VehicleCount key of ADDataStore.sqlitedb indicates the number of connected vehicles.

The Cache.plist file located in the /var/root/Library/Caches/locationd folder stores vehicle information, the last time the vehicle and mobile phone were connected via USB, and the time when the vehicle and Bluetooth connection were disconnected. Apple CarPlay automatically connects to Bluetooth when connected via a USB. Usually, unless the Bluetooth connection is intentionally disconnected, it is disconnected when the vehicle stops engine.

The Cache_encryptedC.db file is in the /var/root/Library/Caches/location folder like the Cache.plist file. This file stores data that can confirm whether the vehicle is moving and whether the driver has been in the vehicle without connecting the iPhone to the vehicle. Table 2 summarizes the data identified in the Cache_encryptedC.db file. 'Start time' means the time the data was recorded, and 'Type' is determined by the ordered pair of 'isVehicular' and 'isMoving' attributes. When the (isVehicular, isMoving) pair is (0,1), it is recorded as 16, (1,0) as 256, and (1,1) as 4096. 'isVehicular' is an attribute indicating whether to board or not, and 1 means boarding and 0 means getting off. The 'isMoving' attribute indicates whether the vehicle is stopped or driven, 1 indicates driving, and 0 indicates stopping. 'vehicleExitState' means whether the driver or passenger gets off. Based on the video captured during the data acquistion process, at

4:09:10 PM, the driver stopped the vehicle and waited for a signal. If we check the table, we can confirm that the driver is in the car and the car stopped. After a while, at 4:10:23 pm, we can confirm that the data in the table and the driver's behavior match.

Table 2. The recorded data of Cache_encryptedC.db file

Start time	Type	Confidence	isVehicular	isMoving	vehicleExitState
4:09:10pm	256	3	1	0	0
4:10:23pm	4096	3	1	1	0

The sms.db file in the /var/mobile/Library/SMS folder records text messages, PreviousConversation.plist in /var/mobile/Library/Assistant records voice commands using Siri functions, /var/mobile/Library/CoreDuet/People. In the ZINTERACTIONS table of the interactionC.db file, the called phone number, call time, and message transmission information are stored.

4 Discussions and Limitations

After connecting Apple CarPlay to the car Palisade via a USB and driving the car, we have collected and analyzed various type of digital data stored in iPhone worked with the car. In the experiment, we could acquire the interesting information such as event timestamps, iPhone connection and disconnection, the GPS coordinates and speeds of the car created during driving, and so on. Figure 6 shows the timestamps, and the coordinates and speeds of the vehicle which have been stored in iPhone during driving. The path and name of the table shown Fig. 6 are private/var/mobile/Library/Caches/com.apple.routined/Cache.sqlite/ ZRT-CLLOCATIONMO. It is possible to accurately reconstruct the travelled routes using the information in the table (please refer to Fig. 5).

Note that the information of the table can be created on an iPhone itself even when the iPhone is not connected to a vehicle. For confirming that the information was the actual coordinates and speeds of the vehicle connected to the iPhone. We must identify the time when the iPhone was connected to the vehicle using the data in knowledgeC.db or Cache.plist of Table 1.

Edwards and Mahalik [3] have also showed a table information of Fig. 7, which is similar to that of the ZRTCLLOCATIONMO table of Fig. 6. The file name and the database name are different. These differences may be due to the different iPhone versions and vehicles used in the experiment. They did not describe how to reconstruct travelled routes in their study [3].

According to the study of Ebbers et al. [1], the scope of the data stored on the smartphone communicating with a vehicle strongly depends on the equipment of the vehicle. Among the ten vehicle assistant apps, Mercedes me Adapter and We Connect Go apps provide extensive data. The Mercedes me Adapter app

TIMESTAMP	COORDINATES	ALTITUDE	COURSE	SPEED (M/S)	SPEED (MPH)	SPEED (KMPH)
2020-08-30 16:05	37.6487802903964, 127.123782154556	0	47.95164	14.71311111	32.91234677	52.9672
2020-08-30 16:05	37.6488672034982, 127.123903345385	0	47.95164	14.30155556	31.99172168	51.4856
2020-08-30 16:05	37.648957070076, 127.124028654515	0	47.95164	14.71311111	32.91234677	52.9672
2020-08-30 16:05	37.6490430048448, 127.12414846221	0	47.90848	14.30155556	31.99172168	51.4856
2020-08-30 16:05	37.6491293765949, 127.1242687155928	0	47.90848	14.30155556	31.99172168	51.4856
2020-08-30 16:05	37.6492135179992, 127.124386155712	0	48.04177	13.47844444	30.15047152	48.5224
2020-08-30 16:05	37.6492946440236, 127.124499567384	0	47.9903	13.427	30.03539338	48.3372
2020-08-30 16:05	37.6493704168358, 127.124605367764	0	47.9903	12.70677778	28.42429948	45.7444
2020-08-30 16:05	37.6494449663796, 127.124709460114	0	47.9903	12.24377778	27.38859626	44.0776
2020-08-30 16:05	37.6495136617188, 127.124805536423	0	48.08317	11.47211111	25.66242423	41.2996
2020-08-30 16:05	37.6495826475339, 127.124902174754	0	48.08146	11.47211111	25.66242423	41.2996
2020-08-30 16:05	37.6496479478515, 127.124993650279	0	48.08146	10.649	23.82117406	38.3364
2020-08-30 16:05	37.6497077069972, 127.125077363489	0	48.08146	10.186	22.78547084	36.6696
2020-08-30 16:05	37.6497667155857, 127.125160025286	0	48.08146	9.825888889	21.97992389	35.3732
2020-08-30 16:05	37.6498249484223, 127.125241600376	0	48.08146	9.362888889	20.94422067	33.7064
2020-08-30 16:05	37.6498832957041, 127.125323335838	0	48.08146	9.774444444	21.86484576	35.188
2020-08-30 16:05	37.6499430242436, 127.125407006121	0	48.08146	9.774444444	21.86484576	35.188
2020-08-30 16:05	37.6500057907909, 127.125494867815	0	48.05526	10.649	23.82117406	38.3364
2020-08-30 16:05	37.6500698537687, 127.125584527459	0	48.05551	10.649	23.82117406	38.3364

Fig. 6. ZRTCLLOCATIONMO table of Cache.sqlite in our work

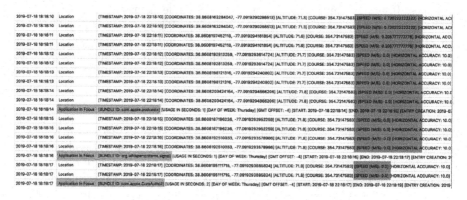

Fig. 7. Location DBs and knowledgeC.db in [3]

provides the largest amount forensic data such as drive log, recent location, parking, refueling, user info, car info, and logout. In the myAudi app, they could not obtain the following data: recent location, parking, user info, car info, logout, and uninstall info. The my BMW app does not store any relevant data on the file system.

The Mercedes me Adapter app was started up by plugging a vehicle adapter into the vehicle's On-Board Diagnostic (OBD) interface not a USB [1]. The adapter interacted with the iPhone via a Bluetooth connection. The database DriverLogbook.sqlite stored the records of the driver logbook. The trips with start and destination addresses were linked to data records from the ZDLCORE-DATRACKPOINTS table, which stored the vehicle location every ten seconds. The adapter or VW DataPlug must be plugged into OBD interface and communicate via a Bluetooth connection. Then, the apps offer trip lists or trip logs [1].

Table 3. Comparison of our work and previous related studies

	Vehicles/Apps	Data acquisition method	Important path	Key digital data
Hick [5]	Nissan/CarPlay	Mobile Device Model : Nexus 5X(Android 8) Rooting by TWRP and Magisk Access '/data' partition for acquisition	.../var/mobile/Library/ .../var/root/Library/	Device connections/disconnections, Name of the vehicles paired with iPhone, Layout of the home screen, Most recently used apps, Siri usage (Conversation with Siri, iMessage, Inquiry/Response), Contacts list, Bluetooth MAC address for vehicle, Cached Locations with GPS coordinates being where driver parked, etc.
Edwards & Mahalik [3]	Audi S3/CarPlay	Mobile Device Model : iPhone X(iOS 12.1.1) : Samsung smartphone Jailbreaking iPhone X Rooting Samsung smartphone	.../var/mobile/Library/	Device connections/disconnections, Name of the vehicles paired with iPhone, Layout of the home screen, Siri usage (messages), SMS chats, Audio input/output, App usage in vehicle, Driving information (location DBs, etc.), Cached Locations with GPS coordinates and speeds of vehicle, etc.
Ebbers [1]	Audi/myAudi, Mercedes/Mercedes me Adapter, Tesla/Tesla, etc.	Mobile Device Model : iPhone 6S(iOS 13) : Xiaomi Redmi Note 4(Android 7) Jailbreaking by Checkra1n Acquisition by iPhone RootFS tool Installing TWRP for acquisition	.../var/mobile/Containers/ Data/Application/<UUID>/.	Drive log, Recent location, Parking, Refueling, User info, Car info, Logout. (Note that different apps provide different types and amounts of available data.)
Our work	Palisade/CarPlay	Mobile Device Model : iPhone 7 Plus(iOS 13.3) Jailbreaking by Checkra1n Acquisition by Final Mobile Forensics tool	.../var/mobile/Library/ .../var/root/Library/	Device connections/disconnections, Name of vehicles, Bluetooth MAC address for vehicle, USB connection time, Layout of the home screen, Most recently used apps, Siri usage (conversation with Siri), Audio input/output, Cached Locations with GPS coordinates and speeds of vehicle, Call logs, SMS chats, etc.

Our study focuses on only Apple CarPlay communicated with the Hyundai Palisade. We did not deal with other smartphone apps for vehicles such as Android Auto, neither in-vehicle infotainment (IVI) systems.

5   Conclusion

In this paper, we connected iOS CarPlay to the vehicle Palisade, generated various events based on a scenario while driving, and then analyzed CarPlay-related data stored in the iPhone. As a result of the analysis, it was possible to grasp the time that CarPlay was connected to the vehicle, the name of Bluetooth on the vehicle, the driving speeds, GPS locations, timestamps, etc. In addition, we analyzed what kinds of searches were conducted using Siri. By merging the analyzed data and composing them based on a timeline, it was possible to acquire information that could be used for vehicle forensics.

In the future, we plan to conduct research on collecting and analyzing data stored in the vehicle when the vehicle is connected to a smartphone and driven. We will then compare the data in the vehicle with those in the smartphone.

Acknowledgment. This research was supported by Basic Science Research Program through the National Research Foundation of Korea (NRF) funded by the Ministry of Science and ICT (no. 2021R1A2C2012574), and also supported by Research Program funded by the Supreme Prosecutors' Office of the Republic of Korea (SPO).

References

1. Ebbers, S., Ising, F., Saatjohann, C., Schinzel, S.: Grand theft app: Digital forensics of vehicle assistant apps. arXiv preprint arXiv:2106.04974 (2021)

2. Edwards, S.: Apple pattern of life lazy output'er (apollo). https://github.com/mac4n6/APOLLO. Accessed 2020

3. Edwards, S., Mahalik, H.: They See Us Rollin, They Hatin-Forensics of iOS CarPlay and Android Auto. SANS DFIR (2019)

4. Final Data: Final mobile forensics. https://finaldata.com/mobile/

5. Hickman, J.: Ridin' with apple carplay. https://thebinaryhick.blog/2019/05/08/ridin-with-apple-carplay/. Accessed 2019

6. Holstein, T., Wallmyr, M., Wietzke, J., Land, R.: Current challenges in compositing heterogeneous user interfaces for automotive purposes. In: Kurosu, M. (ed.) HCI 2015. LNCS, vol. 9170, pp. 531–542. Springer, Cham (2015). https://doi.org/10.1007/978-3-319-20916-6_49

7. Kopencova, D., Rak, R.: Issues of vehicle digital forensics. In: 2020 XII International Science-Technical Conference Automotive Safety, pp. 1–6. IEEE (2020)

8. Kumari, N., Mohapatra, A.K.: An insight into digital forensics branches and tools. In: 2016 International Conference on Computational Techniques in Information and Communication Technologies (ICCTICT), pp. 243–250. IEEE (2016)

9. Le-Khac, N.-A., Jacobs, D., Nijhoff, J., Bertens, K., Choo, K.-K.R.: Smart vehicle forensics: challenges and case study. Futur. Gener. Comput. Syst. **109**, 500–510 (2020)

10. Raji, M., Wimmer, H., Haddad, R.: Analyzing data from an android smartphone while comparing between two forensic tools. In: SoutheastCon 2018, pp. 1–6. IEEE (2018)

11. Rak, R., Kopencova, D.: Actual issues of modern digital vehicle forensic. Internet of Things Cloud Comput. **8**(1), 12–16 (2020)

12. Strayer, D.L., et al.: Visual and cognitive demands of carplay, android auto, and five native infotainment systems. Hum. Factors **61**(8), 1371–1386 (2019)

13. SWGDE: SWGDE Best Practices for Mobile Phone Forensics. https://www.swgde.org/documents/Current%20Documents/2013-02-11%20SWGDE%20Best%20Practices%20for%20Mobile%20Phone%20Examinations%20V2-0. Accessed 2013

14. Ayers, R., Brothers, S., Jansen, W.: Guidelines on Mobile Device Forensics (NIST Special Publication 800–101). US Department of Commerce, Washington, DC (2014)

15. Edwards, S.: Exploring macOS with APOLLO. https://github.com/mac4n6/Presentations/blob/master/Exploring%20macOS%20with%20APOLLO/Exploring_macOS_with_APOLLO.pdf. Accessed 14 Mar 2020

16. checkra1n 0.10.2 beta. https://checkra.in/releases/0.10.2-beta

17. Knox, S., Moghadam, S., Patrick, K., Phan, A., Choo, K.-K.R.: What's really happning? A forensic analysis of android and iOS happn dating apps. Comput. Secur. **94**, 101833 (2020)

18. Bays, J., Karabiyik, U.: Forensic analysis of third party location applications in android and ios. In: IEEE INFOCOM 2019-IEEE Conference on Computer Communications Workshops (INFOCOM WKSHPS), pp. 1–6. IEEE (2019)

Classification and Analysis of Vulnerabilities in Mobile Device Infrastructure Interfaces

Konstantin Izrailov[1,2] , Dmitry Levshun[1] , Igor Kotenko[1] ,
and Andrey Chechulin[1]([✉])

[1] St. Petersburg Federal Research Center of the Russian Academy of Sciences,
39, 14th Line V.O., St. Petersburg 199178, Russia
{izrailov,levshun,ivkote,chechulin}@comsec.spb.ru
[2] Bonch-Bruevich St. Petersburg State University of Telecommunications,
49 Kronverksky Pr., St. Petersburg 197101, Russia
https://www.sut.ru/eng, https://spcras.ru/en/

Abstract. A consequence of the widespread use of mobile devices is the emergence of a threat to information security. One of the reasons for this lies in the vulnerabilities of device interaction interfaces. This area is quite new, so it is not well investigated. The aim of this investigation is to classify and analyze vulnerabilities of infrastructure interfaces. As a part of the results the general classification model is proposed in an analytical form. This model allows one to map vulnerabilities to the interface classes. Interfaces are separated based on infrastructure components they provide interaction between. Additionally, the interactions themselves are separated into subclasses. The categorical division apparatus is used for classification with 64 classes. The relationship between the infrastructure of mobile devices and the vulnerabilities of its interfaces is analysed. An experiment was carried out for a typical scenario of finding the owner of devices in the infrastructure of mobile devices. The experiment showed the efficiency of the proposed model and made it possible to make a number of predictions regarding potential vulnerabilities in the future.

Keywords: Mobile devices · Information security · Interaction · Interface · Model · Categorical division

1   Introduction

One of the most important indicator of the development of modern society is its almost complete transition to information technology. The high mobility of such technologies further enhances the quality of life of people. Providing mobility requires a lot of technical support from assistive devices, both working in conjunction with each other and requiring human support. Thus, we can talk about the need to create a whole Mobile Device Infrastructure (hereinafter – MDI).

The reported study was funded by RFBR, project number 19-29-06099.

I. You et al. (Eds.): MobiSec 2021, CCIS 1544, pp. 301–319, 2022.
https://doi.org/10.1007/978-981-16-9576-6_21

Nevertheless, one of the challenges arising in this case is the appearance in the created technologies and devices that implement them such entities as vulnerabilities, leading to information security breaches [15]. As a result, in a number of cases this is the cause not only of economic damage or political defeat, but even of human losses [13]. The latter is especially important for areas directly related to the life of people.

The devices that ensure the functioning of the main subsystems of the MDI can be considered standard and well studied from the security standpoint (for example, there are extensive databases of vulnerabilities for operating systems, telecommunication equipment, network protocols, etc. [1,19]). However, such a bottleneck as the interfaces of interaction between the elements of the MDI, at the moment, are practically ignored. By interfaces, we mean not an abstract entity that means the separation of two environments, but a real part of the MDI infrastructure, which ensures the exchange of data between two elements [12, 26]. As a result, there is not enough information about the vulnerabilities of such interfaces, which calls into question both the security of existing interface tools and does not allow paying due attention to this in the ones that are still being developed. Thus, the problem of searching for vulnerabilities of interfaces applicable to MDI is especially urgent. The first step towards its solution can be an analysis of the subject area and the creation of a model for classifying interface vulnerabilities, which is what the current research is devoted to. In the features of such a model, it is necessary to indicate that it is suitable not only for searching for already known vulnerabilities (i.e. existing in practice), but also allows predicting those that have not yet been discovered (assumed in theory).

Novelty of the paper lies in the suggested solution assuming the inclusion in the classification model of the requirement of "necessity and sufficiency", which is mean that any, even hypothetical, vulnerability is guaranteed to be attributed to one and only one class. Also, the presented model includes the classification of a variability by the possibility of its expansion and detailing by adding new pairs of categorical separation.

The paper has the following structure. Section 2 provides an overview of the work on methods and models for classifying MDI interfaces and vulnerabilities. Section 3 builds a model for classifying MDI vulnerabilities. Section 4 makes an experiment on the application of the classification model. Section 5 discusses the disadvantages of the proposed paths and solutions. Section 6 summarizes the main findings of the current investigation, as well as describes ways of its future development.

2   Related Work

Let us consider state of the art in the area of methods and models for classification of MDI interfaces and their vulnerabilities in terms of their application and problem solved.

In [24] an adaptive model for detection of vulnerabilities in the interfaces of unmanned vehicles is proposed. The detection process is based on dynamic assessment of information states of resources. The input data represents network traffic that is distributed between the following states: normal state, denial of service, unauthorized access from a remote computer, unauthorized access to privileged user rights, scanning ports to identify vulnerabilities in the system.

In [18] a new class of access control vulnerabilities in GUI-based applications is introduced. Such vulnerabilities can arise through misuse of widget attributes. The classification of vulnerabilities is as follows: (1) unauthorized information disclosure; (2) unauthorized information modification and (3) unauthorized callback execution. Moreover, authors implemented a technique to analyze applications and discovered exploitable security-relevant bugs in user interfaces.

In [17] a method for detecting vulnerabilities of unmanned vehicle interfaces is proposed. Interfaces are divided into the following types: vehicle to device, vehicle to infrastructure, vehicle to pedestrian and vehicle to vehicle. This method is based on continuous discretization of values of unmanned vehicle resources, which include: communication channel, processor, memory. For each of these resources, changes in the degree of resource load and the speed of such changes are evaluated.

In [3] an approach for detection of vulnerabilities in interfaces of unmanned vehicles is proposed. The proposed approach is based on the statistical distance estimation between the probability distributions of a random variable. The Jensen-Shannon information criterion is used as an evaluation criterion. The vulnerability detection is performed on the basis of processing the values of resources state of unmanned vehicles.

In [25] a new classification for side-channel attacks is considered. The classification divides side-channel attacks into passive and active. In turn, both passive and active attacks are divided into physical and logical. Passive and active physical attacks are divided into local, vicinity and remote. The same classification is made for active physical and logical attacks – they both are also divided into local, vicinity and remote.

In [21] a comprehensive review of the state-of-the art in the area of vulnerabilities detection in embedded systems and firmware images is proposed. The analyzed techniques are divided into static analysis, dynamic analysis, symbolic execution, and hybrid approaches. Techniques were compared both quantitative and qualitative. For example, vulnerability detection techniques are applied to embedded systems in 37% of cases, firmware – 21% and binaries – 42%. As unresolved issues of the vulnerability detection the following are mentioned: detection of unknown vulnerabilities, detection of runtime vulnerabilities, identification of inline functions, scalability and lack of semantic insights.

In [9] the process of static analysis on code property graphs is presented. Such graph combines abstract syntax tree, control flow graph, and program dependence graph.There were analyzed different checkers of vulnerabilities, and extracted most commonly used operations as a set of interfaces. After that, the implementation based on the obtained set of interfaces was evaluated on the

Linux kernel source code. Experimental results showed that proposed interfaces can express most vulnerabilities correctly.

In [20] a systematic review of threats and vulnerabilities in embedded systems is conducted. Moreover, authors presented an attack taxonomy for embedded systems. Attacks are divided based on precondition, attack method, vulnerability, target and effect. Preconditions are divided into unknown, miscellaneous, direct physical, physical proximate, Internet facing and local/remote access. Attack methods are divided into unknown, normal use, malware, reversing, eavesdropping/sniffing, control hijacking and injection. Vulnerabilities are divided into unknown, insecure configuration, improper use of cryptography, weak access control/authentication, web and programming errors. Targets are divided into protocol, device, application, operating system/firmware and hardware. Effects are divided into unknown, miscellaneous, degraded levels of protection, financial loss, illegitimate access, information leakage, integrity violation, code execution and denial of service.

In [16] vulnerability research in the area of critical infrastructure security is described. This research is focused on the software for Human-Machine Interfaces that is used on control panels of workstations. The results of this research were used to improve the security of Industrial Control Systems and Supervisory Control and Data Acquisition Systems. Authors taxonomy allows to distinguish vulnerabilities that occur due to design flaws and programming errors, require internal or external attack vector, by difficulty of exploitation, patch status and mitigation effectiveness.

In [28] an overview of existing attacks on virtual and augmented reality interfaces of security systems is provided. Vulnerabilities are divided into vulnerabilities of reality, virtuality and mixed reality. Virtuality vulnerabilities are divided into input, output, data processing and storage. Reality vulnerabilities are divided into sense organs, psyche and perception as well as data transfer. Mixed reality contains vulnerabilities of the intersection of virtual and real environments.

In [2] an exhaustive framework for cyber security threat classifications in mobile devices and applications is proposed. This framework included the classification and principles of cyber threats. Authors propose using this framework to systematically identify cyber security threats and show their potential impacts. It is assumed that such actions will help to draw the mobile users' attention to those threats, and enable them to take protective actions as appropriate.

In [6] the state-of-the-art in the area of hybrid BCI was systematically reviewed and analyzed. As a result, authors developed a systematic taxonomy for classifying the types of hybrid brain-computer interfaces (BCIs) with multiple taxonomic criteria. As a categorization criteria, authors used: (1) diversity of input signal, (2) stimulus modality, (3) signal signature, (4) role of operation and (5) mode of operation. Input signals are divided into homogeneous and heterogeneous. Stimulus modality is divided into visual, tactile, auditory and operant. Signal signature is divided into steady-state, event-related, motion-onset, sensor-motor rhythm, mental speech and m-rhythm. Role of operation is divided into sequential-selector, sequential-switch and simultaneous. Mode of operation is divided into synchronous and asynchronous.

In [8] authors present a unified taxonomy of external human machine interfaces (eHMI) in automated vehicles. This taxonomy is developed for a systematic comparison of the eHMI across 18 dimensions, covering their physical characteristics and communication aspects from the perspective of human factors and human-machine interaction. For example, authors divided eHMI in accordance with vehicle type, communication modality, nature of message, HMI placement, communication strategy, communication resolution, implementation complexity, etc.

The analysis showed that the problem of a unified classification of interfaces of complex information systems still remains not fully solved. Moreover, information security aspects are usually not taken into account. Existing approaches are solving specific tasks and not applicable for classification and analysis of vulnerabilities in interfaces of infrastructure of mobile devices. The proposed approach is based on the vulnerability model that is presented in the following section.

3 Developed Model

Let's analyze the subject area and build an appropriate model, in terms of which it will be possible to define a method for searching for vulnerabilities in MDI.

Proceeding from the fact that there is no uniform classification of interface vulnerabilities, it is advisable to propose our own, based on the following principle. First, since each interface is a part of the MDI that provides information exchange, the vulnerabilities of the interface represent some weakness that leads to violations of such exchange. Therefore, the vulnerability is inextricably linked with the firmware that implements the interface, and therefore the classification of vulnerabilities can be compared with the classification of interfaces. Secondly, the MDI subsystems have certain goals (due to the general concept of mobility and personalization of services during the globalization of exchange), and, therefore, its interfaces solve some specialized tasks for the exchange of information between previously known infrastructure components. Thus, it is possible to classify the interfaces based on their associated MDI components. As a consequence, the classification of interfaces will also affect the classification of their vulnerabilities. Thirdly, the interaction can hypothetically (since not only at the present moment, but also in the future) occur between any pair of components (thereby obtaining the topology of a fully connected graph), which leads to the existence of the same number of interfaces and their classes. Fourthly, the features of information exchange are associated not only with the final components, but also with the data transfer mechanism, which will add another "sub-level" of classification. And, fifthly, since the implementation of interfaces is some relatively standard software and hardware solutions (user input / output devices, exchange with surrounding devices, network exchange with infrastructure, etc.), which themselves have already known vulnerabilities, then with each a certain group of vulnerabilities can be associated with an interface class.

In this case, MDI refers to the structure of ensuring the functioning of devices moving in space, as well as other participants to whom these devices provide services.

3.1 Use Case

As an explanation of this infrastructure, we describe an example of the following scenario of its functioning, which will be used below.

A man-athlete makes a morning jog in the park. He has a mobile phone, sports bracelet and wireless headphones with him. The bracelet monitors the athlete's heart rate and transmits this information via Bluetooth to the athlete's mobile phone. The mobile phone tracks the coordinates of the athlete using its own GPS tracker and builds a route that transmits via GPRS to the athlete's personal account. The bracelet informs the person of the arrival of a call with the help of vibration, to answer which it is necessary to touch it. The headphones are connected to the phone via Bluetooth and play a music track. The athlete controls the sound volume by touching the headphones. Also, the choice of the track they do through the touch screen of the phone. To improve the quality of the Internet connection and improve the positioning of the phone, Wi-Fi towers with free access are provided in the park. And since both cellular, Wi-Fi and other supporting equipment are technically complex, it requires constant checking, tuning and repair – by the maintenance personnel (engineer) from the special services. Thus, in such a fairly simple scenario, the following MDI participants are present: mobile device owner, support engineer, mobile phone, wireless headphones, smart bracelet, mobile tower, GPS satellite or signal booster, wireless local area network (Wi-Fi) tower. At the same time, the following interactions are possible, provided by qualitatively different interfaces: GPS, GPRS, Wi-Fi, Bluetooth, physical presses, photoplethysmography (change in human heart rate), touch presses, vibration, graphic screen, physical and program access (to the software of stationary communication devices). And each of these interfaces can have vulnerabilities, for example, the headphones can connect to someone else's phone, the phone can determine the wrong coordinates, or the bracelet will not make it possible to answer an important call.

Summarizing the above, the idea of the model consists of classes of vulnerabilities that are identical to the classes of the interfaces containing them, which are determined by the classes of MDI components they bind and the purpose of the transmitted data. Each such class (vulnerability or interface) contains a specific and previously known set of vulnerabilities; for example, in NVD (National Vulnerability Database), CVE (Common Vulnerabilities and Exposures), etc.

The predictive features of the proposed model are that only when designing a certain interface it will be possible to determine its class and predict possible actual vulnerabilities, the prevention of which will be carried out at early stages – when creating a conceptual model of a device or its architecture.

Let us describe in more detail the main elements of the model, created taking into account the above principles.

3.2   Components and Their Interactions

One of the main criteria for any correct classification is compliance with the requirements for the necessity and sufficiency of division. First, that any element must be assigned to no more than one class. Second, that for any element there is at least one class. Thus, the simultaneous fulfillment of the conditions will allow to unambiguously classify all the elements.

A workable approach used for this is the use of the apparatus of categorical division by isolating pairs of categories that are antagonists (in a philosophical sense), and then combining them [11]. As a result, the entire set of elements will be split on opposite sides of the conditional start of the middle.

Let us further distinguish categorical pairs using the key features of the MDI, which will allow us to divide the latter into a set of equivalent classes of components. At the same time, in addition to the requirements for the necessity and sufficiency of division, the size of the classes should not differ significantly. Otherwise (for example, if elements are missing in one of the classes) it may be useless. For example, dividing MDI according to the pair Expert vs Intellectual is likely to be effective, since the level of intellectualization of its components is more or less close. As a result, the elements are likely to fall into one of the classes, or the division will be too subjective.

It is on the basis of the above considerations that the subsequent selection of pairs of categories should be based on the key features of the MDI, which have internal interaction and confrontation. Each pair of categories will divide the components into 2 qualitatively different subsets. Thus, the category in this case is identical to one of the classes in the binary classification.

The first feature is that MDI provides services to a specific user. Thus, the 1st pair of the MDI component classifier will consist of the following antagonist categories: 1) The category "Human" (CC_H), corresponding to a subset of human components that have consciousness and are able to set a goal to solve it; 2) The category "Machine" (CC_M), corresponding to a subset of automatic components that are not conscious and cannot set a goal.

Thus, all components of the MDI can be classified into those in which the functioning is based on humans or automata.

The second feature is that there are moving elements within the MDI. Thus, the 2nd pair of the MDI component classifier will consist of the following antagonist categories: 1) Category "Static" (CC_S), corresponding to a subset of static components that are stationary in the infrastructure; 2) Category "Dynamic" (CC_D), corresponding to a subset of dynamic components moving in the infrastructure.

Thus, all components of the MDI can be reclassified as those that are stationary or moving.

Each categorical division is a classification of all MDI components into 2 classes according to qualitatively different characteristics. The use of all 2 indicated divisions into categorical pairs at once will allow to single out $2^2 = 4$ classes. Each of these classes will be defined by a combination of one of the elements of each category pair. Let's give an interpretation of each class (with an example from the script above), denoting them with the symbol "C" and a subscript in the form of a sequence of the first letters of the categories that form them:

1. C_{HS} – stationary people, for example, a service for maintaining GPS towers;
2. C_{HD} – people on the move, for example, the owner of mobile devices;
3. C_{MS} – fixed automatic devices, for example, Wi-Fi-point;
4. C_{MD} – moving automatic devices, for example, a mobile phone or a bracelet.

An important feature of these classes is the difference in their goal-orientation, since pairs of categories were selected based on the features that reflect the MDI. As a result, different interactions are possible between all classes of components, having certain directions and type [4] of data transfer. In this case, the interaction of the components of each class with the components of the same class is possible, since the task-oriented modules included in its composition (as opposed to the goal-orientedness of the entire component) can transfer data to each other.

In a formalized form, the division of MDI into components ($component_i$ from the set $Components$) and their classes ($Class_i^{Component}$ from composition 8, identified earlier) can be written as follows:

$$\begin{cases} Components = \bigcup_{i=1..4} component_i; \\ \forall i = 1..4 | component_i \leftrightarrow Class_i^{Component}; \\ \forall i = 1..4 | Class_i^{Component} \equiv \{C_{HS}, C_{HD}, C_{MS}, C_{MD}\}. \end{cases} \qquad (1)$$

Thus, each component has its own class and vice versa.

These 4 fully connected component classes form $4 \times 4 = 16$ options for interaction between classes (ordered $< component_i | component_j >$ pairs from the $Components$ set) associated with the corresponding $Class_k^{Component}$ classes from a set of 16 classes), which can be written in a formalized form as follows:

$$\begin{cases} Interactions = \bigcup_{i=1..4, j=1..4} < component_i | component_j >; \\ \forall i = 1..4, j = 1..4, k = 1..16 | \\ < component_i | component_j > \leftrightarrow Class_k^{Interaction}. \end{cases} \qquad (2)$$

Thus, with every interaction between the two components, $< component_i | component_j >$ associated class $Class_k^{Component}$ and vice versa. Each interaction is provided with a set of dedicated interfaces.

Let's consider the possibilities of each of the interactions between the components based on the characteristics of the MDI. The first feature is that MDI is not only a source of private goods (i.e. paid, such as mobile communications), but also public (i.e. free, such as GPS signals from satellites). To prevent the free use of commercial services, it is obvious that access restriction mechanisms should be applied. Mechanisms can be built, for example, based on AAA (Authentication, Authorization, Accounting) processes. Or, in the case of physical protection, on the fingerprint on the phone. Thus, the 1st pair of the classifier of interactions of MDI components from the position "availability" (the designation of the a

index below) will consist of the following categories-antagonists: 1) The "Open" accessibility category (CI_O), corresponding to a subset of interactions open to the free exchange of information; 2) The category "Close" of accessibility (CI_C), corresponding to a subset of interactions closed for free exchange of information.

Thus, all interactions between MDI components can be reclassified as those that allow free exchange of information access or are closed and require additional checks.

The second feature is that MDI follows the concept of cyber-physical systems and, therefore, allows combining the functionality of the physical and information world. This also affects the components of the MDI, especially in terms of their interactions and interfaces [27]. Thus, some of the interactions are transmitted during local (i.e. physical) contact; for example, pressing keys or phone sensors. Some of the interactions are transmitted during remote (i.e. logical) contact; for example, voice jitter or receiving network packets. Remote interactions are obtained after converting external physical interactions to local digital ones, for example, by analog-to-digital conversion. Thus, the 2nd pair of the classifier of interactions of MDI components from the position of "contiguity" (denotation of the c index below) will consist of the following categories-antagonists: 1) The category "Locality" of materiality (CI_L), corresponding to a subset of interactions that physically process information; 2) The category "Remote" of materiality (CI_R), corresponding to a subset of interactions that logically process information.

Thus, all interactions of the MDI components can be reclassified into those that physically provide the exchange of information or translate it into logical flows.

Similar to the combination of categorical pairs for component classes, there are 4 combinations of interaction classes. Let's give an interpretation of each class (with an example from the script above), denoting them with the symbol "I" and a subscript in the form of a sequence of the first letters of the categories that form them:

1. CI_{OL} – opening local interaction, for example, turning on the phone by pressing a button;
2. CI_{OR} – open remote interactions, for example, phone access to the Internet through a free Wi-Fi hotspot;
3. CI_{CL} – private local interactions, for example, logging into the phone using a personalized fingerprint;
4. CI_{CR} – closed remote interactions, for example, the transfer of information by the bracelet to the phone only after "pairing" using a password.

This consideration of interactions from the standpoint of accessibility and proximity will increase the detailed classification of interactions between components by $2^2 = 4$ times (i.e., bring their number to $16 \times 4 = 64$).

For convenience, we write the resulting subclassification of interactions in the following form:

$$\forall i = 1..4 | Subclass_i^{Interaction} \equiv \{C_{OL}, C_{OR}, C_{CL}, C_{CR}\} \tag{3}$$

All new oriented interactions $(< component_i | component_j >_{a,m}$ from the set $InteractionsOverral)$ and their classes $(Class_k^{InteractionOverral}$ from the set of 64 classes) can be written in a formalized form as follows:

$$\left\{ \begin{array}{c} InteractionsOverral = \\ \bigcup_{i=1..8, j=1..8, a\in\{CI_O, CI_A\}, c\in\{CI_L, CI_R\}} < component_i | component_j >_{a,c}; \\ \forall i = 1..8, j = 1..8, a \in \{CI_O, CI_C\}, c \in \{CI_L, CI_R\}, k = 1..64| \\ < component_i, component_j >_{a,c} \hookleftarrow Class_k^{InteractionOverral}. \end{array} \right. \quad (4)$$

Thus, for every interaction with a certain accessibility and materiality between two components $< component_i, component_j >_{a,c}$, there is associated its own class $Class_k^{InteractionOverral}$ and vice versa.

3.3 Interfaces and Their Vulnerabilities

As it was said initially, the interface is a means of providing information exchange between the elements of the system (in this case, MDI). Proceeding from the fact that all classes of interactions between the components of the MDI are qualitatively different (since the process of obtaining them is based on the apparatus of categorical division), then the same different classes of interfaces are responsible for the process of information exchange. Otherwise, one interface would contain too heterogeneous functionality and it would be logical to divide it into several; it itself would in this case be a "complex interface". For example, although a mobile phone looks monolithic with a single interface functionality, it logically consists of several interfaces: physically pressed buttons, logical modules for processing GPS signals, etc. interface, which allows you to link their classes as well.

In a formalized form, the division of interfaces $(interface_i$ from the set $Interfaces)$ of MDI into classes $(Class_k^{Interface}$ from a set of 64 classes) can be written as follows:

$$\left\{ \begin{array}{c} Interfaces = \bigcup_{i=1..64} interface_i; \\ \forall i = 1..64 | interface_i \hookleftarrow Class_i^{Interface} \hookleftarrow Class_i^{InteractionOverral}. \end{array} \right. \quad (5)$$

Thus, each interface $interface_i$ has its own class, $Class_i^{Interface}$, associated with an interaction class with a certain availability and materiality $Class_i^{InteractionOverral}$ and vice versa.

Since the interface is actually a software and hardware solution – an "interface tool" that implements some information exchange through itself, errors in such an exchange can occur solely due to vulnerabilities in the tool (naturally, relying on the fact that the data created by the MDI components themselves are absolutely correct). Therefore, each interface can have a set of vulnerabilities associated with it. And since modern software is built on basic sets of modules (for example, program libraries) and vulnerabilities are located in them, the same vulnerability can be present in different classes of interfaces. This statement is legitimate, since interface classes solve the problem of exchanging qualitatively different information, for which, in most cases, specialized design patterns, algorithms and data sets are used, which contain certain vulnerabilities.

In a formalized form, vulnerabilities ($vulnerability_i$ from the $Vulnerabilities$ set) located in the interface modules ($module_j$ from the $Modules$ set) can be written as follows:

$$
\left\{
\begin{array}{l}
Vulnerabilities = \bigcup_i vulnerability_i; \\
Modules = \bigcup_j module_j; \\
\{v_l\}_m \to module_m; \\
\{b_m\}_n \to interface_n; \\
\forall l \geq 1, m \geq 1, x \geq 1, n = 1..64, y = 1..y_{max}, y_{max} < 64| \\
C_n^{Interface} \to \{module_m\}_n \to \{\{vulnerability_l\}_m\}_n \equiv \\
\{vulnerability_x\}_y \to Class_y^{Vulnerability}.
\end{array}
\right.
\tag{6}
$$

Thus, each interface of a certain class $C_n^{Interface}$ is implemented by a subset of firmware modules $\{module_m\}_n$, each of which contains a subset of vulnerabilities $\{vulnerability_l\}_m$; the subset of all vulnerabilities $\{vulnerability_x\}_y$ of a particular interface corresponds to the class $Class_y^{Vulnerability}$. In this case, $Class_y^{Vulnerability}$ is the main result for which a classification model is built and used. At the same time, since different interfaces can be implemented by the same modules potentially containing the same vulnerabilities, then the sets of vulnerabilities of two interfaces can not only overlap, but also coincide and, therefore, the number of interface vulnerability classes should be no more than the number of interface classes ($n = 1..64$ vs $y = 1..y_{max}, y_{max} < 128$).

3.4 Analytical Scheme

The sought-for model of classification of vulnerabilities MDI (Model) in a formalized form can be written as follows:

$$
\begin{array}{c}
Model \equiv< Components, Interactions, \\
InteractionsOverral, Interfaces, Modules, Vulnerabilities > .
\end{array}
\tag{7}
$$

Thus, the model includes all previously introduced sets – $Components$ components, $Interactions$ interactions, $InteractionsOverral$ availability and materiality interactions, $Interfaces$, $Modules$ modules and $Vulnerabilities$ vulnerabilities.

In graphical form, the generalized model has the following analytical scheme (see Fig. 1).

Let us introduce the operation of searching for MDI vulnerabilities – $Detection()$, which, using this model and the features of the $Features$ interface, allows us to determine the classes of vulnerabilities and may underlie the future method:

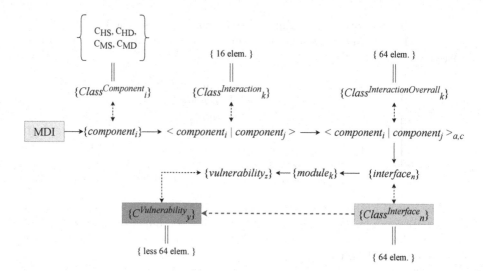

Fig. 1. Scheme of the generalized model for classification of MDI vulnerabilities

$$\begin{cases} \{vulnerability_z\}' = Detection(Model, Features); \\ Features = \bigcup_j feature_j; \\ Detect := Feature \rightarrow Class_n^{Interface} \rightarrow \{module_m\}_n \rightarrow \\ \{\{vulnerability_l\}_m\}_n \rightarrow \{vulnerability_x\}_y \equiv \{vulnerability_z\}'. \end{cases} \quad (8)$$

Thus, the operation of searching for vulnerabilities $Detection()$ as arguments takes the model $Model$ and the attributes of the $Features$ interface, by which the interface class $Class_n^{Interface}$ is then determined, according to the composition of the modules $\{modules_m\}_n$ of which, as well as their vulnerabilities $\{\{vulnerability_l\}_m\}_n$, and the sought set of vulnerabilities of the $\{vulnerability_z\}'$ interface is calculated.

For the operation of the search for vulnerabilities, the signs of interfaces and the method of obtaining the interface class itself from them remain an open question, however, this issue goes beyond the scope of the subject area considered in the current paper, and an attempt to solve it will be undertaken by the authors in the continuation of the investigation.

4   Experiment

To show the performance of the proposed model, we will conduct an experiment to search for vulnerabilities in the interfaces of the MFA elements.

As the initial data for the experiment, we will take the example of the scenario with the athlete in the park discussed earlier.

4.1 Process Description

According to the introduced classification, elements from the example scenario (described earlier) can be attributed to the following classes of MDI components:

1. Components of class C_{HS} – support engineer;
2. Components of class C_{HD} – owner of mobile devices;
3. C_{MS} class components – mobile tower, GPS satellite or signal booster, wireless local area network (Wi-Fi) tower;
4. Components of class C_{MD} – mobile phone, wireless headphones, smart bracelet.

In theory, interactions are possible between all classes of components. Taking into account the introduced division of interactions into 2 categorical pairs, their number in the limit will be equal to 64. Each interaction will be provided with its own interface with its own vulnerabilities. In a real scenario, the number of interaction classes can be much less.

Here are the possible interactions of a certain MDI participant with the rest of the participants from the example scenario. To describe the interaction, we use the following formal notation (for simplicity, omitting the C symbol for classes):

$$
\begin{cases}
Class_i^{Component} \rightarrow Class_j^{Component} \approx Subclass_k^{Interaction}; \\
i \in \{HS, HD, MS, MD\}; \\
j \in \{HS, HD, MS, MD\}; \\
k \in \{OL, OR, CL, CR\}.
\end{cases}
\tag{9}
$$

literally reads as "a component of class C_i interacts with a component of class C_j by way of C_k".

4.2 Results

Let's take the owner of mobile devices as an example of a participant. Then all its interactions with other participants can be represented as shown in Table 1. For simplicity, we will consider only interactions emanating from the owner, we will omit interactions from other participants to the owner.

Alternatively, consider the interactions of a mobile device, a smart bracelet, with other participants (see Table 2).

As can be clearly seen, even for such a fairly simple scenario of finding a person in the MDI, there is a huge number of possible directed interactions from both person and mobile device. Constructing a general diagram of all possible interactions (e.g. in the form of a graph) is a solvable task, since the current investigation proposes the approach for this. The construction of such a scheme is purely technical and goes beyond the current scientific (and, to a greater extent, methodological) research.

Each of these interactions (see Tables 1 and 2, column "Interaction Record") is provided by one of 64 unique interfaces of its own. Each such interface can hypothetically have its own vulnerabilities. So, the interaction between mobile

Table 1. Interactions of the owner of mobile devices with the rest of the participants

Second participant	Description of interaction	Interaction recording
Owner of mobile devices	Absent	
Support engineer	Absent	
Mobile phone	1. pressing the button 2. talk transfer or voice input 3. fingerprint login	1. $Class_{HD}^{Component} \rightarrow Class_{MD}^{Component}$ $\approx Subclass_{OL}^{Interaction}$ 2. $Class_{HD}^{Component} \rightarrow Class_{MD}^{Component}$ $\approx Subclass_{OR}^{Interaction}$ 3. $Class_{HD}^{Component} \rightarrow Class_{MD}^{Component}$ $\approx Subclass_{CL}^{Interaction}$
Wireless headphones	Control by pressing the button	1. $Class_{HD}^{Component} \rightarrow Class_{MD}^{Component}$ $\approx Subclass_{OL}^{Interaction}$
Smart bracelet	1. control by pressing the sensor 2. determining the optical density of the tissue	1. $Class_{HD}^{Component} \rightarrow Class_{MD}^{Component}$ $\approx Subclass_{OL}^{Interaction}$ 2. $Class_{HD}^{Component} \rightarrow Class_{MD}^{Component}$ $\approx Subclass_{OL}^{Interaction}$
Mobile tower	Absent	
GPS satellite or signal booster	Absent	
Wireless local area network tower (Wi-Fi)	Absent	

Table 2. Interactions of the smart bracelet with the rest of the participants

Second participant	Description of interaction	Interaction recording
Owner of mobile devices	Vibration transmission	1. $Class_{MD}^{Component} \rightarrow Class_{HD}^{Component}$ $\approx Subclass_{OL}^{Interaction}$
Support engineer	Absent	
Mobile phone	Send heart rate data	1. $Class_{MD}^{Component} \rightarrow Class_{MD}^{Component}$ $\approx Subclass_{CR}^{Interaction}$
Wireless headphones	Bluetooth control (optional)	1. $Class_{MD}^{Component} \rightarrow Class_{MD}^{Component}$ $\approx Subclass_{CR}^{Interaction}$
Smart bracelet	Absent	
Mobile tower	Data transmission over the Internet (optional)	1. $Class_{MD}^{Component} \rightarrow Class_{MS}^{Component}$ $\approx Subclass_{CR}^{Interaction}$
GPS satellite or signal booster	Absent	
Wireless local area network tower (Wi-Fi)	Absent	

devices after "pairing" with the use of a password sounds like "a component of the class C_{MD} interacts with a component of the class C_{MD} by way of C_{CR}". A vulnerability in the interface associated with the interaction of this class may be the absence or incorrect operation of the AAA security mechanism. As a result, all MDI participants supporting this interface can automatically have this class of vulnerability.

5 Discussion

Analysis of the experimental results allows us to draw the following conclusion. First, the application of the vulnerability classification for the example of the MDI scenario showed the efficiency of the proposed model. Secondly, the obtained classes can be considered correct, since for two MDI components (the owner of mobile devices and a smart bracelet), all their interactions were isolated and reclassified. At the same time, the obtained detailing, on the one hand, can be considered necessary (interactions are clearly related to one class), and on the other hand, sufficient (for each interaction, at least one class was found). Third, the model has rich predictive capabilities. So, the absence of interactions in Tables 1 and 2 may mean that they will appear in the future. For example, the connection of one smart bracelet with another via Bluetooth (which at the moment, if it exists, is not very common) will allow it to convey the danger of the owner's health, thereby attracting attention and possibly saving his life. At the same time, such interaction should be carried out without asking for a password (i.e. remotely and openly). In this case, its record form will be as follows:

$$Class_{MD}^{Component} \rightarrow Class_{MD}^{Component} \approx Subclass_{CR}^{Interaction}. \tag{10}$$

And, fourthly, if new devices appear, even before their direct implementation and implementation in MDI, it will be possible to predict possible vulnerabilities in their interfaces. Thus, it will be possible to immediately prevent security problems. This is done by defining an interface class and examining its inherent vulnerabilities.

Let's compare the obtained solution with analogues.

In [23], it is proposed to use a context-sensitive classification of vulnerabilities. The approach is based on machine learning and uses a textual description of vulnerabilities. The classification model proposed in the current article is more versatile. Our proposed model can be the methodological basis for any machine learning-based solutions.

Paper [22] is close to Work [23] in terms of applying machine learning for classification, although it analyzes the source code and aims to classify commits security. Likewise, our model can be applied to solutions related to security commits.

In [10], the classification of vulnerabilities is based on term frequency-inverse document frequency and deep neural network. The classification efficiency was assessed using records in the National Vulnerability Database. However, this database does not clearly enough allow us to distinguish vulnerabilities associated with interfaces. Thus, our model in the case of interfaces will be more in demand.

Paper [5] is devoted to the automatic classification of vulnerabilities in relation to the Internet of Things. However, unlike our model, the classification of interface vulnerabilities still remains unaffected.

In [14], an attempt is made to predict new vulnerabilities by analyzing historical data in the National Vulnerability Database. For this, machine learning is used in terms of regression models. Our model differs from the one proposed in this paper in that the prediction is more objective and sometimes accurate. This follows from the fact that vulnerabilities are determined by combinations of categorical pairs that do not depend on the previous experience of experts.

Summing up the comparison of our proposed model with analogs, we can say that although it is oriented for the classification of interfaces, it nevertheless has the potential for wider application for classification. However, this will require the creation of an appropriate model-based classification method.

Despite the obvious, both theoretical and practical significance of the investigation, the results themselves and the process of obtaining them have certain disadvantages.

Chapter 2 does not cover all the work that exists in the scientific field. However, the purpose of the review was to show possible approaches to the classification of MDI interfaces and their vulnerabilities, assessing their inherent advantages and disadvantages. Also, the general lack of research on this issue is clearly visible.

In Chap. 3, although the apparatus of categorical division is strict, nevertheless, categorical pairs were chosen subjectively. However, their choice was due to the author's rich experience, and their success was supported by the experiment on the example of the MDI script.

Chapter 3 just mentions the method for vulnerability searching, but its algorithm is not provided. However, the aim of the current investigation was to develop a classification model. The method of vulnerability searching in MDI interfaces will be a logical continuation of the investigation.

In Chap. 4, the experiment was performed on only two of the 8 elements of the sample scenario. However, even such a minimal amount of experiment shows both the performance of the model and its theoretical and practical significance. The authors plan to construct a complete scheme of interactions between MDI participants with full-fledged forecasting of the vulnerabilities of their interfaces in future works with a more practical focus.

Thus, despite a number of shortcomings (the main one of which is the low formalization of decisions), they all have ways to be eliminated.

6   Conclusion

In the interests of the first step in solving the problem of searching for vulnerabilities of MDI interfaces, a review of existing solutions for the classification of interfaces and their vulnerabilities was made. Based on the analysis, a formalization of the model for classifying the vulnerabilities of the MDI components was proposed, the novelty of which is the first established formal relationship between the MDI, its components, their interactions, interfaces, modules that implement the functionality of the interfaces, and the vulnerabilities of the latter. So, all MDI was divided into 4 classes of components. The interaction between the components was also divided into 4 classes. Thus, in general, all interactions between all components in the MDI were divided into 64 classes. Each such class is provided with the same number of interfaces, each of which can contain a certain set of modules with vulnerabilities. A feature of the classification obtained is the satisfaction of the requirements of the necessity and sufficiency of classes, which is justified by the correct application of the scientific and methodological apparatus of categorical division. It is assumed that using the proposed approach it will be possible to enhance the security of existing and developing devices [7].

The authors see the continuation of the investigation as follows. First, on the basis of the model, it is necessary to create a prototype of a software tool for classifying interfaces, which has low values of errors of I and II types, high efficiency and does not require a high level of training from an expert user. Secondly, using the presented model and prototype, it will be possible to synthesize the very method of searching for vulnerabilities in the MDI interfaces, thereby proposing a solution to the initially posed challenge. And, thirdly, it will be necessary to assess the search for vulnerabilities using the created method, which will be the basis for confirming the success of the entire investigation.

References

1. Abhishta, A., van Heeswijk, W., Junger, M., Nieuwenhuis, L.J., Joosten, R.: Why would we get attacked? an analysis of attacker's aims behind DDos attacks. J. Wirel. Mob. Netw. Ubiquit. Comput. Dependable Appl. 11(2), 3–22 (2020)
2. Almaiah, M.A., Al-Zahrani, A., Almomani, O., Alhwaitat, A.K.: Classification of cyber security threats on mobile devices and applications. In: Maleh, Y., Baddi, Y., Alazab, M., Tawalbeh, L., Romdhani, I. (eds.) Artificial Intelligence and Blockchain for Future Cybersecurity Applications. SBD, vol. 90, pp. 107–123. Springer, Cham (2021). https://doi.org/10.1007/978-3-030-74575-2_6
3. Bryukhovetskiy, A., Miryanova, V., Moiseev, D.: Research of the model for detecting UMV interfaces vulnerabilities based on information criterion. In: CEUR Workshop Proceedings, pp. 162–168 (2021)
4. Buinevich, M., Izrailov, K., Kotenko, I., Kurta, P.: Method and algorithms of visual audit of program interaction. J. Internet Serv. Inf. Secur. 11(1), 16–43 (2021)
5. Chen, H., Zhang, D., Chen, J., Lin, W., Shi, D., Zhao, Z.: An automatic vulnerability classification system for IoT softwares. In: 2020 IEEE 19th International Conference on Trust, Security and Privacy in Computing and Communications (TrustCom), pp. 1525–1529. IEEE (2020)
6. Choi, I., Rhiu, I., Lee, Y., Yun, M.H., Nam, C.S.: A systematic review of hybrid brain-computer interfaces: taxonomy and usability perspectives. PLoS ONE 12(4), e0176674 (2017)
7. Desnitsky, V., Kotenko, I., Chechulin, A.: Configuration-based approach to embedded device security. In: Kotenko, I., Skormin, V. (eds.) MMM-ACNS 2012. LNCS, vol. 7531, pp. 270–285. Springer, Heidelberg (2012). https://doi.org/10.1007/978-3-642-33704-8_23

8. Dey, D., et al.: Taming the eHMI jungle: a classification taxonomy to guide, compare, and assess the design principles of automated vehicles' external human-machine interfaces. Transp. Res. Interdisc. Perspect. **7**, 100174 (2020)
9. Du, X., Yin, L., Wu, P., Jia, L., Dong, W.: Vulnerability analysis through interface-based checker design. In: 2020 IEEE 20th International Conference on Software Quality, Reliability and Security Companion (QRS-C), pp. 46–52. IEEE (2020)
10. Huang, G., Li, Y., Wang, Q., Ren, J., Cheng, Y., Zhao, X.: Automatic classification method for software vulnerability based on deep neural network. IEEE Access **7**, 28291–28298 (2019)
11. Izrailov, K., Chechulin, A., Vitkova, L.: Threats classification method for the transport infrastructure of a smart city. In: 2020 IEEE 14th International Conference on Application of Information and Communication Technologies (AICT), pp. 1–6. IEEE (2020)
12. Kim, H.: 5G core network security issues and attack classification from network protocol perspective. J. Internet Serv. Inf. Secur. **10**(2), 1–15 (2020)
13. Kitana, A., Traore, I., Woungang, I.: Towards an epidemic SMS-based cellular botnet. J. Internet Serv. Inf. Secur. **10**(4), 38–58 (2020)
14. Last, D.: Using historical software vulnerability data to forecast future vulnerabilities. In: 2015 Resilience Week (RWS), pp. 1–7. IEEE (2015)
15. Levshun, D., Gaifulina, D., Chechulin, A., Kotenko, I.: Problematic issues of information security of cyber-physical systems. Inform. Autom. **19**(5), 1050–1088 (2020)
16. McGrew, R.W.: Vulnerability analysis case studies of control systems human machine interfaces. Ph.D. thesis, Mississippi State University (2013)
17. Moiseev, D., Bryukhovetskiy, A.: Method for detecting vulnerabilities of unmanned vehicle interfaces based on continuous values discretization, pp. 43–47 (2021)
18. Mulliner, C., Robertson, W., Kirda, E.: Hidden gems: automated discovery of access control vulnerabilities in graphical user interfaces. In: 2014 IEEE Symposium on Security and Privacy, pp. 149–162. IEEE (2014)
19. Nowaczewski, S., Mazurczyk, W.: Securing future internet and 5G using customer edge switching using DNSCrypt and DNSSEC. J. Wirel. Mob. Netw. Ubiquit. Comput. Dependable Appl. **11**(3), 87–106 (2020)
20. Papp, D., Ma, Z., Buttyan, L.: Embedded systems security: threats, vulnerabilities, and attack taxonomy. In: 2015 13th Annual Conference on Privacy, Security and Trust (PST), pp. 145–152. IEEE (2015)
21. Qasem, A., Shirani, P., Debbabi, M., Wang, L., Lebel, B., Agba, B.L.: Automatic vulnerability detection in embedded devices and firmware: survey and layered taxonomies. ACM Comput. Surv. (CSUR) **54**(2), 1–42 (2021)
22. Sabetta, A., Bezzi, M.: A practical approach to the automatic classification of security-relevant commits. In: 2018 IEEE International Conference on Software Maintenance and Evolution (ICSME), pp. 579–582. IEEE (2018)
23. Siewruk, G., Mazurczyk, W.: Context-aware software vulnerability classification using machine learning. IEEE Access **9**, 88852–88867 (2021)
24. Skatkov, A., Bryukhovetskiy, A., Moiseev, D.: Adaptive fuzzy model for detecting of vulnerabilities of unmanned vehicles interfaces based on evaluation of the information state of resources. In: IOP Conference Series: Materials Science and Engineering, vol. 862, p. 052029. IOP Publishing (2020)
25. Spreitzer, R., Moonsamy, V., Korak, T., Mangard, S.: Systematic classification of side-channel attacks: a case study for mobile devices. IEEE Commun. Surv. Tutor. **20**(1), 465–488 (2017)
26. Wong, S.K., Yiu, S.M.: Identification of device motion status via Bluetooth discovery. J. Internet Serv. Inf. Secur. **10**(4), 59–69 (2020)

27. Wong, S.K., Yiu, S.M.: Location spoofing attack detection with pre-installed sensors in mobile devices. J. Wirel. Mob. Netw. Ubiquit. Comput. Dependable Appl. **11**(4), 16–30 (2020)
28. Zhernova, K., Chechulin, A.: Overview of vulnerabilities of decision support interfaces based on virtual and augmented reality technologies. In: Kovalev, S., Tarassov, V., Snasel, V., Sukhanov, A. (eds.) IITI 2021. LNNS, vol. 330, pp. 400–409. Springer, Cham (2022). https://doi.org/10.1007/978-3-030-87178-9_40

5G Virtual Infrastructure, Cryptography and Network Security

Which One is More Robust to Low-Rate DDoS Attacks? The Multipath TCP or The SCTP

Lejun Ji[1], Gang Lei[1(✉)], Ruiwen Ji[1], Yuanlong Cao[1], Xun Shao[2(✉)], and Xin Huang[1]

[1] School of Software, Jiangxi Normal University, 99 Ziyang Avenue, Nanchang 330022, Jiangxi, China
{ji_lejun,leigang,jiruiwen,ylcao,xinhuang}@jxnu.edu.cn
[2] Kitami Institute of Technology, Kitami 0900801, Hokkaido, Japan
x-shao@ieee.org

Abstract. With the vigorous development of mobile Internet technology, real-time streaming media applications such as mobile short video and network live broadcast are becoming more and more popular. As a result, people have higher demand for the transmission rate and service quality of streaming media applications. However, the existing single-path transmission network can not meet the needs of people well. Many researches show that it is an effective measure to improve the transmission performance of network by using multipath transmission protocol. At present, MPTCP and SCTP are two multipath transmission protocols which are widely studied in the academic circle. Even so, the multipath transmission network based on multipath transmission protocol will also be attacked by LDDoS attacks and other network attacks, which will seriously affect the robustness of the transmission system and users' streaming media application experience. Therefore, through the use of NS2 simulation software, this paper mainly studies the performance of MPTCP and SCTP protocols against the LDDoS attack, compares the robustness of the two protocols against LDDoS attacks, enriches the research related to network security of multipath transmission system, and improves the defense ability of multipath transmission system against LDDoS attacks.

Keywords: Multipath TCP · SCTP · Low-rate DDoS · Robustness

1 Introduction

According to the 47th "Statistical Report on Internet Development in China" [1] officially released by China Internet Network Information Center (CNNIC) on February 3, 2021, by December 2020, the number of Internet users in China had reached 989 million, among which the number of mobile Internet users had reached 986 million, and the percentage of Internet users using mobile phones was as high as 99.7%. The report also showed that the number of online video

© Springer Nature Singapore Pte Ltd. 2022
I. You et al. (Eds.): MobiSec 2021, CCIS 1544, pp. 323–334, 2022.
https://doi.org/10.1007/978-981-16-9576-6_22

users (including short videos) and live streaming users accounted for 93.7% and 62.4% of China's total Internet users, respectively. These data show that people have a growing demand for personalized streaming media applications, such as mobile short video and network live broadcast, which have higher requirements for traffic and network transmission performance. Therefore, it is particularly important to improve the transmission rate and service quality of streaming media applications.

Both the commonly used TCP and UDP protocols are single-path transmission protocols, which can no longer well meet users' requirements for high-speed transmission of streaming media applications [2]. With the large-scale application of multi-host terminal devices, the realization of parallel multipath transmission has been widely concerned and discussed. Stream Control Transmission Protocol (SCTP) [3] and Multipath TCP (MPTCP) [4] are the two most classic multi-path Transmission protocols. Figure 1 shows a simple example of parallel multiplexing in the streaming media application, where a multi-hosted terminal device is simultaneously communicating data with the streaming media server through two paths (Path A and Path B). This can improve the transmission performance of streaming media applications and meet the needs of users for personalized streaming media services. At present, the research on the multi-path transmission protocol in current academic circles mainly focuses on data scheduling algorithm optimization [5–7], energy consumption optimization [8–11], fairness problem [12–14] and congestion control mechanism [15–17], etc. Research on MPTCP and SCTP protocols supporting multiple parallel transmission is the future trend.

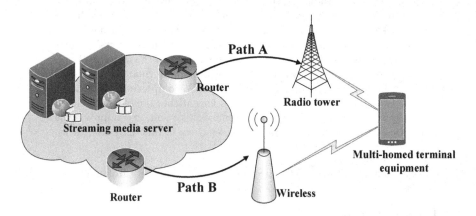

Fig. 1. The schematic diagram of the multiple parallel transmission of streaming media applications.

Although multipath transmission protocols can realize the efficient transmission of streaming media applications, it is also vulnerable to network attacks. In recent years, the network attack presents the rapid development trend [18,19].

Among them, the Low-rate Distributed Denial of Service (LDDoS) attack is one of the fastest developing attack types at present due to its low transmission rate and strong invisibility [20]. LDDoS attacks send a short attack data stream to the target at a low rate, which causes the transmission system to be in a state of timeout retransmission all the time and unable to respond to the normal request of legitimate users, so that the robustness of the transmission system decreases. As mentioned above, researches on network security related issues of multipath transport protocols [21–23] are relatively lacking. However, in a multipath transmission system, if one of the paths is attacked by LDDoS, the performance degradation of this path will cause asymmetry between paths and form a heterogeneous network [24], which will seriously affect the robustness of the multipath transmission system.

According to the current research situation, this paper mainly studies the performance of MPTCP and SCTP against LDDoS attacks, and compares the robustness of the two protocols against LDDoS attacks. By using NS2 (Network Simulator Version 2) simulation software [25], we respectively examine changes in the throughput, delay and jitter rate performances of MPTCP and SCTP transmission systems against LDDoS attacks. By comparing and analyzing the three kinds of performance, the robustness of multipath transmission system against LDDoS attack is obtained. The research conclusions of the paper enrich the research on network security of multipath transmission system and provide a new idea for multipath transmission system to defend against LDDoS attacks.

The remainder of this paper is structured as follows. The second part is the experimental design and analysis, which is divided into experimental design and experimental analysis. The parameter setting of the network topology structure and the performance comparison and analysis of the multipath transmission system are introduced in detail, and the experimental conclusion is finally drawn. The third part is the summary and outlook.

2   Experimental Design and Analysis

2.1   Experimental Design

In the experimental design stage, we used NS2 simulation software to design the basic network topology of a multipath transmission system, as shown in Fig. 2. In this multipath transmission system, the multi-hosted terminal device (Receiver) can communicate with its corresponding streaming media server (Sender) through three links (Path A, Path B and Path C). Three normal data streams are sent from the sending end on their respective transmission paths and forwarded by the router to the receiving end. The entire transmission system adopts the DropTail path management algorithm. The bandwidth between the sender and the router, between the router and the router, and between the router and the receiver is set to 5 Mb, and the transfer delay time is set to 25 ms. Normal data stream starts to send in 0 s and stops to send in 60 s.

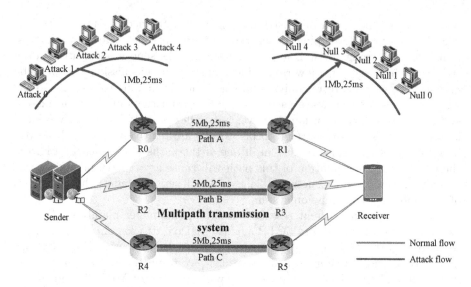

Fig. 2. The network simulation topology of the multipath transmission system under LDDoS attacks.

We set five edge nodes (Attack 0, $\cdots$, Attack 4) is connected to router R0, simulating that five dummy machines are carrying out LDDoS attacks on router R0. In addition, we set up five edge nodes (Null 0, $\cdots$, Null 4) is connected to router R1 to receive incoming attack streams. The bandwidth between the edge node and the corresponding router is set to 1 Mb, and the transfer delay time is set to 25 ms. LDDoS uses the CBR type of attack data streams, which has a fixed transmission rate. LDDoS attack data stream starts to send in 1 s and stops to send in 60 s.

In order to make LDDoS attacks achieve the best attack effect, we adjust the three basic parameters of the LDDoS attack (attack period, attack duration and attack rate). The optimal attack effect can make the normal data flow continue in the timeout retransmission stage, and the congestion window size (cwnd) is always the initial value [26]. Finally, we set the attack cycle of LDDoS attacks as 100 ms, the attack duration as 100 ms, and the attack rate as 1 Mbps. Figure 3 shows the changes of the cwnd of the transmission system under LDDoS attacks. As can be seen from the figure, the initial value of the cwnd is 1, and the cwnd gradually increases as the packets are continuously sent successfully. However, after the LDDoS attack, the cwnd drops sharply to 1. Although the cwnd fluctuates slightly in a period of about 25 s to 35 s, the size of the cwnd is always 1 after that, so as to achieve the best attack effect.

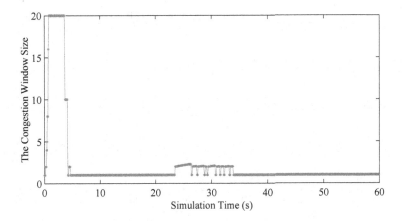

Fig. 3. The changes of congestion window size under LDDoS attacks.

2.2 Experiment Analysis

In the part of experimental analysis, we test the throughput, delay and jitter performances of MPTCP and SCTP transmission systems against LDDoS attacks by using NS2 simulation software. At the same time, the three network performance indexes are compared and analyzed, so as to comprehensively evaluate the transmission performance of multipath transport protocols (MPTCP and SCTP) under LDDoS attacks. Thus, it can indirectly obtain the robustness comparison between MPTCP transmission system and SCTP transmission system under LDDoS attacks of the same intensity [27]. The three network performance indexes can be integrated to evaluate the transmission performance of the multipath transmission system and provide a reliable theoretical basis for the experimental conclusion.

Throughput Performance Comparison. Figure 4, 5 respectively show the throughput performance of MPTCP transmission system and SCTP transmission system under LDDoS attacks. As can be seen from Fig. 4, with the continuous transmission of TCP packets, the throughput of MPTCP transmission system is generally in a state of slow growth, reaching a maximum of 296.98 Mbps at about 19.5 s. Due to repeated LDDoS attacks, it immediately dropped to 8.93 Mbps after reaching the maximum. After the LDDoS attack reached its optimum at about 35 s, the throughput fluctuated slightly around 9 Mbps. As can be seen from Fig. 5, with the continuous successful sending of SCTP packets, the throughput of the SCTP transmission system showed an obvious upward trend, and then fluctuated around 10 Mbps.

Through comparative analysis, it is found that the throughput fluctuation range of SCTP transmission system is less than that of MPTCP transmission system. This is due to the multi-stream nature of SCTP, and there is relative independence between "streams" and "streams", while strict and orderly data

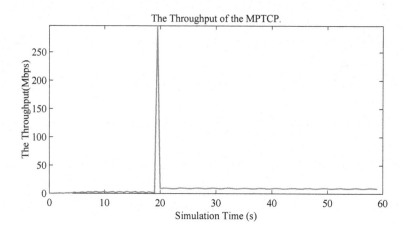

Fig. 4. The MPTCP' s throughput performance under LDDoS attacks.

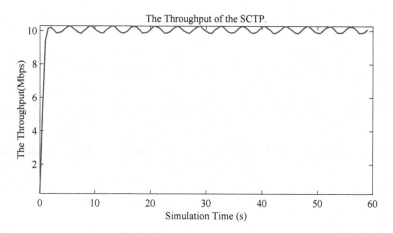

Fig. 5. The SCTP' s throughput performance under LDDoS attacks.

are maintained within "streams" [28]. When the data packets sent in the SCTP transmission system are out of order due to LDDoS attacks, the multi-stream feature can ensure that the data packets can be delivered to the user as long as the data in a certain "stream" arrives in an orderly manner, even in the case of out-of-order between different "streams". This ensures stable throughput performance to a certain extent, whereas transport systems based on the standard MPTCP must deliver packets to the user in an orderly manner. In the MPTCP transmission system, if the data packet of DSN (Data Sequence Number) $i+1$ has reached the buffer, and the data packet of DSN i has not reached the receiving end due to LDDoS attacks, then the data packet of DSN $i+1$ cannot be submitted to the next layer, resulting in low throughput. However, the average throughput of the MPTCP transmission system is better than that of the SCTP transmission system, which also shows that the overall throughput performance of the MPTCP transmission system is better to a certain extent.

End-to-end Delay Performance Comparison. Figure 6, 7 respectively show the end-to-end delay performance of MPTCP transmission system and SCTP transmission system under LDDoS attacks. As can be seen from Fig. 6, there were two large time delay fluctuations in the MPTCP transmission system during the experimental simulation running time. The first time was at the beginning of the attack of LDDoS attacks, and the second time was within the time interval of about 25 s to 35 s. After LDDoS attacks reached the optimal attack, the delay remained stable at 0.08 s. As can be seen from Fig. 7, the delay of SCTP transmission system is always in a state of constant fluctuation, with a maximum value of 0.0274 s.

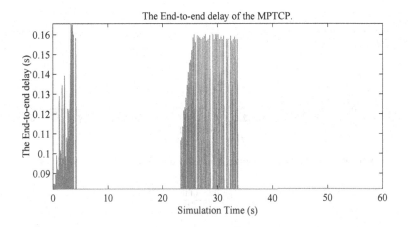

Fig. 6. The MPTCP' s delay performance under LDDoS attacks.

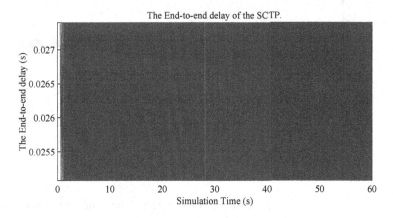

Fig. 7. The SCTP' s delay performance under LDDoS attacks.

Jitter Rate Performance Comparison. Figure 8, 9 respectively show the jitter performance of MPTCP transmission system and SCTP transmission system under LDDoS attacks. As shown in Fig. 8, the jitter rate of MPTCP transmission system is always around 0 s, and even when LDDoS attacks reach the optimal attack effect, it fails to have a significant impact on its jitter rate. As shown in Fig. 9, when the SCTP transmission system was attacked by LDDoS attacks at 1 s, it was obvious that the jitter rate changed significantly around 1 s, and the maximum value could reach about 0.32 s. As the attack time increases, the variation range of jitter rate becomes smaller after about 20 s.

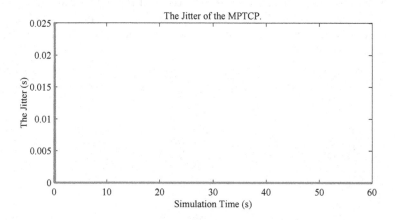

Fig. 8. The MPTCP's jitter performance under LDDoS attacks.

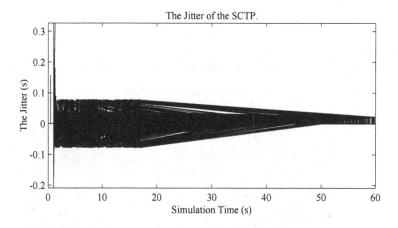

Fig. 9. The SCTP's jitter performance under LDDoS attacks.

Through the comparison and analysis of the delay and jitter rate performance, it is found that the SCTP transmission system has a low delay, but compared with the MPTCP transmission system, it is always in a state of frequent fluctuation. This is caused by the congestion control mechanism of the SCTP. Although the multi-host feature of SCTP enables data transmission through multiple links between multi-host devices, the standard SCTP only selects one path as the primary path to realize data transmission, and the other paths as standby paths for data retransmission [29]. When SCTP remotely detects that the main path has failed due to LDDoS attacks, it will select one of the alternate paths as the new main path for data transmission. Frequent switching of the main path will undoubtedly cause considerable delay jitter variation. In contrast, MPTCP can simultaneously use multiple interfaces of multi-host devices, and use multiple links to send data at the same time to achieve reliable multi-path parallel transmission. When one of the paths fails due to LDDoS attacks, the packet being transmitted on the path can not reach the receiving end normally. After reaching the maximum number of retransmission, the packet can be switched to the other path with good performance for retransmission.

In this experiment, we compared and analyzed the throughput, delay and jitter performance of MPTCP and SCTP transmission systems, so as to obtain the robustness analysis of MPTCP and SCTP transmission systems against LDDoS attacks. To sum up, in terms of throughput performance, the throughput of the SCTP transmission system is relatively stable, but the average throughput is lower than that of the MPTCP transmission system. In terms of delay performance, the SCTP transmission system is always in a state of frequent fluctuation, while the MPTCP transmission system only fluctuates to a certain extent in the two time periods just after being attacked by LDDoS and before reaching the optimal attack. In terms of jitter rate performance, compared with the MPTCP transmission system, the jitter rate of the SCTP transmission system changes greatly.

3   Summary and Outlook

Based on NS2 simulation software, this paper builds MPTCP and SCTP multi-path transmission systems respectively, and simulates the transmission system under LDDoS attacks. Secondly, we evaluate the transmission performance of the two transmission systems by calculating their throughput, delay and jitter performance. At the same time, the performance of the transmission system can directly reflect the robustness of the transmission system.

Through comparison and analysis, we find that MPTCP and SCTP multi-path transmission systems have their own scheduling algorithms and congestion control mechanisms, and have their own good performance in network performance indicators such as throughput and delay performance. But in general, the stability of the MPTCP transmission system against LDDoS attack is better than that of the SCTP transmission system. If the stability performance is poor, the transmission speed of streaming media applications will decrease, which will seriously affect the robustness of the transmission system, and then affect the quality of user experience. In addition, the MPTCP can maintain fairness for single-path TCP connections and can be well compatible with existing network devices [30].

In our future research work, we will improve the data scheduling algorithm [31] and congestion control mechanism of the MPTCP to further improve the robustness of MPTCP transmission system against LDDoS attacks. At the same time, we try to realize the identification and detection of the LDDoS attack in the MPTCP transmission system using machine learning and depth learning [32–34]. The research conclusions of this paper enrich the cross research of multipath transmission system and LDDoS attacks, put forward a new idea for the improvement and application of multipath transmission protocols, and improve the defense ability of multipath transmission system against LDDoS attacks.

Acknowledgments. This work was supported by the National Natural Science Foundation of China (NSFC) under Grant No. 61962026, by the Natural Science Foundation of Jiangxi Province under Grant No. 20192ACBL21031, by the ROIS NII Open Collaborative Research 2021 under Grant no. 21AF03, and by the Cooperative Research Project Program of the Research Institute of Electrical Communication, Tohoku University.

References

1. China Internet Network Information Center (CNNIC), The 47th "Statistical Report on Internet Development in China", February 2021. https://zndsssp.dangbei.net/2021/20210203.pdf
2. Zhang, W., He, Z., Du, B., Luo, M., Zheng, Q.: Deploying external bandwidth guaranteed media server clusters for real-time live streaming in media cloud. PLoS ONE **14**(4), e0214809 (2019)
3. Sun, W., Yu, S., Xing, Y., Qin, Z.: Parallel transmission of distributed sensor based on SCTP and TCP for heterogeneous wireless networks in IoT. Sensors **19**(9), 2005 (2019)
4. Palash, M.R., Chen, K.: MPWiFi: synergizing MPTCP based simultaneous multipath access and WiFi network performance. IEEE Trans. Mob. Comput. **19**(1), 142–158 (2020)
5. Hurtig, P., Grinnemo, K., Brunstrom, A., Ferlin, S., Alay, O., Kuhn, N.: Low-latency scheduling in MPTCP. IEEE-ACM Trans. Netw. **27**(1), 302–315 (2019)
6. Dong, P., Wang, J., Huang, J., Wang, H., Min, G.: Performance enhancement of multipath TCP for wireless communications with multiple radio interfaces. IEEE Trans. Commun. **64**(8), 3456–3466 (2016)
7. Sharma, V.K., Verma, L.P., Kumar, M.: CL-ADSP: cross-layer adaptive data scheduling policy in mobile Ad-hoc networks. Future Gener. Comput. Syst.- Int. J. Escience **97**, 530–563 (2019)
8. Hashimoto, M., Hasegawa, G., Murata, M.: SCTP tunneling: flow aggregation and burst transmission to save energy for multiple TCP flows over a WLAN. IEICE Trans. Commun. **E96B**(10), 2615–2624 (2013)
9. Cao, Y., Chen, S., Liu, Q., Zuo, Y., Wang, H., Huang, M.: QoE-driven energy-aware multipath content delivery approach for MPTCP-based mobile phones. China Commun. **14**(2), 90–103 (2017)
10. Wu, J., Tan, R., Wang, M.: Energy-efficient multipath TCP for quality-guaranteed video over heterogeneous wireless networks. IEEE Trans. Multimedia **21**(6), 1593–1608 (2019)

11. Khedr, A.M., Raj, P.P., Al Ali, A.: An energy-efficient data acquisition technique for hierarchical cluster-based wireless sensor networks. J. Wirel. Mob. Netw. Ubiquit. Comput. Dependable Appl. **11**(3), 70–86 (2020)

12. Xu, C., Li, Z., Li, J., Zhang, H., Muntean, G.: Cross-layer fairness-driven concurrent multipath video delivery over heterogeneous wireless networks. IEEE Trans. Circ. Syst. Video Technol. **25**(7), 1175–1189 (2015)

13. Arianpoo, N., Leung, C.M.V.: A smart fairness mechanism for concurrent multipath transfer in SCTP over wireless multi-hop networks. Ad Hoc Networks **55**, 40–49 (2017)

14. Jin, B., Kim, S., Yun, D., Lee, H., Kim, W., Yi, Y.: Aggregating LTE and Wi-Fi: toward intra-cell fairness and high TCP performance. IEEE Trans. Wirel. Commun. **16**(10), 6295–6308 (2017)

15. Xu, Z., Tang, J., Yin, C., Wang, Y., Xue, G.: Experience-driven congestion control: when multi-path TCP meets deep reinforcement learning. IEEE J. Sel. Areas Commun. **37**(6), 1325–1336 (2019)

16. Wei, W., Xue, K., Han, J., Wei, D.S.L., Hong, P.: Shared bottleneck-based congestion control and packet scheduling for multipath TCP. IEEE-ACM Trans. Netw. **28**(2), 653–666 (2020)

17. Najm, I.A., Ismail, M., Lloret, J., Ghafoor, K.Z., Zaidan, B.B., Rahem, A.A.T.: Improvement of SCTP congestion control in the LTE-A network. J. Netw. Comput. Appl. **58**, 119–129 (2015)

18. Alizadeh, M., Andersson, K., Schelen, O.: A survey of secure Internet of Things in relation to blockchain. J. Internet Serv. Inf. Secur. **10**(3), 47–75 (2020)

19. Abhishta, A., Heeswijk, W., Junger, M., Nieuwenhuis, L.J.M., Joosten, R.: Why would we get attacked? an analysis of attacker's aims behind DDoS attacks. J. Wirel. Mob. Netw. Ubiquit. Comput. Dependable Appl. **11**(2), 3–22 (2020)

20. Agrawal, N., Tapaswi, S.: Low rate cloud DDoS attack defense method based on power spectral density analysis. Inf. Process. Lett. **138**, 44–50 (2018)

21. Cao, Y., Chen, J., Liu, Q., Lei, G., Wang, H., You, I.: Can multipath TCP be robust to cyber attacks with incomplete information? IEEE Access **8**, 165872–165883 (2020)

22. Demir, K., Nayyer, F., Suri, N.: MPTCP-H: a DDoS attack resilient transport protocol to secure wide area measurement systems. Int. J. Crit. Infrastruct. Prot. **25**, 84–101 (2019)

23. Kim, H.: 5G core network security issues and attack classification from network protocol perspective. J. Internet Serv. Inf. Secur. **10**(2), 1–15 (2020)

24. Wu, J., Yuen, C., Cheng, B., Wang, M., Chen, J.: Streaming high-quality mobile video with multipath TCP in heterogeneous wireless networks. IEEE Trans. Mob. Comput. **15**(9), 2345–2361 (2016)

25. Pang, M., Shen, J., Wu, L.: A distributed congestion control strategy using harmonic search algorithm in internet of vehicles. Sci. Program. **2021** (2021)

26. Cao, Y., Song, F., Liu, Q., Huang, M., Wang, H., You, I.: A LDDoS-aware energy-efficient multipathing scheme for mobile cloud computing systems. IEEE Access **5**, 21862–21872 (2017)

27. Jin, X., Liu, Y., Fan, W., Wu, F., Zhang, H.: A throughput improved path selection method based on throughput prediction model and available bandwidth for MPTCP. Int. J. Future Gener. Commun. Netw. **8**(2), 105–114 (2015)

28. Gan, J., Xiong, N.N., Wen, H., Zhu, Q.: Analysis of SCTP concurrent multipath transfer in vehicular network communication. J. Internet Technol. **16**(3), 495–504 (2015)

29. Pan, J.-Y., Chen, M.-C., Lin, P.-C., Lu, K.-L.: Quality-aware SCTP in wireless networks. EURASIP J. Wirel. Commun. Netw. **2010**(1), 1–14 (2010). https://doi.org/10.1155/2010/820578

30. Lee, C., Song, S., Cho, H., Lim, G., Chung, J.: Optimal multipath TCP offloading over 5G NR and LTE networks. IEEE Wirel. Commun. Lett. **8**(1), 293–296 (2019)

31. Khamayseh, Y., Mardini, W., Aldwairi, M., Mouftah, H.: On the optimality of route selection in grid wireless sensor networks: theory and applications. J. Wirel. Mob. Netw. Ubiquit. Comput. Dependable Appl. **11**(2), 87–105 (2020)

32. Colace, F., Santo, M.D., Lombardi, M., Mosca, R., Santaniello, D.: A multilayer approach for recommending contextual learning paths. J. Internet Serv. Inf. Secur. **10**(3), 91–102 (2020)

33. Johnson, C., Khadka, B., Basnet, R.B., Doleck, T.: Towards detecting and classifying malicious URLs using deep learning. J. Wirel. Mob. Netw. Ubiquit. Comput. Dependable Appl. **11**(4), 31–48 (2020)

34. Wong, S.K., Yiu, S.M.: Location spoofing attack detection with pre-installed sensors in mobile devices. J. Wirel. Mob. Netw. Ubiquit. Comput. Dependable Appl. **11**(4), 16–30 (2020)

A Blockchain-Based User Identity Authentication Method for 5G

Zhe Tu[ID], Huachun Zhou[(✉)], Kun Li[ID], Haoxiang Song, and Weilin Wang[ID]

School of Electronic and Information Engineering, Beijing Jiaotong University,
No. 3 Shangyuancun, Haidian District, Beijing 100044, China
{zhe_tu,hchzhou,kun_li,20120099,21111026}@bjtu.edu.cn

Abstract. The massively connected 5G IoT scene brings new challenges
to identity authentication. Existing identity authentication methods have
problems such as high time delay and poor efficiency when mass access is
performed, and it is difficult to meet the situation of the rapid increase in
the number of users. In this paper, we proposed a blockchain-based user
identity authentication method for 5G IoT scenarios. This method builds
the mapping relationship between user attributes and identity, and utilizes blockchain technology to realize the authentication requirements of
mass users in 5G scenarios. In addition, we also deployed a prototype
system to verify the performance of the proposed method. Experimental
results show that the identity authentication method proposed in this
paper has significant advantages in delay and processing efficiency compared with traditional centralized authentication methods and common
distributed authentication methods.

Keywords: Blockchain · Registration · Authentication · Internet of
things

1 Introduction

The rapid development of 5G technology has made the Internet of Everything a
reality, and improving the security of the Internet of Things (IoT) that supports
massive connections has gradually become a research hotspot [3]. The identity
authentication technology can prevent the malicious access of illegal users and
improve the security of the network by identifying the user's identity. However, with the rapid growth of IoT devices, the existing identity authentication
methods are increasingly difficult to meet the identity authentication requests of
massive devices [4]. Therefore, it is urgent to find a user identity authentication
method suitable for the scenario of mass access.

With the rise of Blockchain, it has become a trend to use blockchain technology to construct new user authentication methods [8,9,13]. On the one hand,
a distributed trusted identity authentication platform can be built by storing the user's identity credentials in the blockchain with the immutable feature of the blockchain. On the other hand, using the traceability feature of the

© Springer Nature Singapore Pte Ltd. 2022
I. You et al. (Eds.): MobiSec 2021, CCIS 1544, pp. 335–351, 2022.
https://doi.org/10.1007/978-981-16-9576-6_23

blockchain, by storing the identity authentication information on the chain, the user's identity can be traced to achieve rapid cross-domain authentication. However, due to the complex access devices and massive access users in IoT, the existing blockchain-based identity authentication methods still have shortcomings in terms of authentication delay and response efficiency. Therefore, it is particularly important to find a blockchain-based user identity authentication method in IoT.

Thus, in this paper, based on the Extensible Authentication Protocol (EAP) framework, an identity authentication method based on blockchain is proposed by using the smart contract. The authentication method uses user identification to characterize user identities, realizes mass user identity authentication based on user attributes, and meets the rapid authentication requirements of massive users in IoT.

The rest of the paper is organized as follows. In Sect. 2, we review the related works about authentication methods. In Sect. 3, we introduce the user model and the authentication entities in the proposed authentication method. In Sect. 4, we put forward the user identity registration method and authentication method. Then we analyze the proposed authentication method from the aspects of Safety and efficiency in Sect. 5. In Sect. 6, we evaluate the performance of the proposed method in the prototype system. Finally, In Sect. 7, we summarize the paper.

2   Related Work

With the development of blockchain technology, the features of blockchain, such as non-tampering, distributed storage, and traceability, can meet the security access requirements of mobile application scenarios of IoT devices [10,16]. Therefore, more and more scholars have carried out research on how to build a blockchain-based identity authentication method.

Shen et al. [14] proposed a blockchain-based cross-domain identity management mechanism. The authenticated device will remain anonymous and communicate securely through key negotiation. This solution realizes the establishment of trust between different areas of the alliance blockchain, as well as key storage and privacy protection. Danish et al. [5] proposed a blockchain authentication mechanism for ultra-long-distance spread spectrum communication (LoRaWLAN). The solution uses the blockchain as an independent network to work simultaneously with LoRaWLAN, and uses smart contracts to realize verification information and device information storage in LoRa terminal devices to achieve the purpose of device identity verification. Mohanta et al. [11] proposed a distributed authentication scheme for IoT devices based on Ethereum. This scheme mainly uses smart contracts to store user IDs and their associated wallet addresses and uses blockchain to solve the single point of failure of a single server. Ourad et al. [12] use Ethereum and smart contracts to authenticate devices. Users provide device authentication information to the smart contract.

The smart contract distributes the authentication credentials to the device and the user and then completes the device authentication. The blockchain in this solution is responsible for the management and distribution of credential generation.

The above-mentioned blockchain-based user identity authentication schemes mostly revolve around how to use the blockchain to provide services such as the storage and management of identity authentication credentials, and how to use the distributed nature of the blockchain to prevent a single point of failure. However, the above authentication method is difficult to apply in the IoT scenario with a large number of users. Therefore, there is an urgent need to find a new identity authentication method based on blockchain technology that is suitable for mass connection of the IoT.

3   User Model and Authentication Entities

In this section, we mainly focus on the user model and authentication entity involved in the proposed authentication method.

3.1   User Model

Before introducing the authentication method in a massively connected IoT scenario, the user model in the IoT needs to be defined first. Different from traditional Internet users, IoT users have the characteristics of a large number and multiple types, so the proposed user model needs to be able to fully characterize the characteristics of IoT users. In this subsection, we define the user model from the perspective of user attributes, and characterize the user model as follows:

$$User = \{U_{id}, U_{attri}\} \tag{1}$$

The user model is composed of U_{id} and U_{attri}. U_{id} is the name of the IoT user. In the proposed authentication method, we use U_{id} to distinguish a large number of users in a fine-grained manner; U_{attri} is a set that characterizes user attributes, which can be composed of sub-attributes that characterize users' specific attributes, such as user groups, user roles, and user permissions. In the proposed authentication method, the rapid identity authentication of a large number of users with the same attributes can be realized through the user attribute set U_{attri}.

3.2   Authentication Entities

To better understand the proposed blockchain-based user identity authentication method, we briefly introduce the three entities involved in the authentication method. In this section, we will introduce the three entities involved in the proposed authentication method: User, Gateway, and Blockchain.

User: Considering the diversity of devices and users in IoT, we use a unified user entity to represent users and devices that require identity registration/authentication. This user entity can be represented by the user model proposed above and can send and receive information messages to the gateway during the user identity registration/authentication phase.

Gateway: In the blockchain-based identity authentication method proposed in this paper, the gateway entity acts as the identity authentication device and responds to the registration/authentication request sent by the user entity. Different from the traditional centralized identity authentication method, the distributed identity authentication method is adopted in this paper. By deploying the same blockchain between distributed gateway entities, distributed mass user identity authentication is realized.

Blockchain: Blockchain entities act as trusted authentication centers in the proposed authentication methods by storing user authentication records or providing user authentication credentials. After receiving registration/ authentication request, the gateway entity authenticates the user's identity by calling a third-party interface or smart contract to obtain the identity credentials stored on the blockchain. Gateway entity and blockchain entity can be deployed on the same device or different devices. In the following section, in order to better describe the interaction of gateway entity and blockchain entity, we represent them separately. The gateway entity realizes user identity registration/ authentication by calling relevant functions of the smart contract in the blockchain entity.

4   Registration and Authentication Method

In order to improve the authentication rate and efficiency of the IoT users, in this paper, we use distributed blockchain technology to propose a user identity authentication method based on blockchain. Based on the Extensible Authentication Protocol (EAP) framework, we have endowed the blockchain network with the functions of a traditional authentication server and adopted the authentication method similar to EAP-MD5 to realize user identity authentication. In addition, in order to make the proposed authentication method applicable to the IoT scenario of mass connection, we construct the mapping relationship between attributes and identifiers, and realized rapid authentication of massive users based on user attributes.

Although the devices and users in IoT are complex and diverse, due to the existence of a large number of the same sensor devices in IoT, the devices and users of the IoT can be classified by using the user attributes proposed above, which is the basis of the massive user registration and authentication method proposed in this paper. Next, we will introduce our proposed user identity authentication method based on blockchain from two aspects: registration method and authentication method.

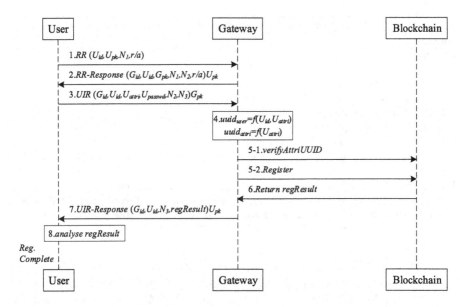

Fig. 1. Blockchain-based user identity registration method

4.1 Registration Method

When an IoT user (or device) accesses the network for the first time, it is necessary to register with a trusted distributed user identity authentication center (gateway). The user (device) sends the information such as user attributes and passwords to the gateway through encrypted packets. Then the gateway invokes a smart contract to store the user information in the blockchain. This section describes the process of user identity registration between user entities, gateway entities, and blockchain entities.

Figure 1 shows the user identity registration method proposed in this paper, which consists of three entities: user, gateway, and blockchain. The registration message is exchanged between the user and the gateway in the form of a packet, and the registration message is exchanged between the gateway and the blockchain entity by calling the smart contract function.

(1) First of all, User sends a registration request (RR) message to gateway, including $(U_{id}, U_{pk}, N_1, r/a)$, to indicate the beginning of the user identity registration. U_{id} represents the user name, U_{pk} represents the user's public key, and N_1 is a random number selected by the User. r/a is the registration/authentication information flag, which is used to distinguish between registration messages and authentication messages. In the registration phase, r/a is set to 0, indicating that the message is a user identity registration message.

(2) When the Gateway receives the RR message, it can extract the user's public key U_{pk} from it. Then, a registration request response (RR-Response) message is sent to the User, including $G_{id}, U_{id}, G_{pk}, N_1, N_2$ and r/a,

---

Algorithm 1. Parameters and function definitions in the user registration smart contract.

---

parameters:

$uuid_{user}$: User identity;

$uuid_{attri}$: User identity;

U_{passwd}: User password;

U_{attri}: User attribute set;

Reg_time: User registration time.

Function: $verifyAttriUUID(uuid_{attri})$

// check whether users with the same attribute set have been registered on the blockchain.

Function: $Register(uuid_{user}, uuid_{attri}, U_{passwd}, U_{attri}, Reg\_time)$

// record the user identity, user attribute identity, user password, user attribute set and registration time in the user registration record, which is stored in the blockchain.

---

where RR-Response message $= (G_{id}, U_{id}, G_{pk}, N_1, N_2, r/a)_{U_{pk}}$. G_{id} represents the gateway name, G_{pk} represents the gateway's public key, and N_1 is a random number selected by the Gateway. $(A)_k$ represens the message A is encrypetd using the key k.

(3) After receiving the RR-Response message, the user decrypts it with his private key U_{sk}. The trusted identity of the gateway is verified by judging the gateway name G_{id} and the random number N_1 in the message. If the gateway identity is trusted, a user identity registration (UIR) message encrypted with the gateway's public key G_{pk} is sent to the gateway. The user identity registration message contains the user name U_{id}, the gateway name G_{id}, the user attribute set U_{attri}, user password U_{passwd}, random number N_2 and the newly generated random number N_3. UIR message $= (G_{id}, U_{id}, U_{attri}, U_{passwd}, N_2, N_3)_{G_{pk}}$.

(4) The gateway receives the UIR message, decrypts it with its private key G_{sk}, and verifies the validity of the registration message by the random number N_2, user name U_{id} and gateway name G_{id}. Then, the gateway maps the user name U_{id} and user attribute set U_{attri} in the UIR message into a user identity $uuid_{user}$ that represents the user's identity. Besides, in order to achieve mass user registration, the gateway maps the user attribute set U_{attri} to the attribute identity $uuid_{attri}$. For the mapping relationship mentioned above, we take $uuid_{attri}$ as an example. $uuid_{attri} = f(U_{attri})$, f represents the mapping function.

(5) The gateway calls the function in the user registration smart contract to register the user's identity in the blockchain entity.

(5-1) Call the $verifyAttriUUID$ function in the smart contract to verify that a user with the same attribute identifier has been registered on the blockchain. If the result is True, it indicates that another user with the same attributes has already registered. This user does not need to register again and jumps to step (6). If the result returned is False, it indicates that the user has not registered the user identity in the blockchain, then proceed to steps (5-2). The function $verifyAttriUUID$ is shown as the pseudocode 1.

(5-2) The gateway calls the $Register$ function in the smart contract to store the user identity $uuid_{user}$, user attributes identity $uuid_{attri}$, and user password U_{passwd} in the blockchain. The function $Register$ is shown as the pseudocode 1.

(6) Blockchain entities generate new transactions that contain user information, and synchronously the new blocks after mining operations. After the user's identity is successfully registered on the chain, the blockchain entity returns the user's registration result information $regResult$ to the gateway.

(7) After receiving the registration result information $regResult$, the gateway sends the user identity registration Response (UIR-Response) message, including (gateway name G_{id}, user name U_{id}, random number N_3 and $regResult$). UIR-Response message $= (G_{id}, U_{id}, N_3, regResult)_{U_{pk}}$.

(8) The user decrypts the UIR-response message with the user's private key U_{sk} and verifies the correctness of the message by verifying the random number N_3, the gateway name G_{id} and the user name U_{id}. After successful message validation, user identity registration is completed.

4.2 Authentication Method

To ensure the validity of the user identity, user identity authentication is required after the user identity registration. In the user identity authentication stage, users only need to send their own attribute set and other information to the access gateway, and the access gateway will authenticate users according to the user attribute set and the user information stored in the blockchain by invoking the smart contract.

The process of the user authentication method based on the blockchain proposed in this paper is shown in Fig. 2. The interaction process between the three entities is consistent with the registration phase, that is, the user and the gateway interact through data messages, and the gateway and the blockchain use smart contracts for information interaction.

(1-2) Except for the difference in the flag r/a, the message content in the authentication phase is the same as the message content in the registration phase, so it will not be explained here. In order to better distinguish between user authentication messages and user registration messages, we use AR to represent user authentication request messages, where the flag r/a is set to 1.

(3) After receiving the authentication request response (AR-Response) message, the user sends a user identity authentication (UIA) message to the gateway, including $(G_{id}, U_{id}, U_{attri}, N_2, N_3)$. UIA message $= (G_{id}, U_{id}, U_{attri}, N_2, N_3)_{G_{pk}}$. N_2 and N_3 represent the received and newly generated random numbers, respectively.

(4) Step 4 is the same as step 4 of the registration process, that is, the $uuid_{user}$ and $uuid_{attri}$ are respectively mapped.

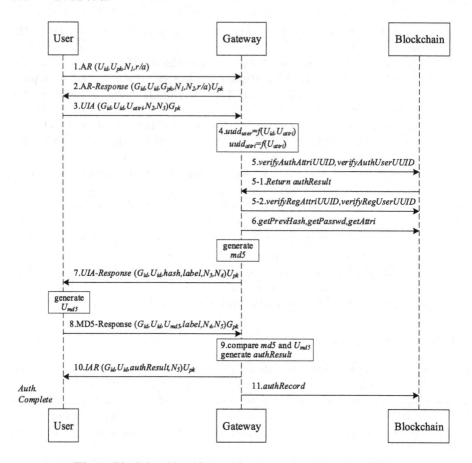

Fig. 2. Blockchain-based user identity authentication method

(5) The gateway calls $verifyAuthAttriUUID$ and $verifyAuthUserUUID$ functions in the authentication smart contract to query whether there is an authentication record with the same $uuid_{user}$ or $uuid_{attri}$ in the blockchain. The function $verifyAuthAttriUUID$ and $verifyAuthUserUUID$ is shown as the pseudocode 2.

(5-1) If there are authentication records with the same $uuid_{user}$ or $uuid_{attri}$, the blockchain entity returns the authentication success message $authResult$ to the gateway entity. The next step is (10).

(5-2) If the records with the same $uuid_{user}$ and $uuid_{attri}$ cannot be found in the authentication record, the gateway calls the functions $verifyRegUserUUID$ and $verifyRegAttriUUID$ in the smart contract to query the blockchain entity for the existence of the registration record with the same $uuid_{user}$ and $uuid_{attri}$. The function $verifyRegAttriUUID$ and $verifyRegUserUUID$ is shown as the pseudocode 2.

Algorithm 2. Parameters and function definitions in the user authentication smart contract.

parameters:

  $uuid_{user}$: User identity;

  $uuid_{attri}$: User attribute identity;

  $authReslut$: User authentication result;

  $Auth\_time$: User authentication time.

Function: $verifyAuthAttriUUID(uuid_{attri})$

  // Check whether the authentication records of users with the same user attribute set are stored in the blockchain.

Function: $verifyAuthUserUUID(uuid_{user})$

  // Check whether the user authentication records is stored in the blockchain.

Function: $verifyRegAttriUUID(uuid_{attri})$

  // Check whether the registration records of users with the same user attribute set are stored in the blockchain.

Function: $verifyRegUserUUID(uuid_{user})$

  // Check whether the user registration records is stored in the blockchain.

Function: $getPrevHash()$

  // Obtain the latest block hash value of the previous block.

Function: $getPasswd(uuid_{user})$

  // Obtain the user password with the same user ID stored in the blockchain.

Function: $getAttri(uuid_{attri})$

  // Obtain the user attribute set with the same user attribute identifier stored in the blockchain.

Function: $authRecord(uuid_{user}, uuid_{attri}, authReslut, Auth\_time)$

  // record the user identity, user attribute identity, user authentication result and authentication time in the user authenticationn record, which is stored in the blockchain.

(5-2.1) If there are registration records with the same $uuid_{user}$ and $uuid_{attri}$ on the blockchain, it indicates that the user has completed identity registration on the blockchain. The next step for identity authentication is (6-1).

(5-2.2) If the registration record with the same $uuid_{attri}$ can be found in the registration record, but the registration record with the same $uuid_{user}$ cannot be found, it indicates that there are users with the same attribute in the blockchain who have completed the registration, while the current user has not completed the identity registration. In order to quickly implement user authentication, we adopt the authentication process of steps (6-2) for such users.

(5-2.3) If neither $uuid_{user}$ nor $uuid_{attri}$ is found in the registration record, the blockchain entity returns the authentication message $AuthResult$ to the gateway that the user's identity requires registration.

(6) The gateway calls the $getPrevHash$ function in the authentication smart contract to obtain the hash value $hash$ of the previous block in order to generate an MD5 challenge message.

(6-1) The gateway calls the $getPasswd$ function in the authentication smart contract to obtain the password U_{passwd} with the same $uuid_{user}$ in the registration record, and generate MD5-challenge message $md5$. $md5 = g(hash, U_{passwd})$, g represents the MD5 challenge function. In addition, the label $label$ representing the type of user authentication is generated, and the $label$ is set to u.

(6-2) The gateway calls the $getAttri$ function in the authentication smart contract to obtain user attributes set U_{attri} with the same $uuid_{attri}$ in the registration record, and generate MD5-challenge message $md5$. $md5 = g(hash, U_{attri})$. In addition, the label $label$ representing the type of user authentication is generated, and the $label$ is set to a.

(7) The gateway sends the user an user identity authentication response (UIA-Response) message, which contains $(G_{id}, U_{id}, hash, label, N_3, N_4)$. UIA-Response message $= G_{id}, U_{id}, hash, label, N_3, N_4)_{U_{pk}}$.

(8) After the user receives the UIA-response message, it decrypts it with its own secret key U_{sk} and queries the $label$ value in the message.

(8-1) If $label$ is u, user generates the MD5 challenge message U_{md5} based on the user password U_{passwd} and the hash value $hash$ received and then sends the MD5 challenge response (MD5-Response) message to the gateway. MD5-Response message $= (G_{id}, U_{id}, U_{md5}, label, N_4, N_5)_{G_{pk}}$. N_5 is the random number newly generated by the user. $U_{md5} = g(hash, U_{passwd})$.

(8-2) If $label$ is a, user generates the MD5 challenge message U_{md5} based on the user attributes set U_{attri} and the hash value $hash$ received and then sends the MD5 challenge response (MD5-Response) message to the gateway. MD5-Response message $= (G_{id}, U_{id}, U_{md5}, label, N_4, N_5)_{G_{pk}}$. $U_{md5} = g(hash, U_{attri})$.

(9) After receiving the MD5-response message, the gateway decrypts it with its private key G_{sk}, and compares the U_{md5} in the message with the $md5$ value generated by step (6). If the two values are equal, the user authentication is successful, and the authentication result $authResult$ message is set to $success$. If the two values are not equal, it indicates that the user authentication has failed, and the authentication result $authResult$ message is set to $failed$.

(10) Gateway sends identity authentication result (IAR) message, which contains $(G_{id}, U_{id}, authResult, N_5)$. IAR message $= (G_{id}, U_{id}, authResult, N_5)_{U_{pk}}$.

(11) Subsequently, gateway calls the $authRecord$ function in the authentication smart contract to store the successfully authenticated user ID $uuid_{user}$, attribute ID $uuid_{attri}$, and authentication result $authResult$ on the blockchain. It should be noted that only the authentication record of the user whose call $verifyAuthAttriUUID$ function returns $False$ will be stored on the chain.

5   Authentication Method Analysis

In this section, we analyze the proposed user identity authentication method from two aspects of security and efficiency.

5.1   Security Analysis

The method proposed in this paper guarantees the security of user registration/authentication in the following aspects: First, in the User-Gateway interaction process, the transmitted message is encrypted by asymmetric encryption to prevent the information from being stolen by malicious users. Secondly, the verification of random number and the identity information of the client and gateway is introduced into the message load information to ensure the legitimacy of the identity of both parties. In addition, using blockchain technology to build a distributed trusted user identity registration/authentication platform can effectively avoid the problem of a single point of failure. At the same time, the smart contract is used to improve the registration/authentication protocol process, and the immutable property is used to ensure the reliability of the registration/authentication process of the gateway entity and blockchain entity. Finally, the matching mapping relationship among user identity, attribute information and identity is built in the gateway node to realize the isolation between the user identity information on the access side and the information stored in the blockchain, to ensure the security of user identity information.

5.2   Efficiency Analysis

In this section, we analyze the authentication efficiency of the proposed authentication method. To analyze the efficiency of qualitative of registration and authentication, we first define the time spent in each part of the registration/Authentication process as shown in Fig. 1 and Fig. 2. In the method proposed in this paper, we define the encryption and decryption time as T_1 and T_2, respectively. The identity mapping time is defined as T_3, and the time taken to generate the md5 challenge massage is defined as T_4. To uniformly describe the response time of the smart contract, we define the time spent calling the smart contract function (such as $verifyRegAttriUUID$) to verify the data stored in the blockchain as T_5, and the time spent calling the smart contract function (such as $getPasswd$) to obtain the data stored in the blockchain as T_6. The time spent for user identity registration and recording authentication user information in the blockchain is defined as T_7 and T_8 respectively.

With the above-mentioned time definition, we can qualitatively express the time spent on user registration and user authentication. For a single user, as shown in Fig. 1, the time T_{rs} it takes to register the user identity for the first time can be expressed as $T_{rs} = 3T_1 + 3T_2 + 2T_3 + T_5 + T_7$, and the time T_{ra} it takes to register a single user with the same attribute set can be expressed as $T_{ra} = 3T_1 + 3T_2 + 2T_3 + T_5$. In the user identity authentication phase, the time T_{as} spent on user authentication for the first authentication as shown in Fig. 2

can be expressed as $T_{as} = 5T_1 + 5T_2 + 2T_3 + 2T_4 + 4T_5 + 2T_6 + T_8$, and the time T_{aa} spent on re-authenticating users or users with the same attributes set can be expressed as $T_{aa} = 3T_1 + 3T_2 + 2T_3 + 2T_5$. For users with the same attribute set, in terms of user authentication and registration time, the method proposed in this paper can save T_7 and $2T_1 + 2T_2 + 2T_4 + 2T_5 + 2T_6 + T_8$ time compared with other blockchain-based user registration and authentication methods.

In a massively connected IoT scenario, it is assumed that there are N users and M users who need identity registration and identity authentication. Among the N users who need identity registration, n_1 users perform identity registration for the first time, and n_2 users have the same attribute set as the users in the registration records stored in the blockchain; Similarly, among the M identity authentication users, m_1 users perform identity authentication for the first time, and m_2 users have the same attribute set as the users of the authentication records stored in the blockchain. The time spent on registration and authentication of a large number of users can be expressed as $n_1 * T_{rs} + n_2 * T_{ra}$ and $m_1 * T_{as} + m_2 * T_{aa}$, respectively. Compared with other blockchain-based user registration and authentication methods, the method proposed in this article can save $n_2 * T_7$ and $m_2 * (2T_1 + 2T_2 + 2T_4 + 2T_5 + 2T_6 + T_8)$ time respectively in the scenario of massive user registration and authentication.

6   Experimental Results

In this section, we verify the performance of the proposed user registration method and user authentication method. First, we introduced the experimental test environment built. Subsequently, we evaluated the performance of the user registration/authentication method proposed in this paper.

6.1   Experimental Environment

We built a prototype system to verify the performance of the proposed blockchain-based authentication method. The prototype system runs in an ESXi-based server management cluster, which contains a total of 8 blockchain nodes and 4 user nodes. These 12 nodes are equipped with a Linux-based Ubuntu 18.04 system at the same time and are allocated 40G of hard disk space and 8G of operating space. Among the 8 blockchain nodes, we built a go language compilation environment and used the Ethereum [6] Geth v1.10.1 client to build an Ethereum private chain based on the POW [7] consensus mechanism. The 4 user nodes are directly connected to the blockchain node as the user entity that initiates authentication/registration. The blockchain node serves as a gateway entity for user request analysis, and as a blockchain entity to complete user authentication/registration.

In the user node, we deployed a user registration/authentication communication script written in Python language to send a user registration/authentication request to the gateway; Similarly, we deploy server-side communication scripts

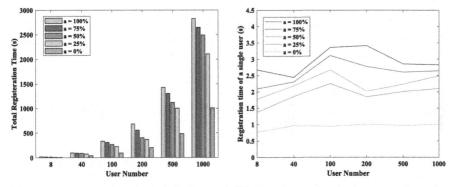

(a) Time spent on registration of all users   (b) Time spent for single user registration

Fig. 3. Time spent in the user registration phase

on blockchain nodes to parse responses to received user requests. In addition, we deployed a user registration/authentication smart contract based on the Solidity [15] language on the blockchain. In the blockchain node, we use the web3.py [1] library to realize the communication between the server script, the Ethereum blockchain, and the smart contract.

6.2 Performance Evaluation

We first verify the performance of the proposed user registration method. We compared the performance of the registration methods proposed by 8, 40, 100, 200, 500, and 1000 users. In addition, we also compared the impact of the proportion a of users who registered for the first time on the proposed registration method. We verified the performance of the user identity registration method under the proportion of 100%, 75%, 50%, 25%, and 0% of the first registered users. It should be noted that when the users are all registered users for the first time, this scenario can be regarded as the same as the common blockchain-based user authentication method. When the proportion of users registered for the first time is 0%, it can be regarded as a user re-registration or a user registration scenario with the same attribute set. The time spent on registration for different users and different proportions of first-time users is shown in Fig. 3. To reduce the error generated by external factors, we evaluated each scene 10 times and took the average of the 10 evaluations for graph display.

Figure 3(a) shows the total time it takes for all users to register under different numbers of users and different proportions of users who register for the first time. Figure 3(b) shows the average registration time of a single user under the premise of the different number of users and different proportions a. It can be seen from Fig. 3(b) that with the increase in the number of users, the registration time of a single user will also increase. And with the increase of the proportion of first-time registered users, the growth of the single user registration time will be more obvious. This is because the increase in the number of users will lead to

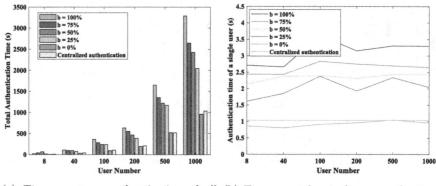

(a) Time spent on authentication of all users

(b) Time spent for single user authentication

Fig. 4. Time spent in the user authentication phase

an increase in the load on the blockchain nodes, which in turn will lead to an increase in the time it takes to parse the user registration request. On the other hand, when the proportion of first-time registered users is relatively high, the increase in user registration time will be more obvious. This is because when a user is registered for the first time, the blockchain node needs to call a smart contract to store the user registration information in the blockchain. The higher the proportion of users who need to register for the first time, the more user registration information the blockchain node needs to store in the blockchain, so the user registration time will significantly increase. In addition, it can be seen from Fig. 3(a) that the method proposed in this paper is well applicable to the IoT scenario of mass users. In the IoT, because there are a large number of IoT devices with the same attributes, the method proposed in this article only needs to register users with the same attribute set on the blockchain and does not need to store identity registration information again, which greatly shortens the registration time.

Secondly, we compare and analyze the performance of the proposed user authentication methods. To avoid the impact of user registration on the user authentication phase, we assume that all users have completed their identity registration on the blockchain. Similar to the user registration performance evaluation, we also compared the time spent on user authentication when the number of users is 8, 40, 100, 200, 500, and 1,000. In addition, we also compared the influence of the proportion b of re-authenticated users (or the proportion of users with the same attribute set) on user authentication. We compared the time required for user authentication when the proportion of re-authenticated users (or the proportion of users with the same attribute set) were 100%, 75%, 50%, 25%, and 0% respectively. It should be noted that when the proportion of re-authenticated users (the proportion of users with the same attribute set) is 0%, the method proposed in this article is the same as the common blockchain-based user authentication method. In addition, we also built a RADIUS-based centralized user authentication server in the prototype system to compare the differences between distributed authentication methods and centralized EAP-MD5 authentication methods. Figure 4 shows the time spent on authentication with different numbers of users and different user proportions. Figure 4(a) shows the total time it takes for all users to authenticate under different numbers of users and different proportions b of re-authenticated users (users with the same attribute set). Figure 4(b) shows the average authentication time of a single user under the premise of different numbers of users and different proportions b.

It can be seen from Fig. 4(b) that the authentication time of a user increases with the increase in the number of users. In this experiment, the blockchain node is used as a user authentication response node, and its load will increase as the number of users increases, which will affect the analysis of user authentication requests. Therefore, compared with the case of a small number of users, the authentication time of a user with a large number of users will increase significantly. In addition, as shown in Fig. 4(a), the user's authentication delay is negatively related to the proportion of re-authenticated users (or the proportion of users with the same attribute set). The higher the proportion of re-authenticated users (or users with the same attribute set) in the total users, the lower the user authentication delay. This is because, in the user authentication process, the blockchain node needs to store the authentication record of the first authenticated user on the chain, while the re-authenticated user (or user with the same attribute set) queries the historical authentication record stored in the blockchain, Blockchain nodes do not need to perform redundant mining operations, which greatly shortens the authentication time.

In addition, we also compared the time delay of the proposed authentication method and the centralized EAP-MD5 [2] user authentication method. In the centralized user authentication method, we deploy the RADIUS server in another domain, and set the cross-domain link delay to 500ms. In the blockchain-based user authentication method proposed in this paper, when the proportion of re-authenticated users (users with the same attribute set) is 100%, the authentication delay of the proposed methods is lower than the centralized cross-domain user authentication method as shown in Fig. 4(b). However, when the proportion of re-authenticated users (or users with the same attribute set) is low, the authentication efficiency is lower than the centralized user authentication method. This is because the constructed blockchain network uses a consensus algorithm based on POW, and blockchain nodes need to mine new blocks to store user authentication information in the blockchain. Therefore, the greater the number of newly authenticated users, the greater the number of blocks that blockchain nodes need to mine, and the time it takes to mine blocks will also increase. However, it should be noted that the performance of blockchain nodes also affects the mining time of the block to a certain extent, which in turn affects the user authentication time.

7   Conclusion

In this paper, we proposed a user identity authentication method based on blockchain. This method uses blockchain to build a credible distributed user authentication platform, and by constructing a mapping relationship between user attributes and attribute identifiers, the rapid identity registration and authentication process of massive user connections in the IoT scene is realized.

In addition, we built a prototype system to verify the performance of the proposed method. The experimental results show that the user identity registration/authentication method proposed in this paper is superior to the common distributed blockchain-based authentication methods in terms of authentication speed and authentication efficiency. In particular, compared to the centralized authentication method, the proposed method also has better performance advantages in terms of authentication time and authentication efficiency.

Acknowledgments. This paper is supported by National Key R&D Program of China under Grant No. 2018YFA0701604. Huachun Zhou is the corresponding author of this paper.

References

1. web3.py. https://web3py.readthedocs.io/en/stable/. 21 July 2021
2. Aboba, B., Blunk, L., Vollbrecht, J., Carlson, J., Levkowetz, H., et al.: Extensible Authentication Protocol (EAP) (2004)
3. Akpakwu, G.A., Silva, B.J., Hancke, G.P., Abu-Mahfouz, A.M.: A survey on 5G networks for the internet of things: communication technologies and challenges. IEEE access **6**, 3619–3647 (2017)
4. Cao, J., Yan, Z., Ma, R., Zhang, Y., Fu, Y., Li, H.: LSAA: a lightweight and secure access authentication scheme for both UE and MMTC devices in 5G networks. IEEE Internet Things J. **7**(6), 5329–5344 (2020)
5. Danish, S.M., Lestas, M., Asif, W., Qureshi, H.K., Rajarajan, M.: A lightweight blockchain based two factor authentication mechanism for LoRaWan join procedure. In: 2019 IEEE International Conference on Communications Workshops (ICC Workshops), pp. 1–6. IEEE (2019)
6. Dannen, C.: Introducing Ethereum and Solidity. Apress, Berkeley (2017). https://doi.org/10.1007/978-1-4842-2535-6
7. Gervais, A., Karame, G.O., Wüst, K., Glykantzis, V., Ritzdorf, H., Capkun, S.: On the security and performance of proof of work blockchains. In: Proceedings of the 2016 ACM SIGSAC Conference on Computer and Communications Security, pp. 3–16 (2016)
8. Hammi, M.T., Hammi, B., Bellot, P., Serhrouchni, A.: Bubbles of trust: a decentralized blockchain-based authentication system for IoT. Comput. Secur. **78**, 126–142 (2018)
9. Lee, Y., Son, B., Park, S., Lee, J., Jang, H.: A survey on security and privacy in blockchain-based central bank digital currencies. J. Internet Serv. Inf. Secur. (JISIS) **11**(3), 16–29 (2021)
10. Li, X., Jiang, P., Chen, T., Luo, X., Wen, Q.: A survey on the security of blockchain systems. Futur. Gener. Comput. Syst. **107**, 841–853 (2020)

11. Mohanta, B.K., Sahoo, A., Patel, S., Panda, S.S., Jena, D., Gountia, D.: Decauth: Decentralized authentication scheme for IoT device using ethereum blockchain. In: TENCON 2019–2019 IEEE Region 10 Conference (TENCON), pp. 558–563. IEEE (2019)
12. Ourad, A.Z., Belgacem, B., Salah, K.: Using blockchain for IOT access control and authentication management. In: Georgakopoulos, D., Zhang, L.-J. (eds.) ICIOT 2018. LNCS, vol. 10972, pp. 150–164. Springer, Cham (2018). https://doi.org/10.1007/978-3-319-94370-1_11
13. Patil, A.S., Hamza, R., Hassan, A., Jiang, N., Yan, H., Li, J.: Efficient privacy-preserving authentication protocol using PUFs with blockchain smart contracts. Comput. Secur. **97**, 101958 (2020)
14. Shen, M., et al.: Blockchain-assisted secure device authentication for cross-domain industrial IoT. IEEE J. Sel. Areas Commun. **38**(5), 942–954 (2020)
15. Wohrer, M., Zdun, U.: Smart contracts: security patterns in the ethereum ecosystem and solidity. In: 2018 International Workshop on Blockchain Oriented Software Engineering (IWBOSE), pp. 2–8. IEEE (2018)
16. Zheng, Z., Xie, S., Dai, H.N., Chen, X., Wang, H.: Blockchain challenges and opportunities: a survey. Int. J. Web Grid Serv. **14**(4), 352–375 (2018)

Cyber-Attack Behavior Knowledge Graph Based on CAPEC and CWE Towards 6G

Weilin Wang⬥, Huachun Zhou(✉), Kun Li⬥, Zhe Tu⬥, and Feiyang Liu

School of Electronic and Information Engineering, Beijing Jiaotong University,
No. 3 Shangyuancun, Haidian District, Beijing 100044, China
{20120122,hchzhou,kun_li,zhe_tu,19120077}@bjtu.edu.cn

Abstract. 6G-oriented network intelligence needs the support of knowledge from inside and outside the network. CAPEC and CWE are network security databases targeting attack patterns and weaknesses respectively, which are relatively complete knowledge from outside the network. Constructing the important entities and relationships in CAPEC and CWE as knowledge graphs is conducive to comprehensively grasping the strategies and behaviors of certain attacks, thus providing a supplement for network internal knowledge and guidance for attack prediction and network situational awareness. Therefore, this paper analyzes the content and organizational structure of CAPEC and CWE, and proposes a method to construct cyber-attack knowledge graph based on CAPEC and CWE, which is implemented in the graph database Neo4j. This paper also introduces the application of the knowledge graph in DDoS flood attack and multi-stage attack.

Keywords: Knowledge graph · Internet security · CAPEC · CWE

1 Introduction

The sixth generation (6G) mobile network will further integrate Information Technology (IT), Communication Technology (CT) and Data Technology (DT) to achieve endogenous intelligence and security [1]. Ubiquity of intelligence is an important feature of 6G network. Artificial intelligence technology has emerged as a new way to design and optimize 6G networks [2]. In the future, Artificial Intelligence technologies, including machine learning and deep learning, will be widely used in the network. These methods need to mine the required knowledge from a large number of complex data to provide decision support. These methods usually model the network as a black box, and provide decision support by extracting features and discovering knowledge from a large number of complex data. Therefore, these methods rely on comprehensive and sufficient data, and the organization and utilization of complex data is the foundation to realize intelligent network. In terms of network security, different from passive interception in the past, we expect 6G network to realize intelligent prediction and detection of malicious network behaviors, and to be able to respond automatically. Therefore, we need to make full use of network security data and knowledge from both

© Springer Nature Singapore Pte Ltd. 2022
I. You et al. (Eds.): MobiSec 2021, CCIS 1544, pp. 352–364, 2022.
https://doi.org/10.1007/978-981-16-9576-6_24

inside and outside the network. The knowledge from the inside of the network refers to the knowledge obtained from the analysis of network infrastructure or traffic data through artificial intelligence, which reflects the characteristics of the real network. The knowledge from outside the network is the technology or experience summarized by experts or organizations according to previous network security incidents, such as the vulnerabilities used by certain attacks, the steps implemented and mitigation measures, etc. CAPEC and CWE are the representatives of them. CAPEC describes the prerequisites, technical requirements and mitigation measures of common attack modes [3], while CWE describes the common vulnerabilities of software and hardware in the network [4]. The knowledge and conclusions summarized by the external knowledge base can be used as a supplement to the network internal security knowledge, and provide high-level basis and guidance for the prediction and detection of network malicious behaviors and the perception of network situation. However, both CAPEC and CWE are described in text format, which makes it difficult for these information to be directly used in the detection and mitigation of network malicious behavior. In order to facilitate the retrieval and utilization of useful information in CAPEC and CWE, this paper considers using knowledge graph to reorganize the structure of the two. As an important branch of artificial intelligence, knowledge graph can represent data as an "entity-relation-entity" structure, help understand big data, or use graph algorithm to analyze the deep correlation of data to provide decision support [5]. Therefore, in order to construct network attack behavior knowledge graph, this paper considers to use knowledge graph to reorganize important entities and relationships in CAPEC and CWE, which can help obtain a comprehensive description of a certain attack in the process of attack prediction, detection and mitigation and supplement the knowledge of network internal security.

The network security knowledge from external data sources and the network security knowledge extracted from network infrastructure data complement each other, which can better describe the network state and network attack scenarios, and is of great significance to attack prediction, intrusion detection and network situation awareness. The interaction between the cypher-attack behavior knowledge graph proposed in this paper and network internal security knowledge is shown in Fig. 1. Network Traffic Features Knowledge Graph is a knowledge graph which is extracted from normal traffic and abnormal traffic by artificial intelligence and reflects the features of different kinds of traffic. The Network Entity Connecting Knowledge Graph consists of hardware and software entities in a real network and their connections. As external knowledge, the knowledge graph of network attack behavior can supplement the characteristics of attack traffic extracted from the network traffic, help to find the vulnerabilities of software and hardware in the network, and provide mitigation measures for attacks or vulnerabilities.

The content structure of this paper is as follows: The second section discusses the related work. The third section introduces the organizational structure and relationships of CAPEC and CWE. In the fourth section, the structure and implementation of the knowledge graph of network attack behavior based on CAPEC and CWE are introduced in detail, and the application of the knowledge graph of network attack behavior is introduced with the example of DDoS flood attack. The fifth section summarizes the whole work and puts forward some suggestions for the future work.

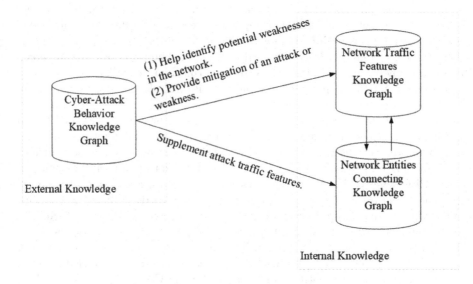

Fig. 1. Interactions between external and internal knowledge

2   Related Work

With the enrichment of communication scenarios, security problems in networks will become more diverse. [6] classified security problems and attacks in 5G networks according to protocols. In order to effectively identify attacks in networks, we need to conduct more comprehensive analysis of attacks and introduce new methods. [7] proposes a hybrid model to analyze 27 distinct DDoS attack events that occurred in 2016 and reveals several motives underlying DDoS attacks.

In terms of creating the network security knowledge graph. [8] puts forward a method to construct the network security knowledge graph. This paper first constructs the ontology in the field of network security, and then describes the Entity extraction and rule-based knowledge reasoning methods based on Named Entity Recognizer (NER). [9] using Malware After Action Reports (AARs) as the data source, NER was also used to extract entities and neural network was used to predict the relationship between entities. The role of this knowledge graph is to provide useful information in AARs to security engineers and reduce the time of manual inspection of Reports. [10]specifically studied the improved method of relationship extraction in the process of creating network security knowledge map, and used deep learning method to extract the possible relationships between entities, so as to ensure the accuracy and integrity of the relationships between entities. [11] proposed the framework of creating Knowledge Graph of Threat Actor, built network security ontology around Threat Actor, and also extracted entities from text data by improving NER. In the creation of the network security knowledge graph, the above paper constructs the network security domain ontology from different perspectives such as assets, attacks and attackers, focusing on the method of entity identification and relationship extraction in the text.

CAPEC and CWE, as complete public databases in the field of network security, have been widely applied in the field of network security. [12] proposed a systematic attack pattern modeling method to analyze the attack strategies of 102 attack modes in CAPEC from the perspective of attackers. This method can effectively identify multi-level attacks. [13] designed a tool for generating random attack sequences and security events based on CAPEC, which can be used for security system testing. [14] based on the hierarchical correlation of vulnerabilities in CWE, PageRank algorithm was used to calculate the severity score of each vulnerability to evaluate the vulnerability, so as to improve the accuracy of vulnerability evaluation. In addition, there is a mapping relationship between the ontology in the network security knowledge graph and the attacks and weaknesses in CAPEC and CWE in some studies. CAPEC and CWE are important data sources of network security ontology [15–17].

In addition, in order to deal with new attack modes and complex attacks, researchers have proposed the kill chain model, ATT&CK and other models to describe multi-stage attacks. The Kill chain model is a model based on the life cycle of an attack, consisting of seven phases in which an attacker typically executes an attack [18]. ATT&CK is based on the real-world attacker's tactical and technical knowledge base and provides a more fine-grained description of the tactics, techniques, and processes at each stage of an attack than the kill chain model [19]. These models describe the attack process from the attacker's point of view and provide guidance for the detection of attacks in each stage. However, the corresponding knowledge is needed to provide guidance for specific attack scenarios. The attack patterns listed in CAPEC correspond to the kill chain model and specific attack techniques in ATT&CK, and the weaknesses listed in CWE correspond to vulnerabilities exploited by attackers during the invasion phase. Therefore, CAPEC and CWE need to provide intellectual intelligence to attack models in an efficient way.

It can be seen that CAPEC and CWE play an important role in attack and vulnerability analysis, network security ontology, knowledge graph construction and attack model intelligence source. This paper mainly studies the construction of network security knowledge graph by using CAPEC and CWE.

3 Structures of CAPEC and CWE

3.1 CAPEC

Since the initial version of CAPEC was released in 2007, it currently contains 541 attack patterns [3]. Each attack pattern includes how the attack is designed, executed and mitigated, which is stored in a hierarchical structure. However, these attack patterns are described in text and are not conducive to automated analysis.

Attack patterns in CAPEC are stored in a hierarchical structure, providing two views, "attack principle" and "attack domain". The "attack principle" view classifies the attack mode according to the attack method, while the "attack domain" view classifies the attack according to the network security domain. There are four levels of abstraction in the hierarchy, which are Category Level, Meta Level, Standard Level and Detailed Level. Category is a collection of attack patterns based on common features; Meta Attack Pattern is a description of the specific methods or techniques used in the Attack, providing a high-level understanding of the Attack methods without any specific techniques or implementations. The Standard Attack Pattern describes the specific methods or techniques used in an Attack and provides a detailed description of the Attack methods. Detailed Attack patterns describe specific techniques and execution processes, usually associated with other Attack patterns of different levels to achieve an Attack target. The hierarchical storage structure makes there exist hierarchical relationships among different attack modes. When the Category is not considered and only the one-way relationship is considered, there are four relationships among different attack modes, which are ChildOf, CanPrecede, PeerOf, and CanAlsoBe.

3.2 CWE

CWE is a list of errors or vulnerabilities that can be exploited by attacks during the deployment and design of network software or hardware. Its goal is to help users of network software or hardware eliminate common vulnerabilities and prevent some attacks from happening at the source. Mitre started this work in 1999, and CWE currently contains a total of 918 weakness records [4]. These weaknesses are also described in text, which is not conducive to automated analysis and use.

Weakness in a CWE is stored in a hierarchy, divided into Pillar, Class, Base, Variant, and Compound according to different levels of abstraction. A Pillar is the most abstract weakness type and represents weaknesses on the same topic with a technical description. Class is also an abstract vulnerability type, independent of a particular language or technology. Base remains independent of resources or technology, but provides specific methods of detection and prevention. Variant is a weakness related to a product that relates to a specific language or technology. It is more specific than a weakness in the Base category. A Compound is a compound of several weaknesses that, when combined, create other potential weaknesses. Without considering the two-way relationship, there are six types of relationships among CWE weaknesses, namely ChildOf, CanPrecede, PeerOf, CanAlsoBe, Requires, and StartsWith.

3.3   Relationship Between CAPEC and CWE

The vulnerability described in CWE is the root cause of an attack, while the attack pattern in CAPEC describes how to exploit a weakness to launch an attack. An attack pattern may be associated with one or more vulnerabilities, and a vulnerability may be exploited by multiple attacks. There are descriptions of related weaknesses and attack patterns in both CAPEC and CWE, but the ID of related weaknesses and attack patterns is only listed under "Related Weakness" and "Related Attack Patterns", which makes it difficult to obtain all the attack information through one-time query. If using the knowledge graph to represent the attack mode, vulnerability and the relationship between them in the form of entities and relationships, the subattacks of a certain type of attack, the vulnerability of a certain type of attack and the mitigation measures of the attack can be obtained more comprehensively and quickly.

4   Cyber-Attack Behavior Knowledge Graph

4.1   Structure of Cyber-Attack Behavior Knowledge Graph

Knowledge graph stores data in the form of "entity-relationship-entity," so entities and relationships need to be defined based on the information provided by CAPEC and CWE. A more intuitive approach is to abstract attack patterns and weaknesses into two types of entities. Once the entity is identified, you need to define its properties, which store important information about the attack pattern or vulnerability. The attack mode attributes and meanings selected from CAPEC are shown in Table 1. The attack pattern entity contains eight attributes, including CAPEC ID, Name, Abstraction, Description, Typical Severity, Requisites, Consequences and Mitigation. The vulnerability attributes selected from the CWE and their meanings are shown in Table 2. The weakness entity contains six attributes, including CWE ID, Name, Abstraction, Description, Consequences and Mitigations.

For the relationship between entities, it is needed to obtain relationships between attack modes, between vulnerabilities, and between attack modes and weak. So the relationship between attack patterns and attack patterns, between attack patterns and weaknesses, and between weaknesses and weaknesses provided by CAPEC and CWE are extracted. The relationships contained in the knowledge graph are shown in Table 3.

Table 1. Attributes and meanings of attack patterns in cyber-attack behavior knowledge graph

Attack pattern attributes	Corresponding term(s) in CAPEC	Meanings
CAPEC ID	ID	Unique identification of the attack pattern
Name	Name	The generic name of the attack pattern
Abstraction	Abstraction	The level of abstraction of an attack pattern, reflecting the hierarchy between attack patterns
Description	Description	A general description of the attack pattern
Typical severity	Typical severity	Reflects the severity of the attack pattern
Requisites	Prerequisites	Reflects the conditions of the attack, can be used for attack prediction.
	Skills required	
	Resources required	
Consequences	Consequences	The consequences of the attack
Mitigations	Mitigations	Attack mitigation measures, mitigation or recovery measures after an attack has occurred

Table 2. Attributes and meanings of weaknesses in cypher-attack behavior knowledge graph

Weakness attributes	Corresponding term(s) in CWE	Meanings
CWE ID	ID	Unique identification of the weakness
Name	Name	The generic name of the weakness
Abstraction	Abstraction	The level of abstraction of a weakness, reflecting the hierarchy between weaknesses
Description	Description	A general description of the weakness
Consequences	Consequences	The consequences of the weakness
Mitigations	Mitigations	Vulnerability mitigation, means of repairing or mitigating a vulnerability

Table 3. Entities and relationships in cyber-attack behavior knowledge graph

Entities 1	Relationships	Entities 2
Attack pattern	Child of, can precede, peer of, can also be	Attack Pattern
Weakness	Child of, can precede, peer of, can also be, requires, starts with	Weakness
Attack pattern	Related weaknesses	Weakness

4.2   Realization of Cyber-Attack Behavior Knowledge Graph

According to the entity and relationship information obtained from CAPEC and CWE, the structure of the cyber-attack behavior knowledge graph is shown in Fig. 2. The cyber-attack behavior knowledge graph contains entities of weakness and attack pattern, which constitute three types of relations among attack modes, among weaknesses, and between attack modes and weaknesses. After designing the knowledge graph of network attack behavior, this paper selects the graph database Neo4j to create the knowledge graph. Neo4j is a stable high-performance graph database, which uses Cypher as a query language and provides multiple development methods [20]. This article uses Neo4j-community-4.3.2 and Java driver package development, Cypher language embedded in Java. First, using Java to read the XML data sets provided by CAPEC and CWE to get the required entities and relationships. The entities and relationships are then created using the CREATE, MERGE, and other statements in the Cypher language. Some of the entities and relationships in the created knowledge graph are shown in Fig. 3. Entities in the knowledge graph include attack patterns and weaknesses, and the relationships between entities are reflected in the form of edges. The "entity-relation-entity" structure in knowledge graph can quickly and intuitively reflect an attack pattern and related weaknesses, so the attack characteristics, attack requirements, attack and related vulnerability mitigation measures of a certain attack can be acquired quickly and comprehensively, which can effectively help attack prevention, attack detection and network situational awareness.

4.3   Application of Cyber-Attack Behavior Knowledge Graph

DDoS attacks prevent computers or networks from providing normal services. The ability to detect and respond to DDoS attacks automatically is the embodiment of the intelligence of 6G network in attack detection. To achieve this goal, information in the knowledge graph should be fully utilized.

DDoS Flood is a common type of DDoS attacks. Next, the information support of knowledge graph for intelligent network will be introduced by taking flood attack as an example. First, enter the query statement "MATCH (a:CAPEC name:" Flooding ")-[r1]-(b:CAPEC) RETURN a,r1,b " in neo4j to obtain the "Flooding" attack pattern and other attack patterns directly related to it. As shown in Fig. 4, the Flooding attacks in CAPEC include TCP Flood, UDP Flood, ICMP Flood, HTTP Flood, SSL Flood, XML Flood, Amplification and BlueSmacking. In order to obtain the related weaknesses of Flooding attacks, the Cypher query statement "MATCH (a:CAPEC name:" Flooding ")-[r1]-(b)-[r2]-(c) RETURN a, r1, b, r2, c" can be entered in Neo4j. Then it can return node sets b and c, which start from CAPEC node "Flooding" and are connected through relationship sets r1 and r2, as shown in Fig. 5. According to the returned results, Flooding attacks are associated with the weaknesses of "Allocation of Resources Without Limits or Throttling" and "Improper Resource Shutdown or Release" in CWE. TCP Flood, UDP Flood, ICMP Flood, HTTP Flood, SSL Flood, XML

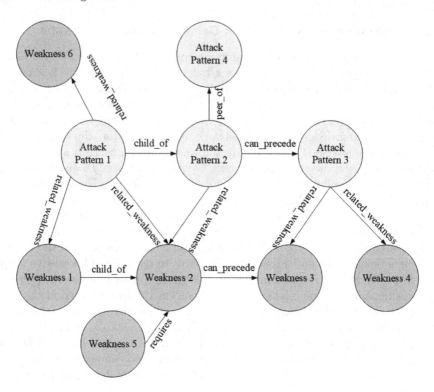

Fig. 2. Entities and relationships of cyber attack behavior knowledge graph

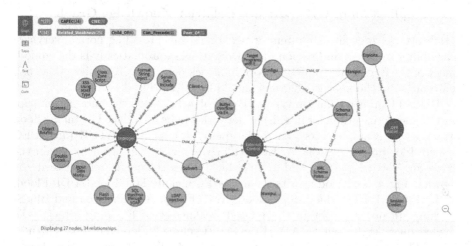

Fig. 3. Some entities and relationships of cyber attack behavior knowledge graph in Neo4j

Flood, and Amplification are caused by "Allocation of Resources Without Limits or Life is precious, and BlueSmacking is caused by "precious Resource Shutdown or Release." XML Flood contains a more detailed attack description, XML Ping of the Death, which is related to the vulnerability "Uncontrolled Resource Consumption". The returned results also show other weaknesses related to the primary weakness ("Allocation of Resources Without Limits or Throttling" and "Improper Resource Shutdown or Release") of the flood attack.

```
neo4j$ MATCH (a:CAPEC {name:"Flooding"})-[r1]-(b:CAPEC) RETURN a,r1,b
```

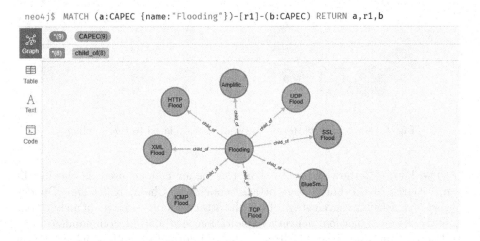

Fig. 4. The attack patterns related to the flooding

It can be seen from the connection between attacks and weaknesses that the weakness "Allocation of Resources Without Limits or Throttling" is associated with a variety of flood attacks and is the key weakness to cause flood attacks. If the weakness is prevented or mitigated according to the information provided by CWE, the impact of Flooding attacks will be effectively mitigated. The causal relationship between various kinds of weaknesses can be seen from the connection between weaknesses and weaknesses, which is conducive to preventing the generation of vulnerabilities from the source. According to the relationship and weakness returned by the knowledge graph, the corresponding attributes can be found to obtain the attack policy, cause and mitigation measures, which can provide basis and guidance for attack detection and mitigation. Compared with the web search methods provided by CAPEC and CWE, the network security knowledge graph proposed in this paper can comprehensively obtain the related attacks and weaknesses of a certain type of attack through a single query and it is easier to find the key weakness.

```
neo4j$ MATCH (a:CAPEC {name:"Flooding"})-[r1]-(b)-[r2]-(c) RETURN a,r1,b,r2,c
```

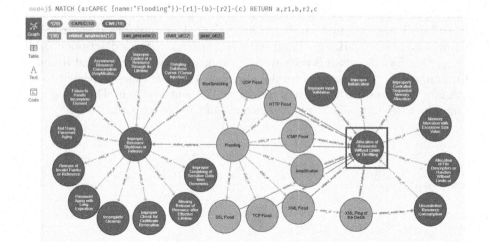

Fig. 5. The attack patterns and weaknesses related to the flooding

The knowledge graph proposed in this paper can be used as the intelligence source of the multi-stage attack model Kill Chain. Kill Chain Divides network attacks into seven stages from the attacker's perspective, namely reconnaissance, weaponization, delivery, exploitation, installation, command&control and actions on objectives [17]. The weakness information and attack execution information in the knowledge graph may be the basis for the attacker to carry out each attack stage. Therefore, after an attacker's action is captured, the vulnerability and possible trend exploited by the attacker can be quickly obtained through the knowledge graph to take appropriate countermeasures. Again, taking flooding attack as an example, in the knowledge graph returned by the above query language, We can see from the attribute information under the flood attack node that the prerequisite for launching the flood attack is "Any target that services requests is vulnerable to this attack on some level of Scale. ", which helps us determine the scope of our defenses against attacks. In the attribute information of "Allocation of Resources Without Limits or Throttling", mitigation measures for different stages of vulnerability exploitation can be obtained, providing guidance for attack prevention and mitigation.

In the era of 6G, artificial intelligence technology will be integrated into the network architecture. The network security knowledge graph facilitates artificial intelligence technology to utilize complex and huge network data, so that the network can use machine learning, deep learning, natural language processing and other technologies to understand and mine the information in the knowledge graph, and feed back to the network decision events. With the help of the knowledge graph, useful information in CAPEC and CWE will be able to be more effectively combined with attack models and artificial intelligence technologies to aid intelligence-driven network security.

5   Conclusion

This paper mainly analyzes the main content and storage structure of CAPEC and CWE, then describes the method of constructing cyber-attack behavior knowledge graph using CAPEC and CWE, and introduces the application method based on Neo4j Cypher language. Compared with other network security knowledge graphs, this paper focuses on the analysis and application of CAPEC and CWE. With the help of the quick query function of the knowledge graph, the comprehensive information of a certain attack can be returned and the key weaknesses of a certain attack can be found. In addition, the knowledge graph proposed in this paper can be used as an intelligence source for multi-stage attack models such as Kill Chain and ATT&CK.

It is the basis of content reasoning and attack prediction to establish knowledge graph with comprehensive content and fast query. At present, the function of knowledge graph proposed in this paper is still based on the query and display function provided by Neo4j. With the development of machine learning and natural language processing technology, machine learning technology can be used to analyze the deep connection between attacks and weaknesses in the graph, and natural language processing can be used to realize automatic query and screening of useful information. The most important work in the future is to improve the interaction between the network attack behavior knowledge graph and the network internal knowledge, and to apply the knowledge of attack patterns and vulnerabilities to attack detection and network situational awareness.

Acknowledgement. This paper is supported by National Key R&D Program of China under Grant No. 2018YFA0701604.

References

1. Liu, G., et al.: Vision, requirements and network architecture of 6G mobile network beyond 2030. China Communications **17**(9), 92–104 (2020)
2. Yang, H., Alphones, A., Xiong, Z., Niyato, D., Zhao, J., Kaishun, W.: Artificial-intelligence-enabled intelligent 6G networks. IEEE Network **34**(6), 272–280 (2020)
3. Mitre. Common attack pattern enumeration and classification (2021). https://capec.mitre.org/
4. Mitre. Common weakness enumeration (2021). https://cwe.mitre.org/
5. Nickel, M., Murphy, K., Tresp, V., Gabrilovich, E.: A review of relational machine learning for knowledge graphs. Proc. IEEE **104**(1), 11–33 (2016)
6. Kim, H.: 5G core network security issues and attack classification from network protocol perspective. J. Internet Serv. Inf. Secur. **10**(2), 1–15 (2020)
7. Abhishta, A., van Heeswijk, W., Junger, M., Nieuwenhuis, L.J.M., Joosten, R.: Why would we get attacked? an analysis of attacker's aims behind DDos attacks. J. Wirel. Mob. Netw. Ubiquit. Comput. Dependable Appl. **11**(2), 3–22 (2020)
8. Jia, Y., Qi, Y., Shang, H., Jiang, R., Li, A.: A practical approach to constructing a knowledge graph for cybersecurity. Engineering **4**(1), 53–60 (2018)
9. Piplai, A., Mittal, S., Joshi, A., Finin, T., Holt, J., Zak, R.: Creating cybersecurity knowledge graphs from malware after action reports. IEEE Access **8**, 211691–211703 (2020)

10. Pingle, A., Piplai, A., Mittal, S., Joshi, A., Holt, J., Zak, R.: Relext: relation extraction using deep learning approaches for cybersecurity knowledge graph improvement. In: 2019 IEEE/ACM International Conference on Advances in Social Networks Analysis and Mining (ASONAM), pp. 879–886 (2019)

11. Hooi, E.K.J., Zainal, A., Maarof, M.A., Kassim, M.N.: TAGraph: knowledge graph of threat actor. In: 2019 International Conference on Cybersecurity (ICoCSec), pp. 76–80 (2019)

12. Li, T., Paja, E., Mylopoulos, J., Horkoff, J., Beckers, K.: Security attack analysis using attack patterns. In: 2016 IEEE Tenth International Conference on Research Challenges in Information Science (RCIS), pp. 1–13 (2016)

13. Kotenko, I., Doynikova, E.: The CAPEC based generator of attack scenarios for network security evaluation. In: 2015 IEEE 8th International Conference on Intelligent Data Acquisition and Advanced Computing Systems: Technology and Applications (IDAACS), vol. 1, pp. 436–441 (2015)

14. Du, Y., Lu, Y.: A weakness relevance evaluation method based on PageRank. In: 2019 IEEE Fourth International Conference on Data Science in Cyberspace (DSC), pp. 422–427 (2019)

15. Syed, Z., Padia, A., Finin, T., Mathews, L., Joshi, A.: UCO: a unified cybersecurity ontology. In: AAAI Workshop on Artificial Intelligence for Cyber Security (2016)

16. Ansarinia, M., Asghari, S.A., Souzani, A., Ghaznavi, A.: Ontology-based modeling of DDoS attacks for attack plan detection. In: 6th International Symposium on Telecommunications (IST), pp. 993–998 (2012)

17. Kiesling, E., Ekelhart, A., Kurniawan, K., Ekaputra, F.: The SEPSES knowledge graph: an integrated resource for cybersecurity. In: Ghidini, C., et al. (eds.) ISWC 2019. LNCS, vol. 11779, pp. 198–214. Springer, Cham (2019). https://doi.org/10.1007/978-3-030-30796-7_13

18. Hutchins, E., Cloppert, M.J., Amin, R.M.: Intelligence-driven computer network defense informed by analysis of adversary campaigns and intrusion kill chains (2010)

19. Strom, B.E., Applebaum, A., Miller, D.P., Nickels, K.C., Pennington, A.G., Thomas, C.B.: Mitre att&ck: Design and philosophy. In: The MITRE Corporation, Tech Rep: MP180360 (2020)

20. Neo4j. Documentation (2021). https://neo4j.com/docs/

A DDoS Detection Method with Feature Set Dimension Reduction

Man Li⬤, Yajuan Qin, and Huachun Zhou⁽✉⁾

School of Electronic and Information Engineering, Beijing Jiaotong University,
Beijing 100044, China
{20111018,yjqin,hchzhou}@bjtu.edu.cn

Abstract. With the advent of fifth-generation network, mobile internet security suffer plenty of DDoS attacks. The number and frequency of occurrence of DDoS attacks are predicted to soar as time goes by, hence there is a need for a sophisticated DDoS detection framework to 5G network without worrying about the security issues and threats. Normally, the neural networks are widely used to detect complex and diversified DDoS attacks. However, feature vectors with high dimensions have a negative effect on detection performance. At present, there is little work on DDoS security dataset dimensionality reduction and verification. This paper proposes a DDoS detection method based on dimensionality reduction security dataset. First, XGBoost and mutual information algorithms are used to reduce the dimensionality of the KDDCup99 and CICDDoS2019 dataset respectively. Futhermore, we collect dataset in the experimental environment. Then, the CNN+LSTM and MLP neural network detectors are used to detect the dataset before and after the XGBoost dimensionality reduction. The experimental results show that using the XGBoost dimensionality reduction dataset, the neural network detector can detect multiclassify DDoS attack types with high accuracy and recall rate.

Keywords: DDoS attack · Mutual information · XGBoost demension reduction · Detection method

1 Introduction

With a large number of devices connected to the Internet, while previous cyber-attacks seem to be less complicated and relatively sophisticated, future attacks such as code hacking, morphing, and bots may be very destructive both to mobile internet security and the entire 5G network if not detected and mitigated [1]. Thus making them vulnerable to cyber-attacks such as Denial of Service and Distributed Denial of Service (DDoS) as the case may be [1].

During 2017–2018, Kaspersky organization quarterly compared DDoS attacks number and frequency [2], which indicate that the attack time continues to increase with quarterly changes. In 2020, NSFOCUS released a report on the

© Springer Nature Singapore Pte Ltd. 2022
I. You et al. (Eds.): MobiSec 2021, CCIS 1544, pp. 365–378, 2022.
https://doi.org/10.1007/978-981-16-9576-6_25

development trend of cyber attacks. The report pointed out that network security incidents was showed a rapid growth trend, and the types of attacks showed diversified characteristics [3].

The researchers utilize neural networks to solve network problem. K.M [4] proposed machine learning algorithms implemented in network intrusion detection. Zhe Tu [5]proposed they will combine artificial intelligence and neural network to analyze spatial routing. Moreover, neural network can find long correlation between features as well as non-linear correlation in the dataset, which is widely applied to detect complex and diversified DDoS attacks. However, excessive DDoS attack features will make the network computational complexity increase, and the high dimensionality feature will have a negative effect on model performance [6].

Researchers have proposed many dimensionality reduction methods that can improve neural network performance. Jie Cai [7] discuss several frequently used evaluation measures for feature selection, and then survey supervised, unsupervised, and semi-supervised feature selection methods, and future challenges. Olsson et al. [8] combined frequency threshold, information gain and chi-square for text classification problems., which did not apply in DDoS detection problem. Kamalov et al. [9] proposed a feature selection method that deal with continuous input features and discrete target values. It can achieve high accuracy in distinguishing between DDoS and benign signals. This method just achieve binary class. Fadi Salo et al. [10] propose combining the approaches of information gain (IG) and principal component analysis (PCA) with an ensemble classifier based on support vector machine (SVM), Instance-based learning algorithms (IBK), and multilayer perceptron (MLP). The performance of this ensemble method was evaluated based on three datasets, namely ISCX 2012, NSL-KDD, and Kyoto 2006. Experimental results show that the proposed hybrid dimensionality reduction method with high accuracy and low false alarm rates. But it does not fit multiclass. Xin Li [11] propose LNNLS-KH algorithm for feature selection of network intrusion detection. Experiments show that the LNNLS-KH algorithm retains 7 features in NSL-KDD dataset and 10 features in CICIDS2017 dataset on average, which effectively eliminates redundant features while ensuring high detection accuracy. Chundong et al. [12] proposed a SU Genetic method to select important features of the original attack data. The SU Genetic method ranks features by the symmetrical uncertainty and then selects features with the genetic algorithm. The experiment show that the efficiency and accuracy were improved with the proposed SU Genetic feature selection method. But this dataset is old. Odnan [13] proposed a feature reduction approach based on the Analysis of Variance (ANOVA), which show that it can reduce the data input, meawhile, increase accuracy. Brian Morris [14] theoretically mentioned that the intrusion detection system captures the data packet flow, and combines the three dimensionality reduction methods with integrated learning, independent component analysis, and principal component analysis with artificial intelligence. The network learns malicious and benign traffic, but this paper lack experimental verification to provide the effectiveness of the proposed dimensionality reduction method. With

ICA(Independent Component Analysis, ICA), PCA(Principle Component Analysis, PCA), SVD(Singular Value Decomposition, SVD) and NMF(Non-negative Matrix Factorization, NMF), Mandikal Vikram et al. [15] use the four method reduce the dimensionality of Tiny-Imagenet, Caltech-256 and MNIST datasets, however, this paper did not verify the performance in terms of network security. Amiri et al. [16] used a feature selection algorithm based on the mutual information to reduce KDDCup99 dataset, selected the maximum mutual information feature, then as a feature subset. Compared to the linearly related feature and forward feature dimensionality reduction method, [16] used false positives, true positive and accuracy rate evaluation method performance, the results show that dimensionality reduction based on mutual information effectively detect R2L (Remote to Local Attack, R2L) and Probe. However, mutual information dimensionality reduction did not consider the correlation and redundancy so as to the neural network do not accurately recognize the DDoS and U2R. In order to compare the mutual information dimensionality reduction proposed by Amiri [16], we propose a detection DDoS method with the reduction dimensionality method.

The major contributions of this paper include: (1) propose a security dataset dimensionality reduction method, and reduced the dimensionality of the CICD-DoS2019 and KDDCup99 datasets, (2) In the tensorflow platform, CNN+LSTM and MLP network detector detect the performance effect of the dataset before and after the dimensionality reduction, (3) In the experiment, we collect the dataset including SYN, ACK, UDP and Benign, (4) we utilize the XGBoost to reduce dimensionality the self-generated dataset and multiclassify the DDoS attack type.

The remainder of this article is organized as follows: Sect. 2 introduces the method of detection dimensionality reduction safety dataset, XGBoost, mutual information dimensionality reduction algorithm and the principle of the neural network detector; Sect. 3 explains the safety dataset reduction dimension method; Sect. 4 performs experimental verification; Sect. 5 summarizes the paper.

2 Detect Safety Dataset Based on the Dimensionality Reduction

First, this section adopts XGBoost and mutual information algorithm to reduce dimensionality KDDCup99 [17] and CICDDoS2019 [18] datasets, secondly, CNN+LSTM (Convolutional Neural Networks, CNN, Long Short Term Memory, LSTM) as well as MLP (Multilayer Perceptron, MLP) separately detect DDoS attacks. Finally, detection method based on dimensionality reduction dataset is achieved.

2.1   DDoS Detection Method Based on Dimensionality Reduction Security Dataset

Figure 1 describe the detection dimensionality reduction dataset method for DDoS attacks. The method consists of dataset acquisition, feature extraction, feature dimensionality reduction and attack detection.

Because there are a large number of irrelevant or redundant feature values in the CICDDoS2019 and KDDCup99 datasets, which fail to identify DDoS attacks [19], therefore, the dataset needs to be preprocessed in the feature extraction stage. In the feature dimensionality reduction stage, first, the number of features is reduced through XGBoost and mutual information. Second, the method will effectively choose the feature subset of DDoS attacks, third, the feature subset is fed to the neural network detector, as well as the CNN+LSTM and MLP neural network detectors learn the relationship between the label and the feature values. Finally, according to the relationship, DDoS attack traffic is detected.

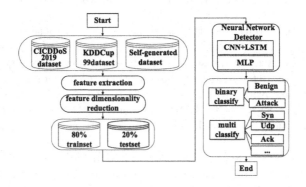

Fig. 1. The dimensionality reduction dataset detection method for DDoS attacks.

We use mutual information and XGBoost algorithms reducing the dimensionality of the security datasets. Mutual information algorithm [20] calculates the correlation between features and label, and the correlation between label and label, then, rank the correlation feature value. In the XGBoost dimensionality reduction algoritm [21], the feature values are sorted at the beginning. During the sorting process, CPU multithread is used to calculate the feature branch points in parallel, find the appropriate split point, repeat calling the feature value, calculate the information gain of each feature, and finally sort information gain value.

2.2   Neural Network Detector

We utilize deep learning to deeply capture the features of long correlation and nonlinear correlation between features. DDoS attacks are detected based on the features in the security dataset. The CNN+LSTM detection DDoS attack model is shown in Fig. 2.

The feature vector in the dataset is fed into the CNN. The attack feature is translated by the convolutional layer, then the pooling layer selects the local features and uses downsampling method to reduce feature complexity. The LSTM unit inputs the important feature sequence extracted by CNN, through the forget gate, input gate and output gate, information flow transmission is adjusted. The LSTM layer use a time window to maintain time series features. Finally, the fully connected layer distinguishes smurf, back, neptune, and teardrop attacks in the KDDCup99 dataset, SYN, UDP attack and benign traffic in the CICDDoS2019 dataset.

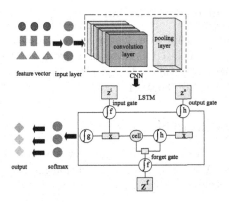

Fig. 2. Detect DDoS based on CNN+LSTM method

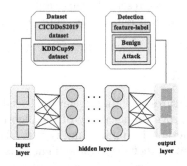

Fig. 3. Detection DDoS based on MLP

As can be seen in Fig. 3, the feature columns of the dataset are fed to the input layer of the MLP neural network. The hidden layer learn the one-way feature information. The output of the output layer is the probability of determining a certain type.

3   Reduce Security Dataset Dimensionality Method

Because of irrelevance and redundancy in the KDDCup99 and CICDDoS2019 dataset, dimensionality reduction algorithm converts high-dimensional data into low-dimensional data, and retains important information. Therefore, it is necessary that we should adpot dimensionality reduction security dataset methods including feature normalization, feature selection, and dataset segmentation.

3.1   Character Feature Digitization

In order to transfer the character features, we adopt LabelBinarizer encoding mapping method. SYN, UDP, Benign correspond to 1,0,0; 0,1,0; 0,0,1. Teardrop, Smurf, Back, Neptune, Benign respectively correspond to 1,0,0,0,0; 0,1,0,0,0;0,0,1,0,0; 0, 0,0,1,0; 0,0,0,0,1.

3.2   Feature Normalization

In order to eliminate the deviation in the dataset, the feature scale method scales the feature value [22]. We adopt the normalization method to process the data. The normalization method is given by

$$X = \frac{X - X_{\min}}{X_{\max} - X_{\min}} \tag{1}$$

According to formula (1), X represents feature value, Xmax represents the smallest number in a certain dimension, Xmin represents the largest number in a certain dimension.

3.3   Feature Selection

By selecting suitable features, deleting irrelevant features, reducing redundant features, three ways improve the accuracy of the algorithm. In this paper, the correlation coefficient method is applied, and the correlation coefficient value is set to 0.8. If the correlation coefficient value higher than 0.8, the feature affect the accuracy of the neural network, thence the feature is removed. Finally, the 26 dimensional feature is composed of KDDCup99+ new dataset, and the 43 dimensional feature is composed of CICDDoS2019+ new dataset.

3.4   Dataset Segmentation

The research objective of this article is to detect DDoS attacks, so the following involves DDoS attacks, teardrop, smurf, back, neptune, and normal samples in the KDDCup99 dataset and UDP, SYN, Benign samples in the CICDDoS2019 dataset.

Because of the dataset oversize, the detection time is prolonged. In order to avoid this situation, according to a certain ratio, teardrop, smurf, back, neptune and normal separately extract 50000 rows, 800 rows, 10000 rows, 400 rows, and 10000 rows which combines into the KDDCup99 train set, as well as extract 20000 rows, 10000 rows, 1000 rows, 20000 rows, and 500 rows which combines into the KDDCup99 test set. UDP, SYN and Benign separately extract 10000 rows, 10000 rows, and 5000 rows which combines into the CICDDoS2019 trainset, as well as extract 15000 rows, 15000 rows, and 30000 rows which combines into the CICDDoS2019 testset.

3.5 Feature Dimensionality Reduction

We use XGBoost and mutual information to reduce KDDCup99 and CICD-DoS2019 trainset dimensionality, and feature set is fed to the neural network, which detect DDoS attack.

First, we use the XGBoost plot feature importance. The gain value measures how important the feature is in the dataset. By the size of the gain value, we select src bytes, dst bytes, flag, diff srv rate, protocol type, dst host count and wrong fragment making up the KDDCup99 train subset. Its importance value and meaning are shown in Table 1. In Table 1, protocol type represents the protocol type of the attack packet. When the host faces attack, attacker request more service from the destination host so as to quickly consume resource. Meanwhile, src bytes, dst bytes, dst host count and diff srv rate will also change significantly. In the KDDCup99 train set, The value of wrong fragment can judge the correct of the datagram fragmentation in the teardrop attack. If the value is high, the connection is likely to be attacked. Since both SYN attacks and UDP attacks send a large number of attack packets during the attack, the number of bytes will increase in the network. The flow bytes can reflect the network traffic. The flow duration reflects the communication time between data packets. If the time

Table 1. KDDCup99 train subset and gain

Feature name	Gain
Src byte	0.33
Flag	0.14
Diff srv rate	0.11
Dst bytes	0.11
Protocol type	0.8
Dst host count	0.5
Wrong fragment	0.4

Table 2. CICDDoS2019 train subset and gain

Feature name	Gain
Destination Port	0.37
Source Port	0.31
Total Length of Fwd Packets	0.22
Flow Duration	0.18
SYN Flag Count	0.15
Flow Bytes/s	0.10
Protocol	0.10

is over long, it means that an attack can be happen. The feature protocol indicates the type of protocol. Different protocol data packets can reflect different attack behaviors, so the protocol field can also be used as a detection feature. Regarding the UDP attack, the source port and destination port number reflect that the attacker can construct malicious messages by setting the specific port number. The feature total length of fwd packets reflect that the attacker send the same length data packet. During a SYN flood attack, the attacker uses a large number of half-open connections to consume the victim resources. Therefore, the SYN flags is one of the selected features. Similarly, in order to avoid increasing the detection time, CICDDoS2019 train subset consist of Destination Port, Source Port, Flow Bytes/s, Flow Duration, SYN Flag Count, Total Length of Fwd Packets, Protocol. Its gain value and meaning are shown in Table 2.

In order to ensure that the trainset is equal to the number of features in the testset, Src bytes, Dst bytes, Flag, Diff srv rate, Protocol type, Dst host count and Wrong fragment compose the KDDCup99 test subset, Destination Port, Source Port, Flow Bytes/s, Flow Duration, SYN Flag Count, Total Length of Fwd Packets, Protocol constitute the CICDDoS2019 test subset.

Secondly, mutual information dimensionality reduction method deletes the high dimensional features. In order to be consistent with the KDDCup99 training subset and the CICDDoS2019 train subset, we take the top seven features, therefore, the protocol type, Src bytes, Destination byte, Urgent, Su attempted, Is hot login, Num outbound cmds form KDDCup99* train subset. Source Port, Fwd Packet Length Max, Flow Bytes/s, Flow Duration, ACK Flag Count, Total Length of Fwd Packets, Protocol compose the CICDDoS2019* train subset.

In order to ensure that the trainset is equal to the number of features in the testset, Protocol type, Src byte, Dst bytes, Urgent, Su attempted, Is hot login, Num outbound cmds compose the KDDCup99 test subset, Destination Port, Source Port, Flow Bytes/s, Flow Duration, SYN Flag Count, Total Length of Fwd Packets, Protocol constitute the CICDDoS2019 test subset.

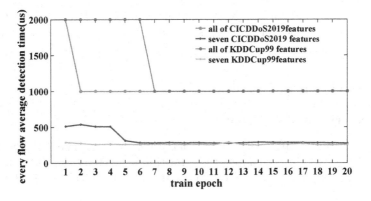

Fig. 4. The contrast of the detect time

Table 3. CICDDoS2019 dataset and false negative rate

Feature number	SYN	UDP
Sevent feature	0.003	0.014
Four feature	0.07	0.08

Table 4. KDDCup99 dataset and false negative rate

Feature number	Teardrop	Smurf	Back	Neptune
Sevent feature	0.0019	0	0.0005	0.004
Four feature	0	0.0004	0	0.016

The Fig. 4 is a comparison diagram of the detect time. It can be seen from Fig. 4 that the train of all features of the neural network detector will increase the average time for detecting each flow in the two data sets of CICDDoS2019 and KDDCup99. Table 3 and Table 4 are the false alarm rate of the CICDDoS2019 data set and the false alarm rate of the KDDCup99 data set respectively. In Table 3, the neural network detection of the four features has a higher false positive rate than the false positive rate of SYN and UDP generated by the detection of seven characteristics. In Table 4, the neural network respectively identify four types of attacks in the KDDCup99 dataset. The experimental results show that the neural network incorrectly identify Smurf and Neptune using the four characteristics with a higher probability. In summary, too many features will increase the time for the neural network detector to detect DDoS attacks, as well as too few features is not conducive to the deep characteristics of the detector learning features, which will cause high false alarms for each type of attack.

The source codes in our work will all be published on GitHub to interested researchers. The source codes is available at https://github.com/liliMpro/dataset.

4   Experimental Results

4.1   Experimental Environment

All experiments adopt the windows operating system. The CPU is Intel-i7 6700K. The keras library compile the algorithm in the tensorflow platform. Similarly, the keras process the KDDCup99 dataset and CICDDoS2019 dataset.

4.2   Evaluation Metric

In order to appreciate the detection quality of the different experiments, we provide the following performance metrics for each experiments: accuracy, precision, recall, and F1 [22]. Accuracy is the correctly classified sample proportion. Precision is all the samples that are predicted to be actually positive. Recall is actually a positive sample which is predicted to be a positive sample. F1 score is a weighted balance between precision and recall. The loss rate represents the difference between the true label and the predict label. There are A and B experiments. Experiment A: this scene uses XGBoost and mutual information to reduce the KDDCup99, CICDDoS2019 dataset dimensionality, then, the CNN+LSTM neural network detect the dataset. Experiment B: this scenario uses XGBoost to reduce the self dataset dimensionality, then the CNN+LSTM, RNN neural networks detect the dataset and multi classification DDoS attack.

4.3   Experiment A

The parameter values of our deep learning network model are shown in Table 5. To overcome overfitting, dropout and weight constraints were utilized. Note that the dropout is randomly dropping units from the neural network during training. Batchnorm speed up the training process and reduce detection time. Hence, the neural network model add batchnorm and dropout parameters. The neural network train 20 rounds. After using the dimensional method, the train feature are fed to the neural network and save the network model. We use detection metrics to compare the effects of different dimensionality reduction methods.

Table 5. CNN+LSTM

Parameter	Parameter value
Convolution kernel	3
Downsampling	1
Optimizer	SGD
Activation function	Relu

In order to avoid the unbalanced distribution of samples, we use precision, recall and F1 score which evaluate the performance of neural network classifiers. In Fig. 5, the neural network is more suitable for detecting the XGBoost dimensionality reduction dataset. Compared with the mutual information method, the neural network detector can identify DDoS attacks after XGBoost dimensionality reduction with higher accuracy.

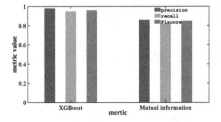
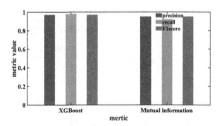

Fig. 5. The KDDCUP99 performance   **Fig. 6.** The CICDDoS2019 performance

The Fig. 6 lists the accuracy, recall and F1 score. The higher the accuracy, the detector can classify most of the samples as DDoS attacks. The F1 score is directly proportional to the performance of the detector. From the values in Fig. 6, it can be seen that the performance of the neural network is equivalent in the two cases. Experiments show that compared to mutual information dimensionality reduction technology, the XGBoost dimension method can not only reduce the feature dimensionality, but also we use the neural network to train the reduced dimensionality dataset, as well as the detector can achieve high accuracy.

4.4   Experiment B

We use the Ubuntu18.04 Server operating system to build an experimental environment, use the hping3 tool to simulate SYN, UDP, ACK DDoS traffic, as well as make use of python to simulate 5G scenarios to generate benign traffic, such as browsers, file transfers, etc. Benign traffic and attack traffic are combined into a self-generated dataset.

In experiment A, the results show that compared with the mutual information dimensionality reduction algorithm. We prefer to choose neural network to detect XGBoost dimensionality reduction dataset. The neural network performance is better.

Therefore, in experiment B, first of all, the XGBoost reduce the self-generated dataset dimensionality, hereafter, the CNN+LSTM and MLP neural network was used to multiclassify the self-generated dataset to verify the neural performance of the network. The MLP neural network structure parameters are shown in

Table 6, and the CNN+LSTM neural network parameters are shown in Table 5. We use CNN+LSTM and MLP neural network to train 20 rounds, and use the softmax classifier to fine grain the traffic in the test subset.

Table 6. MLP

Parameter	Parameter value
Hiden layer	3
Optimizer	Adam
Activation function	Relu

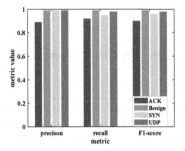

Fig. 7. CNN+LSTM result   **Fig. 8.** MLP result

In Fig. 7, we compare the performance of CNN+LSTM neural network detecting the self-generate dataset. The precision of SYN and UDP attacks is close to 1; the recall of SYN attacks is close to 0.94; the F1 of SYN attacks score is 0.96; the recall of UDP attacks and the F1 scores are 0.98. For the normal traffic, all of the metrics are 0.99. Most of the ACK metric is 0.89. As shown in Fig. 8, the probability that MLP neural network can correctly classify the SYN attack is close to 0.95. The all metric values of the UDP and benign flow are 0.98. The precision of ACK is 0.89 and the rest metrics are 0.90.

In summary, the XGBoost reduce self-generate dataset dimensionality and we use CNN+LSTM and MLP neural network to detect. Experimental results show that the neural network can multiclassify all traffic type, and the metrcis can be close to 0.93 on average.

5   Conclusion and Future Work

Secured communication has always been a problem and that probblem has increased and will continue to increase, especially with the recent adoption of 5G networks. DDoS tops when it comes to security threats for these networks and that precipitated the need for efficient DDoS prevention and detection. We detect

DDoS attacks based on dimensionality reduction security datasets method. This method can reduce the feature dimension of the safety datasets. The experiment A results demonstrate that with XGBoost dimensionality reduction method, the neural network can improve the accuracy of the model. Experiment B results show that different neural networks can detect DDoS attacks in the self-generated feature set after XGBoost dimensionality reduction, and more accurately multiclassify attack types. Next, we will integrate LSTM and attention, which can reduce the dependency of features. And we will compare with traditional methods which verify the effectiveness of the detection method in a real-world network environment.

Acknowledgments. This paper is supported by National Key R&D Program of China under Grant No. 2018YFA0701604.

References

1. Mantas, G., Komninos, N., Rodriuez, J., Logota, E., Marques, H.: Security for 5G Communications. Fundamentals of 5G Mobile Networks (2015)
2. Cheskidov, P., Nikolskaia, K., Minbaleev, A.: Choosing the reinforcement learning method for modeling DdoS attacks. In: Proceedings of the International Multi - Conference on Industrial Engineering and Modern Technologies, pp. 1–4. IEEE (2019)
3. NSFOCUS. Vulnerability development trend (2020). http://blog.nsfocus.net
4. Komisarek, M., Pawlicki, M., Kozik, R., Choraś, M.: Machine learning based approach to anomaly and cyberattack detection in streamed network traffic data. J. Wirel. Mob. Netw. Ubiquit. Comput. Dependable Appl. **12**(1), 3–19 (2021)
5. Zhe, T., Zhou, H., Li, K., Li, G.: DCTG: degree constrained topology generation algorithm for software-defined satellite network. J. Internet Serv. Inf. Secur. **9**(4), 49–58 (2019)
6. Liu, H., Yu, L.: Toward integrating feature selection algorithms for classification and clustering. IEEE Trans. Knowl. Data Eng. **17**(4), 491–502 (2005)
7. Cai, J., Luo, J., Wang, S., Yang, S.: Feature selection in machine learning: a new perspective. Neurocomputing **300**, 70–79 (2018)
8. Lopez, A.D., Mohan, A.P., Nair, S.: Combining feature selectors for text classification. In: Proceedings of the 15th ACM International Conference on Information and Knowledge Management, pp. 798–799 (2006)
9. Firuz, K., Sherif, M., Rita, Z., Omar, M.: Feature selection for intrusion detection systems. In: Proceedings of the13th International Symposium on Computational Intelligence and Design, pp. 265–269 (2020)
10. Salo, F., Nassif, A.B., Essex, A.: Dimensionality reduction with IG-PCA and ensemble classifier for network intrusion detection. Comput. Netw. **148**, 164–175 (2019)
11. Li, X., Yi, P., Wei, W., Jiang, Y., Tian, L.: LNNLS-KH: a feature selection method for network intrusion detection. Secur. Commun. Netw. **1–22**, 2021 (2021)
12. Wang, C., Yao, H., Liu, Z.: An efficient DDoS detection based on SU-genetic feature selection. Clust. Comput. **22**, 2505–2515 (2019). https://doi.org/10.1007/s10586-018-2275-z

13. Sanchez, O.R., Repetto, M., Carrega, A., Bolla, R., Pajo, J.F.: Feature selection evaluation towards a lightweight deep learning DDoS detector. In: IEEE International Conference on Communications, pp. 1–6 (2021)
14. Morris, B.: Explainable anomaly and intrusion detection intelligence for platform information technology using dimensionality reduction and ensemble learning. In: 2019 IEEE Autotestcon, pp. 1–5 (2019)
15. Vikram, M., Pavan, R., Dineshbhai, N.D., Mohan, B.: Performance evaluation of dimensionality reduction techniques on high dimensional data. In: Proceedings of the 3rd International Conference on Trends in Electronics and Informatics (ICOEI), pp. 1169–1174 (2019)
16. Amiri, F., Yousefi, M.R., Lucas, C., Shakery, A., Yazdani, N.: Mutual information-based feature selection for intrusion detection systems. J. Netw. Comput. Appl. **34**(4), 1184–1199 (2011)
17. Yamanishi, K., Takeuchi, J., Williams, G.: On-line unsupervised outlier detection using finite mixtures with discounting learning algorithms. Data Min. Knowl. Disc. **8**, 275–300 (2004). https://doi.org/10.1023/B:DAMI.0000023676.72185.7c
18. Sharafaldin, I., Lashkari, A.H., Hakak, S., Ghorbani, A.A.: Developing realistic distributed denial of service (DDoS) attack dataset and taxonomy. In: Proceedings of the International Carnahan Conference on Security Technology, pp. 1–8 (2019)
19. Chen, F., Ye, Z., Wang, C., Yan, L., Wang, R.: A feature selection approach for network intrusion detection based on tree-seed algorithm and k-nearest neighbor. In: Proceedings of the 4th International Symposium on Wireless Systems within the International Conferences on Intelligent Data Acquisition and Advanced Computing Systems, pp. 68–72 (2018)
20. Battiti, R.: Using mutual information for selecting features in supervised neural net learning. IEEE Trans. Neural Netw. **5**(4), 537–550 (1994)
21. Chen, T., Guestrin, C.: Xgboost a scalable tree boosting system. In: Proceedings of the 22nd ACM SIGKDD International Conference on Knowledge Discovery and Data Mining, pp. 785–794. ACM (2016)
22. Jithu, P., Shareena, J., Ramdas, A., Haripriya, A.: Intrusion detection system for IoT botnet attacks using deep learning. SN Comput. Sci **2**, 1–8 (2021). https://doi.org/10.1007/s42979-021-00516-9

Development of Total Security Platform to Protect Autonomous Car and Intelligent Traffic System Under 5G Environment

WonHaeng Lee[(✉)] [iD], Keon Yun, MyungWoo Chung, JinHyeok Oh, HyunJun Shin, and KwonKoo Kwak

Penta Security System Inc., 115, Yeouigongwon-ro, Yeoungdeungpo-gu, Seoul 07241, Republic of Korea
{whlee,kyun,mwchung,jhoh,hyunjun,kkkwak}@pentasecurity.com
http://www.pentasecurity.com

Abstract. Despite the development of autonomous driving technology, there are still vulnerabilities in security technology. Therefore, this paper proposes a cybersecurity attack response plan that may occur in autonomous driving. First, we propose a C-ITS security structure for autonomous vehicle security in a 5G environment. Subsequently, the latest security technologies applicable to autonomous vehicles are analyzed. Finally, we describe what targets can be achieved by applying these techniques.

Keywords: 5G · Security · Autonomous driving

1 Introduction

From July 2020, the Ministry of Land, Infrastructure and Transport introduced safety standards for level 3 autonomous driving for the first time in the world and allowed them to be applied to actual commercial vehicles [1]. In addition, 28GHz-based high-speed, low-latency 5G communication, which is a necessary condition for autonomous driving, will be introduced in the second half of 2020 [2]. As such, autonomous driving is getting closer to our lives, but security technologies and products to protect autonomous vehicles and Cooperative-Intelligent Transport Systems (C-ITS) from cyber terrorism are lacking. Therefore, in this study, we

This work was partly supported by Institute of Information & communications Technology Planning & Evaluation (IITP) grant funded by the Korea government (MSIT) (No. 2020-0-00304, Development of Total Security Platform To Protect Autonomous Car and Intelligent Traffic System Under 5G Environment, 100% and Korea Evaluation Institute of Industrial Technology (KEIT) grant funded by the Korea government (MOTIE) (No. 2020-0-00304, Development of Total Security Platform To Protect Autonomous Car and Intelligent Traffic System Under 5G Environment, 100%).

© Springer Nature Singapore Pte Ltd. 2022
I. You et al. (Eds.): MobiSec 2021, CCIS 1544, pp. 379–395, 2022.
https://doi.org/10.1007/978-981-16-9576-6_26

propose the following autonomous vehicle security technology in the 5G environment to effectively defend and respond to all possible cyber attacks in the autonomous vehicle and C-ITS environment (Fig. 1).

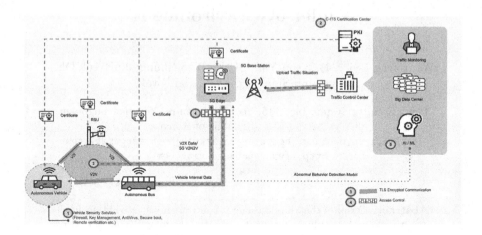

Fig. 1. Proposed autonomous vehicle security technology in 5G environment

1.1 Threatening the Hacking of Self-driving Cars that Threaten Citizens' Property and Life

Recently developed and produced automobiles are equipped with intelligent functions such as RADAR, LiDAR sensors, Smart Cruise Control (SCC), and Advanced Emergency Braking System (AEB), securing network connectivity, making them susceptible to hacking threats [3]. Since hacking of self-driving cars threatens the property and safety of citizens, integrated security products that can secure both hardware and software are needed. Therefore, through this study, we intend to propose security technologies for software such as detection of abnormal behavior as well as hardware security equipment such as embedded system security products for vehicles.

1.2 Analysis and Response of Security Threats to Internal/External Targets of Autonomous Vehicles

In order to analyze and respond to security threats within/outside self-driving cars, we first want to identify domestic and foreign technology trends of the latest automobile hacking technology and design countermeasures. We will investigate known threats internal and external automobiles for self-driving cars and need to investigate trends in self-driving car threat response technologies that can respond to these threats. In addition, it is necessary to develop a secure boot remote verification plan to protect the autonomous vehicle battlefield system.

Integrity verification and OTA communication security environment for software/firmware update files such as navigation updates should be established (Fig. 2).

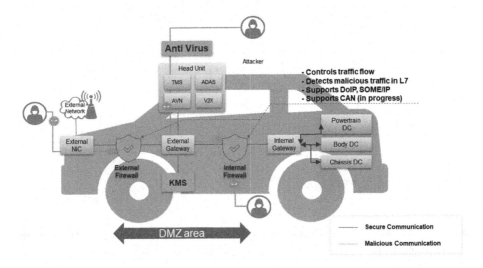

Fig. 2. Security threats and response suites inside self-driving cars

1.3 Establishment of an Autonomous Vehicle and Intelligent Transportation System Certification System

The certification system in autonomous vehicles and intelligent transportation systems proposed in this paper is designed to comply with communication security standards in C-ITS environments such as IEEE 1609.2 [4], SAE J2735 [5], and SAE J3061 [6]. Anonymous certificate technology is applied to protect personal information such as vehicle-specific information, vehicle owner information, and location information. It should include all elements of certificate management, such as Certificate Authority (CA), Registration Authority (RA), and Certificate Revolution List (CRL), and aims to commercialize certification services in an intelligent transportation system through the establishment of a virtualized cloud-based certification system.

1.4 5G Edge Environmental Security

Security standards for 5G communication protocols should be studied to establish a security system for 5G Edge environments. And in order to establish a security system in a 5G autonomous driving environment, it is necessary to establish an enterprise-level security environment for the Edge environment. For security of networks via edge in an autonomous driving environment, access

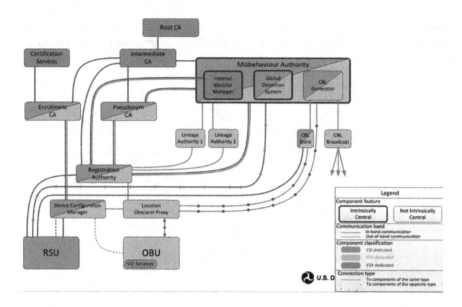

Fig. 3. Structure diagram of autonomous vehicle and intelligent transportation system certification system

control and communication security systems must be established between edge node and vehicle, edge node and ITS infrastructure, and edge node and traffic information centers (Fig. 3).

1.5 Establishment of Malicious Code Response System for Autonomous Vehicle Environment

We intend to establish a malicious code response system for autonomous vehicles and ITS environments through the following methodologies.

- Implementation of communication monitoring technology for L3, L4, and L7 layers used in V2X
- Malicious code and Advanced Persistent Thread (APT) detection through Deep Packet Inspection (DPI)
- Integrated multi-engine inspection systems such as Virus Total, Metalfender, hybrid-analysis, etc.
- Real-time response system for new and variant viruses through machine learning.

1.6 Provide Access Control Measures Through Network Security

We will study network security measures such as applying centralized access control policies, certificate-based self-driving cars, ITS infrastructure classification and access control, and Software Defined Perimeter (SDP) [7] technology.

It is intended to provide access control measures to traffic control centers in autonomous driving environments using network security technology. Figure 4 shows the network security structure through the SDP access control system between the ITS infrastructure such as Road Side Unit (RSU) and the traffic control center.

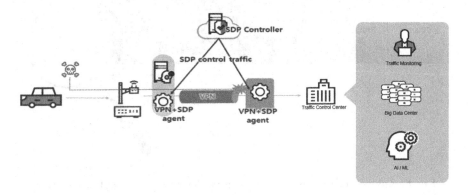

Fig. 4. SDP access control network structure

1.7 Autonomous Car and ITS Data Collection and Behavior Analysis Through Machine Learning

Through this study, we intend to build an anomaly detection model through machine learning by collecting hardware, software, and network security, as well as in-vehicle/external data generated by 5G communication networks and WAVE communication in real time. The data learned in machine learning and deep learning plans to utilize log records of existing legacy equipment, Edge nodes, and V2X data collected from traffic control centers.

2 Technology Trends of Domestic and International Related to Automobile Security

2.1 High Speed Detection Technology for Malicious Packets Through Deep Packet Inspection (DPI)

Deep packet analysis technology is a concept that extends the scope of monitoring to the content (content) of packets coming and going on the network and can determine whether packets are malicious based on much more information than security products used to monitor packet origin and destination or header information in the past [8]. Therefore, DPI technology inevitably results in a decrease in network speed by monitoring a large portion of packets, and the core of the technology is to handle these network loads smoothly. Figure 5 shows the analysis method and DPI application layer according to the packet layer.

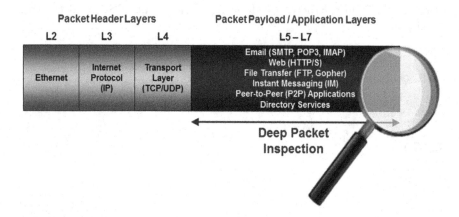

Fig. 5. Analysis method according to packet layer and DPI application layer

Technology Trends in Korea

[Penta Security System Inc.] A representative domestic company with DPI technology is the Penta Security System. The Penta Security System develops and distributes its own web firewall, the No. 1 market share in the Asia-Pacific market. Due to the nature of the web firewall, packets must be detected to the application layer, so the Penta Security System has the element technology necessary for in-depth packet analysis.

Technology Trends in International

According to the 2009 Yankee Group Report, the company's return on investment (ROI) is estimated to increase to more than 25% on average when applying DPI technology, and the need for it is expected to increase further in the future convergence environment. The DPI-related market is expanding to markets in various fields such as security, traffic control platforms, and network optimization (ADC) markets, and is expected to be easy to enter the initial market as it is in the early stages of the business.

[Netscreen Technology] Network security company Netscreen Technology applies DPI technology to its own "Netscreen-5000" firewall to support technologies such as attack on application programs and prevention of protocol ambiance and regression on IP protocols.

[**Top Layer Networks**] The ASIC architecture-based AppSafe 3500^{TM} developed by Top Layer Networks provides DDoS attack mitigation, VPN, IDS functionality, firewall load balancing, VPN load balancing, and server load balancing.

[**Radware**] A company called Radware which mainly develops switch equipment for network load balancing, has adopted DPI technology for its own Radware Security-Switch products.

2.2 Machine Learning/Deep Learning

Recently, companies affected by social engineering hacking techniques have emerged, and security solutions that can respond to them are needed. It is evaluated that the introduction of artificial intelligence techniques is essential to cope with social engineering hacking threats. Gartner Group, an IT market research company, newly defines the Security Intelligence product line and evaluates it as a security technology that will last for the next five to 10 years.

Technology Trends in Korea

[**Penta Security System Inc.**] Penta Security System launched Cloudbric 2.0 an upgraded version of the web hacking blocking service Cloudbric and the core of Cloudbric 2.0 is the installation of machine learning detection engine Catalyst supporting intelligent detection tailored to websites.

[**AhnLab**] AhnLab collects and analyzes malicious codes through cloud-based AhnLab Smart Defense (ASD). AhnLab has collected about 300 million malicious URLs and 10 million cyber threat activities, and detects malicious code and security threats through machine learning about the information.

[**FASOO**] FASOO, a domestic data protection company, has applied the latest machine learning technology to Digital Page an intelligent lifestyle service recently launched. "Digital Page" provides a function that allows you to easily view all related information without having to find each of the previous records by presenting a page related to the written memo at the bottom.

Technology Trends in International

[**DarkTrace**] DarkTrace, an information security company established in 2013 in Cambridge, UK, has developed a model for detecting abnormal and malicious behavior through automated machine learning and is recognized as a $500 million company in four years since its establishment. DarkTrace immediately displays known threats such as Known APT and user account violations in real time and provides the ability to classify detected abnormalities into known and unique threats.

[**Splunk**] Splunk has launched Splunk UBA an immediate support solution for finding known, unknown, and hidden threats using data science, machine learning, behavior analysis, peer group analysis, and advanced correlation analysis.

2.3 Software Defined Perimeter (SDP)

Software Defined Perimeter (SDP) is an advanced form of current Network Access Control (NAC) products as a network security model proposed by the Cloud Security Alliance (CSA) since 2013. SDP performs device certification, user certification, and software certification in the SDP controller with an additional repeater in the existing server-client structure, and performs access control by connecting real servers only for safe requests.

Technology Trends in Korea

[**Mark Any**] Mark Any has launched an SDP solution named Black Port which uses seven stages of security technologies such as Single Packet Authorization (SPA), dynamic firewalls, mutual certification, and TLS.

Overseas, it is known that large companies with large networks such as CoCa-Cola are using some SDPs, but there are no known cases in Korea.

Technology Trends in International

[**Check Point**] Check point, a global conglomerate of firewall products, has developed and sold a product called Software-Defined Protection. The SDP product of Check Point consists of three layers: Enforcement layer, Control layer, and Management layer, providing a convenient user environment.

[**Vidder**] Vidder develops and sells its own SDP product named Precision Access and blocks certification theft and server attacks.

3   The Goals and Contents of the Study

The final goal of this study and end-product are as follows.

Goal

- Establishment of an autonomous vehicle and intelligent transportation system certification system
- Analysis and response of security threats to internal/external targets of autonomous vehicles
- Data collection of autonomous vehicles

- Machine learning to detect abnormal behavior of autonomous vehicles
- Development of a Software Defined Perimeter(SDP) access control system to block network attacks
- Development of network security products for automobiles
- Configuration of a simulation environment reflecting a virtual driving environment and a driving scenario.

End Product

- PKI certificate system for autonomous vehicles and ITS environment
- Key Management system(KMS) for autonomous vehicles
- Firewalls for autonomous vehicles
- SDP solution for network access control
- Autonomous vehicles and ITS data collection systems
- Machine learning based malicious code detection technology
- Machine learning based abnormal behavior detection technology.

3.1   Establishment of an Autonomous Vehicle and Intelligent Transportation System Authorization System

Establishment of PKI Certificate System for C-ITS. We are planning to establish a PKI-based certificate system for C-ITS for certification and communication encryption of lightweight devices such as vehicle-to-vehicle (V2V) and vehicle-to-infrastructure (V2I). Figure 6 shows an example of the configuration of a authorization system and a V2X certificate management system in a C-ITS environment. In addition, the authorization system scheduled to be established in this study will support certification between the ITS infrastructure and the traffic information center.

Service Authorization System for Autonomous Vehicles and ITS Environment. After establishing a authorization system in the C-ITS environment, it is planning to service the authorization system in the ITS environment. By virtualizing the PKI based certificate system into a cloud environment, it is possible to support certification services technically without space constraints. In addition, the authorization system built in a cloud edge environment has the advantage of being able to provide fast and accurate certification services. Figure 7 is a diagram of the authorization system in a V2X environment.

Research is also underway to develop a Key Management System (KMS) for autonomous vehicles to establish a authorization system for C-ITS and safely store certificates for autonomous vehicles.

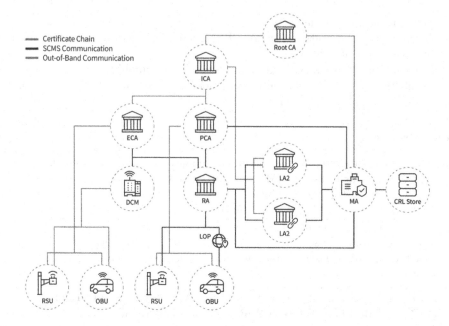

Fig. 6. An example of an authorization system configuration in a C-ITS environment

3.2 Analysis and Response of Security Threats to Internal/External Targets of Autonomous Vehicles

Research is underway to identify and respond to previously known automobile security threats to self-driving cars' battlefield platforms, internal/external networks, and management/diagnosis.

In order to check the integrity of the autonomous driving system, the entire system will be diagnosed at the time of automobile booting (when the system is powered on) safe conditions will be remembered through system image/hash and the process of verifying forgery by comparing ideal conditions with the current system.

Through this study, we intend to develop a Secure Boot system for self-driving cars that includes integrity verification by specifying various elements such as bootloaders, OS images, kernel images, and key setting values [9]. Figure 8 is an example of a Secure Boot architecture design.

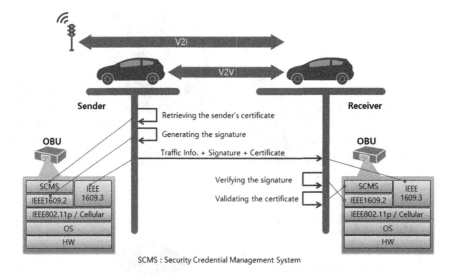

Fig. 7. Certificate system for V2V and V2I

3.3   Data Collection of Autonomous Vehicles

We study how to collect data through the OBD-II system or IVI system and use it to develop an abnormal behavior detection model for internal network of autonomous vehicles. If there is no IVI system or does not provide necessary functions, data inside and outside self-driving vehicles can be collected as a way to collect data from the device after installing a separate OBD-II device. If the IVI system exists and the IVI system is in charge of communication inside and outside the vehicle, data related to self-driving cars can be collected through the IVI system. The collected data will be developed to be collected through edge node to the traffic information center through a dedicated application. Figure 9 shows examples of data collection using OBD-II devices and data collection using IVI systems.

If there is no separate communication module in the vehicle such as OBD-II and IVI systems, the autonomous vehicle must perform V2X communication through the OBU (On Board Unit). Therefore, in order to collect data through OBU, the process of collecting and storing V2X communication data is required.

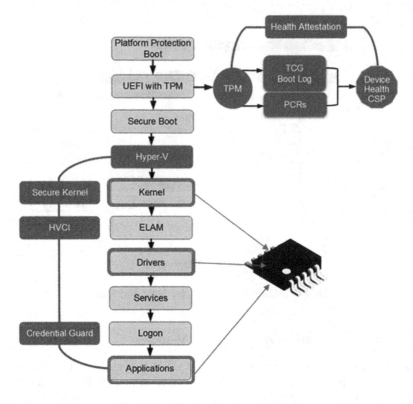

Fig. 8. Architecture of secure boot

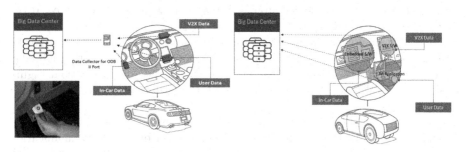

Fig. 9. OBD-II system & IVI system

3.4 Machine Learning to Detect Abnormal Behavior of Autonomous Vehicles

Detection of Abnormal Behavior Based on Collected Autonomous Driving Data. We utilize data from autonomous vehicles obtained from OBD-II devices, IVI systems, and OBU to develop abnormal behavior detection models. Abnormal behavior detection technology includes technology to detect abnormal fault conditions and intrusion of external devices.

In order to maintain the high anomaly detection rate of the abnormal behavior detection model developed through self-driving car data analysis, we plan to conduct periodic learning and minimize additional work of users using the CNN (Convolutional Neural Network) based Innovation Learning model.

See Fig. 10 for CNN network structure for incremental learning.

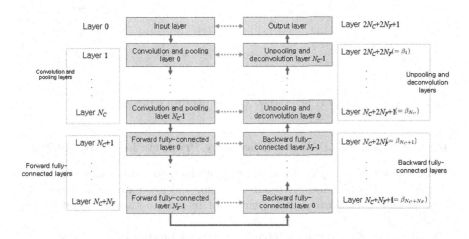

Fig. 10. CNN structure for incremental learning

Certificate Misuse Detection Using Machine Learning. We collect certificate information used for communication with surrounding objects from the PKI server to detect misuse of certificates. And abnormalities in certificates or misuse of certificates are detected based on the collected certification information. We are also studying the certificate management process in which certificates with abnormal behavior detected are registered and managed in the certificate revolution list (CRL).

3.5 Development of a Software Defined Perimeter (SDP) Access Control System to Block Network Attacks

In this study, we would like to establish an ITS network security policy by introducing an SDP access control system that performs dynamic firewall functions into a 5G autonomous driving environment. As shown in Fig. 11, the SDP access control system performs network access control between the ITS infrastructure (e.g., Road Side Unit, RSU) and the traffic information center.

The SDP access control system includes an SDP Host and an SDP Controller. SDP Host supports device, application, and user integrity verification and supports single packet authorization (SPA) technology. And SDP Controller supports server IP non-exposure technology, Dynamic Firewall technology, and single packet authorization (SPA) technology.

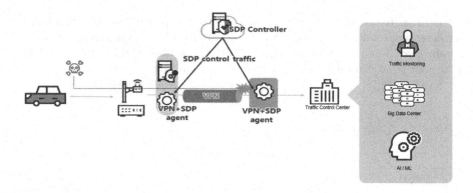

Fig. 11. SDP access control network structure

3.6 Development of Network Security Products for Automobiles

We are trying to develop network security products for autonomous vehicles. It is developing firewalls and intrusion detection and prevention solution (IDPS) as products for monitoring and security of internal networks of autonomous vehicles.

Vehicle firewalls and vehicle intrusion detection products also use open source frameworks such as PF_RING and Snort [10]. Unlike existing web firewall or intrusion detection products, we are making great efforts to simplify the structure and improve performance, considering that firewalls and network products for autonomous vehicles should be built in embedded systems with relatively large resource constraints rather than server environments (Fig. 12).

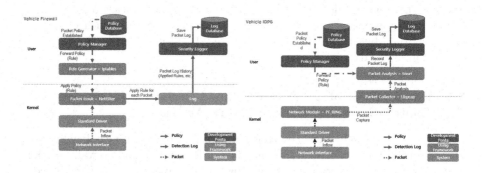

Fig. 12. Vehicle firewall & vehicle IDPS

3.7 Configuration of a Simulation Environment Reflecting a Virtual Driving Environment and a Driving Scenario

In order to verify the validity of the security products applied to the autonomous driving environment developed in this study, we will organize a simulation environment to evaluate the impact of implementing security functions on autonomous vehicles. For this process, a driving scenario is designed and an interface model is being developed that interworks with a virtualization simulation environment (Fig. 13).

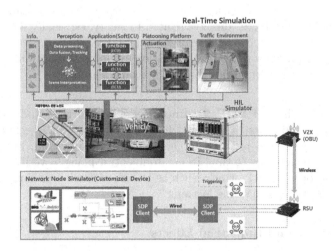

Fig. 13. Network simulation environment of V2X modules

4 Expectation Effectiveness

Automobile security has core tasks at each level of the value chain, and continues to grow in size due to rising public awareness of cybersecurity, increased demand for personal information protection, deepening regulations on cybersecurity issues, and concerns over loss of OEM brand reputation. Therefore, we analyzed the expected effects of building a car security system in an autonomous driving environment by dividing them into technical and economic.

4.1 The Expected Effects of Technology

Development of Integrated Security Products for Autonomous Vehicles. This study aims to build an all-in-one package that provides all necessary security technologies for autonomous driving, such as communication security inside autonomous vehicles, prevention of malicious code infection in IVI systems, and certificates and key management products. In addition, as a result of these studies, we can secure access control ITS systems for infrastructure protection, such as establishing certification systems for communication outside autonomous vehicles such as connected cars and ITS transportation infrastructure and establishing V2X communication security systems.

Solving the Fundamental Causes of Car Security. Recent studies related to the development of automobile security technology in international have cited vulnerabilities in automobile internal networks as the fundamental cause of automobile hacking, and security technology is not applied at all to the current mass-produced automobile networks. And as automobile-ICT convergence accelerates, new types of automobile security problems are expected to arise, and it is clear that security is a key factor directly related to safety, especially for self-driving cars. Therefore, through continuous research and development, we want to solve this problem by protecting ITS transportation infrastructure as well as detecting vehicle and driver abnormalities through machine learning.

Commercialization of SDP Technology. Through this study, the goal is to study the world's first software defined perimeter (SDP) technology at a level that can be commercialized in the transportation system. In addition to applying SDP technology to the ITS environment, it plans to verify efficiency in defending various network attacks such as DDoS, network scanning, and MitM. abnormalities through machine learning.

4.2   Economic and Industrial Effects

Reduction of Property and Human Casualties Through Traffic Safety. As of 2018, the number of deaths in traffic accidents in Korea reached 3,781 and 323,000 were injured. Most of the causes of death in traffic accidents are carelessness, speeding, and non-compliance with driver safety rules such as drunk driving, and vehicle defects are less than 4%, and accidents caused by defects in the vehicle itself are very small in total. Based on these statistics, if human mistakes of the driver are excluded through autonomous driving, it can be expected that human and property damage caused by traffic accidents will decrease sharply. We intend to help reduce traffic accident damage by promoting the introduction of autonomous vehicles by solving security, the biggest concern of autonomous driving.

Securing Competitive Advantage in Export of Autonomous Vehicle with Security Modules. Many foreign countries are demanding cybersecurity and privacy functions when importing vehicles. Vehicles equipped with reliable security modules are expected to have a strong competitive advantage when pioneering overseas markets and can lead to securing a competitive advantage in the domestic automobile industry.

Establish Itself as a Leading Country in 5G Environment Automobile Security Technology. Future cars, represented by self-driving cars, connected cars, and eco-friendly cars, are national growth engines promoted by the government and are high value-added projects that will be responsible for future food. 5G communication is emerging as a next-generation communication technology for high-speed and low-latency, and is emerging as an essential technology for autonomous driving, smart factories, and IoT systems. It is expected that it will be able to establish itself as a new powerhouse in the global security product market by solving both edge cloud security and self-driving car security, which are the core of 5G communication.

5   Proposed Result

We achieve the following objectives through our research: First, it detects more than 10 types of forgery elements in autonomous vehicle systems. Autonomous vehicles and ITS systems achieve 95% malware detection accuracy. In addition, it supports more than 3 types of network firewall protocols for autonomous vehicles, and supports 15 types of external vaccines for cooperative detection. When using HSM, the self-driving car certificate verification speed is developed to 1 ms or less, and when using S/W, the certificate verification speed is developed to 10 ms or less. When using SDP, more than 95% network availability is secured. Finally, machine learning-based anomaly detection accuracy of 90% is achieved.

References

1. Ministry of Land, Infrastructure and Transport. http://www.molit.go.kr/USR/NEWS/m_71/dtl.jsp?id=95083365. Accessed 30 July 2021
2. Chosunbiz. https://biz.chosun.com/site/data/html_dir/2020/01/02/2020010203124.html. Accessed 30 July 2021
3. El-Rewini, Z., Sadatsharan, K., Sugunaraj, N., Selvaraj, D.F., Plathottam, S.J., Ranganathan, P.: Cybersecurity attacks in vehicular sensors. IEEE Sens. J. **2022**, 13752–13767 (2020)
4. IEEE Standard for Wireless Access in Vehicular Environments-Security Services for Applications and Management Messages, IEEE Std 1609.2-2016 (Revision of IEEE Std 1609.2-2013), pp. 1–240 (2016)
5. SAE J2735, Dedicated Short Range Communications (DSRC) Message Set Dictionary. SAE International, pp. 1–267 (2016)
6. SAE J3061, Cybersecurity Guidebook for Cyber-Physical Vehicle Systems, SAE International, pp. 1–128 (2016)
7. Cloud Security Aliance: Software Defined Perimeter. Accessed 29 Jan 2014
8. El-Maghraby, R.T., Abd Elazim, N.M., Bahaa-Eldin, A.M.: A survey on deep packet inspection. In: 2017 12th International Conference on Computer Engineering and Systems (ICCES), pp. 188–197. IEEE, Cairo (2017)
9. Frederic Stumpf and Christian Meves and Benjamin Weyl and Marko Wolf: A Security Architecture for Multipurpose ECUs in Vehicles (25. VDI/VW-Gemeinschaftstagung: Automotive Security), Ingolstadt, Germany (2009)
10. Snort: foremost Open Source Intrusion Prevention System. https://www.snort.org

An Anonymous Communication System Based on Software Defined Architecture

Xinda Cheng, Yixing Chen, Jincai Zou, Yuqiang Zhang, and Ning Hu$^{(\boxtimes)}$

Cyberspace Institute of Advanced Technology, Guangzhou University,
Guangzhou, China

Abstract. The existing low-latency anonymous communication networks represented by Tor and I2P networks are mainly composed of voluntary nodes all over the world, and these nodes use onion routing or garlic routing to implement data hop-by-hop transmission. Due to the high autonomy and randomness of voluntary nodes, the reliability, credibility and availability of the entire anonymous network cannot meet specific QoS requirements. For this reason, based on the advantages of P2P network, this paper proposes an anonymous communication system based on software-defined architecture. The system uses file exchange instead of message exchange, realizes asynchronous communication, realizes the anonymity of transmission path, and introduces The control center performs unified programming on the message forwarding path, which has higher flexibility and reliability. The experimental results show that the entire process is encrypted and different messages cannot be correlated, which can achieve the effect of anti-tracing.

Keywords: Anonymous communication · Software-defined architecture · P2P

1 Introduction

There are many threats to mobile communication in the Internet environment, such as eavesdropping, blocking, and tracking. Due to political or economic reasons, the nodes in the communication may be in a state that is not controlled by the communicating parties. The exposure of "PRISM" [29] and "Einstein Project" [1] indicates that there is indeed a risk of privacy leakage in mobile communications. With the enhancement of hardware computing power and the advancement of artificial intelligence technology, the ability of Internet powers to crack passwords and VPN traffic analysis capabilities are also increasing. Therefore, traditional secure communications based on encryption algorithms and VPNs are facing severe security tests.

In order to better protect user privacy during mobile communication, anonymous communication system was proposed. The current research results mainly

© Springer Nature Singapore Pte Ltd. 2022
I. You et al. (Eds.): MobiSec 2021, CCIS 1544, pp. 396–407, 2022.
https://doi.org/10.1007/978-981-16-9576-6_27

include: traditional anonymous communication networks and blockchain networks. The anonymity principles of traditional communication networks are MIX technology [3] and onion routing technology [5], etc. Its introduction of P2P is to solve the problems of single-agent system trust, excessive traffic concentration, excessive investment by the MIX system server and complicated management. And in the blockchain network, P2P is used to decentralize and realize the collaboration of multiple peer nodes [9,12,13,15,16]. Moreover, the idea of software definition, which has been applied into many domains successfully [10,11], has been proposed to make the anonymous network more flexible.

This paper combines the idea of software definition [19] with P2P technology, views each node in P2P as a forwarding node, and controls the P2P node through a higher-level console server to realize the programmable forwarding path of information, and then realize an anonymous communication scheme that deploys controllable nodes in an uncontrollable network environment to build an ad hoc network, and uses file synchronization between nodes to transmit information.

The paper is divided into five parts: The first part explains the design motivation, presents the existing threats and the goals achieved; Following part gives the model architecture of the anonymous communication scheme, and explains its working mode; The system is analyzed in three aspects: anonymity, health safety and anti-traceability in the third part; the fourth part adopts the self-organizing network mode of the open source software syncthing [25] to simulate the real experimental environment to realize the system; The last part proposes the relevant performance of the system problems to be solved and future work.

2 Motivation

The existing low-latency anonymous communication network represented by Tor and I2P [30] network is mainly composed of voluntary nodes all over the world, and these nodes use the onion routing or the garlic routing to realize the hop-by-hop data transmission. Since the self-protection ability and identity credibility of voluntary nodes cannot be guaranteed, this type of anonymous communication network lacks overall protection and fuse mechanism when facing sybil attacks and node betrayal [7]. In addition, voluntary nodes cannot guarantee a stable online time and transmission capacity, resulting in lower data throughput capacity of the overall network and higher latency.

In addition, the existing anonymous communication network architecture mostly adopts a flat architecture, and a unified networking mechanism is adopted between nodes. The nodes are based on a session communication protocol and lack the necessary anti-tracking and traceability mechanism. Although they can guarantee confidentiality, integrity and reliability in the information sharing process, but there are still deficiencies in resisting traffic association attacks [17] and node betrayal.

In terms of data transmission, taking Tor as an example, its client will send various requests to Tor's server when constructing an onion route. Before the data packet enters the anonymous communication system, it will also face the modification of the header of the data packet such as a third-party network watermark attack [14].

In summary, due to the high autonomy and randomness of voluntary nodes, the reliability, credibility, and availability of the entire anonymous network cannot meet specific QoS requirements. Therefore, this paper proposes a new-architecture anonymous communication system, which transforms the uncontrollable voluntary nodes of the communication system into the controllable nodes of the system owner, and combines software-defined ideas to realize the programmable node and forwarding path. In order to realize the concealment of the network communication relationship, file exchange is used instead of message exchange to realize asynchronous communication. The data to be transmitted is synchronized to each intermediate node in the form of a file, and the intermediate node transmits to the receiver according to the established forwarding path. The encrypted traffic data volume of the point-to-point transmission between the two communication parties is extremely small and there is no real information, while the effective information uses the controllable nodes in the P2P network built by the system for real information transmission.

This system has a better effect on the protection of non-correlation and unobservability, and resistance to traceability attacks.

3   Proposed Scheme

3.1   Architecture

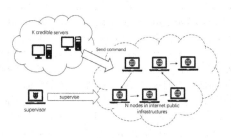

Fig. 1. Architecture

The system is proposed in this paper consists of N nodes and K console servers and shown in Fig. 1. As a communication user, a node also provides file storage and forwarding services for anonymous communication of other nodes. Each node maintains N folders and N-1 backup files, where N folders correspond to each node i. The console server is the core of the system, which controls the IP addresses of all nodes and determines whether each node participates in the communication process. The sender can set the forwarding route through the console server before communication. The console server can also control whether the node performs file synchronization. Due to the large throughput of the console server, the system needs to use multiple console servers to prevent the supervisor from tracing the source.

3.2 Basic Idea

Imagine that there is a supervisor who can monitor the traffic of all nodes except the console server. In this system, the basic idea to realize anonymous communication is as follows:

Pre-communication. The sender Alice sends the relevant information of the communication content directly to the receiver Bob in the form of a file. The information includes the file name, the maximum receiving time and the return receiving flag. In this part, some ways out of bound like SMS [18] or hiding the key information in tiktok [6] could be used [21]. Since the amount of data carried by the traffic is small, when there is a confused traffic, the supervisor cannot perceive whether Alice is communicating with Bob in real data.

Routing. Alice selects a forwarding path through the console server, and the console server sends the synchronization configuration file to each node. Similar to the advance communication, the supervisor here also cannot know whether Alice and various other nodes exchange effective information.

Information Transfer. Alice synchronizes the information to the nodes in the forwarding path in the form of files. Before Bob receives the file and returns the receiving identifier, the nodes on this path are synchronized in turn. In this process, the traffic identified by the supervisor includes Alice communicating with another node Carol, and Bob communicating with another node Dave.

Finally, Alice and Bob realize the complete communication process. Throughout the process, Alice and Bob communicate with multiple nodes with Oblivious Third Party, which obscures the real traffic transmission information. The third party cannot identify the real data traffic.

3.3 Core Mechanism

Fig. 2. Pre-communication

Alice and Bob are independent nodes in the anonymous communication system, corresponding to folders folder A and folder B respectively. Other nodes can be regarded as an Oblivious Third Party, as shown in Figs. 2, 3, 4.

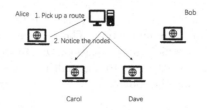

Fig. 3. Routing

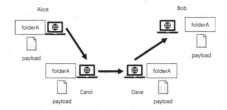

Fig. 4. Information transmission

Pre Communication. Both Alice and Bob maintain a backup file, and the backup file of either party is written to be regarded as initiating communication to the other party. While this file could be various, for example, the exchanged keys but based on Wildcard identity-based encryption [8]. When Alice tries to send Msg_a, she first writes the pre-communication content PreMsg to the Backup file, which includes the three variables in Table 1.

Table 1. Configuration of the edge server

Variables	Class	Meaning
File name	String	File name to be sent, The summary of Msg_a, denoted as $hash(Msg_a)$
Maximum time limit	Time	Maximum duration of file synchronization
Return receive flag	Boolean	After receiving the file, the receiver judges whether it needs to send a return message

The algorithm of the pre-communication process is as follows:

Algorithm 1: Pre-communication
Input: PreMsg, Alice, Bob
Output: Backup
1 PreMsg $<-$ filename, time, returnflag>;
2 **if** $check(Alice,Bob) == True$ **then**
3	filesync(Alice, Bob)
4 **end**
5 hash(Msg_a) = Msg_aPKb
6 **return** result

Routing. The route selection is by the console server randomly selecting m controlled nodes (m < N − 2.) or the sender selecting m nodes to form the path R, as shown in formula (1):

$$R = \{N_1, N_2, N_3, \cdots, N_{m-1}, N_m\} \tag{1}$$

The console server sends configuration files to these controlled nodes to synchronize the nodes with the previous node in turn.

The store-and-forward method here is different from that in traditional anonymous communication networks such as Tor. In this way, every controlled node is synchronizing files. Third parties can only perceive that they are implementing store and forward at the network layer.

Information Transformation. The information transmission process is the file synchronization process. The system adopts TLS1.3 encryption during file synchronization to ensure the security of information at the transmission layer. The entire information transmission process is as follows:

4 Security Analysis

The background of the proposed system is to build an anonymous communication system implemented by controllable nodes at the application layer in an uncontrolled network. It shields all information below the application layer. Except for the two parties of the communication, other users and supervisors cannot obtain the relevant information of the two parties of the communication from the network layer.

Confidentiality, Integrity and Privacy. On the one hand, the proposed method offloads tasks with different security risks to devices in different security domains near the user. Tasks with high security risks are offloaded to the user's private device, which ensures the confidentiality and privacy of data storage and data processing. On the other hand, the decentralized computing paradigm offloads resource-constrained mobile IoT services to multiple devices. This means

---

Algorithm 2: Information transformation

   Input: R, Alice, Bob, PreMsg
   Output: Msg_a
1 **for** $i=0; i<m; i++$ **do**
2 | filesync(Ni, Ni+1)
3 **end**
4 returnflag = PreMsg[3] maxtime = PreMsg[2] **if** *returnflag=1* **then**
5 | **for** $i=m; i>1; i-$ **do**
6 | | Ni->Ni-1:delete file;
7 | **end**
8 **end**
9 **else**
10 | **while** *time>maxtime* **do**
11 | | **for** $i=0; i<m; i++$ **do**
12 | | | Alice->Ni:delete file;
13 | | **end**
14 | **end**
15 **end**
16 Msg_a = SKb$\{\{Msg_a\}$PKb$\}$;
17 **return** Msg_a;

---

that data can be encrypted and signed on some devices with strong computing resources to ensure the confidentiality and integrity of the data transmission process. Besides that, the cost and effectiveness must be two targets for each communication network. Naiwei Liu [20] came up with a method for trustzone, in which way we could get the same way to find out the cost and effectiveness of our node.

4.1 Anonymity

Anonymity includes the anonymity of the sender, the anonymity of the receiver, and the anonymity of the communication relationship. Anonymity of the sender means that a specific message will not be associated with any sender, that is, no message is associated with a specific sender. Recipient anonymity means that a specific message will not be associated with any receiver, that is, no message is associated with a specific sender. Anonymity of communication relationship means that the supervisor cannot determine who is communicating with whom.

    The sender and receiver, console server and other nodes all use encrypted traffic to communicate, and the volume of traffic data is close. Each time the sender sends data, the receiver is different, and with the confusion of other business traffic, it is difficult to distinguish the true end of the information. Since the system is a P2P system, the node is also providing forwarding services for other nodes while acting as the sender, resulting in different sources and types of received data. In addition, the time-based traceability attacks, the system can guarantee the anonymity of the sender and receiver.

From the supervisor's point of view, each node is sending data to multiple other devices and cannot confirm the identity of the sender and receiver, so the anonymity of the communication relationship is still established.

4.2 Security

In terms of security, this article considers several common attacks: Sybil attacks, man-in-the-middle attacks, and Dos attacks.

Sybil attack refers to the fact that a few nodes in a P2P network control the majority of nodes and obtain multiple false identities and making it no longer a peer-to-peer network. In this system, since the console server is credible, the scenario of the Sybil attack is that the node is controlled by the attacker, and all synchronized files are obtained by the attacker. In fact, what distinguishes this system from other P2P networks is that the console server is a trusted central control node that can control and monitor the abnormal traffic of all nodes, and notify the node user when there is an abnormality. Abnormal nodes will be quickly separated from the network, ending the witch attack.

A man-in-the-middle attack means that the information of the communicating parties will be intercepted and forwarded by the attacker. However, this system not only uses TLS1.3 [24] to encrypt the traffic at the network layer, but also uses digital signatures and encryption for valid information at the application layer, so only the receiver can successfully decrypt it and avoid man-in-the-middle attacks.

The possible Dos attacks in this system are that during the communication process. According to Abhishta Abhishta [2], once a node is maliciously controlled, and before the console server takes it offline, a large amount of malicious data would be sent to other nodes which causing the network bandwidth to be occupied and other normal forwarding services can't be performed. In the information transmission of 3.1, this paper has proposed that the system will send a maximum time limit during pre-communication. Therefore, when the sender node in the network does not receive the flag information returned by the node within the maximum time limit, the console server will send data so that all nodes discard the malicious data, thereby preventing Dos attacks.

4.3 Anti-traceability Analysis

Since this article implements routing in the form of file forwarding using software in an uncontrolled network environment, it can better resist traditional network-level traceability attacks, including passive traceability and active traceability.

In passive traceability, all types of attacks come from correlation attacks. Correlation attack refers to that when the attacker can control the nodes of the anonymous channel and can observe the ingress and egress traffic of the anonymous channel at the same time, they can compare the traffic packets and their sequence within a certain time delay, and then analyze the corresponding information to achieve traceability effect. Correlation attacks require that both ends of the communication are under control, but in large-scale network confrontations, the network where the sender and receiver nodes are located is within the supervision of the supervisor, and the traffic at the network layer will be monitored and correlated by the supervisor.

In our system, the sender and receiver have and only exist once in the point-to-point communication at the application layer, the amount of payload data is small, and most of the data is encrypted and transmitted through other nodes. Therefore, within a certain time delay, the supervisor cannot associate the traffic of the two communicating parties from the massive traffic, which guarantees the non-correlation.

Active traceability is mainly based on network watermarking attacks. A network watermarking attack means that when the traffic enters the anonymous channel, the network supervisor inserts specific watermark information into the traffic, and when the traffic is received by the receiver, the two are correlated, thereby destroying the anonymity. According to the watermark form, it can be divided into four forms based on content, delay, packet length and ratio.

The common point of this type of attack method is that the object is a network stream. Therefore, the produced watermark will inevitably be lost in multiple asynchronous forwarding of multiple nodes in different physical environments. The supervisor cannot obtain the relationship between the node and the console server, which guarantees the non-correlation of the system. In addition, due to the different paths used to forward valid data each time, the supervisor cannot distinguish the real recipient, thus ensuring anonymity.

5   Experiment

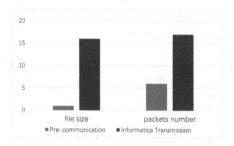

Fig. 5. Comparison of the two packet capture results

Packet content of valid data The testbed consists of a host and three cloud servers. With the help of syncthing's self-organizing network mode, we simulate deployed nodes in an uncontrolled network environment. The routing part has been configured when syncthing is installed.

As shown in Fig. 5, A 1kb Backup file is stored on the host (Alice), and it is set to synchronize the file to a server (Bob). The content in the Backup file is the PreMsg that Alice will pass to Bob.

6   Evaluation

Fig. 6. Comparison of the two packet capture results

First, synchronize another $folder_a$ of Alice to the corresponding $folder_a$ of another server Carol. Then synchronize Carol's same directory $folder_a$ to the corresponding path of the next server Dave. Finally, Dave synchronizes the file with Bob regularly to complete the high-latency asynchronous communication process.

We compare and analyze the data packets captured in the above process. The data packet comparison of two syncthing transmission data is shown in Fig. 3. It is easy to know that the number of data packets is positively correlated with the size, and there is no obvious feature in the size of a single data packet.

The content of the corresponding data packet is shown in Fig. 6. It is impossible to analyze the flow characteristics and information from the encrypted data packet.

7   Related Works

The current anonymous communication solutions using P2P technology have MorphMix [27], Crowds [26], I2P and etc. Their common feature is the realization of the decentralization of the anonymous network. Each node can independently realize functions such as path selection and routing forwarding. New nodes can be added dynamically, and old nodes can be discarded.

I2P improves onion routing and proposes garlic routing to improve conceal-ment and security; Crowds proposes a random node selection mechanism to realize anonymous web browsing. On top of the integrated mix technology and onion routing technology, new anonymous communication technologies such as TARANET [4] and Loopix have also emerged [23].

What's more, besides information in the transport layer or application layer, more views has been put forward. Fulvio Valenza [28] improved an optimized firewall anomaly resolution. Sherifdeen Lawa [22] introduced micro-frontend and it could be used to deploy the micro-service faster and more flexible.

8   Conclusion

This article focuses on building an anonymous communication system that is resistant to eavesdropping under network supervision. We propose to construct an anonymous communication system based on the file synchronization function in the P2P network. The program relies on the idea of software-defined networking. By storing the information such as the header information and payload of the traditional network in the application layer, and handing over the routing information to the software, it can be regarded as an implementation of the software-defined anonymous network. The program is still in its infancy, and the feasibility and safety have been explored temporarily through syncthing. Compared with anonymous communication systems such as Tor and I2P, there is still a lot of room for optimization in details and performance.

Acknowledgments. This work was supported in National Natural Science Foundation of China (Grant No. 61976064), National Defence Science and Technology Key Laboratory Fund (61421190306), Guangzhou Science and Technology Plan Project (202102010471), Guangdong Province Science and Technology Planning Project (2020A1414010370).

References

1. Cisa.einstein[db/ol]. [DB/OL]. https://www.cisa.gov/Einstein. Accessed 31 July 2021
2. Abhishta, A., van Heeswijk, W., Junger, M., Nieuwenhuis, L.J.M., Joosten, R.: Why would we get attacked? An analysis of attacker's aims behind DDoS attacks. J. Wirel. Mob. Netw. Ubiquit. Comput. Dependable Appl. (JoWUA) **11**(2), 3–22 (2020)
3. Chaum, D.: The dining cryptographers problem: unconditional sender and recipient untraceability. J. Cryptol. **1**(1), 65–75 (1988)
4. Chen, C., Asoni, D.E., Perrig, A., Barrera, D., Danezis, G., Troncoso, C.: TaraNet: traffic-analysis resistant anonymity at the network layer. In: 2018 IEEE European Symposium on Security and Privacy (EuroS&P), pp. 137–152. IEEE (2018)
5. Dingledine, R., Mathewson, N., Syverson, P.: Tor: the second-generation onion router. Technical report, Naval Research Lab Washington DC (2004)
6. Domingues, P., Nogueira, R., Francisco, J.C., Frade, M.: Analyzing TikTok from a digital forensics perspective. J. Wirel. Mob. Netw. Ubiquit. Comput. Dependable Appl. (JoWUA) **12**(3), 87–115 (2021)
7. Douceur, J.R.: The sybil attack. In: Druschel, P., Kaashoek, F., Rowstron, A. (eds.) IPTPS 2002. LNCS, vol. 2429, pp. 251–260. Springer, Heidelberg (2002). https://doi.org/10.1007/3-540-45748-8_24
8. Duong, D.H., Susilo, W., Trinh, V.C.: Wildcarded identity-based encryption with constant-size ciphertext and secret key. J. Wirel. Mob. Netw. Ubiquit. Comput. Dependable Appl. (JoWUA) **11**(2), 74–86 (2020)
9. Hu, N., Teng, Y., Zhao, Y., Yin, S., Zhao, Y.: IDV: internet domain name verification based on blockchain. CMES-Comput. Model. Eng. Sci. **129**(1), 299–322 (2021)
10. Hu, N., Tian, Z., Du, X., Guizani, M.: An energy-efficient in-network computing paradigm for 6G. IEEE Trans. Green Commun. Netw. (2021)
11. Hu, N., Tian, Z., Du, X., Guizani, N., Zhu, Z.: Deep-green: a dispersed energy-efficiency computing paradigm for green industrial IoT. IEEE Trans. Green Commun. Netw. (2021). https://doi.org/10.1109/TGCN.2021.3064683

12. Hu, N., Tian, Z., Sun, Y., Yin, L., Zhao, B., Du, X., Guizani, N.: Building agile and resilient UAV networks based on SDN and blockchain. IEEE Netw. **35**(1), 57–63 (2021)
13. Hu, N., Yin, S., Su, S., Jia, X., Xiang, Q., Liu, H.: Blockzone: a decentralized and trustworthy data plane for DNS. CMC-Comput. Mater. Continua **65**(2), 1531–1557 (2020)
14. Iacovazzi, A., Elovici, Y.: Network flow watermarking: a survey. IEEE Commun. Surv. Tutor. **19**(1), 512–530 (2016)
15. Jia, X., et al.: IRBA: an identity-based cross-domain authentication scheme for the internet of things. Electronics **9**(4), 634 (2020)
16. Jia, X., Hu, N., Yin, S., Zhao, Y., Zhang, C., Cheng, X.: A2 chain: a blockchain-based decentralized authentication scheme for 5G-enabled IoT. Mob. Inf. Syst. **2020** (2020)
17. Johnson, A., Wacek, C., Jansen, R., Sherr, M., Syverson, P.: Users get routed: traffic correlation on tor by realistic adversaries. In: Proceedings of the 2013 ACM SIGSAC conference on Computer & Communications Security, pp. 337–348 (2013)
18. Kitana, A., Traore, I., Woungang, I.: Towards an epidemic SMS-based cellular botnet. J. Internet Serv. Inf. Secur. (JISIS) **10**(4), 38–58 (2020)
19. Kreutz, D., Ramos, F.M., Verissimo, P.E., Rothenberg, C.E., Azodolmolky, S., Uhlig, S.: Software-defined networking: a comprehensive survey. Proc. IEEE **103**(1), 14–76 (2014)
20. Liu, N., Yu, M., Zang, W., Sandhu, R.: Cost and effectiveness of TrustZone defense and side-channel attack on arm platform. J. Wirel. Mob. Netw. Ubiquit. Comput. Dependable Appl. (JoWUA) **11**(4), 1–15 (2020)
21. Narteni, S., Vaccari, I., Mongelli, M., Aiello, M., Cambiaso, E.: Evaluating the possibility to perpetrate tunneling attacks exploiting short-message-service. J. Internet Serv. Inf. Secur. (JISIS) **11**(3), 30–46 (2021)
22. Pavlenko, A., Askarbekuly, N., Megha, S., Mazzara, M.: Micro-frontends: application of microservices to web front-ends. J. Internet Serv. Inf. Secur. (JISIS) **10**(2), 49–66 (2020)
23. Piotrowska, A.M., Hayes, J., Elahi, T., Meiser, S., Danezis, G.: The loopix anonymity system. In: 26th {USENIX} Security Symposium ({USENIX} Security 17), pp. 1199–1216 (2017)
24. Pohlmann, N.: Transport layer security (TLS)/secure socket layer (SSL). In: Pohlmann, N. (ed.) Cyber-Sicherheit, pp. 407–438. Springer, Wiesbaden (2019). https://doi.org/10.1007/978-3-658-25398-1_11
25. Quinn, C., Scanlon, M., Farina, J., Kechadi, M.-T.: Forensic analysis and remote evidence recovery from syncthing: an open source decentralised file synchronisation utility. In: James, J.I., Breitinger, F. (eds.) ICDF2C 2015. LNICST, vol. 157, pp. 85–99. Springer, Cham (2015). https://doi.org/10.1007/978-3-319-25512-5_7
26. Reiter, M.K., Rubin, A.D.: Crowds: anonymity for web transactions. ACM trans. Inf. Syst. Secur. (TISSEC) **1**(1), 66–92 (1998)
27. Rennhard, M., Plattner, B.: Introducing MorphMix: peer-to-peer based anonymous internet usage with collusion detection. In: Proceedings of the 2002 ACM Workshop on Privacy in the Electronic Society, pp. 91–102 (2002)
28. Valenza, F., Cheminod, M.: An optimized firewall anomaly resolution. J. Internet Serv. Inf. Secur. (JISIS) **10**(1), 22–37 (2020)
29. Verble, J.: The NSA and Edward Snowden: surveillance in the 21st century. ACM SIGCAS Comput. Soc. **44**(3), 14–20 (2014)
30. Zantout, B., Haraty, R., et al.: I2P data communication system. In: Proceedings of ICN, pp. 401–409. Citeseer (2011)

Security Association Model: Interdisciplinary Application of 5G Positioning Technology and Social Network

Haoran Tao[1] , Ning Ding[2] , Tianhui Huang[3] , Kehan Yu[4] ,
Dongsheng Qian[5,6] , Yan Luo[5,6] , and Yuyin Ma[5(✉)]

[1] Beijing Key Lab of Petroleum Data Mining, College of Information Science
and Engineering, China University of Petroleum-Beijing, Beijing, China
2020211269@student.cup.edu.cn
[2] Central University of Finance and Economics, Beijing, China
2020212346@email.cufe.edu.cn
[3] Data Company of XinJiang Oilfield Company, Karamay, China
hth2020@petrochina.com.cn
[4] Southwest Jiaotong University, Chengdu, China
YuKhan@my.swjtu.edu.cn
[5] School of Electronic Information Engineering, Beijing Jiaotong University,
Beijing, China
mayuyin@bjtu.edu.cn
[6] Beijing Key Lab of Petroleum Data Mining, College of Information Science
and Engineering, China University of Petroleum, Beijing, China
{2018015230,2018015337}@st.cupk.edu.cn

Abstract. Mobile communication technology is an important information science and technology. With the development and wide application of mobile communication technology, the security of mobile communication has become an important research field, and its security connotation is constantly enriched. First of all, this paper introduces the current situation of people's life safety and the development of 5G communication technology in the face of COVID-19. Based on this situation, a positioning method is proposed and a method of constructing the association graph between mobile communication devices is designed. A health and safety monitoring system based on mobile communication positioning technology is designed. This paper applies mobile communication positioning technology to health and safety monitoring, and expands the security technology scope of mobile communication technology.

Keywords: Security · Mobile · Location · Base-station · Association

Supported by China University of Petroleum, Beijing and Beijing Jiao Tong University. Y. Ma—National Engineering Laboratory for Next Generation Internet Technology and the School of Electronic and Information Engineering, Beijing JiaoTong University, Beijing, China.

© Springer Nature Singapore Pte Ltd. 2022
I. You et al. (Eds.): MobiSec 2021, CCIS 1544, pp. 408–419, 2022.
https://doi.org/10.1007/978-981-16-9576-6_28

1   Introduction

The continuous development of mobile communication technology is a symbol of the historical development of science and technology [1]. Network is widely used in industrial production and life services. 5G has higher base station density than 4G. Therefore, the high-density characteristics of 5G base stations can be used to further explore mobile security applications. At present, the spread of covid-19 is the most serious security incident in the world. At present, 194608040 people have been infected with covid-19,4170155 people have died of the spread of the virus, tens of millions of people have died, lost their relatives and hundreds of millions of people have lost their jobs. COVID-19 has changed the life of everyone on earth [2].

5G has the characteristics of high bandwidth and low delay, so it has a wide range of application scenarios [3]. The rapid development of mobile communication technology provides new ways and application ideas for the security problems in the field of public safety and health [4]. This paper applies mobile communication positioning technology to the field of public safety and health, and expands the security scope of mobile communication (Fig. 1).

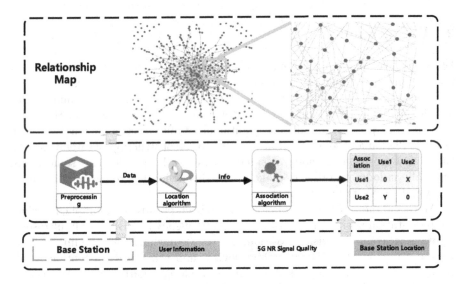

Fig. 1. Health security association model

Mobile communication technology not only has a wide range of application scenarios in industry, but also can play an important role in the field of public medical and health security [5]. When an infected person is found in a certain area, a reliable range can be located based on the person's activity range. The devices in the area calculated by the location algorithm can describe the correlation between devices, so the location algorithm can be used to achieve finer grained epidemic prevention and control. Location information can also be used to analyze the preference of equipment for a specific area, the track of equipment walking in the area, the time of equipment staying in some areas.

The research focus of this paper is not the network security of mobile Internet, but how to solve the security problem through mobile Internet. It expands the boundary of mobile network security and applies mobile network to the field of security. This paper proposes a practical method to protect public and personal security, which is the same as the essence of mobile Internet network security. In addition, if the method proposed in this paper is used by criminals, it will lead to the network security problem of mobile Internet.

In Sect. 2, the current research status of localization algorithm and the global impact of the new crown pneumonia epidemic are introduced in the paper. In Sect. 3, the positioning idea based on 5G base station is also introduced. This paper introduces a method based on the least square method, and proves the solvability of this method in mathematics. In Sect. 4, this paper proposes a device association method, which constructs the association mapping between different devices combined with the epidemiological infection model. In Sect. 5, this paper makes a specific analysis combined with a case. In Sect. 6, this paper introduces the architecture of the associated system.

2   Background

With the development of communication technology in the new era, the network not only provides communication services for people [6], but also provides space location services through satellites and base stations. Location technology for mobile devices has always been one of the research hot spots all over the world [7]. Outdoors, people generally use traditional satellite positioning methods, such as GPS, Beidou and so on [8]. However, due to the obstruction of satellite signal, the precise positioning mode of satellite can not be provided in some areas, especially indoors. In order to make up for this deficiency, researchers began to study indoor positioning technology.

More and more related technologies have been proposed and applied, including base station positioning, Wi-Fi, wireless frequency tag, Bluetooth, ultrasonic positioning, computer vision positioning, etc. Meanwhile, with the miniaturization and intelligentization of mobile devices and the world's attention to 5G communication technology [9], the number of global smartphone users above 3 billion in 2020. The large number of mobile devices and the dense coverage of mobile communication base stations make the mobile device positioning method based on base stations stand out in many research directions.

The picture shows the base station nodes in a region of Asia and Korea. Different colors represent different base station types. It can be seen that the base station cover density is high, which provides the foundation for the positioning of the equipment. And compared with WiFi, base stations that are mostly run by one or more operators, the interaction between data is more convenient. Compared with Bluetooth, UWB positioning and other positioning methods, the

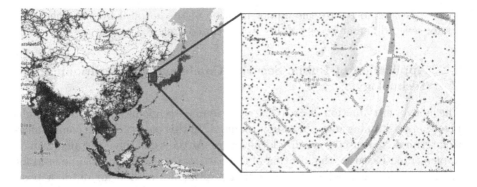

Fig. 2. Regional base station distribution

large-scale coverage of base stations around the world has laid a solid foundation for the positioning method based on base stations (Fig. 2).

Researchers only need to focus on how to achieve accurate positioning without additional consideration of how to popularize the technology, which also makes the implementation of base station based positioning technology more flexible. And the device access to a variety of mobile communication base stations is an active behavior, which is better than WiFi, Bluetooth and other positioning technologies. Compared with Wi-Fi, because most base stations are operated by one or more operators, the data interaction between base stations is more convenient.

2.1 Introduction to Wireless Positioning Technology

Although the location method based on base station has high advantages, it has high requirements for the quality of the algorithm. This paper Proposed using circular polarization (CP) antenna to alleviate multipath effect and using uncertain data mapping (LUDM) algorithm to improve positioning accuracy. The location algorithm based on fingerprint location algorithm uses the difference of signal strength between regions to locate the equipment. This paper proposed to integrate neighborhood clustering into the positioning reference of fingerprint positioning algorithm, which improved the effectiveness of the algorithm and the positioning accuracy of edge positioning points [10]. This paper introduced the improved method based on ant colony algorithm into fingerprint positioning algorithm to improve the positioning accuracy. This paper proposed k-nearest neighbor (KNN) The fingerprint identification algorithm directly processes the measured received signal strength indication (RSSI) value and matches it with the latest value in the fingerprint database [11]. This paper proposed the WiFi location algorithm based on the location fingerprint algorithm, which can generate the probability graph and further improve the reference information of the location information through the probability density function [12]. In addition, this paper proposed the location detection method based on machine learning method is used to realize the indoor location of the hospital by using the data sets of seven different access points in the closed area [3].

2.2 Application of Public Security Combined with Positioning Technology

The above introduction to wireless positioning technology can obtain high-precision positioning in an ideal environment. In this paper, mobile communication technology is used to realize localization. At the same time, the algorithm is implemented based on the location of the base station, so it can also be used for outdoor positioning, which is a common positioning method for outdoor positioning and indoor positioning. Location technology has a wide range of applications in today's industry and life. Its main goal is to expand people's information perception ability. At present, indoor positioning technology has been used to detect the flow of people, monitor sensitive locations, track the logistics information of goods in warehouses, factories and stores. Precise positioning is used in battlefield soldier position discovery, robot motion tracking and so on. In this paper, location technology is used to describe the approximate location between people, and provide data basis for population association algorithm.

3   Positioning Algorithm

Table 1. Base station acquisition equipment information.

Field name	Data type	Allow null	Primary key	Remarks
rowid	int	No	Yes	Line number
time	data	No	No	Time
Userid	varchar	No	No	Equipment information
rssi	int	No	No	Received signal strength

As shown in the Table 1, the mobile device information and storage mode collected by the base station. On the basis of the above, this paper proposes a mobile communication base station group location algorithm based on least square method.

As shown in the Fig. 3 the signal range of the signal base station is approximately A circle. In the Fig. 3, two circles O_1 and O_2 intersect at A and B, and the other two circles O_1 and O_3 intersect at C and D.

The algorithm steps are as follows:

1. identifies base stations with a distance below 3000 m in this area.
2. Find the base station group composed of base stations whose distance from the user is less than 3000 m.

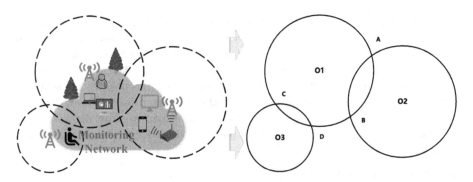

Fig. 3. Relationship between equipment and mobile communication base station

The coordinates of $BS_1, BS_2, \cdots, BS_n$ are $(x_1, y_1), (x_2, y_2), \cdots, (x_n, y_n)$.
Customer's location is (X, Y), distance (X, Y) between $BS_1, BS_2, \cdots, BS_n$
is $d_1{}^2, d_2{}^2, \cdots, d_n{}^2$.

The following equations can be obtained.

$$(x_i - X)^2 + (y_i - Y)^2 = d_i{}^2 \tag{1}$$

Let all other formula minus the first formula:

$$2(x_1 - x_i) X + 2(y_1 - y_i) Y = d_i{}^2 - d_1{}^2 + x_1{}^2 + y_1{}^2 - x_i{}^2 - y_i{}^2 \tag{2}$$

Transform the above formula:

$$m_i X + n_i Y = s_i \tag{3}$$

Except by n_i

$$X k_i + Y = c_i \tag{4}$$

Set $\hat{c} = X k_i + Y$, when $(\hat{c} - c_i)^2 = (X k_i + Y - c_i)^2$ to obtain the minimum,
the best fitting effect

$$\frac{\partial f}{\partial X} = 0 \tag{5}$$

$$\frac{\partial f}{\partial Y} = 0 \tag{6}$$

Seeking the partial guide for the above two variables, the results are as follows:

$$X = \frac{(n-1)\sum\limits_{i=1}^{n-1} k_i c_i - \sum\limits_{i=1}^{n-1} k_i \sum\limits_{i=1}^{n-1} c_i}{(n-1)\left(\sum\limits_{i=1}^{n-1} k_i\right)^2 - \sum\limits_{i=1}^{n-1} k_i \sum\limits_{i=1}^{n-1} k_i} \tag{7}$$

$$Y = \frac{\sum\limits_{i=1}^{n-1} c_i - X \sum\limits_{i=1}^{n-1} k_i}{(n-1)} \tag{8}$$

The optimal solution of the device position (X, Y) under the set conditions can be obtained. The method can get a more accurate position under the current condition. However, this paper notes the limitations of base station signal positioning, although the positioning accuracy based on 5G signal is greatly improved compared with 4G. However, in most cases, the positioning accuracy using the signal base station can not reach the decimeter level. However, at this stage, the positioning accuracy of 5G base station can roughly determine the location of people, and provides a data basis for subsequent association rules.

4   Association Rules

After obtaining the location information of devices, you can describe the degree of association between devices based on the distance between devices and the association duration of devices.

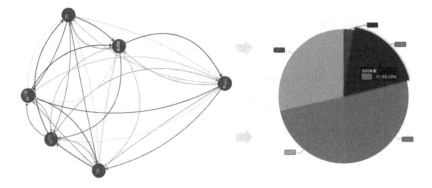

Fig. 4. Describing interpersonal relationships based on association rules

This picture Fig. 4 illustrates the relationship between people. Each dot in the left half of the picture represents a different person, and the lines between the circles represent the relationship between people. The pie chart on the right half of the picture represents the relationship with other people. The larger the sector, the stronger the degree of connection to others.

$$Con = \sum_{z=1}^{n-1} Con\,(t, i) \tag{9}$$

Con describes the strength of the relationship between two devices. When two devices are in the same defined area, the value of the individual association strength is determined by distance and duration. The shorter and longer the distance, the stronger the connection between the two. A person's degree of relevance to others is formed by the superposition of several degrees of relevance.

$$Con\left(t, i\right) \propto \left\{T_z\left(t\right), L_z\left(i\right)\right\} \tag{10}$$

T_z marks the time variable in an association. The longer two people spend in the same designated area, the greater the time variable. L_z marks the distance variable in an association. The closer two people are within the same defined area, the greater the distance variable. Depending on the infectivity of different COVID-19 strains, different parameters can be used to describe the influence of distance and time on the degree of association. For example, the basic coefficient of infection of the original COVID-19 virus is 2.5, while that of the Delta variant is 5. Thus, the original COVID-19 virus had a lower association strength than the Delta variant virus at the same distance and duration parameters.

Data is stored based on a graph data structure that stores the strength of associations between all devices. In this way, the storage space of data can be compressed and the retrieval efficiency can be improved.

5 Case Study

This chapter describes in detail how to determine the correlation parameters when there is a patient. Firstly, the clustering algorithm is used to describe the association relationship between different points in space, and finally the cyclic clustering in periodic time is used to describe the association relationship between different points in time. After obtaining the correlation relationship before different points, a two-dimensional table is constructed to record the relationship between any two points, with the help of the correlation table to achieve accurate epidemic prevention and control, and quickly locate the people in close contact according to the correlation index.

After obtaining the location and time information of different devices, the location information can be clustered based on density clustering algorithm. If there are new crowns in a category, then the shortest path algorithm is used to get the correlation degree between the members in this category and the new crown patients in a certain period. This algorithm based on density clustering, which assumes that the category can be determined by the tightness of sample distribution. In the same category sample, there is a special correlation between them, so they are closely connected in data characteristics. This means that samples of the same category exist not far from any sample of this category. By dividing the compact samples into one class, a clustering class is obtained. By dividing all groups of closely connected samples into different categories, the final clustering results are obtained.

The transmission of COVID-19 strain is related not only to the contact distance between people, but also to the contact time. Here, it is assumed that density cluster analysis is performed on the population every T (T is a constant time) minutes. When a clustering is completed, if there are confirmed patients in a cluster, take each patient as the source point, obtain the shortest path from the source point to each point in the class, and use the reciprocal of the weight of the shortest path to describe the association degree $Con\left(u, v, t\right)$. Where u is the source point, v is the other point in the class cluster, and t is the point set collection for the t time. α is the infection coefficient. $w\,(u, v, t)$ is the shortest path value of device u and device v in the t-th cycle. Therefore, $Con\,(u, v, t)$ is defined as:

$$Con\,(u, v, t) = \frac{\alpha}{w\,(u, v, t)} \tag{11}$$

In the first point set collection, if there is a new crown patient in the cluster, all personnel in the cluster shall be classified as close connected personnel. Taking the equipment of the new crown patient as the source point u_1, the shortest path from the source point to each point in the class is obtained. $ConT\,(u_1, v, 1)$ is obtained through the weight of the shortest path, and its association degree is defined as:

$$ConT\,(u_1, v, 1) = Con\,(u_1, v, 1) \tag{12}$$

If a device v is still in the same category as the source device u_1 when collecting information for the second time, the association degree calculated for the second time is $Con\,(u_1, v, 2)$, and the association degree of the second time and the first time is the association degree of device u_1 and device v, which is defined as:

$$ConT\,(u_1, v, 2) = Con\,(u_1, v, 2) + ConT\,(u_1, v, 1) \tag{13}$$

Similarly, if device v and source device u_1 are in the same category during the third acquisition, the association degree calculated for the third time is $Con\,(u_1, v, 3)$, and the association degree of the first three times is the association degree between device u and device v, which is defined as:

$$ConT\,(u_1, v, 3) = Con\,(u_1, v, 3) + ConT\,(u_1, v, 2) \tag{14}$$

According to Eq. 12, 13, 14, when $t > 1$, it can be concluded that:

$$ConT\,(u_1, v, t) = Con\,(u_1, v, t) + ConT\,(u_1, v, t - 1) \tag{15}$$

Assuming that there are n COVID-19 patients in this cluster instead of one, it can be concluded that:

$$ConTandN\,(u, v, t) = ConT\,(u_1, v, t) + \cdots + ConT\,(u_n, v, t) \tag{16}$$

Through the above process, this paper describes the generation process of correlation parameters in detail. The parameter system considers the influence of space and time on the correlation parameters. This method does not cluster space and time in a two-dimensional setting, but clusters in the cycle time in a circular way. Each calculation depends on the previous results, not the previous data. This method reduces the computational workload and improves the efficiency of the algorithm, and the model can be updated online.

6   System Architecture Design

As shown in Fig. 5, this system is mainly composed of information collection module, data management and storage module, calculation and analysis module and front-end user interface module.

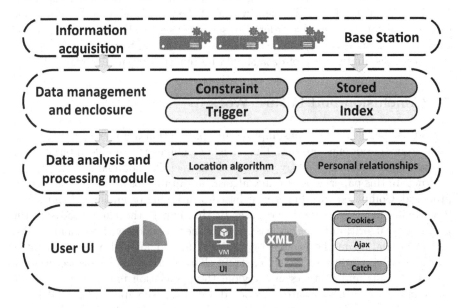

Fig. 5. System architecture design

1. Data collection module: The collected information includes the position of the base station, signal strength and signal power. In the process of collecting data, the data source must obtain the consent of the relevant personnel and meet legal, ethical and technical requirements. The collected data shall be reviewed by the specialized agencies.
2. Data management and storage module: In order to ensure the validity and accuracy of the collected data, the data is cleaned and denoised to delete redundant values, low signal values and irregular device information.
3. Calculation and analysis module: Based on the association rule algorithm, the association graph between devices is constructed. Design a mobile communication base station group positioning algorithm based on least squares method to obtain the position of different devices.
4. Device visualization interface: The above information is uploaded to the data visualization interface in JSON data format, and the page is dynamically refreshed according to the Ajax framework. In the data visualization interface, the system will ensure everyone's privacy and do not display unauthorized personal information.

The methods proposed in this paper need the following three basics: 5G equipment provided by communication equipment manufacturers, equipment information provided by mobile operators, and personal information provided by national administrative departments. This paper only proposes a crowd association method based on device positioning, and uses the program in the attachment description to simulate it. This article does not use real data. This article also suggests strengthening the supervision of the use of positioning information through legislation, executive orders and social consensus. Balancing privacy and security is a global issue. Therefore, citizens' data should be managed by special state agencies, and the use of data should be reported to citizens regularly.

7   Conclusion and Future Work

Nowadays, people's lives, consumption and production are increasingly inseparable from the mobile Internet. This article combines the mobile Internet with security and health technology to expand the security boundary of the mobile Internet. In this paper, a positioning algorithm suitable for multi-base stations is proposed. Compared with fingerprint-based positioning technology, it can locate faster without preset knowledge base. In this paper, the effectiveness of the positioning algorithm based on least squares method is derived mathematically, and a correlation method based on COVID-19 epidemiological characteristics is proposed. According to the time, strain characteristics and distance between infected people and contacts in a region, the association index is constructed, and a matching data structure is proposed. Finally, we completed the COVID-19 transmission infection association system. The system consists of an information acquisition module, a data management and storage module, a computing and analysis module, and a front-end user interface module.

However, the research on COVID-19 and its infectious disease characteristics in this paper is not enough. For example, time, strain characteristics and transmission distance, it is difficult to accurately construct infectious disease association models according to the above variables. How to closely integrate epidemiological models and how to further improve the accuracy of indoor positioning algorithms will be the next research direction.

This article does not use any real personal information for the research of positioning algorithms and association algorithms. The application of the technology proposed in this paper must be based on respect for morality and law. This article calls on organizations and individuals to respect the privacy rights of every citizen, and should establish a privacy protection organization represented by citizens to organize the review and supervision of the use of personal privacy data. Organizations cannot decide anything on behalf of citizens. Organizations should let every resolution pass the supervision of citizens.

References

1. Zhang, W., et al.: Deep reinforcement learning based resource management for DNN inference in industrial IoT. IEEE Trans. Veh. Technol. **70**(8), 7605–7618 (2021)
2. Worldometer: COVID Live Update: 198,200,314 Cases and 4,228,299 Deaths from the Coronavirus - Worldometer. https://www.worldometers.info/coronavirus/
3. Song, F., Zhu, M., Zhou, Y., You, I., Zhang, H.: Smart collaborative tracking for ubiquitous power IoT in edge-cloud interplay domain. IEEE Internet Things J. **7**(7), 6046–6055 (2019). https://doi.org/10.1109/JIOT.2019.2958097
4. Zhang, W., et al.: Optimizing federated learning in distributed industrial IoT: a multi-agent approach. IEEE J. Sel. Areas Commun. (2021). https://doi.org/10.1109/JSAC20213118352
5. Song, F., Li, L., You, I., Zhang, H.: Enabling heterogeneous deterministic networks with smart collaborative theory. IEEE Netw. **35**(3), 64–71 (2021). https://doi.org/10.1109/MNET.011.2000613
6. Song, F., Zhou, Y.T., Wang, Y., Zhao, T.M., You, I., Zhang, H.K.: Smart collaborative distribution for privacy enhancement in moving target defense. Inf. Sci. **479**, 593–606 (2019). https://doi.org/10.1016/j.ins.2018.06.002. https://www.sciencedirect.com/science/article/pii/S0020025518304468
7. Sabah, L., Argun, Ü.İ.D.: An approach to the use of Wi-Fi signals for hospital indoor location detection: performance comparison of classification algorithms. In: 2019 Scientific Meeting on Electrical-Electronics Biomedical Engineering and Computer Science (EBBT), pp. 1–4, April 2019. https://doi.org/10.1109/EBBT.2019.8741769
8. Fang, X., Chen, L.: An optimal multi-channel trilateration localization algorithm by radio-multipath multi-objective evolution in RSS-ranging-based wireless sensor networks. Sensors **20**(6), 1798 (2020)
9. Song, F., Ai, Z., Zhang, H., You, I., Li, S.: Smart collaborative balancing for dependable network components in cyber-physical systems. IEEE Trans. Ind. Inf. **17**(10), 6916–6924 (2020). https://doi.org/10.1109/TII.2020.3029766
10. Bagherinia, A., Minaei-Bidgoli, B., Hossinzadeh, M., Parvin, H.: Reliability-based fuzzy clustering ensemble. Fuzzy Sets Syst. **413**, 1–28 (2020)
11. Wang, S., Ma, R., Li, Y., Wang, Q.: A bluetooth location method based on kNN algorithm. In: 2019 15th International Computer Engineering Conference (ICENCO), pp. 1–4, December 2019. https://doi.org/10.1109/ICENCO48310.2019.9027408. iSSN 2475-2320
12. Jian, H.X., Hao, W.: WIFI indoor location optimization method based on position fingerprint algorithm. In: 2017 International Conference on Smart Grid and Electrical Automation (ICSGEA), pp. 585–588, May 2017. https://doi.org/10.1109/ICSGEA.2017.123

Author Index

Alcarria, Ramón 16
Aleksandrova, Elena B. 211
Astillo, Philip Virgil 30

Bharti, Monika 107
Bordel, Borja 16

Cao, Yuanlong 323
Chechulin, Andrey 301
Chen, Li-Woei 3
Chen, Lulu 44
Chen, Yixing 396
Cheng, Xinda 396
Cho, Seong-je 289
Choudhary, Gaurav 93, 222, 236
Chow, Yang-Wai 195
Chung, MyungWoo 379

D'Angelo, Gianni 171
Dakhnovich, Andrei 79
Ding, Ning 408
Du, Chu 44
Duguma, Daniel Gerbi 30, 236

Gao, Xianming 122, 139
Gao, Yueqing 44
Gebremariam, Yonas Engida 30
Gharat, Paresh Sajan 93
Go, Myong-Hyun 263
Guan, Jianfeng 122, 139

Hsu, Hsiung-Chieh 3
Hu, Ning 65, 396
Huang, Tianhui 408
Huang, Xiaoting 155
Huang, Xin 323

Izrailov, Konstantin 301

Ji, Lejun 323
Ji, Ruiwen 323

Kang, Hae Young 263
Khisaeva, Guldar 248

Kim, Bonam 30
Kim, Hanmin 52
Kim, Jongkil 195
Kim, Juwon 289
Kim, Minhwan 52
Kim, Yu-kyung 263
Kotenko, Igor 248, 301
Kumar, Rajesh 107
Kwak, KwonKoo 379

Lan, Zejun 122
Lee, Jemin Justin 263
Lee, Junsu 289
Lee, Keonyong 289
Lee, Kyungho 263
Lee, WonHaeng 379
Lei, Gang 323
Leu, Fang-Yie 3
Levshun, Dmitry 301
Li, Kun 335, 352
Li, Man 365
Liu, Feiyang 352
Luo, Yan 408

Ma, Yuyin 408
Moad, Deepali 236
Moskvin, Dmitrii 79

Oh, JinHyeok 379

Palmieri, Francesco 171
Park, Gyudong 52
Park, Minkyu 289
Park, Younjai 289
Poltavtseva, Maria A. 211

Qian, Dongsheng 408
Qin, Yajuan 365

Ren, Lanfang 155
Robustelli, Antonio 171

Saxena, Sharad 107
Seong, Hojun 289

Shandilya, Shishir Kumar 93
Shao, Xun 323
Sharma, Vishal 107
Shen, Yuting 44
Shi, Benhui 44
Shi, Yuyuan 139
Shin, HyunJun 379
Shmatov, Vadim S. 211
Sihag, Vikas 93, 222, 236
Singh, Pradeep 222
Sinha, Rahul 222
Sohn, Mye 52
Song, Haoxiang 335
Su, Li 155
Susilo, Willy 195

Tao, Haoran 408
Tsai, Kun-Lin 3
Tu, Zhe 335, 352

Vardhan, Manu 222
Vorobeva, Alisa 248

Wang, Weilin 335, 352
Wu, Chuan-Tian 3

Yang, Bo 155
You, Ilsun 30, 236
Yu, Kehan 408
Yun, Keon 379

Zakoldaev, Danil 248
Zegzhda, Dmitrii 79
Zhang, Tianhong 122
Zhang, Yuqiang 65, 396
Zhao, Yan 65
Zhou, Huachun 44, 155, 335, 352, 365
Zong, Wei 195
Zou, Jincai 65, 396

Printed in the United States
by Baker & Taylor Publisher Services